(continued on back cover)

The Musician's Guide
to Theory and Analysis

W. W. NORTON & COMPANY

NEW YORK · LONDON

The Musician's Guide to Theory and Analysis

Jane Piper Clendinning
Florida State University School of Music

Elizabeth West Marvin
Eastman School of Music

W. W. Norton & Company has been independent since its founding in 1923, when William Warder Norton and Mary D. Herter Norton first began to publish lectures delivered at the People's Institute, the adult education division of New York City's Cooper Union. The Nortons soon expanded their program beyond the Institute, publishing books by celebrated academics from America and abroad. By mid-century, the two major pillars of Norton's publishing program—trade books and college texts—were firmly established. In the 1950s, the Norton family transferred control of the company to its employees, and today—with a staff of four hundred and a comparable number of trade, college, and professional titles published each year—W. W. Norton & Company stands as the largest and oldest publishing house owned wholly by its employees.

Copyright © 2005 by W. W. Norton & Company, Inc.

Editor: Maribeth Payne
Developmental editor: Susan Gaustad
Managing editor, college books: Marian Johnson
E-media editor: Steve Hoge
Editorial assistant: A. Courtney Fitch
Manufacturing by Quebecor World, Taunton
Production manager: JoAnn Simony
Music and page composition: Music by Design
Art director: Rubina Yeh

Library of Congress Cataloging-in-Publication Data

Clendinning, Jane Piper.
    The musician's guide to theory and analysis / by Jane Piper Clendinning and Elizabeth
  West Marvin
        p. cm.
    Includes bibliographical references (p.) and index.
    ISBN 0-393-97652-1
        1. Music theory. 2. Musical analysis. I. Marvin, Elizabeth West, 1955– II. Title.

MT6.C57 2004
781--dc22   2004049508

W. W. Norton & Company, Inc., 500 Fifth Avenue, New York, N. Y. 10110
                    www.wwnorton.com
W. W. Norton & Company Ltd., Castle House, 75/76 Wells Street, London W1T 3QT

5   6   7   8   9   0

To our teachers, colleagues, and students—
with whom we have shared the joy of music,
and from whom we continue to learn—
and, with thanks, to our families
for their patience and support

Brief Contents

Contents

Chapter 16   Further Expansions of the Basic Phrase: Tonic Expansions, Root Progressions, and the Mediant Triad   276

Chapter 17   The Interaction of Melody and Harmony: More on Cadence, Phrase, and Melody   298

Part IV   Further Expansion of the Harmonic Vocabulary

Part V Musical Form and Interpretation

Preface

We have entered a new century. Today's students will be performing, teaching, composing, recording, and marketing music in its first decades. Perhaps you (or the student sitting beside you in class) will compose popular music for recordings or broadcast; write music for films, video games, or advertising; or create new forms of jazz, rock, or electronic dance music. Or you might find your place in the orchestra, concert hall, or recording studio, performing art music of the seventeenth century to today. What will you, as a twenty-first-century musician, need to know to prepare for music making in this new era? We believe the answer to that question is "as much as possible, and in as many styles as possible." The more you know about many kinds of music, the better prepared you will be to perform, compose, teach, and advocate for music throughout your career.

The *Musician's Guide* series is perhaps the most comprehensive set of materials available today for learning music theory. The *Theory and Analysis* portion of the series includes a textbook with coordinated Workbook—covering wide-ranging topics, from music fundamentals to music of today—plus an Anthology of core repertoire for study. Every work in the Anthology can be heard on the accompanying three-CD set, which features many performances newly recorded for this collection by artists from the Eastman School of Music. A coordinated Web site offers sound files of all music examples in the text that are not included on the CDs (as well as "Analysis" examples from the Workbook), flashcards of Glossary definitions, "WebFacts" to challenge and interest you, and additional exercises; its URL is www.wwnorton.com/web/musictheory.

The *Aural Skills* portion of the package, published in two volumes, is coordinated with the theory text and covers dictation, sight-singing, keyboard, improvisation, composition, and contextual music listening. Each volume comes with a CD of music examples for listening and dictation. In addition, through a partnership with MacGamut software (www.macgamut.com), you can acquire a special edition of the MacGamut ear-training and dictation program organized to correspond chapter-by-chapter with our texts.

Why Study Music Theory?

Have you ever tried to explain something without having the right words to capture exactly what you mean? It can be a frustrating experience. Part of the process of preparing for a professional career is learning the special language of your chosen field. To those outside the profession, the technical language may seem like a secret code intended to prevent the nonspecialist from understanding. For example, a medical doctor might speak of "cardiac infarction," "myelocardia," or "angina" when referring to conditions that we might call (inaccurately) a "heart attack." To those who know the technical terms, however, one or two words capture a wealth of associated knowledge—years of experience and pages' or even books' worth of information.

Words and symbols not only let us name things, they also help us to communicate how separate elements work together and group into categories. Music theory provides useful terms and categories, but it does more than that: it also provides a framework for considering *how* music is put together, *what* musical elements are in play, *when* particular styles were prevalent, and *why* music sounds the way it does. Understanding the vocabulary for categorizing and explaining musical events will prepare you to develop your own theories about the music you are playing and studying.

The purpose of this book is to introduce you to the technical language of music. In the first part, you will learn (or review) basic musical terminology and notation. Mastery of terminology will allow you to communicate quickly and accurately with other musicians; mastery of notation will allow you to read and write music effortlessly. You will next learn about small-to-medium-scale musical progressions and how they work. Mastery of these progressions will help you compose music in particular styles, structure improvisations on your instrument, make interpretive decisions in performance, and improve your sight-reading skills.

Later parts of the book deal with larger musical contexts: how medium-to-large sections of music fit together to make musical form. You will learn how to write in standard musical forms, how to divide the pieces you perform into musical sections, and how to convey your understanding of form in performance. In the final chapters, we explore ways that these concepts are transformed (or abandoned) in music of the twentieth century, and consider new theories that have arisen to explain music structure in this repertoire. We will apply this information in the same musical ways as in previous chapters—with direct links to performance, analysis, and writing.

One of the most important things to remember about music theory is that it is all about sounds—how and why music sounds the way it does. You will be listening to music in every chapter so that you can associate terms and notation with sounding music. We want you to make connections every day between what you are learning in this book and the music you are playing, singing, hearing, and writing.

Music theory is absolutely relevant to the music making we do—whether it's performing, analyzing, or composing. You will see references in every chapter to the way its content might inform your music making. Use this information! Take it to the practice room, the studio, and the rehearsal hall to make the connection between your coursework and your life as a practicing musician. We hope that the concepts you learn here will impact the ways you think about music for many years to come.

Using This Book

This book is organized to make it as easy as possible for you to learn about music theory and analysis. The narrative is accompanied by many useful features that will facilitate your study. These features are described below.

CHAPTER 26 Popular Song and Art Song

Outline of topics covered

The musical language of the popular song
- Quaternary and verse-refrain forms
- Chord extensions: Added-sixth and ninth chords
- Pentatonic and blues scales
  The twelve-bar blues
- Mixture chords
- Suspensions and rhythmic displacement
- Chords with altered fifths

Analysis of songs
- The relation between text and song structure
- Text painting
- Motivic analysis

Other song forms

Overview

Having studied chromatic harmony and modulation, we now turn to short, complete compositions in which these musical elements come into play: songs. Because the repertoire is vast, we will limit ourselves to two types, early twentieth-century American popular song and the nineteenth-century German Lied. We will consider standard song forms, musical interpretation of the text, and new harmonic features typical of popular songs.

Repertoire
Johannes Brahms, "Die Mainacht" (CD 1, track 63)
George Gershwin, "I Got Rhythm," from *Girl Crazy* (CD 1, track 87)
John Lennon and Paul McCartney, "Eleanor Rigby," from *Revolver*
James Myers and Max Freedman, "Rock Around the Clock"
Franz Schubert, "Erlkönig" (CD 3, track 25)
Clara Schumann, "Liebst du um Schönheit" (CD 3, track 34)
Robert Schumann, "Im wunderschönen Monat Mai," from *Dichterliebe* (CD 3, track 38)
Meredith Willson, "Till There Was You," from *The Music Man* (CD 3, track 63)

508

Along the left margin of each chapter's opening page is an **Outline of topics covered**, which can serve as a chapter preview and also a review once you have completed your study.

To the right, you will find a short **Overview** that gives a general description of what you will learn in the chapter.

Beneath the overview, the **Repertoire** list tells you which pieces are featured in the chapter, along with the relevant CD and track numbers if the piece is included in the Anthology.

In this example, you will see that the repertoire draws generously from the art music tradition, but also from popular music and show tunes. If you get to know the pieces in the Anthology as they are discussed chapter by chapter, you will finish the text knowing a good cross-section of music repertoire, from J. S. Bach to Steve Reich and Meredith Willson. Any composition discussed in a chapter can be heard either on one of the Anthology CDs or in a MIDI rendition on the *Musician's Guide* Web site.

Following are aids designed to help you identify key information and remember it.

Boldface signals a new and important term you should remember. Most such terms are defined in the Glossary in Appendix 2 at the back of the book, as well as on the Web site (in the form of flashcards).

Key Concept and **Summary** boxes identify the most important ideas to remember.

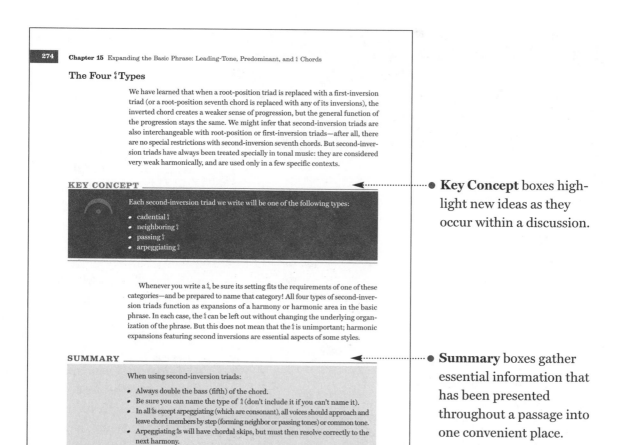

274   **Chapter 15** Expanding the Basic Phrase: Leading-Tone, Predominant, and ⁶⁄₄ Chords

The Four ⁶⁄₄ Types

We have learned that when a root-position triad is replaced with a first-inversion triad (or a root-position seventh chord is replaced with any of its inversions), the inverted chord creates a weaker sense of progression, but the general function of the progression stays the same. We might infer that second-inversion triads are also interchangeable with root-position or first-inversion triads—after all, there are no special restrictions with second-inversion seventh chords. But second-inversion triads have always been treated specially in tonal music: they are considered very weak harmonically, and are used only in a few specific contexts.

KEY CONCEPT

Each second-inversion triad we write will be one of the following types:

- cadential ⁶⁄₄
- neighboring ⁶⁄₄
- passing ⁶⁄₄
- arpeggiating ⁶⁄₄

Whenever you write a ⁶⁄₄, be sure its setting fits the requirements of one of these categories—and be prepared to name that category! All four types of second-inversion triads function as expansions of a harmony or harmonic area in the basic phrase. In each case, the ⁶⁄₄ can be left out without changing the underlying organization of the phrase. But this does not mean that the ⁶⁄₄ is unimportant; harmonic expansions featuring second inversions are essential aspects of some styles.

SUMMARY

When using second-inversion triads:

- Always double the bass (fifth) of the chord.
- Be sure you can name the type of ⁶⁄₄ (don't include it if you can't name it).
- In all ⁶⁄₄s except arpeggiating (which are consonant), all voices should approach and leave chord members by step (forming neighbor or passing tones) or common tone.
- Arpeggiating ⁶⁄₄s will have chordal skips, but must then resolve correctly to the next harmony.

● **Key Concept** boxes highlight new ideas as they occur within a discussion.

● **Summary** boxes gather essential information that has been presented throughout a passage into one convenient place.

Another Way

Here are two other methods for spelling triads.

1. If you like to visualize triads on the keyboard or staff, memorize the generic triads from just the white keys or plain note heads on the staff:
- triads on C, F, and G are major;
- triads on D, E, and A are minor;
- triads on B are diminished.

Then use this information to build other-quality triads.

- Triads on C, F, and G remain major if all the accidentals match (e.g., C♯-E♯-G♯). To make a minor triad, lower the middle accidental a half step (e.g., change C-E-G to C-E♭-G, or change C♯-E♯-G♯ to C♯-E-G♯).
- Triads on D, E, and A remain minor if all the accidentals match (e.g., D♭-F♭-A♭). To make a major triad, raise the middle accidental a half step (e.g., change D-F-A to D-F♯-A, or change D♭-F♭-A♭ to D♭-F-A♭).
- Triads on B remain diminished if all the accidentals match (e.g., B♯-D♯-F♯). To make a major triad, lower the accidental of the root a half step (e.g., B♭-D-F or B-D♯-F♯). To make a minor triad, raise the accidental of the fifth a half step (e.g., B-D-F♯ or B♭-D♭-F).

2. You may also spell triads using only major key signatures. First, build a major triad (referring to the key signature of the triad's root), then
- for a minor triad, lower the third a half step;
- for a diminished triad, lower the third and fifth each a half step;
- for an augmented triad, raise the fifth a half step.

Try it #3

Spell the following triads.

minor triad above B♭: _____

major triad above F: _____

minor triad above G: _____

minor triad above G♯: _____

augmented triad above E♭: _____

minor triad above D: _____

diminished triad above B♭: _____

major triad above D: _____

major triad above A: _____

Often one voice-leading error will create other problems as well. In Example 14.6b, for example, we see not only overlapping between the tenor and alto, but also contrary fifths between the alto and bass voices.

Check your understanding of these guidelines in Example 14.7, a complete chorale phrase with numerous voice-leading errors. Sing or play through the phrase, circle and label the mistakes, then rewrite the phrase with correct voice-leading. (*Try it #4*)

EXAMPLE 14.7: A chorale phrase with errors

c: i V⁶ i — ⁶ V — ⁷ i

Since many music theory concepts can be learned in more than one way, **Another Way** boxes offer alternative explanations. Use whatever method works best for you.

Try it exercises provide opportunities for you to practice a concept that's just been explained. They may range from spelling chords to working out a harmonic or phrase analysis in a music example, and they give you immediate feedback on your understanding. You can check your work in Appendix 1 at the back of the book, where all *Try it* answers are given.

Many of these exercises are not self-contained boxes, but rather questions posed in the text. When you see a "(*Try it #1*)," "(*Try it #2*)," and so on in the text, that means you can answer the questions posed at that spot in the text and check your work by looking up that *Try it* number in Appendix 1.

When you come to one of the exercises, try it! Only then will you know that you have understood the new concept and can apply it in your music making.

WF1

- **WebFacts** explain how certain ideas (such as the musical staff) came to be, fill in background for composers and pieces featured in the chapter (for example, Bach's composing methods, the story behind a Mozart aria), or supply more advanced information (in case you're curious!). The numbered icons in the margin (like the one at left) point you to the appropriate "facts" on the Web site that are linked to the passages you are reading. WebFacts aren't required reading, but are rather a source of enrichment (why are some trumpets and clarinets in B♭? what peculiar circumstances resulted in Kern's "Smoke Gets in Your Eyes"?). Some of these facts are actually included in the text chapter, in the form of shaded boxes. As for those on the Web, check them out—they are designed to be interesting and entertaining!

Every chapter ends with a list of **Terms You Should Know** and **Questions for Review** to help you study and test your knowledge.

In addition to the *Try it* answers and Glossary, the **Appendixes** include a summary of part-writing guidelines, a summary of instrumental ranges, and a table of set classes.

Finally, there are two **indexes**: one for composers and pieces studied, another for terms and concepts.

Using the Workbook

While *Try it* exercises provide handy checkpoints to test your understanding along the way, you will need additional practice to really master the concepts in each chapter. Many more exercises, for homework and additional class work, are provided in the **Workbook**.

Each Workbook chapter follows the same plan:
- **Basic Elements** provide practice of fundamental concepts, with short exercises such as chord spelling and two- or three-chord connections.
- **Writing Exercises** include such tasks as harmonizing melodies, realizing figured basses, and writing short compositions. Most of the writing exercises are based on passages from music literature rather than practice exercises.
- The **Analysis** portion of each chapter begins with brief excerpts, followed by longer examples or complete works. The longer analyses are often drawn from the works in the Anthology, allowing you to revisit the core repertoire and to hear these works again on your CD. Each analysis exercise directs your attention to specific aspects of the passage; some ask you to answer questions in the form of a short essay.

Using the Anthology and CD Set

In order to use the *Musician's Guide* package, you need to purchase the coordinated **Anthology** and CD set. The study of these Anthology works is integral to the book's approach to learning music theory. We have chosen music that we like and that our students have enjoyed. Some of the works should be familiar to you ("Greensleeves," "The Stars and Stripes Forever"), while others will probably be new (Edgard Varèse's *Density 21.5*). There are pieces for varied performing ensembles (flute, trumpet, guitar, violin, chamber orchestra, and string quartet, among others) and in contrasting musical styles—from American popular songs to German Lieder, from piano ragtime to sonatas to minimalist music, from marches for band to hymns and anthems for choirs. While the Anthology includes gems of familiar repertoire (Mozart and Beethoven sonatas, Schubert Lieder, Bach chorales, and so on), we also aim to stretch your ears with representative works by women and African-American composers (Fanny Mendelssohn Hensel, Scott Joplin), as well as diverse works written within the last century.

2.33 🎧   We begin every chapter by listening to one or two works from the Anthology. You will see a headphone icon in the margin (like the one at left) that gives you the relevant CD and track number every time we want you to listen to a musical example (the icon at left refers you to CD 2, track 33). Please take the time to listen and follow the Anthology score—it will increase your enjoyment of this text, make your music theory study more relevant to your performance studies, and broaden your knowledge of music literature. (CD tracks are also given in the Anthology scores themselves.) Our spiral-learning approach revisits the Anthology's core repertoire from chapter to chapter as you learn new concepts—thus, a single piece might be used to illustrate scales, triads, cadence types, secondary dominants, common-chord modulation, sequence, and binary form. By the third or fourth time you "visit" a particular work, it will seem like an old friend. We hope you will get to know the works on the CDs until you can hear each one in your head, the same way you can hear familiar songs from the radio, TV, or movies just by thinking about them.

To the Instructor

The *Musician's Guide* is a comprehensive teaching and learning package for undergraduate music theory classes that integrates technological resources with a traditional textbook and CD set. Numerous support mechanisms help you efficiently prepare for class. We know that not all theory classes are taught by professional music theorists, and we have designed these materials specially with teaching assistants and performance faculty in mind.

- The **Teacher's Edition** of *The Musician's Guide to Aural Skills* and the **Teacher's Edition** of the Workbook that accompanies *The Musician's Guide to Theory and Analysis* include answers to all exercises, including fundamentals drills, part-writing, analysis questions, and dictation exercises. The *Aural Skills* manual also offers helpful teaching strategies for conveying new concepts to your students.
- Our coordinated **Web site** includes additional assignments or examination questions for your use (www.wwnorton.com/nrl), along with the features (music examples, Glossary flashcards, WebFacts) described above.
- **Compact discs**: No longer will you need to plan for a trip to the library before class to find a recording of the work you will be studying; this package includes recordings of the entire core repertoire studied, as well as all dictation exercises, in high-quality professional performances. Highlights of the repertoire in the anthology/CD set, 62 works or movements, include the following.

  - 22 twentieth-century compositions, ranging from pre-1950 (Stravinsky, Bartók, Schoenberg, Webern) to post-1950 (Penderecki, Reich, Corigliano, Tavener)
  - Music by women and African-American composers (Clara Schumann, Fanny Mendelssohn Hensel, Scott Joplin)
  - Music in popular genres (ragtime and popular songs by Gershwin and Willson)
  - Music for band, wind ensemble, and orchestra (Bach, Chance, Sousa, Penderecki)
  - Music for choir (Bach, Tavener)
  - Music featuring solo instruments (flute, clarinet, trumpet, guitar, violin)
  - Keyboard performances on piano, fortepiano, harpsichord, organ
  - "Bonus tracks" demonstrating performance-practice issues (Purcell, Joplin)

Our Thanks to . . .

A work of this size and scope is helped along the way by many people. We are especially grateful for the support of our families—Elizabeth and David Clendinning and Glenn, Russell, and Caroline West. Our work together as co-authors has been incredibly rewarding, and we are thankful for that collaboration and friendship. We also thank Joel Phillips (Westminster Choir College) for his many important contributions—pedagogical, musical, and personal—to our project, and especially for *The Musician's Guide to Aural Skills*. While working on the project, we have received encouragement and useful ideas from our many colleagues and students at Florida State University and the Eastman School of Music as well as from music theory teachers across the country.

We thank Jon Piersol (dean of Florida State University's School of Music) for his enthusiasm and unfailing support. For pedagogical discussions over the years, we thank Steve Laitz, Bob Wason, Dave Headlam, and William Marvin at Eastman, and James Mathes and Judy Bowers at Florida State University. For editorial assistance, especially the compilation of the Glossary and CD track list plus numerous hours of careful proofreading, our gratitude to Phil Chang. We thank Mary Arlin (Ithaca College), whose meticulous review of the Workbook led to improvements in the main text as well. We are indebted to the thorough and detailed work of our prepublication reviewers, whose careful reading of our manuscript inspired many improvements, large and small; Mary Arlin, Steve Bruns (University of Colorado), Walter Everett (University of Michigan), Richard Hermann (University of New Mexico), Janis Kindred (Stetson University), Joe Kraus (University of Nebraska), and J. Kent Williams (University of North Carolina, Greensboro). We also acknowledge that the foundation for this book rests on writings of the great music theorists of the past, from the sixteenth to twentieth century, from whom we have learned the "tricks of our trade" and whose pedagogical works have inspired ours.

For subvention of the compact disks, we thank James Undercofler (director and dean of the Eastman School of Music), as well as Eastman's Professional Development Committee. For CD engineering, we are grateful to recording engineer extraordinaire John Ebert. For CD production work, thanks to Glenn West and Christina Lenti, who assisted Elizabeth Marvin in recording sessions. We also thank the faculty and students of the Eastman School who gave so generously of their time to these recordings. The joy of their music making contributed mightily to this project.

We are indebted to the W. W. Norton staff for their commitment to *The Musician's Guide* and their painstaking care in producing these volumes. Most notable among these are former music editor Suzanne LaPlante, who originally commissioned the project, and current music editor Maribeth Payne, who saw it through to completion and whose vision has helped launch it with great enthusiasm. We are grateful for the amazingly detailed work of developmental editor Susan Gaustad, and for the forward-thinking technology editor Steve Hoge, who helped refine our ideas for the book's Web site. Rubina Yeh created the wonderful design for all parts of the *Musician's Guide* package, Allison Benter coordinated the production of the CD sets for both the *Theory and Analysis* and *Aural Skills* texts, Courtney Fitch pursued copyright permissions, and JoAnn Simony oversaw the production of these multifaceted texts through to completion. Our gratitude to one and all.

Jane Piper Clendinning
Elizabeth West Marvin

PART I

Building a Musical Vocabulary: Basic Elements of Pitch and Rhythm

CHAPTER 1

Pitch and Pitch Class

Outline of topics covered

Introduction to pitch notation
- Letter names
- Pitch classes and pitches

Flats and sharps
- The piano keyboard: Naming white keys
- Naming black keys
- Enharmonic equivalents
- Half steps and whole steps
- Double flats and sharps

Reading pitches from a score
- Staff notation
- Clefs
   Reading pitches in different clefs
   C-clefs
- Ledger lines
- Naming registers

Dynamics

Overview

When we read a page of music, we translate its symbols into sound—sung, played on an instrument, or heard in our heads. We will begin our study of music theory by learning to read and write the symbols that represent pitch, one of music's basic elements.

Repertoire

Johann Sebastian Bach, *Brandenburg Concerto* No. 4, second movement (CD 1, track 3)

John Lennon and Paul McCartney, "Eleanor Rigby," from *Revolver*

"On Top of Old Smoky" (folk tune, arranged by Norman Lloyd)

o o o o o o o o o o o o o o o o o o o o o o o o o o o o o o o o o o o o o o o o o o o o o o o o o o

Introduction to Pitch Notation

1.3 Listen to the beginning of the second movement of Bach's *Brandenburg Concerto* No. 4 (mm. 1–18a). Try to follow along with the score in your anthology; the first few measures are also shown in Example 1.1. Some of the musical symbols may be unfamiliar to you. For example, you may never have seen how music for full orchestra is written. When we read scores like these, or write scores of our own, we need to understand the meaning of many music-notation symbols. We begin with the symbols associated with pitch.

EXAMPLE 1.1: Bach, *Brandenburg Concerto* No. 4, second movement, mm. 1–5a

Letter Names

In Western music notation, we name musical tones using the first seven letters of the alphabet: A, B, C, D, E, F, G. This **musical alphabet** repeats endlessly. We "count" up or down in the series by reciting its letters forward or backward. To count up beyond G, start over with A: . . . E–F–G–A–B. . . . To count down below A, start over again with G: . . . C–B–A–G–F–E. . . . Practice counting backward and forward in the musical alphabet from A to A, C to C, G to G, and so on, until you feel as comfortable counting backward as forward.

Learning to count in letter names is a fundamental musical skill. Think of the movement as "upward" when you count forward, and "downward" when you count backward. For example, 5 above C is G: C–D–E–F–G. (Always count the first and last letter names of your series.) To discover what is 6 below E, you must count backward: the answer is again G (E–D–C–B–A–G).

Try it #1

Find the letter name requested.

What is 7 above G?	_____	5 below A?	_____
6 above F?	_____	3 above E?	_____
2 above D?	_____	8 below C?	_____
4 below B?	_____	1 below A?	_____

Pitch Classes and Pitches

What is 8 below C? The answer is another C. In this seven-name system, each letter name reappears every eighth position. Tones eight letter names apart make up an **octave**. The repetition of letter names reflects the way listeners familiar with Western music hear. Tones an octave apart sound similar. This principle is known as **octave equivalence**. Octave-related notes have the same letter name and belong to the same **pitch class**. The pitch-class F, for example, consists of every F on a piano or other instrument.

WF1   What, then, is a **pitch**? A pitch is a tone sounding in a particular octave. In the Bach concerto, you may have noticed that the first three pitches of the lowest string parts all sound similar. Listen again, as you follow the lowest line of Example 1.1. This musical line begins with three notes belonging to pitch-class E, all sounding in different octaves.

Flats and Sharps

The Piano Keyboard: Naming White Keys

Throughout this text, we will reinforce concepts with the help of the keyboard. As a musician, you will find keyboard skills essential, even if the piano is not your primary instrument. Because of the piano's great range and its ability to sound numerous pitches simultaneously, keyboard skills allow you to play simple accompaniments, demonstrate musical ideas, and harmonize melodies.

The white keys of the piano correspond to the seven letters of the musical alphabet. We name them on the keyboard in relation to the two- and three-note groupings of black keys. Immediately to the left of any group of two black keys is pitch-class C; immediately to the left of any three black keys is pitch-class F. **Middle C**, the C closest to the middle of the piano keyboard, is identified in Figure 1.1: a close-up segment of the piano keyboard (see Figure 1.2 on p. 15 for a full keyboard). Write in the pitch labels for the white keys above (to the right of) middle C in the figure, using the black-note groupings to find your place. The white keys on the piano that have no black keys between them are E–F and B–C. For extra practice, choose several pitch-class letter names, then play pitches that correspond with these letter names on a real piano in four different octaves.

KEY CONCEPT

No black key appears between white keys E and F or between B and C.

FIGURE 1.1: Piano keyboard, with middle C marked

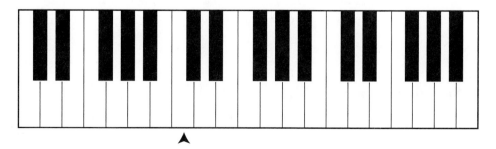

Middle C

Naming Black Keys

The black-key pitches are named in relation to adjacent white-key pitches. The key immediately *above* any white note gets the white note's name plus a **sharp** (♯). The keyboard group of two black keys is therefore called C♯ and D♯, and the group of three black keys is F♯, G♯, and A♯. Write the sharp note names at the top of each of the black keys above middle C in Figure 1.1.

The key immediately *below* (to the left of) any white key gets the white note's name plus a **flat** (♭). That means the keyboard group of two black keys can also be called D♭ and E♭, and the three black keys can be called G♭, A♭, and B♭. In fact, every black key has two possible names: one with a sharp and one with a flat. The two names are called **enharmonic** spellings. Now write the enharmonic spelling for each black key you labeled in Figure 1.1, this time with flats.

The sharp and flat symbols are called **accidentals** (although there is nothing "accidental" about their use or placement). There is a third common accidental called a **natural** (♮): a natural cancels a sharp or flat. It returns the pitch name to its "natural" state and to its white-key location on the keyboard. (If you see an E♭ followed by an E♮, for example, you first play the black key E♭ and then the white key E.)

Enharmonic Equivalents

Enharmonic pitches have the same sound, but different names (B♭ = A♯). They belong to the same pitch class. On the keyboard, you play enharmonic pitches by depressing the same key. The "spelling" a composer chooses is determined by the musical context in which the pitch appears (we will learn more about spelling choices in Chapters 6 and 7).

Not all sharped or flatted pitches are black keys. If you raise an E or B to the closest possible note on the keyboard, you get a white key, not a black one. That means E♯ is a white key and is enharmonic with F, just as B♯ is white and enharmonic with C. On the flat side, C♭ is enharmonic with B, and F♭ is enharmonic with E. Find these pitches on the piano or in Figure 1.1, then practice finding enharmonic spellings for other pitches.

Try it #2

Name the enharmonic equivalent.

G♭ enharmonic:	<u>F♯</u>	B enharmonic:	<u>C♭</u>
B♯ enharmonic:	<u>C</u>	A♭ enharmonic:	<u>G♯</u>
A♯ enharmonic:	<u>B♭</u>	E♯ enharmonic:	<u>F</u>
D♭ enharmonic:	<u>C♯</u>	C♭ enharmonic:	<u>B</u>

Half Steps and Whole Steps

The distance between any two notes is called an **interval**, and the two fundamental intervals that serve as basic building blocks of many musical structures are half steps and whole steps. A **half step** (or **semitone**) is the interval between any pitch and the next-closest pitch on the keyboard. Usually a half step will span a white note to a black note (or black to white)—except in the case of B to C and E to F, which naturally span a half step.

WF2   The combination of two half steps together forms a **whole step**. Usually whole steps span two piano keys the same color: black to black (like F♯ to G♯) or white to white (like A to B). The exceptions to this color rule are the white-to-white half steps: E to F and B to C. A whole step above E is not F, but F♯. A whole step below C is not B, but B♭.

Try it #3

Name the pitch requested, and give an enharmonic equivalent where possible.

Half step above G♭: ___G___ or ___A♭♭___

Half step below C♯: ___C___ or ___B♯___

Half step below B: ___B♭___ or ___A♯___

Half step above E: ___F___ or ___G♭♭___

Half step above D: ___E♭___ or ___D♯___

Half step below B♭: ___A___ or ___B♭♭___

Half step above B♯: ___C♯___ or ___D♭___

Specify whether the two pitches named span a whole step or a half step.

F♯ to E: ___whole step___

C♯ to D: ___half step___

B♭ to A♭: ___whole step___

C to B♭: ___whole step___

E to F: ___half step___

F to G: ___whole step___

B♯ to C: ___no step___

An Accidental Invention

It was because of whole and half steps that accidentals were invented in the first place. In the Middle Ages (from about 800 to 1430) and the Renaissance (roughly 1430 to 1600), musical relationships were understood in terms of a musical structure called a hexachord ("hexa" means "six"), built in a standard pattern of whole and half steps: W–W–H–W–W. Accidentals were invented when musicians needed to transpose this hexachord's pattern of whole and half steps. The first accidental they came up with was B♭, which allowed the hexachord on C (C–D–E–F–G–A) to begin on F instead (F–G–A–B♭–C–D) with the same whole-step and half-step pattern. To indicate the hexachord's B♭, they developed the rounded flat symbol.

Musicians called the hexachord beginning with C the "natural" hexachord, and the one beginning with F the "soft" hexachord. When they played the pattern on G (G–A–B–C–D–E), they called it the "hard" hexachord. If a song moved from the soft hexachord to the hard one, composers needed to show that B♮, not B♭, was to be played. They wrote the letter "h" to indicate B♮ (a usage that continues today in German-speaking countries), but over the years this symbol evolved into both the natural sign and the sharp sign. After these symbols had been in use for some time to indicate B♭ and B♮, they came to be linked with other letter names as well.

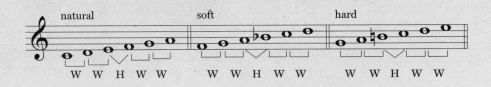

SUMMARY

Follow the guidelines below when identifying half and whole steps at the piano.

1. Half steps usually span keys of different colors: white to black or black to white.

   - The exceptions to the half-step rule are E–F and B–C, the white-note half steps.

2. Whole steps usually span keys the same color: white to white or black to black.

   - The exceptions to the same-color rule for whole steps are E♭–F, E–F♯, B♭–C, and B–C♯.

3. Double-check the spelling of any half or whole step that includes E, F, B, or C.

Double Flats and Sharps

The way we spell a note determines its musical meaning. Occasionally, we see accidentals called **double sharps** (×) or **double flats** (♭♭) in a musical score. We use a double sharp to raise a note that is already sharp; we use a double flat to lower a note that is already flat. A double sharp raises a pitch two half steps (or one whole step) above its letter name; a double flat lowers a pitch two half steps below its letter name. For example, the pitches G♭♭ and F are enharmonic, and the pitches A× and B are enharmonic.

○ ○

Reading Pitches from a Score

Staff Notation

Perhaps you once made up a tune, or improvised a piece of music on your instrument, then created your own system of music notation so you could play the piece again another day. Your system may have consisted of lines slanting up or down to show the shape of the melody or drawings to show fingerings. These are exactly the ways that the earliest forms of Western music notation were invented.

WF3   Early notation of melodies merely showed rising or falling melodic lines, and did not identify pitches by letter name. With the invention of the **staff** (the plural is "staves"), specific pitches could be notated by placing them on lines or spaces. The modern staff consists of five lines and four spaces, which are generally read from bottom to top, with the bottom line called the first:

Clefs

We cannot read notes on the staff's lines and spaces without a **clef**, the symbol that appears to the far left of every staff. The clef tells which line or space represents which pitch (in which octave). Listen again to the opening of the *Brandenburg Concerto* movement while following the score in Example 1.1 (p. 3). How many different clefs do you see? You should find three, which we call the treble (𝄞), bass (𝄢), and alto (𝄡) clefs.

1.3

Reading Pitches in Different Clefs   The clefs you will encounter most are the bass and treble clefs. The **treble clef** is sometimes called the G-clef: its shape somewhat resembles a cursive capital G, and the end of its central curving line rests on the staff line for G. Look at Example 1.2 to see how all other pitches can be read from G, by counting up or down in the musical alphabet: one pitch for each line and space. We rarely count letter names in music reading, however; it is much quicker simply to memorize the pitch names for each line and space. One way to memorize the lines and spaces is to make up sentences whose words begin with the letters you are trying to remember. The treble-clef lines (E-G-B-D-F), for example, might be "Every Good Bird Does Fly." The spaces of the treble clef simply spell a word: F-A-C-E. Make up your own sentences!

EXAMPLE 1.2: Treble clef (G-clef)

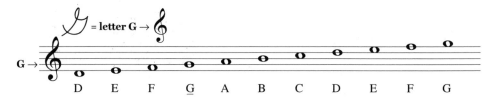

When we read and write letter names with accidentals, the accidental comes after the note name, as with C♯ or A♭. When these notes are written on the staff, however, the accidental is placed before the note.

Try it #4

(*a*) Lennon and McCartney, "Eleanor Rigby," mm. 9–11

Play a recording or sing this passage, if you are familiar with it, while looking at the notation. Use the placement of the notes on the lines or spaces of the staff to determine the letter names of its pitches. Write them beneath the staff.

(*b*) Identify the pitches on the treble staff below.

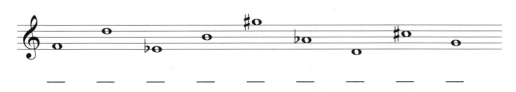

The **bass clef** is also known as the F-clef: it resembles a cursive capital F. As Example 1.3 shows, its two dots surround the line that represents F. Other pitches may be counted from F or, more likely, memorized according to their position on the bass-clef staff. Two common ways to remember the bass-clef spaces (A-C-E-G) are "All Cows Eat Grass" and "All Cars Eat Gas." Make new ones up for yourself. One sentence for the bass-clef lines (G-B-D-F-A) might be "Great Big Doves Fly Away."

EXAMPLE 1.3: Bass clef (F-clef)

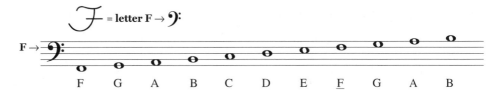

Try it #5

(*a*) Bach, *Brandenburg Concerto* No. 4, second movement, mm. 24–26 (cello part)

Write the letter name for each pitch beneath the bass-clef staff.

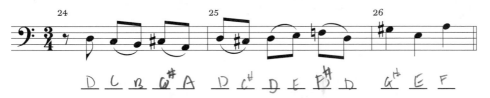

D C B G# A   D C# D E F# D   G# E F

(*b*) Identify the pitches on the bass staff below.

F#   G   Db   B   F#   Ab   C   G

C-Clefs   The third clef represented in Example 1.1, the alto clef, is one of five possible placements of a **C-clef**. Music reading starts with knowledge of the treble and bass clefs, but it is good to learn how to read the C-clefs as well, since you will encounter them in orchestral and chamber music scores. The C-clef may appear in different positions on the staff, to identify any one of the five lines as middle C. WF4 (In Bach's time, the treble and bass clefs could move as well.) Its distinctive shape— 𝄡 — identifies middle C by the point at which the two curved lines join together in the middle, as Example 1.4 shows. Depending on its position, the clef may be called a soprano, mezzo-soprano, alto, tenor, or baritone clef. Although the only C-clefs you will probably see in modern scores are the alto and tenor clefs, you may WF5 come across multiple C-clefs in older editions.

EXAMPLE 1.4: Names for C-clefs

Soprano clef   Mezzo-soprano clef   Alto clef   Tenor clef   Baritone clef

Try it #6

(*a*) Bach, *Brandenburg Concerto* No. 4, second movement, mm. 36–39 (viola part)

This passage is written in the alto clef. Beneath the example, write the letter name for each pitch, then play it at the keyboard.

(*b*) Identify the pitches on the C-clefs below; play them at the keyboard.

Why do orchestral scores include so many different clefs? We need different clefs because each one transforms the staff's range to span the pitches needed for a particular instrument or voice type. Look back at Example 1.1 to see Bach's instrumentation. The higher instruments, like the flute and violin, generally read treble clef. Lower instruments, like the cello and bass, generally read bass clef. Other instruments, like violas, use C-clefs. Some players regularly read more than one clef: for example, pianists read both bass and treble clefs; bassoonists and cellists read both bass and tenor clefs.

The tenor part in vocal scores is often notated using a treble clef with a small "8" attached beneath it; these pitches are read down an octave. How do we know which clefs to use in instrumental or vocal compositions? That's why composers and arrangers study orchestration!

WF6

Ledger Lines

Sing through the familiar folk tune "On Top of Old Smoky," given in Example 1.5. Beneath the singer's melody line is a **grand staff**—two staves, one in treble clef and one in bass clef, connected by a curly brace. Some pitches are circled. In these spots, the music's range extends below what can be written on the staff, and extra lines have been drawn to accommodate the circled notes. We call these lines **ledger lines**.

EXAMPLE 1.5: Ledger lines and grand staff in "On Top of Old Smoky"

We read ledger lines just like other staff lines: by counting forward or backward in the musical alphabet. In "On Top of Old Smoky," for example, the first pitch of the vocal line is a C. Remember to count backward in the alphabet: the bottom line of the treble-clef staff represents E, the space below it is D, and the first ledger line represents C. The lowest note of the first piano chord is also a C. The bottom line of the bass-clef staff represents G, the space below it is F, and the first ledger line is E; the space below that ledger line is D, and the pitch below D (on the second ledger line below the bass staff) is C.

Try it #7

(*a*) What are the circled pitches between the two piano staves in measures 4 and 7 of Example 1.5?

m. 4: ___ ___   m. 7: ___ ___ ___

(*b*) Identify the pitches in each clef.

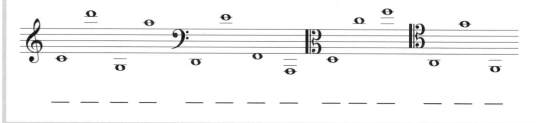

Notes higher than the staff have ledger lines drawn through them or beneath them, but never above them; notes below the staff have ledger lines through them or above them, but never beneath. We draw ledger lines the same distance apart as staff lines. Example 1.6 shows ledger lines correctly and incorrectly drawn. You will find notes on ledger lines between the treble and bass staves as well, including middle C, as Example 1.7 shows (and as we saw in Example 1.5).

EXAMPLE 1.6: Correct and incorrect ledger lines

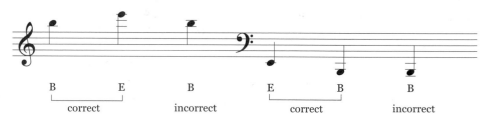

EXAMPLE 1.7: Ledger lines between staves

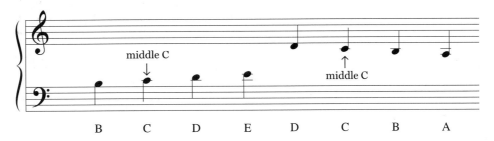

B   C   D   E   D   C   B   A

An alternative to ledger lines is the *ottava* sign. An "8va" above the staff means to play an octave higher (the 8v stands for "octave," and the a stands for *alta*, Italian for "above"). An "8vb" beneath the staff means to play an octave lower (the b stands for *bassa*, or "below").

Try it #8

(*a*) Some instruments routinely read ledger lines. Name the three instruments in Bach's *Brandenburg Concerto* (check the score in your anthology) that read the most ledger lines.

(*b*) For extra practice, read aloud the letter names for the flute line in the first four measures (1–5a), given in Example 1.1. Play this line on your own instrument (move it to a comfortable octave).

Naming Registers

WF7   Because pitches sound in a particular octave, we sometimes want to specify the octave placement. In this book, we will use the numeric system shown with the piano keyboard in Figure 1.2. The lowest C on the piano is C1 and the highest is C8; middle C is C4. The number for a particular octave includes all the pitches from C up to the following B. The B above C4 is B4; the B below C4 is B3. What of the three notes below the C1 on the piano? They are A0, B♭0, and B0.

FIGURE 1.2: Full piano keyboard, with octave designations

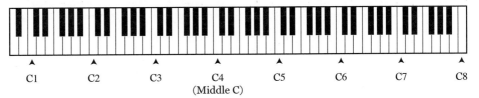

C1   C2   C3   C4   C5   C6   C7   C8
                     (Middle C)

Try it #9

(*a*) Bach, *Brandenburg Concerto* No. 4, second movement, mm. 68–71

For practice identifying pitches with their octave numbers, name all the pitches that occur in the final chord of this excerpt—the final chord of the movement.

(*b*) Identify the following pitches by letter name and octave number.

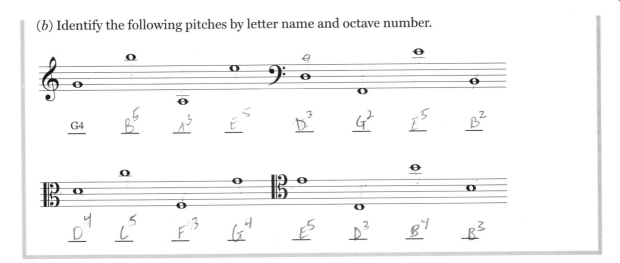

G4 B⁵ A³ E⁵ D³ G² E⁵ B²

D⁴ C⁵ F³ G⁴ E⁵ D³ B⁴ B³

Dynamics

Look again at the Bach excerpt in *Try it #9a*. This passage begins with a flute flourish marked *piano*, followed by two chords marked *forte*. *Piano* and *forte* are **dynamic** indications, which tell performers how soft or loud to play. They also help musicians make decisions about the character or mood of a piece.

Piano (abbreviated *p*) is a soft dynamic; *forte* (abbreviated *f*) is a loud dynamic. You will also sometimes see the abbreviations *mp* (for *mezzo piano*) and *mf* (for *mezzo forte*), indicating "medium soft" and "medium loud." The chart below shows a typical range of dynamics. The indication that tells you to get louder is *crescendo*, while *decrescendo* or *diminuendo* means to get softer. When performing, pay careful attention to the dynamics marked in the score. They will contribute greatly to shaping a musical and sensitive performance.

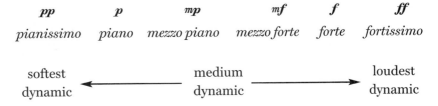

pp	*p*	*mp*	*mf*	*f*	*ff*
pianissimo	*piano*	*mezzo piano*	*mezzo forte*	*forte*	*fortissimo*

softest dynamic ← medium dynamic → loudest dynamic

TERMS YOU SHOULD KNOW

accidental	double flat	interval	pitch class
clef	double sharp	ledger line	sharp
• alto clef	dynamics	musical alphabet	staff
• bass clef	enharmonic	natural	whole step
• C-clef	flat	octave	
• tenor clef	grand staff	octave equivalence	
• treble clef	half step	pitch	

QUESTIONS FOR REVIEW

1. How do the staff and clefs work together to identify letters of the musical alphabet?
2. How can we distinguish between pitches and pitch classes when we name notes?
3. What is the function of (a) C-clefs, (b) accidentals, (c) ledger lines?
4. How do the piano's white and black keys help us determine whole and half steps?
5. What special relationship do B and C have? E and F?
6. Find a melody from music in your repertoire. Identify the register of its pitches by octave number, then name any pitches that appear on ledger lines.

Beat, Meter, and Rhythm:
Simple Meters

CHAPTER 2

Outline of topics covered

Dividing musical time
- Pulse, beat, and beat divisions
- Simple and compound meters

Metric organization
- The grouping of beats
- Conducting patterns
- Hearing meter
- Metrical accent
- Rhythm and meter
- Rhythmic values in simple meters
- Signatures for simple meters
- Other metric symbols

Rhythmic notation in simple meters
- Beat divisions and subdivisions
- Less common beat units
- Rests
- Dots and ties
- Syncopations

Notation guidelines
- Stems and flags
- Common beat-unit patterns and beaming
- Upbeats

Implications for performance
- Metrical hierarchy
- Tempo indications

Overview

We turn now to the organization of music in time. In this chapter, we will hear how musical beats are grouped and divided to create meter. Then we will learn to conduct, read, write, and perform rhythms in simple meters.

Repertoire

Johann Sebastian Bach, *Brandenburg Concerto* No. 4, second movement (CD 1, track 3)

Stephen Foster, "Oh! Susanna"

"Greensleeves" (folk tune) (CD 1, track 94)

George Frideric Handel, "Rejoice greatly," from *Messiah* (CD 2, track 10)

Scott Joplin, "Pine Apple Rag" (CD 2, track 28)

John Philip Sousa, "The Stars and Stripes Forever" (CD 3, track 41)

Dividing Musical Time

Pulse, Beat, and Beat Divisions

2.28 🎧
2.10 🎧
We begin by listening to portions of two lively works in contrasting styles: Joplin's "Pine Apple Rag," for piano solo, and Handel's "Rejoice greatly," from *Messiah*. As you listen, tap your foot in time. This tap represents the work's primary pulse. Can you hear a secondary pulse moving twice as fast as your foot tap? Try tapping the secondary pulse in one hand while your foot continues with the primary pulse. The interaction between primary and secondary pulse is the first component of musical **meter**. We call the primary pulse the **beat** and the secondary pulse the **beat division**.

Simple and Compound Meters

1.94 🎧
Beats typically divide into two or three parts. In the Joplin and Handel, the beat divides into twos. Now listen to the English folk tune "Greensleeves" on your CD. Tap your foot along with the beat. The "speed" of this beat is called the **tempo.** When you add the beat division in your hand, you'll notice that the beat divides not into twos, but into threes. As you listen to other compositions, practice listening for the beat division into twos or threes.

If you have trouble distinguishing between beat divisions in twos or threes, try walking in time to the music: your feet will show the primary pulse. You might think of the motion for simple-time divisions like marching—down, up; down, up. In contrast, the motion for compound-time divisions might feel like waltzing or skating—stroke, glide, glide; stroke, glide, glide.

KEY CONCEPT _____

Music written in **simple meters** have beats that divide into twos. Music written in **compound meters** have beats that divide into threes.

When we begin learning a new piece, we often count aloud or write counts into our scores. There are many counting systems, and most distinguish between simple and compound meters. You may have learned to count simple meters as "1-and, 2-and," and compound meters as "1-and-a, 2-and-a." Another system uses "1-te, 2-te" for simple and "1-la-li, 2-la-li" for compound. Still another counts "du-de, du-de" and "du-da-di, du-da-di," respectively. (See "Another way" box below for details.) Practice with the counting system that you or your instructor chooses to determine whether pieces you hear are examples of simple or compound meters.

Another Way

The following system of rhythmic counting is adapted from the methods of music educator Edwin Gordon. For simple time, read the onset of every beat as "du" and the beat division (or offbeat) as "de" (pronounced "day"). In a meter with a quarter-note beat, for example, a string of eighths would be read: "du-de, du-de, du-de." These syllables stay in these positions, and any other subdivisions are read as "ta." For example, groups of four sixteenths in this meter would be read "du-ta-de-ta, du-ta-de-ta." A chart of common rhythmic patterns is given below, with the rhythm syllables and an alternate counting system for each:

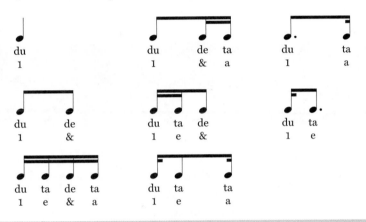

Try it #1

Listen to each of the following musical excerpts on your CD. Which is *not* in a simple meter?

PIECE	CD	METER TYPE
Joplin, "Solace"	CD 2, track 33	_____
Sousa, "The Stars and Stripes Forever"	CD 3, track 41	_____
Hensel, "Nachtwanderer"	CD 2, track 19	_____
Gershwin, " 'S Wonderful!" (refrain)	CD 1, track 93	_____

○ ○

Metric Organization

The Grouping of Beats

 3.41

Beats are grouped into larger units called **measures**, or **bars**, separated by **bar lines**. Listen to the opening of Sousa's "The Stars and Stripes Forever" while tapping only the primary pulse or beat unit. If we were to march along with the music, we would step left-right, left-right, or in groupings of two beats.

KEY CONCEPT _____

> When beats *group* into units of two, the meter is called **duple** (as in the Sousa march). When beats group into units of three, the meter is **triple**; when they group into units of four, the meter is **quadruple**.

A work's **meter** tells how its beats are divided (simple, compound) and how they are grouped (duple, triple, or quadruple). For example, "The Stars and Stripes Forever" has beats that divide into twos (simple) and group into twos (duple). We call this meter simple duple. "Greensleeves," on the other hand, has beats that divide into threes (compound) and group into twos (duple). We therefore call its meter compound duple. (We will learn more about compound meters in Chapter 5.)

Conducting Patterns

Conductors outline specific patterns for each meter to convey a tempo and interpretation to performers. Look at the conducting patterns for duple, triple, and quadruple meters given in Figure 2.1. These basic patterns are the same whether the piece is in a simple or compound meter, although the conductor may articulate divisions (and perhaps subdivisions) within the basic pattern. Practice these conducting patterns until you feel comfortable using them.

FIGURE 2.1: Conducting patterns

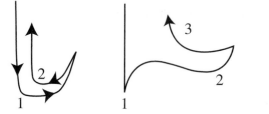
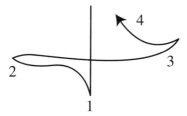

Hearing Meter

Determining the meter of a musical composition by ear is a basic skill that musicians must master. We hear meter by (1) listening for the beat, (2) listening for the beat division (simple or compound), then (3) listening for groupings of the beat (duple, triple, or quadruple). Sing "My Country, 'Tis of Thee" to yourself. Tap the beat with your foot and beat division with your hand to decide whether the piece is in a simple or compound meter. Then try using the conducting patterns from Figure 2.1 to help you determine whether the grouping is duple, triple, or quadruple.

The meter is simple triple. Practice this skill with the works we are studying and with works you hear on other recordings, in rehearsal rooms, and concerts.

Try it #2

Listen to each of these simple-meter compositions on your CD, and decide whether the grouping of beats is duple, triple, or quadruple by conducting along.

PIECE	CD	METER TYPE
Gershwin, " 'S Wonderful!" (refrain)	CD 1, track 93	_____
Bach, "O Haupt voll Blut und Wunden"	CD 1, track 7	_____
Mozart, Piano Sonata in C Major, K. 545, second movement	CD 2, track 69	_____
Joplin, "Pine Apple Rag"	CD 2, track 28	_____
Bach, *Brandenburg Concerto* No. 4, second movement	CD 1, track 3	_____

Metrical Accent

As you practice each conducting pattern, you will feel a certain physical weight associated with the **downbeat**—the motion of the hand down on beat 1 of the pattern. You will probably feel anticipation with the **upbeat**—the upward lift of the hand for the final beat of each pattern. Such hand motions date from the Baroque era.

WF1

The "weight" of the downbeat and the "lift" of the upbeat reflect metrical accent. We sometimes use symbols from poetry analysis to diagram strong and weak metrical beats: / ∪ represents strong-weak.

WF2

KEY CONCEPT

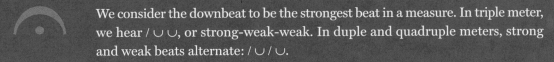

We consider the downbeat to be the strongest beat in a measure. In triple meter, we hear / ∪ ∪, or strong-weak-weak. In duple and quadruple meters, strong and weak beats alternate: / ∪ / ∪.

Meter is considered hierarchical because we can perceive it simultaneously at different levels. In simple time, for example, the relationship between the beginning of a beat and its offbeat ("1-and") is strong-weak. Within a measure, beats may alternate strong-weak. Then, at a higher level, full measures may also alternate strong-weak (see Chapter 16). For this reason, you may sometimes have trouble hearing the difference between duple and quadruple meters by ear; you may hear one measure in quadruple meter as two bars of duple. It is also possible to hear two measures of simple triple meter as one measure of compound duple. Don't worry that you are "wrong"—you are simply identifying the meter at a different level of the hierarchy. Tempo can provide an important clue. If you perceive a very fast beat in three, for example, perhaps you are hearing the beat divisions (in compound meter).

Rhythm and Meter

Rhythm and meter are two different, but related, aspects of musical time. **Rhythm** refers to the durations of pitch and silence (notes and rests) used in a piece. Meter sets up expectations of strong and weak beats against which the rhythms are heard.

SUMMARY

In metric music:

Meter defines
- how musical beats are divided (simple or compound), and
- how beats are grouped (duple, triple, or quadruple).

Rhythm consists of
- durations of pitch and silence (notes and rests) heard in the context of the underlying meter.

In **common-practice** tonal music, roughly 1600 through the early twentieth century, rhythms usually occur within the framework of meter. But **nonmetric pieces**—pieces without meter—are found in non-Western music and in Western music of the twentieth century.

Rhythmic Values in Simple Meters

Each part of a note has a name; these are labeled in Figure 2.2. The round portion is the note head, the straight line is the stem, the wavy line is the flag, and the horizontal line connecting two or more notes is the beam.

FIGURE 2.2: Parts of a note

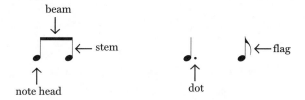

Now look at Figure 2.3 for a chart of common rhythmic values in simple meters. The chart is organized to reflect the beat division in simple time: a whole note divides into two half notes, a half note divides into two quarters, and so on. You can create smaller note values by adding flags or beams to the note stem; in the chart, for example, beams have been added to eighth notes to create sixteenths (a thirty-second note has three flags or beams, and a sixty-fourth note has four).

FIGURE 2.3: Rhythmic values in simple time

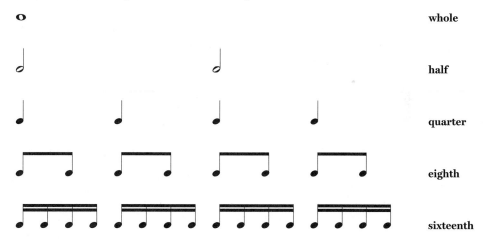

Signatures for Simple Meters

A **meter signature** (or **time signature**) at the beginning of a musical score establishes the meter and beat unit.

KEY CONCEPT

In simple meters:

- The upper number of the signature is 2, 3, or 4 to show that the meter is simple duple, triple, or quadruple; this number also tells us how many beats are in each measure.

- The lower number can be any number that represents the beat unit; generally we find 2 (half note), 4 (quarter note), 8 (eighth note), or 16 (sixteenth note).

For example, in $\frac{2}{4}$ there are two beats per measure, and the quarter note is the beat unit. In $\frac{3}{2}$ there are three beats per measure, and the half note is the beat unit. A signature of $\frac{4}{16}$ shows that the meter is simple quadruple (four beats per measure) and that the sixteenth note is the beat unit.

Try it #3

For each meter signature given below, name its meter type (e.g., simple quadruple) and beat unit.

METER SIGNATURE	METER	BEAT UNIT
$\frac{2}{2}$	_____	_____
$\frac{3}{16}$	_____	_____
$\frac{4}{8}$	_____	_____
$\frac{3}{4}$	_____	_____

Other Metric Symbols

You may see other symbols in scores to represent meter signatures. For example, ℂ, called "common time" (a symbol dating back to the fourteenth century), is frequently used to represent $\frac{4}{4}$, and ¢ (*alla breve*, sometimes called "cut time") can take the place of $\frac{2}{2}$.

In twentieth-century scores, composers and arrangers sometimes substitute a note value for the bottom number of the signature.

SUMMARY

Meter signatures you are most likely to see in simple time include the following:

- Simple duple: $\frac{2}{2}$ ¢ $\frac{2}{4}$ $\frac{2}{8}$

- Simple triple: $\frac{3}{2}$ $\frac{3}{4}$ $\frac{3}{8}$ $\frac{3}{16}$

- Simple quadruple: $\frac{4}{2}$ $\frac{4}{4}$ c $\frac{4}{8}$ $\frac{4}{16}$

○ ○

Rhythmic Notation in Simple Meters

Beat Divisions and Subdivisions

2.10 🎧 Look at the music notation for the Handel aria "Rejoice greatly" in the anthology while listening to the opening section. If you are a singer, you know that the most challenging measures in this piece are the repetitions of the word "Rejoice," with long, drawn-out lines of quick-moving sixteenth notes.

KEY CONCEPT

In simple meters, the beat divides into twos and subdivides into fours.

In this $\frac{4}{4}$ movement, the quarter-note beat divides into two eighths and subdivides into four sixteenths or a combination of eighths and sixteenths. Look at the first page of the aria in the anthology: in this single page of music, Handel uses almost all possible combinations of eighths and sixteenths within the quarter-note beat unit. This variety helps create the driving rhythm and exuberant mood of the passage. Circle as many different ways as you can find that Handel has filled one beat. What other combinations of eighths and sixteenths are possible within one beat, but not seen here? *(Try it #4)*

Less Common Beat Units

The way we count the rhythm in a passage of music depends on its meter. Even the idea that "a whole note gets four beats" is correct only in certain meters—such as $\frac{4}{4}$, where quarter notes get one beat, half notes get two beats, and whole notes get four beats. But in $\frac{4}{2}$, the half note gets just one beat, whole notes get two beats, **3.41** 🎧 and quarter notes get a half beat. Listen again to the opening of Sousa's "The Stars and Stripes Forever" while following the piano reduction in Example 2.1. The ¢ ($\frac{2}{2}$) meter instructs the performers to think of these measures in two (two beats per measure). To develop good sight-reading skills, practice reading rhythms with the less common half-note or eighth-note beat units, as in the Sousa, as well as the more familiar quarter-note unit.

EXAMPLE 2.1: Sousa, "The Stars and Stripes Forever," mm. 1–12 (piano reduction)

Try it #5

One way to practice less common beat units is to begin with a pattern of counts, then write the correct rhythmic notation in meters with differing beat units. For example, take the counting pattern "1-and, 2 (3) | 1, 2, 3 | 1-and, 2-and, 3 | 1 (2 3)"; it is notated below in $\frac{3}{4}$, $\frac{3}{2}$, and $\frac{3}{8}$.

Now look at the counts written below. Write rhythms for which these counts would be correct, in at least two different meters.

(*a*) 1-and, 2-and, 3, 4 | 1-e-and-a, 2-and, 3-and, 4 | 1 (2), 3 (4)
  or du-de, du-de, du, du | du-ta-de-ta, du-de, du-de, du | du (du), du (du).

(*b*) 1-and, 2-e-and-a, 3 | 1, 2, 3-and | 1-e-and-a, 2-and, 3 | 1 (2 3)
  or du-de, du-ta-de-ta, du | du, du, du-de | du-ta-de-ta, du-de, du | du (du du).

There are various reasons why you might see compositions written with one of these less common beat units. Sometimes these meters are used to remind the performer of a particular compositional type or character—such as *alla breve* for marches. Sometimes rhythms are notated with a longer beat unit for ease of reading, so that quick-moving or complex rhythms need not be notated in small note values. In the Sousa, for example, the *alla breve* signature allows the quick-moving pitches to be notated as eighths rather than sixteenths.

Sometimes the reason for a less common beat unit has historical roots. To eigh-
WF4 teenth-century musicians, for example, a beat unit in longer values often indicated a slower tempo and a more stately character; a signature of $\frac{3}{16}$ would indicate a sprightly jig, while $\frac{3}{4}$ would suggest the slower tempo of a minuet.

Rests

Rests represent durations of silence. Each rest lasts just as long as the note value with the same name. Figure 2.4 shows each type of rest with its corresponding note value in simple time. Be careful when you read and write whole and half rests, because they resemble each other. The difference is not in their shape, but in their placement on the staff: the half rest "sits" on top of the third staff line; the whole rest "hangs" from the fourth line. (You might think of the whole rest as "heavier" and thus having to hang from the line, while the "lighter" half rest can sit on top.) A whole rest may represent four quarter-note beats or two half-note beats. A whole rest is sometimes used for a whole measure, regardless of how many beats are in that measure. (In music with a half-note beat unit, you may see a double whole note or rest, which lasts four half-note beats.)

FIGURE 2.4: Note values and rests

𝅜	𝄺	double whole
𝅝	𝄻	whole
𝅗𝅥	𝄼	half
𝅘𝅥	𝄽	quarter
𝅘𝅥𝅮	𝄾	eighth
𝅘𝅥𝅯	𝄿	sixteenth

Dots and Ties

A **dot** adds to a note half its own value, as Figure 2.5 shows. That is, a dotted-quarter note equals a quarter plus an eighth; a dotted eighth equals an eighth plus a sixteenth.

FIGURE 2.5: Use of dots

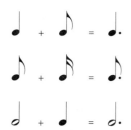

In simple meters, dotted notes are usually grouped with another note to fill out the beat unit: for example, dotted quarter plus eighth, dotted eighth plus sixteenth. Learn these pairings as a unit. **Double dots**, which emerged in the Baroque period (1600–1750), add to a note half its rhythmic value plus a quarter of its value. However, composers did not always write the double dot when they intended it to be played. In performance practice, double-dotted rhythms are often performed in French Overtures even when single dots are notated.

We use a **tie** to add the duration of note values together—for example, two quarter notes tied together equal a half note. (Both quarter notes are the same pitch; the second note is not articulated separately.) Ties can also work like dots: a quarter tied to an eighth equals a dotted quarter. Ties look like small arcs connecting the note heads of two identical pitches.

Arcs that connect two (or more) *different* pitches are **slurs**. Slurs affect performance articulation—bowing or tonguing, for example—but not duration.

Try it #6

Write the counts beneath each note in the melodies below, then perform their rhythms until you can read them fluently. Use parentheses for counts that are not played.

(*a*) Bach, *Brandenburg Concerto* No. 4, second movement, mm. 13–18 (solo violin)

(*b*) Gershwin, "'S Wonderful!" mm. 29–36 (vocal line)

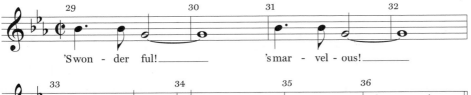

(*c*) Joplin, "Pine Apple Rag," mm. 1–4 (right hand)

Now look at the excerpt from Bach's *Brandenburg Concerto* below while listening. Circle two ties and at least two slurs.   **1.3**

(*d*) Bach, *Brandenburg Concerto* No. 4, second movement, mm. 1–5a (violin and cello)

KEY CONCEPT

Ties and dots should be notated in a way that clarifies the meter rather than obscuring it. For example, an eighth tied to a quarter would be clearer than a dotted quarter in the rhythmic context shown below.

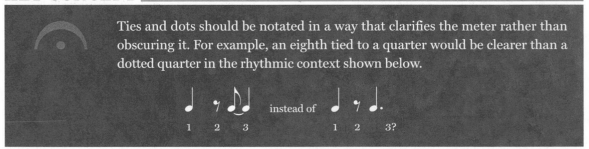

Syncopations

WF5

2.28

Syncopations are rhythmic displacements of expected metrical accents, created by dots, ties, rests, dynamic markings, or accent marks. Syncopations occur in all types of music (a special kind is found in cadences in Baroque-era works), but they are especially common in popular music, jazz, and ragtime. In the excerpt from Joplin's "Pine Apple Rag" shown in Example 2.2, we find syncopations within the beat (m. 1) and across the beat (m. 2). Listen to the piece: such syncopations occur throughout. They are effective because the "stomp bass," or "jump bass," accompaniment in the left hand (heard later in the piece) creates a strong sense of the beat and its division. Syncopations can only be perceived if there is a strong sense of the underlying beat for them to play against.

EXAMPLE 2.2: Joplin, "Pine Apple Rag," mm. 1–4 (syncopations circled)

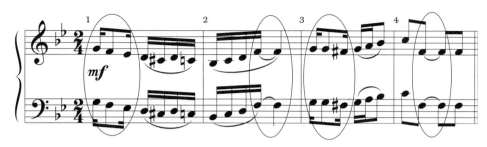

Notation Guidelines

Stems and Flags

When writing music, you may attach a stem to the note head in two possible ways: either on the right side extending upward (somewhat like a letter d) or on the left side extending downward (like a letter p). For single pitches above the middle line of the staff, draw the stems downward; for those below the middle line, draw the stems upward. (Stems for pitches on the middle line may go either way.) This keeps the stems primarily on the staff. Draw the flag on the right-hand side of the stem, regardless of whether the stem goes up or down.

Try it #7

Locate the incorrectly notated stems and flags.   Notate them correctly here.

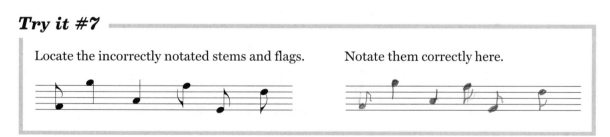

Common Beat-Unit Patterns and Beaming

Your ability to sight-read, remember, and write music will be greatly enhanced by learning all the common rhythmic patterns that can occur within a beat. As a start, learn the patterns in Figure 2.6 for meters with a quarter-note beat unit. Your ability to read beat-unit groupings quickly and accurately will be improved when you notate rhythms correctly.

FIGURE 2.6: Note values in one beat unit

1	&		du	de				
1	e	&	a	du	ta	de	ta	
1	&	a	du		de	ta		
1	e	&	du	ta	de			
1	e	a	du	ta		ta		
1	a	du		ta				
1	e	du	ta					
1	a	du		ta				
1	a	du	ta					

KEY CONCEPT

Rhythmic patterns should be grouped by beaming to reflect the beat unit.

This notational rule generally holds for any meter, although you can certainly find exceptions in printed music. For now, in $\frac{3}{4}$ beam four eighth notes into two groups of two eighths to reflect the quarter-note beat unit. In contrast, in $\frac{3}{2}$ beam all four eighths into a single unit to reflect the half-note beat. The primary exception to the beaming rule occurs in vocal music, where beaming frequently corresponds to syllabic subdivisions in the text (see Chapter 10).

Finally, when beaming pairs of notes together, determine stem direction by the pitch of the second note. For groups of three or more, determine stem direction by the direction of the majority of pitches.

Try it #8

Circle beats that are beamed incorrectly. Then renotate with the correct beaming.

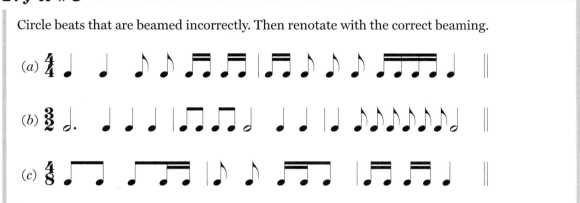

Upbeats

Not all music begins on the downbeat. Some works begin with an upbeat that precedes the first downbeat. The upbeat may also be called an **anacrusis** or **pick-up**. In a simple duple piece, for example, the music might begin on beat 2 of an incomplete measure, in preparation for the stronger downbeat of the first complete measure. Sing or play a verse of Foster's "Oh! Susanna," which is given in Example 2.3. This American popular song begins with an anacrusis of two sixteenth notes.

EXAMPLE 2.3: Foster, "Oh! Susanna," mm. 1–8

In music that begins with an upbeat, we notate the last measure of the piece as an incomplete bar to "balance" the upbeat. We do this by subtracting the value of the upbeat from the last measure of the piece. For example, in $\frac{4}{4}$ a quarter-note upbeat is balanced at the end of the piece by a final measure with only three beats. In Example 2.3, the final pitch in the melody is notated as a dotted-quarter note, to balance the two-sixteenth-note anacrusis.

○ ○

Implications for Performance

Metrical Hierarchy

One of the most important concepts that you may glean from this chapter is that musical structure is hierarchical—that some pitches carry more structural weight than others. When you perform passages with continuous eighth-note motion, remember that not every eighth note is equally important. Carefully studying a work's metric and harmonic organization can help you determine the relative importance of each pitch, and thus shape an effective performance.

Let's return briefly to Handel's setting of the word "Rejoice" in Example 2.4 from this vantage point. The continuous sixteenth-note motion of the syllable "-joice" can be sung with a slight emphasis on the first note of each grouping of four sixteenths (/ ∪ ∪ ∪). If you think of the first and third beats of each measure as metrically stronger than the second and fourth beats, you will create more goal-oriented motion to each measure's downbeat. Handel in fact begins the words "daughter" and "Zion" on strong beats three and one, which helps the singer to stress these words musically.

EXAMPLE 2.4: Handel, "Rejoice greatly," from *Messiah* (vocal part), mm. 12–14

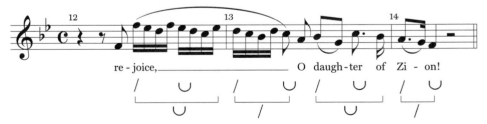

You might find it helpful sometimes to think "one to the bar" to create a large-scale alternation between strong and weak measures at a higher level of the metric hierarchy. This will help contribute to a performance with broad sweep, one that is not bogged down by rhythmic detail. Try comparing several recordings; listen for weak and strong measures. Do the recordings "agree" as to which is weak and which strong?

Tempo Indications

When we perform pieces of music, one way we can convey the character of the work is by selecting the proper tempo. Tempos are customarily notated with markings in Italian or other languages. Slower tempos are indicated by the terms *grave*, *largo*, *larghetto*, and *adagio*; medium tempos by *andantino*, *andante*, *moderato*, and *allegretto*; and faster tempos by *allegro*, *vivace*, *presto*, and *prestissimo*.

TERMS YOU SHOULD KNOW

alla breve	downbeat	meter signature	syncopation
anacrusis	eighth note	note head	tempo
bar line	flag	quarter note	tie
beam	half note	rest	time signature
beat	measure	rhythm	upbeat
common time	meter	simple meter	whole note
compound meter	• duple meter	sixteenth note	
cut time	• quadruple meter	slur	
dot	• triple meter	stem	

QUESTIONS FOR REVIEW

1. What is the difference between (a) simple and compound meters, (b) rhythm and meter, (c) beat division and subdivision, (d) a flag and a beam, (e) a tie and a slur?
2. How does the meter signature reflect metric organization of music in simple meters?
3. For each of the following meter signatures, provide the number of beats per measure and the beat unit: $\frac{3}{2}$, $\frac{4}{8}$, $\frac{2}{4}$. For each of these meters, write three measures of rhythm using correct notation.
4. What are the notation rules for (a) stem direction, (b) beaming beat divisions, (c) upbeats?
5. How are syncopations created? Write two syncopated rhythmic patterns.
6. Find a piece of music from your repertoire in each of the following meters: simple duple, simple triple, simple quadruple. Choose at least one with a less common beat unit, and practice chanting its rhythm while conducting the meter.
7. Choose a phrase from your repertoire. Try to perform the phrase with equal stress on each beat, then mark the strong and weak beats and perform again.

CHAPTER 3

Pitch Collections, Scales, and Major Keys

Outline of topics covered

Chromatic and diatonic collections

Scales
- Ordered collections
- Scale degrees

Major keys and major scales
- Whole-step and half-step pattern
- Spelling pitches within scales
- Accidentals and key signatures
- The circle of fifths
- Identifying a key from a key signature
- Writing key signatures
- Scale-degree names

The major pentatonic scale

Implications for performance

Overview

The concept of key is fundamental to Western tonal music. In this chapter, we will learn about keys by building and playing major scales. We will memorize the major key signatures and scale-degree names as foundations for our future study of harmony.

Repertoire

Johann Sebastian Bach, Invention in C Major

Stephen Foster, "Camptown Races"

Alan Menken and Tim Rice, "A Whole New World," from *Aladdin*

"Michael Finnigin" (folk tune)

Wolfgang Amadeus Mozart, Piano Sonata in C Major, K. 545, first movement (CD 2, track 57)

John Philip Sousa, "The Stars and Stripes Forever" (CD 3, track 41)

Richard Sherman and Robert Sherman, "Feed the Birds," from *Mary Poppins*

Anton Webern, Variations for Piano, Op. 27, second movement (CD 3, track 62)

Chromatic and Diatonic Collections

2.57 🎧
3.62 🎧

We begin by listening to the opening of two piano compositions, written about 150 years apart: Mozart's Piano Sonata in C Major, K. 545, first movement (Example 3.1), and Webern's Variations for Piano, Op. 27, second movement (Example 3.2). Below the examples, write out the letter names of the pitch classes in each excerpt. Write each letter name you find just once, without duplications. When you have finished, you will have written a pitch-class **collection** for each excerpt—that is, a group of pitch classes with no ordering or duplications.

EXAMPLE 3.1: Mozart, Piano Sonata in C Major, K. 545, first movement, mm. 1–4

EXAMPLE 3.2: Webern, Variations for Piano, Op. 27, second movement, mm. 1–11

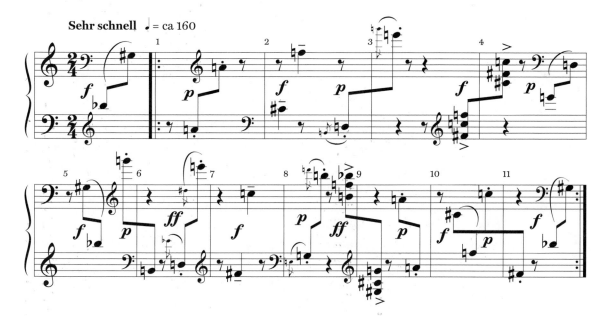

Webern includes all twelve pitch classes—what we call the complete **chromatic** collection. Mozart uses only seven: the **diatonic** collection C D E F G A B.

Since the seven-note diatonic collection is included in the chromatic collection, the diatonic collection is a **subset** of the chromatic (see Chapter 30). Because collections are unordered, you could have listed C E G B D F A or any other order for the diatonic collection. Compare this collection with the one used by Sherman and Sherman in "Feed the Birds." Write the pitch-class collection beneath Example 3.3. Does it differ from Mozart's? *(Try it #1)*

EXAMPLE 3.3: Sherman and Sherman, "Feed the Birds," mm. 1–4

Colorful Roots

Where does the word "diatonic" come from? This and many other music terms derive from the music theory of the ancient Greeks (although the modern meaning of some terms often differs from the original). Looking to the Greek roots of these words can help you remember what they mean. "Diatonic" begins with the prefix *dia -*, meaning "through" or "across" (like "diagonal"); if you think "across" the piano's white keys, you've got a diatonic collection. "Tonic" comes from the same root as "tone." The word "chromatic" comes from the Greek *chroma*, meaning "color"; chromatic collections include all twelve possible pitch-class colors.

○ ○

Scales

Ordered Collections

Listen again to the Mozart sonata and compare it with "Feed the Birds." Can you sing any one pitch that seems to be more stable than the rest in these examples? In both excerpts, the pitch C provides a grounding for a special type of collection called a scale. **Scales** differ from collections in that scales are ordered. When you play or sing a scale, there is a beginning pitch and an order to the remaining notes that corresponds to the musical alphabet—in this case, C D E F G A B C.

When the chromatic collection is ordered, it becomes the chromatic scale. We often see portions of chromatic scales in showy music as a decorative or virtuosic element. Listen to the Trio section of "The Stars and Stripes Forever" while following the score in Example 3.4. Try to find the chromatic scale segments (look for lots of accidentals). Where are they, and how many consecutive pitches of the chromatic scale does Sousa include? *(Try it #2)*

3.45 🎧

EXAMPLE 3.4: Sousa, "The Stars and Stripes Forever," mm. 77–84a (melody)

We write the chromatic scale, as in Example 3.5a, with adjacent pitches equally spaced a half step apart. That means the chromatic scale is **symmetrical**. A symmetrical scale divides the entire octave into a pattern of whole (W) and/or half (H) steps that is the same from start to middle as from middle to end. In contrast, the pattern of whole and half steps marked in Example 3.5b is **asymmetrical**: W-W-H-W-W-W-H.

WF1

EXAMPLE 3.5: Symmetrical and asymmetrical scales

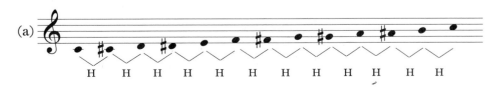

(a)   H   H   H   H   H   H   H   H   H   H   H   H

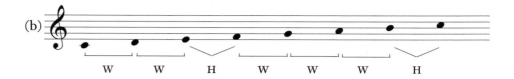

Scale Degrees

WF2

The word "scale" comes from the Latin *scalae* (or the Italian *scala*), meaning "stairs" or "ladder." We call each pitch of the scale a **scale degree** or **scale step**, in keeping with the stairs image. When you write or play a scale, its beginning tone—called the **tonic**—is usually repeated one octave higher at the end. The tonic scale degree is very important both aurally and structurally in scales and musical passages. The other scale steps vary in structural weight, depending in part on the musical context. Compare, for example, the melodies of the Mozart sonata in Example 3.1 and "Feed the Birds" in Example 3.3. Do you see any similarities? *(Try it #3)*

As you begin to analyze music, it is helpful to refer to specific scale degrees by number or name. Scale-degree numbers are customarily written with a caret above: $\hat{1}, \hat{2}, \hat{3}, \hat{4}$, and so on. Some sight-singing methods encourage singing on scale-degree numbers. Another method, **movable-do solfège**, or **solfège** for short, gives each scale degree a syllable—*do, re, mi, fa, sol, la, ti, do*—as shown in Example 3.6a. Example 3.6b gives scale-degree numbers and solfège syllables for the beginning of "Twinkle, Twinkle, Little Star."

EXAMPLE 3.6: Solfège syllables and scale-degree numbers

(a) Scale beginning on C

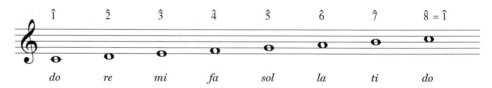

(b) "Twinkle, Twinkle, Little Star" (first part)

Try it #4

For practice with scale-degree relationships, take some familiar children's songs or popular tunes and try to sing them on scale-degree numbers or solfège "by ear." Some possibilities include "Frère Jacques" ("Are You Sleeping?"), "Pop Goes the Weasel," "Clementine," and "My Country, 'Tis of Thee." More challenging are "Hickory, Dickory Dock," "Happy Birthday to You," and "Over the Rainbow." (Answers to "Frère Jacques" and "Happy Birthday" are given in Appendix 1.)

Major Keys and Major Scales

Whole-Step and Half-Step Pattern

WF3

You are probably familiar with **major scales** from playing and singing them as technical warm-ups. All major scales share the same pattern of whole and half steps between adjacent notes: W-W-H-W-W-W-H. One way to remember this is to divide the scale into two four-note groups (or **tetrachords**; *tetra* means "four"), which are a whole step apart. Each tetrachord, called a **major tetrachord**, consists of the pattern W-W-H. Try playing major tetrachords, beginning on various pitches, on a keyboard or other instrument to get this sound into your ears. You can build a major scale on any pitch following the W-W-H-W-W-W-H pattern, as shown in Example 3.7.

KEY CONCEPT

To write an ascending major scale from any given pitch:

1. Write the given pitch on the staff.
2. Write "bare" pitches (with no accidentals) on every line and space from the given pitch, up to and including that same pitch class an octave higher.
3. Label the space *between* each pair of consecutive pitches, from bottom to top, W-W-H-W-W-W-H.
4. Evaluate each pair of pitches, adding the appropriate accidental (♯ or ♭) needed to make it match its whole- or half-step label.

As a short cut, you can replace step 3 with just an angle bracket to show where each half step falls. You may also build the major scale by playing a major tetrachord followed by another major tetrachord one whole step above it.

EXAMPLE 3.7: Steps in constructing a major scale (D Major)

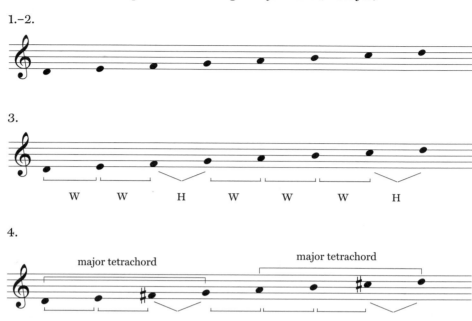

Any major scale you write should have eight pitches—all seven letters of the alphabet plus the repeated tonic pitch class—and the accidentals should be either all sharps or all flats, not a mixture of sharps and flats. Make sure you do not change the first note from the pitch given. If your scale doesn't conform to these guidelines, go back and check your work. Another way to practice major scales is at the piano. Choose random pitches on which to begin, then use the pattern of whole and half steps (and your ear) to play a complete scale.

Spelling Pitches Within Scales

The "spelling" of a scale refers to the enharmonic letter names you give to pitches in that scale. In B♭ Major, for example, it would be incorrect to write D♯ instead of E♭, as Example 3.8a demonstrates. Why? Because this spelling does not include all seven letter names.

In chromatic scales, we do use some letter names more than once. When we write chromatic scales, we normally use sharps when ascending and flats when descending, as shown in Example 3.8b. Intervals like D–D♯ are called **chromatic half steps**; they take the same letter name plus a chromatic alteration. Intervals like D–E♭ are called **diatonic half steps**; they take different letter names and are adjacent pitches in the diatonic scale.

EXAMPLE 3.8:

(a) Notation of the B♭-Major scale

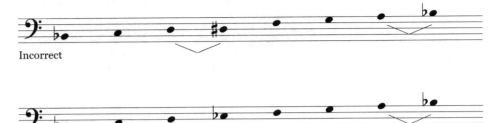

(b) Notation of the chromatic scale

In practical terms, seeing the correct spelling helps you sight-read better. Once you are used to the look and feel of a particular key, you will find unusual spellings distracting and confusing. If you spell any musical structure incorrectly—even if your spelling "sounds" the same—you change the musical meaning. Eventually your training in correct spelling will pay off, in both sight-reading and composition skills, and it will help others perform your music with fewer errors.

Accidentals and Key Signatures

In writing scales so far, we have placed an accidental next to any note that needed it. In musical scores, however, this type of notation is not standard practice for tonal music. Look at the beginning of Menken and Rice's "A Whole New World," given in Example 3.9. You may want to find a recording or perform this excerpt with classmates.

EXAMPLE 3.9: Menken and Rice, "A Whole New World," mm. 1–6

I   can show— you the   world,

This work is in D Major, whose scale has two sharps, yet not a single accidental is notated next to any pitch in the example. Instead, the **key signature** instructs the players to sharp every F and C.

KEY CONCEPT

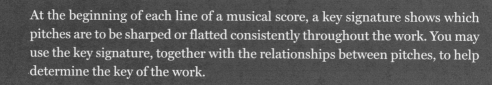

At the beginning of each line of a musical score, a key signature shows which pitches are to be sharped or flatted consistently throughout the work. You may use the key signature, together with the relationships between pitches, to help determine the key of the work.

When we say a piece of music is "in" a key, we mean that its pitches are drawn primarily from a single scale, and that the pitches of the scale have predictable relationships of stability and instability in that piece. For example, the first note of the scale is generally the most stable.

Figure 3.1 gives all the major key signatures. You should memorize them, since many music-theoretical skills we will learn in future chapters build on this knowledge.

FIGURE 3.1: Major key signatures

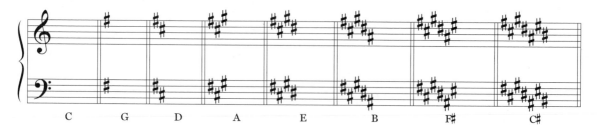

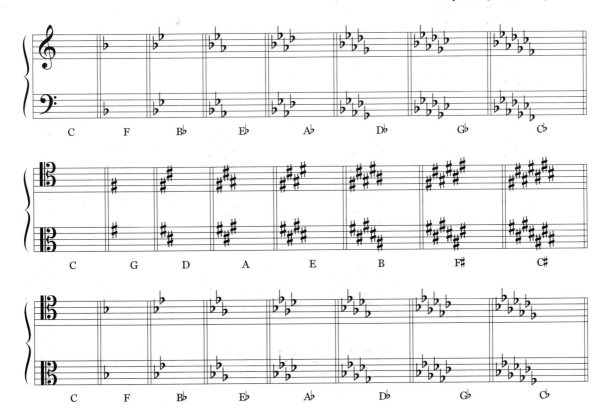

Look again at the score to "The Stars and Stripes Forever" —this time in the anthology—and identify the key using the chart in Figure 3.1. Look through the movement. Does the key change anywhere in the piece? If so, to what key does it change? *(Try it #5)*

The Circle of Fifths

You may have noticed in Figure 3.1 that as a new sharp is added, each key is five steps higher than the last; and as a new flat is added, each key is five steps lower than the last. That is, C Major has no sharps or flats, G Major (five steps higher) has one sharp, D Major (five higher than G) has two sharps, and so on. This relationship between keys is sometimes represented around a circle, like the one in Figure 3.2, called the **circle of fifths**. The keys that require sharps appear around the right side of the circle, with each key a fifth higher. The keys that require flats appear around the left side of the circle, with each key a fifth lower. You may find the circle of fifths a helpful aid as you learn the key signatures. In fact, students have used the circle of fifths to learn about musical structure since the eighteenth century.

WF4

FIGURE 3.2: Circle of fifths

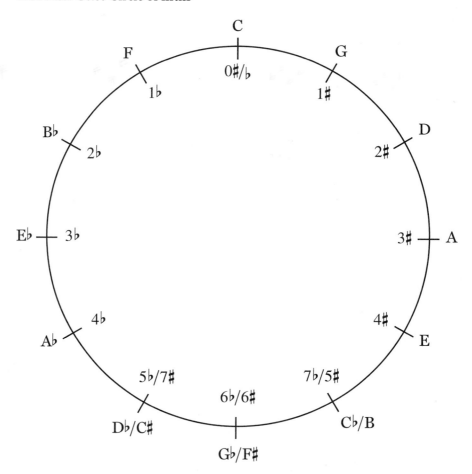

Identifying a Key from a Key Signature

Although you should memorize which key goes with which signature, you can also calculate the name of the key from looking at the signature.

KEY CONCEPT _____

For sharp keys, imagine that the last sharp of the signature is *ti* (or scale-degree $\hat{7}$) of the key. To find the tonic, just go up a half step.

For example, look at the key signature with four sharps (F♯, C♯, G♯, D♯): if D♯ represents *ti* (or $\hat{7}$), then E must be *do* (or $\hat{1}$), and the key is E Major.

KEY CONCEPT

For flat keys, consider the last flat of the signature to be *fa* (or $\hat{4}$) of the key. Shortcut: Since the flats are spaced a fourth apart (the same number of steps as *do* up to *fa*), the next-to-last flat of the signature will always represent the name of the key.

For example, given the key signature with three flats (B♭, E♭, A♭), E♭, the next-to-last flat, is the name of the key. The shortcut always works for flat keys except in the case of F Major's one flat, B♭ (because there is no next-to-last flat in the signature).

Writing Key Signatures

As you begin to compose music or take music dictation, you will need to write key signatures. The key signature is placed between the clef sign and meter signature.

KEY CONCEPT

The sharps and flats are an ordered collection of accidentals; learn to write them in the correct order and octave. The order of the sharps on the staff is F–C–G–D–A–E–B; the order of the flats is the same, only backward: B–E–A–D–G–C–F.

The placement of sharps on the staff alternates directions "down-up," with one exception. Because accidentals are not notated on ledger lines, the sharp on A (which would fall on a ledger line in the treble clef) is written in the lower octave, so there are two "downs" in a row. The flats alternate "up-down" without exception.

Another Way

Most people use mnemonic (or memory) devices to help them learn music fundamentals. One way to remember the order of symbols at the beginning of the staff is that they occur in alphabetical order: clef, key, meter. A common mnemonic to remember the first four flats is that they spell the word "bead." One handy sentence to remember for the order of sharps and flats is "Father Charles Goes Down And Ends Battle." When you read it forward, the first letter of each word gives you the order of sharps; when you read it backward ("Battle Ends And Down Goes Charles's Father"), it gives you the order of flats.

Try it #6

Practice writing key signatures for the major keys specified below, in both the treble and bass clefs.

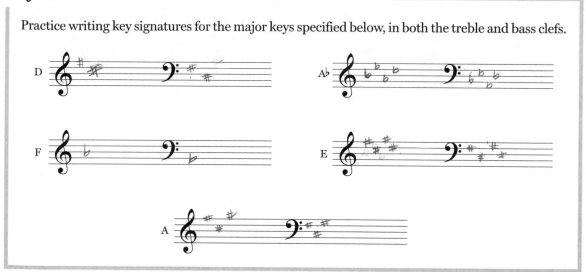

Scale-Degree Names

In addition to numbers, scale-degrees also have names. These names commonly indicate the harmony built on each scale degree, and we will use them extensively when we begin our study of chords. It is helpful to remember a meaning for each label. We call scale-degree $\hat{1}$ **tonic**, since it is the "tone" upon which the scale is built. Scale-degree $\hat{5}$ is the **dominant**, since its musical function "dominates" tonal music, as we will see in future chapters. Scale-degree $\hat{2}$ is called **supertonic** because the prefix *super-* means "above" (as in "superhuman" or "superior"). This label shows the relationship of $\hat{2}$ above $\hat{1}$.

Scale-degree $\hat{3}$ is called the **mediant**, since it falls in the "medial" position midway between $\hat{1}$ and $\hat{5}$. Scale-degree $\hat{4}$ is the **subdominant**; the prefix *sub-* means "below" (as in "submarine" or "subordinate"). This label originates from the idea that scale-degree $\hat{4}$ lies the same distance *below* tonic as the dominant lies *above* tonic. Similarly, the **submediant**, scale-degree $\hat{6}$, falls a third *below* tonic (as the mediant falls a third above). Finally, the **leading tone**, or seventh degree of the scale, gets its name from its tendency to "lead" upward toward resolution on the tonic pitch. In fact, $\hat{7}$ is sometimes called a "tendency tone" because of its strong pull toward tonic.

SUMMARY

Following are the scale-degree names in major keys.

$\hat{1}$—tonic $\hat{5}$—dominant

$\hat{2}$—supertonic $\hat{6}$—submediant

$\hat{3}$—mediant $\hat{7}$—leading tone

$\hat{4}$—subdominant

Try it #7

Given the scale and scale degree, supply the correct letter name. (Remember that incorrect spellings are incorrect answers!) You may do this exercise in your head or at an instrument, by playing (or singing) the full scale.

SCALE	SCALE DEGREE	LETTER NAME
F Major	$\hat{4}$	B♭
G Major	leading tone	F♯
A♭ Major	$\hat{5}$	F
E Major	mediant	A
B Major	supertonic	D♭
D♭ Major	$\hat{6}$	B♭

○ ○

The Major Pentatonic Scale

Sing Example 3.10, Foster's "Camptown Races," on solfège or scale-degree numbers. Although this melody sounds major, it includes only a subset of the major scale: *do, re, mi, sol, la* (scale-degrees $\hat{1}$, $\hat{2}$, $\hat{3}$, $\hat{5}$, and $\hat{6}$). It is missing *fa* and *ti* ($\hat{4}$ and $\hat{7}$). Because this collection includes only five of the seven diatonic pitches, we call it a **pentatonic** collection (*penta* means "five"; a pentagon, for example, has five sides). There are a number of pentatonic collections found in folk and popular music, world music, rock, and jazz. We call the type used in "Camptown Races" the **major pentatonic** collection because it begins with the first three degrees of the major scale.

EXAMPLE 3.10: Foster, "Camptown Races," mm. 1–8

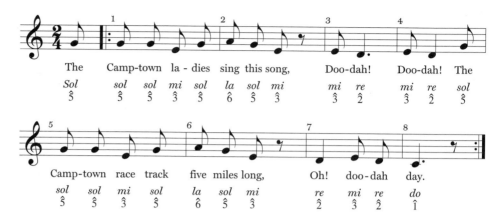

Implications for Performance

What are scales "used" for? For one thing, practicing scales on your instrument helps you gain finger facility in many keys to prepare you for the technical demands of works that include scalewise musical passages. It also helps you to "think" in different keys, which in turn helps with memorization and improvisation in those keys. But music doesn't always use complete scales. Melodies often feature segments of the scale. The scale's first five notes (W–W–H–W) are called the major pentachord (P); scale-degrees $\hat{5}$, $\hat{6}$, $\hat{7}$, and $\hat{8}$ (W–W–H) are called the major tetrachord (T). Melodies may sometimes feature a combination of the major pentachord and major tetrachord: for example, the pentachord beneath the tetrachord (PT) or above it (TP). These two combinations are shown in Examples 3.11 and 3.12. Learning to identify and play segments of the major scale has important musical benefits, including better sight-reading and memorization.

Scales can also be considered an analytical tool: an abstraction from the composition that helps musicians understand the function of pitches and scale degrees within it—especially the tendency tones and their expected resolutions. Eventually you may choose to bring out these particular tones and their resolutions in performance. You should be able to play all the major scales on your instrument in preparation for the work we will do in future chapters; singers should practice playing the scales at the piano to accompany their singing. Work with your performance teachers for correct fingering and technique.

EXAMPLE 3.11: Bach, Invention in C Major, m. 1 (PT model)

EXAMPLE 3.12: "Michael Finnigin" (TP model)

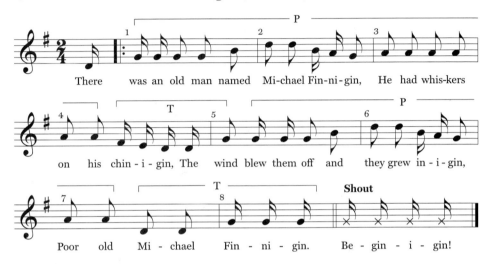

TERMS YOU SHOULD KNOW

chromatic	dominant	mediant	subdominant
chromatic half step	key signature	pentatonic	submediant
circle of fifths	leading tone	scale	supertonic
collection	major pentachord	• major scale	tetrachord
diatonic	major pentatonic	scale degree	tonic
diatonic half step	major tetrachord	solfège	

QUESTIONS FOR REVIEW

1. How do the whole- and half-step patterns differ in the diatonic and chromatic scales?
2. How can we identify the key of a work from its key signature for flat keys? for sharp keys?
3. What notation rules are important for writing the key signatures? What is the order of the sharps? of the flats?
4. Name three systems for identifying scale degrees. Why do we name scale degrees?
5. Find a passage of music for your instrument or voice that includes a portion of a chromatic scale. Do the same for a diatonic scale.

CHAPTER 4

Minor Keys and the Diatonic Modes

Outline of topics covered

Parallel keys
- The "forms" of minor

Relative keys
- Relative minor: Shared key signatures
- Finding the relative minor
- Finding the relative major
- Identifying the key of a musical passage

Writing minor scales

Scale degrees in minor
- Scale-degree names
- Mixture of major and minor
- Modal scale degrees

Modes of the diatonic collection
- Examples of modes
- The "relative" identification of modes
- The "parallel" identification of modes
- Spelling modal scales

The minor pentatonic scale

Twentieth-century modal practice

Overview

In this chapter, we will continue our key and scale study by building and playing scales in minor keys and the six diatonic modes. Then we will apply what we have learned toward identifying keys and modes in musical scores.

Repertoire

Johann Sebastian Bach, *Brandenburg Concerto* No. 4, second movement (CD 1, track 3) and first movement

Bach, Chaconne, from Violin Partita No. 2 in D minor (CD 1, track 23)

"Greensleeves" (folk tune) (CD 1, track 94)

John Lennon and Paul McCartney, "Eleanor Rigby," from *Revolver*

Wolfgang Amadeus Mozart, "Voi, che sapete," from *The Marriage of Figaro* (CD 2, track 82)

"Old Joe Clark" (folk tune)

Franz Schubert, "Der Lindenbaum," from *Winterreise* (CD 3, track 16)

"Wayfaring Stranger" (folk tune)

Parallel Keys — shares the same tonic

3.16

3.19

You know from your own listening and performing that not all music is composed in major keys. If this were the case, the palette of musical colors would be very limited. Listen to the opening of Schubert's song "Der Lindenbaum" (mm. 1–16). Now listen to measures 25–36, where the melody is transformed. How do these passages differ? Examples 4.1a and b show the first measures of the vocal melody from each passage (each is preceded by a piano introduction).

EXAMPLE 4.1: Schubert, "Der Lindenbaum," from *Winterreise*

(a) Mm. 8b–12a   3.17

Translation: By the fountain in front of the gate, there stands a linden tree.

(b) Mm. 28b–32a   3.20

Translation: I had to pass it again today in the dead of night.

do   re   me   fa   sol

The two passages are written in **parallel keys**: E Major and E minor. Each melody is a pentachord. The first is the familiar major pentachord. The second differs from the first by just one pitch: its third scale degree is lowered. We call the pentachord in Example 4.1b the **minor pentachord**. We can also build a minor pentachord from whole and half steps: W-H-W-W. We sing the major pentachord (Example 4.1a) in solfège as *do-re-mi-fa-sol*; we sing the minor pentachord (Example 4.1b) as *do-re-me-fa-sol*.

KEY CONCEPT

- Parallel keys share the same tonic.

- Parallel-key pentachords share four scale degrees ($\hat{1}$, $\hat{2}$, $\hat{4}$, and $\hat{5}$).

- Scale-degree $\hat{3}$ of the minor pentachord is a half step lower than in the major pentachord (the solfège syllable *me* instead of *mi*).

Key signatures for parallel keys differ by three accidentals—for example, B Major has five sharps and B minor two sharps. To find the parallel minor of a major key, move three "steps" counterclockwise around the circle of fifths. Even D Major (two sharps) and D minor (one flat) follow this rule, if you think of the three accidentals as three steps to the left around the circle of fifths. (See Fig. 4.1 on p. 64.)

Try it #1

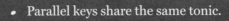

Provide key signatures (give the number of sharps or flats) for these parallel keys.

KEYS	SIGNATURES	
B Major — B minor	5♯	2♯
F Major — F minor	1♭	4♭
C Major — C minor	N	3♭
F♯ Major — F♯ minor	6♯	3♯
A Major — A minor	3♯	N

The "Forms" of Minor

1.25 Example 4.2 gives a passage from Bach's stately Chaconne in D minor. If you can, play the example on your instrument. On the staves below the example, write the scales Bach uses in measures 41 and 45. Now write the pitch classes found in measure 49 and arrange them as a scale. How do these collections differ?

EXAMPLE 4.2: Bach, Chaconne, from Violin Partita No. 2 in D minor, mm. 41–53

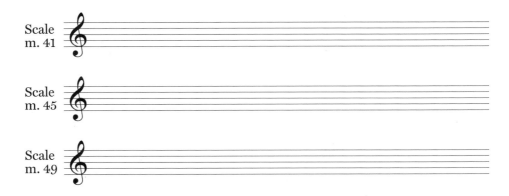

Scale
m. 41

Scale
m. 45

Scale
m. 49

All three collections share the same minor pentachord, but the upper tetra-chords differ. Sing the ascending A–B♮–C♯–D from measure 41 and the descending D–C♮–B♭–A from measure 45. This variability in scale-degrees $\hat{6}$ and $\hat{7}$ is typical in minor-key compositions: in D minor, scale-degree $\hat{6}$ may appear as B♭ or B♮, while scale-degree $\hat{7}$ may appear as C♮ or C♯.

Play all of Example 4.2 again, paying special attention to scale-degrees $\hat{6}$ and $\hat{7}$. Which spelling of these scale degrees is more common as the line ascends? Which is more common as the line descends? In musical contexts, rising lines are usually associated with the raised forms of scale-degrees $\hat{6}$ and $\hat{7}$: B♮–C♯ in Bach's measure 41. These raised pitches follow the tendency of the upward line toward tonic; the A–B♮–C♯–D tetrachord is sung to the same syllables as in the parallel major *sol–la–ti–do*. Falling lines, on the other hand, are usually associated with the low-ered forms of scale-degrees $\hat{6}$ and $\hat{7}$: C♮–B♭ in measure 45. The lowered pitches follow the tendency of the line to descend toward tonic; the descending D–C♮–B♭–A tetrachord is sung with the syllables *do–te–le–sol*.

Because of this variability in the upper tetrachord, some musicians distinguish between different "forms" of the minor scale: melodic, harmonic, and natural minor. We can write any of these minor scales by combining a minor pentachord with one of three different tetrachords. The scales we heard in measures 41 and 45 of the Chaconne illustrate **melodic minor**. This scale differs in its ascending and descending forms, as shown in Example 4.3a. In the ascending form, we hear the minor pentachord followed by the major tetrachord (W-W-H). In its descend-ing form, the major tetrachord is replaced by the **Phrygian tetrachord**. We build Phrygian tetrachords (from low to high) with the pattern H-W-W. A scale with the same pitches as the descending form of melodic minor, both ascending and descending, is **natural minor** (Example 4.3b). We saw an example of this form of minor in measure 49 of the Chaconne.

EXAMPLE 4.3: D-minor scale

(a) Melodic minor

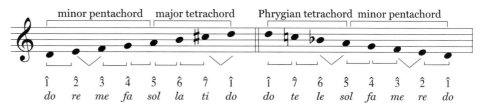

(b) Natural minor

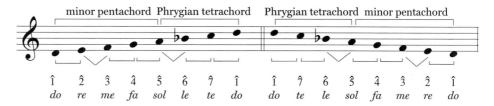

1.24

Now play an earlier passage from the Chaconne, given in Example 4.4. This passage features the half-step relation between D and C♯; scale-degree $\hat{7}$ is raised, but not $\hat{6}$. This form of the scale is sometimes known as **harmonic minor**. It is less commonly found as a "scale" in musical compositions, primarily because the distance between $\hat{6}$ and $\hat{7}$—B♭ to C♯ in Example 4.5—is larger than a whole step. It is an **augmented second** (A2), equivalent to a step and a half (see Chapter 6). We write a harmonic minor scale by combining a minor pentachord with a **harmonic tetrachord** (H-A2-H).

EXAMPLE 4.4: Bach, Chaconne in D minor, mm. 25–29

EXAMPLE 4.5: D-minor scale (harmonic minor)

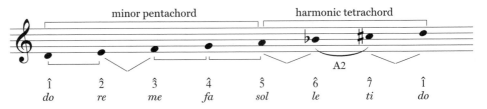

Try it #2

For the key of G minor, write out the minor pentachord.

Then add the major tetrachord above it to make the ascending melodic-minor scale.

Now add the Phrygian tetrachord above the minor pentachord to make the natural-minor form.

Add the harmonic tetrachord above the minor pentachord to make the harmonic-minor form.

Relative Keys

Relative Minor: Shared Key Signatures

1.3 Listen to a portion of the expressive, minor-key second movement of Bach's *Brandenburg Concerto* No. 4 while following the score excerpt given in Example 4.6a. Why is this concerto called *Brandenburg Concerto* No. 4 in G Major when the movement we hear is in minor? To answer this question, compare the key signatures of the first and second movements (Examples 4.6a and b). Both movements have a signature of one sharp—yet the first movement is in G Major and the second is in E minor. These two movements are said to be in **relative keys**: although they have different tonics, they share the same key signature. (A multi-movement work like this one is generally known by the key of its first movement.)

EXAMPLE 4.6: Bach, *Brandenburg Concerto* No. 4

(a) Second movement (E minor), mm. 1–5a

(b) First movement (G Major), mm. 1–7a

Finding the Relative Minor

Look at Example 4.7 to compare the scales for the relative keys G Major and E natural minor. The **relative minor** scale is made from the same pitch-class collection as its **relative major**, but it begins on scale-degree $\hat{6}$ of the major key.

EXAMPLE 4.7: Finding the relative minor

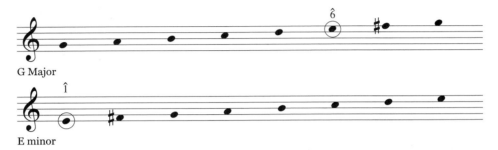

G Major

E minor

To find the relative minor of any major key, identify scale-degree $\hat{6}$ of the major scale: that pitch class is the tonic of the relative minor.

A shortcut for finding the relative minor is to count *down* three half steps from the major-key tonic, but be careful to choose the correct spelling: it should conform to the key signature of the major key and span three different letter names. To find the relative minor of A Major, for example, we know we must span three letter names (A–G–F). Now count half steps: A to G♯, G♯ to G, G to F♯. The answer is F♯ minor. (It would be incorrect to answer G♭ minor, since A Major has no flats and since that answer would span only two letter names: A–G.)

For speed and facility in sight-reading and analysis, you will want to memorize the minor key signatures, just as you have the major ones. The circle of fifths, with the relative keys added in Figure 4.1, may help you.

FIGURE 4.1: Circle of fifths with minor keys added

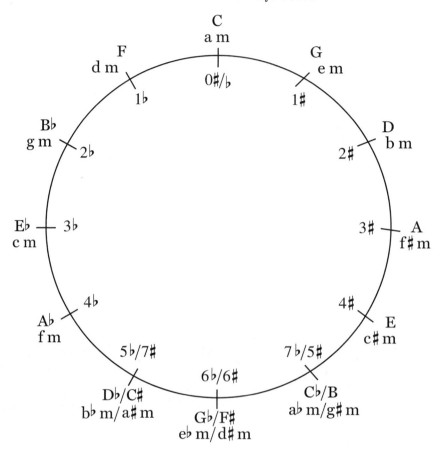

Try it #3

Given the major key or key signature below, supply the name of the relative minor.

KEY OR KEY SIGNATURE	RELATIVE MINOR
E Major	_____
Four flats	_____
D Major	_____
E♭ Major	_____
Five sharps	_____
One flat	_____

Finding the Relative Major

What if we are given a minor key—how do we find the relative major? Look at Example 4.8 to find out.

EXAMPLE 4.8: Finding the relative major

G minor

B♭ Major

KEY CONCEPT _____

> To find the relative major of any minor key, identify scale-degree $\hat{3}$ of the minor scale: that pitch is the tonic of the relative major.

You may also find the relative major by counting up three half steps from the minor-key tonic. When you count up by half steps, choose a spelling for scale-degree $\hat{3}$ that spans three letter names from the minor-key tonic. For example, when finding the relative major of G minor, counting G to G♯, G♯ to A, and A to A♯ produces an *incorrect* answer since it does not span three letter names (G–A–B). The relative-major key is B♭ Major, not A♯.

Try it #4

Given the minor key, supply the name of its relative major. Then at the keyboard or on your own instrument, play each minor-major scale pair, noting that they share the same pitch classes.

MINOR KEY	RELATIVE MAJOR
A minor	_____
G♯ minor	_____
C minor	_____
D minor	_____
C♯ minor	_____
F minor	_____

Identifying the Key of a Musical Passage

Look back at the scores in Examples 4.6a and b. How do we know that the first example is in E minor and the second is in G Major, when both share the same key signature? We interpret clues given to us by the scale degrees of the melodic lines.

KEY CONCEPT

To determine the key of a work:

1. Look at the key signature.

2. Look at the beginning of the melody for motion to and from the tonic ($\hat{1}$).

3. Look at the end of the melody for motion to the tonic.

4. Look for a repeated accidental to raise scale-degree $\hat{7}$ in minor.

Similar clues can be found by looking at the **bass** line—the lowest-sounding part.

In Example 4.6b, the first movement's G-Major key is clearly stated by the opening violin line: G, A, B (scale-degrees $\hat{1}, \hat{2}, \hat{3}$ in G Major). In addition, the bass line (continuo) supports G Major with G, D, G ($\hat{1}$, $\hat{5}$, $\hat{1}$). In contrast, the expressive violin melody of the second movement (Example 4.6a) is supported by a bass line that clearly states E minor with its octave leaps E–E–E–D♯–E ($\hat{1}$–$\hat{1}$–$\hat{1}$–$\hat{7}$–$\hat{1}$ in E minor). The D♯ is another important clue, since D would be natural in G Major. Remember, when you look at a score, always imagine two possible tonics for its key signature: one for major, one for minor. Then look at the melody and bass lines at the beginning and end for clues in the form of scale degrees.

Try it #5

Look at the score for each of the following pieces in the anthology to determine whether the piece is in major or minor. Once you think you have the answer, listen to the works for an aural hint!

EXCERPT	SCORE	CD	KEY
Joplin, "Solace"	p. 131	CD 2, track 33	_____
Purcell, "Music for a While"	p. 183	CD 3, track 5	_____
Handel, Chaconne, Variations 15–16	p. 104	CD 2, track 8	_____
Gershwin, "'S Wonderful!"	p. 94	CD 1, track 91	_____

o o o o o o o o o o o o o o o o o o o o o o o o o o o o o o o o o o o o o o o o o o o o o o o o o o o o o o

Writing Minor Scales

We can write minor scales either by focusing on their pentachord-tetrachord structure or by drawing on our knowledge of key signatures. For the key-signature method, begin by writing note heads on the staff extending from tonic to tonic (for example, B to B), then determine the relative-major key by counting up three half steps from the tonic (being sure to span three letter names as well; B–C, C–C♯, C♯–D). Add that key signature (for D Major: two sharps) to the staff. If needed, add accidentals to your note heads for the proper "form" of the minor scale. (These forms, incidentally, have been taught only during the last century or so; they were unknown in Mozart and Beethoven's time.)

WF1

SUMMARY

- Natural minor
  = minor pentachord + Phrygian tetrachord (H-W-W)
  = same key signature as relative major, no additional accidentals

- Harmonic minor
  = minor pentachord + harmonic tetrachord (H-A2-H)
  = same key signature as relative major, but $\hat{7}$ is raised a half step

- Melodic minor
  Ascending:
  = minor pentachord + major tetrachord (W-W-H)
  = same key signature as relative major, but $\hat{6}$ and $\hat{7}$ are raised a half step
  Descending:
  = same as natural minor

o o o o o o o o o o o o o o o o o o o o o o o o o o o o o o o o o o o o o o o o o o o o o o o o

Scale Degrees in Minor

Scale-Degree Names

The scale-degree names in minor are identical to those in major with only a few exceptions. We call the raised scale-degree $\hat{7}$ in harmonic or melodic minor the **leading tone**. Otherwise we call it the **subtonic**, to show its placement a whole step beneath tonic. (This label is analogous to the supertonic, which lies a whole step above tonic.) When scale-degree $\hat{6}$ is raised in melodic minor, it is simply known as the **raised submediant**.

Mixture of Major and Minor

2.82 🎧
2.85 🎧
WF2

Listen to Mozart's "Voi, che sapete," from *The Marriage of Figaro*, while following the score in the anthology. In the passage reproduced as Example 4.9, Cherubino sings of his desire for, and fear of, women. In what key is he singing? Although the two flats of the key signature would suggest B♭ Major, the E♭ has been consistently canceled with a natural sign to establish a short F-Major passage. So Cherubino begins singing of his excitement in F Major—but what happens in measures 35–36, when the text turns to despair? Mozart alters scale-degrees $\hat{3}$ and $\hat{6}$ from A and D to A♭ and D♭ in the accompaniment, and includes a poignant A♭ in the singer's vocal line. This sudden mixture of the parallel minor with major is a time-honored and effective method by which composers interpret the meaning of a text (see Chapter 12).

EXAMPLE 4.9: Mozart, "Voi, che sapete," from *The Marriage of Figaro*, mm. 29–36

Translation: I have a feeling, full of desire, which is by turns delightful and miserable.

Modal Scale Degrees

As we know, major scales and their relative-minor scales are made of the same pitch classes arranged to begin in two different places. These are only two of several possible starting points for this collection of pitch classes, as we shall see. The different arrangements of a collection of pitch classes are called **modes**. For this reason, we sometimes refer to a piece as being in the "major mode" or "minor mode." Because the major and parallel-minor scales differ only by scale-degrees $\hat{3}$, $\hat{6}$, and $\hat{7}$, we sometimes call these scale degrees the **modal scale degrees**.

o o o o o o o o o o o o o o o o o o o o o o o o o o o o o o o o o o o o o o o o o o o o

Modes of the Diatonic Collection

Examples of Modes

1.94 🎧

Perhaps you know pieces whose underlying scales do not fit neatly into any of the major or minor scale types we have studied thus far. The tune "Greensleeves," given in Example 4.10, is one such melody. Sing or play this melody, or listen to the arrangement for guitar on your CD. It appears to be in A minor, since it begins and ends on the pitch A. Yet its key signature (F♯) suggests a raised scale-degree 6̂. The tune thus uses the same pitch collection as G Major (or E minor), but with a scale that begins and ends on A.

This type of scale is neither major nor minor, but is **modal**—in this case, the mode we call **Dorian**. In the example, the Dorian melody is altered at the end (with an added G♯) to create a tonal cadence. We typically find modal melodies in music of the Renaissance and early Baroque, folk and popular music of many eras, world musics, and some rock and jazz.

EXAMPLE 4.10: "Greensleeves," mm. 1–8 (melody)

As another example, sing through Example 4.11, the tune "Old Joe Clark." This melody sounds major (with D as the tonic) but has a prominent lowered seventh (C♮). This mode, similar to major but with a lowered seventh scale degree, is called **Mixolydian**.

EXAMPLE 4.11: "Old Joe Clark" (melody)

Old Joe Clark, he had a house, fif - teen sto - ries high.

Ev - 'ry sto - ry in that house was filled with chick - en pie.

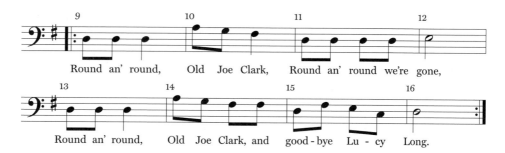

Round an' round,   Old   Joe   Clark,   Round an' round we're gone,

Round an' round,   Old   Joe   Clark, and   good-bye   Lu - cy   Long.

The "Relative" Identification of Modes

WF3 There are six diatonic modes, sometimes called the "church" modes. These modes share the same diatonic collection as the major and natural minor scales, but each mode begins with a different starting pitch of that collection. As you listen to each mode, you will discover that the new arrangement of whole and half steps gives it a distinctive sound. Example 4.12 shows the pitches of the major scale, and the six "rotations" of these pitches so that each diatonic mode begins on a different scale degree. Sing or play each mode.

KEY CONCEPT

The diatonic collection from C to C (with no sharps or flats) may be rotated to begin with any pitch. Each rotation is a diatonic mode.

C to C: Ionian   F to F: Lydian

D to D: Dorian   G to G: Mixolydian

E to E: Phrygian   A to A: Aeolian

(We applied the D-to-D pattern of whole and half steps to conclude that "Greensleeves" is in the Dorian mode, even though its scale begins and ends on A; similarly, the scale used in "Old Joe Clark," with D as the tonic, fits the G-to-G pattern of whole and half steps and is thus Mixolydian.)

EXAMPLE 4.12: Rotations of the C diatonic collection (modes)

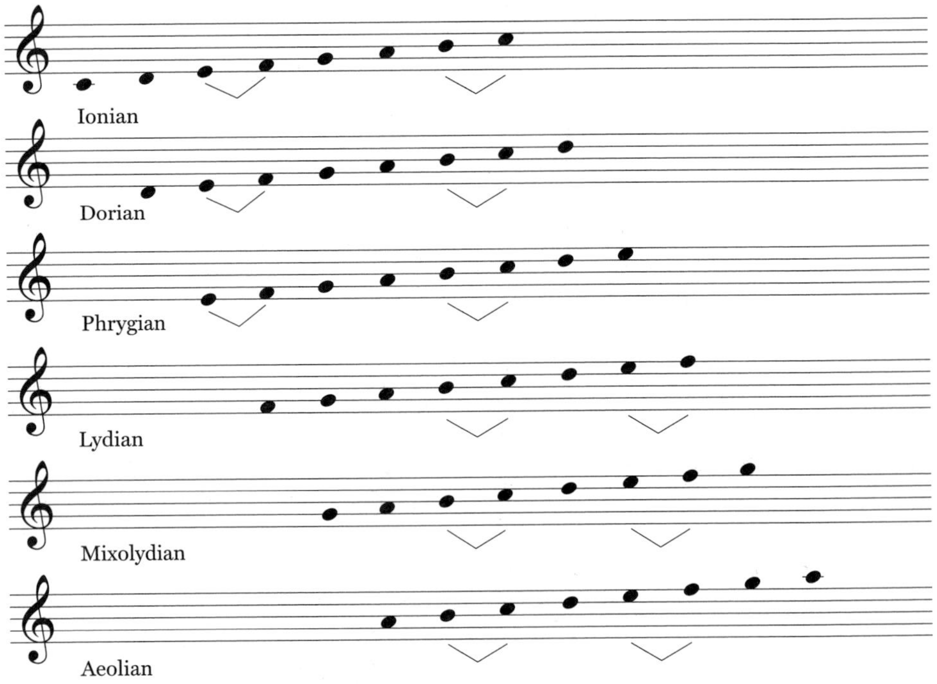

Ionian

Dorian

Phrygian

Lydian

Mixolydian

Aeolian

The "Parallel" Identification of Modes

Because our twentieth-century ears are accustomed to the major and minor scales, we sometimes hear the modes as alterations of these more familiar scales (even though this approach is historically inaccurate). We can group the modes into two families, according to whether their third scale degree comes from the major or minor pentachord. Example 4.13 summarizes this approach.

KEY CONCEPT

Modes that begin with the major pentachord (or with what sounds like the major pentachord):
- Ionian (scale is identical to major)
- Mixolydian (scale has a lowered $\hat{7}$)
- Lydian (scale has a raised $\hat{4}$)

Modes that begin with the minor pentachord (or with what sounds like the minor pentachord):
- Aeolian (scale is identical to natural minor)
- Dorian (scale has a raised $\hat{6}$)
- Phrygian (scale has a lowered $\hat{2}$)

EXAMPLE 4.13: Modes grouped by families on C

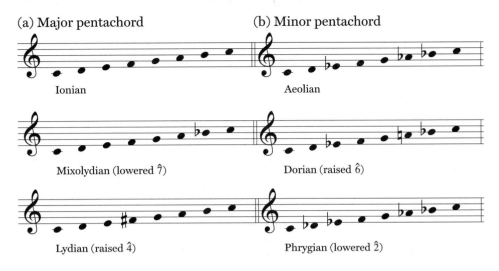

(a) Major pentachord

Ionian

Mixolydian (lowered $\hat{7}$)

Lydian (raised $\hat{4}$)

(b) Minor pentachord

Aeolian

Dorian (raised $\hat{6}$)

Phrygian (lowered $\hat{2}$)

Church Modes

In the seventeenth century, music teachers in France began to teach a variant of the modal system where modes might begin on a different pitch from the norm (for example, Dorian beginning on G instead of D). We call such variants "transpositions," or "transposed modes." The first transpositions introduced B♭ and F♯ as scale tones. These transposed modes were called the "ecclesiastical modes," from which came our modern reference to church modes. (The terms "church" and "ecclesiastical" refer to the association of modes with sacred music, from the Gregorian chant of the medieval era to the modal polyphony of the Renaissance.) The ecclesiastical modes traditionally included eight modes, and several of them were transpositions of Ionian and Dorian.

In the early eighteenth century (during the lifetimes of Johann Sebastian Bach, George Frideric Handel, and Franz Joseph Haydn), writers argued over whether the old modes should be taught or whether they should be replaced by the more modern major and minor scales. Those wishing to retain the modes lamented the possible loss of their beauty and richness; those in favor of major and minor observed that the scales worked better with the functional harmonies of tonal music. You may be surprised to learn that in the early eighteenth century, the model minor scale was not our Aeolian (or natural minor) but Dorian! Manuscripts of music in minor from that time often show one less flat in their key signature than we would expect; the extra flat (for the sixth scale degree) was carefully written in every time that pitch class appeared in the music.

Spelling Modal Scales

There are two methods you can use to spell a mode correctly beginning on any given starting note. One is the "relative" scale method. Say you want to write Dorian beginning on G.

1. Remember that from C major, Dorian is the mode beginning on $\hat{2}$.
2. To write Dorian on G, we ask, "What is tonic, if G is $\hat{2}$?"
3. The answer is F, so we use the key signature of F but begin the scale on G: G–A–B♭–C–D–E–F–G.

You can also use the "parallel" scale method.

1. Remember that Dorian sounds like minor with a raised $\hat{6}$.
2. Take the key signature for G minor (two flats, B♭ and E♭).
3. Raise scale-degree $\hat{6}$ by adding a natural to the E: G–A–B♭–C–D–E♮–F–G.

Try it #6

Spell each of the following modes.

MODE	SPELLING
E Dorian	
B♭ Lydian	
B Aeolian	
A Mixolydian	
F♯ Phrygian	
E♭ Ionian	

○ ○

The Minor Pentatonic Scale

Sing Example 4.14, the folk tune "Wayfaring Stranger," on solfège or scale-degree numbers. Although this melody sounds minor, it features only a subset of the natural minor (or Aeolian) scale. Which scale degrees are missing?

EXAMPLE 4.14: "Wayfaring Stranger" (melody)

The melody includes only *do, me, fa, sol, te* (the minor-key scale degrees $\hat{1}$, $\hat{3}$, $\hat{4}$, $\hat{5}$, and $\hat{7}$); it is missing *re* and *le* ($\hat{2}$ and $\hat{6}$). Because it is made up of only five of the seven diatonic pitches, it is another of the pentatonic collections. We call the type used in "Wayfaring Stranger" the **minor pentatonic** collection because it features the first and third degrees of the minor scale.

○ ○

Twentieth-Century Modal Practice

The diatonic modes were the subject of renewed interest in the twentieth century (after years of neglect in the late eighteenth and nineteenth centuries, outside of folk music), as jazz and popular musicians—as well as "classical" composers—rediscovered their beauty. (See Chapters 30 and 32.) In modern usage, the six diatonic modes can be transposed to begin on any pitch class—even so, the modes are most commonly seen in their white-key versions and transpositions with one flat or one sharp. Musicians of the twentieth century occasionally drew on the **Locrian** mode—the B-to-B scale—as well, making it a seventh diatonic mode.

Just as composers mix major and minor for expressive effect, musical passages can express one mode and then shift to another. For example, consider Lennon and McCartney's "Eleanor Rigby." Its key signature of one sharp and repeated Es in the cello and second violin suggest E minor. Yet in the melody of measures 9–12, reproduced in Example 4.15, we see a C♯ alteration—a raised $\hat{6}$ that temporarily invokes the Dorian mode.

EXAMPLE 4.15: Lennon and McCartney, "Eleanor Rigby," mm. 9–12a

TERMS YOU SHOULD KNOW

Aeolian	melodic minor	parallel minor
Dorian	minor pentachord	Phrygian
harmonic minor	minor pentatonic	Phrygian tetrachord
harmonic pentachord	Mixolydian	raised submediant
Ionian	modal scale degree	relative major
Locrian	mode	relative minor
Lydian	natural minor	subtonic

QUESTIONS FOR REVIEW

1. What similarities do the relative and parallel minors share with major? How do the relative and parallel minors differ from each other?
2. What are the scale-degree differences between the three minor scale types? How do these differences affect the scale-degree names?
3. Given a key signature, how do you know which minor key it represents?
4. Given a minor key, how do you find the relative major?
5. How do the modes differ from major and minor? Describe the relative and parallel methods for identifying modes.
6. Given a pitch and a mode to build upon it, what steps should you follow?
7. Find a piece, in your own repertoire if possible, with two movements related by relative or parallel key.

CHAPTER 5

Beat, Meter, and Rhythm:
Compound Meters

Outline of topics covered

Compound meter
- Compound meters defined
- Meter signatures
    Interpreting meter signatures
- Conducting patterns

Rhythmic notation in compound meters
- Notation of the beat, divisions, and subdivisions
- Notation guidelines
- Upbeats
- Less common beat units
- Syncopations

Mixing simple and compound meters
- Triplets
- Duplets and quadruplets

Metrical accent and implications for performance

Overview

In this chapter, we focus on groupings and divisions of the beat in compound meters. We will learn typical rhythmic patterns in compound meters, how to notate these patterns, and how to perform them.

Repertoire

Johann Sebastian Bach, Gigue, from Violin Partita No. 2 in D minor

Bach, Fugue in E♭ Major for Organ (*St. Anne*)

Johannes Brahms, Trio in E♭ Major for Piano, Violin, and Horn, Op. 40, second movement

Frédéric Chopin, Nocturne in E♭ Major, Op. 9, No. 2

"Down in the Valley" (folk tune, arranged by Norman Lloyd)

"Greensleeves" (folk tune) (CD 1, track 94)

Fanny Mendelssohn Hensel, "Nachtwanderer" (CD 2, track 19)

John Lennon and Paul McCartney, "Norwegian Wood," from *Rubber Soul*

Jerry Livingston, Mack David, and Al Hoffman, "Bibbidi-Bobbidi-Boo," from *Cinderella*

Franz Schubert, "Der Lindenbaum," from *Winterreise* (CD 3, track 16)

Compound Meter

Compound Meters Defined

1.94 🎧
2.19 🎧
WF1

First, listen to the beginning of two contrasting songs: the folk song "Greensleeves" and a German art song by Fanny Mendelssohn Hensel, "Nachtwanderer." Find the primary beat in each, then listen for a quick-paced secondary beat that helps establish each work's musical character.

WF2

Now try conducting along with each song—"in two" for "Greensleeves" and "in three" for "Nachtwanderer"—while tapping the beat division. Can you identify the meter? Recall that when the beat divides into twos, the movement is in a simple meter, and when the beat divides into threes, the work is in a compound meter (terms that may have been unknown to Bach). Both songs are in compound meters. "Greensleeves"'s meter is compound duple, since there are two beats per bar; the Hensel is compound triple, with three beats per bar.

If we were to count along, we could use one of the counting systems introduced in Chapter 2: 1-and-a, 2-and-a; 1-la-li, 2-la-li; or du-da-di, du-da-di. Counting with any of these systems captures the triple division of the beat, and conducting along with the music shows the grouping of beats within the measure. We associate a "lilting" quality with music in compound time. It is often chosen by composers for pastoral or folk-like music, lullabies, and certain types of dances.

Meter Signatures

We learned to read simple-meter signatures in Chapter 2. Now we follow a different set of guidelines to read compound-meter signatures.

KEY CONCEPT _____

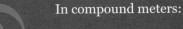

In compound meters:

- The upper number of the meter signature is 6, 9, or 12, representing duple, triple, or quadruple meter, respectively. Divide the top number by three to get the number of beats per measure (two, three, or four).

- The lower number is usually 4, 8, or 16. This number shows the **division** of the beat. Add together three of these note values to get the beat unit, which will always be a dotted note.

The compound meters you are most likely to see are summarized in the table below.

METER	METER SIGNATURE (BEAT UNIT)		
compound duple:	$\frac{6}{4}$ (♩.)	$\frac{6}{8}$ (♩.)	$\frac{6}{16}$ (♪.)
compound triple:	$\frac{9}{4}$ (♩.)	$\frac{9}{8}$ (♩.)	$\frac{9}{16}$ (♪.)
compound quadruple:	$\frac{12}{4}$ (♩.)	$\frac{12}{8}$ (♩.)	$\frac{12}{16}$ (♪.)

Interpreting Meter Signatures   We now practice interpreting compound-meter signatures by looking at (and listening to) several pieces. How does the $\frac{9}{8}$ meter signature of the folk song "Down in the Valley," shown in one possible transcription as Example 5.1, tell us the number of beats per measure and the beat unit? First, divide the top number by three to get three beats per measure. To find out the beat unit, add together three eighth notes—from the 8, the bottom number—to get a dotted quarter. The beat unit in compound meters is always a dotted note.

EXAMPLE 5.1: "Down in the Valley," mm. 1–4a

Follow the same procedure for Lennon and McCartney's "Norwegian Wood" (in $\frac{12}{8}$, Example 5.2) and the middle section of Bach's *St. Anne* Fugue, for organ (in $\frac{6}{4}$, Example 5.3). What are the number of beats per measure and the beat unit for each? *(Try it #1)*

EXAMPLE 5.2: Lennon and McCartney, "Norwegian Wood," mm. 13–14

EXAMPLE 5.3: Bach, Fugue in E♭ Major for Organ (*St. Anne*), mm. 38–40

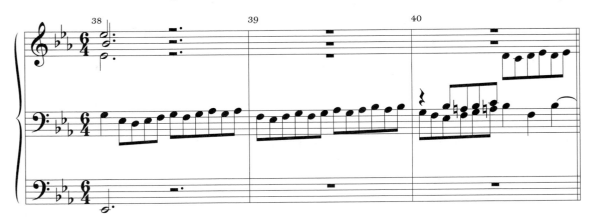

Another Way

Another way to look at compound meters is to think of them as though they are built from combinations of measures in simple meter. For example, we could see $\frac{6}{8}$ as a "compound," or combination, of two measures of $\frac{3}{8}$—hence the term "compound meter." When we look at compound meters this way, we need to remember to shift the level of the beat unit from the eighth note of $\frac{3}{8}$ to the dotted quarter of $\frac{6}{8}$.

Conducting Patterns

Conducting patterns remain the same for compound meters as they are for simple. That is, duple meters are conducted in two, triple meters in three, and quadruple in four. Only in very slow tempi would the conducting pattern correspond with the upper number of the meter signature (for example, $\frac{9}{8}$ conducted "in nine"). In that case, the conducting pattern is considered a "subdivided" pattern.

Rhythmic Notation in Compound Meters

Notation of the Beat, Divisions, and Subdivisions

In compound meters, the beat divides into threes and subdivides into sixes. (When counting subdivisions, we add the syllable "ta" between each syllable of the beat division; for example, "1-la-li" becomes "1-ta-la-ta-li-ta," and "du-da-di" becomes "du-ta-da-ta-di-ta.") We already have a good idea of the "look" of compound meters with dotted-quarter beat units from the "Down in the Valley" and "Norwegian Wood" examples. Take a moment to circle each of the different ways these composers have filled one dotted-quarter beat unit in these examples, in both the vocal and instrumental parts. *(Try it #2)*

As in simple meters, you can use the beaming of rhythmic units as a guideline to find the beat unit, except in a vocal line. What other combinations of eighths and sixteenths are possible within one beat but not seen in these scores? *(Try it #3)*

Notation Guidelines

As mentioned in Chapter 2, your ability to sight-read, remember, and write rhythms is greatly enhanced by learning the possible combinations of notes that can occur within a beat. Figure 5.1 gives a chart of the most common patterns for a dotted-quarter beat unit. The beaming helps identify the beat unit.

KEY CONCEPT

Correct notation reinforces the beat unit. Notes should be beamed to reflect the beat. Rests should also be notated to clearly reflect the beat units.

This beaming rule holds true in the accompaniment to "Down in the Valley" (Example 5.1), but not in the vocal line, where flags replace beams when a word's syllable changes. Most of the eighths in the vocal line are notated with flags because the syllable changes on each pitch.

FIGURE 5.1: Common beat units in compound meters

Upbeats

Example 5.4 shows the first and last measures of the Gigue from Bach's Violin Partita No. 2 in D minor. Play through these measures on a piano or on your own instrument. We learned in Chapter 2 that when pieces begin with an anacrusis (sometimes called an upbeat or pick up), the notation of the final measure reflects this fact. This is true in compound meters as well. The final measure of this movement is missing an eighth note's duration to make up for the eighth-note anacrusis.

EXAMPLE 5.4: Bach, Gigue, from Violin Partita No. 2 in D minor

(a) Mm. 1–2

(b) Mm. 39–40

Less Common Beat Units

Although we use beaming to show the beat unit, this is harder when the bottom number of the meter signature is a 4. Why? Look at Example 5.5, drawn from Bach's *St. Anne* Fugue. Here, the compound duple meter is $^6_4$, with a beat division of three quarter notes (see, for example, the right hand of m. 81). Beaming the three quarters together to reflect the beat would turn them into eighths—it cannot be done without altering their duration. In this example, only the beaming of the eighth notes into groups of sixes shows the dotted-half beat unit clearly.

You may find that compound meters with dotted-half beat units are more difficult to sight-read. It is up to you, the performer, to group the rhythms correctly in your mind to reflect the proper accentuation of the meter. In Example 5.5, circle all the different ways Bach has filled one beat unit in measures 77–80 (ignore any ties). When you are finished, make sure you can perform each rhythmic pattern accurately. *(Try it #4)*

EXAMPLE 5.5: Bach, *St. Anne* Fugue, mm. 77–82a

Syncopations

As in simple meters, ties can create offbeat accents, or syncopations, within the beat. Typical syncopations in compound meters are shown in Figure 5.2, using a dotted-quarter beat unit. As the figure shows, ties are commonly renotated so that an eighth note substitutes for two sixteenths tied together, in order to create syncopations within the beat. Syncopation may also be created by placing an accent mark on a weak beat or the weak part of the beat, by placing ties across two beats, or by placing a rest on the strong part of a beat.

FIGURE 5.2: Typical syncopations in compound time

du ta   ta di   du da ta   ta   du ta   ta   ta

WF3 A special type of syncopation, called a **hemiola**, occurs in compound meters when the accent structure of a measure is displaced so that the "normal" three-part beat division is temporarily regrouped into twos. As the passage from the *St. Anne* Fugue in Example 5.6 shows, this regrouping creates a temporary simple-triple meter (three half notes, in this case) imposed upon the normal compound duple.

EXAMPLE 5.6: Bach, *St. Anne* Fugue, mm. 58–59 (with hemiola)

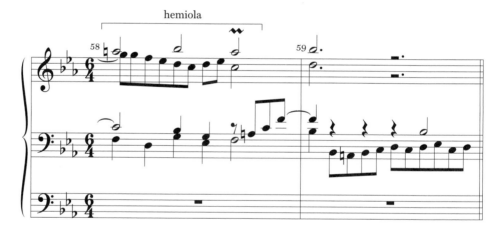

Mixing Simple and Compound Meters

Triplets

3.17 You can mix duple and triple beat divisions in one composition. One way is to "borrow" a beat unit from a compound meter in a simple-meter piece. These borrowed units are called **triplets.** Listen to the excerpt from Schubert's song "Der Lindenbaum" given in Example 5.7a. In Chapter 4, we studied Schubert's shifts between the major and minor modes in this song to see how he interpreted the mood of the poem. The melody in Example 5.7a moves primarily in quarter and eighth notes, except for the last beats of measures 11 and 15, where the quarter-note beat duration is divided into three instead of two (indicated with a small 3 above the grouping). We notate the group with eighth notes because they take the place of one quarter-note beat (the eighth is one duration unit "smaller" than the quarter). We can simply borrow our counting from compound time to account for the triplet. Measure 11 is counted "1, (2)-and, 3-and-a" or "du, (du)-de, du-da-di." (The numbers or syllables in parentheses account for the dotted-quarter note.)

EXAMPLE 5.7: Schubert, "Der Lindenbaum," from *Winterreise*

(a) Mm. 8b–16a

Translation: By the fountain in front of the gate, there stands a linden tree.

3.20 Now compare Example 5.7a with 5.7b, the second verse of the song. How has Schubert developed the triplet idea? He has changed the piano accompaniment to feature the triplet on the first beat of each measure. The triplet in the piano part is beamed correctly to reflect the quarter-note beat unit, but in the vocal line (m. 31), the beaming reflects the placement of the syllables of text: the first two pitches of the triplet are beamed for the syllable "tie-," and the final eighth receives a flag (not beamed to the triplet group) for the syllable "-fer."

(b) Mm. 28b–32a

Translation: I had to pass it again today in the dead of night.

3.16 Listen now to the piano introduction to this song, given in Example 5.7c. Here, we hear sixteenth-note triplets—each triplet divides the eighth-note beat division into thirds. In measure 5, you can see and hear how the sixteenth-note triplets in the right hand align with the eighth notes in the left. We notate these triplets as sixteenths because they divide the eighth-note duration into threes (the sixteenth is one duration unit "smaller" than the eighth). These sixteenth-note triplets create a wonderful effect, depicting the rustle of the tree's leaves.

(c) Mm. 1–7 (piano introduction)

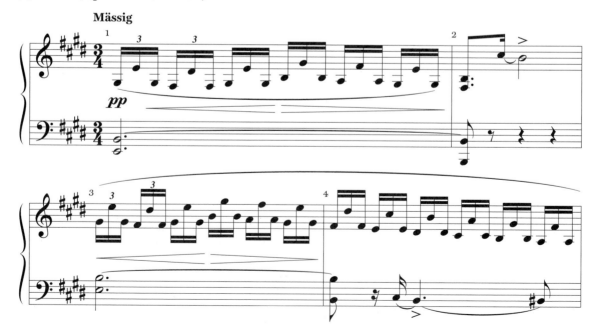

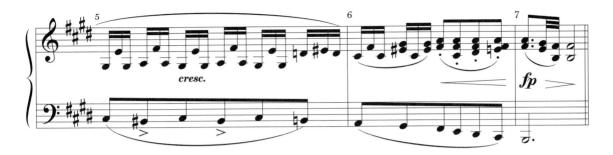

For a final example of triplet notation, look at Example 5.8 and sing the vocal line. In this song, Livingston, David, and Hoffman's "Bibbidi-Bobbidi-Boo," the triplets are so pervasive that the song sounds like compound quadruple. This type of notation is common in popular-music scores. In some performances, the dotted-eighth-plus-sixteenth units may be performed with a triplet feel, as quarter notes followed by an eighth.

EXAMPLE 5.8: Livingston, David, and Hoffman, "Bibbidi-Bobbidi-Boo," mm. 3–6a

Duplets and Quadruplets

In compound meters, we can also borrow beat units from simple meters. These borrowings are called **duplets** or **quadruplets**. With triplets, duplets and quadruplets are sometimes referred to collectively as "tuplets." Other types of tuplets are possible as well, such as quintuplets (groups of five), sextuplets (groups of six), and septuplets (groups of seven).

Look at the beginning of the second movement of Brahms's Trio in E♭ Major for Piano, Violin, and Horn, given in Example 5.9. The movement begins with quarter-note motion in a quick $\frac{3}{4}$. Given its tempo, you would probably count "one to the bar," with groupings into two-bar units—"1-and-a, 2-and-a"—as though the movement were in a compound meter like $\frac{6}{4}$. But in measures 14–16, the groupings into threes are replaced by groupings of two, marked with a bracket and a 2 to show the duplet. At measure 14, you would switch from "1-and-a, 2-and-a" to "1-and, 2-and."

EXAMPLE 5.9: Brahms, Trio in E♭ Major for Piano, Violin, and Horn, Op. 40, second movement, mm. 9–18

Now look at the excerpt from Chopin's Nocturne, Op. 9, No. 2, given in Example 5.10. The piece is in a lyrical $\frac{12}{8}$ meter, but in measure 18 a group of four eighth notes appears, with a 4 beneath to mark the quadruplet. Again, shifting from counting compound-time beat divisions to simple-time divisions will help you practice the right-hand part in this passage. What about the forbidding-looking second beat of measure 16? Rhythmic figures like these in Romantic-era music mimic the freedom of improvisation.

EXAMPLE 5.10: Chopin, Nocturne in E♭ Major, Op. 9, No. 2, mm. 16–18

Metrical Accent and Implications for Performance

At the beat level, compound meters have the same patterns of metrical accentuation as simple meters: that is, duple and quadruple meters alternate strong and weak beats, while compound triple follows a strong-weak-weak pattern. Each beat division also has a lower-level strong-weak-weak relationship between the beginning of the beat and the other two parts of the beat. If we let poetic symbols diagram this relationship, / ∪ ∪ represents strong-weak-weak.

When learning a new piece in a compound meter, marking the score with the metrical symbols can help you identify the implied accentuation. Take, for example, the opening measures of the Bach Gigue, which is marked with metrical symbols in Example 5.11. The metrical pattern of / ∪ ∪ within each beat lends a dance-like quality to the movement, while the larger alternation of strong and weak beats helps give the movement a larger shape and a sense of motion toward metrical goals.

EXAMPLE 5.11: Bach, Gigue, from Violin Partita No. 2 in D minor, mm. 1–5a

Rhythmic notation only approximates a truly musical performance. The performer's interpretation will usually include tempo fluctuations that speed or broaden the tempo as the work approaches an important musical goal. This type of temporary change of tempo is called **rubato**.

Try it #5

Try singing or playing Example 5.11 on your own instrument, giving equal stress to each note. Play it again with the metrical accents diagrammed in the example. Which performance do you find more musically satisfying?

TERMS YOU SHOULD KNOW

anacrusis	duplet	rubato
compound duple	hemiola	triplet
compound triple	quadruplet	tuplet
compound quadruple	metrical accent	upbeat

QUESTIONS FOR REVIEW

1. How are compound meters distinguished from simple meters?
2. What guidelines should we use in reading a compound-meter signature to determine (a) the number of beats per measure and (b) the beat unit?
3. For each of the following meter signatures, provide the number of beats per measure and the beat unit: $\frac{12}{4}$, $\frac{9}{16}$, $\frac{6}{8}$.
4. What guidelines should we follow in beaming rhythms together? What makes this difficult when the dotted half is the beat unit?
5. What is the relationship between a hemiola and a syncopation in compound meters?
6. How do the guidelines for metrical accent compare in simple and compound meters?
7. If possible, find a piece of music from your repertoire in each of the following meters: compound duple, compound triple, compound quadruple. Choose at least one with a less common beat unit, and practice chanting its rhythm while conducting the meter.

CHAPTER 6

Pitch Intervals

Outline of topics covered

Combining pitches
- Generic pitch intervals
- Melodic and harmonic intervals
- Compound intervals

Pitch-interval qualities
- Major, minor, and perfect intervals
- Using scales to spell pitch intervals
- Spelling pitch intervals beneath a given note
- Another way to spell pitch intervals
- The tritone
- Spelling diminished and augmented intervals
- Enharmonically equivalent intervals

The relative consonance and dissonance of intervals

The inversion of intervals
- Interval classes as families of intervals

Overview

In this chapter, we will combine pitches to form pitch intervals, and learn several ways to name these intervals. We will see and hear how intervals are used by composers in various styles to structure their works.

Repertoire

George Gershwin, "'S Wonderful!" (CD 1, track 91)

George Frideric Handel, Chaconne in G Major, from *Trois Leçons* (CD 2, track 1)

○ ○

Combining Pitches

Generic Pitch Intervals

In Chapter 1, we learned how to name and write pitches, and we identified pairs of pitches that made whole or half steps. As we also learned, whole and half steps are examples of intervals.

KEY CONCEPT _____

An interval measures the musical space between two pitches or pitch classes. The intervals between pitches are called **pitch intervals**. The intervals between pitch classes are called **pitch-class intervals**.

Unless otherwise stated in this book, the term "interval" refers to pitch interval.

2.3 Listen to Example 6.1, a passage from a keyboard composition by Handel, while focusing on the treble-clef melody. Some of the intervals are familiar half or whole steps; bracket them on the example, and label them H or W. How do we name the larger intervals? The first step in naming an interval is to count the letter names spanned from one pitch to the next. For example, we refer to both half and whole steps as seconds, since both span two adjacent letter names. The interval between D5 and C5 in the treble clef of measure 57 is a whole step, and the interval between G5 and F♯5 in measure 59 is a half step, but both may also be called seconds because they span two letter names.

When we name intervals this way, we are using **generic pitch-interval names**. The terms "third," "fourth," "fifth," "sixth," and "seventh" refer to generic pitch intervals encompassing three, four, five, six, and seven letter names. For example, in measure 57, the interval from B4 up to D5 is a third (B–C–D); the interval from G4 up to D5 is a fifth (G–A–B–C–D; again, always count the first and last letter names). You may also count intervals downward: in measure 58, D5 down to E4 is a seventh (D–C–B–A–G–F–E). What are the generic-interval names for the intervals in measure 60 (treble clef)? *(Try it #1)*

EXAMPLE 6.1: Handel, Chaconne in G Major, Variation 7, mm. 57–64

In Chapter 1, we also learned the name for an interval spanning eight letter names: the octave, from the Latin *octavus*, or "eight"; related words are "octopus" (eight legs) and "octagon" (eight sides). There are octave intervals in the treble-clef part of Example 6.1 in measures 58 and 59. The interval 1 is commonly known as a **unison** (from the Latin *unus*, or "one"; "unit" is a related word) and abbreviated U. This term may be familiar to you from choral singing: when all voice parts sing a line together, they are singing "in unison."

Try it #2

Name the generic interval spanned by each pair of pitches.

A5 down to G5:	_____	E5 up to A5:	_____
G5 up to A5:	_____	A5 down to D5:	_____
A5 down to F♯5:	_____	D5 up to A5:	_____
F♯5 up to A5:	_____	A5 down to C5:	_____
A5 down to E5:	_____	C5 up to A5:	_____

Melodic and Harmonic Intervals

We call pitch intervals measured between successive pitches, like those in Example 6.1, **melodic intervals**. Listen again to the example, and now follow the bass-clef part. In measure 57, there are three pitches that sound all at once: G3, B3, and D4. We call pitch intervals between simultaneous pitches (two pitches sounding at once) **harmonic intervals**, and name them the same way we do melodic intervals—by counting the letter names encompassed by the interval. There are thirds between G3 and B3 and between B3 and D4, and a fifth between G3 and D4. What generic intervals are made by the pitches in the bass clef in measure 58? What about measure 60? *(Try it #3)*

Example 6.2 shows all the types of generic intervals up to an octave. Learn these landmarks so that you are able to identify generic intervals quickly: thirds, fifths, and sevenths always have both pitches either on lines or on spaces. For thirds, the lines or spaces are adjacent; for fifths, one line or space is skipped between the notes; for sevenths, there are two skipped spaces or lines in between. Look at measures 61–64 in Example 6.1—where are the thirds? fifths? sevenths? Learning to identify interval sizes quickly and accurately by eye and by ear is an essential step in reading music fluently.

EXAMPLE 6.2: Generic intervals up to the octave

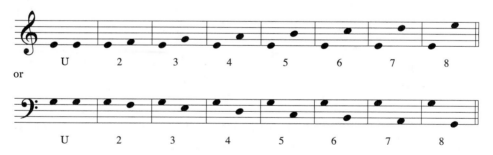

Compound Intervals

In Example 6.1, the first interval in measure 63 in the treble clef actually spans an octave plus a second. This interval is sometimes called a ninth, since it spans nine letter names. Pitch intervals larger than an octave are called **compound intervals**. Most common are ninths, tenths, elevenths, and twelfths—which correspond to an octave plus a second, third, fourth, and fifth, as shown in Example 6.3. We can also think of compound intervals as octave expansions of simple intervals: when naming compound intervals, we add seven to the simple interval. (This is because we begin numbering the unison with 1 rather than 0.) For example, a second plus an octave equals a ninth, and a fourth plus an octave equals an eleventh.

EXAMPLE 6.3: Compound intervals

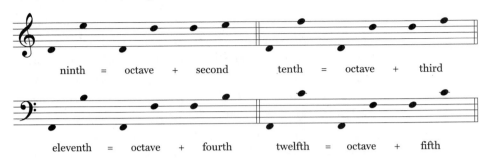

The exact musical space spanned by an interval is important to the way it sounds—we know, for example, that an octave from C5 to C6 played by two flutes is very different from the interval C2 to C6 played by a tuba and a flute, and that a melodic third is easier to sing than a melodic tenth. There are times when we need to label the span of an interval exactly. More often, however, we invoke octave equivalence for one of the pitches—that is, we label the interval without regard for the "extra" octaves between pitches. We use octave equivalence when we refer to intervals either by generic name (such as thirds and fifths) or generic-interval numbers (1 to 8). We will return to generic-interval names and numbers when we learn to combine musical lines in later chapters.

Pitch-Interval Qualities

1.91 Listen to the Gershwin song "'S Wonderful!" while following the score in your
1.92 anthology. A portion of the melody line is shown in Example 6.4a. This melody is made up of repeated pitches and only a few types of generic intervals—which ones? (*Try it #4*)

EXAMPLE 6.4: Gershwin, "'S Wonderful!"

(a) Mm. 5–20 (melody)

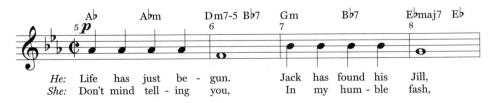

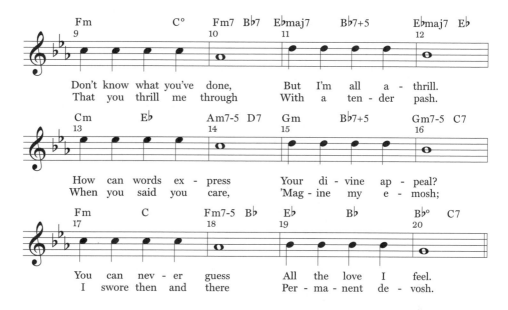

(b) Thirds from mm. 5–20

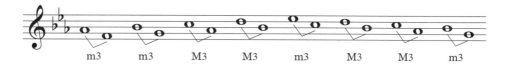

All the thirds from Gershwin's melody are isolated in Example 6.4b. They may all be thirds, but are they all exactly the same size? Play or sing them. If we locate these thirds on a keyboard and count the half steps they span, we find that some of them span three half steps (for example, the thirds from mm. 5–6 and 7–8), and some span four half steps (the thirds in mm. 9–10 and 11–12). Our generic-interval name "third" gives the general size of these intervals, but it does not express the differences in size between them.

KEY CONCEPT

When two generic pitch intervals share the same interval number but are not the exact same size, the difference in size is called the **interval quality**.

In this case, the intervals that span three half steps are called **minor thirds**; those that span four half steps are called **major thirds**. Both are thirds, but their quality (major vs. minor) differs.

Major, Minor, and Perfect Intervals

In tonal music, we express exact interval sizes with a combination of the generic-interval number plus another term (**major, minor, perfect, diminished,** or **augmented**) that specifies the interval quality. We can draw on our knowledge of major and minor scales to identify pitch intervals and their qualities. Look at the F-Major scale and its parallel minor, F-minor, shown in Example 6.5. Compare scale-degrees $\hat{1}$, $\hat{4}$, $\hat{5}$, and $\hat{8}$ between the major and parallel minor. These scale degrees feature the same pitches in both scales. The interval from $\hat{1}$ to $\hat{4}$ is known as the perfect fourth (abbreviated P4), from $\hat{1}$ to $\hat{5}$ is the perfect fifth (P5), and from $\hat{1}$ to $\hat{8}$ is the perfect octave (P8). (From the time of the earliest writings about music, around the fifth century B.C., these intervals were considered the purest, hence the term "perfect.")

WF1

EXAMPLE 6.5: Perfect intervals in major and minor scales

(a) F Major

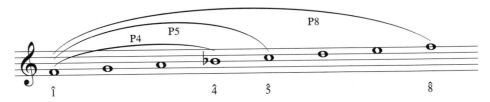

(b) F minor

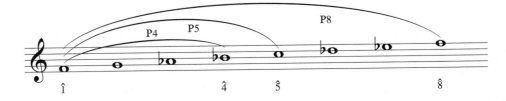

Now compare the intervals between $\hat{1}$ and $\hat{3}$, between $\hat{1}$ and $\hat{6}$, and between $\hat{1}$ and $\hat{7}$ in Example 6.6. In the major scale (Example 6.6a), these form a major third, major sixth, and major seventh, respectively (abbreviated M). In the minor scale (Example 6.6b), each of these intervals is labeled "minor" (abbreviated m).

KEY CONCEPT _____

Major intervals are a half step larger than minor intervals.

EXAMPLE 6.6: Major and minor intervals within scales

(a) F Major

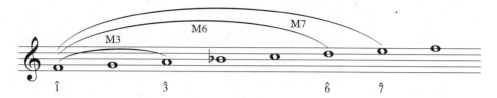

(b) F minor

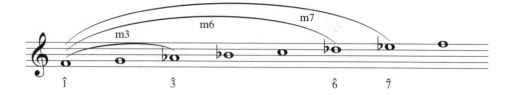

As discussed in Chapter 4, scale-degrees $\hat{3}$, $\hat{6}$, and $\hat{7}$ are sometimes called the modal scale degrees because they are different between parallel major and minor keys, and the intervals they form help give major and minor keys their characteristic sound. Thirds, sixths, and sevenths derived from the minor scale are called minor; those found in the major scale are called major. Seconds also come in major and minor: the whole step is also known as the major second; the half step (when spelled diatonically, with two different letter names), as the minor second.

Using Scales to Spell Pitch Intervals

Because the half- and whole-step patterns of all major scales are the same, the intervals between scale degrees are always the same size no matter which major scale you choose. This is also true of minor scales. We can thus use scales to help us spell pitch intervals quickly and accurately. For example, if we want a major third above G, we can think of scale-degrees $\hat{1}$ to $\hat{3}$ in G Major—so the second note of the interval is B. For a minor sixth above A, think of A (natural) minor. The key signature of A minor has no flats or sharps, and the sixth scale degree is F; therefore a minor sixth above A is F. (Continue to practice memorizing key signatures. The better you know them, the faster you will be able to spell intervals.)

KEY CONCEPT

One quick way to spell a pitch interval is to imagine that the interval is in a key, where the bottom note is the tonic and the upper note lies somewhere in the scale.

1. Always begin by writing the generic interval first (by counting lines and spaces).
2. If the interval you want is perfect (unison, fourth, fifth, or octave) or major (second, third, sixth, or seventh), add an accidental to the upper note so that it conforms to the major key signature of the bottom note.
3. If the interval you want is a minor third, sixth, or seventh, add an accidental to the upper note that conforms to the *minor* key signature of the bottom note.
4. If the interval you want is a minor second, follow step #1, then add an accidental to the upper note if needed to make the interval a half step.

Let's try spelling some more intervals using major and minor key signatures. If we were asked to spell a major sixth above E, we would place E on the staff and a bare note head six lines and spaces above it, on C (E–F–G–A–B–C). We ask: What is the key signature of E Major? Since E Major has four sharps and one of those sharps is C, we must sharp the C in this interval: a major sixth above E is C♯. What is a perfect fifth (P5) above E♭? Spell the generic interval first by counting up five: E–F–G–A–B. Now add the accidentals: since E♭ Major has three flats and one of them is B♭, we must spell this perfect fifth as E♭–B♭.

Try it #5

Name the following notes.

m6 above D: _____	m3 above F: _____
M7 above A: _____	M2 above E♭: _____
P5 above B♭: _____	m7 above C: _____

We also can use scales to identify a given interval. To name the interval from F to B♭, think of the F-Major scale: B♭ is the fourth scale degree of F Major. Therefore the interval is a perfect fourth (P4), since the interval between $\hat{1}$ and $\hat{4}$ in any major or natural minor scale is a P4. What is the interval from E to C? If you think of the E-Major scale, you'll quickly realize that C must be sharped in that key. Try E minor: C is scale-degree $\hat{6}$ of E minor. The interval is therefore a minor sixth.

Try it #6

Name the following intervals.

G up to F♯: _____   A up to C: _____

C up to A♭: _____   C♯ up to G♯: _____

B♭ up to D: _____   B up to E: _____

Spelling Pitch Intervals Beneath a Given Note

What if we want to spell a major sixth *below* C? We begin by counting the generic interval downward: C–B–A–G–F–E. E now becomes the tonic of our scale. (We always consider the lowest note as the tonic of the scale.) We must imagine a major scale, since we're spelling a major interval. We ask: Does C fit in an E-Major scale? No, since E Major includes C♯. We cannot change the given note C, so let's try changing the lower note, the tonic of the scale. Would C fit in an E♭-Major scale? Yes. A major sixth below C is E♭.

What is a minor third below A? Count down three: A–G–F. F is our tonic; does A fit in an F-minor scale? No, because F minor includes A♭. But A does fit in an F♯-minor scale. A minor third below A is F♯.

Try it #7

Name the following notes.

m6 below D: _____   m3 below F: _____

M7 below A: _____   M2 below E♭: _____

P5 below B♭: _____   m7 below C: _____

As you become more familiar with intervals and scales, you will find other ways of quickly identifying and spelling intervals using scales. For example, recognizing that an interval is scale-degree $\hat{7}$ up to $\hat{1}$ in a major scale is another way to identify the interval as a minor second; thinking of *re* to *fa* in a major scale is another way of writing a minor third.

Another Way to Spell Pitch Intervals

We can also spell pitch intervals by counting up the lines and spaces of the generic interval from the first pitch of the interval to the second, then counting the number of semitones spanned. For example, to write a minor third above G4, you must first know that a minor third spans three semitones. To spell the interval, write the generic interval first, by drawing a note head on the third line of the treble staff (B4, the next line above G4). Count the semitones from G4 to B4; does the interval span three semitones? Since it spans four semitones, add a flat to lower the B4 to B♭4. You have correctly spelled the minor third above G4.

The table below summarizes the information we need to know to spell diatonic pitch intervals.

SUMMARY

You can identify pitch intervals by knowing the number of scale steps they span and the number of semitones they encompass.

INTERVAL NAME	ABBREVIATION	NUMBER OF SCALE STEPS	NUMBER OF SEMITONES
unison	U	1	0
minor second	m2	2	1
major second	M2	2	2
minor third	m3	3	3
major third	M3	3	4
perfect fourth	P4	4	5
tritone (see p. 105)	A4 or d5	4 or 5	6
perfect fifth	P5	5	7
minor sixth	m6	6	8
major sixth	M6	6	9
minor seventh	m7	7	10
major seventh	M7	7	11
octave	P8	8	12

Sometimes in twentieth-century music, where the spelling of intervals and chords does not indicate function within a major or minor scale, we name intervals only by the number of semitones they span (see Chapters 30–32).

The Tritone

You may have noticed that we have not yet considered one type of pitch interval listed in the SUMMARY box above: the **tritone**. This interval has six semitones, which places it between a perfect fourth and perfect fifth in size. The *tri* in the word simply means "three" (as in "tricycle" or "triangle"), and refers to the three whole steps (or tones) that make up a tritone. The tritone may be spelled as a diminished fifth (abbreviated d5) or an augmented fourth (abbreviated A4), depending on where it is positioned within the scale and its musical function. In the major scale, all the fifths made between pairs of scale degrees ($\hat{1}$–$\hat{5}$, $\hat{2}$–$\hat{6}$, etc.) are perfect fifths except one: between $\hat{7}$ and $\hat{4}$ (E and B♭ in the scale of F Major, for example; see Example 6.7). When $\hat{4}$ is lower than $\hat{7}$, the tritone is spelled as an augmented fourth (B♭–E); when $\hat{7}$ is lower than $\hat{4}$, it is a diminished fifth (E–B♭).

EXAMPLE 6.7: The augmented fourth and diminished fifth in F-Major context

Spelling Diminished and Augmented Intervals

The augmented fourth and diminished fifth are the only *diatonic* augmented and diminished intervals—that is, they are the only diminished or augmented intervals that fall within the diatonic collection (major or natural minor scales). But others can be made by raising or lowering diatonic scale degrees by a half step. Many types of augmented and diminished intervals are possible, but only a few—including the A4, d5, A2, A6, and d7—are commonly encountered in tonal music.

KEY CONCEPT

When a major or perfect interval is made one chromatic half step larger, we call it **augmented**. When a minor or perfect interval is made one chromatic half step smaller, we call it **diminished**.

When a major or perfect interval is made one whole step larger (without changing the letter names of the pitches), we call it **doubly augmented**. When a minor or perfect interval is made one whole step smaller (without changing the letter names of the pitches), we call it **doubly diminished**.

Don't be surprised to see doubly augmented or doubly diminished intervals spelled with double sharps or double flats or with one note sharped and the other flatted.

If we were asked to spell the interval of an A4 above D, we would first spell a P4: D to G. Since an augmented interval is one chromatic half step larger than perfect (or major), we would raise the G one half step: D to G♯ is an A4. What is a d3 above F♯? First we spell a minor third: F♯–A. Since a diminished interval is one chromatic half step smaller than minor (or perfect), we would lower the A one half step: F♯–A♭ is a d3. We cannot call the upper note G♯, because that would make a second instead of a third. Finally, to spell an A6 below C, we would first spell a M6 below: C to E♭. Now we make this one chromatic half step larger: C to E♭♭. Writing a D♮ instead of an E♭♭ would result in a minor seventh below C. Example 6.8 shows the steps we have just taken to spell these intervals.

EXAMPLE 6.8: Spelling augmented and diminished intervals

Another Way

Diminished and augmented pitch intervals may also be identified by the number of scale steps they span combined with the number of semitones they encompass. Less common augmented and diminished intervals are marked with an *. There is no diminished unison.

INTERVAL NAME	ABBREVIATION	NUMBER OF SCALE STEPS	NUMBER OF SEMITONES
*augmented unison	AU	1	1
*diminished second	d2	2	0
augmented second	A2	2	3
*diminished third	d3	3	2
*diminished fourth	d4	4	4
augmented fourth	A4	4	6
diminished fifth	d5	5	6
*augmented fifth	A5	5	8
*diminished sixth	d6	6	7
augmented sixth	A6	6	10
diminished seventh	d7	7	9

Enharmonically Equivalent Intervals

Intervals that span the same number of semitones but have different interval names are said to be **enharmonically equivalent**. For example, the minor third F to A♭ spans three semitones, and the augmented second F to G♯ spans the same three semitones. Any interval can have four possible spellings, all of them enharmonic.

Although intervals spanning the same number of semitones sound the same, when writing pitch intervals in tonal music, we need to be very careful to select the correct spelling of an interval based on how it functions in the music. In tonal music, we usually write intervals using pitches from the piece's major or minor key. When we see intervals that are not spelled as we would expect in the key, the spelling may indicate how the interval functions in the musical context. As shown in Example 6.9, an interval spanning ten semitones spelled A♭ to G♭ (as a minor seventh) does not resolve the same way as one spelled A♭ to F♯ (as an augmented sixth). (See Chapters 12 and 25.) The correct spelling also makes the interval easier to read for performers. Incorrect notation causes confusion and may waste rehearsal time!

EXAMPLE 6.9: Resolutions of m7 and A6

m7   A6

The Relative Consonance and Dissonance of Intervals

Over the course of music history, intervals have been characterized as **consonant** if they sound pleasing to the ear or tonally stable, and **dissonant** if they sound tonally active (as if they need to move somewhere else to find a resting point) or jarring or unpleasant. Consonance and dissonance are relative terms based on properties of sound and on the norms of compositional practice: what sounds consonant to us today may have sounded dissonant to a Renaissance musician.

As a rule of thumb, consider the following intervals to be consonant: unison, third, fifth, sixth, octave. Of the consonant intervals, the unison, fifth, and octave are considered **perfect consonances** because of their pure acoustic properties, while the third and sixth are **imperfect consonances**. Dissonances include the second, seventh, and any augmented or diminished interval, such as the tritone. (Theorists in the Middle Ages sometimes called the tritone the "devil in music" because of its dissonant sound.) As we saw earlier, the perfect fourth is usually grouped among the perfect consonances because of its acoustic properties, yet composers after the Renaissance tended to treat the harmonic fourth (but not the melodic fourth) as a dissonance in their writing. We will learn more about this as we begin writing counterpoint and harmony.

One of the critical elements that define a given musical style is the way composers handle consonant and dissonant intervals. As we will see in later chapters, Anton Webern (in the first half of the twentieth century) uses sevenths differently than J. S. Bach (in the first half of the eighteenth century) or Johannes Brahms (in the nineteenth century).

SUMMARY

- Consonant intervals: unison, third, fifth, sixth, octave

- Dissonant intervals: second, seventh, any augmented or diminished interval

- Special case: fourth (acoustically consonant; melodic interval is usually a consonance, harmonic interval is usually a dissonance)

Now that we are familiar with interval quality, and with consonance and dissonance, let's return to the passage from the Handel keyboard piece in Example 6.1 and look again at the intervals in measure 58. Label each melodic interval with both interval size and quality, then circle any interval that is dissonant. *(Try it #8)*

The Inversion of Intervals

Earlier in the chapter, we saw how the augmented fourth and diminished fifth could be made from scale-degrees $\hat{4}$ and $\hat{7}$ of the major scale. If $\hat{4}$ is lower than $\hat{7}$, it is spelled as an augmented fourth; when $\hat{7}$ is lower than $\hat{4}$, it is a diminished fifth. Pairs of intervals like these, made from the same scale degrees but with the order reversed, we call **inversionally related intervals**. The A4 and d5 are the only inversionally related tonal intervals that are exactly the same in size and sound identical if not in a musical context. The perfect fourth and the perfect fifth are another pair of inversionally related intervals (Example 6.10a); both share the name "perfect," and both are perfect consonances. A major interval will invert to a minor-quality interval: for example, a major third inverts to a minor sixth (Example 6.10b). The possible combinations for inversionally related intervals are shown in the KEY CONCEPT box below.

EXAMPLE 6.10: Inversionally related intervals

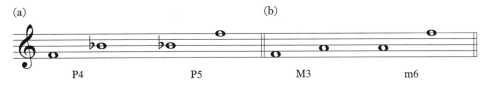

(a)   (b)

        P4   P5   M3   m6

KEY CONCEPT

Things to keep in mind when determining the quality and size of an interval inversion.

1. Quality:
   - perfect intervals remain perfect;
   - major intervals invert to minor, and vice versa;
   - diminished intervals invert to augmented, and vice versa.

2. Size:
   - the two numbers always sum to 9; for example 1 inverts to 8, 3 inverts to 6, 4 inverts to 5, etc.

Try it #9

For each pair of pitches below, name the interval. Then write the inversion, and name the new interval. The first one has been completed for you.

PITCHES	INTERVAL	INVERSION	NAME OF INVERTED INTERVAL
D up to F♯:	M3	F♯ up to D	m6
A up to G♯:			
G up to D♭:			
E♭ up to B♭:			
C♯ up to A:			
B up to D:			

Interval Classes as Families of Intervals

Because of octave equivalence, inversionally related intervals tend to sound more like each other than they do like other intervals. As noted above, compound intervals also sound more like the basic interval (within the octave) than they do other, unrelated, intervals. We use the term **interval class** for all pitch intervals that can be made from the same pair of pitch classes or transpositions of these pitch classes. For example, the interval formed between any C and E, in any octave and any order, belongs to interval-class 4 (because the smallest interval formed between C and E spans four semitones). Likewise, the interval formed between any D and F♯, in any octave and any order, also belongs to interval-class 4. When we group the pitch intervals this way, each of them falls into one of six basic interval classes, named for the number of semitones in its smallest-size interval.

KEY CONCEPT

All intervals (and their related inversions, compound intervals, or enharmonic equivalents) fall into one of these interval-class families:

interval-class 1: m2 and M7

2: M2 and m7

3: m3 and M6

4: M3 and m6

5: P4 and P5

6: tritone

TERMS YOU SHOULD KNOW

augmented interval	generic pitch interval	perfect consonance
compound interval	imperfect consonance	pitch interval
consonance	interval class	tritone
diminished interval	interval quality	unison
dissonance	inversionally related interval	

QUESTIONS FOR REVIEW

1. What information is missing from generic pitch-interval names? What is the difference between melodic intervals and harmonic intervals?
2. Which generic intervals are considered consonances? dissonances?
3. What is the difference in size between a major interval and a minor interval with the same generic number (for example, M6 and m6)?
4. What is the interval called that is one half step smaller than a minor interval? one half step larger than a major interval?
5. What is the interval called that is one half step smaller than a perfect interval? one half step larger?
6. Write out an interval. What intervals can you think of that are enharmonically equivalent to it? What are the names of each of the different enharmonically equivalent intervals?
7. Examine the melodic intervals between pitches in a song of your choosing. Are most of the intervals one generic size? What is the largest interval in the melody?
8. What qualities do intervals share that are in the same interval class?

CHAPTER 7

Triads and Seventh Chords

Outline of topics covered

Chords and triads
- Spelling triads above a scale
- Triad qualities in major keys
- Triad qualities in minor keys
- Spelling isolated triads

Scale-degree triads in a tonal context
- Roman numerals for scale-degree triads
- The inversion of triads
- Analyzing triads
- Figured bass
- Triads in musical contexts

Seventh chords
- Diatonic seventh chords in major keys
- Roman numerals and figures for seventh chords
- Diatonic seventh chords in minor keys
- Spelling isolated seventh chords

Triads and seventh chords in popular styles
- Other types of seventh chords
- Seventh chords and musical style

Overview

In this chapter, we will combine intervals to form triads and seventh chords, and learn several ways to label them. We will also consider how triads and seventh chords function in musical contexts.

Repertoire

George Frideric Handel, Chaconne in G Major, from *Trois Leçons* (CD 2, track 1)

Wolfgang Amadeus Mozart, "Voi, che sapete," from *The Marriage of Figaro* (CD 2, track 82)

Jimmy Van Heusen and Johnny Burke, "Here's That Rainy Day," from *Carnival in Flanders*

○ ○

Chords and Triads

2.1

Scales, intervals, and chords are basic elements of tonal music. In the previous chapters, we learned about scales and intervals; chords are the subject of this chapter. Listen to the theme and first four variations of Handel's keyboard Chaconne in G Major while following the score in your anthology. In each variation, try to identify—by ear and eye—which hand carries the melody and which plays mostly chords.

KEY CONCEPT

A **chord** is a group of pitches that form a single harmonic idea. When we write chords, their pitches may sound all at once, or they may sound in succession.

In the Handel example, you heard left-hand chords in the theme and Variations 1 and 3, and right-hand chords in Variations 2 and 4. You may also have noticed variations in which the two hands are notated in different meters (see Example 7.1). This **polymetric** notation is an alternative to writing all triplets in one hand.

In the right hand of Variation 4, given in Example 7.1, the chord in measure 33 (G-B-D) is made of two thirds, one on top of the other. Three-pitch chords that can be represented like this—as two thirds, one above the other—are called **triads**. When triads are written in this spacing, you can recognize them easily by their position on the staff as line-line-line or space-space-space. Use this guideline to find at least three triads in the left hand of Variation 1, given in Example 7.2.

EXAMPLE 7.1: Handel, Chaconne in G Major, Variation 4, mm. 33–40

EXAMPLE 7.2: Handel, Chaconne, Variation 1, mm. 9–16

While there are many triads in Example 7.2 to choose from, those that fit the line-line-line or space-space-space model may be found on the downbeats of measures 9 (G-B-D), 11 (E-G-B, plus an "extra note," D), 12 (D-F♯-A), 13 (G-B-D), and 14 (C-E-G).

KEY CONCEPT

When triads are spelled in thirds, the interval between the lowest pitch of the triad (called the **root**) and the highest pitch (called the **fifth**) is a fifth. The middle member of a triad is called the **third**, because it is a third above the root. Because the root is on the bottom, this triad position is called **root position**.

We can speak of the "root," "third," and "fifth" of a triad even when the triad is not arranged in thirds. We will return to the Handel variations later in this chapter to analyze non-root-position chords.

Spelling Triads Above a Scale

Since the Chaconne is in G Major, we can anticipate which triads Handel is more likely to include by writing out triads above each note of the G-Major scale (Example 7.3). In musical practice, as we shall see in future chapters, triads built on some scale degrees are much more common than others. Compare the triads in Example 7.3 with the root-position chords we found in Example 7.2. Handel's triads are built on which degrees of the scale? *(Try it #1)*

EXAMPLE 7.3: Triads above each scale degree in G Major

$\hat{1}$ M $\hat{2}$ m $\hat{3}$ m $\hat{4}$ M $\hat{5}$ M $\hat{6}$ m $\hat{7}$ d

Triad Qualities in Major Keys

For some of the triads built on a major scale, the bottom third of the triad is a major third and the top third is a minor third—these are called **major triads**. In major keys, major triads are made on scale-degrees $\hat{1}$, $\hat{4}$, and $\hat{5}$. For other triads in a major scale, the bottom third of the triad is a minor third and the top third is a major third—these are called **minor triads**. The triads on scale-degrees $\hat{2}$, $\hat{3}$, and $\hat{6}$ in major keys are minor triads. What about the triad built on $\hat{7}$? It has a diminished fifth between the root and fifth, and both of its thirds are minor. It is called a **diminished triad**. In Example 7.3, the **triad qualities** are labeled below the staff—M for major, m for minor, and d for diminished.

Triad Qualities in Minor Keys

If we build triads above the scale degrees of a natural minor scale, as shown in Example 7.4a, the triads on scale-degrees $\hat{1}$, $\hat{4}$, and $\hat{5}$ are minor, those on scale-degrees $\hat{3}$, $\hat{6}$, and $\hat{7}$ are major, and the triad on scale-degree $\hat{2}$ is diminished. As we learned in Chapter 4, though, the seventh scale degree in minor is often raised to create a leading tone. When we include the raised $\hat{7}$ in our triads, the triads on scale-degrees $\hat{5}$ and $\hat{7}$ become major and diminished in quality, respectively (shown in Example 7.4b). These are all commonly used triads in minor keys.

EXAMPLE 7.4: Triads above each scale degree in G minor

What happens to the triad on scale-degree $\hat{3}$ when $\hat{7}$ is raised? Look at Example 7.4c. When $\hat{7}$ is raised in minor keys, a triad built on the third scale degree has major thirds between the root and third and between the third and fifth. Since the interval between the root and fifth is an augmented fifth, this type of triad is called an **augmented triad** (labeled A). This triad is not commonly found. In music analysis, you will occasionally encounter other altered degrees of the minor scale (for example, the raised $\hat{6}$). We will discuss the effect of these alterations in Chapter 24.

Spelling Isolated Triads

You will improve the speed with which you analyze and sight-read music by learning to spell and identify triad qualities quickly.

KEY CONCEPT

We can spell triads with the help of intervals, as Example 7.5a shows.

1. Write the root of the triad.

2. Write a fifth above the root. For a major or minor triad, write a P5 above the root. For a diminished triad, write a d5. For an augmented triad, write an A5.

3. Write a third above the root. For a major or augmented triad, make it a M3. For a minor or diminished triad, make it a m3.

Example 7.5b shows another way to spell triads by means of intervals. You can write a major triad as a major third beneath a minor third; a minor triad as a minor third beneath a major third; a diminished triad as two minor thirds; and an augmented triad as two major thirds.

EXAMPLE 7.5:

(a) Spelling triads as fifths and thirds

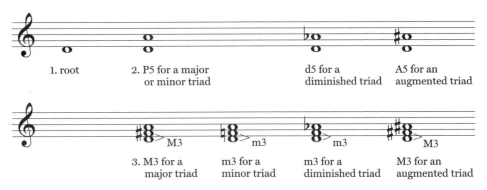

1. root

2. P5 for a major
   or minor triad

   d5 for a
   diminished triad

   A5 for an
   augmented triad

3. M3 for a
   major triad

   m3 for a
   minor triad

   m3 for a
   diminished triad

   M3 for an
   augmented triad

(b) Spelling triads as stacked thirds

Major triad is M3
beneath m3.

Minor triad is m3
beneath M3.

Diminished triad is
m3 beneath m3.

Augmented triad
is M3 beneath M3.

We can also let major- and minor-key signatures help us, just as we did for interval spelling. To spell a major or minor triad, imagine it in a key, where the root of the triad is tonic and the upper notes lie in the scale. Always begin by writing the generic triad first, putting root, third, and fifth on the staff (line-line-line or space-space-space). Then think about the accidentals needed. For a major triad, take the major-key signature of the bottom note. For a minor triad, take the minor-key signature of the bottom note. Use this method to spell an E-Major triad and a C-minor triad. *(Try it #2)*

To spell diminished triads, either (1) follow the instructions for a minor triad above and lower the fifth, or (2) think of the root of the triad as the leading tone of a major scale, and determine from those scale members the other two notes of the triad. For example, E diminished could be spelled (1) by making an E-minor triad (E-G-B) and then lowering the fifth (E-G-B♭), or (2) by writing the thirds on the staff (E-G-B), then thinking of the major key where E is the leading tone—F Major, which has one flat (B♭)—to make E-G-B♭. Augmented triads are spelled by writing a major triad on the given root and raising the fifth a half step.

Another Way

Here are two other methods for spelling triads.

1. If you like to visualize triads on the keyboard or staff, memorize the generic triads from just the white keys or plain note heads on the staff:
- triads on C, F, and G are major;
- triads on D, E, and A are minor;
- triads on B are diminished.

Then use this information to build other-quality triads.

- Triads on C, F, and G remain major if all the accidentals match (e.g., C♯-E♯-G♯). To make a minor triad, lower the middle accidental a half step (e.g., change C-E-G to C-E♭-G, or change C♯-E♯-G♯ to C♯-E-G♯).
- Triads on D, E, and A remain minor if all the accidentals match (e.g., D♭-F♭-A♭). To make a major triad, raise the middle accidental a half step (e.g., change D-F-A to D-F♯-A, or change D♭-F♭-A♭ to D♭-F-A♭).
- Triads on B remain diminished if all the accidentals match (e.g., B♯-D♯-F♯). To make a major triad, lower the accidental of the root a half step (e.g., B♭-D-F or B-D♯-F♯). To make a minor triad, raise the accidental of the fifth a half step (e.g., B-D-F♯ or B♭-D♭-F).

2. You may also spell triads using only major key signatures. First, build a major triad (referring to the key signature of the triad's root), then
- for a minor triad, lower the third a half step;
- for a diminished triad, lower the third and fifth each a half step;
- for an augmented triad, raise the fifth a half step.

Try it #3

Spell the following triads.

minor triad above B♭:	_____
major triad above F:	_____
minor triad above G:	_____
minor triad above G♯:	_____
augmented triad above E♭:	_____
minor triad above D:	_____
diminished triad above B♭:	_____
major triad above D:	_____
major triad above A:	_____

Scale-Degree Triads in a Tonal Context

In tonal music, the harmonic function of a triad is associated with the scale degree on which it is built. For example, in a piece in G Major, we call the triad built on $\hat{1}$ (G) the tonic harmony (like the tonic scale degree) because G is the tone that serves as a "home base" for harmonies in that key. Similarly, we refer to each triad built on the other scale degrees by the name of its root, as Examples 7.6 and 7.7 show. Keep in mind that not all triads carry equal functional weight in musical contexts, and some appear much more often than others. Not all triads are equal!

Roman Numerals for Scale-Degree Triads

As we begin to learn more about the harmonic structure of music, it will be helpful to have one label for each harmony that indicates both the quality of the triad and its placement within a key. We thus write capital Roman numerals (I to VII) for major triads, and lowercase Roman numerals (i to vii) for minor triads. For augmented triads, we add a small raised plus sign to an uppercase Roman numeral (III⁺); for diminished triads, we add a small raised circle to a lowercase Roman numeral (vii°). The Roman numerals for each triad in G Major and G minor are shown in Examples 7.6 and 7.7, along with the scale-degree names for each. When

WF1 | analyzing music with Roman numerals, indicate the key at the beginning of your analysis, as the examples show (an uppercase letter for major keys, a lowercase letter for minor).

EXAMPLE 7.6: Triads in G Major, with scale-degree names and Roman numerals

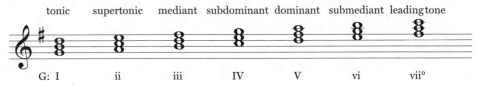

EXAMPLE 7.7: Triads in G minor, with scale-degree names and Roman numerals

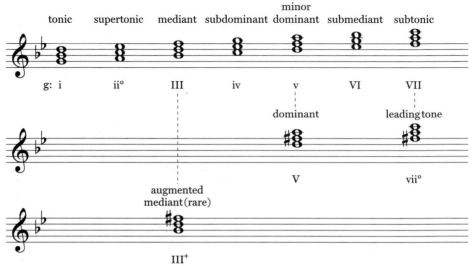

The Inversion of Triads

Let's return now to the passage from the Handel Chaconne shown in Example 7.2. On the downbeat of measure 12, the root of the bass-clef triad is repeated, or **doubled**, in two octaves—we hear both D3 and D4 in this chord. On the second beat of the measure, the D3 is no longer sounded; this triad is no longer in root position, but is inverted. Triads in **inversion** have some chord member other than the root in the lowest-sounding voice (or **bass**). Any member of a triad—root, third, or fifth—may sound in the bass voice. Can you find other inverted triads in this passage? *(Try it #4)*

KEY CONCEPT

Things to keep in mind when determining a triad's inversion.

- If the root of the triad is lowest, it is in **root position**.
- If the third of the triad is lowest, it is in **first inversion**.
- If the fifth of the triad is lowest, it is in **second inversion**.

2.1

Listen now to the Chaconne's third variation, shown in Example 7.8, to find triads in root position and in inversion. Measure 25 expresses a single G-Major harmony, with G in the bass. Since this piece is in G Major, we can label this measure with Roman numeral I. Because the root is in the bass, this chord is in root position. Measure 26 is a D-F♯-A harmony, but with the F♯—the third of the chord—

in the bass. This is a V chord in first inversion. In measure 31, beat 2, there is another G-Major chord—but this time with the fifth, D, in the bass. This position is called second inversion.

EXAMPLE 7.8: Handel, Chaconne, Variation 3, mm. 25–32

Analyzing Triads

WF2

As a first step when analyzing triads, think about how the pitches of the chords would be notated if they were in root position. (This was the method of French composer Jean-Philippe Rameau [1683–1764], who is often given credit for the idea of chord inversion.) If you need to, you can "collect up" the pitch classes on a separate sheet of staff paper and write them in thirds to identify which scale degree the triad is built on. Eventually, you'll be able to do this quickly in your head.

KEY CONCEPT

To identify the root in an inverted chord, look for the interval of a fourth. The upper note of the fourth is the root.

For example, the second chord in measure 30 of the Chaconne's third variation (Example 7.8) includes pitch-classes A-C-F♯. The F♯ (at the top of the fourth) is the root. Rearranged in thirds, the chord is F♯-A-C: an F♯-diminished chord, or vii° in the key of G Major. What Roman numeral and inversion represent the triad on the downbeat of measure 31? (*Try it #5*)

Figured Bass

When a triad is arranged with its root in the bass, the intervals formed above the root are a fifth and a third. In the Baroque era (1600–1750), musicians indicated this chord with the numerals 5 and 3, written one over the other below the bass note (see Example 7.9a). This shorthand type of chord labeling is called **figured bass**. Figured bass consists of a bass line with numbers written under it (or over it); the numbers represent the generic intervals to be played above the bass to make the chords. In a musical context, the fifth and third might be spaced as a compound interval, the third might be a major or minor third, and one of the pitches might be doubled an octave higher to make four parts (Example 7.9b), but these details were not specified in the basic label for the chord. The voicings of each chord and the connections between them were determined by stylistic conventions learned by anyone who studied figured bass.

When the triad is arranged with the third in the lowest part, the intervals above the bass are a sixth and a third; the figured-bass representation was thus 6 and 3 written beneath the bass note, as Example 7.9 shows. If the fifth is in the bass, the intervals are a sixth and a fourth, represented in figured-bass notation by 6 and 4.

EXAMPLE 7.9:

(a) Triads and inversions in three voices

5 3	6 3 or 6	6 4	arrow denotes the root

Remember: When a triad is inverted, the root lies at the top of the fourth.

(b) Triads and inversions in four voices

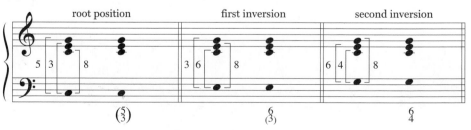

The Birth of Figured Bass

Around 1600, composers in Italy began experimenting with a new, radical style. While music of the previous century had been written by putting many equal, independent musical lines together (called counterpoint), the new style featured one solo musical line with a background chordal accompaniment (called **monody**). But rather than writing out the entire accompaniment, which was much less important than the melody, composers wrote out a bass line and indicated some of the intervals to be played in the upper parts, with Arabic numerals under that bass line—the method we call figured bass. A performer on harpsichord or lute would then know which intervals to play by reading the figures. The earliest pieces in this style only had a few numbers indicated; the other chords were realized as root-position triads. (The first extant publication that featured figured bass, Italian composer Lodovico Viadana's *Cento concerti ecclesiastici* [*One Hundred Sacred Concerti*, 1602], is an example.) Later composers added more types of figures as the variety of chords increased.

Figured bass was employed in much the same way as **lead-sheet notation** (a popular-music notation with chord symbols above the melody line) is today: keyboard players looked at the bass line and figures and knew from them which chords to play in the upper parts. Because players read the chords directly from the bass and figures, the figures were made as simple as possible to allow musicians to read them quickly. Since the $\frac{5}{3}$ figure was the most common, it was often left out. When performers saw a bass note without a figure, they assumed $\frac{5}{3}$. The figure $\frac{6}{3}$ was frequently shortened to just 6 (with 3 implied), but for $\frac{6}{4}$, which was less common, the full figure was given to avoid confusion. (The figures shown in Example 7.9b in parentheses were thus often not notated.) In each case, the numbers represent intervals above a bass line.

WF3 We will sometimes use figures the way Baroque musicians used them—to represent intervals over a bass line. But we can also write figures to represent inversions of chords—$\frac{5}{3}$ (or nothing) for root position, $\frac{6}{3}$ or ^{6} for first inversion, and $\frac{6}{4}$ for second inversion. Unless a figure is altered, we draw from the pitches in the key signature of the piece. When these symbols are combined with Roman numerals, they identify the chord's scale degree, quality, and inversion—providing a lot of information in a space-saving label.

Triads in Musical Contexts

2.82 In some pieces of music, all members of a chord sound at the same time. In others, a chord may be **arpeggiated**—played one pitch at a time—as in the bass-clef part of the accompaniment to Mozart's "Voi, che sapete," shown in Example 7.10a. (Mozart chose to arpeggiate the chords here because a singer onstage is pretending to accompany the aria on a guitar; the arpeggiated staccato in the left hand is intended to mimic the sound of a guitar.) There are many possible arpeggiation patterns. To analyze the chords in this piece, we need to collect up the pitches for the whole chord (Example 7.10b) before arranging them in root position so that we can identify the chord (Example 7.10c). In the first measure, a B♭-Major triad is played one chord member at a time: B♭–D–F–B♭. In the following measure, an F-Major chord (V$^6_3$ in the key of B♭ Major) is arpeggiated A–C–F–A. Why would Mozart use a first-inversion chord here? The A in the bass, instead of the root F, makes a smooth bass connection between the B♭s of measures 1 and 3.

EXAMPLE 7.10: Mozart, "Voi, che sapete," from *The Marriage of Figaro*, mm. 1–4

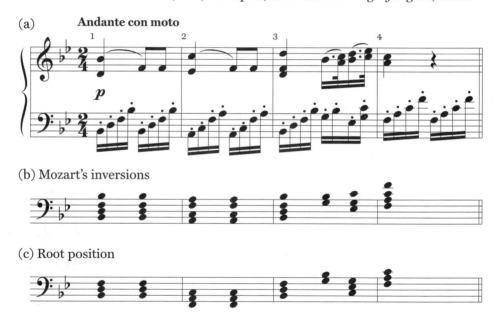

(a) **Andante con moto**

(b) Mozart's inversions

(c) Root position

2.6 For another accompaniment pattern common in the Classical period (1750–1830), listen to the passage shown in Example 7.11, a minor-key variation from Handel's Chaconne. The first two beats of the variation express a G-minor triad—i in the key of G minor. The left-hand accompanimental pattern arpeggiates the harmony with an "up-down-up" contour that is typical of an **Alberti bass**. In

WF4 an Alberti bass, the pitches at the beginning of each harmony change are typically the lowest notes of the chord (not necessarily the root) and form a bass line.

EXAMPLE 7.11: Handel, Chaconne, Variation 12, mm. 97–100

Seventh Chords

Diatonic Seventh Chords in Major Keys

If we add another third on top of a root-position triad, a seventh is formed between the root and the top note. This type of chord is called a **seventh chord**. We can build seventh chords above each scale degree in a major scale by adding a third above each scale-degree triad (see Example 7.12). Seventh chords are named by the quality of their triad plus the quality of the seventh measured from the root to the seventh. For example, the seventh chord built on $\hat{1}$ is a major triad with a major seventh; it is called a "major-major seventh chord" (MM7); the seventh chord on $\hat{2}$ is a minor triad with a minor seventh; it is called a "minor-minor seventh chord" (mm7); and so on.

EXAMPLE 7.12: Seventh chords built above the G-Major scale

Triad quality:	M	m	m	M	M	m	d
7th quality:	M	m	m	M	m	m	m
Name:	major-major 7th	minor-minor 7th	minor-minor 7th	major-major 7th	major-minor 7th	minor-minor 7th	diminished-minor, or half-diminished, 7th
Abbreviation:	MM^7	mm^7	mm^7	MM^7	Mm^7	mm^7	$ø7$
Roman numeral:	I^7	ii^7	iii^7	IV^7	V^7	vi^7	$vii^{ø7}$

Roman Numerals and Figures for Seventh Chords

Like triads, seventh chords may be labeled with Roman numerals to indicate their scale-degree placement (and function) in the key. Because the major-minor seventh chord appears only once, on $\hat{5}$, we call it a "dominant seventh chord" and label it V^7. The leading-tone seventh chord is the only one that has a diminished triad with a minor seventh. We call this type of chord a "half-diminished seventh chord" and write it as follows: $vii^{\varnothing 7}$. These are two of the most common seventh chords in music literature.

Like triads, seventh chords can appear in root position or in an inversion. The intervals above the bass are shown in Examples 7.13a and b for root position and each of the inversions. Like the figured-bass symbols for triads, these figures are usually simplified: ^{7} for root position, $^6_5$ for first inversion, $^4_3$ for second inversion, and $^4_2$ or ^{2} for third inversion.

EXAMPLE 7.13:

(a) A seventh chord and its inversions in three voices

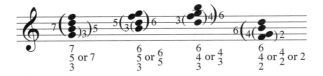

(b) A seventh chord and its inversions in four voices

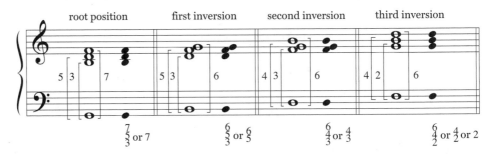

Try it #6

Spell each of the following seventh chords from bass to soprano. Then identify the type of seventh chord. The first one has been completed for you.

SEVENTH CHORD	SPELLING	CHORD TYPE
A Major: V$^4_3$	B-D-E-G♯	Mm7
B♭ Major: ii$^6_5$	_____	_____
D Major: V$^4_2$	_____	_____
E♭ Major: IV$^6_5$	_____	_____
E Major: V$^4_3$	_____	_____
G major: ii$^6_5$	_____	_____

Diatonic Seventh Chords in Minor Keys

The seventh chords built from a minor scale (G minor) are shown in Example 7.14. Since scale-degree $\hat{7}$ is typically raised in minor, the seventh chords on scale-degrees $\hat{5}$ and $\hat{7}$ are written in the example with an F♯. The seventh chord built on the leading tone in minor introduces another seventh-chord type: it has a diminished triad and a diminished seventh. This chord is called a "fully diminished seventh chord," or "diminished seventh chord" for short, and is labeled vii$^{\circ 7}$. Together, Examples 7.12 and 7.14 list all the commonly used diatonic seventh chords.

EXAMPLE 7.14: Seventh chords built above the G-minor scale

Triad quality:	m	d	M	m	M	M	d
7th quality:	m	m	M	m	m	M	d
Name:	minor - minor 7th	diminished - minor, or half-diminished, 7th	major - major 7th	minor - minor 7th	major - minor 7th	major - major 7th	diminished- diminished, or fully diminished, 7th
Abbreviation:	mm^7	⌀7	MM^7	mm^7	Mm^7	MM^7	∘7
Roman numeral:	i^7	ii$^{\varnothing 7}$	III^7	iv^7	V^7	VI^7	vii$^{\circ 7}$

Spelling Isolated Seventh Chords

To spell a specific quality of seventh chord above a given root, first spell the correct-quality triad. Say you want to write a minor seventh chord above F; first spell a minor triad, F-A♭-C. Then write in the seventh by drawing a note head a third above the fifth of the triad (E). Check the interval between the root and the note you just added—is it the correct quality of seventh? If not, add an accidental to make the correct seventh. F to E is a major seventh, so you would make the E an E♭.

It may be easier to check the quality of the seventh by inverting the interval. Imagine the root of the seventh chord up an octave, making a second with the seventh of the chord. If the second is minor (half step), the seventh is major; if the second is major, the seventh is minor; if the second is augmented, the seventh is diminished.

Try it #7

Spell the following seventh chords.

QUALITY	ROOT	THIRD	FIFTH	SEVENTH
(*a*) major-minor	G			
(*b*) minor-minor		E♭		
(*c*) half-diminished			C	
(*d*) fully diminished		D		
(*e*) major-major	F			
(*f*) half-diminished		B♭		
(*g*) major-minor			B	
(*h*) fully diminished				B♭

○ ○

Triads and Seventh Chords in Popular Styles

If you play in studio, rock, or jazz bands, you may be familiar with another labeling system for triads and seventh chords. This system is found in lead sheets and may be combined with guitar-chord symbols, as shown in Example 7.15. Chord symbols in popular music use a capital letter for the chord's root—a capital letter alone indicates a major triad (for example, G). In Van Heusen and Burke's "Here's That Rainy Day," the first three harmonies accompanying the tune are all major triads. Play through this example.

EXAMPLE 7.15: Van Heusen and Burke, "Here's That Rainy Day," mm. 5–12

We add a small letter m (Gm) to indicate a minor triad (you may also see this written Gmi or with a minus sign as G–). We write augmented triads with the root plus a small plus sign (G⁺), and diminished with a small circle (G°) or sometimes Gdim or Gmin(♭5). To notate an inverted triad, we first write the triad type followed by a slash, then the letter name of the pitch to appear in the bass. For example, a first-inversion G-minor triad is notated Gm/B♭.

Look at the seventh chords in Example 7.15. In popular-music symbols, a letter name plus 7 assumes a Mm7 (dominant seventh) quality. Thus, the D7 chord in measure 10 is a D Mm7 (V⁷). Measure 11 shows a MM7 (major seventh) chord on G; it could be labeled Gmaj7 (as here), GM7, or G⁺7 (the system is not completely standardized, and these symbols are used interchangeably). We also see a mm7 (minor seventh) built on A in measure 9, labeled Am7. Example 7.16 shows various seventh chords on C with their possible labels.

EXAMPLE 7.16: Seventh chords in C Major and C minor, with lead-sheet labels

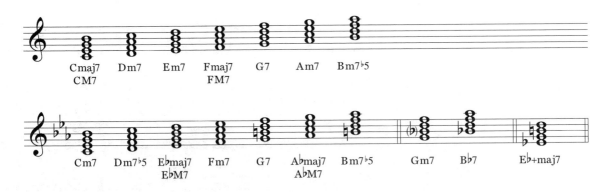

Other Types of Seventh Chords

You may have noticed that Examples 7.12 and 7.14 do not exhaust the possible combinations of triads and sevenths. For example, what about a seventh chord made from an augmented triad with a major seventh, or an augmented triad with a minor seventh, or a minor triad with a major seventh? Although these seventh chords are not found in common-practice tonal music, they add harmonic richness in some styles of jazz as substitutes for diatonic seventh chords.

Play through Example 7.17, another excerpt from "Here's That Rainy Day." Most of the chords in this passage are seventh chords. In measure 15, a B♭maj7 (on the word "told") is followed by a B♭⁺ (on "a-"). At the end of measure 16, we hear a B♭maj7(♯5) (on "And"). The chords in both Examples 7.14 and 7.16 are notated with guitar tablature (a miniature diagram of the strings and frets with dots showing where you place your fingers) as well as lead-sheet chord symbols.

EXAMPLE 7.17: Van Heusen and Burke, "Here's That Rainy Day," mm.13–20

Seventh Chords and Musical Style

The treatment of seventh chords is an important aspect of musical style. For example, only seventh chords built on scale-degrees $\hat{2}$, $\hat{5}$, and $\hat{7}$ are frequently used in Classical-period music; yet seventh chords on all scale degrees are common in jazz writing and in some popular styles. In some styles, the seventh of the seventh chord must be approached and resolved carefully by stepwise motion; in others, the dissonant interval of the seventh may be left unresolved for dramatic effect, or the entire chord may simply slide up or down by step to another seventh chord. As you identify seventh chords in music you are playing, consider what type of seventh chord each is, and how the chord is connected to those around it. We will note some special uses of seventh chords in later chapters as a part of our study of harmony and style.

TERMS YOU SHOULD KNOW

Alberti bass
arpeggiated bass
chord
chord members
fifth
first inversion
inversion
lead-sheet chord notation
root

root position
second inversion
seventh chord
- diminished seventh
- dominant seventh
- fully diminished seventh
- half-diminished seventh
- major seventh
- minor seventh

third inversion
triad
- augmented
- diminished
- major
- minor
triad quality

QUESTIONS FOR REVIEW

1. What are the differences between the following ways of labeling triads: chord quality, figured bass, Roman numeral, lead sheet? What aspects of chordal or key structure does each emphasize?

2. What are the different ways to label seventh chords? (Hint: Refer to question #1.) What aspects of chordal or key structure does each emphasize?

3. Find a piece in your repertoire with a fairly simple rhythmic texture (preferably chordal, possibly with an arpeggiated bass) and no accidentals. Choose four measures to analyze three ways: (a) chord root, quality, and inversion; (b) Roman numeral and inversion; (c) lead-sheet symbols.

PART II

Linking Musical Elements in Time

Intervals in Action (Two-Voice Composition)

Overview

In this chapter, we will learn how to connect intervals to make two-voice note-against-note counterpoint. We also consider melodic embellishments in two-voice counterpoint and four-voice chorales.

Repertoire

"Auld Lang Syne" (Scottish folk song)

Johann Sebastian Bach, Prelude in C Major, from *The Well-Tempered Clavier*, Book I (CD 1, track 17)

Bach, "Ein feste Burg ist unser Gott" (Chorale No. 20)

Bach, "Wachet auf" (Chorale No. 179) (CD 1, track 9)

Wolfgang Amadeus Mozart, Variations on "Ah, vous dirai-je, Maman" (CD 2, track 86)

"My Country, 'Tis of Thee" (CD 2, track 97)

Andrew Lloyd Webber and Tim Rice, "Don't Cry for Me Argentina"

Counterpoint: Intervals in Action

In the two previous chapters, we focused on the basic building blocks for tonal music: melodic and harmonic intervals, triads, and seventh chords. In this chapter, we begin to learn how to make the two dimensions of melody and harmony work together to create **counterpoint**.

The word "counterpoint" comes from the Latin *punctus contra punctum,* meaning "point against point." When we write counterpoint, we set two or more melodic lines of music together so that the lines form harmonies, or we set harmonies one after another so that the individual voices make good melodic lines.

Most composers from the Middle Ages until the early twentieth century began their composition studies with counterpoint. Many famous composers, such as Bach and Mozart, also taught counterpoint. We will learn about counterpoint for the same reason their students did: writing two-voice counterpoint encourages the young musician to focus on specific problems that come up in working with lines and harmonies, without the complexity of several parts going on at once. In a way, learning counterpoint is like learning scales and arpeggios on your instrument—both practices isolate and develop basic musical skills.

| WF1 |

Counterpoint is also a way of seeing the relationships between the underlying melodic/harmonic framework of a composition and its more elaborate musical surface. We will begin with a simple framework and add elaboration; later, in analyzing music, we will use our knowledge of counterpoint to discover the hidden underlying framework and how it is embellished. We will not consider everything a musician should know about counterpoint in this textbook—many colleges and universities offer in-depth study of counterpoint as a separate advanced course—but focus instead on the basic contrapuntal skills needed for writing and analyzing tonal music.

Connecting Intervals: Note-Against-Note Counterpoint

2.86

We begin our study with note-against-note counterpoint in two parts. Listen to Mozart's Variations on "Ah, vous dirai-je, Maman." You will recognize this theme as "Twinkle, Twinkle, Little Star." Familiar tunes like this one are often chosen as the basis for a set of variations because listeners know the theme, and can recognize it even when "hidden" in the varied versions. The theme of Mozart's variations is the most basic type of two-voice counterpoint: note-against-note.

It is called "note-against-note," or 1:1, because each note in the top part is matched with a single note in the lower part. This type of counterpoint, sometimes called **first species**, was the first type of music-writing young musicians learned in the Renaissance and Baroque eras.

WF2   In traditional first-species counterpoint exercises, both lines were notated with whole notes, as shown in Example 8.1, from Johann Joseph Fux's *Gradus ad Parnassum* (1725), a counterpoint textbook that was a best-seller in its day. In our note-against-note writing, we will use any duration (not just whole notes) as long as both voices have the same duration. Throughout our studies, we will follow

WF3   guidelines designed for writing eighteenth-century-style counterpoint. This style is less strict about some dissonances than Fux was. For example, while Fux restricts first species to consonant intervals only, we will learn how to connect consonances with chordal dissonances (see p. 143). We will also use tonal endings in our contrapuntal writing, rather than the modal endings of traditional first species.

EXAMPLE 8.1: A first-species counterpoint from *Gradus ad Parnassum*

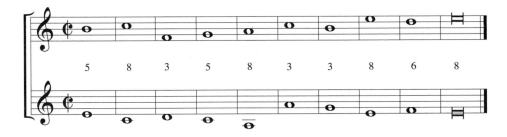

Labeling Intervals in Counterpoint

Since counterpoint is the interaction of melodic and harmonic intervals, we need to think about both types of intervals. When we analyze melodic intervals in counterpoint, we consider the melodic connections between intervals, rather than specific pitch-interval names. We will thus refer to a melodic interval of a half or whole step as a **step** and an interval of a third or fourth as a **skip** (these intervals can be thought of as "skipping" between adjacent members of a triad). An interval of a fifth or larger will be called a **leap** (these intervals "leap" over members of a triad); leaps, though, will be used sparingly in contrapuntal melodic lines.

Look at the melodic intervals in Mozart's counterpoint in Example 8.2a. Listen to this passage, or play it through at the keyboard. The upper line opens with a leap of a fifth. Otherwise, it is mostly stepwise, with a skip at the end (from $\hat{3}$ to $\hat{1}$). The bass line includes more skips than the melody; the skips are mostly thirds, but there is a leap of an octave at the beginning and a leap of a fifth at the end.

Species Counterpoint

The practice of counterpoint as a compositional technique predates the term. The earliest written account of the technique is an anonymous treatise called *Musica enchiriadis*, from about 900. This textbook for musicians describes how to add counterpoint to a preexisting melody, called a **cantus firmus**, by doubling the melody at the fifth to make two parts, then doubling both of those parts at the octave to get four parts. Curiously, by the time the term "counterpoint" itself came into common use, around the fourteenth century, the technique was rarely note-against-note ("point against point") because florid **organum**, a type of counterpoint with many notes to one of the slow-moving cantus firmus, was the style. Counterpoint was the primary compositional technique in the Middle Ages (800–1430) and Renaissance (1430–1600), but its fundamental principles remain the foundation of tonal practice right up to the present day.

During the seventeenth and eighteenth centuries, teachers of counterpoint developed step-by-step methods to teach each compositional task in order, from simplest to most elaborate. These methods came to be called **species counterpoint** ("species" simply means "type" or "kind," as in "plant species" or "animal species"). The first species, or the first type of counterpoint, was the easiest—note-against-note in two voices, using consonant intervals only; students then progressed to other types as their skills grew. Most textbooks presented detailed instructions for two-voice counterpoint (one line was given, and the student was to write the other), followed by a little instruction in three-voice, but very sketchy explanations of four- or five-voice. Young composers were supposed to figure out four-voice writing on their own, based on the previous guidelines.

In the Baroque era (1600-1750), setting a preexisting melody in counterpoint was a typical task for accomplished composers, as well as for students. For example, Bach and other church musicians often wrote contrapuntal settings of preexisting chorale melodies to perform in their churches.

EXAMPLE 8.2: Mozart, Variations on "Ah, vous dirai-je, Maman," theme

(a) Mm. 1–8

When a melody moves primarily by step, like the upper line, we call this type of motion **conjunct**. When a melody moves primarily by skips and leaps, like the bass line, we call this motion **disjunct**.

To show harmonic intervals, we write generic-interval numbers (without specifying perfect, major, or minor) between the upper and lower parts. (For a review of generic intervals, see Chapter 6.) We analyze harmonic intervals from the lowest part upward, and reduce any interval greater than 10 to within the octave: thus, we write 4, not 11. Sometimes 10 is reduced as well, to 3. The first four harmonic intervals of Mozart's theme are 8–8–3–5. Write in the numbers of the remaining intervals between the treble and bass staves. *(Try it #1)*

The one exception to the use of generic harmonic intervals is the diminished fifth (d5) or augmented fourth (A4). Most fifths and fourths in a key are perfect, but the diatonic intervals made with scale-degrees $\hat{4}$ and $\hat{7}$ form the dissonant tritone. Since these dissonances are not treated the same as the consonant P5 or P4, they need to be labeled either d5 or A4, reminding us to check for the correct resolution. There is one tritone between the parts in Example 8.2a. To what interval does it move? *(Try it #2)* We will consider motion from the tritone in more detail shortly.

Four Types of Contrapuntal Motion

Examine the intervals in Mozart's theme (Example 8.2a) again. The first harmonic interval, a double octave, is followed by an octave: one voice stays on the same pitch, and the other leaps an octave. This type of motion—in which one voice stays the same (is repeated or sustained) and the other moves by leap, skip, or step—is called **oblique motion** and labeled with an O. The second and third harmonic intervals in the example are connected by both parts moving up by skip or leap. This type of motion is called **similar motion** (labeled S)—both intervals move in the same direction. From the third to fourth measure, an A5 in the top part moves down to G5, while the C4 of the lower part moves up to E4. This type of motion is known as **contrary motion** (C)—the two voices move in opposite directions.

The fourth type of motion is illustrated in Example 8.2b, from later in Mozart's theme. On the second beat of measure 15, the upper and lower parts are separated by a harmonic third; both move up a step to another harmonic third. When a harmonic interval moves in the same direction to another interval of the same generic size, it creates **parallel motion** (P).

(b) Mm. 9–16

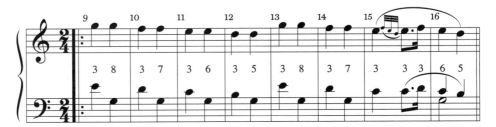

SUMMARY

There are four types of motion between pairs of voices.

- Oblique motion (O): one part repeats or sustains a single pitch, the other moves by leap, skip, or step.
- Contrary motion (C): the two parts move in opposite directions.
- Similar motion (S): both parts move in the same direction, but not by the same generic interval.
- Parallel motion (P): both parts move in the same direction by the same generic interval.

Writing Note-Against-Note Counterpoint

Composers occasionally say in jest that there are three main problems in writing a piece of music: how to start, what to do in the middle, and how to end. As we will see in later chapters, a composer has more choices to make than these three, but still, these are basic issues in composing almost any type of music. We will consider each in turn.

Writing a Good Contrapuntal Line

When we write counterpoint to a given melody, we need to pay attention both to the intervallic relationships between the lines and to the beauty of the melody we are composing.

KEY CONCEPT

When writing a contrapuntal line:

- Use mostly stepwise motion, with a few skips and leaps artfully placed to give your melody an interesting shape.
- Aim for a melodic contour with one high point and several smaller peaks.
- Follow leaps with steps in the opposite direction.
- Avoid more than two skips in a row.

Start by writing the beginning and end of your melodic line. Next, choose and notate a possible high point. Finally, go back and fill in between these melodic landmarks, revising as necessary to make good harmonic and melodic sense.

Beginning a Note-Against-Note Counterpoint

The opening harmonic interval in counterpoint usually establishes the tonic harmony of the key. The most common opening interval is an octave on $\hat{1}$. In traditional modal counterpoint, the opening interval was limited to an octave or fifth, but in eighteenth-century style we can use intervals from the tonic triad: an octave, fifth, third, or sixth built from scale-degrees $\hat{1}$, $\hat{3}$, or $\hat{5}$. (We do not include the fourth, because it is considered a dissonant interval in two-voice counterpoint.)

To practice writing note-against-note counterpoint, let's take the first part of a familiar tune, given in Example 8.3 below. Our first step is to determine the key and mode. Sing through the melody. What is the key and mode? *(Try it #3)*

EXAMPLE 8.3: "My County, 'Tis of Thee," mm. 1–6 (melody)

We refer to the melodic units of these examples as **phrases**. For now, think of a phrase as a complete musical thought (we will learn a more precise definition in Chapter 12). The first phrase of Mozart's theme (Example 8.2a) begins with an octave (Î in both parts), and the second and third phrases (Example 8.2b, mm. 9 and 13) begin with a third (5̂ in the upper part, 3̂ in the lower). In our setting of "My Country, 'Tis of Thee," placing Î in both voices is the best choice; a less common possibility is to put 3̂ in the bass, to open the counterpoint with a sixth. Since Î is repeated in the melody, we can use both intervals—the octave and the sixth—to create some variety: either Î to 3̂ or 3̂ to Î in the bass (see Example 8.4).

EXAMPLE 8.4: Opening gestures for "My Country, 'Tis of Thee"

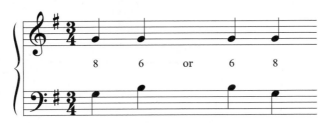

A phrase may begin with an anacrusis (upbeat). In that case, the first downbeat interval usually establishes the tonic harmony of the key, while the anacrusis will usually imply the dominant. When setting melodies with an anacrusis, consider both the anacrusis and the first downbeat to select the opening intervals. Sing through "Auld Lang Syne," shown in Example 8.5. This melody begins with a 5̂ to Î anacrusis and presents several choices. We can set the 5̂ with an octave to imply a dominant chord, then set Î with a sixth (3̂ in the bass), to imply tonic (Example 8.6a). If we wish to set the downbeat with an octave, the 5̂ in the melody must be set with a sixth (leading tone in the bass; Example 8.6b) in order to avoid following an octave with another octave—a practice that was avoided in this style. (See KEY CONCEPT box on p. 144.) Sometimes in folk song settings, the anacrusis is unaccompanied—we may begin the counterpoint with Î in both parts on the downbeat of the first full measure (Example 8.6c).

EXAMPLE 8.5: "Auld Lang Syne," mm. 1–2a (melody)

EXAMPLE 8.6: Opening gestures for "Auld Lang Syne"

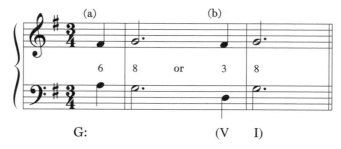

Ending a Note-Against-Note Counterpoint

WF4

The last two intervals in strict species counterpoint are written with scale-degrees $\hat{7}$ to $\hat{1}$ in one voice and $\hat{2}$ to $\hat{1}$ in the other, ending the counterpoint on a unison or octave. Since this phrase of the "My Country" tune ends $\hat{7}$ to $\hat{1}$, a traditional species ending would have $\hat{2}$ to $\hat{1}$ in the lower part, making intervals 6 to 8 (Example 8.7a). We will instead choose a typical tonal close for this phrase: $\hat{5}$ to $\hat{1}$ in the bass line, which makes intervals 3 to 8 and implies the roots of the dominant and tonic triads (Example 8.7b).

EXAMPLE 8.7: Closing gestures for "My Country, 'Tis of Thee"

The strongest phrase endings in eighteenth-century-style note-against-note counterpoint are to an octave or a unison, but a third or fifth is also possible. The first phrase in the Mozart theme (mm. 7–8 of Example 8.2a) demonstrates the strongest tonal closing pattern in two voices: a falling fifth in the bass part from $\hat{5}$ to $\hat{1}$, and a step from $\hat{2}$ to $\hat{1}$ in the upper part (for the moment, ignore the E5). Some typical closing patterns are shown in Example 8.8.

EXAMPLE 8.8: Closing patterns

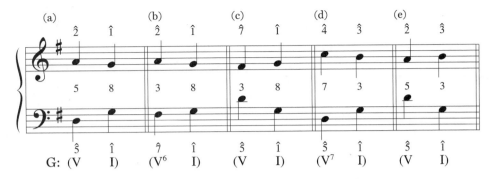

We can see another type of ending in measure 12 of the Mozart theme: the melody ends on D5 and the bass line on G3, implying a dominant chord. This does mark a resting point in the melody line, but it is not a final ending (we will learn more about phrases ending on the dominant in Chapter 12).

WF5

Chordal Dissonance

Dissonant intervals from the dominant seventh chord are found in eighteenth-century-style two-part counterpoint. The intervals m7 to 3—implying dominant-tonic motion—are useful in closing a phrase (see Example 8.8d), but they may also appear within a phrase as long as the rhythmic flow of the line does not stop. This motion is found in the Mozart theme in Example 8.2b between measures 10 and 11 and between 14 and 15.

The third and seventh of a dominant seventh chord ($\hat{7}$ and $\hat{4}$ in the key) also form a dissonant interval: the tritone. We have seen that Mozart includes this interval in Example 8.2a, measure 5. The tritone may be spelled as an augmented fourth ($\hat{4}$ in the lower part and $\hat{7}$ in the upper part) or as a diminished fifth ($\hat{7}$ in the lower part and $\hat{4}$ above).

KEY CONCEPT

We call the dissonant intervals of a dominant seventh chord **chordal dissonances**. Resolve these intervals as follows.

- d5 → 3: both voices move in by a step.
- A4 → 6: both voices move out by a step.
- m7 → 3: the lower voice moves up a P4 or down a P5; the upper voice moves down by a step.

Dissonant intervals are treated carefully in two-part counterpoint: they are traditionally approached by step in both voices, and resolved immediately. As we will see in later chapters, composers do not always follow the guidelines of strict counterpoint in approaching and resolving these dissonant intervals. However, when composers of the tonal era strayed from the guidelines, they assumed their listeners knew how the music was "supposed to go" and heard the departure from the traditional approach and resolution as musically daring and dramatic.

Completing the Counterpoint

To complete the note-against-note counterpoint, observe the following guidelines.

KEY CONCEPT

1. When you connect harmonic intervals, consider the melodic intervals that are created.
   - If one line skips or leaps, the other should step or remain on the same pitch.
   - If one line repeats or sustains the same pitch, the other should step, skip, or leap.
   - Both parts may step.

2. Use contrary motion the most, followed by similar, then oblique.
   - Both lines should be singable.
   - Both should have an interesting contour with a single melodic highpoint.

3. Use parallel motion carefully.
   - Parallel motion between two perfect fifths or octaves is not permitted in this style.
   - Use parallel motion freely with thirds or sixths, but
   - avoid too many parallel thirds or sixths in a row (remember, we are aiming for independent contrapuntal lines).

4. Approach and leave perfect intervals carefully.
   - Aim for contrary or oblique motion into and out of P5 and P8.
   - Avoid parallel motion into and out of P5 and P8.
   - Use similar motion into or out of P5 and P8 only if the soprano moves by step; otherwise avoid.
   - Include perfect intervals less often than thirds and sixths.
   - Avoid harmonic perfect fourths altogether.

5. Use mostly consonant intervals. When you write a chordal dissonance,
   - approach it by repeated pitch in one voice or by step in at least one of the voices;
   - resolve it correctly.

6. Make sure the opening and closing establishes the tonic chord.
   - End the counterpoint with a unison or octave (possibly a fifth or third).
   - Begin the counterpoint with a unison, octave, or fifth (possibly a third or sixth).

7. Close the counterpoint with a phrase ending that suggests dominant-to-tonic harmonic motion.

Almost all of the guidelines above maintain the rules of strict species according to Fux, except that for Fux point #5 would read "Use only consonant intervals," and point #6 would omit the information in parentheses. Point #7 would differ as well: the only cadence patterns allowed in strict first species are the 6–8 and 3-unison (scale-degrees $\hat{7}$ and $\hat{2}$ moving to scale-degree $\hat{1}$ as octave or unison).

Example 8.9 shows two note-against-note settings of the first phrase of "My Country, 'Tis of Thee." Play them at the keyboard, or sing them with your class. The intervals between the parts are labeled between the staves, and the type of motion (C, P, S, O) is labeled above the treble staff. Both (a) and (b) are correct note-against-note settings according to our tonal counterpoint guidelines.

EXAMPLE 8.9: Two note-against-note settings of the first phrase of "My Country, 'Tis of Thee"

Reduction to a Note-Against-Note Framework

Most tonal pieces are more rhythmically elaborate than "My Country" or Mozart's simple theme setting. It is rare to find entire Baroque- or Classical-period pieces in note-against-note counterpoint throughout. For many pieces, however, we *can* find a note-against-note framework behind the elaborate surface. For example, Bach's Prelude in C Major (in your anthology) has an active and elaborate musical surface of sixteenth notes, yet the outer voices (highest and lowest) follow the guidelines for two-part note-against-note counterpoint. The basic outer intervals only change once per measure—they can be notated in whole notes to show the note-against-note framework (as in Example 8.10; follow the example as you listen

1.17

Bach Reduced

We know that Bach and other composers of the Baroque era were aware of the idea of reduction—that there is a basic harmonic or contrapuntal framework underneath the decorative surface of music—because we have eighteenth-century manuscripts of pieces that show only the figuration (decorative patterning) for several measures and give the harmonic framework for the rest. One piece notated like this is Bach's Prelude in C Major, where the arpeggiation is written out in the manuscript only for the first few measures. Several textbooks, including Friedrich Niedt's *Musikalische Handleitung* (*Musical Handbook*, completed in 1717), show a composer how to take a basic harmonic progression and elaborate it into a prelude. From Niedt's time onward, this idea has continued to play a role in writings about music.

WF6 to the Prelude). This way of analyzing music is called **reduction**: separating the elaboration from the underlying framework, naming the types of elaboration, and examining the framework. Compare the reduction with Bach's score in the anthology, to see how the reduction was made.

EXAMPLE 8.10: Bach, Prelude in C Major, mm. 1–11 (outer-voice framework)

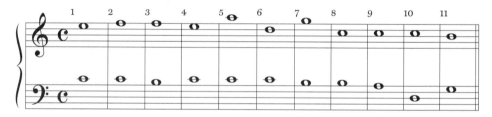

Which of the four types of intervallic motion are found in the outer-voice framework in Example 8.10? Label these above the example, with O (for oblique), S (similar), C (contrary), and P (parallel). *(Try it #4)*

Melodic Embellishment in Chorale Textures

The next step in learning species counterpoint is to focus on **second species**, or 2:1. In traditional second-species exercises, one part has a slower-moving line written in whole notes; the other has a faster one in half notes. Example 8.11 shows a second-species counterpoint exercise from Fux's *Gradus ad Parnassum*. Play it through, or sing with your class. Write in the intervals between the two voices to determine where Fux's counterpoint rules allow consonances and dissonances.

EXAMPLE 8.11: Second-species counterpoint from *Gradus ad Parnassum*

We will write an eighteenth-century-style 2:1 counterpoint, which is most commonly notated with eighth notes against quarter notes. Both voices alternate in taking the slower and faster rhythms. This texture, with both voices in quarter notes and eighth notes, is typical of **chorale style**, or hymn settings, on which we focus in this chapter.

In 2:1 counterpoint, when both voices change pitch on the beat, we usually follow the guidelines of note-against-note counterpoint. Between these framework intervals (on the offbeat), we can incorporate passing tones, neighbor tones (not allowed by Fux), and chordal skips, all of which are defined below.

Passing Tones

The first two phrases of Bach's setting of Martin Luther's chorale tune "Ein feste Burg ist unser Gott" ("A Mighty Fortress Is Our God") illustrate the most common dissonance in 2:1 counterpoint: the passing tone.

KEY CONCEPT

Passing tones (labeled P) are melodic embellishments that fill in between chord members by stepwise motion. The passing tone is approached by step and left by step in the same direction.

The soprano and bass parts of measures 1–4 are shown in Example 8.12; sing one part and play the other. Both parts feature a mix of quarter and eighth notes. The first eighth notes, in the bass anacrusis to the downbeat of measure 1, form the intervals 8–9–3 (including the downbeat) with the soprano. The framework for these two beats is 8–3; the 9 is a dissonant passing tone, which fills in between the consonant intervals on the beats by stepwise motion in one direction.

In the example, the intervals between the voices are labeled, along with two other dissonant passing tones. Do the remaining offbeat eighth notes also make dissonant passing tones? Circle and label them. *(Try it #5)*

EXAMPLE 8.12: Bach, "Ein feste Burg ist unser Gott," mm. 1–4a (soprano and bass)

You probably noticed that two of the eighth-note patterns are different. In measure 1, beat 2 (in the bass), the dissonant passing tone falls on the beat. We call this an **accented passing tone**. (Accented passing tones are not permitted in Fux's second species, but they do occur in eighteenth-century style.) In measure 3, beat 2, the passing tone in the bass maintains consonant intervals: 6 and 5. We call this a **consonant passing tone**. Both of these types of passing tones are possible in tonal 2:1 counterpoint, but they are less common than the unaccented dissonant passing tone. (We usually do not label consonant passing tones.)

Neighbor Tones and Chordal Skips

Sing or play through the soprano and bass lines of Bach's "Wachet auf," given in Example 8.13. Then label all the harmonic intervals between the voices.

EXAMPLE 8.13: Bach, "Wachet auf," mm. 32b–36 (soprano and bass)

The three dissonant passing tones are circled in the soprano and bass voices. What type of dissonance occurs in measure 33? The bass's G3 on the beat is consonant with the E♭5 of the soprano, but the F3 that follows is dissonant. This dissonance is not a passing tone, but a neighbor tone. Neighbor tones temporarily displace the chord tone they decorate, and usually form dissonant intervals with other members of the harmony.

KEY CONCEPT

Neighbor tones (labeled N) are melodic embellishments that decorate a melody pitch by moving to a pitch a step above or below it, then returning to the original pitch. Neighbor tones are approached and left by step, in opposite directions.

The remaining quarter-note motion in the bass line of measure 33 makes intervals 3 and 5 with the soprano: both consonances. Both of these bass pitches are members of the E♭-Major triad. This type of melodic elaboration is called a chordal, or consonant, skip.

KEY CONCEPT

Chordal skips (labeled CS) are melodic embellishments made by skipping from one chord member to another. The harmonic intervals formed are consonances.

Although we have confined our discussion to mostly eighteenth-century style, some of the principles of 2:1 counterpoint can be found in popular music of our time as well. Look at the passage from Lloyd Webber and Rice's "Don't Cry for Me Argentina" shown in Example 8.14a. Mark the intervals and melodic embellishments (CS, P, or N) in the rhythmically simplified soprano-bass reduction given in Example 8.14b. Does this passage follow our 2:1 counterpoint guidelines? *(Try it #6)*

EXAMPLE 8.14: Lloyd Webber and Rice, "Don't Cry for Me Argentina"

(a) Mm. 33–40

(b) Reduction of mm. 33–40

Writing 2:1 Counterpoint

Up to this point, we have looked at examples of 2:1 writing in the free style of chorale composition. When we write our first 2:1 counterpoints, we will follow the simpler rhythmic structure of species instruction, employing the quarter notes and eighth notes typical of eighteenth-century music. In Example 8.15, the bass line consists entirely of quarter notes, and the soprano line of eighths. Analyze the harmonic intervals by writing the correct interval numbers between the staves. Then circle and label all passing tones (P), neighbor tones (N), and chordal skips (CS). Does this counterpoint follow all our guidelines for 2:1 writing? (*Try it #7*)

EXAMPLE 8.15: A sample two-part counterpoint

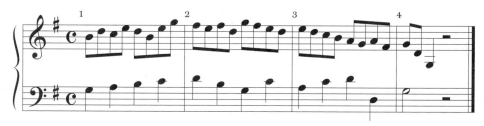

When you write 2:1 counterpoint, follow the same procedures as in 1:1 writing: compose the opening and cadential measures first to ensure that they make good harmonic and contrapuntal sense, then fill in the middle section.

KEY CONCEPT

When writing 2:1 counterpoint:

1. Continue to follow the guidelines for 1:1 counterpoint with respect to
   - types of motion (contrary, similar, oblique, and parallel) and
   - phrase beginnings and endings.

2. Incorporate chordal skips, passing tones, and neighbor tones on the offbeats.

3. Treat the P4 as a dissonance—use it only as a passing or neighbor tone.

4. Avoid similar motion into perfect intervals unless the upper voice moves by step.

5. Don't write parallel perfect consonances (P5 to P5, P8 to P8) on an offbeat to beat or on consecutive beats.

This last guideline (#5) needs special mention, since the addition of melodic embellishments in 2:1 writing provides new opportunities for forbidden parallels. Be sure to check for parallels not only from beat to beat, but also from offbeat to beat. When you have finished writing your counterpoint, perform it (at the keyboard or with a partner) so that you can use your ears to check for parallels, accented dissonances, or other errors.

TERMS YOU SHOULD KNOW

1:1	disjunct	passing tone
2:1	first species	second species
chordal skip	leap	similar motion
conjunct	neighbor tone	skip
consonant skip	note-against-note	step
contrary motion	oblique motion	
counterpoint	parallel motion	

QUESTIONS FOR REVIEW

1. Why do we learn counterpoint?
2. What sizes of intervals are called steps? skips? leaps?
3. What are the four types of melodic intervallic motion?
4. What are some differences between traditional first-species counterpoint (Fux) and the tonal counterpoint we learned in this chapter?
5. What is permitted in 2:1 counterpoint but not in note-against-note?
6. What are the guidelines for composing 1:1 counterpoint? 2:1?
7. Find a piece, in your repertoire if possible, that was written in the eighteenth century and moves in mostly 2:1 rhythm. Choose one phrase, and analyze the bass-soprano counterpoint by labeling intervals and melodic elaborations (CS, P, or N).

Melodic and Rhythmic Embellishment in Two-Voice Composition

CHAPTER 9

Outline of topics covered

Melodic embellishment
- Neighbor tones
  Incomplete neighbors
  Double neighbors
- Consonant skips
- More on passing tones
- Chromatic embellishment

Writing 4:1 counterpoint

Rhythmic embellishment: Suspensions
- Types of dissonant suspensions
- Consonant suspensions
- Chains of suspensions

Free counterpoint

Overview

In this chapter, we return to Mozart's set of variations on "Ah, vous dirai-je, Maman" to learn how melodic embellishments—neighbor tones, passing tones, and chordal skips—are used in 3:1 and 4:1 two-voice counterpoint. We will also see how suspensions can elaborate a two-voice framework. Finally, we will explore ways that musical compositions can be reduced to two-voice frameworks.

Repertoire
Wolfgang Amadeus Mozart, Variations on "Ah, vous dirai-je, Maman" (CD 2, track 86)

○ ○

Melodic Embellishment

As we saw in Chapter 8, the types of melodic embellishment found in compositions from the eighteenth century differ from those taught in species-counterpoint teaching manuals, such as Fux's *Gradus ad Parnassum*. As you read this chapter, refer to the WebFacts to learn which types of embellishment patterns you should leave out of your counterpoint if you want to write in the style taught by Fux.

2.86 For our continued study of melodic embellishment, we return to Mozart's Variations on "Ah, vous dirai-je, Maman." The complete score is given in your anthology. You may want to begin by listening to the entire work. Classical-period variations are excellent for this study because we know (from the theme) what the composer considered a starting point. Mozart's variations include a variety of melodic embellishments and draw on several contrapuntal techniques for their elaborations of the familiar theme. While studying these melodic embellishments and counterpoint, we will also learn a little about variation form.

Neighbor Tones

Listen to Mozart's first variation (mm. 25–48). The melody in this variation, like the theme, is based on the "Twinkle, Twinkle, Little Star" tune, but some additional pitches have been added. Compare measures 25–32 (Example 9.1a) with the first eight measures of the theme (Example 9.1b). Listen to these two excerpts, one right after the other, or play through them at the keyboard. In measures 25–26, an example of **4:1 counterpoint**, added dissonances circle around the pitches C5 and G5 of the theme: each is preceded by the diatonic pitch a step above, then decorated by the pitch a half step below. This type of dissonance is familiar from our study of 2:1 counterpoint—these are neighbor tones. In 4:1 counterpoint, the four notes of this neighbor pattern may be completed against a single pitch in the slower-moving part. Here, the added pitches form the intervals 9 and 7 with the first bass pitch in measure 25, and 4 and 2 with the first bass pitch in measure 26.

Sometimes in music analysis, we may want to specify whether the neighbor is above or below the main melody pitch: those neighbors above are called **upper neighbors** (sometimes marked UN), and those below, **lower neighbors** (sometimes marked LN).

EXAMPLE 9.1: Mozart, Variations on "Ah, vous dirai-je, Maman"

(a) Variation I, mm. 25–32

(b) Theme, mm. 1–8

In 4:1 counterpoint, neighbor tones may appear in accented or unaccented positions, although unaccented neighbors are more common. Look again at Example 9.1a. In measure 25, the consonant interval is the repeated octave on C. The B4 in the third sixteenth-note position of beat 1—a relatively weak rhythmic position—is an example of an **unaccented neighbor tone**. In contrast, the B4 neighbor at the beginning of beat 2 displaces the C5 in a strong rhythmic position; this is an example of **an accented neighbor tone**. Both are lower neighbors. Play this measure to compare the effect of each neighbor tone. Accented neighbor dissonances generally have a more striking aural effect because of the strong-beat dissonance, and performers sometimes add a rhythmic or dynamic stress for expressive effect.

Incomplete Neighbors   Complete neighbor-note patterns involve three notes: the main melody pitch (a consonance that fits with the harmony), the upper or lower neighbor a step away (usually a dissonance), and the return to the main melody pitch. Sometimes one of the consonant elements of this three-part pattern is left out; in this case, we call the dissonance an **incomplete neighbor** (abbreviated IN). In Example 9.2, two incomplete neighbors are circled. The D5 with which measure 25 begins is an incomplete neighbor: the main melody pitch C5 does not precede the neighbor tone D5. This incomplete neighbor, in an accented position, makes sense aurally because we know the tune, and hear the D5 as temporarily displacing the C5 that belongs there. On the downbeat of measure 26, the melody leaps away from C5 to A5, another accented incomplete neighbor. Accented incomplete neighbors like the D5 and A5, both of which form dissonances and resolve down by step, are sometimes known as "appoggiaturas."

EXAMPLE 9.2: Mozart, Variations, Variation I, mm. 25–26

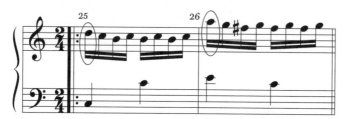

KEY CONCEPT

To write an incomplete neighbor,

- skip or leap to the dissonant neighbor tone, then resolve to the main melody pitch a step away (usually in the opposite direction from the approach); or
- approach the dissonant neighbor tone by step, then leave it by skip or leap in the opposite direction.

2.87 **Double Neighbors**   Listen to Variation II, and circle the neighbor tones in your anthology (a portion is given later in this chapter as Example 9.12). Neighbor tones also embellish this variation—but they decorate the bass line instead of the upper part. In measure 49, we hear both a lower neighbor B3 and an upper neighbor D4.

KEY CONCEPT

We call the combination of successive upper and lower neighbors (in either order) around the same main pitch a **double neighbor**. Sometimes the repetition of the main pitch between the upper and lower neighbor is left out, with the melody skipping from one neighbor to the other before returning to the main pitch.

Double neighbors are the main type of embellishment in this variation. There are also some "single" lower neighbors in measures 53–55 and 68–71.

The opening measures of Variations I and II both include neighbor tones for melodic embellishment, but in opposite parts (I in the melody; II in the bass). These two variations make a pair within the variation set (a typical way Classical-period composers organized sets of variations). Both variations have sixteenth notes in the decorated voice against the basic quarter notes of the original theme.

WF1 This type of rhythmic setting is called **4:1 counterpoint**, or **third species**. Which other variations in this set have a quarter note to four sixteenth notes as a rhythmic combination? Check the complete score in your anthology. (*Try it #1*)

Consonant Skips

What happens in Variations III and IV? These have quarter-note motion in one part, like the others, but the embellished part consists of triplets. This **3:1** rhythmic pat-

WF2 terning is considered a type of second species in Fuxian counterpoint, but in eighteenth-century practice it is more closely related to third species in its use of dissonance (neighbor and double-neighbor patterns are common). Listen to the

2.88 🎧 opening measures of Variation IV, shown in Example 9.3a. The "Twinkle" melody is there, but chords have been added in the treble staff. These chords are shown in Example 9.3b: a C-Major triad in measures 97, 98, and 100 and an F-Major triad in measure 99 (for the moment, ignore the dissonant G5 in m. 99 and the dissonant F5 in m. 100). C and F Major are the harmonies that usually accompany this melody. What is the relationship of the embellished bass part to these chords? The bass line is an arpeggiation made from consonant skips between chord members—the same chords as in the treble staff.

EXAMPLE 9.3: Mozart, Variations, Variation IV

(a) Mm. 97–100

(b) Reduction of the treble-clef part, mm. 97–100

2.88 Now consider Variation III. This variation pairs with IV, in that both are examples of 3:1 counterpoint. In Variation IV, the bass part has the embellishments; in Variation III, the embellishments are in the upper part. Some measures and beats in this variation have arpeggiations—which ones? In measures 75 and 81, shown in Example 9.4, the first beats feature another type of melodic embellishment we have studied in this chapter. What is it? *(Try it #2)*

EXAMPLE 9.4: Mozart, Variations, Variation III, mm. 75, 81

More on Passing Tones

Look at measures 73–76 in Example 9.5. What other familiar embellishment do you find in measures 74–75? The main melody pitch in measure 74 is G5, and the harmony for this measure is a C-Major triad. The C6, G5, E5 and C5 in measure 74 all fit into that harmony. What about the F5 and D5? These are passing tones that fill in the skips between the chord members, making a stepwise scalar line. If we left them out, the melody would be embellished with an arpeggiation of the C-Major triad. These passing tones make dissonant intervals with the C4 (the root of the C-Major triad): the F5 and C4 make a fourth; the D5 and C4, a ninth. As the line passes through these dissonances, the 4 resolves to a 3 and the 9 resolves to 8. On what beats of the measure may passing tones occur? As we learned in Chapter 8, passing tones may be accented or unaccented, and therefore may appear on any beat or portion of a beat in this style. (In strict Fuxian third species, passing and neighbor dissonances are permitted only on the second and fourth parts of the beat.)

WF3

EXAMPLE 9.5: Mozart, Variations, Variation III, mm. 73–76

2.91

Passing tones often fill in the skip of a third, but they can also fill in larger intervals in this style. In the beginning of Variation VIII, given in Example 9.6, the opening melodic skip C5 to G5 of the "Twinkle" tune is filled in with a scale, C–D–E♭–F–G. We can think of this scale as filling in the interval of a fifth from C to G. Alternatively, we could think of this passage as filling in the thirds from C to E♭ and from E♭ to G, but in this case we know that the "Twinkle" tune opens with a fifth.

EXAMPLE 9.6: Mozart, Variations, Variation VIII, mm. 193–194

2.90

In Variation VII, the first two measures are a C-Major scale (mm. 169–170, shown in Example 9.7a). Because the main harmony for the measure is C Major, the scales can be considered arpeggiations of C Major filled in with passing tones (Example 9.7b). Sometimes two passing tones are needed to fill in between chordal skips of a fourth, as in measure 169, beat 2, to measure 170, beat 1, where A4 and B4 fill in the skip from G4 to C5.

EXAMPLE 9.7: Mozart, Variations, Variation VII

(a) Mm. 169–170

(b) Reduction of mm. 169–170, showing arpeggiation with passing tones

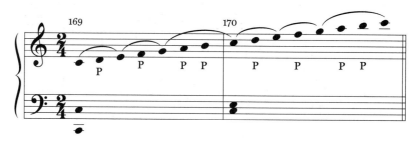

KEY CONCEPT

When scales are used in compositions, they often represent arpeggiations of the main harmony of that measure, filled in with passing tones.

Sometimes in music analysis we label arpeggiations filled in by scales with slurs to connect the members of the chord and the letter P to designate the passing tones (as in Example 9.7b). These slurs are simply analytical symbols to show how the pitches are organized in the music; they do not mean that the scale is to be performed with slurs.

We can now consider one of the more elaborate variations in this set: Variation VI (mm. 145–152 are shown in Example 9.8). In this variation, the "Twinkle" tune is in the treble-clef upper part, with the chords of the harmonization filled in below it. The bass line is embellished in 4:1 counterpoint with the melody. We have studied all of the embellishment types found in this bass line. Listen to the variation, then label the neighbor tones with an N and the passing tones with a P. *(Try it #3)*

2.89

EXAMPLE 9.8: Mozart, Variations, Variation VI, mm. 145–152

Chromatic Embellishment

You may have noticed accidentals before several notes in Example 9.8. Chromatic embellishment is not permitted in species counterpoint as Fux taught it, but you will find it frequently in music of eighteenth- and nineteenth-century composers. In measure 149 of the Mozart example, there is a C♯ followed by a C♮. The C♯4 neighbor tone is a half step lower than D4, rather than the whole step that would have been formed with the diatonic C♮.

KEY CONCEPT

> A half-step neighbor tone created by a nondiatonic accidental is called a **chromatic neighbor tone**.

A chromatic neighbor makes a more striking effect than a diatonic neighbor. The chromatic C♯ neighbor tone draws our attention to the D. Then when the line continues, Mozart changes back to the diatonic C♮, resulting in a downward pull to the next main note of the line. This is a temporary chromaticism, and does not disturb the sense of the key. The G♯ and F♯ in the following measures are also chromatic neighbor tones.

2.91

In the second half of Variation VIII, we see a lot of accidentals (Example 9.9). The corresponding portions of the original theme are shown in Example 9.10. Most of the theme is stepwise—it would not be possible to put *diatonic* passing tones between the pitches. But it is possible to include *chromatic* passing tones on the half steps between the whole steps of the melody, which is what Mozart has done here. Listen to the chromatic minor-mode setting of the tune.

KEY CONCEPT

A passing tone that divides a whole step in the key into two half steps is called a **chromatic passing tone**.

The F♯5 in measure 202 is a chromatic passing tone, as is the E♮ in the following measure (the E♭ may look like a chromatic passing tone, but it is $\hat{3}$ in this minor-mode setting).

EXAMPLE 9.9: Mozart, Variations, Variation VIII, mm. 201–208

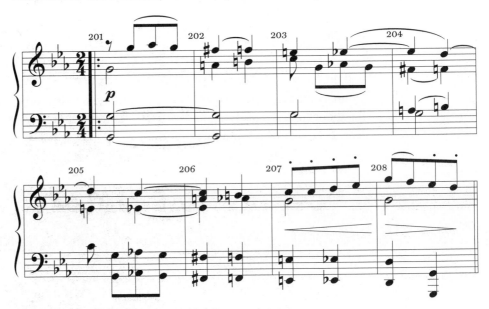

EXAMPLE 9.10: Mozart, Variations, theme, mm. 9–16

2.92  This chromatic scale segment appears in the alto part in measures 204–205, and in the bass part in measures 206–207. This "echoing" of a line in counterpoint is called **imitation**. In the following variation (IX), which is much simpler in texture, the opening fifth of the "Twinkle" tune is imitated in the soprano, alto, tenor, and bass parts in turn. If we heard Variation VIII or IX by itself, we might not recognize the "Twinkle" theme, since it is altered so much; but after hearing the theme and seven variations, the tune is recognizable even in these highly embellished versions.

Writing 4:1 Counterpoint

Good 4:1 counterpoint has a correct framework of note-against-note or 2:1 writing underneath it. Start with a soprano-bass framework like those we wrote in Chapter 8. Then follow the guidelines below to make a 4:1 counterpoint from your note-against-note or 2:1 framework. Remember to write in the intervals between the lines to check for correct use of dissonance and for parallels!

KEY CONCEPT

When writing 4:1 counterpoint:

1. Think in groups of five rather than four. Connect each group of four smoothly to the next beat.
2. Use consonant skips. Decorate a repeated pitch in your 2:1 framework with a skip to a consonance and back. In a note-against-note framework, first add a skip to a consonance and back, then fill in one of the skips with a passing tone (Example 9.11a). Avoid too many skips in one direction (two are usually sufficient).
3. Fill in consonant skips in your 2:1 framework with passing tones (Example 9.11b).
4. Use neighbor tones to decorate a repeated pitch in your 2:1 counterpoint. Use a double neighbor to turn one beat of note-against-note into 4:1, but avoid too many double neighbors because they create a "circular" melodic line. Combine a neighbor pattern with a passing tone (in either order) to fill in a third in a note-against-note framework (Example 9.11c).
5. Every dissonant interval should be a passing tone or neighbor tone. Make sure the dissonant pitch "passes" or "neighbors" correctly!
6. Watch out for forbidden parallels. Check each pair of beats for parallel octaves or fifths in three places: on consecutive beats (beat-to-beat parallels), on the third part of a beat to the next beat (offbeat-to-beat parallels), and from the fourth part of the beat to the next beat (adjacency parallels). Examples 9.11d–f show all three types of parallels.

7. Check the contour. Make sure your counterpoint has an interesting melodic contour, rising to a single high point.

8. Listen. Always sing or play your counterpoint—each line separately and the two lines together—to check your work. If it sounds wrong, it probably is. (The reverse—if it sounds right, it probably is—does not always work for students new to counterpoint. As you learn more about counterpoint, your ability to hear correct and incorrect progressions will improve.)

EXAMPLE 9.11:

(a) Consonant skips

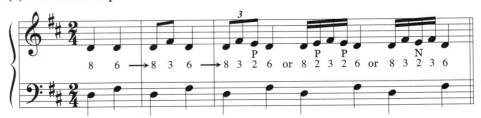

(b) Passing tones

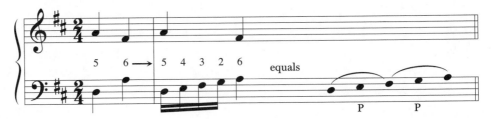

(c) Neighbor tones

(d) Beat-to-beat parallels (e) Offbeat-to-beat parallels

(f) Adjacency parallels

Rhythmic Embellishment: Suspensions

In the melodic elaborations we have considered thus far, we have added consonant or dissonant pitches to decorate a basic note-against-note soprano-bass framework. A second general category of embellishment—rhythmic elaboration—involves shifting consonant pitches of the basic framework forward or backward in time to create a dissonance. The dissonance created by this rhythmic displacement must resolve to complete the embellishment pattern. The most common type of rhythmic embellishment is the suspension, which is taught in **fourth species** in Fux's method. We will consider other types of rhythmic embellishment in the context of four-voice composition in Chapter 13.

WF4

2.87

Listen again to the first part of Variation II (Example 9.12a). When we examined this variation previously, we focused on the outer voices; this time, look at the intervals between the second-highest line and the bass (Example 9.12b).

EXAMPLE 9.12: Mozart, Variations, Variation II

(a) Mm. 49–56

(b) Second-highest-part-and-bass framework, mm. 49–56

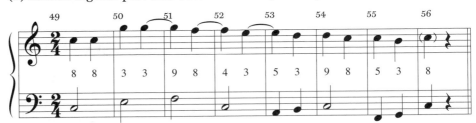

(c) Note-to-note framework, mm. 49–56

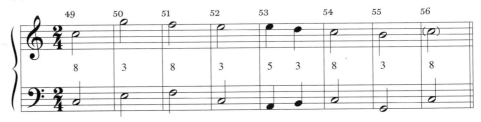

In measures 50–54, the rhythm is similar to 2:1 counterpoint, but the second pitch in each measure is either tied over or repeated to become the first pitch of the next. In some cases, the reiterated pitch creates a dissonance with the bass on the downbeat of the next measure; in some cases, it makes a consonance. Now compare Examples 9.12b and c. What is the relationship between these two examples? (*Try it #4*)

The reiterated pitches in Example 9.12b are suspensions. We can think of suspensions as consonant intervals of a note-against-note basic framework that do not move to the next pitch on time—they are held past their time so that the next pitch arrives late. Not every pitch of the basic framework can be treated this way: we can only make suspensions when one line of the note-against-note framework moves down by step to form a consonance with the other voice.

KEY CONCEPT

A **suspension** is a rhythmic embellishment that occurs when a consonance of the basic framework is held over to the next beat, creating a dissonance until one voice moves down by step to the next pitch. We can think of suspensions as having three parts:

- a consonance (sometimes called the "preparation");
- that consonance held over into the next beat to make an accented dissonance (the suspension);
- the resolution of that dissonance down by step to a consonance (the "resolution").

Suspensions are usually connected to their consonant preparation by a tie, as shown in Example 9.13. When the suspended note is not tied to its preparation, it is called a **rearticulated suspension**.

Types of Dissonant Suspensions

There are only a few types of suspensions. Two of the most common are shown in Example 9.12b: the 9–8 suspension in measure 51 and the 4–3 suspension in measure 52.

KEY CONCEPT

Suspensions are named by the interval numbers of the dissonance and resolution. The most common types of suspensions made by rhythmic displacement of an upper voice are 4–3, 7–6, and 9–8.

Example 9.13 shows each common suspension type, with its three-part structure labeled: preparation, suspension, and resolution.

EXAMPLE 9.13: Suspension types: 4–3, 7–6, and 9–8

A less common suspension, 2–1, is sometimes found between the two lowest parts in four-part writing. There is only one common suspension made by displacement of the bass: a 2–3. As we know, the bass voice usually supports any change in harmony. Sometimes, however, the upper voice signals the change, with the bass voice lagging behind; this creates the 2–3 bass suspension (see Example 9.15b).

Consonant Suspensions

We can also make suspensions from the consonant intervals 6–5 (with the suspension in the upper part) and 5–6 (with the suspension in the lower part). Although these suspensions do not feature the dissonance treatment of those discussed above, we consider them suspensions because they are created by rhythmic displacement. These suspensions are prepared by a consonance, are delayed across the strong beat, and resolve down by step. The opening of Mozart's Variation VIII (Example 9.14) is similar to the comparable measures of Example 9.12a, but some of the suspension patterns are different because the bass line differs. Look at (and listen to) measure 197 for an example of a 6–5 suspension. With the main bass pitch G3, the suspended E♭5 (6) creates a consonant suspension. In this particular case, the E♭ still sounds like a suspended tone since it is not a part of the underlying harmony (G Major).

2.91

EXAMPLE 9.14: Mozart, Variations, Variation VIII, mm. 193–200

Chains of Suspensions

When one part features a stepwise descending line, we can write a chain of suspensions in the other part. For example, a note-against-note series of descending parallel thirds or sixths (Example 9.15a) can be made into a series of suspensions, with the consonant resolution of each preparing the next (Example 9.15b). Only 4–3, 7–6, and 2–3 are used in chains of suspensions. Why? *(Try it #5)*

EXAMPLE 9.15:

(a) Parallel thirds and sixths

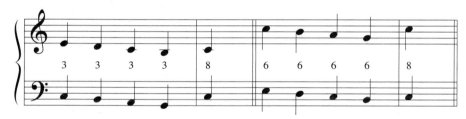

(b) Chain of suspensions

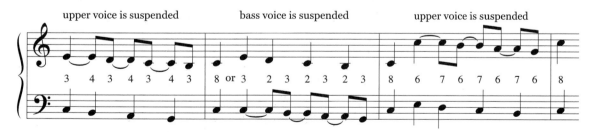

Suspensions—and especially chains of suspensions—can be very expressive musical gestures. It is common when performing suspensions to *crescendo* slightly into the dissonance and pull away from the resolution. Try this (subtly!) for a more effective performance.

Free Counterpoint

Strict species counterpoint exercises, especially those of Fux with the cantus firmus in whole notes, may not seem at first to have much connection to common-practice-period music. But as we have seen in the music examples from this chapter and the previous one, the underlying principles of two-part counterpoint are found in music much more elaborate than the species exercises. In Fux's system, after learning the first through fourth species, students went on to combine the individual patterns of each species to create a counterpoint with varied rhythm; this was called **fifth species**. In fifth species, shown in Example 9.16, one of the voices is the slow-moving cantus firmus in whole notes; the other includes quarter notes (from third species), half notes (second species), half notes tied over the bar (fourth species), and whole notes (first species) mixed together. Play through the example, or sing it with your class.

EXAMPLE 9.16: Fux, *Gradus ad Parnassum*, fifth species

In most compositions, however, melodic and rhythmic embellishments are not isolated in one voice—the species are all mixed together in all the parts. This mixing is sometimes called "free counterpoint," although that does not mean that we are free to do just anything with dissonances. Instead, we are free to choose where, how, and with what note values we will use melodic and rhythmic elaboration. We will be learning about free counterpoint throughout the rest of this book. As musicians, learning to play and interpret melodic and rhythmic embellishments of tonal music is a goal we pursue for a lifetime.

SUMMARY

SPECIES	DISSONANCE TYPE	RHYTHM	
		FUX	EIGHTEENTH CENTURY
First (1:1)	no dissonance	o to o	♩ to ♩, ♩ to ♩, or ♪ to ♪
Second (2:1)	passing tones; neighbor tones in eighteenth-century style	o to ♩	♩ to ♫, ♩ to ♩♩, or ♪ to ♬
Third (4:1)	passing tones; neighbor tones; double neighbors	o to ♩♩♩♩	♩ to ♬♬, ♩ to ♬♬, or o to ♩♩♩♩
Fourth	4-3, 7-6, 9-8, 2-3 suspensions (also consonant suspensions, 6-5 and 5-6)	o to ♩|♩ ♩	♩ to ♩|♩ ♩ or ♩ to ♩|♫
Fifth	all of the above	all of the above	all of the above

TERMS YOU SHOULD KNOW

3:1 (second species, Fux; third species, eighteenth-century practice)
4:1 (third species)

arpeggiation
chromatic neighbor
chromatic passing tone
double neighbor
fifth species

fourth species
imitation
incomplete neighbor
suspension

QUESTIONS FOR REVIEW

1. Which dissonances are used in 4:1 counterpoint? 3:1?
2. How is a neighbor tone approached and resolved? a passing tone? a double neighbor? an incomplete neighbor?
3. What do we do to add embellishments to a note-against-note or 2:1 framework?
4. What are the three parts of a suspension?
5. Which suspensions can be used in chains? Which are not used in chains? Why not?
6. Find a piece with rich melodic and rhythmic elaboration. Choose a phrase or two in which to identify and label all the embellishments you can find. Try writing out the melody with the embellishments removed (like the "Twinkle" theme). Can you still recognize the tune?

Notation and Scoring

Overview

In this chapter, we will examine score notation for solo melody with keyboard accompaniment, for SATB choir, for keyboard, and for guitar. We will learn how to use staves, clefs, beaming, and stemming to make scores that are easy to read for instruments and for voices.

Repertoire

Johann Sebastian Bach, Cantata No. 140 ("Wachet auf"), seventh movement

Bach, "Wachet auf" (Chorale No. 179) (CD 1, track 9)

Ludwig van Beethoven, Variations on "God Save the King"

"Greensleeves" (folk tune, arranged for guitar by Norbert Kraft) (CD 1, track 94)

Charles Ives, Variations on "America" for Organ

Wolfgang Amadeus Mozart, Piano Sonata in C Major, K. 545, first movement (CD 2, track 57)

"My Country, 'Tis of Thee" (CD 2, track 97)

Henry Purcell, "Music for a While" (CD 3, track 5)

"Rich and Rare" (traditional, arranged by Joel Phillips)

The Notation of Melodies

Stems

3.6 Look at the melody of Purcell's song "Music for a While" given in Example 10.1, while listening to the opening phrase. Does the notation of the melody follow the guidelines we learned in Chapter 2 for adding stems to notes? Most of the stems attached to pitches higher than the middle line of the treble staff (B4) extend downward from the left side of the note head; those attached to pitches lower than B4 extend upward from the right side of the note head. What happens when a note is written on the middle line? Such a note may have a stem extending up or down, with the choice depending on the pitches around it. In each case here, however, the notes on the middle line have downward stems. Groups of beamed notes that span the middle of the staff are stemmed in the direction of the melodic line's continuation (see "beguile" in mm. 6–7).

EXAMPLE 10.1: Purcell, "Music for a While," mm. 4–7a (vocal line)

Beams in Instrumental Music

We usually beam notes smaller than a beat unit together to make it easy to see the beats within a measure of music. In most cases, all of the notes in a beamed beat unit will have stems extending in the same direction, with the beam connecting the stem ends. (There are exceptions for very wide skips.) Beaming indicates to performers where to place the slight metric accent that each beat receives. When we are sight-reading, correct beaming helps us quickly scan the measure for beat groupings.

Beams and Flags in Vocal Music

Sometimes we choose not to beam beat units together. In some vocal music, the distribution of beams and flags tells the singer which syllables of text are sung to which notes. For example, in measure 5 of the Purcell song, the four sixteenth notes on beat 4 would have been beamed together in an instrumental part to show that they form a single beat unit. Here, however, the sixteenth notes are beamed in pairs to indicate that the first two fit with the word "for" and the second two are sung to "a."

Listen again to the excerpt from "Music for a While," and put brackets over the notes and rests in Example 10.1 that make up each beat. Are there other places where the beaming reflects the text rather than the beat unit? *(Try it #1)*

KEY CONCEPT

Although it is customary to beam together the durations that make up a beat, in some vocal music the need to indicate the placement of text takes precedence over beat beaming.

Modern editions and contemporary composers often favor "instrumental" notation for vocal lines, however, since beaming beat units together helps singers sight-read rhythms better.

○ ○

The Notation of Two or More Parts on a Staff

Stems can indicate more than one part on a single staff. In the keyboard part of Example 10.2, the accompaniment to Purcell's song is shown on the grand staff with three distinct parts, as indicated by the stemming and beaming: a bass line in the bass staff; an alto line in the treble staff, stems down; and a **countermelody** in the treble staff, stems up. Notes that are a part of both the soprano and alto lines show two stems. Although this passage is played on a single instrument, the accompanist can bring out its independent lines (shown by the stems) in performance, through choices in articulation (such as playing *legato* or *non legato*) and dynamics (such as making a moving part louder).

The Continuo

In the Baroque era (1600–1750), many compositions included a **continuo** part. The notation of the continuo part consisted of a bass line and a series of numbers, called figured bass, that showed which intervals to play above the bass line. Typically, this part was played by a keyboard instrument (harpsichord or organ), with the bass line reinforced by a cello or some other low-pitched melody instrument, such as a bass viol. The continuo part also could be played by a lute or guitar. The keyboard accompaniment to Purcell's "Music for a While" (in your anthology) is one **realization**, or filling in, of the chords above the bass line, following the instructions of the figured bass. It is just one of many possible realizations. For more on figured bass, see Chapter 14.

EXAMPLE 10.2: Purcell, "Music for a While," mm. 4–7a (full texture)

Mu - sic, mu - sic for_ a_ while shall all your_ cares be - guile,_

○ ○

The Notation of Four-Part Harmony SATB

One traditional way of writing four-part harmony is in **SATB** (soprano, alto, tenor, bass) chorale style. This type of notation is found in hymns, chorales, and other settings for chorus. We also use SATB textures to learn principles of harmony and voice-leading. The hymn setting of "My Country, 'Tis of Thee" in Example 10.3 is in SATB chorale-style notation. Listen to this passage to hear the spacing and register of the four distinct vocal parts.

2.97

EXAMPLE 10.3: "My Country, 'Tis of Thee," mm. 1–6

My coun - try, 'tis of thee, Sweet land of lib - er - ty,

Of thee I sing;

Staff, Clefs, and Stems

In SATB style, we notate the soprano and alto voices on the treble staff of a grand staff and the bass and tenor voices on the bass staff.

KEY CONCEPT

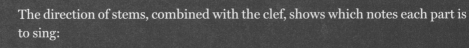

The direction of stems, combined with the clef, shows which notes each part is to sing:

- the soprano part is in the treble staff with stems up;
- the alto part is in the treble staff with stems down;
- the tenor part is in the bass staff with stems up; and
- the bass part is in the bass staff with stems down.

If the soprano and alto are to sing the same note in unison at the same time, the note will have two stems: one up for soprano, and one down for alto. (See the unison soprano and alto in Example 10.3, measure 4, beat 3.) This rule holds for the tenor and bass singing in unison as well. When alto and tenor sing in unison, however, each receives its own note—one for each staff. When either soprano and alto or tenor and bass have a unison in whole notes, we must write two whole notes right next to each other, since there are no stems to show that both parts are to sing the same pitch.

SATB in Open Score

The same four parts could be notated with a staff for each part, in what is called **open score**. Look at Bach's setting of the seventh movement from his cantata "Wachet auf" in Example 10.4. In open-score notation, we write the tenor part with a treble clef, but an octave higher than it is sung (the small 8 under the treble-clef sign shows the octave transposition). We will notate our chorale settings on two staves, however, since it saves paper and space, helps vocalists see how their part fits with the others, and makes it easier for an accompanist to play along with the voices. (The bottom bass staff of Example 10.4 provides the figured bass. Listen to the version of this tune in your anthology, sung to verse 1, to hear an unaccompanied setting of the music.)

1.9

EXAMPLE 10.4: Bach, Cantata No. 140 ("Wachet auf"), seventh movement, mm. 1–5

Translation: Let glory be sung to thee.

The Basic Principles of SATB Settings

When you write an SATB setting for vocalists, keep four basic concepts in mind: range, spacing, voice crossings, and doubling. We will examine "My Country" and the chorale "Wachet auf" (in your anthology) to see whether these settings correspond to the guidelines for range, spacing, and voice crossing given below. (We will learn about **doubling**—changing a three-voice triad to a four-voice texture by representing one chord member twice—in Chapter 11.)

Range   To make an SATB setting easy to sing, the pitches in each part need to conform to the traditional range for the singers, shown in Example 10.5. These ranges are somewhat flexible, but for SATB settings for general use, you should stay within these guidelines. Do "My Country" and "Wachet auf" conform to these range expectations? (*Try it #2*)

EXAMPLE 10.5: SATB vocal ranges

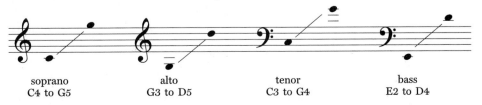

Voice ranges vary depending on the age and maturity of the singer, as well as on the type of composition. Music for children or teens, for example, requires smaller vocal ranges; and the four men's voices in a barbershop quartet have their own special ranges. Choral settings for skilled or professional adult singers may exceed the standard SATB range guidelines.

WF1

WF2

Spacing   Four-part chords usually sound best if the interval between adjacent parts is an octave or less, to allow the parts to blend together with a balanced harmony.

KEY CONCEPT

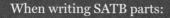

When writing SATB parts:

- Check to see that the interval between soprano and alto and the interval between alto and tenor is an octave or less.
- The interval between the tenor and bass may exceed an octave, but usually remains within a tenth.

Do "My Country" and "Wachet auf" follow the spacing guidelines? *(Try it #3)*

Voice Crossings   When we write in four voices, we need to maintain the independence of each voice line. One way to do this is to avoid **voice crossings**—crossing one voice higher than the part above it or lower than the part below it.

KEY CONCEPT

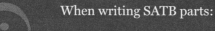

When writing SATB parts:

- Check to see that no alto pitch is higher than soprano or lower than tenor,
- and that no tenor pitch is higher than alto or lower than bass.

However, in some of the Bach chorale settings, voice crossings are included on occasion to create a more interesting line for the alto or tenor. Is this the case in "Wachet auf"? *(Try it #4)* When you find voice crossings, variations in spacing, and other departures from the guidelines given here in music you are studying, consider which concerns may have motivated the composer's choices.

Notation for Keyboard

When we write for the keyboard, we can take advantage of ten fingers and a large range. That means many types of settings are possible. We will examine a wide variety of keyboard textures in the course of this book, but for now we look at those most closely linked to four-part harmonization. When we write four-part harmonizations for keyboard, we need to think about assigning the four voice-leading strands to the two hands, spacing within each hand, and spacing between the hands. Of course, when we write specifically for keyboard, we can include pitches higher or lower than the ranges suggested for voices.

Two Parts in Each Hand

We can set four parts for keyboard with two voices in the treble staff for the right hand and two in the bass staff for the left hand. Keyboard players can play from SATB hymnbook settings like our setting of "My Country, 'Tis of Thee" (Example 10.3)— church musicians and chorus accompanists do this frequently—but four-part textures written specifically for piano usually stem the two parts together on each staff for easy reading, as Example 10.6a shows. We can also set four parts for organ, with the upper two voices stemmed together for the right hand, the tenor played alone in the left hand, and the bass line assigned to the pedal. This type of four-voice texture is shown in Ives's Variations on "America" for Organ (Example 10.6b).

EXAMPLE 10.6: (a) "My Country, 'Tis of Thee," notation for piano

(b) Ives, Variations on "America" for Organ, mm. 1–6 of theme

Three Parts in One Hand, One in the Other

Play through the theme from Beethoven's Variations on "God Save the King," given in Example 10.7. This example illustrates yet another method of setting four parts for keyboard: three parts in the treble staff for the right hand and one in the bass staff for the left (see mm. 3–6). We will see this texture frequently in future chapters, particularly in realizations of figured bass.

EXAMPLE 10.7: Beethoven, Variations on "God Save the King," mm. 1–6

You may have written the opposite—three parts in the left hand and one in the right—in keyboard harmony classes to provide block-chord accompaniments to a melody in the right hand or for popular-music performance. This texture also serves as a model for arpeggiated left-hand patterns, such as Alberti bass (see Chapter 7). For an example of Alberti bass, listen to the passage shown in Example 10.8a, the opening measures of Mozart's Piano Sonata in C Major, K. 545. The underlying block-chord model in Example 10.8b shows the harmonic source of the left-hand arpeggiation.

2.57

EXAMPLE 10.8: Mozart, Piano Sonata in C Major, K. 545, first movement

(a) Mm. 1–4

(b) Reduction of mm. 1–4

Spacing

For keyboard settings, we need to consider spacing—both within each hand and between the hands. When you assign pitches to each hand, be sure that they fall within a hand's reach—usually an octave. (Some pianists with large hands may reach a tenth or more, but we will consider the octave the largest span for our purposes.) You should limit the number of pitches per hand to three (possibly four) to allow the keyboard player a comfortable hand position and a coordinated attack. Try to avoid writing chords for the two hands with more than a tenth between the lowest pitch in the right hand and the highest in the left. This spacing would create the effect of two different chords, one in each hand, instead of a single chord distributed between two hands.

Notation for Guitar

Classical Guitar Notation

1.95 🎧

Guitars are played both as melody instruments and to supply harmonies. Music for guitar is normally notated in a treble staff but sounds one octave lower than written. Example 10.9, an excerpt from "Greensleeves," shows characteristic voicing of guitar chords. Because of the string tuning (the strings are tuned to E2, A2, D3, G3, B3, and E4) and limits on the spans that a hand can reach, some chord spacings are easy to play, while others are quite difficult. Keyboard or vocal spacings of chords stacked in close thirds may not transfer directly to guitar. Nonguitarists should consult with performers when writing for this instrument.

EXAMPLE 10.9: "Greensleeves" (arranged by Norbert Kraft), mm. 29–32

Popular-Music Notation

In popular music, you may notate harmonies for guitar with chord symbols above the melody line. In this case, your performers will choose the spacing and voice-leading from chord to chord. Look at the opening of "Rich and Rare" in Example 10.10. This score includes both chord symbols and diagrams of finger positions

WF3

on the guitar fretboard to assist players with chord fingering and spacing. These diagrams are a type of **tablature**, a traditional method of notation for lutes and guitars that depicts the strings and shows the performer where to place fingers to produce the pitches of each harmony.

EXAMPLE 10.10: "Rich and Rare," mm. 1–4a

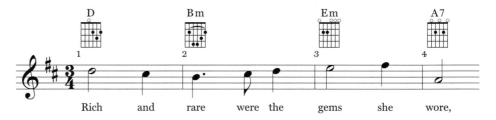

Rich   and   rare   were the   gems   she   wore,

TERMS YOU SHOULD KNOW

alto	SATB	tenor
bass	soprano	vocal range
grand staff	spacing	voice crossing
open score	tablature	

QUESTIONS FOR REVIEW

1. What determines whether stems should go up or down?
2. How do you decide whether notes should be beamed together or flagged? Is your answer the same in vocal music as in instrumental music?
3. How are stems used to show voice parts in an SATB setting?
4. What is the standard range for soprano voices? alto? tenor? bass?
5. What is the standard spacing between adjacent voices in SATB settings? How does spacing differ for keyboard settings? for guitar?
6. What are three ways chords can be notated for guitar?

Voicing Chords in Multiple Parts:

Instrumentation

CHAPTER 11

Outline of topics covered

From two-part counterpoint to four or more parts

- How to make four parts from three chord members

Notation for instrumental trio, quartet, or quintet

- Range, technique, and tessitura
- Timbre and volume

Setting music for transposing instruments

- B♭ instruments
- Other transposing instruments
- Transposing by key signature and interval
- Transposing by scale degree
- Transposing music without key signatures

Setting music for larger ensembles

Overview

In this chapter, we will learn how to set triads and seventh chords in four parts and how to transpose music for band and orchestral instruments.

Repertoire

Johann Sebastian Bach, "Wachet auf" (Chorale No. 179) (CD 1, track 9)

Johannes Brahms, Symphony No. 1 in C minor, Op. 68, first movement

"My Country, 'Tis of Thee" (CD 2, track 97)

Richard Rodgers and Lorenz Hart, "My Funny Valentine," from *Babes in Arms*

John Philip Sousa, "The Stars and Stripes Forever" (CD 3, track 41)

From Two-Part Counterpoint to Four or More Parts

We can take the two-part counterpoint of Chapter 8 as a model for intervallic relationships between voices in a three- or four-part harmonic setting. Listen to the closing measures of Bach's chorale "Wachet auf," given in Example 11.1. We examined the intervals between the soprano and bass voices in Chapter 8. What about the alto-bass and tenor-bass pairings—do they also follow our species guidelines? *(Try it #1)*

EXAMPLE 11.1: Bach, "Wachet auf," mm. 32b–36

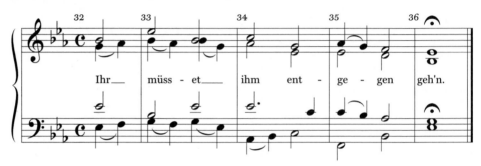

Translation: You must go out and meet him [the bridegroom].

KEY CONCEPT

- Smooth voice-leading in four-voice harmony is based on connections by step or skip, as in species counterpoint.
- Intervals between pairs of voices in four-part harmony follow many of the guidelines for consonance and dissonance treatment we learned in Chapter 8.

How to Make Four Parts from Three Chord Members

In Chapter 7, we learned the various types of triads and seventh chords and how these chords can be inverted without losing their basic identity. Because triads consist of only three chord members (a root, a third, and a fifth), one of the members must be represented twice, or **doubled**, to make four-part harmony. Below are general guidelines for doubling, but you will probably find exceptions in some pieces, where the doubling differs because of the musical context and voice-leading factors.

KEY CONCEPT

Keep in mind the following doubling guidelines for triads.

1. If the triad is in *root position* (and major or minor quality), we usually double the root. Sometimes we double the third or fifth, but these doublings are much less common.

2. If the triad is in *first inversion*, double any chord member that is not a **tendency tone** (a scale degree or chord member that must be resolved) or other altered tone. Doubling the soprano is a common strategy (for major or minor triads only).

3. If the triad is in *second inversion*, double the fifth (the bass). This is the only standard doubling for second-inversion chords.

4. Never double a tendency tone. This guideline applies most frequently to the leading tone of the key ($\hat{7}$) and to the seventh of the dominant seventh chord ($\hat{4}$), but includes any tones that must be resolved, such as chromatic passing tones and altered tones.

5. For diminished triads (which typically appear in first inversion), double the third of the chord. Doubling the root emphasizes the dissonance and causes voice-leading problems (see Chapter 14). Occasionally, the fifth may be doubled.

2.97 Now listen to and look at the four-voice setting of "My Country, 'Tis of Thee" in the anthology. Examine the doubling in all of the triads (ignore seventh chords and passing tones for now). Can you find any exceptions to these guidelines? *(Try it #2)*

Seventh chords generally do not require doubled chord members. In four parts, write each chord member once. In some musical contexts, however, we may want a doubling. A fairly common voicing of the root-position dominant seventh chord omits the fifth and doubles the root (see Chapter 12). For example, play through the series of chords in Example 11.2: all except the first and last are seventh chords. As is typical when seventh chords appear in a series like this, those marked with an x are incomplete—their root is doubled and the fifth left out. We will learn more about seventh chords in sequences like this one in Chapter 18.

EXAMPLE 11.2: Seventh-chord sequences

In popular-music styles, the guidelines for doubling are more flexible. Look at the opening of the Rodgers and Hart song "My Funny Valentine," given in Example 11.3. Play through the excerpt at the piano. The harmonic rhythm (rate of chord change) for measures 1–6 is one chord per measure. Can you find any seventh chords with a doubled or missing chord member? Are there chords with notes added? Do the doublings conform to our guidelines? Look at the guitar chord symbols to check your analysis. *(Try it #3)*

EXAMPLE 11.3: Rodgers and Hart, "My Funny Valentine," mm. 1–8

○ ○

Notation for Instrumental Trio, Quartet, or Quintet

In the same way that four singers may combine to perform four-part harmony, instruments may also be combined in small groups. Settings may be written originally for a specific ensemble of instruments, or an **arrangement** may be made from a composition originally written for other types of performers. In the following chapters, you may be asked to set some of your assignments for three, four, or five instruments instead of voices or keyboard. In some cases, the instrumentation is specified; in others, you may choose to prepare a setting for instruments to be performed by students in your class or other musician friends. You may also want to make arrangements of pieces that you like; you might arrange vocal compositions for groups of instruments, or set instrumental pieces for voices with words added.

In the following sections, we will consider the steps involved in arranging the SATB setting of "My Country, 'Tis of Thee" for a brass quartet. Some considerations when setting four-part harmony for instruments include range, technique, tessitura (the most-used part of the range), timbre, volume, and transposition.

Range, Technique, and Tessitura

Know the range of the instruments you write for. Also, consider the performer's abilities as you write: inexperienced or younger players may have a more limited range on some instruments than more advanced performers. Check the ranges for instruments in Appendix 4. These ranges are just guidelines—advanced players can sometimes extend beyond them.

You may have noticed that some instruments change in timbre over the course of their range. You may also know that on some instruments, particular intervals or combinations of pitches are difficult to play in sequence, even though they fall within the normal range. For example, an interval on a stringed instrument may require a change of string. On a woodwind, an interval may span a "break" between the instrument's upper and lower registers. You will need to consider **tessitura**— how an instrument's or voice's sound quality is different in high, middle, and low portions of its range—when setting music in an arrangement.

Orchestration courses teach the ranges and characteristics of the instruments. Instrumental methods courses, like those required for music education majors, are also good sources of information on basic instrumental technique. When you prepare a score for instrumental performance, consult performers about the special problems associated with their instruments. When you attend live performances, listen and watch carefully to learn about how each instrument is played and how it sounds in various registers.

Timbre and Volume

While it is possible for any group of instruments to play together, some combinations work better than others when the goal is balanced (all parts sounding at the same volume) four-part harmony. Some traditional combinations consist of instruments of the same family, such as string quartets (two violins, viola, and cello), woodwind quintets (flute, oboe, clarinet, horn, and bassoon), saxophone quartets (two alto saxes, tenor sax, and baritone sax), and brass quintets (two trumpets, horn, tenor trombone, and bass trombone or tuba). These groups share a basic timbre and include instruments capable of the same range of volume. Many instrumental combinations are possible, however, if the instruments can play in the range needed for the parts and the performers listen carefully for balance.

For our arrangement of "My Country," we choose two instruments that play in the treble clef to take the soprano and alto parts: trumpets will work. The tenor part of the original (in the anthology) is written in the bass clef with ledger-line pitches. Since the French horn's sounding range lies between the bass and treble clefs, it is an ideal choice to play those pitches. For the bass part, we can use a trombone or euphonium (the bass line goes a little high for tuba). Since all are brass-family instruments—all have similar timbres and volume—they should blend and balance beautifully. After writing the parts, we will check to see if there are any technique problems that we need to adjust before completing our arrangement.

o o o o o o o o o o o o o o o o o o o o o o o o o o o o o o o o o o o o o o o o o o o o o o o

Setting Music for Transposing Instruments

Some instruments are called **C instruments**: in music for these instruments, the pitch you see notated is the pitch you hear. Common C instruments include the piano, flute, oboe, bassoon, trombone, tuba, harp, and most of the string family. Some

WF1

wind and brass instruments, referred to as **transposing instruments**, play from a part whose notated pitches are not the same as the pitches that sound.

Look at Example 11.4 to see transposing instruments in the score to Brahms's Symphony No. 1 in C minor, first movement. You are probably not used to reading a **full score**. Full scores traditionally place the woodwinds at the top, brass and percussion in the middle, and strings at the bottom. You can tell which of the parts are written for transposing instruments by checking the instrument list and the key signatures on each line. How many different key signatures do you see in the Brahms score? *(Try it #4)*

This type of score—one that shows the notes the instruments play rather than the sounding pitches—is called a **transposed score**. You can identify a transposed score by key signatures that are not the same in all instruments.

EXAMPLE 11.4: Brahms, Symphony No. 1 in C minor, first movement, mm. 1–3

B♭ Instruments

We begin our study of transposition with the B♭ instruments: the most common are the B♭ trumpet, B♭ clarinet, bass clarinet, and tenor saxophone. With B♭ instruments, when the player sees a notated pitch and plays it, the sound is a whole step lower than the notated pitch (the bass clarinet and tenor saxophone sound a whole step plus an octave lower). When we write for B♭ instruments, we therefore notate pitches a whole step higher.

KEY CONCEPT

To remember how to transpose for scores, imagine that the notated pitch is C. When the performer reads a C, the resulting **sounding pitch** (or **concert pitch**) is that associated with the name of the instrument—in the case of the B♭ clarinet, the sounding pitch is B♭. When you write for transposing instruments, you need to transpose the players' parts so that the notes are heard at concert pitch. What you see is the notated pitch; what you hear is the concert (sounding) pitch.

Other Transposing Instruments

Some instruments come in several possible transpositions. Trumpets and clarinets, for example, may be pitched in several keys, including C, B♭, A, E♭, or D. Other transposing instruments include:

- E♭ instruments—most commonly the alto and baritone saxophones and E♭ clarinets;
- F instruments—primarily French horns and English horns; and
- A instruments—most commonly A clarinets.

For other instruments pitched at these levels, consult an orchestration text.

Some instruments play octave transpositions. The contrabassoon, string bass, and guitar sound an octave below the range in which the pitches are notated. The piccolo, xylophone, celeste, and orchestra bells (chimes) sound an octave above their notated pitch, while the glockenspiel sounds two octaves above its notated pitch.

Look back at the Brahms symphony in Example 11.4. We have already noted the three different key signatures. The instrument with one flat is the B♭ clarinet. Its part is written a step higher than the sounding pitch; therefore the key signature is D minor rather than the C-minor concert pitch. The brass instruments and timpani present a different case: by convention in the eighteenth and nineteenth centuries, these instruments are often notated without key signatures at all, but with accidentals where needed. Look at the instrumentation at the left of the score to see which of the brass featured in this symphony are transposing instruments: most are pitched in C (first and second horns, trumpets, and timpani). The third and fourth horns are pitched in E♭. Horn parts not in C always sound lower than the notated pitches—in this case, a major sixth below. The E5-G5 in measure 1 will sound as G4-B♭4.

Transposing by Key Signature and Interval

There are several methods for transposing parts from concert pitch to notated pitch. The most common way is by means of key signatures: write in the correct key signature for the transposed part, then transpose all the pitches by a generic interval—that is, for example, by a second or third without concern for whether its quality is major or minor. For example, to transpose a melody in D Major for a B♭ instrument, write the key signature one whole step above D (E Major), then renotate the melody up one generic step. (Remember, when the player of a B♭ instrument reads a C, he plays a B♭; C is a whole step above B♭, so that is why we write the key signature of the B♭ instrument's part [E Major] a whole step above the original key [D Major].)

Let's return now to our arrangement of "My Country." We will use two B♭ trumpets; their parts need to be transposed up a whole step from concert pitch. If the original SATB setting is in F Major, the trumpet parts need to be notated in G Major. Example 11.5a shows the first two measures of the SATB setting in F Major. Example 11.5b has four blank staves (arranged in open score) for the brass quartet parts: trumpet 1, trumpet 2, horn, and trombone. To make your arrangement for brass, first write in the key signature (G Major) for the trumpet parts, then copy the soprano and alto pitches of the SATB version transposed up a second. (Don't worry about the sizes of seconds; the key signature will take care of adjusting the size.) When you add the stems, follow the stem guidelines for single melodies on a staff. *(Try it #5)* We will get to the tenor and bass voices of our SATB arrangement soon, but first we explore other methods and intervals for transposition.

EXAMPLE 11.5: (a) "My Country, 'Tis of Thee," mm. 1–2

(b) Staves for open score, mm. 1–2

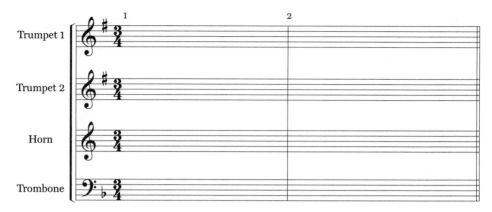

We can employ the same key-signature method for other transposing instruments. For E♭ instrument lines, we write the key signature a minor third below the concert-pitch key, then transpose the melody as follows: for the E♭ clarinet, we transpose down a generic third; for the E♭ alto saxophone, we transpose up a generic sixth (or down a third, then up an octave); and for the baritone saxophone, we transpose up an octave and a generic sixth. For other transpositions, see the SUMMARY table below.

SUMMARY

- B♭ instruments: notated key is a whole step above concert-pitch key.
- E♭ instruments: notated key is a minor third below concert-pitch key.
- F instruments: notated key is a perfect fifth above concert-pitch key.
- A instruments: notated key is a minor third above concert-pitch key.

Another Way ◄

Another way to locate the key signature for transposing instruments is to refer to the circle of fifths.

- For B♭ instruments: move two places to the right on the circle of fifths.
- For E♭ instruments: move three places to the right on the circle of fifths.
- For F instruments: move one place to the right on the circle of fifths.
- For A instruments: move three places to the left on the circle of fifths.

Try it #6

Given the concert key and instrument type below, try to determine the key of the transposed part.

CONCERT KEY	INSTRUMENT TYPE	KEY OF TRANPOSED PART
E♭	B♭ instrument	_____
C	F instrument	_____
B♭	E♭ instrument	_____
G	A instrument	_____
F	F instrument	_____
C	B♭ instrument	_____
E♭	F instrument	_____
C	E♭ instrument	_____

Transposing by Scale Degree

Once you know the key signature, you can use scale degrees of the melody or solfège, rather than intervals, to notate the new part. For example, $\hat{1}$ in the concert key is notated as $\hat{1}$ in the transposed key; $\hat{5}$ in the concert key is notated as $\hat{5}$ in the transposed key. Be careful to place the scale degrees in the correct octave! If you start with the first pitch in the correct octave and follow the contour of the melody when transferring scale degrees, you will avoid octave-placement problems.

To make a horn part for our setting of "My Country," we will transpose the tenor line of the SATB version following the scale-degree method. Our horn is an F instrument. Since the original SATB setting is in F Major, the horn part needs to be notated a perfect fifth above F Major: in C Major. The horn part will thus have a key signature with no flats or sharps and will be written in the treble clef. (Although horns occasionally play from parts in the bass clef, they usually read treble clef. As mentioned previously, horn parts in older scores also omit key signatures altogether and write in each accidental as needed; but modern scores typically include the key signature.)

Above the staff for horn in Example 11.5b, write in the scale-degree numbers or solfège for the SATB tenor part. *(Try it #7)* Now write the corresponding pitches in the key of C Major on the horn's staff. Make sure that the pitches you write are a perfect fifth *above* the original pitches in the SATB setting by checking the first pitch and following the correct contour. When you add the stems, follow the stem guidelines for single melodies on a staff. *(Try it #8)*

Another Way

Another way to transpose is by the clef method. In this technique, you visualize a different clef from the notated one, and also imagine a different key signature. For example, to play from an E♭ part (notated in treble clef) on a concert-pitch (C) instrument, you could imagine a bass clef and use the concert-pitch key signature, then transpose up an octave. To play from a B♭ part (such as a clarinet part) on a concert-pitch instrument, visualize a tenor clef and use the concert-pitch key signature.

The trombone is a C instrument—its part thus does not need to be transposed. Copy the bass line in the SATB setting to the lowest line of the open score. Check the stems! Now the brass quartet setting for the first two measures of "My Country" is complete. This setting is in a comfortable, medium range for the brass instruments, which should be suitable for younger or less experienced players. For expert players, the entire setting could be transposed up a perfect fourth to the concert key of B♭ Major to make a bright, sparkling sound suitable for this patriotic hymn. In that case, what would the key signatures be? *(Try it #9)*

Transposing Music Without Key Signatures

When transposing parts in nontonal music without key signatures, you must transpose each part by specific interval (not generic), since you will not have the key signature to correct the interval qualities. That is, for B♭ instruments, transpose the melody up a major second; for E♭ instruments, transpose down a minor third; and so on. You need to place accidentals in front of each pitch as needed, rather than relying on a key signature.

Setting Music for Larger Ensembles

Setting music for larger ensembles is called **orchestration.** Even an introductory study of orchestration is a semester course on its own; such a study is not included in this book, but we will consider specific details of orchestration in pieces we are analyzing. We will also study larger instrumental ensemble pieces by making reductions from full score to four parts.

In preparing a setting of a four-part harmonization for a larger ensemble, problems of balance, timbre, and variations in instrumental technique become more pronounced because of the variety of instruments in the orchestra or concert band.

3.41 🎧

The composer or arranger must select the right combinations of instruments and doubling to produce a balanced harmony and to provide variety within the setting.

Listen to Sousa's "Stars and Stripes Forever" while following the piano score, then compare the piano score and the conductor's **short score** (both in your anthology). This short score is different from the full score for the Brahms symphony in that it does not have individual staves for each part—several parts are shown on each staff. Although the band includes transposing instruments, like B♭ clarinets and trumpets, this score shows all of the parts in the concert key. This type of non-transposed score is also called a **C score**, or **concert-pitch score**.

Where are parts on the piano score doubled in octaves in the instrumental parts of the short score? What did you notice that was different in the short score as compared with the piano score? *(Try it #10)* How do those differences affect the sound of the march? In Chapter 10, we considered the limitations the span of a player's hands place on keyboard settings. In contrast, the large ensemble setting allows multiple octave doublings and a variety of simultaneous activities.

If you are interested in trying settings for larger numbers of instruments, study the scores in the anthology for orchestra, band, and other large ensembles, and ask your band director or orchestra conductor for suggestions of pieces to study—then try it out!

TERMS YOU SHOULD KNOW

arrangement	concert pitch	short score
B♭ instruments	doubling	tendency tone
C (concert-pitch) score	E♭ instruments	transposed score
C instruments	F instruments	transposing instruments
concert key	orchestration	

QUESTIONS FOR REVIEW

1. What triad member (or chord member) is usually doubled in triads in root position? in triads in first inversion? in triads in second inversion?
2. What chord member is usually doubled in seventh chords? What are the exceptions to this general guideline?
3. How would you transpose a flute melody for B♭ clarinet? a trombone part for tenor saxophone?
4. What is the difference between a concert-pitch score (or C score) and a transposed score? a short score and a full score?

PART III

The Phrase Model

CHAPTER 12

The Basic Phrase Model:
Tonic and Dominant Voice-Leading

Overview

In this chapter, we will learn the fundamental harmonic pattern that serves as a foundation for most tonal music, from phrases to entire movements. We will use this pattern to compose phrases and to accompany melodies.

Repertoire

Johann Sebastian Bach,
  "Aus meines Herzens Grunde" (Chorale No. 1) (CD 1, track 5)
  "Ach Gott, vom Himmel sieh' darein" (Chorale No. 253)
  "Wachet auf" (Chorale No. 179) (CD 1, track 9)

Ludwig van Beethoven, Piano Sonata in D minor, Op. 31, No. 2 (*Tempest*), third movement

Muzio Clementi, Sonatina in C Major, Op. 36, No. 1, first movement (CD 1, track 74)

"Clementine" (folk tune, arranged by Norman Lloyd)

George Frideric Handel, "Rejoice greatly," from *Messiah* (CD 2, track 10)

Franz Joseph Haydn, Scherzo, from Piano Sonata No. 9 in F Major (CD 2, track 17)

"Merrily We Roll Along" (folk tune)

Franz Schubert, "Die Forelle"

Robert Schumann, "Im wunderschönen Monat Mai," from *Dichterliebe* (CD 3, track 38)

Parts of the Basic Phrase

WF1

A **phrase** is a basic unit of musical thought, similar to a sentence in language. The typical phrase—like most sentences—has a beginning, a middle, and an end. The end is marked by a **cadence**: the harmonic, melodic, and rhythmic features that make the phrase sound like a complete thought. Phrases may end conclusively (like a sentence punctuated with a period) or inconclusively (like a clause punctuated with a comma or semicolon). For examples of cadence and phrase, we will listen to the beginnings of two piano movements, a Haydn Scherzo and a Clementi Sonatina, while following the score excerpts below. The Haydn example expresses two complete phrases; the Clementi expresses one. Which of these phrases ends less conclusively than the others, as though the music must continue after the phrase ends?

2.17
1.74

EXAMPLE 12.1: Haydn, Scherzo, from Piano Sonata No. 9 in F Major, mm. 1–8

EXAMPLE 12.2: Clementi, Sonatina in C Major, Op. 36, No. 1, first movement, mm. 1–4a

Conclusive cadences, like the final cadence of Example 12.1, sound finished. They generally end on scale-degree $\hat{1}$ in both the soprano and bass. While the first cadence of Example 12.1 (in m. 4) also sounds conclusive—it ends with $\hat{1}$ in the bass—it is weaker than the final cadence because its soprano ends on $\hat{3}$ rather than $\hat{1}$.

Inconclusive cadences, like the cadence in Example 12.2, sound incomplete—as though the musical thought needs to continue further—because they do not end with $\hat{1}$ in either the soprano or the bass. Recognizing phrase types can help us shape our performances. In particular, we can think of the musical phrase as motion toward the cadence. We can use expressive timing techniques in performance (called **rubato**) to emphasize the arrival on the tonic in a conclusive phrase, or to bring out the suspense or surprise of avoiding the tonic in an inconclusive phrase.

○ ○

Defining the Phrase Model

Conclusive phrases include at least three tonal areas, which form what we call a **basic phrase**: an opening **tonic area** (I), a **dominant area** (V), and **tonic closure** (a cadence on I). Find each of these areas in the two phrases of Example 12.1. (*Try it #1*) An inconclusive phrase usually begins with the tonic and dominant areas, then may cadence in the dominant area or on a chord substituting for the tonic. In Example 12.2, three measures of tonic harmony are followed by a measure of dominant harmony, where the phrase ends.

The I–V–I progression of the basic phrase structures both large- and small-scale harmonic motion in much common-practice music.

The Tonic Area

As we learned in Chapter 7, we write the tonic triad with scale-degrees $\hat{1}$, $\hat{3}$, and $\hat{5}$. The tonic at the beginning of the basic phrase establishes a stable home base, since there are no dissonant intervals in the tonic triad to resolve. Example 12.3 shows the tonic triad in the context of the basic progression I–V^7–I in an SATB texture. We see in this example that the tonic chord is sometimes complete and sometimes incomplete—here, the third chord consists of three roots and a third.

KEY CONCEPT

The tonic triad is usually represented at the beginning or in the middle of a phrase by a complete chord. In root position at a cadence, it can also be represented by just the root and third of the chord, without the fifth.

EXAMPLE 12.3: SATB setting of I–V⁷–I

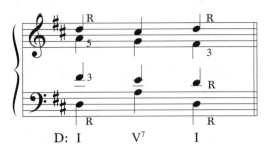

Establishing the Sense of Tonic

To shape a phrase properly, you need to establish a strong sense of tonic at the beginning. You can do this most simply by selecting a root-position tonic triad as the first chord of the phrase, but the tonic area usually extends for more than a single block chord. You may expand the tonic area by repeating or arpeggiating the tonic triad, as in measures 1–2 and 5–6 of the Haydn Scherzo (Example 12.1), by combining root-position and inverted tonic triads, or by adding passing tones or neighbor tones between chord members.

Example 12.4, drawn from a Beethoven sonata, features both arpeggiation of the tonic and passing tones. The tonic triad may even be extended over many measures, as shown in Example 12.5, the opening of Schubert's song "Die Forelle" ("The Trout"). Here, Schubert's piano figuration depicts the text's brook and fish through its sextuplet flourishes and upward skips, while repeating just the tonic triad throughout the entire introduction (mm. 1–6) and half of the first vocal phrase.

EXAMPLE 12.4: Beethoven, Piano Sonata in D minor, Op. 31, No. 2 (*Tempest*), third movement, mm. 1–3

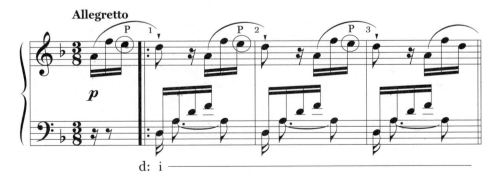

EXAMPLE 12.5: Schubert, "Die Forelle," mm. 1–10a

Translation: In a bright little brook, there shot by in happy haste [a capricious trout].

Example 12.6 illustrates Bach's skillful handling of repeated tonic triads in the chorale "Wachet auf." Listen to the opening phrase (part a): Bach uses a new voicing of the chord on each beat of measures 1–2a. In measures 32–33 (part b), a phrase beginning later in the chorale, he adds passing and neighboring tones in parallel tenths between the bass and alto to add musical interest.

EXAMPLE 12.6: Bach, "Wachet auf"

(a) Mm. 1–3

Translation: Wake up! the [voice] calls to us.

(b) Mm. 32b–33

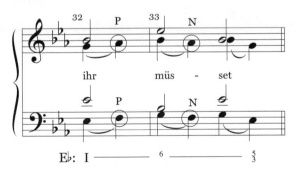

Another way to establish a strong sense of tonic is to precede the initial downbeat by a dominant anacrusis, or "pickup." When you begin the tonic area with a dominant anacrusis, you do not weaken the tonic function. The tendency tones (the leading tone and chordal seventh) of the dominant actually strengthen the initial tonic, as you can hear in the first phrase of Bach's chorale setting "Ach Gott, vom Himmel sieh' darein" ("O God, Look Down on Us from Heaven"), given in Example 12.7. Sing each line of this chorale, and listen for the resolutions of the tendency tones.

EXAMPLE 12.7: Bach (adapted), "Ach Gott, vom Himmel sieh' darein," mm. 4b–6a

g: V   i

The Dominant Area

In Chapter 7, we learned to spell the dominant triad (scale-degrees $\hat{5}$, $\hat{7}$, and $\hat{2}$) and the dominant seventh chord (scale-degrees $\hat{5}$, $\hat{7}$, $\hat{2}$, and $\hat{4}$).

KEY CONCEPT

The dominant harmony almost always appears in music literature as a major triad (V) or major-minor seventh (V^7). When you write in minor keys, remember to use an accidental to raise this chord's third (so that it becomes a leading tone in the key).

3.38

3.39

The dominant-seventh-chord quality is so distinctive that it will imply a tonic (and key) even if nothing else is played. Imagine the tension a performer can create by lingering on a chordal seventh! Robert Schumann used just this effect in the final cadence of his song "Im wunderschönen Monat Mai." Listen to the final verse of this song (score and translation are in your anthology). The piano postlude, shown in Example 12.8, ends on an unresolved V^7. Can you hum the implied tonic? What might be the symbolism of this unresolved chord? (The text, "Sehnen und Verlangen," means "longing and desire"; see box on p. 205.)

EXAMPLE 12.8: Schumann, "Im wunderschönen Monat Mai," from *Dichterliebe*, mm. 22–26

The Versatile Dominant Seventh

What might be the symbolism of the unresolved chord at the end of Example 12.8? Schumann's song comes from his cycle *Dichterliebe* (*The Poet's Love*), Op. 48 (1840). *Dichterliebe* is filled with imagery of unrequited love; perhaps the lack of resolution in the V^7 depicts this longing for love musically.

This song belongs to the great tradition of the German Romantic Lied. Nineteenth-century Lieder (plural) were often composed in cycles of multiple songs, written to poetry filled with imagery that included themes of nature—birdsong, rain or snow, forests or streams, the moon or stars—as well as tales of love and love lost, alienation, and death. The year this song was written, 1840, was Schumann's great song year, in which he wrote over a hundred. Many attribute this flowering of song to the composer's love for Clara Wieck, whom he eventually married. (Clara was herself a composer and one of the foremost concert pianists of the nineteenth cen-

tury. Her song "Liebst du um Schönheit" appears in your anthology.)

Schumann's focus on the tension in the dominant seventh chord is not unique. Composers and performers in various eras have given this harmony special attention. In music of the Baroque era, performers often highlight the dominant with a trill on $\hat{2}$ before its resolution to $\hat{1}$. In Classical-era concertos, a virtuosic cadenza may prolong the harmonic tension of the dominant area (again, with a trill on $\hat{2}$) before the orchestral closing. The dominant seventh chord is also used to build tension just before the main theme returns in the first movement of an eighteenth- or nineteenth-century sonata or symphony and at the end of a contrasting section in a twentieth-century pop song. In performance, you may choose to bring out the dominant area's tension by lingering on this harmony longer than the notated duration, by increasing the volume slightly before resolution, or by other musical means.

Resolutions of V and V⁶

The active ingredient in dominant-function triads is the leading tone: scale-degree $\hat{7}$.

KEY CONCEPT

Scale-degree $\hat{7}$ has a strong linear pull upward toward resolution on the tonic. When V resolves to I, $\hat{7}$ will almost always resolve up by half step to $\hat{1}$.

The dominant triad (V) provides the strongest resolution to tonic when it is in root position. It is frequently found in first inversion as well, since the bass line between V⁶ and I is stepwise: $\hat{7}$–$\hat{1}$. Look at Example 12.9 to see how different SATB voicings of the dominant and tonic are resolved in D Major and D minor. In each case, scale-degree $\hat{7}$ resolves up by half step to $\hat{1}$. Remember that in D minor, we must raise $\hat{7}$ to create the leading-tone pull toward tonic.

EXAMPLE 12.9: Resolutions of V–I

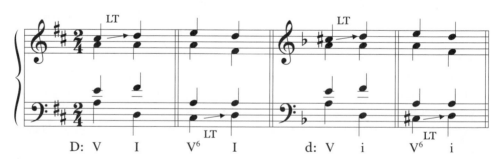

Resolutions of V⁷ and Its Inversions

When you use the V⁷, you add an additional active ingredient to the dominant harmony: the chordal seventh (scale-degree $\hat{4}$). The seventh creates a dissonance with the chord's root that, in common-practice style, almost always resolves down by step. Voice-leading principles for music of this period require that the dissonant tritone between the third and seventh of the V⁷ (scale-degrees $\hat{7}$ and $\hat{4}$) also be resolved.

WF2

SUMMARY

When V^7 moves to I, two tendency tones resolve at once:

- the chordal seventh moves down by half step (major) or whole step (minor) (scale-degree $\hat{4}$ moves to $\hat{3}$); and
- the leading tone resolves up by half step (scale-degree $\hat{7}$ resolves to $\hat{1}$).

Examples 12.10a–d give four SATB settings of the V^7–I progression, featuring each inversion of the dominant harmony. Each shows the typical resolution of the leading tone up and chordal seventh down. In Example 12.10e, $\hat{7}$ does not resolve to $\hat{1}$. You may use this type of resolution only at the end of a phrase, when $\hat{7}$ appears in an inner voice; resolve it down to $\hat{5}$ to complete the final tonic chord. (The resolution here works in part because our ears hear the $\hat{7}$ in the alto voice resolving up to $\hat{1}$ in the soprano.) Example 12.10f shows another resolution of the V$^4_2$, with a skip between scale-degrees $\hat{2}$ and $\hat{5}$ in the soprano. In this example, both the leading tone and chordal seventh resolve as expected.

In Chapter 14, we will learn one voice-leading context in which composers of this era resolve the chordal seventh up. For now, however, you should always resolve the tendency tones according to these guidelines when you write in common-practice style.

EXAMPLE 12.10: Six SATB settings of V^7–I

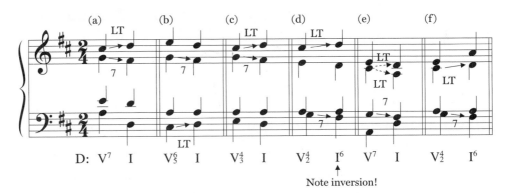

As we learned in Chapter 7, the V^7 may appear in root position ($\frac{7}{5}$), first inversion ($\frac{6}{5}$), second inversion ($\frac{4}{3}$), or third inversion ($\frac{4}{2}$). Root-position dominant sevenths create the strongest progression; first-inversion dominant sevenths are the next strongest. We use second and third inversions when we want to write weaker progressions—for example, at the beginning or the middle of a phrase. Look again at the SATB realizations in Example 12.10; follow the resolution of the leading tone and chordal seventh for each inversion. Why must the V$^4_2$ resolve to a I^6?

KEY CONCEPT

In common-practice composition, the only correct resolution of a V_2^4 is to a I^6. This voice-leading allows $\hat{4}$ to resolve properly down to $\hat{3}$ in the bass voice.

When you compose, you may include more than one dominant chord in the dominant area, as Example 12.11a shows. You may want to write different inversions and spacings to maintain musical interest. If you do, place the strongest dominant function (usually root-position V^7) just before the resolution to tonic harmony. Scale-degree $\hat{7}$ or the chordal seventh (scale-degree $\hat{4}$) may change from one voice to another within the dominant area before they resolve; this is called a **transferred resolution**. Example 12.11b shows the transfer of the leading tone in a V chord from the bass to the soprano before it resolves.

EXAMPLE 12.11: Extension of the dominant harmony

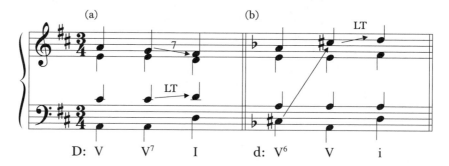

Dominant Seventh Resolutions in Music Literature

We have seen how tendency tones $\hat{4}$ and $\hat{7}$ resolve in SATB contexts, but what happens in freer musical textures? Consider another excerpt from Beethoven's *Tempest* Sonata, given in Example 12.12. How does the leading tone (C♯4) resolve in measure 8? How does the chordal seventh (G5) resolve in this same measure? (*Try it #2*)

EXAMPLE 12.12: Beethoven, *Tempest* Sonata, third movement, mm. 4–8a

d: V⁷ —————————————————————————————————— i

2.10 Finally, listen to the introduction to Handel's "Rejoice greatly" while following the keyboard score in Example 12.13. Find two V$^4_2$ chords, and consider how they resolve. Does Handel resolve them as our guidelines predict? (*Try it #3*)

EXAMPLE 12.13: Handel, "Rejoice greatly," from *Messiah*, mm. 1–9a

Doubling Guidelines

When you write SATB or other four-voice arrangements of triads and sevenths in common-practice style, keep the following doubling guidelines in mind.

KEY CONCEPT

- In the V chord, double the root.
- In the V^7, no doubling is necessary (it has four pitches).
- If the V^7 is in root position at a cadence, you may omit the fifth and double the root.
- Never double tendency tones, such as the leading tone or chordal seventh.

Play through Example 12.14. The third chord is missing the fifth. The fifth can be omitted because it is not an active ingredient; it is not essential to the sound of the root-position dominant seventh, but is implied by the rest of the chord.

EXAMPLE 12.14: Doublings in V and V^7

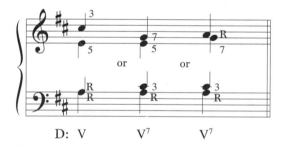

We avoid doubling the leading tone in the dominant harmony because it is a tendency tone. If we double it, we get one of the two voice-leading problems shown in Example 12.15: either (1) both leading tones will resolve correctly, resulting in parallel octaves (labeled ‖ 8), or (2) one of the leading tones will resolve incorrectly. As we discovered in Chapter 8, when two voice-leading parts move in parallel octaves, the parallel voices lose their independence and sound instead like a strongly emphasized single part. We also avoid doubling tendency tones in pieces with more or fewer voices than the four we have seen in our SATB model.

WF3

EXAMPLE 12.15: Voice-leading problems caused by incorrect doubling

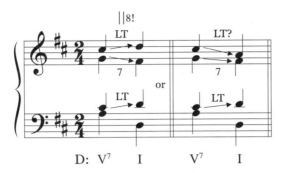

○ ○

Ending the Phrase

Authentic Cadences

To write a strong conclusive cadence, use a root-position V or V⁷ progressing to a root-position I (or i). This type of cadence is most definitive when the soprano moves from scale-degree $\hat{2}$ or $\hat{7}$ to $\hat{1}$, as it does in Example 12.16a. We call this type of cadence a **perfect authentic cadence** (abbreviated PAC). The word "authentic" refers to the harmonic progression V–I, and "perfect" tells us that the soprano and bass are in their strongest positions: root-position harmonies ending with scale-degree $\hat{1}$ in the soprano. Because motion between root-position V or V⁷ and I has such a pronounced cadential sound, we usually reserve this chord sequence for cadences and use it less often mid-phrase.

You can weaken an authentic cadence by (1) placing either harmony in inversion (as shown in Example 12.16b), or (2) ending the soprano on a scale degree other than $\hat{1}$ (part c). A combination of these factors weakens the progression even further. We call such a cadence an **imperfect authentic cadence** (IAC)—it is "authentic" because, again, it involves V and I, but it is no longer "perfect." Use IACs when you want to end a phrase with less finality—for example, in the middle of a piece. Listen again to the orchestral opening of Handel's "Rejoice greatly" while following the keyboard score in Example 12.13. Can you find both an IAC and a PAC? (*Try it #4*)

EXAMPLE 12.16: Cadence types

(a) Perfect authentic   (b) Imperfect authentic   (c) Imperfect authentic
(bass inverted)   (soprano $\hat{4}$–$\hat{3}$)

D: V⁷   I   V⁶   I   V⁷   I

KEY CONCEPT

When we write a perfect authentic cadence (with V or V⁷ in root position), all voice-leading rules for resolving the dominant to tonic remain true except one: sometimes at the cadence we ignore the voice-leading tendency of $\hat{7}$ in an inner voice to resolve up to $\hat{1}$. Instead, $\hat{7}$ skips down to create a complete tonic triad (see Example 12.10e).

Other Cadence Types

Another type of inconclusive cadence occurs when the phrase ends on the dominant: the basic phrase model is incomplete or interrupted (the dominant area does not move to the tonic), as shown in Example 12.17. We call these **half cadences** (abbreviated HC). Half cadences typically end on a root-position V chord, and often (though not always) feature $\hat{2}$ in the soprano. Look at Example 12.18 for a Bach chorale phrase that ends with a half cadence and $\hat{2}$ in the soprano. Listen to this example on your CD, and note its inconclusive ending. For a HC that ends with $\hat{5}$ in the soprano, look back at the first vocal phrase of Schubert's "Die Forelle" in Example 12.5 (m. 10).

1.6

EXAMPLE 12.17: Basic phrase ending with half cadence

EXAMPLE 12.18: Bach, "Aus meines Herzens Grunde," mm. 7b–10a

Translation: O God, upon your throne.

Half cadences function like a comma in a sentence, and must be followed by a continuation phrase. Folk songs often follow this format: four measures ending on scale-degree $\hat{2}$ (and harmonized with a half cadence) followed by four measures ending on $\hat{1}$ (with an authentic cadence). Think of the familiar tunes "Clementine" (shown in Example 12.19) and Foster's "Oh! Susanna," which follow exactly this pattern. Pieces rarely end with a half cadence; those that do are usually multimovement works, where the expected resolution to tonic comes at the beginning of the next movement.

We will learn other types of cadences in future chapters, as new harmonies are introduced. In addition, we will learn new ways to prolong the tonic and dominant tonal areas (see Chapters 14 and 15). With just the tonic and dominant harmonies, however, we have all the necessary tools we need to begin harmonizing melodies and writing simple phrases.

o o o o o o o o o o o o o o o o o o o o o o o o o o o o o o o o o o o o o o o o o o o o o o o

Harmonizing Melodies

Harmonic Rhythm

When harmonizing a melody of any type, we need to determine its **harmonic rhythm**—that is, how quickly the chords need to change to fit with the melody. For folk songs and some dance forms, a typical harmonic rhythm is one chord per measure. Pitches that do not belong to the harmony of the measure we interpret as passing or neighboring tones (or other embellishing tones). For chorale melodies, on the other hand, the typical harmonic rhythm is usually one chord per beat.

You can identify the harmonic rhythm of a melody by singing it on scale-degree numbers (or solfège) and listening for the implied chords, by visually scanning the measures to see how often the implied chords change, and by considering the musical style of the melody. In your own work, once you have established a harmonic rhythm, keep it fairly consistent throughout your harmonization. The one exception is at the cadence, where the harmonic rhythm often speeds up.

Folk Song Harmonization

We can harmonize a number of simple melodies with just tonic and dominant harmonies in the basic phrase model. Folk melodies and children's songs are particularly good choices. Let's look at how an accompaniment might be written to "Clementine," whose melody is given as Example 12.19.

KEY CONCEPT _____

Before you begin a harmonization, always sing or play through the melody. Ask yourself whether it is in a major or minor mode, determine its key, and decide where each phrase ends and what type of cadence is implied there.

Identify the key and mode of "Clementine," then sing the melody with scale-degree numbers or solfège syllables. Let the syllables or numbers guide your decisions about which phrases should end on I or on V. Then choose one harmony (I or V) per measure for the accompaniment, and write the Roman numeral for each beneath the staff and words in Example 12.19. (_Try it #5_)

EXAMPLE 12.19: "Clementine" (melody)

We could write popular-music chord symbols above the staff to show our chord choices for a guitarist or folk instrument performer, who would improvise an accompanimental pattern. The chord symbols would be F, F, F, C7 for the first phrase, and C7, F, C7, F for the second phrase.

Now play through the piano accompaniment to the first two verses of "Clementine" given in Example 12.20. The arranger has used root-position tonic chords through the half cadence that ends the first phrase (m. 6). Then he weakens the strength of the V–I progression by beginning phrase two with an inverted V⁴₃ moving to I (mm. 7–8), before the strong root movement of the PAC. This piano arrangement doubles the melody in the right hand, while the left hand mimics the sound of a guitar arpeggio.

EXAMPLE 12.20: "Clementine," mm. 1–10a

1. In a cav-ern, in a can-yon, Ex-ca-vat-ing for a
2. Light she was and like a fair-y, And her shoes were num-ber

mine, Dwelt a min-er, for-ty-nin-er, And his daugh-ter Clem-en-tine.
nine, Her-ring box-es with-out top-ses, Sand-als were for Clem-en-tine.

Piano Textures

You can turn SATB chorale progressions into piano pieces or into melodies with piano accompaniment. We will work with many types of piano textures in this book, but we begin with two simple patterns, known (informally) as "jump bass" and arpeggiation. The jump-bass pattern works well for accompanying folk and children's songs. We will write a simple accompaniment for the tune "Merrily We Roll Along" by beginning with the SATB block-chord harmonization of Example 12.21a. Sing the tune while playing the block-chord accompaniment.

EXAMPLE 12.21: "Merrily We Roll Along"

(a) Arrangement

For a jump-bass accompaniment, take the bass line of the SATB progression and place it in the left hand of the piano on each downbeat. Write the soprano, alto, and tenor parts (maintaining correct voice-leading) in the right hand on beat two of each measure, as Example 12.21b shows. Now experiment at the piano to turn this arrangement into an arpeggiated accompaniment. You can also turn SATB progressions into compositions for piano solo by means of arpeggiation patterns like those of Example 12.21c. Here, the "Merrily We Roll Along" chords appear in a simple arpeggiated pattern that preserves the voice-leading of the original (with the melody as the highest pitch of the arpeggiation), but creates a very different style and mood.

(b) With jump-bass accompaniment

Mer - ri - ly we roll a - long, roll a - long, roll a - long!

Mer - ri - ly we roll a - long, O - ver the deep blue sea.

(c) Arpeggiated setting

TERMS YOU SHOULD KNOW

basic phrase	half cadence	perfect authentic cadence
cadence	harmonic rhythm	resolution
conclusive phrase	imperfect authentic cadence	tendency tone
dominant area	inconclusive cadence	tonic area

QUESTIONS FOR REVIEW

1. What elements make up the basic phrase? Name and define three possible cadences with which the phrase might conclude.
2. Within the dominant harmony, how do we treat the leading tone when doubling? What about in minor keys?
3. What tendency tones must resolve in the V^7? Do they resolve differently when the dominant appears in an inversion? Do they resolve differently at the cadence? If so, how?
4. Describe the steps you would take in harmonizing a folk melody.
5. Find at least one example in pieces that you are playing of each cadence type considered in this chapter. Did you also find cadences that do not fit the basic phrase model guidelines?
6. Listen to one of your favorite songs—can you hear when the harmony changes? Do the harmonies change at an even rate all through the song? Does the song have a fast or slow harmonic rhythm.

CHAPTER 13

Embellishing Tones

Overview

In this chapter, we will examine ways that melodic lines can be embellished in SATB chorales, and we will see how the same principles can apply when we write in freer textures in common-practice and popular styles.

Repertoire

Johann Sebastian Bach,
    "Christ ist erstanden" (Chorale No. 197)
    "Heut' ist, o Mensch" (Chorale No. 168)
    "Liebster Jesu" (Chorale No. 131)
    "O Haupt voll Blut und Wunden" (Chorale No. 74) (CD 1, track 7)

Bach, Organ Sonata No. 5 in C Major, first movement

Bach, Prelude in E♭ Major for Organ (*St. Anne*)

George Frideric Handel, Chaconne in G Major, from *Trois Leçons* (CD 2, track 1)

Andrew Lloyd Webber and Tim Rice, "Don't Cry for Me Argentina," from *Evita*

Alan Menken and Tim Rice, "A Whole New World," from *Aladdin*

Henry Purcell, "Music for a While" (CD 3, track 5)

o o o o o o o o o o o o o o o o o o o o o o o o o o o o o o o o o o o o o o o o o o o o o o o o o o

Embellishing Tones in Three and Four Voices

Despite the emphasis we place on simple chordal textures when we learn about harmony, very few pieces—not even chorales—rely solely on a succession of block chords. Indeed, much of the beauty and inventiveness of musical composition lies in how composers embellish melodic lines or chord successions. Listen, for example, to the opening of Purcell's "Music for a While," while following the score in your anthology. This work draws much of its expressive power from the interplay of the vocal line with a repeated bass melody—and especially the occasional dissonances between them. These dissonances embellish the underlying harmony and counterpoint.

3.5 🎧

We first encountered embellishing tones in two-voice textures; we now revisit them in textures consisting of full triads and seventh chords. Because the pitches that embellish a musical line are usually not members of the underlying harmony, some textbooks call them "nonharmonic" or "nonchord" tones. The term "embellishing tone," on the other hand, focuses on musical function. Why identify embellishing tones? One reason is that they have expressive potential for performance, as we hear in the Purcell example. We can add stress accents or subtle changes in timing to emphasize the tension of a dissonant embellishment. Another reason to identify them is to clarify a harmonic analysis; you may find it difficult to supply a Roman numeral to a harmony that includes unexplained extra pitches!

As we move now to consider musical phrases in context, we will learn to recognize some harmonies as carrying more structural weight than others. Some harmonies have a strong function within the tonic-dominant-tonic phrase model, while other chords embellish them. In fact, some "chords" are simply collections of embellishing tones. For this reason, beware of analyzing music by taking vertical "snapshots" of each beat, stacking the pitches in thirds, and then applying a Roman numeral. This procedure can be misleading (and not very musical). Instead, spend some time listening to the passage you are analyzing to decide which pitches are structural and which are embellishing in the musical context of what comes before and after. Remember that stepwise motion will often involve at least one embellishing tone. If in doubt, try leaving out the pitch in question—embellishing tones can be omitted without damaging the harmonic logic of a phrase. Above all, learn to use your ears as your guide.

Common Embellishing Tones

Passing tones (P), neighbor tones (N), double neighbors (DN), and incomplete neighbors (IN) function in three- and four-voice textures in much the same way as they do in two-voice counterpoint. We follow the same guidelines in writing them, but now we may place them in any voice within the chordal texture. Listen again to the first vocal phrase of Purcell's "Music for a While," given in Example 13.1a. Some embellishing tones are circled, in both the vocal part and the accompaniment. Label them in the example. (As you complete more musical analyses and discuss them with other musicians, you will discover that not everyone uses the same terminology to name embellishing-tone types. Your instructor may prefer that you substitute other terms.)

WF1

Example 13.1: Purcell, "Music for a While"

(a) Mm. 4–7a

In Purcell's vocal line in measure 5, we hear descending stepwise motion, doubled in the keyboard a third lower. Here, unaccented passing tones embellish a B-diminished triad in both melodic lines, creating parallel thirds between the two voices. In textures of more than two voices, we may place embellishing tones in more than one voice at once, resulting in parallel passing or neighboring motion. Parallel motion of this type may only be written in sixths or thirds, following the principles of good counterpoint.

The example also illustrates several types of consonant skips (CS), including consonant skips filled in with passing tones. Most striking are Purcell's settings of the words "your" and "(be)-guile" in the vocal line of measures 6–7. "Your" is a consonant skip from B4 to D5, within a B-D-F-A seventh chord; "-guile" is a consonant skip from C5 down to A4, within an A-C-E triad. In each case, the skip is filled in with an unaccented passing tone. Can you find other consonant skips in the accompaniment in this passage? (*Try it #1*)

When there are consonant skips in the bass line, we need to consider whether our analysis should indicate a change in inversion. Generally, if the skip is on a weak beat, or if another skip returns to the initial pitch, we do not change inversion. Look at the bass line of measure 4, for instance. The leap to E3 is on the offbeat, with a return to A2 in the next beat. We therefore do not analyze the second half of beat 1 as i⁶₄.

While the chromatic embellishments in the bass line of measures 4 and 5 (F♯, G♯, and C♯) may at first appear to function as incomplete neighbor tones, we could also interpret these pitches as chromatic passing tones. Sing or play through the bass line in this example. The bass in measures 4–5 seems to split into two separate lines, one in the lower register (A2–A2, B2–B2, C3–C♯3, D3–D3) and one in the upper register (E3–F3, F♯3–G3, G♯3–A3, A3–B3). This type of melodic line is called a **compound melody**: it expresses two distinct musical lines embedded within a single melody (see Chapter 20). The line is renotated in Example 13.1b to show its two parts. When viewed as elements of a compound melody, the chromatic pitches we previously identified would instead be interpreted as chromatic passing tones.

WF2

(b) Reduction of mm. 4–5

upper line

lower line

Circled tones function as chromatic passing tones in upper or lower line.

Suspension Types

We have already seen and heard the most common dissonant suspension types (9–8, 7–6, and 4–3) in two-voice contexts. Remember that the suspension, in common-practice style, is prepared by and resolves to a consonance in a three-stage process: preparation, suspension, resolution. While the suspended tone is usually tied to its preparation, suspensions without ties are also possible: these are called rearticulated suspensions.

In music with more than two voices, the intervals specified by the suspension names suggest appropriate triadic resolutions and inversions. For example, the 7–6 suspension usually resolves to a first-inversion chord (hence the "6" in the name). The 4–3 and 9–8 usually resolve to a root-position chord, though first inversion is possible. The 4–3 suspension is frequently placed over the dominant harmony in authentic cadences, where it temporarily displaces (and thus draws attention to) the leading tone. Listen to Example 13.2, an expressive passage from "Music for a While," and identify each of the suspensions. Does Purcell prepare and resolve the suspensions as our guidelines would suggest? (*Try it #2*)

3.8 🎧

EXAMPLE 13.2: Purcell, "Music for a While," mm. 12b–14a

In most dissonant suspensions, one of the upper voices is suspended and resolves to its chord tone after the bass and other voices have changed to the next chord, but the opposite is also possible. That is, the bass may be suspended against the upper voices of a chord, then resolve (late) to its chord tone. The most common bass suspension is a 2–3, or 9–10, suspension. As in two-voice textures, consonant suspensions above the bass—such as the 6–5—are possible as well. In a 6–5 suspension, the sixth above the bass is not a member of the underlying root-position triad.

Voice-Leading in Suspensions Many of the same guidelines for the treatment of suspensions in two voices apply also in fuller textures, including the three-step process for writing them: (1) consonant preparation of the tone to be suspended, (2) retention of that tone as a dissonance on a strong beat, and (3) resolution of the tone down by step to a consonant interval. As in two-voice writing, the suspended note may be tied to its preparation or rearticulated. We will look at suspensions in one of Bach's SATB settings of the chorale tune "O Haupt voll Blut und Wunden." Listen to Example 13.3 on your CD, or sing it with your class on solfège syllables. We concentrate first on the suspension over the dominant seventh harmony at the cadence. Find this suspension and label its type. (*Try it #3*)

EXAMPLE 13.3: Bach, "O Haupt voll Blut und Wunden," mm. 2b–4

Translation: Full of sorrow and object of scorn!

Listen again to the cadence. On beat 3 of measure 3, the pitches sounding at the onset of the beat are (bass to soprano) A-D-A-E. What kind of triad is that? It is an incomplete triad (with a dissonant extra note); the complete triad appears on the next beat: A-C♯-E. The D on beat 3 has been suspended over from the previous harmony on beat 2: the tonic triad D-F-A. The suspended D conforms to the suspension guidelines: (1) it is prepared as a consonant member of the tonic triad, (2) it is repeated (rearticulated) on a strong beat as a dissonant "nonchord" tone, and (3) it resolves down by step to C♯, a consonant chord member. The chord on beat 3 (A-D-A-E) is incomplete because the tone of resolution of this 4–3 suspension is displaced by the suspended tone. If C♯ had been present in that beat, the dissonance of C♯ with the suspended D would have been too harsh. In addition, the C♯ would have anticipated the tone of resolution, interfering with the suspension's effect.

KEY CONCEPT

When writing a suspension in a piece with three or more voices, it helps if you plan the doubling in the chord of resolution first. Make sure that the chord with the dissonant suspension does not also include the suspension's tone of resolution—except in a 9–8 suspension when the resolution tone is in the bass.

Suspensions with Change of Bass Listen to or perform Example 13.3 again to find another suspension. On the first two beats of measure 3, we hear another suspension in the tenor voice. The suspended tone, E4, is prepared by the dominant anacrusis (in m. 2b), of which it is a member. Bach suspends E into the tonic harmony on the downbeat. On beat 2, when the suspension resolves, the supporting tonic harmony changes inversion: the bass moves from D3 via passing tone to F3. This happens often in Baroque music, but it does not disrupt the effect of the suspension. This suspension includes the tone of resolution in the bass (D3), which conforms to our guidelines, but the change of bass results in a doubled third in the chord of resolution.

One way to label this type of suspension is by thinking of both intervals from the initial bass pitch—this suspension is a 9–8 with change of bass. Baroque musicians, however, read each chord as intervals above the bass. They would therefore label this suspension a 9–6: the 9 stands for the suspended dissonant tone, and the 6 represents the interval between the tone of resolution and the new bass note.

Combining Suspensions The opening of Bach's Prelude in E♭ Major for Organ, given as Example 13.4, is characterized by dotted rhythms and prominent suspensions. Circle and label the suspensions and other embellishing tones in the example. (*Try it #4*)

EXAMPLE 13.4: Bach, Prelude in E♭ Major for Organ (*St. Anne*), mm. 1–4

The accented dissonance in measure 4 is a double suspension—simultaneous 9–8 and 4–3 suspensions. In fact, the 9–8 suspension may be used in combination with either the 4–3 or 7–6 in a double suspension; the suspended pitches will move in parallel sixths or thirds above the bass. In the Bach example, we could hear this cadence as having an entire dominant seventh harmony suspended over the tonic bass before resolving to tonic. In one special type of double suspension, common over the dominant at authentic cadences, a consonant 6–5 suspension is combined with a dissonant 4–3. We will see how this works in Example 13.8 below.

Suspensions may be combined successively in suspension chains, as in two-voice composition. Listen to Handel's chain of 7–6 suspensions (between the tenor and bass voices) in Example 13.5. This type, along with the chain that alternates 4–3 with 9–8 suspensions (Example 13.6, between the bass and alto), are the most common. We will return to the voice-leading patterns of suspension chains when we study harmonic sequences (Chapter 17).

EXAMPLE 13.5: Handel, Chaconne in G Major, Variation 9, mm. 73–76 (chain suspension, 7–6)

EXAMPLE 13.6: Bach, "Heut' ist, o Mensch" ("This Day, O Mankind"), mm. 3b–6a (alternating 4–3 and 9–8 suspensions)

Embellishing Suspensions   Suspensions may be embellished before resolution. Example 13.7 is drawn from Bach's setting of "Liebster Jesu" ("Dearest Jesus"), one of many chorales with a 4–3 suspension above the dominant harmony at the cadence. Play through the chorale excerpt, or sing it with your class. In measure 14, Bach embellishes the suspended tone, G4 in the alto, by skipping down to E4 before the suspension's resolution. Although the E4 might be understood as an incomplete neighbor to the tone of resolution, its primary role is as an embellishment of the 4–3 suspension that resolves the dissonant G4 to F4.

EXAMPLE 13.7: Bach, "Liebster Jesu," mm. 11–15

Measures 9–10 of Bach's chorale "Christ ist erstanden" ("Christ Is Arisen"; Example 13.8) present a cadence highly embellished with suspensions. At the cadence (m. 10), Bach employs a double suspension: a dissonant 4–3 in the tenor voice and a consonant 6–5 in the alto, resulting in parallel thirds between these two voices. The dissonance and resolution of the suspension occur on the strong beats 1 and 3. (Imagine the resolution as if beat 2 were missing.) The eighths on beat 2, preceding the resolution, embellish and intensify the dissonant suspension.

EXAMPLE 13.8: Bach, "Christ ist erstanden," mm. 9–10

double suspension

KEY CONCEPT

When we embellish suspensions, we decorate the dissonant suspended tone rather than the tone of resolution.

Retardations In eighteenth-century music, you may encounter a rhythmic embellishment that looks like a suspension, but resolves *up* by step instead of down. This is called a retardation.

KEY CONCEPT

A **retardation**, like a dissonant suspension, begins with a consonance that is held over—tied or rearticulated—to the next beat to make a dissonance. It then resolves up by step. The most common dissonant retardation is made of intervals 7–8, with scale-degrees $\hat{7}$ and $\hat{8}$ above the tonic pitch in the bass.

Retardations are usually found at a cadence: the tonic arrives in the bass, but part of the dominant harmony is sustained or rearticulated in one or more of the upper voices before resolving to tonic, as is the case in Example 13.9 (m. 205, the D4 in the top voice). Retardations are often combined with descending suspensions. In this example, the retardation is combined with a 4–3 suspension (A♭3–G3).

EXAMPLE 13.9: Bach, Prelude in E♭ Major for Organ (*St. Anne*), mm. 204–205 (final cadence)

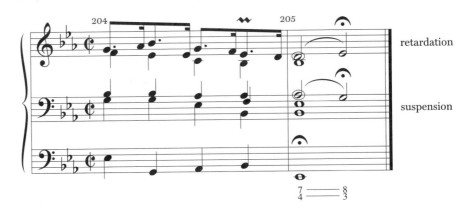

Anticipations With suspensions and retardations, one part of a two-voice framework is delayed and resolves "late." In an **anticipation**, the opposite happens: one part of the framework arrives "early." Listen again to Purcell's "Music for a While"; there are anticipations in the vocal line at many of the cadences. Look at the final measures of the song, given in Example 13.10. Each time the vocalist sings the word "beguile," she arrives on the A4 tonic pitch one sixteenth note ahead of the tonic chord, anticipating the resolution of scale-degree $\hat{2}$ to tonic. Anticipations are unaccented—they appear on the offbeat or weak beat of a measure—and are usually dissonances. They do not need to resolve; they are simply repeated on the next beat, where they "belong" in the counterpoint. Anticipations are not included in strict species counterpoint, but they are frequently used by eighteenth-century composers to decorate cadences.

EXAMPLE 13.10: Purcell, "Music for a While," mm. 35–39 (final cadence)

This Purcell example features remarkable embellishments in the accompaniment, including chromatic lower neighbor tones and ornamented suspensions. Look at measure 37, beat 3, for an ornamented suspension. Here the underlying chord is D minor, but the E4 tied across from the previous beat creates a 9–8 suspension beneath the word "all." Rather than resolving directly by step, however—E4 to D4—the suspension is ornamented with a skip to C♯4. Look for a similar technique in measure 36.

Before we leave the topic of anticipations, look again at Example 13.9, from the Bach Prelude in E♭ Major. Is the final D4 of measure 204 an anticipation? (*Try it #5*)

Pedal Points   Pedal points get their name from passages in organ music, like Example 13.11, in which the organist's foot rests on a single pedal for measures at a time while the harmonies change above this note. Pedal points do not decorate a musical line or framework in the way that passing or neighboring tones do, but they are common nonchord tones that you will come across in music analysis. Like suspensions, pedal points may be rearticulated from beat to beat.

When you encounter a pedal point in music, consider carefully the larger context. Most often, the pedal prolongs a single harmony (usually tonic or dominant), and the voices above it are embellishing. Sometimes the upper harmonies are functional and can be analyzed with Roman numerals (in that case, ignore the "non-harmonic" pedal in your analysis). Pedal points are not limited to the bass line, but may appear in any voice. When in upper voices, they are sometimes called "inverted pedals."

EXAMPLE 13.11: Bach, Organ Sonata No. 5 in C Major, first movement, mm. 35–38

○ ○

Embellishing Tones in Popular Music

Embellishing tones are found in popular music as well, though some of the guidelines for preparation and resolution are more relaxed in this repertoire. Perform the passage from Menken and Rice's "A Whole New World" given in Example 13.12. The phrase opens with a triplet whose middle note is a passing tone between D7 chord members. The downbeats of measures 33 and 34 feature dissonant incomplete neighbors (A4 and C♯5), which add expressive accentuation to the text at these points. The chord symbols in measures 35 and 36 include a "sus" notation (E7sus and A7sus). "Sus chords" are popular-music notation for 4–3 suspensions. Look first at the piano realization of the E7sus chord in measure 35. Is the dissonant fourth prepared and resolved according to common-practice guidelines? (*Try it #6*) The A7sus in measure 36 has no consonant preparation for the dissonant fourth, D4. However, it does resolve down by step to the chord tone, as we would expect.

EXAMPLE 13.12: Menken and Rice, "A Whole New World," mm. 32b–37a

Now perform the opening of Lloyd Webber and Rice's "Don't Cry for Me Argentina," given in Example 13.13. Here is a clear example of a pedal point—C3 in the bass line of the piano arrangement—that is maintained throughout the entire excerpt through several arpeggiated chord changes. The cadence provides an example of an ornamented suspension, similar to that of Bach's "Christ ist erstanden" (Example 3.8). Which type of suspension do you hear? (*Try it #7*)

EXAMPLE 13.13: Lloyd Webber and Rice, "Don't Cry for Me Argentina," mm. 3–10a

TERMS YOU SHOULD KNOW

anticipation	incomplete neighbor	suspension
compound melody	neighbor tone	suspension chain
consonant skip	passing tone	suspension with
double neighbor	pedal point	change of bass
double passing tone	retardation	

QUESTIONS FOR REVIEW

1. What are the three steps necessary to write a suspension?
2. What are the most common suspension types? How might they be ornamented?
3. What embellishments are available in four voices that we did not use in two voices?
4. Try to find an example of an ornamented suspension, an anticipation, and a pedal point in music literature that you know.

Chorale Harmonization and Figured Bass

CHAPTER 14

Outline of topics covered

Chorale harmonization
- Writing the bass-soprano counterpoint
- Special treatment of perfect intervals
- Completing the inner voices
- Voice-leading summary

Realizing figured bass
- About figured bass
- Guidelines for realization
- A figured-bass example
- Checking your work

Overview

In this chapter, we will learn the basic voice-leading principles of four-part chorale composition in the style of the Baroque era (1600–1750). We will also learn the guidelines for realizing Baroque-style figured bass.

Repertoire
Johann Sebastian Bach, "Ach Gott, vom Himmel sieh' darein" (Chorale No. 253)

Bach, Cantata No. 140 ("Wachet auf"), second movement

Bach, "O Haupt voll Blut und Wunden" (Chorale No. 74) (CD 1, track 7)

o o o o o o o o o o o o o o o o o o o o o o o o o o o o o o o o o o o o o o o o o o o o o o o o o o o

Chorale Harmonization

At this point, we place ourselves in the position of Baroque musicians. We will study chorales from that era to learn basic voice-leading principles, to which we will return later when we compose in other styles. You might be surprised to discover how many elements of chorale-style composition are shared with freer compositions. Composers of many eras and styles have followed similar principles to control their use of dissonance, to make harmonic choices, to lead from one harmony to the next, to score for instruments or voices, and to compose pleasing melodies and bass lines. Throughout this text, common features (and differences) between musical styles will be pointed out.

Our study begins with a phrase from one of Bach's settings of "O Haupt voll Blut und Wunden." (See box below for more about Bach's work as a church musician and the context for chorale settings.) The melody given in Example 14.1 is the second phrase of this eight-phrase tune. Sing the melody to yourself to determine the key, mode, and cadence type. (*Try it #1*)

Bach's Way with Hymns

Johann Sebastian Bach, considered by many the foremost composer of the early eighteenth century, at times worked as a church musician—a position that in those days required him to perform as a choirmaster, an organist, and a composer. He often set hymn tunes written by earlier composers, such as "O Haupt voll Blut und Wunden," a famous tune written by Hans Leo Hassler in 1601. Bach harmonized this chorale tune numerous times to several different texts—some with a somber Crucifixion text for use around Easter and others with words that were comforting and cheerful. His various settings show many ways a single tune can be harmonized.

Chorale settings were an important musical hallmark of the Protestant Reformation in Germany. For this reason, many of the chorales we will encounter in our studies are set to German texts. Most include multiple verses of text, which in modern editions are aligned between the staves for singing. Chorales are scored for four voices, SATB, with homophonic textures—that is, each voice moves from chord to chord at the same time, for the most part.

Today we think of Bach's chorales as being like hymns, pieces to be sung in church by everyone. Although congregations did sing chorale melodies in Bach's day, these elaborate chorale harmonizations were movements of the composer's cantatas, passions, and other church music, and were usually sung by the choir or soloists. "O Haupt" comes from Bach's *St. Matthew Passion* (1729).

EXAMPLE 14.1: Bach, "O Haupt voll Blut und Wunden," mm. 2b–4 (melody)

Begin your harmonization by thinking about the solfège or scale-degree numbers you just sang: *re–me–me–re–do–re–do*, or $\hat{2}$–$\hat{3}$–$\hat{3}$–$\hat{2}$–$\hat{1}$–$\hat{2}$–$\hat{1}$. Because chorales usually have a harmonic rhythm of one chord per beat, we can use the scale degrees to plan which harmony to write on each beat: tonic for *me* and *do* (scale-degrees $\hat{3}$ and $\hat{1}$) and dominant for *re* ($\hat{2}$). We will plan a perfect authentic cadence because of the melody's $\hat{2}$–$\hat{1}$ ending. Since the phrase begins with an anacrusis, we will also plan a dominant harmony before the tonic downbeat. On a grand staff, write out the soprano melody, and add these Roman numerals beneath the bass staff.

Writing the Bass-Soprano Counterpoint

We now need a bass line in counterpoint with the melody—one that supports the harmonies we have chosen, but includes inversions to create a singable melodic bass line. Begin by writing the *sol–do* ($\hat{5}$–$\hat{1}$) bass for the perfect authentic cadence. Now return to the beginning of the melody. The second pitch of the melody, F5 ($\hat{3}$), begins the basic phrase on the downbeat. We choose a root-position tonic chord to begin the tonic area. Then, since the F5 repeats, we vary the bass line by moving to i^6 on beat 2, as Example 14.2a shows.

EXAMPLE 14.2: "O Haupt voll Blut und Wunden," mm. 2b–4

(a) Soprano with partial bass line

d: i — 6   V   i

KEY CONCEPT _____

When you write a bass line to a given melody, follow the basic phrase model—but you need not work "left to right": one way is to start with the cadence, then go back to the beginning to write the tonic opening. Finally, fill in the middle of the phrase.

We want the dominant anacrusis to prepare the tonic, but since this is the second phrase of the chorale, we do not necessarily need a strong root-position progression. We choose V^6 for a stepwise bass: *ti–do*, or $\hat{7}$–$\hat{1}$. We now have a bass note for every beat except the soprano's *re–do* ($\hat{2}$–$\hat{1}$) eighth notes. Which of the two pitches should we harmonize? Whatever pitch we do not harmonize is an embellishing tone. We might interpret scale-degree $\hat{2}$ (E) as a passing tone between F and D, or we might think of $\hat{1}$ as a neighbor tone between the two Es. To maintain a consistent harmonic rhythm, we write dominant chords on beats 3 and 4 to balance the tonic chords of beats 1 and 2.

We will see in many musical examples that the dominant harmony at the cadence often extends over two beats, with an octave leap of $\hat{5}$ in the bass, as shown in Example 14.2b. This permits us to add suspensions or other strong-beat dissonances to intensify the motion to tonic. Our choice makes scale-degree $\hat{1}$ a neighbor tone to the repeated $\hat{2}$, E, over a dominant harmony. Finally, we add passing tones to make the bass line easier to sing.

(b) Soprano and bass

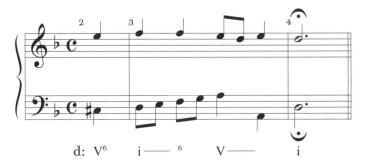

$$\text{d: V}^6 \quad \text{i} —— {}^6 \quad \text{V} —— \quad \text{i}$$

KEY CONCEPT

> Write the soprano-bass counterpoint first before filling in the inner voices. Make sure both voice parts have singable melodic lines, and that they make good contrapuntal and harmonic sense.

Special Treatment of Perfect Intervals

Before we add the alto and tenor lines to our chorale harmonization, we should review voice-leading guidelines for perfect intervals in common-practice style. In both two- and four-voice writing, parallel motion between imperfect consonances like sixths and thirds is common (Example 14.3a), provided that the parallel motion does not continue so long that the voices lose their independence. In fact, parallel thirds and sixths are found in all styles of tonal music.

On the other hand, parallel motion between perfect octaves or fifths (Examples 14.3b and c) is not found in most common-practice compositions; do not use it **WF2** when you write in this style. (Parallel fifths, though, can appear in popular and folk music.) Incidentally, simple repetition of fifths or octaves is common, and not to be confused with parallel motion. In passages like Example 14.3d, there are no parallel fifths—only repeated fifths.

EXAMPLE 14.3: V–I voice-leading guidelines

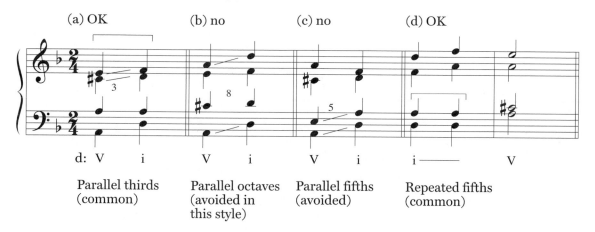

Common-practice composers treated voice-leading into and out of perfect intervals with care. When you write in this style, watch for the following situations. To avoid them, and achieve voice-leading that is more appropriate to the style, you can usually change a chord's doubling or spacing.

1. Direct octaves and fifths When you approach perfect intervals by similar motion, you are writing "direct" (or "hidden") octaves or fifths. We know from our study of first-species counterpoint that similar motion to perfect intervals was not permitted unless the soprano moved by step. Common-practice composers also avoided this type of voice-leading, shown in Example 14.4a. Do not use direct octaves or fifths in the outer voices when writing in this style. They may appear in the inner voices, however, or in any voice paired with a stepwise soprano line (Example 14.4b).

2. Contrary octaves and fifths You cannot disguise the negative effect of parallel octaves or fifths by spacing the chords to create contrary motion between the perfect intervals (Example 14.4c). Motion from one perfect interval to another of the same size is not allowed in this style, whether the voices move in the same or opposite directions.

3. Unequal fifths When you move from a diminished fifth to a perfect fifth by similar motion, you create unequal fifths (Example 14.4d). Similar motion from a d5 to a P5 violates proper voice-leading of the tendency tones, since the d5 (usually scale-degrees $\hat{7}$ and $\hat{4}$) normally resolves by contracting inward to a third ($\hat{1}$ and $\hat{3}$). In Chapter 15, we will consider a few progressions where d5 to P5 is permitted, but for now, avoid it when writing in common-practice style. On the other hand, similar motion from a P5 to a d5 is allowed, because perfect fifths do not have the tendency tones of the d5 (Example 14.4e). The d5 must then resolve, however, or the P5–d5 motion will sound like parallel fifths.

EXAMPLE 14.4: Additional voice-leading guidelines

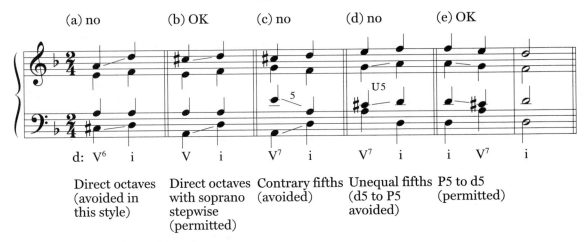

(a) no	(b) OK	(c) no	(d) no	(e) OK
d: V⁶ i	V i	V⁷ i	V⁷ i	i V⁷ i
Direct octaves (avoided in this style)	Direct octaves with soprano stepwise (permitted)	Contrary fifths (avoided)	Unequal fifths (d5 to P5 avoided)	P5 to d5 (permitted)

SUMMARY _____

When you write in common-practice style, do not use

1. direct octaves or fifths: similar motion into a perfect interval in the soprano-bass pair (permitted only in inner voices or if the soprano moves by step);

2. contrary octaves or fifths: contrary motion from one perfect interval to another of the same size; or

3. unequal fifths: motion from a diminished fifth to a perfect fifth, especially in the soprano-bass pair, since this interferes with proper resolution of the tendency tones ($\hat{7}$ resolving up to $\hat{1}$ and $\hat{4}$ resolving down to $\hat{3}$).

Completing the Inner Voices

Let's return now to our chorale composition "O Haupt voll Blut und Wunden." We need to add alto and tenor lines to our soprano-bass counterpoint (Example 14.2b), keeping in mind the voice-leading guidelines we have learned. Remember, we needn't always work left to right. Scan the soprano-bass counterpoint to see whether there are places that might present special challenges (for example, places where the outer voices are particularly close together). In the case of "O Haupt," we don't anticipate any particular problems. We therefore begin with the first chord: the anacrusis, V^6.

KEY CONCEPT

Before voicing the first chord of a phrase, scan the soprano and bass lines for motion up or down. Plan your first chord's spacing with this motion in mind. For example, if the bass moves upward, place the other voices in a higher range to allow them room to move down in contrary motion.

Because the bass line moves up by step from C♯3 to A3, we should begin the alto and tenor lines fairly high in their vocal range. The V^6 chord, A-C♯-E, already has its third and fifth (bass and soprano, respectively). Either the alto or tenor should have an A, the root of the chord. The other voice may double the E (the fifth) or A (the root) but not the C♯ (the third, the leading tone). If we give the alto an E4, this places a full octave between soprano and alto. Since the soprano is about to move upward, however, this may cause spacing problems in the following chords. We place the root, A4, in the alto. Either A3 or E4 is possible for the tenor, but we choose E4, keeping the alto and tenor high enough for contrary motion with the ascending bass.

We now connect V^6 to a root-position tonic, D-F-A, on the downbeat. Since the tonic and dominant share a chord tone (scale-degree $\hat{5}$), we keep this tone in the same voice: A4 in the alto. We now have a complete triad, but need to double one pitch in the tenor voice. In a root-position tonic triad like this one, the usual procedure is to double the root ($\hat{1}$), placing D4 in the tenor. Try doubling something else, to see whether it causes any voice-leading problems. (*Try it #2*) On the next beat, the simplest voice-leading into the i^6 is to keep the same alto and tenor pitches, A4 and D4. A change in voicing is not necessary, since the inversion and the stepwise bass line provide sufficient musical interest.

How shall we connect i⁶ with V on beat 3? Again, keep the common tone in the alto: A4. This gives us two As and an E in this root-position V. The chord is missing the leading tone, C♯, which we place in the tenor for beats 3 and 4. For variety—and to intensify the dominant function at the cadence—we write a V⁷ on the fourth beat, and place a G4 in the alto. We conclude by resolving the V⁷ correctly into the perfect authentic cadence: first, resolve $\hat{7}$ (C♯4) up to $\hat{1}$ in the tenor; then resolve the chordal seventh (G4, or $\hat{4}$) down by step to $\hat{3}$ in the alto. This resolution gives us a tonic triad with tripled root and one third, which is common at a cadence.

1.8   Now compare our completed harmonization in Example 14.5a with Bach's in Example 14.5b. What differences do you see? (*Try it #3*)

EXAMPLE 14.5:

(a) "O Haupt voll Blut und Wunden," mm. 2b–4, with inner voices

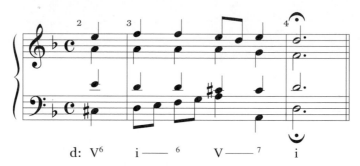

(b) Bach, "O Haupt voll Blut und Wunden," mm. 2b–4

Translation: Full of sorrow and object of scorn!

Voice-Leading Summary

In completing our harmonization of "O Haupt," we have abided by a number of voice-leading principles that are summarized below. Example 14.6 illustrates points 2 and 3.

SUMMARY

Keep in mind the following guidelines when connecting SATB chords.

1. **Work to achieve smooth voice-leading:**
   - Resolve tendency tones correctly, and never double them.
   - If two chords share a common tone, keep the common tone in the same voice.
   - Move each voice to the closest possible member of the following chord (without creating parallel perfect intervals).
   - Avoid skipping down to a chordal seventh.

2. **Aim for independence of the four voices:**
   - Keep each within its own characteristic vocal range.
   - Avoid moving all four voices in the same direction.
   - Avoid placing a pitch in one voice part so that it crosses above or below the pitch sung by an adjacent voice part—either within a single chord (voice-crossing) or between two consecutive chords (overlapping) (see Examples 14.6a and b).
   - Avoid prolonged parallel or similar motion; balance with contrary and oblique motion.

3. **Make each voice a singable melody:**
   - Avoid large leaps (except bass leaps between chord members).
   - Avoid melodic motion by augmented or diminished intervals (e.g., the augmented second between scale-degrees $\hat{6}$ and $\hat{7}$ in harmonic minor; see Example 14.6c).
   - Include passing or neighboring tones to create a smooth line or add melodic interest.

4. **Pay careful attention to voice-leading to and from perfect intervals:**
   - Use contrary or oblique motion when you approach and leave any perfect interval (unison, octave, fifth), since parallel perfect intervals are prohibited in this style.

5. **Remember to write musically:**
   - When a harmony is repeated, create some variety by changing the soprano pitch, the inversion, and/or the spacing of the chord.
   - Where possible, avoid static or repetitive melodic lines.

EXAMPLE 14.6: Avoid in common-practice style

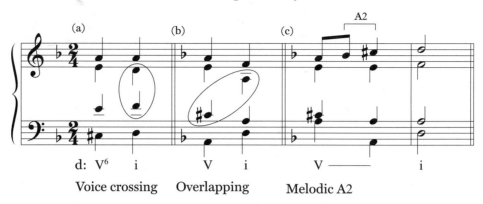

Voice crossing   Overlapping   Melodic A2

Often one voice-leading error will create other problems as well. In Example 14.6b, for example, we see not only overlapping between the tenor and alto, but also contrary fifths between the alto and bass voices.

Check your understanding of these guidelines in Example 14.7, a complete chorale phrase with numerous voice-leading errors. Sing or play through the phrase, circle and label the mistakes, then rewrite the phrase with correct voice-leading. (*Try it #4*)

EXAMPLE 14.7: A chorale phrase with errors

o o o o o o o o o o o o o o o o o o o o o o o o o o o o o o o o o o o o o o o o o o o o o o o

Realizing Figured Bass

About Figured Bass

Improvisation was an everyday part of performance in the Baroque and Classical eras. Singers and solo instrumentalists were expected to add melodic embellishment to melodies (as you will hear in some pieces on your CD). Baroque performers on keyboards, lutes, and other harmony instruments had to be able to improvise harmonic progressions based on a given bass line with figures (Arabic numbers indicating some of the intervals to be played above the bass line) written above or below the notes. As we saw in Chapter 7, this combination of bass line and figures—usually called **figured bass**—was a way of indicating the chords without notating them fully.

Figured-bass was also used to teach the principles of harmony and voice-leading to musicians in the seventeenth and eighteenth centuries. Keyboard players learned a vocabulary of progressions and voicings by practicing standard figures in various keys. In this way, they became familiar with most conventional chord sequences and the usual voice-leading possibilities. Roman numerals for harmonic analysis (and even the concept of inversion as we know it today) were not originally part of this system; they came into use at the end of the eighteenth century.

WF3

The most common chord in the early figured basses was symbolized by the figures $\frac{5}{3}$ above the bass—to indicate what we call a root-position triad—and these intervals were assumed when no figures were given. Composers generally wrote a ^{6} to represent what we call a first-inversion triad. Sometimes they needed to warn the keyboard player to add an accidental to create a leading tone or some other altered tone. At first, they wrote the number of the interval with the sharp or flat in front of it or behind it ($^{\#6}$ or $^{6\#}$, $^{\flat3}$ or $^{3\flat}$). Later they began to write the accidental alone if it was intended for the third above the bass (the most common placement). They also added a slash or a plus to indicate a raised tone (for example, $^{\emptyset}$ or $^{4+}$).

WF4

Example 14.8 shows a figured bass by Bach in a recitative movement for tenor. In this movement, from Cantata No. 140, a tenor soloist is accompanied by either harpsichord or organ, with a cello reinforcing the bass line. The keyboard player performs chords based on the figures, choosing durations that fit with the bass line and an appropriate accompaniment pattern. The singer might add embellishments, including appoggiaturas at appropriate points, such as a D5 on the downbeat of measure 4. The opening measures provide an example of pedal point in recitative style. Here the figures imply changes of pitches in the upper voices, while the bass stays on a single pitch.

EXAMPLE 14.8: Bach, Cantata No. 140 ("Wachet auf"), second movement, mm. 1–6

Translation: He comes, he comes, the bridegroom comes! Come out, you daughters of Zion, he hastens his departure from heaven to your mother's house.

Guidelines for Realization

Why study figured bass? When you create a full musical texture from a figured bass—called **realizing** a figured bass—you demonstrate your ability to compose in common-practice style without having to make the chord choices yourself. Your role is to link these chords as musically as possible within the guidelines of the style. Through working with figured basses, you gain a sense of what skills were expected of performing musicians in that era, while internalizing the principles of voice-leading and dissonance treatment that can inform your musical interpretations and compositions today.

WF5

We will learn basic guidelines here of the figured-bass system from the late Baroque (rather than earlier systems) and examine these principles more fully in future chapters. Remember, figures show *diatonic intervals above the bass.* Embellishing tones in the bass are not included in the figures, except for suspensions. A few chords are realized for you in Example 14.9.

KEY CONCEPT _____

When realizing a figured bass:

- Sing the given line(s) to help orient yourself tonally.
- An accidental next to a number means to raise or lower the pitch associated with that number by one half step (Example 14.9a).

- An accidental by itself means to raise or lower the third *above the bass* (Example 14.9b)—not necessarily the third of the chord.
- Place pitches above the bass in an appropriate octave according to the generic intervals given in the figured-bass symbols (Example 14.9c).
- Use pitches diatonic in the key (Example 14.9d).
- A slash through a number means to raise the pitch associated with that number by a half step (Example 14.9e).
- Accidentals in the figure apply only to that single chord.
- Figured bass does not list all intervals above the bass—some, like octaves and thirds, may be implied by the figures.
- Follow the doubling and voice-leading guidelines when voicing or connecting chords.
- A dash between two numbers means that those intervals belong in the same voice-leading strand (as in a 4–3 suspension; Example 14.9f).
- Melodic embellishing tones (other than suspensions) are not shown in the figures because they are not a part of the main harmonic framework. Musicians realizing the bass would be expected to add them according to their taste.

EXAMPLE 14.9: Realization of common figures

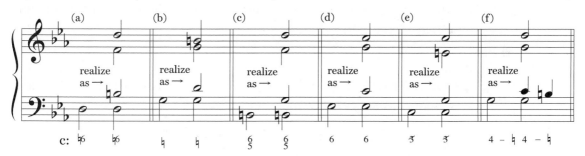

After you study the guidelines, return to Example 14.8 to find the figured-bass symbols that require an added accidental in the realization. Where are these located, and what pitches are implied? (*Try it #5*)

A Figured-Bass Example

We now turn to one of Bach's harmonizations of "Ach Gott, vom Himmel sieh' darein" ("O God, Look Down on Us from Heaven"). Bach composed this harmonization for a melody written in 1524 by German Protestant reformer Martin Luther. The G-minor setting is shown in Example 14.10 as a figured bass (in a version slightly altered from Bach's) beneath the chorale melody. We will complete the alto and tenor parts based on the figures. Always begin by singing through the soprano and bass lines on solfège or scale-degree numbers to orient yourself. This phrase ends on a half cadence. Its soprano-bass counterpoint features beautiful contrary motion in the first measure (G3–A3–B♭3 in the bass against B♭4–A4–G4 in the soprano). We will learn more about this contrapuntal pattern in Chapter 15.

The ♯ beneath the first and last bass notes indicates that the third above the bass is to be raised (from F to F♯). (Remember that the absence of other figures implies a ⅗ chord.) Write an F♯4 in the alto and double the root (D4) in the tenor voice. (This spacing between bass and tenor allows room for the bass ascent that comes in m. 1.) In measure 1, the initial chord has no figures: another ⅗ chord. Fill in the Roman numerals and the alto and tenor voices for this and the following chords, as we work through the figures together.

The second chord of measure 1 has ⁶₄ beneath it. We place a sixth and fourth above this bass note, but we must raise the sixth to F♯ as the slash indicates. The third chord of the measure shows a ⁶ in the figured bass; ⁶ implies ⅗, so we place a sixth and third above this pitch. Because the sixth above the bass is also the melody note (and the root of the triad), you will want to double it in the soprano and alto by drawing stems extending both above and below the G4.

Compose the inner voices for the next few beats on your own, according to our common-practice voice-leading guidelines. At the cadence, the figures direct us to supply a dissonance: a 9–8 suspension. Be sure to prepare and resolve the suspended pitch correctly. Finish the figured bass, then check your solution against the one given in *Try it #6.*

WF6

EXAMPLE 14.10: Bach (modified), "Ach Gott, vom Himmel sieh' darein," mm. 1–2a (soprano and figured bass)

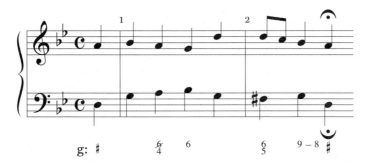

SUMMARY

No figure implies $\frac{5}{3}$.   ♯ implies raised third above the bass.

^{6} implies $\frac{6}{3}$.   ⚹ implies raised sixth above the bass.

Checking Your Work

When you finish an SATB melody harmonization or figured-bass realization, always go back and proofread your work. One of the easiest ways to do this is at the piano—often your ear will pick out mistakes that your eye will not. Read through your work slowly; listen and look for specific types of errors. Scan through once for the resolution of the tendency tones: check every leading tone and chordal seventh. You might want to label the tendency tones with arrows (an up arrow for leading tones and a down arrow for chordal sevenths) to remind yourself not to change those resolutions once you have checked them. If you are writing in a minor key, be sure that each leading tone has the proper accidental. Do one scan each for parallel octaves and fifths: find each perfect fifth or octave, and check the voice-leading into and out of it. Sing each line to yourself on scale degrees or solfège to check again for the resolution of tendency tones, for awkward leaps, and for a musical line.

TERMS YOU SHOULD KNOW

contrary octaves/fifths   figured bass   unequal fifths

direct octaves/fifths   realization

QUESTIONS FOR REVIEW

1. Summarize the steps for melody harmonization. Why not move from left to right, filling in complete chords as you go?
2. What are you going to check for in approaching and leaving perfect fifths and octaves?
3. What do figures in a figured bass represent? How do you know which pitches to place in the upper parts above the bass?
4. Name two different ways a raised third might be notated in figured bass.

CHAPTER 15

Expanding the Basic Phrase:
Leading-Tone, Predominant, and $\frac{6}{4}$ Chords

Outline of topics covered

Dominant substitutes: Leading-tone chords

- Doubling in the vii°⁶
- Resolving vii°⁶
- The viiø⁷ and vii°⁷
- Resolving viiø⁷ and vii°⁷
- Special considerations in resolving viiø⁷, vii°⁷, and their inversions

Predominant harmonies

Dominant expansion with the cadential $\frac{6}{4}$

- Writing cadential $\frac{6}{4}$ chords

Other expansions involving $\frac{6}{4}$s

- The neighboring $\frac{6}{4}$
- The passing $\frac{6}{4}$
- The arpeggiating $\frac{6}{4}$
- The four $\frac{6}{4}$ types

Overview

In this chapter, we will consider new dominant-function chords: leading-tone triads and seventh chords. We will also expand the basic phrase to include predominant harmonies, and learn how $\frac{6}{4}$ chords can function in predominant and dominant areas.

Repertoire

Johann Sebastian Bach,
> "Aus meines Herzens Grunde" (Chorale No. 1) (CD 1, track 5)
> "O Haupt voll Blut und Wunden" (Chorale No. 80) (CD 1, track 7)

Jeremiah Clarke, *Trumpet Voluntary* (CD 1, track 69)

Stephen Foster, "Camptown Races"

Andrew Lloyd Webber and Tim Rice, "Don't Cry for Me Argentina"

Wolfgang Amadeus Mozart,
> Piano Sonata in B♭ Major, K. 333, first movement
> Piano Sonata in C Major, K 545, first movement (CD 2, track 57)
> Piano Sonata in D Major, K. 284, third movement (CD 2, track 48)

"My Country, 'Tis of Thee" (CD 2, track 97)

Henry Purcell, "Music for a While" (CD 3, track 5)

John Philip Sousa, "The Stars and Stripes Forever" (CD 3, track 41)

Dominant Substitutes: Leading-Tone Chords

We begin with a famous work for trumpet and continuo, once attributed to Henry Purcell but now known to have been composed by Jeremiah Clarke. The accompaniment for this Baroque-era piece was originally notated with figured bass; our example shows one possible realization. Listen to the first two phrases of Clarke's *Trumpet Voluntary* (also known as *Prince of Denmark's March*), given in Example 15.1. Where are dominant-function harmonies in the first phrase? Identify each chord in measures 1–4, with Roman numerals and figures. (*Try it #1*)

1.69

EXAMPLE 15.1: Clarke, *Trumpet Voluntary*, mm. 1–8

In Clarke's first phrase, we hear two dominant-function harmonies: V and vii°⁶. Measures 2 and 3 have vii°⁶ chords, while measures 1 and 4 feature V (and V⁶) chords.

KEY CONCEPT

V and V⁷ are not the only chords with the essential active ingredient for dominant function: the leading tone. The diminished triad vii° and the diminished seventh chords vii°⁷ and vii°⁷ are built on the leading tone and can substitute for V or V⁷.

The V and vii°⁶ chords are roughly equivalent in function: they share two scale degrees ($\hat{7}$ and $\hat{2}$) and can substitute for each other. (At one time, leading-tone chords were thought of as incomplete V⁷ chords; see box on p. 253.) The vii°⁶ conveys less harmonic strength than the V, since it is missing scale-degree $\hat{5}$. In the Clarke passage, both of the vii°⁶ chords function in a similar way: as a voice-leading link between a root-position and first-inversion tonic chord; they help expand the tonic area of the phrase. We will use leading-tone triads and seventh chords at the beginning and middle of phrases, or in other places where we do not want as strong a dominant function.

Doubling in the vii°⁶

Because the leading-tone triad includes the dissonant tritone $\hat{7}$ to $\hat{4}$, pay careful attention to its doubling and inversion. Example 15.2 shows possible SATB arrangements of the voices.

EXAMPLE 15.2: Voicings and spacings for vii°⁶

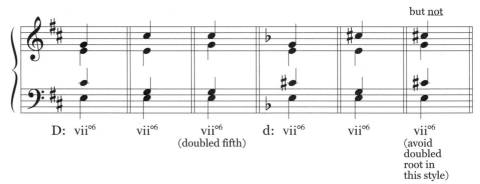

KEY CONCEPT

When using the leading-tone triad:

- Write vii° in first inversion—this inversion softens the tritone by placing at least one member of the dissonant tritone in an inner voice.
- Double the third of the vii°⁶ (the bass note, or scale-degree $\hat{2}$), since this scale degree is not part of the tritone; if this doubling is not possible, double the fifth ($\hat{4}$).
- Never double the root ($\hat{7}$, the leading tone).

We avoid doubling the leading tone because its doubled resolution would create parallel octaves or incorrect voice-leading in one of the lines. Look back at the doubling of the vii°⁶ chords in Example 15.1. Does this harmonization conform to our doubling guidelines? (*Try it #2*)

Resolving vii°⁶

We resolve vii°⁶ as a dominant-function harmony—to I or I⁶ (i or i⁶ in minor). Because V⁷ and vii° share the tendency tones $\hat{7}$ and $\hat{4}$, their normal resolutions follow the same principles: $\hat{7}$ resolves up to $\hat{1}$, and $\hat{4}$ down to $\hat{3}$. The resolution of $\hat{4}$ can vary in the leading-tone chord, however, depending on its spacing and context. Example 15.3 gives several correct resolutions, corresponding to points (a)–(d) in the KEY CONCEPT box below.

The Root of the Matter

Some textbooks from the 1950s to the 1970s describe leading-tone triads as dominant seventh chords without a root (see Walter Piston, *Harmony* [New York: Norton, 1941, 1969]). These chords were labeled V°⁷. While this view led to jokes about whether or not to double the missing root, there is a grain of truth to it—the leading-tone chord often appears in progressions where a V or V⁷ could have been used instead.

The idea of vii° as a V⁷ without a root is an old one, dating back to Jean-Philippe Rameau's theories of chord progression in the early eighteenth century. When Rameau wrote a *fundamental bass* (an analytical bass line written on a staff under the music's bass line, indicating the roots of each chord) for vii°, he showed the root as $\hat{5}$—the root of V⁷.

KEY CONCEPT

When resolving vii^{o6}:

(a) If the tritone is spelled as a diminished fifth—$\hat{7}$ below $\hat{4}$—it normally resolves inward to a third: $\hat{1}$-$\hat{3}$ (Example 15.3a).

(b) If the tritone is spelled as augmented fourth—$\hat{4}$ below $\hat{7}$—it may follow the voice-leading of the tendency tones and resolve outward to a sixth (Example 15.3b), or

(c) it may move in similar motion to a perfect fourth ($\hat{5}$-$\hat{1}$) (Example 15.3c).

(d) When the tritone is spelled as a diminished fifth, you may resolve scale-degree $\hat{4}$ up to $\hat{5}$ in only one context: when the soprano-bass counterpoint moves upward in parallel tenths ($\hat{2}$ to $\hat{3}$ in the bass, and $\hat{4}$ to $\hat{5}$ in the soprano). The strength of the parallel motion in this contrapuntal pattern overrides the voice-leading tendency of scale-degree $\hat{4}$ to resolve down (Example 15.3d).

EXAMPLE 15.3: Resolutions of vii^{o6}

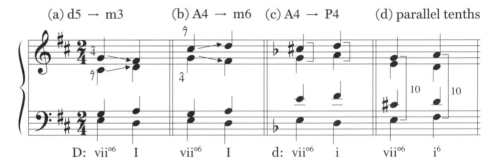

Consider now a second Bach setting of "O Haupt voll Blut und Wunden," a chorale melody we harmonized in Chapter 14. The first three chords of phrase two are given as Example 15.4. Here, Bach chooses to harmonize $\hat{2}$—the dominant-function anacrusis—with a vii^{o6} instead of a V. His doubling of the third in this chord is normal; he also doubles the third in the root-position tonic triad that follows, to create parallel thirds between the bass and alto.

EXAMPLE 15.4: Bach, "O Haupt voll Blut und Wunden," mm. 2b–4

Translation: Full of sorrow and object of scorn!

The vii$^{\varnothing7}$ and vii$^{\circ7}$

When you add a minor or diminished seventh to vii$^{\circ}$, you create the seventh chord vii$^{\varnothing7}$ (half-diminished) or vii$^{\circ7}$ (fully diminished). These chords have the same active ingredients as the diminished triad, but with the added scale-degree $\hat{6}$. Since $\hat{6}$ is one of the modal scale degrees, the quality of diminished seventh chord will change depending on the form of the scale used. Look at Example 15.5 to see how vii$^{\varnothing7}$ and vii$^{\circ7}$ are spelled in major and minor keys. In major keys, the leading-tone seventh chord is half-diminished (vii$^{\varnothing7}$), with the interval of a minor seventh between its root and seventh. In minor keys, it is fully diminished (vii$^{\circ7}$), with the interval of a diminished seventh between the root and seventh. Remember: When you spell a leading-tone harmony in a minor key, the root is the raised seventh scale degree—it will require an accidental.

EXAMPLE 15.5: Spelling vii$^{\varnothing7}$ and vii$^{\circ7}$ in major and minor keys

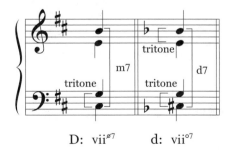

KEY CONCEPT

The fully diminished leading-tone seventh chord appears more commonly in music literature than the half-diminished, possibly because of the half-step voice-leading between the lowered scale-degree $\hat{6}$ to $\hat{5}$. In fact, the fully diminished vii°⁷ is sometimes found in major keys, with an accidental to lower scale-degree $\hat{6}$.

Another Way

Another way to think of the half-diminished seventh is as a diminished triad with a major third on top, and the fully diminished seventh as a diminished triad with a minor third on top. You can also spell a fully diminished seventh chord by stacking three minor thirds on top of each other.

Try it #3

Practice spelling the leading-tone seventh chord in the following keys.

KEY	SPELLING	CHORD TYPE
G minor	F♯-A-C-E♭	vii°⁷
B Major		
D minor		
F♯ minor		
E♭ Major		

Leading-Tone Chords in Two Eras

Music examples from the Baroque and Classical eras show two ways to think of leading-tone triads and seventh chords. During the early eighteenth century (the end of the Baroque era), composers considered harmony from the viewpoint of counterpoint; they thought of music as combined melodic lines, and the music they wrote has many chords that were conceived linearly (made from melodies in each of the SATB parts). Leading-tone chords were frequently used linearly, as tonic extensions, in Baroque chorales.

In the late eighteenth century, composers continued to pay careful attention to counterpoint, but some began to think of chords as thirds above a root. As a result, they chose chords to make particular harmonic progressions. Although linear leading-tone chords can be found in Classical compositions, they were less suited to the Classical Alberti bass and slower harmonic rhythm (in comparison with Baroque chorales). Instead, Classical composers tended to employ leading-tone chords as dominant substitutes. In later chapters, we will learn how leading-tone chords function in the chromatic harmonies of Romantic-period works, as well as in modern tonal contexts.

Resolving vii$^{\varnothing7}$ and vii$^{\circ7}$

Like all seventh chords, we usually write vii$^{\varnothing7}$ and vii$^{\circ7}$ with all four chord members present, in root position or any inversion. The leading-tone seventh chords share with V^7 scale-degrees $\hat{7}$, $\hat{2}$, and $\hat{4}$. The normal resolutions of the tendency tones $\hat{7}$ and $\hat{4}$ are the same as for the V^7. In addition, the chordal seventh, scale-degree $\hat{6}$, typically resolves down to $\hat{5}$.

SUMMARY

We normally resolve the tendency tones of vii$^{\varnothing7}$ and vii$^{\circ7}$ like those of V^7:

- resolve $\hat{7}$ up to $\hat{1}$,
- resolve $\hat{4}$ down to $\hat{3}$, and
- resolve the chordal seventh down ($\hat{6}$ to $\hat{5}$).

Try it #4

Spell the resolutions of $\hat{7}$ up to $\hat{1}$ and $\hat{4}$ down to $\hat{3}$ in the following keys.

KEY	$\hat{7}$–$\hat{1}$	$\hat{4}$–$\hat{3}$
C minor	_____	_____
A Major	_____	_____
B minor	_____	_____
E minor	_____	_____
A♭ Major	_____	_____

Special Considerations in Resolving vii^{ø7}, vii^{o7}, and Their Inversions

Look at Example 15.6a for a typical resolution of a root-position vii^{ø7} to tonic. In this example, all the tendency tones resolve correctly. Scale-degree $\hat{2}$ resolves up to $\hat{3}$, which results in a tonic triad with two thirds. This a common voice-leading and doubling. Why can't scale-degree $\hat{2}$ resolve down to $\hat{1}$? (*Try it #5*)

EXAMPLE 15.6: Resolutions of root-position vii^{ø7}-i and vii^{o7}-i

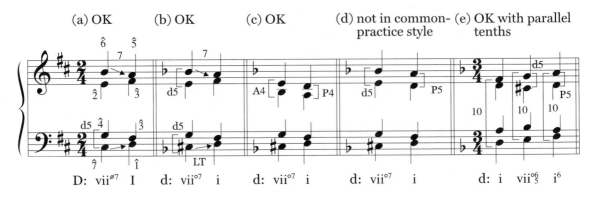

(a) OK   (b) OK   (c) OK   (d) not in common-practice style   (e) OK with parallel tenths

In addition to the familiar tritone between scale-degrees $\hat{7}$ and $\hat{4}$, the fully diminished leading-tone seventh chord, vii^{o7}, contains a second tritone: between $\hat{2}$ and $\hat{6}$. (Remember that this is the lowered $\hat{6}$ of minor keys.) This second tritone introduces the potential for unequal fifths: similar motion from a diminished fifth to perfect fifth.

KEY CONCEPT

In resolving vii°⁷ and its inversions:

- Resolve the d5 (in Example 15.6b, between $\hat{2}$ in the alto and $\hat{6}$ in an upper voice) inward to a third, $\hat{3}$-$\hat{5}$. This results in a tonic triad with a doubled third.
- When scale-degree $\hat{2}$ is voiced higher than $\hat{6}$ (as in Example 15.6c), $\hat{2}$ may resolve down to $\hat{1}$. The resulting augmented fourth to perfect fourth is permitted in this style.
- Avoid motion from a d5 to P5 in root-position leading-tone seventh chords (as in Example 15.6d); the d5 usually contracts to a third in this style.

There is one common exception to the "Avoid motion from a d5 to P5" guideline: when the soprano voice moves $\hat{3}$–$\hat{4}$–$\hat{5}$ to a bass line $\hat{1}$–$\hat{2}$–$\hat{3}$ in parallel tenths (as in Example 15.6e). Listen to Example 15.7, from Bach's setting of "Aus meines Herzens Grunde," which illustrates this progression in a musical context. The strong counterpoint of the soprano-bass parallel tenths overrides the d5 tendency tones. Does Bach's harmonization conform to our doubling guidelines? (*Try it #6*)

EXAMPLE 15.7: Bach, "Aus meines Herzens Grunde," mm. 7b–10a

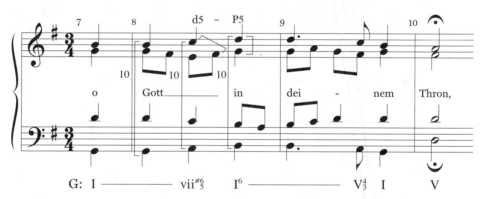

Translation: O God, upon your throne.

Leading-tone seventh chords are typically found in root position, first inversion, and second inversion. Third inversion is not common, because it resolves to a tonic second-inversion triad.

KEY CONCEPT

Typical resolutions of the leading-tone seventh chords to tonic:

$$\text{vii}^{\varnothing 7} \to \text{I} \qquad\qquad \text{vii}^{\circ 7} \to \text{i}$$
$$\text{vii}^{\varnothing \,6}_{5} \to \text{I}^6 \qquad\qquad \text{vii}^{\circ \,6}_{5} \to \text{i}^6$$
$$\text{vii}^{\varnothing \,4}_{3} \to \text{I}^6 \qquad\qquad \text{vii}^{\circ \,4}_{3} \to \text{i}^6$$

Some common voicings and resolutions of these chords are given in Example 15.8. Example 15.9 shows the less common usage in third inversion. Here, because the chordal seventh is in the bass, the bass must resolve down to $\hat{5}$, usually to a tonic second-inversion triad. The tonic second-inversion triad then must resolve as either a cadential or passing $^6_4$ (both of which are discussed later in the chapter).

EXAMPLE 15.8: Common resolutions of vii$^{\varnothing}$ and vii$^{\circ 7}$ in inversion

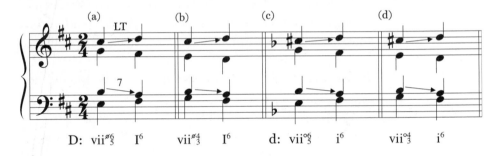

EXAMPLE 15.9: Resolutions of vii$^{\varnothing 4}_{2}$ and vii$^{\circ 4}_{2}$ to cadential $^6_4$

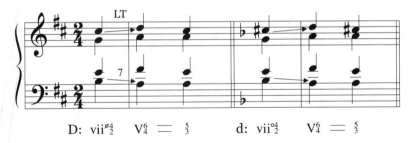

Predominant Harmonies

Play through the excerpt of Mozart's Piano Sonata in B♭ Major, K. 333, given in Example 15.10. As you listen, try to identify chords that we have not yet studied in the context of the basic phrase. Thus far, we have learned how to begin and end the basic phrase—how to establish the tonic at the beginning and how to write an authentic cadence at the end. We know how to use some of the diatonic triads and seventh chords—including I (i in minor), V, V⁷, vii°, vii°⁷, vii⁰⁷, and their inversions—but we know from Chapter 7 that there are many more diatonic chords than these! Which chords have we not considered yet? (*Try it #7*) Are any of these found in the Mozart example?

EXAMPLE 15.10: Mozart, Piano Sonata in B♭ Major, K. 333, first movement, mm. 1–4a

Start by identifying the harmonies at the beginning and end of Example 15.10, then write these Roman numerals beneath the staff. This phrase begins with an unaccompanied anacrusis, followed by the initial tonic triad. It ends with an authentic cadence: V⁷–I. What is the chord in measure 2? This is the supertonic triad: ii. This triad, together with the subdominant, IV, belongs to a class of harmonies called predominants.

Predominant harmonies—ii and IV (ii° and iv in minor keys)—are so named because they typically lead to the dominant harmony within the basic phrase. (Some teachers may refer to this functional area as the "dominant preparation area"; others may call it the "subdominant area.") The predominant triads share scale-degrees $\hat{4}$ and $\hat{6}$ (the supertonic seventh chord also shares $\hat{1}$ with the IV or iv chord).

KEY CONCEPT

We can now expand our basic phrase model to include a predominant area that precedes the dominant: T–PD–D–T. Following are typical Roman numerals for the basic phrase.

- In major keys: I – (ii, ii⁶, or IV) – V⁷ – I

- In minor keys: i – (ii°⁶ or iv) – V⁷ – i

Any of the chords in these progressions may be inverted. In the predominant area, although any triad may be replaced with a seventh chord, the seventh chords ii[7] and ii[ø7] (and their inversions) are the most typical. As we have seen in previous chapters, inversions usually weaken the sense of harmonic motion between chords but may strengthen linear connections between them. When you write these progressions, place the subdominant triad in root position for now. The supertonic triad is more common in first inversion, but it may appear in root position in major keys. Why can't we use the root-position supertonic triad in minor? (*Try it #8*)

The progressions outlined above (in the KEY CONCEPT box) are some of the most common chord patterns in styles of music with a slow harmonic rhythm, such as Classical-period pieces, folk songs, and some contemporary popular music. To compose a basic four-measure phrase typical of these styles, write any of these progressions with one chord per measure. We saw a typical Classical-style phrase in the T–PD–D–T model in Example 15.10. Example 15.11 shows a phrase from a Stephen Foster tune, "Camptown Races," that follows the same model. We can expand the predominant area by a change in inversion or by motion from one predominant to another (IV to ii, for example).

EXAMPLE 15.11: Foster, "Camptown Races," mm. 12b–16

The chord on the second beat of measure 15, known as the "cadential $^6_4$," serves as an embellishment of the dominant harmony. We will explore this embellishment in the next section.

○ ○

Dominant Expansion with the Cadential $^6_4$

2.48 🎧

The dominant harmony may be expanded through a combination of chords that extend its dominant function. For instance, a typical cadence in Classical style involves the **cadential** $^6_4$. Listen to the opening of the third movement of Mozart's Piano Sonata in D Major, K. 284 (Example 15.12), which illustrates the use of this voice-leading chord. In this very typical-sounding Mozart cadence (m. 4), the dominant triad is preceded by what appears to be a tonic harmony in second inversion (A-D-F♯). This tonic, however, does not function like the tonic at the beginning of the phrase. In fact, it does not have a tonic function at all; rather, it displaces and embellishes the V chord by simultaneous 6–5 and 4–3 intervallic motions above the sustained bass note. The F5 and D4 are approached as passing tones from the previous chord. In this example, the intervals of 6 and 4 above the bass occur on the downbeat to create the $^6_4$, which resolves on the following beat to $^5_3$.

EXAMPLE 15.12: Mozart, Piano Sonata in D Major, K. 284, third movement, mm. 1–4a

If you doubt the dominant function of the cadential $^6_4$, try singing the chord roots as you listen to Example 15.12. Chances are, you will sing $\hat{5}$ on both beats of measure 4. The cadential $^6_4$ in this example is preceded by a ii^6 chord, labeled PD in the contextual analysis. This contextual analysis shows the large-scale motion of the phrase to the dominant (the half cadence in m. 4). Measures 1–3a actually express a smaller-scale T–PD–D–T motion, but when such motions are embedded within a larger phrase, we interpret them as expanding the tonic area. (We will return to tonic expansions in Chapter 16.)

KEY CONCEPT _____

We interpret the cadential $^6_4$ as a dominant function, despite the fact that it is built of tones from the tonic triad. It expands the dominant area of the basic phrase.

Like most embellishing chords, the cadential $^6_4$ can be removed from the cadence without changing the general harmonic plan of the phrase, but we use it for the smooth voice-leading it provides from the predominant area. Cadential $^6_4$s are almost always preceded by a predominant harmony, as in Example 15.12, rarely by the tonic harmony. For now, we will primarily consider approaches by ii, ii^7 (and their inversions), and IV (or, in minor, ii°, ii^{ø7}, and iv).

Writing Cadential $^6_4$ Chords

KEY CONCEPT _____

When you write a cadential $^6_4$:

1. Always double the bass. Any other doubling will result in voice-leading problems and is not idiomatic to the use of these chords.
2. Hold any common tones between the chord of approach and the $^6_4$, and move other voices the shortest distance.
3. Write the cadential $^6_4$ chord on a strong beat in the measure; it displaces the V or V^7 to a weaker beat. In triple meter, sometimes the cadential $^6_4$ appears on the second beat, resolving to V or V^7 on the third beat.

4. Resolve the "suspended" tones of the $^6_4$ downward: the sixth above the bass moves to a fifth, and the fourth above the bass moves to a third (shown in Example 15.13a). Always resolve the chord this way.

5. If there is a seventh in the dominant harmony that follows the cadential $^6_4$, the doubled bass note (an octave above the bass) moves to the seventh of the dominant seventh chord (Example 15.13b).

EXAMPLE 15.13: Resolutions of the cadential $^6_4$

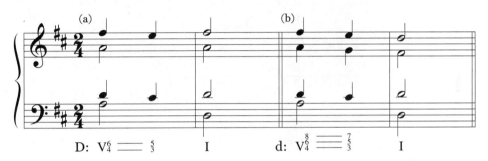

The $^{6-5}$ and $^{4-3}$ are figures like those we write for suspensions. The ^{6} and ^{4} are simply intervals above the bass that displace the chord tones 5 and 3 of the dominant triad. The dashes in the $^{6-5}$ and $^{4-3}$ indicate that the figures represent voice-leading. Don't write V$^6_4$ alone as a symbol for the cadential $^6_4$ (that would make no sense, since the cadential $^6_4$ contains the wrong pitches to be labeled V$^6_4$). Think instead of the label V$^{6-5}_{4-3}$ as a single analytical symbol that shows voice-leading above a dominant harmony. Likewise, it's best not to use the symbol I$^6_4$—even though many older textbooks do—because that symbol obscures the chord's dominant function at the cadence.

KEY CONCEPT

Write voice-leading patterns $^{6-5}_{4-3}$ combined with Roman numerals (V$^{6-5}_{4-3}$) where no independent chord is created by the voice-leading embellishments.

Another Way ◀

You may be confused at first by the V$^{6-5}_{4-3}$ and unsure about which pitches to place in the V$^6_4$. The key is not to read these numbers as inversion symbols. The label "V$^6_4$" in the context of the cadential $^6_4$ does not represent the pitches of the V chord at all: the first numbers ($^6_4$) represent the notes that displace and delay, like suspensions, the chord tones $^5_3$. Remember: A cadential $^6_4$ is spelled with the pitches of a tonic triad, but it functions like a dominant.

Other Expansions Involving $^6_4$s

The Neighboring (or Pedal) $^6_4$

The cadential $^6_4$ is not the only typical use of the second-inversion triad. When a second-inversion triad is created by two simultaneous upper-neighbor tones embellishing a continuing harmony, we call this the **neighboring** $^6_4$. One of the most common types is the IV$^6_4$ between two root-position tonic chords, as shown in Example 15.14.

EXAMPLE 15.14: A neighboring $^6_4$ progression

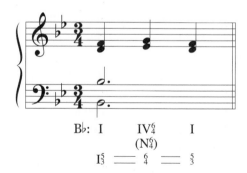

B♭:　I　　　　IV$^6_4$　　　I
　　　　　　　(N$^6_4$)

　　　I$^5_3$ ⸺ $^6_4$ ⸺ $^5_3$

KEY CONCEPT

The neighboring $^6_4$ embellishes and prolongs the chord it neighbors—usually a tonic- or dominant-area chord—and is usually metrically unaccented. It shares its bass note with the harmony it embellishes, while two upper voices move in stepwise neighboring motion above that bass. This progression is also called a **pedal** $^6_4$ because the bass stays on the same pitch, providing a foundation for the simultaneous neighbor tones.

The neighboring ⁶₄ works particularly well on the second beat of the measure in triple meters, for example, or on the second subdivision of the beat in compound meters. You may also find a neighboring ⁶₄ on strong beats in music literature, as Examples 15.15 and 15.16 show. Listen to the Mozart passage while following the contextual analysis beneath. Note that the IV⁶₄ in its neighboring role to the tonic is too weak to carry a structural PD label. This basic phrase expresses T–D–T only.

EXAMPLE 15.15: Mozart, Piano Sonata in C Major, K. 545, first movement, mm. 1–4

EXAMPLE 15.16: Lloyd Webber and Rice, "Don't Cry for Me Argentina," mm. 33–34a

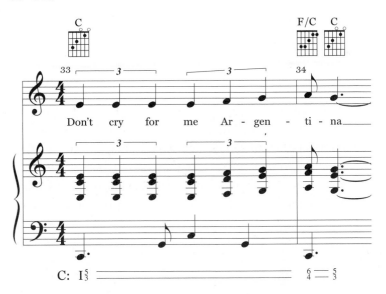

In the Lloyd Webber example, the neighboring ⁶₄ again carries little harmonic function; the chord sounds like accented neighbor tones on the downbeat, prolonging the tonic.

KEY CONCEPT

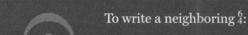

To write a neighboring $^6_4$:

1. Decide which chord you want to prolong.
2. Write that chord twice in the same position, leaving a space in-between for the neighboring $^6_4$ (Example 15.17a).
3. Fill in the bass of the neighboring $^6_4$ first—the same bass as the chords on either side—and double it in the same voice as the chords on either side (Example 15.17b).
4. Write in upper neighbors decorating the other two voices (Example 15.17c).

EXAMPLE 15.17: Steps in writing a neighboring $^6_4$ chord

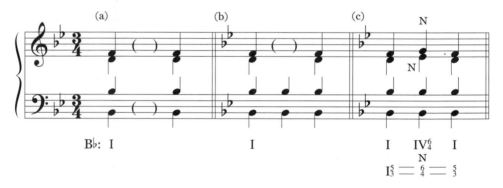

Neighboring $^6_4$ progressions may be indicated by Roman numerals in a vertical analysis, with an N written beneath the neighboring $^6_4$. To show the neighboring function most effectively, write the Roman numeral of the prolonged structural harmony, with figures $^5_3$–$^6_4$–$^5_3$ (as shown in Example 15.17c). Although these neighboring $^6_4$ examples illustrate a common expansion of the tonic harmony, the same technique may be applied to dominant or predominant harmonies as well.

The Passing $^6_4$

In eighteenth-century compositions, the tonic area is often expanded by motion from a root-position I to I⁶ or the reverse. This chord connection may involve a **voice exchange**, in which two parts exchange chord members. Look at Example 15.18a to see a soprano-bass voice exchange: in the first chord, the bass has scale-degree $\hat{1}$ and the soprano has $\hat{3}$. In the second chord, a I⁶, these chord members have swapped positions: the bass has scale-degree $\hat{3}$ and the soprano has $\hat{1}$. We indicate a voice exchange in music analysis by crossed lines connecting the exchanged pitches, making an X between the chords.

As Example 15.18b shows, you may embellish a voice exchange by placing passing tones in the two voices, typically on metrically unaccented positions. Passing tones introduce an element of dissonance and rhythmic motion that decorates and adds interest to the underlying expansion of the tonic harmony.

EXAMPLE 15.18: Voice exchanges between I and I[6]

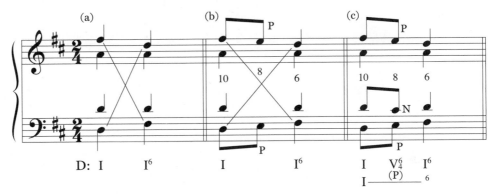

When you connect the two tonic chords of a voice exchange with passing tones, you produce counterpoint in contrary motion: in Example 15.18b, scale-degrees $\hat{1}$–$\hat{2}$–$\hat{3}$ in one voice and $\hat{3}$–$\hat{2}$–$\hat{1}$ in the other. The passing tone—scale-degree $\hat{2}$—can be harmonized, as in Example 15.18c, with a **passing $^6_4$ chord**. Passing $^6_4$ chords are defined by their bass-line passing motion. In this case, the passing chord of part c is created from part b by adding a lower neighbor tone to the tenor voice to yield a V chord in second inversion. Because of its inversion and context, the passing V does not convey its usual strong dominant function. Instead, it plays a voice-leading role: it serves to expand the tonic area in a way that is much more interesting than merely repeating the tonic or moving directly from I to I[6].

KEY CONCEPT _____

Passing $^6_4$s connect root-position and first-inversion chords of the same harmony. We call them "passing" because the $^6_4$ harmonizes a bass-line passing tone.

Passing $^6_4$s can expand other harmonies as well. The subdominant harmony, for example, can be expanded by a passing I$^6_4$—making the progression IV–I$^6_4$–IV[6] or IV[6]–I$^6_4$–IV, as shown in Example 15.19. The progressions featuring passing $^6_4$s are usually "reversible": the root-position harmony can come first or last. Unlike the cadential $\frac{6}{4}$, we place passing $\frac{6}{4}$s on relatively unaccented positions in the measure. We generally label each chord in the vertical first-level analysis, then write a P beneath to show the passing function, or simply indicate by a long dash in the contextual level of analysis that the structural chord in the progression is prolonged. Example 15.19 shows how to label these chords; a voice exchange is also marked.

EXAMPLE 15.19: Subdominant prolonged with passing $\frac{6}{4}$

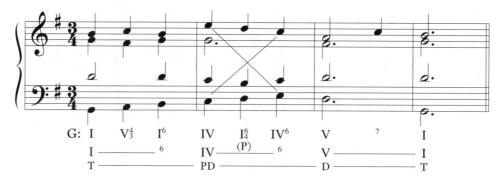

The passing $\frac{6}{4}$ may also connect two *different* chords, as long as these chords serve the same function. For example, in the progression IV^6–I^6_4–IV, the last chord may be replaced with ii^6—a triad with the same function and the same bass as the IV chord, as shown in Example 15.20. This type of progression, sometimes with chromatic chords substituted for the diatonic ones, is a mainstay of Romantic-era harmony, as we will see in later chapters.

EXAMPLE 15.20: Passing $\frac{6}{4}$: IV^6–I^6_4–ii^6

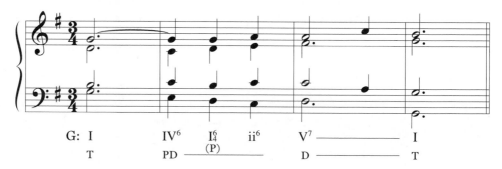

KEY CONCEPT

To write passing $^6_4$s:

1. Decide which harmony you want to prolong.
2. Set up root-position and first-inversion chords of that harmony, with a voice exchange between the bass and one of the upper parts (often the soprano part, but it doesn't have to be). (See Example 15.21a.)
3. Fill in skips of a third with stepwise motion in both voices that are participating in the voice exchange; this automatically doubles the fifth of the $^6_4$, making the correct doubling (Example 15.21b).
4. Complete the other voice-leading strands. All voices should connect by common tone or by step, making neighbor or passing patterns (Example 15.21c).

EXAMPLE 15.21: Steps in writing a passing $^6_4$

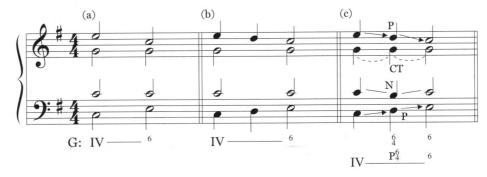

The Arpeggiating $^6_4$

The **arpeggiating** $^6_4$ is a little different from the types we have considered up to now, in that it requires only a change of bass note within a single harmony, and thus does not involve dissonances. This type of second-inversion triad is typical of freer textures with a relatively slow harmonic rhythm but several changes of bass note per harmony. For example, the bass line may arpeggiate a triad, sounding first the root, then the third, then the fifth, as in measures 7 and 9 of "My Country, 'Tis of Thee," shown in Example 15.22. When the bass reaches the fifth of the triad, an arpeggiating $^6_4$ has been created.

2.98

EXAMPLE 15.22: "My Country, 'Tis of Thee," mm. 7–10

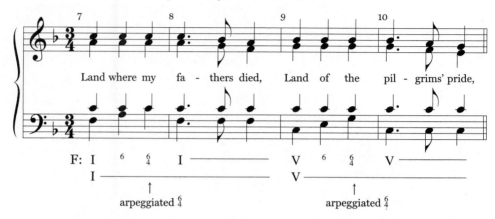

A bass instrument may alternate between the root and fifth of the chord, as in Sousa's "Stars and Stripes Forever," shown in Example 15.23. In addition to marches, we also typically find bass-line alternation of the root and fifth in rags, waltzes, and some popular songs, as Example 15.24 ("Don't Cry for Me Argentina") illustrates. Walking bass lines, made from arpeggiations and passing tones, also may create apparent $\frac{6}{4}$s, as in Example 15.25, Purcell's "Music for a While." In this example, the bass line is a compound melody, and the "$\frac{6}{4}$ chords" (marked with arrows) are really an inner part.

3.45

3.5

EXAMPLE 15.23: Sousa, "The Stars and Stripes Forever," Trio, mm. 37–40a

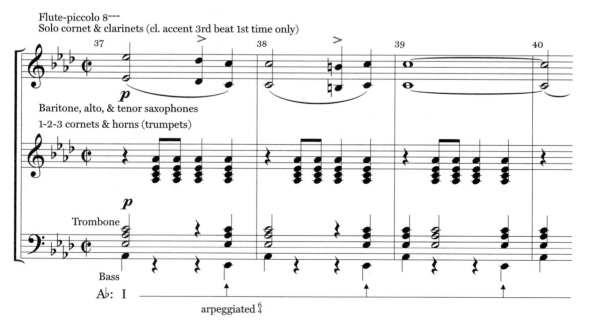

EXAMPLE 15.24: Lloyd Webber and Rice, "Don't Cry for Me Argentina," mm. 33–34a

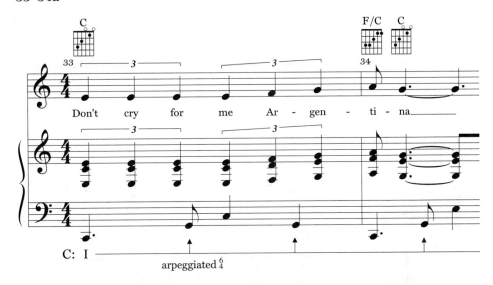

EXAMPLE 15.25: Purcell, "Music for a While," mm. 1–3a (walking bass)

In each case shown above, the $^6_4$s are ephemeral: the bass line quickly "walks" or arpeggiates to other chord members. You need no special voice-leading rules to write an arpeggiating $^6_4$, other than the recommendation that it be placed on a weak beat in a context where the primary bass note of the chord (something other than the fifth) is clear. When you make a reduction, consider carefully what the main bass note of the measure is—usually the lowest-sounding chord tone—and examine the progression with that note in mind. When you analyze an arpeggiated $^6_4$ with Roman numerals, you may label the chord with its Roman numeral and $^6_4$ in a first-level vertical analysis, with "arp" written beneath the $^6_4$ to show its type. In a second-level contextual analysis, you need not mark the arpeggiated $^6_4$ at all; simply supply the Roman numeral for the primary bass note of the measure and the appropriate figured bass.

The Four $^6_4$ Types

We have learned that when a root-position triad is replaced with a first-inversion triad (or a root-position seventh chord is replaced with any of its inversions), the inverted chord creates a weaker sense of progression, but the general function of the progression stays the same. We might infer that second-inversion triads are also interchangeable with root-position or first-inversion triads—after all, there are no special restrictions with second-inversion seventh chords. But second-inversion triads have always been treated specially in tonal music: they are considered very weak harmonically, and are used only in a few specific contexts.

KEY CONCEPT

Each $^6_4$ chord we write will be one of the following types:

- cadential $^6_4$
- neighboring $^6_4$
- passing $^6_4$
- arpeggiating $^6_4$

Whenever you write a $^6_4$, be sure its setting fits the requirements of one of these categories—and be prepared to name that category! All four types of second-inversion triads function as expansions of a harmony or harmonic area in the basic phrase. In each case, the $^6_4$ can be left out without changing the underlying organization of the phrase. But this does not mean that the $^6_4$ is unimportant; harmonic expansions featuring second inversions are essential aspects of some styles.

SUMMARY

When using second-inversion triads:

- Always double the bass (fifth) of the chord.
- Be sure you can name the type of $^6_4$ (don't include it if you can't name it).
- In all $^6_4$s except arpeggiating (which are consonant), all voices should approach and leave chord members by step (forming neighbor or passing tones) or common tone.
- Arpeggiating $^6_4$s will have chordal skips, but must then resolve correctly to the next harmony.

TERMS YOU SHOULD KNOW

arpeggiating $^6_4$

cadential $^6_4$

contextual analysis

diminished seventh

dominant substitute

half-diminished seventh

leading-tone chord

passing $^6_4$

neighboring $^6_4$

predominant

prolongation

tonic expansion

vertical analysis

voice exchange

QUESTIONS FOR REVIEW

1. How are the d5 and A4 treated in the resolution of the vii°⁷ chord?
2. What contrapuntal soprano-bass pattern influences the normal resolution of the tendency tones in dominant-function harmonies? How does it do this?
3. Why do we label the cadential $^6_4$ as we do? Discuss the pros and cons of other possible labeling systems.
4. Why do we study the voice exchange? What type of $^6_4$ is associated with it?
5. In common-practice style, which chords are typically chosen if only one pre-dominant is needed in a phrase? How does this chord function within the phrase?
6. Which type of $^6_4$ is usually preceded by a predominant harmony?
7. In music for your own instrument, find an example of three of the four $^6_4$ types.

CHAPTER 16

Further Expansions of the Basic Phrase:

Tonic Expansions, Root Progressions, and the Mediant Triad

Outline of topics covered

Tonic expansions
- Prolonging tonic with the submediant
- Prolonging tonic by 5–6 motion
- Prolonging tonic with the subdominant
- Prolonging tonic with the dominant
- Typical soprano-bass counterpoint
- Passing and neighboring dominants in freer textures

Basic root progressions
- Root motion by falling fifth
  - Part-writing progressions
- Root motion by falling third
- Root motion by ascending third
  - Part-writing progressions
- Root motion by second
  - Part-writing progressions

About mediant triads
- Mediants in music analysis
- Writing mediant triads

Overview

In this chapter, we look at ways that counterpoint and harmony interact to expand the tonic area of the basic phrase. We also consider three common root motions—by fifth, by third, and by second—and where each may fit in the basic phrase. We conclude by learning about the mediant triad.

Repertoire

Johann Sebastian Bach, Chaconne, from Violin Partita No. 2 in D minor (CD 1, track 23)

Stephen Foster, "Camptown Races'

Don McLean, "Vincent"

Wolfgang Amadeus Mozart,
  Piano Sonata in B♭ Major, K. 333, first movement
  Piano Sonata in D Major, K. 284, third movement (CD 2, track 48)
  Piano Sonata in C Major, K. 545, second movement (CD 2, track 69)

Modest Mussorgsky, "The Great Gate of Kiev," from *Pictures at an Exhibition*

Jimmy Owens, "Doxology," from *Come Together*

Richard M. Sherman and Robert B. Sherman, "Feed the Birds," from *Mary Poppins*

"Wayfaring Stranger" (folk song, arranged by Norman Lloyd)

Tonic Expansions

Prolonging Tonic with the Submediant

 We begin by revisiting the third movement of Mozart's Piano Sonata in D Major, K. 284, given in Example 16.1. Fill in the Roman numerals underneath to see how Mozart expands the tonic area of the basic phrase model. As before, begin by labeling the beginning and end of the phrase. The excerpt begins with an unaccompanied dominant anacrusis, followed by a tonic triad. Because the phrase ends with a half cadence on V, the phrase model is incomplete: only T–PD–D. The ending is decorated by a cadential $^6_4$ progression.

EXAMPLE 16.1: Mozart, Piano Sonata in D Major, K. 284, third movement, mm. 1–4a

What about the chords midphrase? You may have already spotted the V⁷–I harmonic progression in measures 2–3. Why does this strong harmonic gesture not create a phrase-ending cadence? (*Try it #1*) Label the chords between the opening tonic and the V⁷ in measure 2. They are vi and ii⁶, a common chord succession for the middle of phrases.

KEY CONCEPT _____

> The vi chord represents a new way to expand the tonic area. Because I and vi share scale-degrees $\hat{1}$ and $\hat{3}$, vi can prolong or substitute for I in certain musical contexts.

The I and vi chord express the tonic area, and the ii⁶ chord functions as a predominant to the following V⁷. What does this progression mean in terms of the phrase as a whole, especially since it ends with another predominant-dominant progression—ii⁶ to V in measures 3–4?

KEY CONCEPT

When small-scale T–PD–D–T progressions are embedded within a larger phrase, they serve to prolong the tonic area.

We can therefore hear a tonic expansion from measure 1 through the first half of measure 3, followed by predominant (m. 3b) and dominant (m. 4) at the cadence. Write a contextual analysis to show this beneath your vertical analysis.

Prolonging Tonic by 5–6 Motion

We continue our study of the submediant triad's role in expanding the tonic area with another Mozart phrase, from his B♭-Major Sonata (Example 16.2). Here the tonic chord in the first half of measure 1 is subtly transformed in the second half of the measure by moving F4 to G4 in the left hand (G5 appears in the right hand melody as well). The F–G motion above the bass, B♭3, forms the intervals 5–6. A vertical approach to Roman numeral analysis might label the second half of the measure a vi⁶. However, the "submediant" is so fleeting, that we hardly hear it as a new chord. When I moves directly to ii (m. 2), the 5–6 linear motion prevents the parallel fifths that would otherwise occur between the root-position triads.

EXAMPLE 16.2: Mozart, Piano Sonata in B♭ Major, K. 333, first movement, mm. 1–4a

KEY CONCEPT

The tonic area may be expanded by 5–6 motion above scale-degree $\hat{1}$. We generally label this as I$^{5-6}$ rather than I–vi⁶.

Prolonging Tonic with the Subdominant

We may also place the subdominant, in any inversion, between two tonic chords to prolong the tonic area. This is a common compositional technique in most styles of tonal music. Examples 16.3 and 16.4 show root-position i–iv–i and I–IV–I successions expanding the tonic area at the beginning of phrases in folk- and popular-music styles.

EXAMPLE 16.3: "Wayfaring Stranger," mm. 1–4a

EXAMPLE 16.4: Sherman and Sherman, "Feed the Birds," mm. 1–4

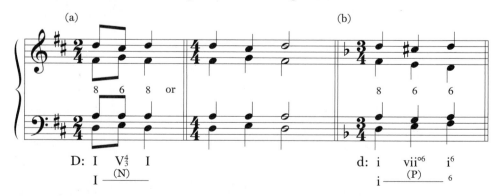

Prolonging Tonic with the Dominant

In Chapter 15, we harmonized scale-degree $\hat{2}$ with a passing V^6_4. We could also have used V^4_3, vii^{o6}, or vii$^{ø6}_5$, each of which shares the dominant function and scale-degree $\hat{2}$ in the bass. When dominant chords prolong the tonic area, other types of outer-voice counterpoint work just as well as the passing motion we saw in the voice exchange. Some inversions, in fact, only work with specific voicings. Example 16.5a shows neighboring motion in both soprano and bass, producing the outer-voice counterpoint 8–6–8. The N in the contextual analysis represents the bass line's neighboring motion in the I–V$^4_3$–I tonic expansion. This example is notated in two different rhythmic contexts to show how passing or neighboring chords are usually placed metrically. For now, write them on the offbeat or in a weak metrical position—such as beats 2 or 4 in quadruple meter or beat 2 in duple or triple meter.

EXAMPLE 16.5: Tonic expansions with neighbor motion

Example 16.5b combines neighboring motion in the soprano with passing motion in the bass (through a passing vii°⁶), which yields the outer-voice counter-point 8–6–6. What other chords could have harmonized 2̂ in the bass line of parts a and b? Which pitches would have to be changed in the upper voices? (*Try it #2*)

Typical Soprano-Bass Counterpoint

When you harmonize a melody or bass line, look for melodic patterns that imply tonic expansion. Tonic expansions usually begin on a strong beat.

KEY CONCEPT

Patterns that imply tonic expansion include

- stepwise motion between members of the tonic triad (1̂–2̂–3̂, 3̂–2̂–1̂, 3̂–4̂–5̂, or 5̂–4̂–3̂);
- neighboring motion above or below a member of the tonic triad (1̂–2̂–1̂, 1̂–7̂–1̂, 3̂–2̂–3̂, 3̂–4̂–3̂, or 5̂–4̂–5̂).

Harmonize these patterns with stepwise contrary motion in the other voice. You could also combine passing motion in one voice with neighboring motion in the other, resulting in outer-voice counterpoint of 8–6–6 (as shown in Example 16.5b) or 10–10–8. In general, avoid soprano-bass patterns that result in parallel perfect intervals or a poor resolution of tendency tones. There is one exception to the normal resolution of tendency tones: when the soprano moves 3̂–4̂–5̂ against a bass line 1̂–2̂–3̂, the outer voices of a tonic expansion move in parallel motion: 10–10–10. In this context, we resolve the chordal seventh of the V⁷ *upward* (4̂ to 5̂) in the soprano, as shown in Example 16.6.

EXAMPLE 16.6: Tonic expansion with passing motion

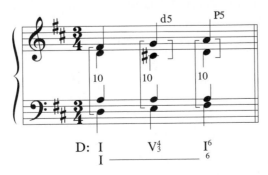

Other bass-soprano combinations are possible as well. For example, with any of the passing or neighboring soprano patterns discussed above, the bass might skip from a member of the tonic triad to an incomplete neighbor tone in the dominant harmony before resolving to tonic (for a review of incomplete neighbor tones, see Chapter 9). Examples 16.7a and b show two such progressions: I–V$^4_2$–I^6 and i^6–V$^6_5$–i. As is typical with incomplete neighbors, the bass note G3 in part a could have been approached by step from the chord tone F had the initial tonic chord been in first inversion; this implied stepwise connection is what makes the incomplete neighbor work. Part b shows an incomplete neighbor in the bass line creating a skip of a diminished fourth, which is normally avoided in eighteenth-century voice-leading. Use skips like this only in the bass, and only where the function of the skip (here, as tonic expansion) is clear.

EXAMPLE 16.7: Incomplete and double neighbor patterns

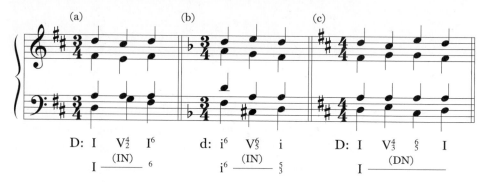

Double neighbor tones are also possible in the bass, as Example 16.7c illustrates, especially if you move from one inversion of the dominant to another, as in the progression I–V$^4_3$–V$^6_5$–I. A good exercise to prepare for melody harmonization is to imagine various soprano-bass contrapuntal patterns, and to supply possible Roman numerals for their harmonization.

Try it #3

What two harmonizations are possible for the following patterns? Try working out each solution at the piano until you are satisfied with the voice-leading and chord choice.

KEY	SOPRANO	BASS	HARMONIZATION 1	HARMONIZATION 2
major	$\hat{3}$–$\hat{2}$–$\hat{1}$	$\hat{1}$–$\hat{2}$–$\hat{3}$	I–V$^6_4$–I^6	I–V$^4_3$–I^6
major	$\hat{1}$–$\hat{2}$–$\hat{1}$	$\hat{1}$–$\hat{7}$–$\hat{1}$		
minor	$\hat{1}$–$\hat{7}$–$\hat{1}$	$\hat{1}$–$\hat{4}$–$\hat{3}$		
major	$\hat{3}$–$\hat{4}$–$\hat{5}$	$\hat{1}$–$\hat{2}$–$\hat{3}$		
minor	$\hat{3}$–$\hat{4}$–$\hat{3}$	$\hat{1}$–$\hat{7}$–$\hat{1}$		

Passing and Neighboring Dominants
in Freer Textures

2.69

We study SATB textures because they provide a simple way to show basic voice-leading principles. As we have seen in previous chapters, however, instrumental figuration can often be reduced to the same chord progressions and voice-leading patterns. Look, for example, at the excerpts given in Example 16.8 from the second movement of Mozart's C-Major Sonata, K. 545. Both passages a and b are embellished versions of the progression I–V$^4_3$–I. We can reduce the left-hand Alberti bass to the block chords given in c, with a bass line of scale-degrees $\hat{1}$–$\hat{2}$–$\hat{1}$ against an ornamented melodic ascent of $\hat{3}$–$\hat{4}$–$\hat{5}$ in the soprano line. The bass-line neighbor-tone pattern helps us hear the V$^4_3$ not as a strong dominant function, but as a neighboring chord that prolongs the tonic. The dominant function is further weakened by the absence of the leading tone.

EXAMPLE 16.8: Mozart, Piano Sonata in C Major, K 545, second movement

(a) Mm. 1–2

(b) Mm. 9–10

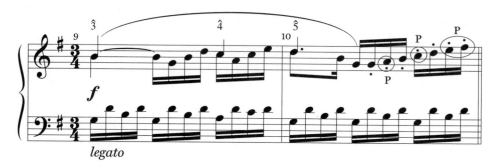

(c) Reduction

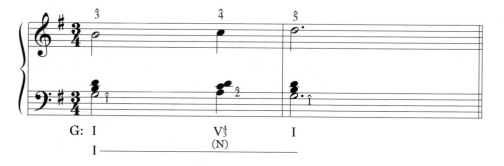

○ ○

Basic Root Progressions

We learned in Chapter 15 that the predominant harmonies ii and IV (ii° and iv in minor) can be thought of as functionally interchangeable. Yet the progression IV to ii is common, but ii to IV is not. Why is this so? Because IV to ii represents a common root progression—the falling-third progression—while ii to IV does not. When we include more than one chord in a single functional area of the basic phrase, such as ii and IV in the predominant area, root progressions can help us remember the customary ordering. Root progressions are also useful in helping us move between areas of the basic phrase.

Most of the connections between chords in tonal music fall into one of three basic root movements: falling fifth, falling third, and ascending second. If we think back to progressions we have learned already, we can see this in action: the authentic cadences (V to I or i) show a root movement from $\hat{5}$ to $\hat{1}$. The roots of these chords may not be in the bass—either the dominant or tonic or both may be inverted—but the authentic cadences as a group can be thought of as **falling-fifth root progressions** because of the descending fifth between the chord roots.

In Chapter 15, we considered connections between vii° and I; these are examples of an **ascending-second root progression**. Connections between IV and V and I and ii are also ascending-second root progressions. The third type, the **falling-third root progression**, is typically found in the tonic and predominant areas of a phrase, and will be introduced in this chapter (as well as the less common ascending-third root progression). Each of these root-progression types appears at specific points in the basic phrase; we now consider each in turn.

Root Motion by Falling Fifth

The strongest root motion in tonal music is by falling fifth (or ascending fourth—we can think of those as interchangeable). This root motion underlies the cadences we studied in Chapter 12 and many other typical progressions. While we often include a single falling-fifth connection between chords, it is useful to think of them in a chain, beginning with I (or i), then moving downward by fifth (or up by fourth) to other diatonic chords in the key:

I–IV–vii°–iii–vi–ii–V–I in major keys, or
i–iv–vii° (or VII) –III–VI–ii°–V–I in minor.

All of the fifths in each falling-fifth chain are perfect except one—which? (*Try it #4*)

Sometimes we connect only two chords in this chain, sometimes three or four, or we may include it in its entirety to circle through all of the diatonic chords in a key. Look back at Example 16.1: beginning on the third beat of measure 1, Mozart employs the progression vi–ii⁶–V⁷–I, a four-chord segment from the end of the falling-fifth chain.

Not all of the links in the falling-fifth chain are equally strong: for example, the connections involving either the leading-tone or mediant triad rarely appear without the rest of the chain. We do not typically find root motion by *ascending* fifth in tonal music, other than between tonic and dominant.

KEY CONCEPT

Some of the most common falling-fifth progressions:

- I–IV (or i–iv)
- vi–ii (or VI–ii°)
- ii–V (or ii°–V)
- IV–vii°⁶ (in minor, to set $\hat{6}$–$\hat{7}$–$\hat{1}$ in the melody)
- V–I (or V–i)

This root motion can connect the tonic and predominant areas (as in I–IV or vi–ii, where vi is a tonic expansion), the predominant and dominant areas (as in ii–V), and the dominant and final tonic areas (as in V–I). We find these progressions in all styles of tonal music.

Part-Writing Progressions When we connect triads with roots a fifth apart, the triads will share one chord member. For example, G-B-D and C-E-G share pitch-class G. Example 16.9 shows how to connect these two chords.

EXAMPLE 16.9: Connecting chords a fifth apart

C: V   I   V   I   V   I⁶   V⁶   I

KEY CONCEPT

A typical method of connecting triads with roots a fifth apart is to hold the common tone in the same voice, and move all of the other parts to the closest possible chord member.

As always, observe the guidelines for doubling and resolution of tendency tones within the key.

In some falling-fifth progressions, we typically substitute seventh chords for some of the triads: we may write ii⁷ (or ii°⁷) and its inversions instead of ii (or ii°), or V⁷ and its inversions instead of V, as shown in Example 16.10. (While it is possible to substitute the subdominant or submediant seventh chords in place of their triads, these seventh chords are much less common in eighteenth- and nineteenth-century music outside of root-progression chains.) In part-writing these seventh chords, the chordal seventh should be approached by common tone or by step, and must be resolved down. Unlike V⁷ and vii°⁷, which have two tendency tones (the seventh of the chord and the leading tone), the nondominant seventh chords (such as ii⁷, vi⁷, or IV⁷) have no leading tone to resolve.

EXAMPLE 16.10: Progressions featuring ii⁷ and ii°⁷

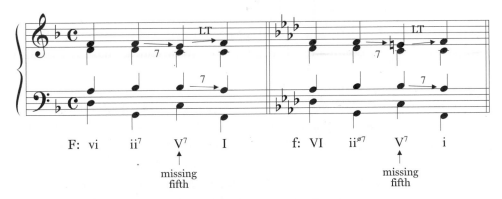

F: vi   ii⁷   V⁷   I   f: VI   ii°⁷   V⁷   i

missing   missing
fifth   fifth

KEY CONCEPT

Resolve the seventh of the nondominant seventh chord down by step, then move the other two upper voice parts the shortest distance to members of the next chord. Check for parallels, doubling, and spacing. In SATB textures, when one seventh chord follows another, one of the two will be incomplete, missing the fifth.

Root Motion by Falling Third

While root motion by fifth refers almost exclusively to *falling*-fifth progressions, root motion by third is possible both ascending and descending, with the latter the most typical. Root motion by falling third can also be repeated to make a chain:

I–vi–IV–ii–vii°–V–iii–I in major keys, or
i–VI–iv–ii°–vii° (or VII)–V–III–i in minor.

1.23 Some parts of this chain are commonly used progressions—for example, I–vi, vi–IV–ii, and ii–vii°. Bach includes the first three chords of the falling-third chain in his Chaconne in D minor, shown in Example 16.11. As we have already seen, the descending-third progression I–vi may also be heard as an expansion of the tonic area. Seventh chords are not typically found in falling-third progressions.

EXAMPLE 16.11: Bach, Chaconne in D minor, mm. 3–4

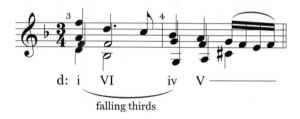

In Chapter 15, we learned how vii°, vii°⁷, and vii°⁷ and their inversions can act as dominant substitutes. Since these chords share $\hat{7}$, $\hat{2}$, and $\hat{4}$ with V⁷, they can make cadences like V⁷, but with a weaker sense of closure. If we replace V with vii° in the progression ii–V, we create a falling-third approach to the cadence.

The last parts of the chain, around the mediant chord (V–iii and iii–I), are rarely heard in common-practice music: when the phrase reaches the dominant area, a cadence usually follows. The descending-third progression vii°–V is also rarely found if the texture of the music is chordal and the harmony changes on each chord. In pieces with a freer texture, such as guitar or piano accompaniments, you may encounter a dominant area that begins with vii° (or vii°⁷ or vii°⁷), then brings in $\hat{5}$ to make V or V⁷.

Root Motion by Ascending Third

The chains made by repeated ascending-third motion are

I–iii–V–vii°–ii–IV–vi–I in major keys, or
i–III–V–vii° (or VII)–ii°–iv–VI–i in minor.

Only a few of these connections are typical in tonal music, and each has a special role. These are: I–iii as a tonic expansion (discussed later in the chapter); vi–I as a kind of "backward" tonic expansion; and V–vii°, usually found in freer textures where the root of the V drops out temporarily during a dominant-area expansion. The others are considered **retrogressions** (backward progressions) of descending-third chains and are not often found in common-practice music, but they may appear in contemporary tonal pieces. For example, the chord progression in the verse of "Vincent," by Don McLean, is I–ii–IV– V⁷–I, as shown in Example 16.12. The parallel fifths from the second half of the measure to the following measure are characteristic of popular styles.

EXAMPLE 16.12: McLean, "Vincent," mm. 4–11a

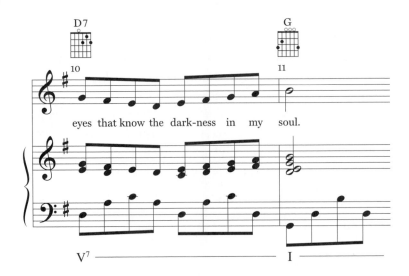

eyes that know the dark-ness in   my   soul.

V⁷ ─────────────── I ───────

Part-Writing Progressions Triads whose roots are a third apart share two pitch classes. For example, C-E-G and A-C-E share pitch-classes C and E. These progressions are usually voiced with the root of the chords in the bass and the root doubled in an upper part to make at least one common tone between each pair of chords, as Example 16.13 shows.

EXAMPLE 16.13: Connecting chords by thirds

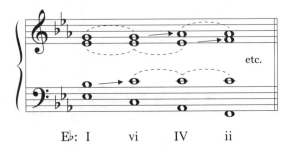

E♭: I   vi   IV   ii

KEY CONCEPT _____

When connecting chords with roots a third apart, hold the common tones and move the other parts to the next-nearest chord member.

Root Motion by Second

Root movement by second typically connects functional areas in the basic phrase.

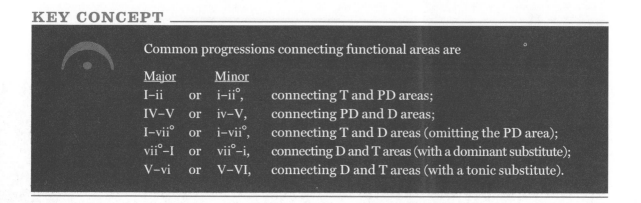

Common progressions connecting functional areas are

Major		Minor	
I–ii	or	i–ii°,	connecting T and PD areas;
IV–V	or	iv–V,	connecting PD and D areas;
I–vii°	or	i–vii°,	connecting T and D areas (omitting the PD area);
vii°–I	or	vii°–i,	connecting D and T areas (with a dominant substitute);
V–vi	or	V–VI,	connecting D and T areas (with a tonic substitute).

Other than the progression I–vii°, all of these common progressions feature root motion by ascending second.

Part-Writing Progressions   When we write the ascending-second progression, we need to pay careful attention to voice-leading between chords. The most direct way to connect chords with roots a second apart is to simply shift the entire chord up or down a step. While this type of connection is sometimes found in twentieth-century music, folk-style accompaniments, and popular music, common-practice-period composers usually avoided it because it creates parallel fifths and octaves between the two chords, as shown in Example 16.14. With these parallels, it is possible to hear only one melodic line, doubled by triads, rather than four fully independent voice-leading strands.

EXAMPLE 16.14: Chord progressions with parallel fifths and octaves

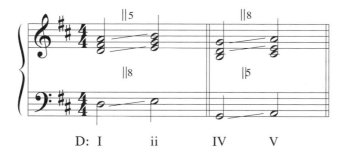

KEY CONCEPT

Chords with roots a second apart are responsible for most parallel-fifth and -octave errors in student part-writing! When we write root-position chords a second apart, we move the upper parts in contrary motion to the bass line, as shown in Example 16.15, to avoid unwanted parallels.

EXAMPLE 16.15: Voice-leading for chords with roots a second apart

Inverting one or more of the chords makes it easier to avoid the parallels, but we still need to check the voice-leading carefully for parallel fifths and octaves. If you have written parallels in a progression with inversions, changing the doubling in one of the chords may correct the voice-leading.

Because of its propensity to create parallel voice-leading, root movement by second is not usually found in chains without some sort of voice-leading procedure to break up the fifths and octaves. We will learn more about root-progression chains moving by second in Chapter 18.

○ ○

About Mediant Triads

Mediants in Music Analysis

The mediant triad is made up of scale-degrees $\hat{3}$, $\hat{5}$, and $\hat{7}$, sharing two scale degrees with the tonic ($\hat{3}$ and $\hat{5}$) and two with the dominant ($\hat{5}$ and $\hat{7}$). Mediant triads do not often appear in tonal music as freestanding chords. Why not? Perhaps because they do not fit cleanly into either the tonic- or dominant-function areas; they sound a little like both.

Progressions connecting a mediant and V^7 or vii° are relatively rare. Sometimes you may come across what seems to be one of these progressions; in most cases, however, closer inspection reveals that the apparent mediant triad is not a "real" chord, but a dominant-function harmony where not all of the chord tones sound at the same time. Look again at the opening of Bach's Chaconne in D minor, shown in Example 16.16. Some of the chords were labeled in Example 16.11; what are the other chords in these measures? What is unusual about these chords? (*Try it #5*)

The chord on beat 2 in measure 4 may seem at first to be a III, progressing to vii° on the next beat. A closer inspection of the context reveals otherwise: this piece is based on a four-measure repeating harmonic pattern that starts with an anacrusis. If you compare the corresponding measures (compare measure 4, beats 2–3, with measure 8, beats 2–3), it becomes clear that the apparent III–vii° is really a V^7 in which all the chord members simply do not arrive at the same time. Some listeners may also hear beat 2 in measure 4 as a cadential $^6_4$ (without scale-degree $\hat{1}$), which would make it a dominant prolongation.

EXAMPLE 16.16: Bach, Chaconne in D minor, mm. 1–8

Example 16.17 gives another example, in a more popular style, of a "iii" chord that is really a dominant. In Foster's "Camptown Races," the downbeat of measure 3 seems to suggest a iii⁶ (E-G-B). Since the harmonic rhythm is one chord per bar, think of the whole measure as a single chord: its bass note is G, and its function is V⁷. The "Doo-dah!" exclamation is consonant 6–5 motion above the bass, and should not be analyzed as iii⁶–V.

EXAMPLE 16.17: Foster, "Camptown Races," mm. 1–4a

Writing Mediant Triads

The mediant in minor keys has a special relationship with VI (submediant) and VII (subtonic)—what is it? (Hint: Think about these chords in the relative-major key.) (*Try it #6*) One of the mediant's more common positions is in a falling-fifth relationship with VI. Sing or play the opening of "Wayfaring Stranger" from the score in Example 16.18. Write in the Roman numeral analysis at the beginning and end. The first four measures express a i–iv–i tonic expansion, while the cadence is iv–v–i, enlisting the minor dominant for this modal folk tune. What are the two chords midphrase, in measures 5–6? They are the III–VI (falling-fifth) pattern. We will look more closely at this relationship later in the book, when we learn about applied dominants and modulation.

We have not encountered the minor dominant before. Where may it be used?

EXAMPLE 16.18: "Wayfaring Stranger," mm. 1–8a

KEY CONCEPT

> Minor dominant chords (v) are occasionally found midphrase in tonal music, where they temporarily evoke the sounds of modal composition. Write them sparingly (or not at all) in common-practice style, and not at a cadence (where the leading tone is a necessary ingredient).

The mediant triad sometimes functions as a dominant substitute in late nineteenth-century Russian nationalistic music, which draws on the modal scales of the Russian Orthodox chant tradition. For example, in the "Great Gate of Kiev" movement from Mussorgsky's *Pictures at an Exhibition*, shown in Example 16.19, iii stands in for V in the progression ii§–iii–I.

EXAMPLE 16.19: Mussorgsky, "The Great Gate of Kiev," from *Pictures at an Exhibition*, mm. 18–22

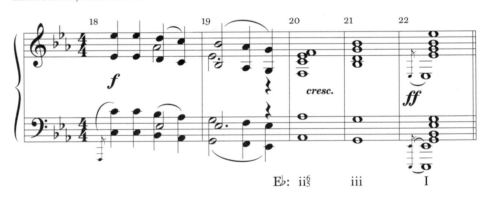

The mediant may also be part of a tonic expansion at the beginning of a phrase: I–iii (or i–III). Like the submediant in the more typical tonic expansion I–vi (or i–VI), the mediant shares two scale degrees with tonic; but because $\hat{1}$ is not shared, the mediant triad is less effective as a tonic substitute than the submediant, and rarely constitutes an independent chord in common-practice style.

In twentieth-century pop styles, I–iii may serve as a substitute for I–I⁶. Look, for example, at a late twentieth-century setting of the "Doxology" text from the musical *Come Together*, given in Example 16.20. As Example 16.21 shows, the mediant triad as a tonic extension may be produced by linear motion from $\hat{1}$ to $\hat{7}$ in an upper part, accompanied by a bass motion from I to I⁶—the tonic note "disappears" temporarily because of these simultaneous activities. Any predominant chord that can follow a I⁶ may follow the apparent iii, but take care to avoid parallels in connecting iii–IV (as Example 16.21 does).

EXAMPLE 16.20: Owens, "Doxology," mm. 1–4a

EXAMPLE 16.21: Voice-leading for I–iii–IV

TERMS YOU SHOULD KNOW

falling-fifth chain	linear chords	root progression
falling-third chain	retrogression	tonic substitute

QUESTIONS FOR REVIEW

1. Name several soprano-bass patterns that could support tonic expansions.
2. What are the chords in a falling-fifth chain? Where are the "weak links"?
3. What are the chords in a falling-third chain? Where are the "weak links"?
4. Why are root progressions in seconds not generally found in chains? Where might we see them?
5. How are mediant triads used? How can you distinguish an apparent mediant from a real one?
6. In what contexts may minor dominant chords appear in common-practice style? In what other styles might you hear them.

CHAPTER 17

The Interaction of Melody and Harmony:

More on Cadence, Phrase, and Melody

Outline of topics covered

New cadence types

- The deceptive cadence: V–vi (or VI)
- The plagal cadence: IV–I (iv–i)
- The Phrygian cadence: iv^6–V

Phrase and harmony

- Phrases revisited
- Phrase analysis
- Subphrases, motives, and the sentence

Phrases in pairs: The period

- Parallel and contrasting periods
- Phrase groups and asymmetrical periods
- Double periods

Motives

- The transposition of motives
- Melodic sequences

Writing melodies

Overview

In this chapter, we explore new types of cadences with which phrases may conclude. In addition, we will use what we have learned about harmony to discover more about phrases, including ways that melodies and phrases may be composed and grouped. We also consider how melodic and phrase analysis can inform musical interpretation.

Repertoire

Johann Sebastian Bach, "Wachet auf" (Chorale No. 179) (CD 1, track 9)

Bach, *Brandenburg Concerto* No. 4, second movement (CD 1, track 3)

Muzio Clementi, Sonatina in C Major, Op. 36, No. 1, first movement (CD 1, track 74)

Stephen Foster, "Oh! Susanna"

George Frideric Handel, "Hallelujah!" from *Messiah*

John Lennon and Paul McCartney, "Nowhere Man," from *Rubber Soul*

Wolfgang Amadeus Mozart, Kyrie, from *Requiem*

Mozart, Piano Sonata in C Major, K. 545, first movement (CD 2, track 57)

Mozart, "Voi, che sapete," from *The Marriage of Figaro* (CD 2, track 82)

"My Country, 'Tis of Thee" (CD 2, track 97)

Meredith Willson, "Till There Was You," from *The Music Man* (CD 3, track 63)

New Cadence Types

1.11

As we know from previous chapters, a cadence is the harmonic and melodic conclusion of a phrase. What options do we have when we begin to compose a phrase and decide we don't want either the inconclusive ending of a half cadence (HC) or the strong conclusive effect of a perfect authentic cadence (PAC)? Listen to two phrases from Bach's chorale "Wachet Auf," given in Example 17.1, to see his solution. Bach repeats the same melody in each phrase, but his harmonization creates a very different effect at the two cadences. In what other ways does Bach vary the two phrases? *(Try it #1)*

EXAMPLE 17.1: Bach, "Wachet auf," mm. 17b–24 (cadences)

Translation: Wake up, the bridegroom comes; stand up, take up your lamps!

The Deceptive Cadence: V–vi (or VI)

Bach's solution at the end of the first phrase (m. 20) is to replace the expected final tonic harmony with a tonic substitute, the submediant triad, to make a **deceptive cadence**: V⁷–vi. The name of this cadence is appropriate, since the drama of this harmonic "deception" can be striking. The most effective deceptive cadences are voiced just like PACs, except that the final chord is a vi (or VI) instead of I (or i). For the strongest deceptive effect, use V or V⁷ in root position, leading to a root-position vi (or VI), as shown in Example 17.2. Resolve the V or V⁷ normally, with $\hat{7}$ moving up to $\hat{1}$ and $\hat{4}$ (if present) resolving down to $\hat{3}$. This voice-leading usually results in a doubled third in the vi (or VI) chord. (The Ts in the contextual analysis stands for "tonic substitutes.")

EXAMPLE 17.2: Deceptive cadence model

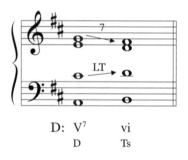

Other types of deceptive cadences are possible as well, most commonly V–IV⁶. Look at the cadence in Mozart's Kyrie shown in Example 17.3 (m. 50). This cadence, in the key of D minor, includes the pitch-classes D and F of the tonic triad, but also G♯ and B♮, making a fully diminished seventh chord that is not diatonic in the key of D minor. We consider this cadence deceptive because V does not move to the tonic triad as expected. We could also call this an "evaded" cadence.

EXAMPLE 17.3: Mozart, Kyrie, from *Requiem*, mm. 49–52

Translation: Lord, have mercy.

2.97 🎧 The submediant triad may also follow V or V⁷ in the middle of a phrase, when a cadence is not desirable, allowing the phrase to circle back to the tonic or predominant area before progressing to the final cadence. Listen to (or sing through with your class) Example 17.4a, an SATB setting of the beginning of "My Country, 'Tis of Thee." In measure 4, the V⁷ on beat 2 is followed by a vi, preventing the phrase from ending on "liberty"; the cadence is repeated in measures 5–6, concluding this time on the tonic. The submediant in midphrase creates a **deceptive resolution** of the V chord and allows the phrase to expand further before it concludes. When you connect V or V⁷ to vi or VI in the middle of a phrase, you may want to weaken the dominant chord by inverting it. This makes the progression less likely to sound like a firm cadence and implies harmonic continuation.

EXAMPLE 17.4: "My Country, 'Tis of Thee"

(a) Mm. 1–6

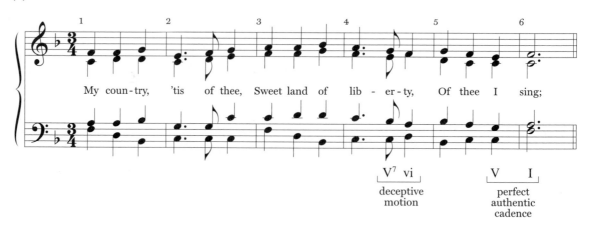

The Plagal Cadence: IV–I (iv–i)

2.99 Sing the final measures of "My Country, 'Tis of Thee," given in Example 17.4b, with your class. This setting includes an "Amen," as is typical in some American hymnbooks. The word is set with the root-position chords IV–I; these chords form a **plagal cadence.** Because of their association with hymns, plagal cadences are sometimes called "Amen" cadences.

(b) Mm. 13–14, plus "Amen" plagal cadence

We know that the progression I–IV–I prolongs the tonic area; this suggests that plagal motion at the end of a composition (after the final dominant-tonic cadence) might be interpreted as an expansion or prolongation of the final tonic. A famous instance is shown in Example 17.5, from the end of Handel's "Hallelujah Chorus." The final PAC is in measures 87–88, but the choir continues to sing I^6–IV–I repeatedly in a closing section that ends with a forceful plagal cadence on the final "Hallelujah." Some conductors interpret this structure musically with a sense of arrival at the PAC in measure 88 before launching into the closing plagal extension. The extension allows the rhythmic energy of the piece to unwind while reaffirming the tonic with the repeated D5s in the soprano. Instead of referring to a IV–I ending as a plagal cadence, some musicians speak of a "plagal resolution" or "plagal expansion of the tonic."

EXAMPLE 17.5: Handel, "Hallelujah!" from *Messiah*, mm. 86–94

The plagal harmonic motion has found another use in some styles of popular music. Look at the opening of Lennon and McCartney's "Nowhere Man" in Example 17.6. If you have a recording, listen to this song while following the chord symbols above the staff. In some rock and blues styles, the progression I–V–IV–I is a basic ingredient of the harmonic structure. While this progression would not have been permitted in music of the eighteenth century, it makes a common and distinctive chord succession in popular styles. In "Nowhere Man," we might hear the first four measures (chord symbols E–B–A–E, or I–V–IV–I) as prolonging the tonic. The next three measures end with a plagal cadence.

You may use plagal cadences freely when writing in a contemporary or popular style. When composing in common-practice style, consider placing an authentic cadence first and then expanding the final tonic with plagal motion.

EXAMPLE 17.6: Lennon and McCartney, "Nowhere Man," mm. 1–7

The Phrygian Cadence: iv⁶–V

When you write a half cadence in a minor key, with a first-inversion iv chord as the predominant to V, you have written a special type of cadence we call the **Phrygian cadence**. This cadence, always iv⁶–V in minor, is named for its characteristic bass line: the half-step descent from $\hat{6}$ to $\hat{5}$. Such a descent evokes the Phrygian mode, with its half step from $\hat{2}$ to $\hat{1}$. Listen to Example 17.7, from the second movement of Bach's *Brandenburg Concerto* No. 4; here, an entire movement ends on a Phrygian cadence. This inconclusive "conclusion" on V sets up expectations on the part of the listener for the lively final movement. The example gives both the orchestral score and a reduction of the final two chords, so the iv⁶–V progression is clear.

1.4

EXAMPLE 17.7: Bach, *Brandenburg Concerto* No. 4, second movement

(a) Mm. 65–71

(b) Reduction of mm. 70–71

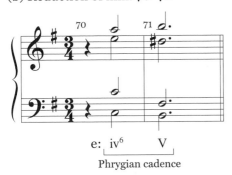

e: iv⁶   V

Phrygian cadence

When you write a Phrygian cadence, do not move from $\hat{6}$ to the raised $\hat{7}$ (*le* to *ti*), because that motion creates a melodic augmented second. A common voicing is to place scale-degrees $\hat{4}$ to $\hat{5}$ in the soprano.

SUMMARY

New cadence types we have learned:

- The deceptive cadence (V–vi or VI) avoids the expected tonic resolution.
- The plagal cadence (IV–I or iv–i) prolongs the tonic area ("Amen" cadence).
- The Phrygian cadence (iv^6–V) is a special type of half cadence.

Phrase and Harmony

Phrases Revisited

Having explored some of the harmonic underpinnings of musical phrases, including cadence types, we turn now to some musical examples. In your instrument or voice lessons, you have probably discussed "phrasing" with your teacher. An important part of preparing a piece for performance is determining how it divides up, where the goals are, and how to perform it with directed motion toward these goals. For our purposes, the word "phrase" will not be used as a verb—we will not learn how to "phrase" a melody (at least not in those terms). Instead, we will use this word only as a noun, one with a distinct meaning.

3.63 Listen to the first sixteen measures of the beautiful love song from Meredith Willson's musical *The Music Man*: "Till There Was You," shown in Example 17.8. (If you listen to "oldies" radio stations, you may know this song from a 1960s Beatles recording!) Pay careful attention to where you think the phrases end. If you sing the melody through to yourself, you will see that the tune and text seem to fall into four-measure groups. Are those units phrases?

EXAMPLE 17.8: Willson, "Till There Was You," mm. 1–16a

KEY CONCEPT

A **phrase** expresses a musical idea and moves toward a goal: the cadence. It is the smallest musical gesture that ends with a cadence. This means, for example, that a four-measure unit makes a phrase only when it concludes with a cadence.

Where does the first phrase end in "Till There Was You"? You may be tempted to answer that it ends in measure 4, with the word "ringing." After all, a sentence of text ends there, and the singer will take a breath. But what type of cadence would this phrase ending represent? Instead of doing an exhaustive Roman numeral analysis, look at the harmonies that support the beginning and end of each vocal unit to get a sense of the broad harmonic motion. (For now, disregard the sevenths and added notes that give these harmonies the character of the popular-song genre. We will revisit these in Chapter 26.) The first vocal unit extends from E♭ to F♯ in measure 4, but there is no true cadence here. In fact, there is no phrase ending until measure 8, with the arrival on a B♭7 chord representing a half cadence (somewhat weakened by the seventh chord).

The first phrase of the song therefore spans measures 1–8. These long, soaring phrases are almost "operatic" in their eloquence and may symbolize the character's admission that she has indeed fallen in love at long last. Where does the second phrase end? It begins the same as the first, with only a slight change in text. As before, there is no cadence at measure 12 ("winging"); rather, the phrase continues to measures 14–16, where we hear a perfect authentic cadence on the words "till there was you."

Phrase Analysis

When we analyze phrases, we label them with lowercase alphabet letters, generally from the beginning of the alphabet. Phrases that sound different get different letters—**a**, **b**, **c**, and so on—while phrases that are identical are labeled with the same letter. Phrases that are similar—based on the same musical ideas or variants of each other but not identical—receive the same alphabet letter with a prime mark (´) after them: **a** and **a´**, for example. When you use a prime mark, be sure to indicate what is alike about the phrases (why they have the same letter) and also what is different (why the ´). Because the first two phrases of "Till There Was You" begin identically but end differently, we would label them **a** and **a´**. If you find the prime marks cumbersome, you may also analyze similar phrases as **a¹**, **a²**, **a³**, etc.

Some analysts like to represent phrase structure with charts that show the measures spanned, thematic repetitions, and cadence types. A phrase chart for the first sixteen measures of "Till There Was You" would look like this:

	16	
	a	**a´**
	8	8
mm.	1–8	9–16
E♭:	HC	PAC

How might you think about this phrase analysis if you were going to perform the song? One strategy for the singer would be to consider the interaction of text and harmony, knowing that even though a sentence of the text ends in measure 4, the harmony continues to move the line forward. The singer and pianist should look together for points of repose. Even interpreting the half cadence at this first phrase end is somewhat tricky, since the singer's line arrives on scale-degree $\hat{5}$ in measure 7, while the piano does not reach its dominant until midway through measure 8. At this first vocal cadence, the performers will probably want to take some time as the singer arrives on the word "you," then let the pianist push the tempo forward a bit on the way to the keyboard's dominant harmony.

In thinking about the second phrase, performers will want to keep a hierarchy of cadences in mind: their arrival on the PAC in measure 16 should be stronger than the arrival on the HC in measure 8. From the beginning of the song, they should already be thinking forward to measure 16 as their first big harmonic and formal goal.

Subphrases, Motives, and the Sentence

We call melodic units that are smaller than phrases **subphrases**. A subphrase is a musically coherent gesture that does not end with a cadence (like mm. 1–4 of the Willson song). Even smaller than a subphrase is a motive.

KEY CONCEPT

A **motive** is the smallest recognizable musical idea. Motives may be characterized by their pitches, contour, and/or rhythm, but they rarely contain a cadence. For a musical segment to qualify as a motive, it must be repeated either exactly or in varied form.

In musical analysis, we generally identify motives with lowercase alphabet letters from the end of the alphabet: **w, x, y, z.** You can be more creative than this if you wish. Some analysts like to name motives by their musical or symbolic characteristics: the scale motive, the arpeggiated motive, the neighbor-note motive, the weeping motive, and so on. What motives can you identify in the Willson song? *(Try it #2)*

WF1

Symbolic Motives

Perhaps the most famous motives named for their symbolic associations are the *leitmotivs* used by Richard Wagner (1813–1883) in his operas. Each leitmotiv represents a character, idea, or object in the opera; thus we hear motives in the composer's four-opera cycle *Der Ring des Nibelungen (The Ring of the Nibelung)* representing the ring, the giants, the Valkyries, the Tarnhelm (a magic cloak), fire, and Valhalla (residence of the gods), among others. Wagner himself did not coin this term—it was popularized by a friend of his—but it has now come into common usage. While locating statements of each motive is only one part of an analysis of these masterworks, learning to identify them by ear can add to your enjoyment of the operas. To learn more about Wagner's musical style, read the essays in the Norton Critical Score *Prelude and Transfiguration from Tristan and Isolde*, edited by Robert Bailey (New York: Norton, 1985). To learn more about Wagner's life, consult Ernest Newman's *Life of*

Richard Wagner (London: Cassell, 1933–47; reprinted 1976).

Another famous instance of motives interpreted for their symbolic associations can be found in Albert Schweitzer's two-volume *J. S. Bach* (original in French, 1905; reprinted in 1980 by Paganiniana). Throughout the book, but particularly in Chapters 22 ("The Musical Language of the Chorales") and 23 ("The Musical Language of the Cantatas"), Schweitzer categorizes musical motives from Bach's works according to their Christian symbolism, as well as interpreting motives to represent emotions such as peace, grief, joy, tumult, exhaustion, terror, and so on. While we have no evidence that Schweitzer's analyses present an accurate picture of Bach's compositional intention, you may find that identifying these motives in compositions you perform colors your interpretations of the composer's works in interesting and musical ways.

Let's look now at an example from the beginning of Clementi's Piano Sonatina in C Major, Op. 36, No. 1. Begin by listening to the opening eight measures, given in Example 17.9. Identify any motives you might find, as well as their repetitions. Mark these in the example.

1.74

EXAMPLE 17.9: Clementi, Sonatina in C Major, Op. 36, No. 1, first movement, mm. 1–8a

The first two phrases (mm. 1–4 and 5–8) are related by their use of the same opening motive. We could call this the "arpeggiated motive"; it appears in measures 1–2 and 5–6. We might call the five-note descending scale that begins measure 3 the "scale motive"; it reappears in measure 4. Finally, we might call the repeated two-note pattern that permeates measure 7 the "falling-thirds motive"—it comes from the second and third pitches of the arpeggiated motive, which is a falling third.

What does this motivic analysis tell us? First, it demonstrates real compositional economy and unity; nearly all of the piece is derived in some way from these three motives and one other. Second, it shows us how the piece all fits together, which can help us in memorizing it. Third, the motivic analysis reveals another structural feature that the two first phrases share: each has a 1 + 1 + 2 design, where the numbers refer to measure groupings. The design of the first phrase is thus arpeggio (1 m.) + arpeggio (1 m.) + scale (2 mm.); the design of the second phrase is arpeggio (1 m.) + arpeggio (1 m., transposed) + falling thirds (2 mm.). This 1 + 1 + 2 design is so common in Classical-era melodies that it has a name: **sentence**.

The second phrase of the Clementi example (mm. 5–8) is the better illustration of typical sentence structure. In the first unit of a sentence, a motive is stated; in the second unit, the motive is repeated, often with variation (here it is transposed) or a change in harmony. (One typical sentence design expresses the motive first in the tonic harmony, then in a dominant harmony.) In the third unit, the motive is broken up and developed with accelerated harmonic rhythm as the phrase moves toward the cadence (here, the descending third is extracted from the motive and repeated with stepwise descending transpositions, creating a variation on the descending-scale motive of the first phrase). Sentence structure is associated with

WF2 the music theories of Arnold Schoenberg, who was a theorist as well as a composer.

A phrase diagram for the first eight measures of the Clementi sonatina would look like this:

		8	
	a		**a´**
	4		4
	1+1+2		1+1+2
mm.	1–4		5–8
C:	HC		PAC

○ ○

Phrases in Pairs: The Period

Play and sing through the melody of Stephen Foster's "Oh! Susanna," given in Example 17.10; then diagram its phrase structure.

EXAMPLE 17.10: Foster, "Oh! Susanna," mm. 1–8

knee,   I'm_ going to Loui - si - a - na, My Su - san - na for to   see.

This melody has a harmonic structure that is common in music from the Classical era and in some American folk songs: motion in the first phrase from I to V (half cadence), followed by motion in the second phrase from I to V–I (authentic cadence).

KEY CONCEPT

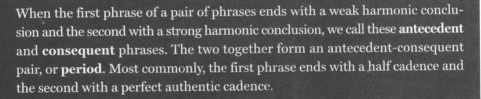

When the first phrase of a pair of phrases ends with a weak harmonic conclusion and the second with a strong harmonic conclusion, we call these **antecedent** and **consequent** phrases. The two together form an antecedent-consequent pair, or **period**. Most commonly, the first phrase ends with a half cadence and the second with a perfect authentic cadence.

The melodic structure of "Oh! Susanna" is typical: the first phrase comes to rest on scale-degree $\hat{2}$ over a half cadence, and the second concludes with $\hat{2}$–$\hat{1}$ over a perfect authentic cadence. Can you name other folk tunes with this melodic structure? *(Try it #3)* Some musicians restrict the label "antecedent-consequent" to the HC-PAC relationship we see in "Oh! Susanna," but we will adopt a more liberal definition based on the weaker cadence/stronger cadence relation. For our purposes, an antecedent-consequent pair, or period, may contain IAC-PAC cadences, for example.

Look back at the sonatina phrases in Example 17.9. Does Clementi employ antecedent and consequent phrases? His first phrase ends with a half cadence, the melody ending on scale-degree $\hat{5}$; the second phrase begins with a repetition of material from the first (as the Foster song does), but then changes key—the cadence is perfect authentic in G Major! We will learn more about phrases that change key in Chapter 22, but for now you should know that this is a possibility in antecedent-consequent pairs. In the Clementi case, the first phrase is known as the antecedent and the second as the "modulating consequent."

Parallel and Contrasting Periods

Thus far we have looked at the harmonic structure that shapes musical periods, but there are thematic elements of the melody that work to shape periods as well. When the two phrases that make up a period begin identically, or when the second phrase is a variant of the first, we call this structure a **parallel period (a a´)**. When the two phrases are quite different from each other, we call this structure a **contrasting period (a b)**. Look back at Examples 17.9 and 17.10—which type of period is each? *(Try it #4)*

Phrase Groups and Asymmetrical Periods

2.84

We define a **phrase group** as three or more phrases whose tonal and/or thematic elements group them together as a unit, but which end with an inconclusive cadence. They sometimes, but not always, repeat a phrase or motive to create **a b a**, **a a´ b**, or **a b b´** patterns. Listen now to the opening of Mozart's aria "Voi, che sapete," from *The Marriage of Figaro*. Measures 9–20 are given in Example 17.11. Does this passage express a phrase group? Does it repeat a phrase or motive?

EXAMPLE 17.11: Mozart, "Voi, che sapete," from *The Marriage of Figaro*, mm. 9–20

Don - ne, ve - de - te,____ s'io l'ho__ nel__ cor.

Translation: You who know what love is, ladies, see if I have it in my heart.

Here are three phrases that clearly form a unit: the first ends with a half cadence (m. 12), the second (mm. 13–16) prolongs the tonic for two bars and then the dominant for two bars, while the third states the complete basic phrase model (T–PD–D–T) to bring the passage to tonal closure. In addition, the third phrase ends with a cadential motive that came from the first (compare mm. 11–12 with 19–20), which ties the unit together. But because this group of three phrases ends with a perfect authentic cadence, we view the passage not as a phrase group but as a special type of period. (The three phrases *would* have made a phrase group if the third cadence had also been inconclusive.)

KEY CONCEPT

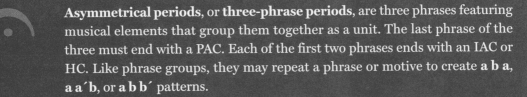

Asymmetrical periods, or **three-phrase periods**, are three phrases featuring musical elements that group them together as a unit. The last phrase of the three must end with a PAC. Each of the first two phrases ends with an IAC or HC. Like phrase groups, they may repeat a phrase or motive to create **a b a**, **a a′ b**, or **a b b′** patterns.

Phrase groups are sometimes found in Baroque-era pieces with continuous motion, such as the Bach C-Major Prelude in your anthology. In that piece, inconclusive cadences create a temporary sense of arrival, yet the continuous flow of the arpeggiation pattern emphasizes the music's continuity rather than its phrase structure. Transition and development sections of Classical-era works may also form phrase groups, with each phrase ending in an inconclusive cadence to make these passages feel as though they are pushing forward. There are whole short Romantic-era pieces that consist of a phrase group, without a definitive cadence, but they are rare; most pieces of tonal music end with a conclusive cadence. We will learn more about phrase groups as we study musical form in later chapters.

Double Periods

A **double period** is a group of four phrases in which the only PAC appears at the conclusion of the fourth phrase. The first two phrases form the antecedent, and the second two form the consequent. Several cadential patterns are possible: one of the most common is IAC–HC, IAC–PAC (the IAC–HC phrases are the antecedent, the IAC–PAC the consequent). If a group of four phrases is melodically structured as **a b a´ b´** (or **a b a b**), with the cadences arranged HC–PAC, HC–PAC, we call this a **repeated period**.

Motives

In addition to melodic motives, composers might include motives that are purely rhythmic or that consist simply of a melodic contour (shape). A **rhythmic motive** maintains its rhythm but changes its contour and interval structure. Think, for example, of the triplet motive we identified in "Till There Was You." Another example is the dotted-eighth-sixteenth motive in "Oh! Susanna." A **contour motive** maintains its contour, or musical shape, but changes its intervals; its rhythm may or may not be altered (see Example 17.12).

The Transposition of Motives

As we saw in the Clementi sonatina, motives may be transposed. When this happens, they usually retain their rhythm, contour, and generic interval structure—that is, a third remains a third, but the interval may change in quality from major to minor or vice versa. Look at Examples 17.12a–c to see how Clementi transforms the arpeggiated motive.

EXAMPLE 17.12: Clementi, Sonatina in C Major, Op. 36, No. 1, first movement

(a) M. 1   (b) Mm. 5–6a   (c) Mm. 16–17

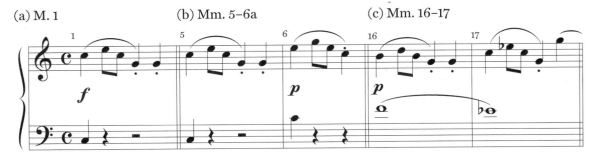

Here, the original motive's major third (C5–E5) is transposed and transformed to a minor third in measure 6 and again in measures 16–17. Even more striking is the fact that the motive's final interval, originally a perfect fourth, becomes a major third in measures 6 and 16. It then returns to a perfect fourth in measure 17—all without disrupting its identity as the arpeggiated motive. Since the motive's identity rests heavily on contour and rhythm, slight changes in interval size do not disrupt our recognition of it. This motive functions as a contour motive as well as a melodic motive.

Melodic Sequences

Sometimes composers incorporate transposed motives in a **melodic sequence**. A melodic sequence begins with a motive followed by its transposition—often up or down by step—and repeats this process several times. Listen to the excerpt from the first movement of Mozart's Piano Sonata in C Major, K. 545, shown in Example 17.13a, to hear a melodic sequence.

2.58

EXAMPLE 17.13: Mozart, Piano Sonata in C Major, K. 545, first movement

(a) Mm. 5–9a

The repeated motive is the "pattern" of the sequence. In this example, the pattern is one measure long, and each repetition is transposed down by a step. Now look at Example 17.13b, another passage from the same sonata. How long is the pattern of the sequence in this example? *(Try it #5)*

2.62

(b) Mm. 18–21

A melodic sequence is often paired with a corresponding harmonic pattern that repeats as well, making it a harmonic sequence as well as a melodic one (as the Mozart sequences were in Example 17.13; we will learn more about harmonic sequences in Chapter 18). Alternatively, a melodic sequence may appear without a harmonic sequence. Composers often use melodic sequences in transitional passages, sometimes leading to a change of key. You may find that melodies with melodic sequences are less likely to appear in balanced phrases of equal duration (4 + 4 or 8 + 8), since the sequence sometimes extends the phrase beyond its expected duration.

WF3   The musical development of motives is a topic that has fascinated music analysts and composers for generations. You may want to pursue motivic analysis on your own in the pieces you perform. Knowing where a motive is located (especially when it appears in an inner voice or in the bass line) can help you articulate it more clearly to your audience.

○ ○

Writing Melodies

Because there are many types of melodies in diverse styles, as we have seen, no single list of instructions can really capture the principles of melody writing. We would need one list for Classical sonata themes, another for Baroque fugue subjects, another for ragtime, yet another for nineteenth-century Lieder melodies, and so on. Although some writers take pains to describe characteristic shapes for melodies, these shapes are few in number. Melodies often begin in a middle register, ascend to a single high point, then descend to tonic. This is a good principle to follow, but you will find examples of melodies that generally descend from beginning to end, or ascend to a high point near the conclusion. For now, write melodic shapes that are fairly simple.

Before beginning to compose a melody, you should have a style in mind. If you choose Classical-style antecedent-consequent phrases, you will write better melodies if you first immerse yourself in examples from the literature. Find melodies for your instrument, and play through a good number before beginning to write your own; then follow these guidelines for your composition.

KEY CONCEPT

To write an antecedent-consequent pair of phrases:

1. Begin by mapping out eight blank measures on two lines of staff paper. Place four on the top line, and align four more beneath them on the second line.
2. Sketch in an approach to each cadence: one that ends on $\hat{3}$–$\hat{2}$ at the end of the first line to suggest an HC, and one that ends on $\hat{2}$–$\hat{1}$ or $\hat{7}$–$\hat{1}$ on the second line for a PAC.
3. Begin in measure 1 on a member of the tonic triad ($\hat{1}$, $\hat{3}$, or $\hat{5}$). If you want to include an anacrusis, try writing one that suggests a dominant harmony.
4. Start composing a melody in the first four measures whose outline implies an incomplete phrase model (T–PD–D). Plan your progression with a harmonic rhythm of one to two chords per measure. Melodies often begin with a slower harmonic rhythm that speeds up near the cadence.
5. Now write a melody that expresses your progression by including arpeggiation or passing and neighboring embellishments around chord tones. Create at least two memorable motives: melodic, rhythmic, or contour. If rhythmic, you may want to use the rhythm more than once. You may want to try a sentence structure (1 + 1 + 2).
6. Copy one to one and a half measures of your first phrase into the beginning of the second phrase. Write a continuation of the phrase that cadences on tonic. Where possible, continue developing one of your motives as you complete the phrase.
7. Most melodies have one high point or climax. Try to build your melody so that its highest note is stated only once—probably in the second phrase.

TERMS YOU SHOULD KNOW

antecedent phrase	motive	Phrygian cadence
consequent phrase	period	plagal cadence
contour motive	• contrasting period	rhythmic motive
deceptive cadence	• parallel period	sentence
deceptive resolution	phrase	subphrase
melodic sequence	phrase group	

QUESTIONS FOR REVIEW

1. Where are deceptive cadences typically found? What type of effect do they create?
2. Where are plagal cadences typically found? What type of effect do they create?
3. Find an example of a deceptive and plagal cadence in music for your instrument.
4. How do Phrygian cadences differ from other types of half cadences? What gives them their distinctive sound (and their name)?
5. In how many different ways might phrases be paired to form periods? Can more than two phrases be grouped together?
6. In music for your own instrument, find an example of (a) an antecedent-consequent pair, (b) a rhythmic motive, (c) a contrasting period, (d) a melodic sequence.
7. In performance, how might you differentiate between an antecedent phrase and its consequent?

Diatonic Sequences

CHAPTER 18

Outline of topics covered

Sequences
- Sequences in a musical context
- Types of sequences

Harmonic sequences based on root progressions
- Falling-fifth sequences
    With seventh chords
    In popular music
- Ascending-fifth sequences
- Falling-third sequences
    With alternating root movements
- About sequences based on seconds
    Parallel § chords
    7–6 and 5–6 motion

Reducing elaborated sequences

Overview

In this chapter, we consider how basic root movements may be used to form harmonic and melodic sequences—repetitions of musical material at different pitch levels. We also investigate several linear sequences, and learn how linear and harmonic elements interact in diatonic sequences.

Repertoire

Johann Sebastian Bach, Prelude, from Cello Suite No. 2 in D minor

Bach, Inventions in D minor (CD 1, track 14) and F Major

Archangelo Corelli, Allemanda, from Trio Sonata, Op. 4, No. 5 (CD 1, track 78)

George Frideric Handel, Chaconne in G Major, from *Trois Leçons* (CD 2, track 1)

Fanny Mendelssohn Hensel, "Neue Liebe, neues Leben" (CD 2, track 22)

Jerome Kern and Oscar Hammerstein II, "All the Things You Are," from *Very Warm for May*

Wolfgang Amadeus Mozart, Rondo in E♭ Major for Horn and Orchestra, K. 371

Mozart, Dies Irae, from *Requiem*

Johann Pachelbel, Canon in D for Three Violins and Keyboard

Robert Schumann, "Ich grolle nicht," from *Dichterliebe* (CD 3, track 35)

Sequences

1.14 To begin our study of sequences, listen to the opening of Bach's Invention in D minor, shown in Example 18.1. In this invention, the first two measures introduce a musical idea, or motive. As we know from Chapter 17, a motive is the smallest recognizable musical idea; it must be repeated exactly or in varied form in order to be called a motive. Is this the case in the Bach example? Listen again to the example, paying special attention to the motive as it appears in either the right- or left-hand part, and draw a bracket over the motive each time you hear this musical idea (even if transposed or slightly varied). Now compare each reappearance with the original in measures 1–2. *(Try it #1)*

EXAMPLE 18.1: Bach, Invention in D minor, mm. 1–18a

You probably bracketed the initial motive in the left hand in measures 3–4 and in the right hand in measures 5–6. These statements are simply repetitions of the motive—one down an octave and one up an octave—with counterpoint added in the other hand. We do not consider such octave-related repetitions part of a sequence. Sequences restate musical materials at other pitch levels.

KEY CONCEPT

In its most basic sense, the term **sequence** refers to a musical pattern that is restated immediately in the same voice at different pitch levels.

WF1

What happens to this melodic idea next? It sounds five more times in measures 7–16—two times in the right hand (mm. 7–10) and three in the left (mm. 11–16). Measures 7–10 and 11–16 are sequences: a musical pattern restated at different pitch levels. If you listen to the rest of the invention, you will hear that this main motive appears many more times.

You may have noticed that the rhythm and contour of the invention's main melodic idea remain consistent, for the most part, in each restatement. The pitch level of the pattern changes in measure 7, however: it begins to move down by step. This restatement of a motive at a different pitch level, down or up, makes a **melodic sequence**. The pattern in these measures, though, includes not only the melodic idea but also the accompanying counterpoint—both hand parts move down by step together. A continuous eighth-note counterpoint accompanies the motive in measures 7–10, then the counterpoint changes in mm. 11–16. When the entire harmonic or contrapuntal framework is a part of the sequential pattern, it is known as a **harmonic sequence**.

1.16

While a melodic sequence may appear without a repeated harmonic pattern, and vice versa, the combination of a melodic motive and a harmonic framework, as is the case here, is the most common. Listen again to the opening of the invention, this time through measure 29 (Example 18.2). You will hear that the motive from measures 1–2 does appear in a purely melodic sequence in measures 18–21, with an upper-voice pedal point.

EXAMPLE 18.2: Bach, Invention in D minor, mm. 18–29a

The sequences in measures 7–16 are **diatonic sequences**: the featured pitches all belong to the diatonic collection of D minor. (**Chromatic sequences**, in contrast, would contain accidentals outside the key of D minor.) The melodic sequence in measures 18–21 of Example 18.2 is also a diatonic sequence, but in the key of F Major. This example also includes a chromatic sequence—where is it? (*Try it #2*)

KEY CONCEPT

In diatonic sequences, generic melodic intervals stay the same when the pattern moves to another pitch level, but pitch-interval qualities change (for example, major to minor, or perfect to diminished).

In Example 18.1, the initial right-hand minor third of measure 7 becomes a major third in measure 9. Likewise, the last left-hand interval in measure 8 is a m2, but when this generic interval reappears in measure 10, it becomes a M2. In the overall tonal organization of the invention, these sequences serve to lead from one tonal area to another: from the opening D minor in measures 1–6 to a cadence in F Major in measures 17–18. (Sequences and form are discussed further in Chapters 23 and 28.)

Sequences in a Musical Context

Sequences are like subways, buses, or trains: you get on at one location, ride for a while, and get off when you reach your destination. In musical contexts, sequences are usually preceded by a chord or harmonic progression that sets up the tonic and key of the starting location, and they usually connect at their termination to a harmonic progression that reestablishes the tonic and key. Such sequences thus "travel" within one key area (like a bus within a city). Others may move from one key to another (like a train that runs between cities, as those in the Bach examples do).

Some sequences, especially harmonic sequences based on the falling-fifth root progression, may be composed of progressions that make sense when analyzed with Roman numerals. Others seem to suspend the sense of progression from the point at which they begin until they connect to a regular harmonic progression at their end. We can think of these as acting like suspension bridges: there are pillars at both ends holding up the bridge, but taut cables strung between them hold up the middle of the bridge. The sequence patterns with no clear sense of root progression typically have strong intervallic progressions underlying their voice-leading.

Sequences may also serve to expand melodies and phrases. While phrases in many compositions tend to be of a consistent length—four measures is typical—sequences tend to subvert these regular phrase subdivisions. The placement of sequences depends on the style of the piece. In Classical-period pieces with regular four-measure phrases, sequences are often used in transitions between groups of regular phrases and in developmental passages. In Baroque-era works, there may be few four-measure phrases at all—instead, a piece may be composed of a series of sequences. In nineteenth- and twentieth-century songs, entire portions of a song may be based on harmonic sequences. We will learn more about sequences in musical forms in later chapters; for now, we focus on how to write and analyze diatonic sequences.

Types of Sequences

A sequence may be based on a root-progression chain combined with an intervallic pattern in the upper voice (a harmonic sequence) or simply on a repeated melodic pattern (a melodic sequence). While all harmonic sequences have an underlying intervallic framework between the highest and lowest voices, some sequences are best thought of in terms of this framework of intervals, without reference to a root progression. These intervallic frameworks are called **linear intervallic patterns**, or **LIPs** for short. As we will see, some sequences, like those in Examples 18.1 and 18.2, include surface elaboration that makes it easy to hear and follow the sequence's pattern; others may hide the repeating intervallic framework under a nonpatterned surface elaboration.

When we analyze sequences, we need to determine (1) what type of pattern they are based on (a root progression, a melodic idea that's restated, an intervallic pattern, or a combination of those) and (2) the intervals of restatement (both the melodic interval and the time interval between restatements). In this chapter, we focus on harmonic sequences with root progressions or intervallic patterns, but it is important to notice whether each musical example features a melodic sequence as well, since melodic patterns make sequences easier to hear.

Harmonic Sequences Based on Root Progressions

In Chapter 16, we learned how to use root progressions to link chords within the basic phrase. In the progressions we considered, we usually saw no more than three or four chords linked by a particular root progression (falling-third, for example) before the chain was interrupted by a chord (or chords) linked by another root progression (such as falling-fifth). We also noted the "weak links" in the chains of root progressions—the chord connections that tend not to be used. These weak points center around diminished triads (vii°) and triads whose function is ambiguous (iii).

When root-progression chains are found in a sequence, the pattern of repetition—whether the entire texture is repeated or only the underlying intervallic framework—smooths over these weak harmonic links with strong linear voice-leading, making it possible to travel through the entire root-progression chain or at least through long sections of it.

KEY CONCEPT

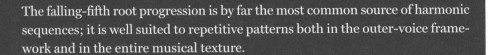

The falling-fifth root progression is by far the most common source of harmonic sequences; it is well suited to repetitive patterns both in the outer-voice framework and in the entire musical texture.

While root progression by third and second do not generate good outer-voice frameworks for sequences (because of the special way chords need to be connected to avoid parallel fifths and octaves), later in the chapter we will learn how these progressions can be adapted, by means of linear intervallic patterns, to make acceptable sequences.

Falling-Fifth Sequences

Many sequences have a falling-fifth root progression, the strongest progression in tonal music, as their foundation. Throughout music of the common-practice era, you will find falling-fifth sequences with root-position triads or with alternating root-position and first-inversion triads. In making sequences, we use longer segments of the chain—four or five chords, or even the entire chain from an initial tonic to an ending one—and we combine the root progression with a soprano-bass linear intervallic pattern. You should memorize the pattern of Roman numerals in the chain (I–IV–vii°–iii–vi–ii–V–I) and some of the common LIPs associated with it.

Example 18.3 shows voice-leading frameworks for basic falling-fifth sequences, both root position and with alternating $^6_3$ chords. These examples are labeled with Roman numerals beneath and with the outer-voice linear intervallic pattern (10–10, 10–6, or 6–10, the generic intervals between the highest and lowest parts) between the staves. The brackets above the staff indicate the repeated pattern, and the ties highlight common tones between the chords. Although the examples show the entire course of a sequence, in musical contexts only a portion may appear—as few as two or three repetitions may represent the sequence.

For each framework, you may use any of these upper-voice strands as the soprano line in an SATB setting. Your choice will determine which linear intervallic pattern (between soprano and bass) you create. In music literature, you may also encounter sequences with only three of the four voices shown here; one of the upper parts (usually a part that would have been doubled in another voice) will have been omitted.

EXAMPLE 18.3: Falling-fifth sequence frameworks

(a) All root position (10–10 LIP)

(b) Alternating root position and first inversion (10–6 LIP)

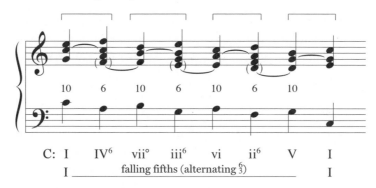

C: I   IV⁶   vii°   iii⁶   vi   ii⁶   V   I
   I _____ falling fifths (alternating ⁶₃) _____ I

(c) Alternating first inversion and root position (6–10 LIP)

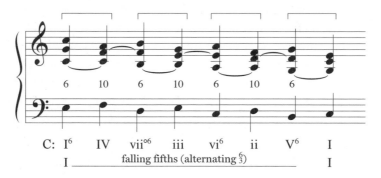

C: I⁶   IV   vii°⁶   iii   vi⁶   ii   V⁶   I
   I _____ falling fifths (alternating ⁶₃) _____ I

KEY CONCEPT

In falling-fifth sequences, a pair of chords connected by falling-fifth root motion usually constitutes the repeated "pattern." These pairings may link the first two chords of the chain, or the second and third (as bracketed in Example 18.3a). The second chord of the pattern then connects to the first chord of the next pattern by a falling-fifth root motion as well.

1.15 🎧

If we pay attention to every other chord, then falling-fifth sequences sometimes sound instead like descending seconds, and repetitions of the melodic sequence may reinforce that perception. Listen again to the first sequence in the Bach invention, where the two-measure melodic motive moves down by a second (mm. 5–10). Example 18.4 shows measures 7–10 (a), with a chordal reduction beneath Bach's counterpoint (b). The chordal reduction was made by removing all embellishing tones from the right hand and presenting the remaining pitches all at once, as a chord. The bass line consists of the lowest-sounding chord tone of each measure. Now the falling-fifth (root-position) pattern is clear: roots D–G–C–F, or chords i–iv–VII–III.

EXAMPLE 18.4: Bach, Invention in D minor

(a) Mm. 7–10

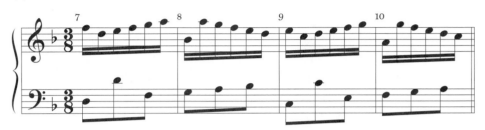

(b) Reduction of mm. 7–10

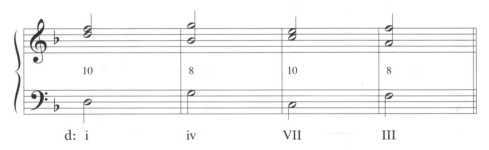

The frames shown in Example 18.3 also work in minor keys if you change the key signature to the parallel minor and pay careful attention to $\hat{6}$ and $\hat{7}$. You should generally use the natural-minor versions of $\hat{6}$ and $\hat{7}$ in the middle of a sequence, then raise these scale degrees at the cadence to create a strong close.

2.5   Listen to Variation 11 from Handel's Chaconne in G Major, the beginning of which is given in Example 18.5a. This variation, from the middle of the set of twenty-one variations, is in the parallel minor. Look at the SATB chordal framework shown beneath (b), to see how these measures are based on a falling-fifth root progression with alternating $\frac{6}{3}$ chords. Here, the harmony changes on the first and third beats, but the melodic sequence extends for a full measure, moving down one step with each restatement. Thus, at one level, the sequence progresses on beats 1 and 3 of each measure, while on another, it progresses once per measure—depending on whether you are following the melodic sequence or the underlying harmonic sequence.

EXAMPLE 18.5: Handel, Chaconne in G Major, Variation 11

(a) Mm. 89–92

(b) Framework for mm. 89–92 (10–8 LIP)

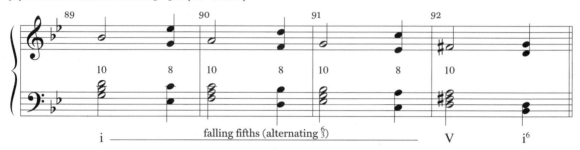

Look now at the intervals between bass and soprano, shown in Example 18.5b, to see the linear intervallic pattern of these measures. Compare measure 89 in both examples: circle and label the embellishing tones in part a to show how the framework relates to the music. *(Try it #3)*

The outer-voice linear intervallic pattern for this passage, 10–8, acts as a framework in many pieces with falling-fifth sequences alternating root-position and first-inversion triads. The LIP 10–8 is only one of several possible outer-voice patterns with a falling-fifth sequence; others are shown in Example 18.3. With most of the sequence frameworks in this chapter, you may place any of the upper-voice strands in the soprano part. Moving an inner voice to the soprano part does not change the basic root progression of the sequence, but it will change the outer-voice LIP.

2.6 🎧

Listen now to Variation 12 of the Chaconne, given in Example 18.6. This variation, also in the parallel minor key, is built from the same framework as Example 18.5, but elaborates the framework with different melodic motives.

EXAMPLE 18.6: Handel, Chaconne in G Major, Variation 12, mm. 97–100

EXAMPLE 18.7: Handel, Chaconne in G Major, Variation 13, mm. 105–108

Finally, listen to Variation 13, shown in Example 18.7. This passage continues with many elements of the previous two variations, but the chords in the falling-fifth sequence are now all in root position. One of the compositional problems of the root-position falling-fifth sequence in minor is how to treat the dissonant tritone in the ii° chord. How does Handel set up the figuration on the third beat of measure 105 in order to avoid the problem in measure 107, where the ii° triad would appear? His solution is that none of the triads on beat 3 includes the fifth.

EXAMPLE 18.7: Handel, Chaconne in G Major, Variation 13, mm. 105–108

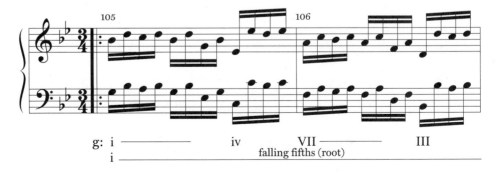

VI ——————— ii° V⁷ ———————

(i) ——————————————— V⁷

KEY CONCEPT

When you write falling-fifth sequences:

- Follow the same part-writing guidelines as for any two chords with roots related by fifth.
- In most cases, the two-chord patterns will include one voice part with a common tone. Keep the common tone, and move the other voices to the closest chord member.
- If the sequence alternates first-inversion triads, the two-chord patterns may or may not have these common tone connections, depending on what you have doubled.

With Seventh Chords   Example 18.8 shows another work by Bach, the opening of the Prelude from his Cello Suite No. 2. Play through this passage on a keyboard or your own instrument. Can you find a falling-fifth sequence? Identify the two-measure pattern by marking it with a bracket, and provide Roman numerals beneath the sequence. (Remember that the pattern in a falling-fifth sequence typically spans two chords.) How does this sequence differ from those we saw in the Handel Chaconne? *(Try it #4)*

EXAMPLE 18.8: Bach, Prelude, from Cello Suite No. 2 in D minor, mm. 1–13a

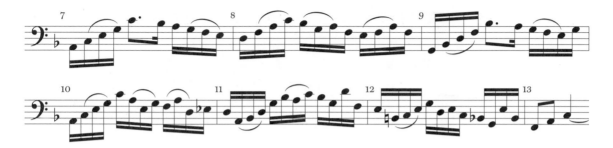

In addition to sequences based on triads, like those we saw in the Handel Chaconne, falling-fifth sequences may include seventh chords: all seventh chords, alternating triads and seventh chords, or alternating inversions of seventh chords. Some basic frameworks for falling-fifth sequences with seventh chords are shown in Examples 18.9a–d.

KEY CONCEPT

In common-practice style:

- When you write a falling-fifth sequence with all root-position seventh chords (Example 18.9a), parallel fifths and octaves can easily result. To avoid them, alternate complete and incomplete seventh chords (omit the fifth). Remember to resolve all of the chordal sevenths down, according to their tendency. In this case, the leading tones need not resolve up, but may be pulled down by a descending voice-leading line.
- When you write a falling-fifth sequence with alternating triads and seventh chords (Examples 18.9b, c), every chord should be complete, with standard doubling.
- Seventh-chord sequences may alternate between two inversions (Example 18.9d). Inverted seventh chords are usually complete in four-part settings.

EXAMPLE 18.9: Frameworks for falling-fifth sequences featuring seventh chords

(a) All root-position chords

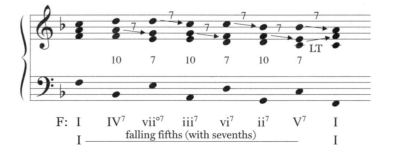

(b) Alternating triad and root-position seventh chords

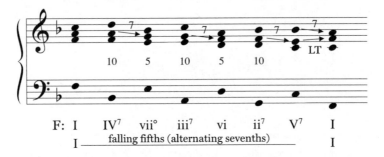

F: I   IV⁷ vii° iii⁷ vi   ii⁷ V⁷   I
   I _____ falling fifths (alternating sevenths) _____   I

(c) Alternating triad and first-inversion seventh chords

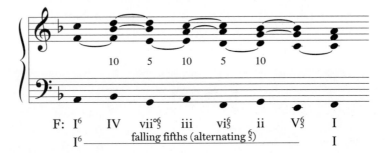

F: I⁶   IV   vii°⁶₅ iii vi⁶₅ ii   V⁶₅   I
   I⁶ _____ falling fifths (alternating ⁶₅) _____   I

(d) Alternating first-inversion and third-inversion seventh chords

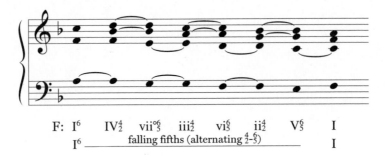

F: I⁶   IV⁴₂ vii°⁶₅ iii⁴₂ vi⁶₅ ii⁴₂ V⁶₅   I
   I⁶ _____ falling fifths (alternating ⁴₂-⁶₅) _____   I

Many of the seventh chords shown in these sequences—for example, iii⁷, IV⁷, vi⁶₅, and iii⁴₂—are rarely found outside one of these frameworks. There are, however, other possible variations on the falling-fifth seventh-chord sequence; you may find others in pieces you are performing or use these as a model to write out others on your own.

1.81 Listen to another typical setting of the falling-fifth sequence, given in Example 18.10, an excerpt from a Corelli trio sonata. This is a sequence with seventh chords, as the figured bass clearly shows, all in root position like the model in Example 18.9a. (We consider the bass pitches on each beat to be the primary bass line, ignoring the consonant skips.) Observe how the chordal sevenths are prepared and resolved: they are a string of 7–6 suspensions, with change of bass, alternating between first and second violin. We find a close link between sequences—even those associated with a strong root progression like this one—and the resolution of dissonant intervals in counterpoint.

EXAMPLE 18.10: Corelli, Allemanda, from Trio Sonata, Op. 4, No. 5, mm. 22b–24

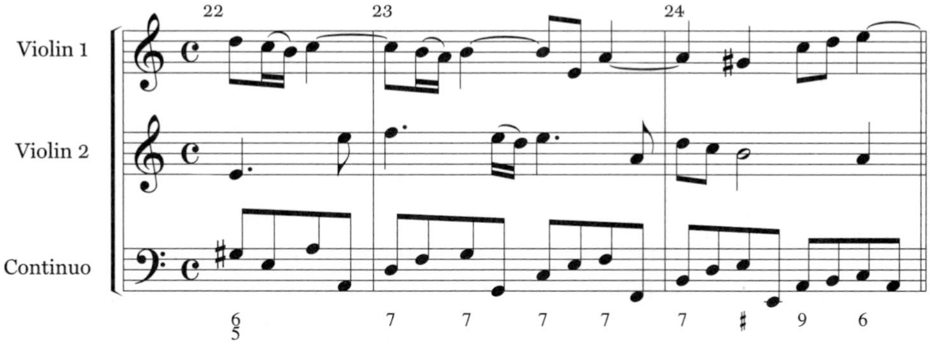

Occasionally you may encounter a sequence in a transitional passage where Roman numerals (or a stable tonic key) are hard to determine. In a case like this, you may simply use popular-music symbols or other shorthand notation to identify the chord roots and qualities. Look at Example 18.11, which is drawn from Bach's Invention in F Major. Here, the two-chord pattern takes place within a single measure, with a change of chord on the second beat of each measure. Mark each repetition of the pattern with brackets, and write the chord roots and qualities beneath.

Your analysis might look something like this: g C^7 | F $b^{ø7}$ | e A^7 | d. From this analysis, we can identify the sequence by its root motion down by fifths and by the pattern of alternating seventh chords, without necessarily assigning Roman numerals. We would need to consider a larger musical context to determine the role of this falling-fifth sequence in the work as a whole.

EXAMPLE 18.11: Bach, Invention in F Major, mm. 21–24

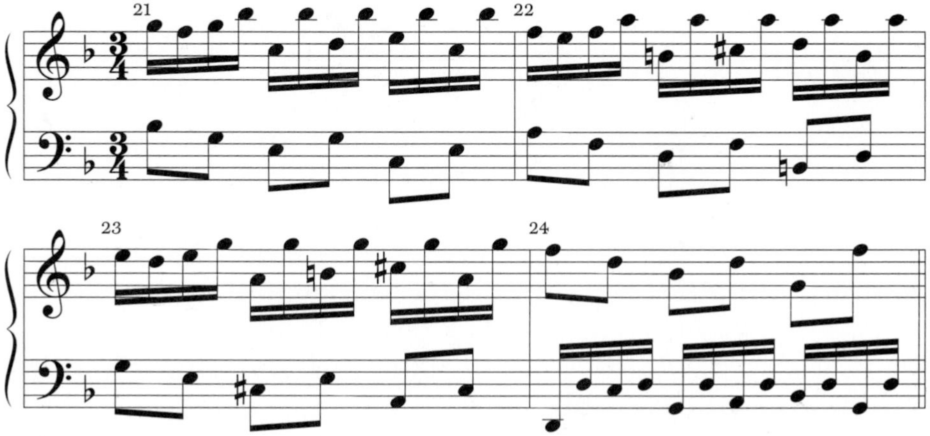

In Popular Music   You may also find falling-fifth seventh-chord sequences in some twentieth-century popular music. Play through the first phrase of Kern and Hammerstein's "All the Things You Are," given in Example 18.12. This song features chords with a third added above the seventh (called **ninth chords**) and harmonies with chromatic alterations. The verse begins in F minor (the chord before m. 5 is a V^7, setting up the F-minor chord as i). The chord progression written in under the staff should be familiar for the most part. Instead of triads, Kern has written seventh and ninth chords to elaborate the falling-fifth progression i^7–iv^7–VII^9–III^7–VI^7 through measure 9. The pattern of the root motion is reflected through measure 11 in the fourth up, fifth down in the bass line (the lowest pitch in a measure is always the chord root) and in the melodic framework of the solo and piano parts (A♭4–D♭5–G4–C5–F4–B♮–E♮).

In this piece, the harmonic framework is sequential, even though the surface decoration is not the same in each pattern. As you probably heard, not all of the chords in this falling-fifth sequence are diatonic. Where do you hear differences from the expected diatonic sequence? *(Try it #5)*

EXAMPLE 18.12: Kern and Hammerstein, "All the Things You Are," mm. 5–12 (falling-fifth sequence with seventh chords)

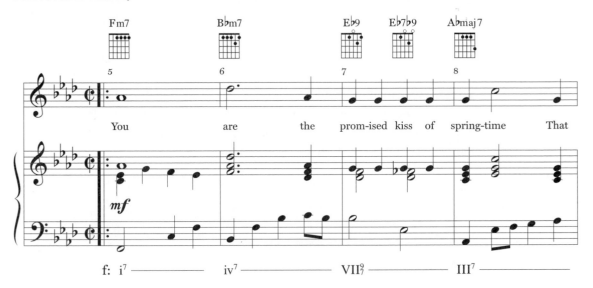

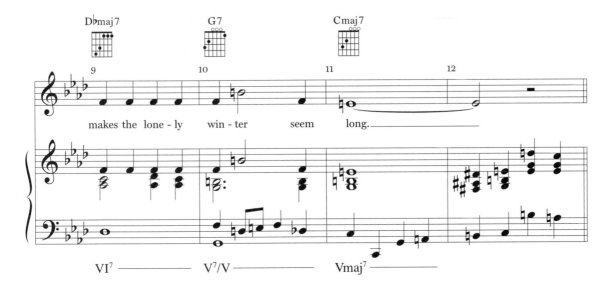

Ascending-Fifth Sequences

We observed in our previous study of root progressions that the ascending-fifth chain generated few commonly used chord progressions. However, with the addition of a soprano-bass pattern, the ascending-fifth chain occasionally appears in harmonic sequences. Typical frameworks are shown in Example 18.13.

EXAMPLE 18.13: Frameworks for ascending-fifth sequences

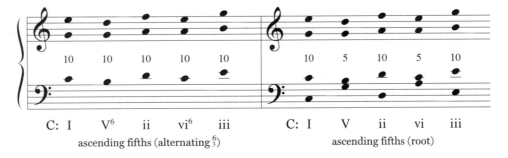

Falling-Third Sequences

Look at Example 18.14a, from Mozart's Rondo in E♭ Major for Horn and Orchestra, shown here in a keyboard reduction. This excerpt, a melodic arpeggiation of falling-third chords, reveals a problem with pairing a linear intervallic pattern with falling thirds: we run into parallel fifths or octaves, as we can see if we stack up the chords (Example 18.14b).

EXAMPLE 18.14: The problem with falling-third progressions

(a) Mozart, Rondo in E♭ Major for Horn and Orchestra, K. 371, mm. 20–24a

(b) Reduction of mm. 20–24a

With Alternating Root Movements   Some falling-third progressions *can* be combined with linear intervallic patterns to create sequences, with the help of intervening chords. For example, in music literature we sometimes find falling-third progressions in a variant that provides a stepwise descending bass line, with the falling-third progression appearing in every other chord. This progression alternates root-position chords (for the falling thirds) with first-inversion (for the intervening chords): usually I–V⁶–vi–iii⁶–IV–I⁶–ii, where ii serves as a predominant to prepare the cadence.

2.22   Listen, for an example, to the opening of Fanny Hensel's "Neue Liebe, neues Leben" (Example 18.15a), which employs this variant of the falling-third sequence, with a stepwise bass. The entire texture—melody, bass line, and accompaniment upper voices—follows a sequential pattern, repeating down a third each measure (the pattern begins in the middle of the measure), and breaking off after the third statement of the pattern just before the half cadence in measures 3–4. Example 18.15b shows the underlying voice-leading framework for the song.

EXAMPLE 18.15: Hensel, "Neue Liebe, neues Leben"

(a) Mm. 1–4a

Translation: Heart, my heart, what does this mean? What is besieging you so?

(b) Framework: Falling-third sequence with stepwise bass

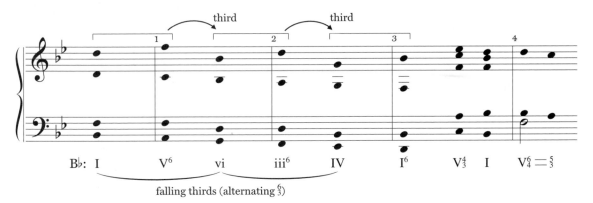

Like falling-fifth sequences, falling-third sequences may incorporate seventh chords. Listen to the opening of Schumann's "Ich grolle nicht" for a poignant example. Here, the singer has been disappointed in love ("I will not complain, even if my heart breaks. Love forever lost . . . "), and the descending bass line and dissonant sevenths add to the sense of loss. As you listen, follow the score excerpt in Example 18.16. Mark Roman numerals and figures in measures 5–9, and name the sequence type. (*Try it #6*)

3.35

EXAMPLE 18.16: Schumann, "Ich grolle nicht," from *Dichterliebe,* mm. 1–12a

Translation: I bear no grudge, even if my heart is breaking. Love lost forever!

Look now at one of the most famous harmonic-sequence-based pieces of all—Pachelbel's Canon in D. (If you are not familiar with this work, listen to it in the library.) The opening chord progression for the continuo part is given in Example 18.17 (mm. 1–2). What type of sequence is this? Analysis of the chords reveals a root-progression pattern of down a fourth, then up a second, until just before the cadence: I–V–vi–iii–IV–I–ii⁶₅–V⁷–I. This may be considered a falling-third sequence because every other chord is a member of the falling-third progression; it takes two chords to complete the repeated harmonic pattern.

Because of the chords inserted between the falling thirds, this progression (unlike the regular root-position falling-third progression) is quite amenable to sequential melodic patterning. In Pachelbel's setting, the bass line stays the same throughout the piece, as does the harmonic progression (with slight changes in voicing). The upper parts, however, explore the many possible melodic lines that can be generated from these chords, beginning with scalar patterns and becoming increasingly elaborate. As the example shows, the violin 1 part introduces each new strand, which is answered in canon after two measures by violin 2, then two measures later by violin 3.

EXAMPLE 18.17: Pachelbel, Canon in D, mm. 1–8

About Sequences Based on Seconds

Parallel $^6_3$ Chords   When we learned about root progressions in Chapter 16, we observed that a chain of root progressions by second can easily result in parallel fifths and octaves. While this voice-leading problem is more of a concern in common practice than popular styles, most sequential root progressions a second apart feature some sort of intervallic pattern to break up the parallels. One of the most common is a parallel series of $^6_3$ chords—ascending or descending—as shown in Example 18.18. The example also shows some of the typical linear intervallic patterns for this kind of sequence.

EXAMPLE 18.18: Parallel $^6_3$ chord sequences by (falling and ascending) second

(a) Falling seconds with
   parallel $^6_3$ chords

(b) Ascending seconds with
   parallel $^6_3$ chords

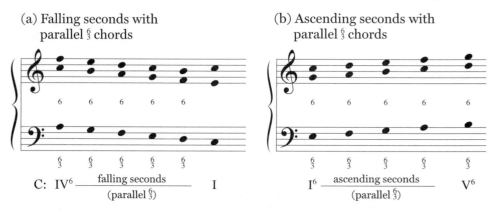

We did not consider this type of root progression by seconds in Chapter 16, because in musical contexts, parallel $^6_3$ chords work more like sequences than harmonic progressions. In music literature, a series of first-inversion triads functions as a linear succession, spanning harmonic pillars, without a strong sense of root motion. In fact, a succession of first-inversion triads is more closely related to doubling a melody in thirds and sixths than it is to independent voice-leading. Further, if we add Roman numerals under this progression, they will not conform to the phrase or root-progression models with which we are familiar.

WF2

Look, for example, at the passage from Mozart's Dies Irae, from the *Requiem*, given in Example 18.19. Beginning with the last beat of measure 27, Mozart employs a succession of $^6_3$ chords: v^6–iv^6–III^6–♭II^6, preceding the half cadence in measure 29. (We will learn more about this altered form of the ii chord in Chapter 25.) This progression clearly does not "make sense" according to the principles of harmonic progression we have learned thus far; however, the linear pattern of parallel $^6_3$ chords makes the succession perfectly acceptable, even typical, in common-practice style.

EXAMPLE 18.19: Mozart, Dies Irae, from *Requiem*, mm. 27–29 (parallel $^6_3$ chords)

Translation: As foretold by David and the Sibyl.

7–6 and 5–6 Motion   Another way to break up the parallel motion when writing root-position sequences by step is to delay the arrival of one of the chord members with a suspension-like or retardation-like figure. We have already observed that falling-fifth sequences feature linear patterns such as 7–6 suspensions; these same intervals can be used with a series of ⁶₃ chords moving down by step as well, as shown in Example 18.20 (a variant on the framework of Example 18.18a) and in Example 18.21, from Handel's Chaconne in G Major. Again, if we analyze the "chords" in these two examples with Roman numerals, as in Example 18.19, the root progression does not make much sense; the interval succession does make sense, however, because of the resulting linear sequence. (This pattern of intervals predates the use of root progressions.) The chain of 7–6 suspensions is often prepared by a 5–6 intervallic motion to set up the first suspension, as shown in measure 73 of the Handel variation. Listen to this passage to hear how the 7–6 suspensions break up potential parallel motion.

2.4

WF3

EXAMPLE 18.20: Falling seconds with parallel ⁶₃ chords (7–6 LIP)

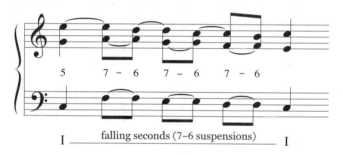

EXAMPLE 18.21: Handel, Chaconne in G Major, Variation 9, mm. 73–76

Another sequence framework based on root motion by second is shown in Example 18.22. Here, we start with a series of root-position triads moving up by step, then delay the arrival of the sixth above the bass one half beat, making a 5–6 linear intervallic pattern. Listen to measures 69–71 of Hensel's "Neue Liebe, neues Leben" (Example

2.26

18.23a) to hear this pattern; the upper part of the three-voice frame is doubled by the voice. Ascending sequences like this one, along with the ascending-fifth sequence, though beautiful, are not frequently found in music literature—they divert the harmonic progression from its traditional goal-directed motion from tonic to dominant.

EXAMPLE 18.22: Ascending seconds (5–6 LIP)

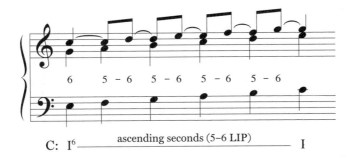

EXAMPLE 18.23: Hensel, "Neue Liebe, neues Leben"

(a) Mm. 69–71

Translation: Love, let me free!

(b) Reduction of mm. 69–71

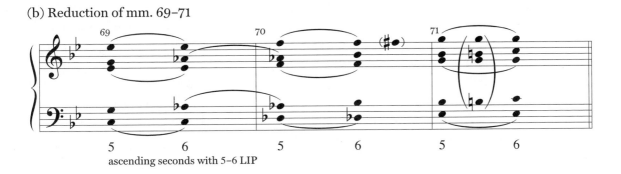

SUMMARY

When you come across a sequence in a piece of music, a contextual analysis beneath your Roman numerals will help clarify the harmonic function and goal of the passage. You may substitute for beat-by-beat Roman numerals a label on the beginning and ending chord, plus a label that describes the sequence type from among the following:

- falling fifth (root position or root alternating with inversions, possibly with sevenths)
- ascending fifth (root position or root alternating with $^6_3$)
- falling third (stepwise bass or alternating root movements)
- parallel $^6_3$ chords (roots moving by seconds)
- 7–6 motion (roots descending by seconds)
- 5–6 motion (roots ascending by seconds)

Reducing Elaborated Sequences

Many of the sequences we have examined in this chapter display elaborate surfaces, with embellishing tones between members of the framework. When you hear a sequential pattern in a piece of music, listen carefully to determine which pitches are embellishments. In some cases, it helps to determine the roots of the triads or seventh chords in the sequence and write out the root progression. In others, the Roman numerals for the root progression may not make sense based on what we know about harmony so far. In the latter type, think about the intervals used—does the sequence match one of the frames we have studied? If there are layers of embellishments (as is usually the case), start by marking passing tones and neighbor tones; these are usually the most superficial embellishments. When considering chordal skips and arpeggiations, it is sometimes helpful to stack up the chord as a simultaneity. In addition, considering the chord members that fall on the beat or coincide with the change of bass may reveal the structural framework.

Analyzing all of the embellishments in an elaborate sequence is a challenge; for our purposes, it is often enough to identify the general type of the sequence (falling fifth, for example) and whether or not seventh chords or inversions are present. If Roman numerals are difficult to determine, just identify the chord root and quality. You will be able to further develop your skills in analysis in later chapters as we learn more about sequences.

TERMS YOU SHOULD KNOW

> linear intervallic pattern (LIP)
> sequence
> > • diatonic sequence
> > • harmonic sequence
> > • melodic sequence
> sequence pattern

QUESTIONS FOR REVIEW

1. What are sequences? Where do we find them?
2. What do we look for in analyzing a sequence pattern?
3. Which root progressions work well as sequence frames? Which need alteration?
4. What is the link between harmonic sequences and voice-leading? between harmonic sequences and dissonance resolution?
5. How do we tell which frame is used in an embellished sequence?
6. If you were to write your own sequential progression with one of the frames in this chapter, what steps would you take?
7. In music for your own instrument, find two different sequences and label their types.

CHAPTER 19

Intensifying the Dominant:

Secondary Dominants and Secondary Leading-Tone Chords; New Voice-Leading Chords

Outline of topics covered

Overview

In this chapter, we consider two topics: (1) how to intensify motion toward the dominant and (2) how to embellish the basic phrase with new voice-leading chords. Both skills build on those we have developed in previous chapters and expand the range of musical examples we will be able to write and analyze.

Repertoire

Johann Sebastian Bach, Prelude in C Major, from *The Well-Tempered Clavier*, Book I (CD 1, track 17)

Bach, "Wachet auf" (Chorale No. 179) (CD 1, track 9)

Frédéric Chopin, Prelude in C minor, Op. 28, No. 20

Scott Joplin, "Pine Apple Rag" (CD 2, track 28)

Wolfgang Amadeus Mozart, Rondo in E♭ Major for Horn and Orchestra, K. 371

Robert Sherman and Richard Sherman, "Feed the Birds," from *Mary Poppins*

Franz Schubert, "Gute Nacht," from *Winterreise*

Intensifying the Dominant

1.9 🎧

1.10 🎧

WF1

Listen to Bach's setting of "Wachet auf" while following the score in your anthology. We will concentrate our analysis here on measures 6b–16, shown in Example 19.1. Beneath the staff, write a Roman numeral analysis, leaving blank any chords you are unable to identify. (*Try it #1*)

EXAMPLE 19.1: Bach, "Wachet auf," mm. 6b–16

Translation: The guard on the high walls cries to us: wake up, city of Jerusalem!

The first phrase begins with a prolonged tonic (mm. 7–8) and ends with a half cadence. What are the harmonies leading up to the cadence, and how do they help intensify the arrival on the dominant harmony? You probably noticed the two A♮s in measures 9 and 10—they represent a raised scale-degree $\hat{4}$. We refer to this scale degree as $\sharp\hat{4}$, to symbolize the chromatic inflection of $\hat{4}$ up by half step, even in flat keys (as in this case) where the score notation calls for a natural rather than a sharp. Each A♮ functions as a temporary leading tone to $\hat{5}$, and it resolves properly as a leading tone should, up by half step.

In what type of chord does the #$\hat{4}$ appear? Look at the last chord of measure 9: F-A♮-C-E♭ (in first inversion; the B♭ in the bass is an accented passing tone). This chord is built on $\hat{2}$ in E♭ Major, but it is not a ii$^6_5$ chord, because its bass is the non-diatonic pitch A♮ instead of A♭. The quality of the chord reveals its local function: it is a major-minor (or dominant) seventh chord. When we encounter a dominant seventh chord—whether built on $\hat{5}$ or not, whether diatonic or not—we can generally assume that it acts like a dominant, even if only in a localized context.

Whose dominant is it? If we found this dominant seventh chord (F-A♮-C-E♭) written without a key context, we could determine its implied tonic in one of two ways. We could count a P5 down (or P4 up) from its root, or we could move a m2 up from the chord's third (the temporary leading tone). Both methods tell us that this V^7 should resolve to either B♭ Major or B♭ minor as its tonic—does it? Does the F-Major triad at the end of measure 10 resolve to B♭ as well? *(Try it #2)*

These chords are called **secondary dominants**, since they act like dominants in their spelling and resolution, but in relation to a scale degree and harmony other than the tonic—in this case, in relation to V.

KEY CONCEPT

The V^7/V (read "V^7 of V") acts as a temporary dominant to the V chord that follows. Triads may also serve as secondary dominants (V/V).

Music analysts have a number of ways of naming and notating secondary dominants. They are sometimes called "applied dominants" (a type of **applied chord**, because they are "applied" to a chord other than tonic) or "secondary-function" chords. Look again at Example 19.1. We can now provide all the Roman numerals for measures 9 and 10: V^6 V$^6_5$/V | V V/V.

Secondary Dominants and Leading-Tone Chords to V

About Secondary Dominants

To understand secondary dominants to V, think of V as a temporary tonic key (rather than a chord). Now imagine what the dominant (or dominant seventh) chord would be in that temporary key. This chord is the secondary dominant: V/V (or V^7/V). For example, if we started in C Major, the temporary tonic key would be

G Major and its V chord D Major (remember: G Major's key signature has F♯, and this sharp is crucial in spelling the secondary dominant correctly). In sum, V/V in C Major is a D-Major chord. Keep in mind that we have not really left the primary key of the movement at all, but are using the idea of a temporary new tonic to help us spell the secondary dominant correctly. While secondary dominant triads (V/V) are possible, secondary dominant seventh chords (V^7/V) are more typical in music literature, since their Mm7 chord quality marks them unambiguously as having a dominant function. In our example, then, V^7/V in C Major would be D-F♯-A-C.

Another way to think of the secondary dominant is as an altered predominant chord. In order to spell it correctly, we would need to raise the third of the diatonic ii chord to give it a major or dominant seventh quality (II or II^7). The chord quality resulting from this chromatic alteration, together with the voice-leading and resolution of the chord, define it as a secondary dominant.

KEY CONCEPT

All V^7/V (or V/V) chords are spelled by chromatically altering a pitch. The alteration is always ♯$\hat{4}$ of the primary key, which functions as the leading tone in the temporary key of V.

The chromatic adjustment you need is part of the key signature of the temporary key. Recall that when we spelled V^7/V in C Major, we noted that the F♯ belonged to the temporary key of G Major. To spell a secondary dominant in minor keys, we need two chromatic alterations to change the diatonic ii° to a dominant seventh quality. Which scale degrees will be altered? *(Try it #3)*

KEY CONCEPT

When you spell a secondary dominant to V, double-check that

- the chord is built on $\hat{2}$,
- the triad quality is major (with ♯$\hat{4}$; in minor, you also need to raise $\hat{6}$), and
- the chordal seventh (if present) is minor.

Secondary dominants to V intensify the dominant harmony so well that we find them in many styles, including rock music, popular songs, and show tunes. Example 19.2 shows the opening of Sherman and Sherman's "Feed the Birds." Because of the popular style, we see a freer use of dissonance than in much of the repertoire we will examine in this chapter, but the secondary dominant is clear. Look at the bass note in measure 7, plus the pitches on the last beat of that bar: a clear V^7/V in C Major. (You can also get a snapshot of the harmonic motion from the chord symbols above the staff.) This temporary intensification of V does not signal a new key, since the next phrase of the song is almost identical to the first—solidly in C Major.

EXAMPLE 19.2: Sherman and Sherman, "Feed the Birds, " mm. 1–8

The secondary dominant to V is one of the most common chromatic chords. You often find it at phrase endings, preceding the dominant of an authentic or half cadence, as we have seen in both examples thus far, or in other passages where the dominant harmony is prolonged. Practice spelling V⁷/V in various keys, and look for them in pieces you play (the presence of ♯4̂ is an important clue). While applied chords to the dominant are by far the most common, secondary dominant chords can make a temporary tonic of other chords as well. (We will consider other possibilities for applied dominants in Chapter 21.) You can also use secondary dominants to modify falling-fifth sequences (more about that in Chapter 29).

Try it #4

For each of the keys below, build a secondary dominant seventh chord by imagining first the V chord as a key area, and then finding the dominant of this key area. (Remember, you can double-check your answer by means of the altered ii chord method.)

KEY	DOMINANT KEY AREA	V⁷/V CHORD
B♭ Major	F Major	C-E♮-G-B♭
E minor		
A Major		
D Major		
G minor		

Tonicization and Modulation   When a secondary dominant resolves, making its chord of resolution seem like a temporary tonic, this effect is called **tonicization**. When a harmony like V is tonicized, the key of the passage does not really change, except in a very temporary sense. After its tonicization by the secondary dominant, the temporary tonic returns to its normal functional role in the primary key and progresses as usual.

Tonicizations of greater structural significance are called **modulations**. If we choose to analyze a passage with a secondary dominant as a modulation, we look for such musical indications as a continuation of the passage in the new key, or the presence of a predominant harmony in the new key. We will learn more about modulation in Chapter 22.

Let's return once more to the Bach chorale in Example 19.1 for an example of tonicization. Although the dominant harmony is tonicized in measures 9–11, the music continues firmly in the tonic key after the fermata. A vertical analysis of the passage is given below, along with a contextual analysis that shows the tonicization of the dominant.

Vertical: E♭: V($\frac{4}{2}$) | I⁶ | I | V⁶ V⁶₅/V | V V/V | V | I | IV⁶ I | IV vi | ii⁷ V⁷ | I |
(V tonicized)
Contextual: T — D ————————— T —— PD —— D T
(HC)   (PAC)

You could also indicate the tonicization of V in measures 9–11 with "bracket notation": list the tonicized chords as though temporarily in the key of V, with a bracket beneath to show the temporary key. Thus, V⁶ V⁶₅/V | V V/V | V becomes
⌐I⁶ V⁶₅ | I V | I⌐.
      V

One characteristic of this chorale setting is Bach's addition of a chordal seventh on the offbeat, such as the offbeat to the opening anacrusis in measure 6b. Our analysis shows a $\frac{4}{2}$ in parentheses, since we could interpret this bass note as a passing tone as well as a chordal seventh, and Bach resolves the V$\frac{4}{2}$ properly to a I⁶ on the downbeat of measure 7. (Extra challenge: In two places, measures 12 and 13, Bach adds a chromatic pitch as chordal seventh; what type of secondary dominant is created if the D♭ is considered a chord tone rather than a passing tone?) *(Try it #5)*

Secondary Dominants to V in the Basic Phrase   The most common role for V⁷/V or V/V in the basic phrase is to replace a predominant-function harmony immediately preceding the dominant area, as shown in Example 19.3. We could think of V⁷/V like a supercharged ii⁷: the raised $\hat{4}$ combined with the falling-fifth root progression (already present between ii⁷ and V) makes a very strong pull toward V. But because the V⁷/V "belongs to" the dominant, its temporary key, we place it in the dominant area of our phrase model. As in progressions from V to I, we can control the strength of the harmonic progression between the secondary dominant and temporary tonic by our choices of inversion and whether to include the seventh.

EXAMPLE 19.3: Typical context for a secondary dominant

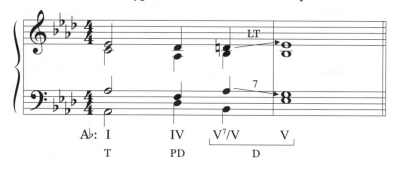

Sometimes a secondary dominant is preceded by a diatonic ii, ii⁷, or IV (in root position or in inversion), as shown in Examples 19.3 and 19.4. In the latter example, the diatonic ii chord is altered chromatically to create the secondary dominant. One way to produce a strong and smooth connection between the predominant harmony and V⁷/V is by writing a **chromatic voice exchange**. For a voice exchange to be considered chromatic, at least one pitch must appear in both its diatonic form and its chromatically inflected form. Most typically, the voice exchange occurs between the bass and an inner voice. Example 19.5a shows a diatonic version of the voice exchange (with scale-degrees $\hat{6}$ and $\hat{4}$), embellished by a passing $^6_4$ chord. In Example 19.5b, the voice exchange again features scale-degrees $\hat{6}$ and $\hat{4}$, then moves to the chromatically inflected pair: $\hat{6}$ and $\sharp\hat{4}$.

EXAMPLE 19.4: Secondary dominant as an altered ii⁷ chord

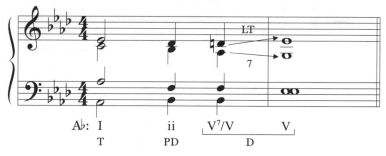

EXAMPLE 19.5: Secondary dominant with a voice exchange

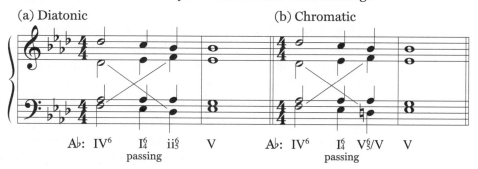

2.28 🎧

2.29 🎧

The V⁷/V may also be expanded by a cadential $^6_4$ in the tonicized key. For an example, listen to the opening section (mm. 1–20) of Joplin's "Pine Apple Rag" while following the score in your anthology. The first four measures, an introduction, are followed by two eight-measure phrases. With what Roman numerals and cadence type does the first eight-measure phrase end? (Example 19.6 shows this phrase, with embellishing tones in mm. 10–11 identified for you.) The chord on beat 2 in measure 10 is I⁶, followed by a V$^{8-7}_{4-3}$/V in measure 11. The voice-leading of this cadential $^6_4$ in the tonicized dominant key is the same as it would be in the tonic key. The secondary dominant then resolves to V in measure 12, making a half cadence. How do we know this is only a half cadence and not a modulation to the key of V (F Major)? The phrase that begins in measure 13 starts out the same as the first one, firmly in the key of B♭ Major.

EXAMPLE 19.6: Joplin, "Pine Apple Rag," mm. 5–12

B♭:   I⁶   V$^8_6$ ⎯ $^7_3$ I   (HC)

Secondary Dominants to V in Common-Practice Style   Since you already have experience writing dominant-to-tonic progressions, you may find it helpful to think of the two-chord secondary-dominant progression as being in a new key—that of the temporary tonic—for just those two chords. This method automatically gives you the correct chromatic alterations you need to spell the secondary dominant correctly. Try imagining that the two chords have a box around them: the boundary for the temporary key. Spell and resolve the chords inside this imaginary "tonicization box" as though they were in that temporary key. Remember, however, that the effect of a tonicization is temporary; outside the tonicization box, you will still be writing in the main key of the phrase.

You do not need to learn any new part-writing procedures to resolve V^7/V, V/V, or their inversions. We write them just like the $V^{(7)}$–I progressions we first learned in Chapter 12. All aspects of this chord connection—doubling, resolving tendency tones, and voicing—remain the same for secondary dominants, as shown in Example 19.7. The main thing you need to remember is to spell the secondary dominant chord with the necessary chromatic changes to pitches.

KEY CONCEPT

When you write and resolve a V^7/V in common-practice style, be sure you

- avoid doubling the $\sharp\hat{4}$ (because of its leading-tone function),
- resolve the temporary leading tone up ($\sharp\hat{4}$ resolves up to $\hat{5}$), and
- resolve the chordal seventh down ($\hat{1}$ resolves down to $\hat{7}$).

When you write in popular styles or in freer textures, these guidelines may be relaxed. Look back, for example, at the secondary dominant in measure 11 of "Pine Apple Rag" in Example 19.6. Do the tendency tones resolve as our guidelines predict? *(Try it #6)*

When we studied authentic cadences in Chapter 12, we learned some special voice-leading guidelines for root-position V–I and V^7–I progressions at the cadence. These guidelines also hold here.

KEY CONCEPT

Resolving root-position chords:

1. When moving from a V/V to a V, both chords are complete and resolve normally (Example 19.7a).
2. If you resolve a complete root-position V^7/V to a root-position V, the chord of resolution will be incomplete (with three roots and a third) if you resolve all of the tendency tones correctly (Example 19.7b).
3. If you want to resolve a root-position V^7/V to a complete V chord, then use an incomplete V^7/V (missing its fifth; Example 19.7c); alternatively,
4. the temporary leading tone may skip instead to the fifth of the next chord to fill out a complete dominant chord (Example 19.7d). The note to which the leading tone should resolve is usually in another voice, as shown by the dotted arrow in this example.
5. The V chord to which the secondary dominant resolves may be embellished by a cadential $\begin{smallmatrix}6\\4\end{smallmatrix}$ (Example 19.7e).

EXAMPLE 19.7: Resolutions of V/V and V^7/V

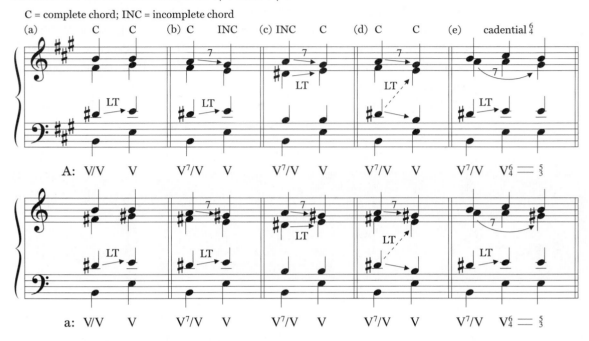

The approach to the V^7/V depends on where it appears in the progression. If you precede the secondary dominant by one of the predominant chords, IV or ii, then the chromatic alteration of $\hat{4}$ to $\sharp\hat{4}$ will need to be handled carefully.

KEY CONCEPT

The sudden introduction of $\sharp\hat{4}$ in one voice right after the diatonic $\hat{4}$ sounds in another voice is called a **cross relation** (Example 19.8a), a technique generally avoided in common-practice music. When you write secondary dominants that are prepared by their diatonic counterparts, keep the diatonic pitch in the same voice as the chromatically altered pitch (Example 19.8b): $\hat{4}$–$\sharp\hat{4}$–$\hat{5}$.

Although generally we avoid cross relations when writing in eighteenth-century style, there are two permissible contexts for a cross relation. The first is the chromatic voice exchange (Example 19.8c). The second occurs when the bass leaps to $\sharp\hat{4}$, creating a cross relation with an inner voice in the previous chord (Example 19.8d). Common-practice composers use this particular type of cross relation so long as it does not involve the soprano voice. For composers in other styles, cross relations may not seem so objectionable—indeed, they are rather common in some chromatic styles, such as barbershop harmony.

EXAMPLE 19.8: Avoiding cross relations

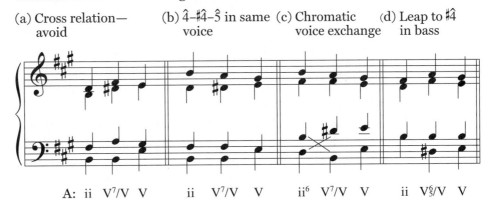

(a) Cross relation—avoid (b) $\hat{4}$–$\sharp\hat{4}$–$\hat{5}$ in same voice (c) Chromatic voice exchange (d) Leap to $\sharp\hat{4}$ in bass

A: ii V⁷/V V   ii V⁷/V V   ii⁶ V⁷/V V   ii V⁶₅/V V

Be careful when you write secondary dominants in minor keys: if V⁷/V is introduced by i or VI, then scale-degrees $\hat{3}$ to $\sharp\hat{4}$ produce a melodic augmented second. You can avoid this by approaching the chromatic tone from above. We will discover many more approaches for V⁷/V when we learn about chromatic predominants (see Chapter 25). For now, when writing secondary dominant progressions, aim for smooth voice-leading connections (by step or common tone) where possible, and follow our usual procedure of checking for doubling and parallel fifths and octaves.

About Secondary Leading-Tone Chords

We learned in Chapter 15 how leading-tone chords may substitute for V chords in many progressions where a dominant function is desired. Secondary leading-tone chords to V can substitute for secondary dominants as well, in any progression where a weaker sense of dominant function is desired. The triad vii°/V may be used as well as vii°⁷/V. Less common is the viiø⁷/V. Like secondary dominants, secondary leading-tone chords are sometimes referred to as "applied chords" since they are also applied to a harmony other than tonic.

KEY CONCEPT

We may use vii°/V, vii°⁷/V, or viiø⁷/V as secondary leading-tone chords to V. The diminished triad and fully diminished seventh chord are the most common choices, because these qualities are associated with leading-tone function. The half-diminished quality is possible as well, but only if the temporary tonic is a major chord.

Secondary Leading-Tone Chords to V in Common-Practice Style

The vii°/V or vii°⁷/V and their inversions connect to V just like leading-tone-to-tonic progressions. All aspects of the connection between the secondary leading-tone chord and its temporary tonic—doubling, resolving the tendency tone(s), and voicing—are the same as for vii°⁷ to I. The one element to which you need to pay close attention is the spelling of the secondary leading-tone seventh chord. Make ♯$\hat{4}$ (the temporary leading tone) the root of the chord, then be sure that the chord you spell has a half-diminished or fully diminished seventh quality. If you write a fully diminished seventh, you can spell the chord as a stack of minor thirds above ♯$\hat{4}$ (in major keys, scale-degree $\hat{3}$ needs to be lowered one half step); for a half-diminished seventh, the top third will be a major third. Example 19.9 shows some characteristic resolutions of secondary leading-tone chords.

KEY CONCEPT

When you resolve a secondary leading-tone chord to V:

- Resolve ♯$\hat{4}$ up to $\hat{5}$.
- Resolve the chordal seventh ($\hat{3}$ or lowered $\hat{3}$) down to $\hat{2}$.
- Avoid parallel fifths and d5 to P5 unless you can place them in inner voices (Examples 19.9 b and f) or unless you write parallel tenths between soprano and bass (Examples 19.9 a and e), but you may write A4 to P4.
- Be sure not to double the third in the chord of resolution (V)—that's the leading tone in the primary key!

EXAMPLE 19.9: Resolutions of vii°/V and vii°⁷/V

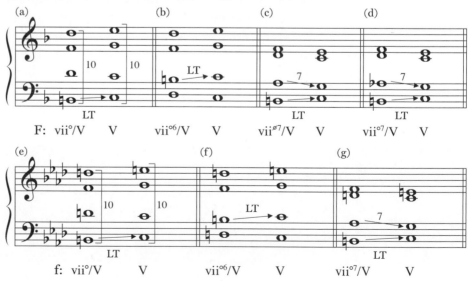

Try it #7

For each of the keys below, build a secondary fully diminished seventh chord by imagining first the V chord as a key area, and then finding the seventh chord built on its leading tone.

KEY	DOMINANT KEY AREA	vii°7/V CHORD
E♭ Major	B♭ Major	A♮-C-E♭-G♭
A minor		
E Major		
F Major		
G minor		

Secondary-Function Chords in Dominant Expansions

In Chapter 16, we learned about progressions that prolong the tonic with V chords: I–V–I progressions embedded within a larger basic phrase, and passing or neighboring harmonies (like passing V$^6_4$ chords). You can use those same progressions with secondary dominant or leading-tone chords to expand V. Write these new progressions exactly like those in Chapter 16, but replace the prolonged I chords with V, and replace the embellishing V$^{(7)}$ or vii°$^{(7)}$ chords with secondary dominants, V$^{(7)}$/V or vii°$^{(7)}$/V.

Example 19.10 shows a dominant expansion from Mozart's Rondo in E♭ Major for Horn and Orchestra, K. 371. The excerpt begins with a strong E♭-Major tonic arpeggiation, followed by the dominant. In measure 90, with the introduction of ♯4 (A♮), V^7/V chords begin to alternate with V chords, and this dominant expansion continues until measure 97. At that point, the dominant harmony becomes V^7 and is arpeggiated until its eventual resolution to tonic in measure 101, where the rondo's first theme is restated. (Note that this passage is scored for horn in E♭.)

EXAMPLE 19.10: Mozart, Rondo in E♭ Major for Horn and Orchestra, K. 371, mm. 88–104

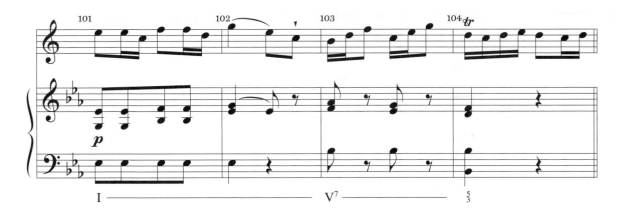

One way to expand V with secondary dominants is to think about the dominant prolongation temporarily in the key of the dominant—think of the "tonicization boxes" described above. For example, to write V^6–V^6_4/V–V in the key of F, think of the familiar progression I^6–V^6_4–I in the key of C, adding a natural to make B♮ instead of B♭ (to match the key signature of C Major), as shown in Example 19.11. To write V–vii°⁶/V–V^6 in the key of D, you could write I–vii°⁶–I^6 in the key of A. Thinking temporarily in the key of A Major will remind you to add the G♯ needed for the ♯$\hat4$ of the secondary leading-tone chord, as shown in Example 19.12.

Of course, these progressions are really an expansion of the dominant, not a change of key. When you analyze dominant expansions, either use the secondary dominant notation (for example, V–vii°⁶/V–V^6), or place a bracket beneath the Roman numerals I–vii°⁶–I^6 and then write a V beneath the bracket. This notation, also illustrated in Examples 19.11 and 19.12, indicates that V is briefly tonicized.

EXAMPLE 19.11: Spelling a V^6–V^6_4/V–V dominant expansion

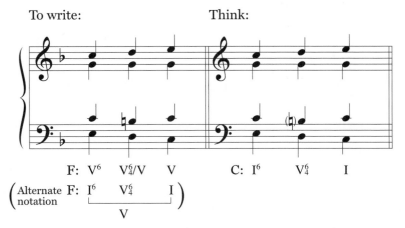

EXAMPLE 19.12: Spelling a V–vii°⁶/V–V⁶ dominant expansion

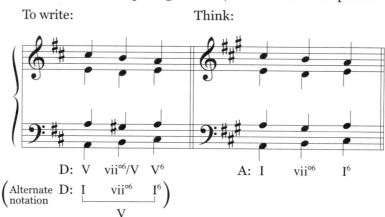

Identifying Secondary Dominant and Leading-Tone Chords to V in Analysis

Secondary dominant and leading-tone chords to V possess distinctive features that will help you identify them quickly when you prepare a harmonic analysis. The first is their location within the phrase: V/V and vii°/V often appear immediately after the predominant area, followed by the dominant or cadential ⁶₄. As we've seen, secondary dominant and leading-tone chords may also be found between two dominants as voice-leading chords expanding the dominant area.

A second clue is the chromatically altered ♯4̂: if you spot this scale degree, check for its resolution to 5̂. Then check the quality and resolution of the chord—a dominant seventh chord or fully diminished seventh chord that is not the diatonic V⁷ or vii°⁷ may be functioning as a secondary dominant or leading-tone chord.

o o o o o o o o o o o o o o o o o o o o o o o o o o o o o o o o o o o o o o o o o o o o o o

New Types of Voice-Leading Chords

Passing ⁴₂ Chords

We learned in Chapter 16 that we can use passing and neighboring ⁶₄ chords to embellish and prolong a structural harmony. Because these expansions occur so frequently in music literature, musicians have named and taught them explicitly as such. But ⁶₄ chords are not the only chords that can fulfill these voice-leading functions. For example, one common chord succession is I–I♯⁴₂–IV⁶ (or, less commonly, vi), shown in Example 19.13. The passing $^4_2$ is created when a passing tone fills in between $\hat{1}$ and $\hat{6}$ in the bass as the chords move from I to IV^6. Some analysts label the passing chord I$^4_2$, especially if it lasts as long as the chords surrounding it. Alternatively, we could simply label the bass note as passing, without a new Roman numeral, to show the voice-leading function of this chord as a tonic expansion.

EXAMPLE 19.13: The passing $^4_2$ chord

Neighboring $^4_2$ Chords

The neighboring $^4_2$ chord can expand the tonic: I–ii$^4_2$–I. Although other diatonic chords may also be decorated with a neighboring $^4_2$ chord, the embellishment of the tonic harmony is most common. This tonic expansion is perhaps best understood as neighbor tones in all three upper parts above a pedal point (see Example 19.14); we could thus call the ii$^4_2$ a "pedal $^4_2$" chord. The individual root progressions shown by Roman numerals, like I–ii–I, do not make much sense; the placement of the ii chord becomes clear only when we consider the three chords as a group. The fact that the $^4_2$ does not resolve its seventh properly (downward by step) is another clue to the neighboring function of this chord.

EXAMPLE 19.14: The neighboring $^4_2$ chord

In the I–ii$^4_2$–I tonic expansion, the ii chord may be chromatically altered with ♯$\hat{4}$, as in the Schubert example shown in Example 19.15 (mm. 88, 90). This poignant dissonance adds considerably to the musical effect. The excerpt shows one chromatically altered ii$^4_2$ in the short piano interlude between the end of one phrase and the beginning of the next (mm. 87–89a) and another accompanying the words "Schreib' im Vorübergehen" (where the character describes tacking a farewell note to his lover's door). This chromatically inflected chord includes the same pitches as the V^7/V we have studied in this chapter, yet its voice-leading does not imply a secondary dominant function but instead merely neighbors the tonic harmony.

EXAMPLE 19.15: Schubert, "Gute Nacht" ("Good Night"), from *Winterreise*, mm. 87b–93a

Translation: On my way out, I will write on your door: good night.

Other $\frac{4}{2}$ Chords

1.17 Listen to Bach's C-Major Prelude while looking at the score in your anthology. (In Chapter 8, we considered this prelude's outer-voice counterpoint.) While listening, you may have noticed that the piece is not divided into clear-cut phrases: definitive cadences are few, and there are no breaks in the rhythmic flow until the

WF3 final cadence at the end. This work is a Baroque **figuration prelude**: it is based on a chord progression that is decorated throughout by a consistent figuration pattern of chord arpeggiation.

The prelude has a definite sense of forward motion created by the harmonic choices and dissonant intervals above the bass. There is one such dissonance in
1.18 measures 5–9 of Example 19.16. Provide a Roman numeral analysis for this passage (observing the secondary dominant to V in $\frac{4}{3}$ position that resolves correctly to V^6). How shall we analyze the $\frac{4}{2}$ chord in measure 8? This chord really derives from voice-leading, from the descending stepwise motion in the bass—we could therefore call it a voice-leading $\frac{4}{2}$ (or linear $\frac{4}{2}$). Another interpretation would read this as a 2–3 bass suspension. When you find unexplained dissonances in your analysis, consider whether they may have a contrapuntal or voice-leading explanation.

EXAMPLE 19.16: Bach, Prelude in C Major, mm. 5–9

Other Voice-Leading Chords

In addition to the relatively common chord successions mentioned in this chapter, a wide variety of passing and neighboring chords may be created by combining embellishing tones vertically into voice-leading chords that expand a structural harmony. Since there are too many possible chords of this type for each one to have a specific name, we refer to them as a category by the term **voice-leading chords** (as we found in the Bach example). In your reading, you may also see the terms "linear chord," "apparent chord," or "embellishing chord" used to describe these sonorities. There are times when it makes sense simply to label the individual embellishments, instead of considering the "chord" they make—particularly if the duration of the embellishments is less than the prevailing harmonic rhythm, or if the embellishments are metrically unaccented.

Let's now consider one possible voice-leading chord from Chopin's Prelude in C minor, Op. 28, No. 20, given in Example 19.17. The chords on beats 1, 2, and 4 are unambiguous—they are i^{5-6} and v^6 (or alternatively, i–VI^6–v^6; see Chapter 16 for a review of 5–6 motion). But what is the third chord? We can best explain this chord by considering the relationship of each of its pitches to those of the chords on either side. We begin with the bass, which is an octave-doubled chromatic passing tone. The soprano and tenor parts are shared with the chord that follows, and the alto part skips from A♭ (a pitch in the previous chord) to F♯, making a kind of double neighbor around the G to which it resolves on beat 4. Each individual voice makes sense in the context, but if we stack this simultaneity in thirds, we get B-D-F♯-A♭, a very bizarre seventh chord.

EXAMPLE 19.17: Chopin, Prelude in C minor, Op. 28, No. 20, m. 5

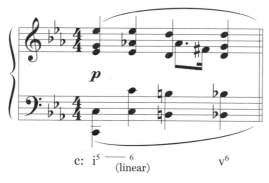

Such progressions work, nevertheless, because of the voice-leading connections between the embellishments and the harmonies they decorate. Harmonic analysis with Roman numerals in these cases may not provide much useful information beyond what is gleaned from analyzing the embellishments. If you like, you may write "linear" (for "voice-leading") in the analysis, and then label the embellishments in the score. One voice-leading interpretation of the Chopin chord is to hear the embellished motion from A♭ to G in the alto as a 7–6 suspension with a chromatic change of bass.

Voice-leading chords like these are particularly common in the chromatic harmony of Romantic-era compositions: the incorporation of chromatically altered scale degrees opens up many additional possibilities for passing tones, neighbor tones, and other embellishments. We will consider some of the more common passing and neighboring chord types later in the book, but there are too many to cover all of them. With persistence and careful consideration of the context, you should be able to determine "What is that? And what is it doing there?" for voice-leading chords you come across in music you are performing and studying.

TERMS YOU SHOULD KNOW

applied chord	neighboring $^6_4$	temporary tonic
chromatic voice exchange	passing $^6_4$	tonicization
cross relation	secondary dominant	voice-leading chord
modulation	secondary leading-tone chord	

QUESTIONS FOR REVIEW

1. Where are secondary dominants used? secondary leading-tone chords?
2. What do we need to remember when spelling secondary dominants? secondary leading-tone chords? Are there special voice-leading guidelines?
3. In what instances are cross relations permitted in common-practice style?
4. In music for your own instrument, find two examples of secondary dominants (in two different pieces or keys). What guidelines can help you scan the score and find them quickly?
5. What are the most common passing and neighboring $^6_4$ progressions?
6. How might we label chords for which no Roman numeral analysis seems quite right?

CHAPTER 20

Phrase Rhythm and Motivic Analysis

Outline of topics covered

Phrase rhythm
- Phrase structure and hypermeter
- Connecting phrases
- Phrase expansion

Baroque melody
- *Fortspinnung*
- Compound melody and step progressions

Motivic analysis
- Transformations in a musical context

Overview

In this chapter, we continue our study of melody, motive, and phrase. We will learn how these elements of musical form interact with metric accent. We will also look at some of the ways in which melodies from different historical eras are distinguished from each other.

Repertoire

Johann Sebastian Bach, Fugue in D♯ minor, from *The Well-Tempered Clavier*, Book I

Bach, Prelude, from Cello Suite No. 2 in D minor

Muzio Clementi, Sonatina in C Major, Op. 36, No. 1, first movement (CD 1, track 74)

Fanny Mendelssohn Hensel, "Nachtwanderer" (CD 2, track 19)

Wolfgang Amadeus Mozart, Piano Sonata in C Major, K. 545, first and second movements (CD 2, tracks 57 and 69)

Robert Schumann, "Widmung"

○ ○

Phrase Rhythm

Phrase Structure and Hypermeter

2.69 Listen to the second movement of Mozart's Piano Sonata in C Major, K. 545, while following the score in your anthology. Divide the first sixteen measures, shown in Example 20.1, into phrases, and identify the cadences and period type. Then think about the following questions, to be discussed below: How long is the first phrase—two, four, or eight measures? And what exactly defines a phrase in this musical context, where melodic units are in clear two-measure groups? How can we, as performers, give the musical line a directed motion without the performance sounding choppy?

EXAMPLE 20.1: Mozart, Piano Sonata in C Major, K. 545, second movement, mm. 1–16k

As we learned in Chapters 12 and 17, a phrase is defined by its harmonic plan: tonal motion (generally away from an initial tonic) followed by a cadence. Shorter musical units—those that complete only a portion of the basic phrase progression and do not conclude with a cadence—we call subphrases. A close look at the harmonic progression in the first four measures of the Mozart example reveals that the first two measures merely prolong tonic by a I–V$^4_3$–I succession. The next two measures continue the prolongation by means of a neighboring $^6_4$ chord. These two-bar units are subphrases. Not until measure 8 do we hear a true cadence: a half cadence that ends this first phrase inconclusively. The next eight measures are a varied repetition of the first eight, concluding with a perfect authentic cadence. This entire **A** section of the movement, measures 1–16, is a parallel period with antecedent-consequent phrases.

As performers, we need to think of measures 1–16 as one large unit with two parts, and not be distracted by trying to shape each two-measure subphrase. There are two general strategies for projecting this interpretation, one harmonic and one metric. The harmonic strategy is to keep in mind the goal of each phrase: the cadence. Envision the cadence as you begin the phrase, move through the harmonies that form the middle of the phrase, then finally reach the harmonic goal.

Some performers compare the harmonic motion of a phrase to the arc of a ball in the game of "Catch"—the phrase beginning is analogous to the throwing of the ball, the internal harmonies represent the arc of the ball's travel, and the final catch is the cadence. The arc of the ball may translate musically into hairpin dynamics, with a slow *crescendo* to the high point of the phrase and a tapering at the cadence. Unlike the catch of a ball, however, we also associate arrival at the cadence with a slight *ritard*, or slowing of tempo.

WF1

At a higher level, try to imagine a hierarchy of cadences, where, for example, a half or deceptive cadence is weaker than an authentic one. When we think of two phrases together as a period, we can minimize the sense of arrival on the half cadence in favor of a stronger arrival on the authentic cadence. In this case, we would need to think of a larger arc for our ball—at the half cadence, the ball is still in midair; only with the authentic cadence does it end its flight.

Our second strategy for performance is a metric one. Until now, we have mostly thought of meter as it applies to individual measures. In pieces like this one, however, we can also think of meter at larger levels. This idea, called "hypermeter," allows us to group whole measures together in a metrical organization with accented and unaccented elements.

KEY CONCEPT

Hypermeter interprets groups of measures as though they were groups of beats within a single measure.

WF2

Just as we hear four beats as strong-weak-strong-weak within a measure, we can also interpret four measures as strong-weak-strong-weak at a higher hypermetric level. While other hypermeters are possible, four-bar hypermeters are by far the most common. Since Classical-era music is often structured from small one-, two-, or four-measure units that combine to make four- or eight-measure phrases, and then combine into eight-, sixteen-, or thirty-two-measure sections, it is not surprising that some of these larger structures replicate the accentual pattern of the smaller ones. This "nesting" of smaller structural units in similarly structured larger ones helps give Classical-era music its feeling of balance and unity.

Most Classical themes fall into four-bar hypermeters, but transitions, sequences, or other less stable musical passages generally do not. In fact, in Classical music, the departure from the four-bar norm is one way listeners can tell that the primary thematic material has ended and a developmental passage has begun. In music of the Baroque era, the four-bar hypermeter is much less common; it occurs most frequently in small binary forms and dance movements. Other Baroque genres employ a technique of "spinning out" that we will consider in more detail below. In music from the Romantic era, composers expanded the four-bar model to create much longer melodies.

We call the interaction of hypermetric structure with phrase structure **phrase rhythm**. When we look at phrase rhythm, we consider how harmonic, melodic, or motivic aspects of the musical phrase fit (or do not fit) within the context of its hypermeter. If you attune your ear to listening for phrase rhythm, you can call on your knowledge of the norms for each historical era to help you decide when a piece was written.

When analyzing the hypermetric structure of a musical phrase, first determine whether the music suggests four-measure groups. Then number the measures 1–4, again 1–4, again 1–4, and so on, as shown in Example 20.2. If some of the phrase endings do not coincide with the groups of four you have labeled, you may have located deviations from the four-measure norm that are of interest!

If you are performing the piece, hypermetric analysis might translate into "thinking in one"—one large beat per measure—which can help give your performance a broad sweep and sense of direction. This strategy is particularly helpful for movements in fast tempi, where performers can get bogged down in all the fast passagework and lose their sense of metrical flow. As you play, try thinking of the strong-weak metric alternation from bar to bar. Don't simply accent the strong bars, however—that would make the performance ungraceful. Rather, think of a gentle ebb and flow of alternating strong and weak, as within a single measure.

EXAMPLE 20.2: Mozart, Piano Sonata in C Major, K. 545, second movement, mm. 1–8 (with hyper-measures marked)

SUMMARY

> There are two aspects to an analysis of phrase rhythm: hypermetric analysis and phrase analysis. Hypermeter refers to the regular metric alternation of strong and weak measures. When we speak of a phrase, we are talking about the harmonies and melodies that conclude with a cadence.

Connecting Phrases

Listen to the second movement of the Mozart sonata again, and mark in your anthology where the **A** section (mm. 1–16) returns. Is it the same as before? *(Try it #1)* After measure 64, we hear music different from the **A** section—a coda of ten measures. A **coda** is a section of music at the end of a movement, generally initiated after a strong cadence in the tonic, that serves to extend the tonic area and bring the work to a close. Codas sometimes consist of energetic cadential flourishes; alternatively, a coda may dissipate energy and bring the work to a quiet close. We will learn more about codas in Chapter 28.

2.70 🎧

Example 20.3 shows the coda, along with several preceding measures. Beginning in measure 61, we hear the final four-measure phrase of the **A** section's repetition, with its conclusive PAC on the downbeat of measure 64. As we know, the **A** section of this movement has set up an expectation of four-bar hypermeasures. Two hypermeasures are marked in the example: measures 61–64 and 65–68. Measure 64 has a PAC that ends the **A** section on the downbeat, but the cadence does not rest long—the music pushes forward, beginning with the second sixteenth note of the downbeat, making a smooth connection to the phrase beginning in measure 65. We

WF3

call this type of phrase connection a "lead-in," or link (the former term dates from the eighteenth century).

KEY CONCEPT

> A **lead-in** is a musical passage that connects the end of one melodic phrase with the beginning of the next. Sometimes the lead-in has an improvisational feel. Its ending generally overlaps with the downbeat of the new phrase.

EXAMPLE 20.3: Mozart, Piano Sonata in C Major, K. 545, second movement, mm. 61–74

In what other ways might phrases be connected? Listen to the opening section of Clementi's Sonatina, Op. 36, No. 1, given in Example 20.4. As you listen, concentrate on the cadence at the end of the first period, in measures 7–8. This cadence includes an ornamented version of the D–C–B–A–G descent that ends the antecedent phrase in measure 4. Where does one period end and the next begin?

EXAMPLE 20.4: Clementi, Sonatina in C Major, Op. 36, No. 1, first movement, mm. 1–15

You may have noticed that the passage changes key; it begins in C Major and ends in G Major. We will learn more about modulating phrases in Chapter 22. What is important for our discussion now is the fact that one phrase ends in measure 8, while another begins simultaneously—indeed, on the same pitches, which serve double duty as the end of one phrase and the beginning of the next. When one phrase ends and another begins at the same time, this is called **elision**, or **overlap**. Some musicians prefer the term "elision" when the end of one phrase and the beginning of the next are articulated by the same pitches, like this Clementi example. Overlap, in contrast, involves more than one musical layer: while one or more voice parts finish the first phrase, one or more other voice parts simultaneously begin the next. Besides linking complete phrases, elisions may link a phrase with a subphrase, or other musical element.

SUMMARY

When phrases are elided, the last note or chord of one phrase simultaneously functions as the first note or chord of the next phrase. When phrases overlap, one or more voices conclude the initial phrase at the same time that other voices begin the next phrase. In a diagram for either of these phrase connections, draw the end of the first phrase arc so that it overlaps with the beginning of the next.

How do phrase elision and overlap interact with hypermeter? In fact, there are two possible ways: one in which the hypermeter is undisturbed and one in which the hypermeasures must be reinterpreted. We will see an illustration of the first type in Example 20.7b; the second type is illustrated by the Clementi example.

In Example 20.4, mark the hypermetric groups by numbering the measures 1–4, 1–4, and so on. As we know, this hypermetric organization implies an alternation of strong-weak-strong-weak measures. But what happens when we reach measure 8? The last measure of one hypermeasure simultaneously functions as the first measure of the next—what was a "weak" measure becomes "strong." This special case—where phrase elision causes a disruption in the regular hypermeter—is sometimes called **metric reinterpretation**. In performance, phrase overlaps with metric reinterpretation are unexpected. Play the reinterpreted measure as a strong new beginning, and enjoy the sense of surprise.

WF4

Phrase Expansion

Even in the context of four-bar hypermeasures, not all phrases extend for exactly four or eight bars. Part of the interest in musical analysis (and performance!) lies in conveying how composers thwart our expectations by deviating from the norm. One way they do this is by extending phrases beyond normal phrase lengths, a technique called **phrase expansion**. Phrases may be expanded at the beginning, middle, or end.

The most common way to expand beyond the four-bar norm is to add material either before or after the phrase. Added material at the beginning is called an **introduction**, or a **prefix**. A short introduction may simply provide an accompanimental pattern before the entry of the primary thematic idea, as shown in Example 20.5, or it may carry some thematic material, as in Example 20.6. Introductions may also be longer than these examples, with several phrases.

2.19

EXAMPLE 20.5: Schumann, "Widmung" ("Dedication"), mm. 1–3

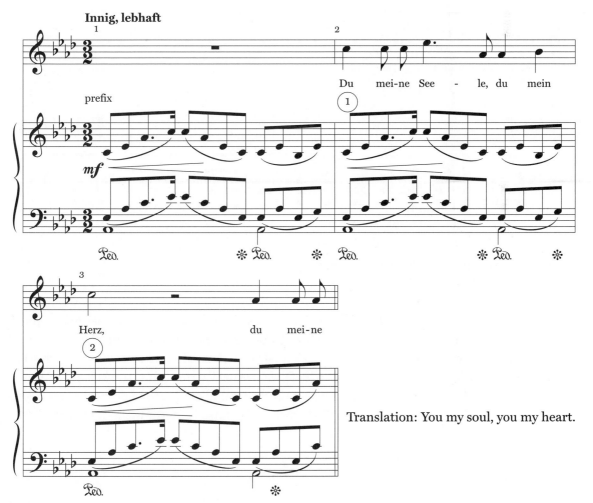

Translation: You my soul, you my heart.

EXAMPLE 20.6: Hensel, "Nachtwanderer," mm. 1–4

Translation: I wander through the quiet night.

2.60

Prefixes are not restricted to the beginning of a movement; they may connect phrases later in a work as well. Example 20.7a gives an excerpt from the first movement of Mozart's Piano Sonata in C Major, K. 545. The example begins with the conclusion of one phrase, on a half cadence in C Major (mm. 11–12), and continues with the beginning of the next, in G Major. While the second phrase proper begins in measure 14, a short prefix in measure 13 introduces the theme and confirms the new key.

EXAMPLE 20.7: Mozart, Piano Sonata in C Major, K. 545, first movement

(a) Mm. 11–17

Expansions at the end of a phrase are known as **suffixes**, or **cadential extensions**. These often begin with an elision. Look back at Example 20.3 for a typical example. Beginning in measure 65 (after a lead-in in m. 64), Mozart introduces a four-measure phrase, which is repeated with alterations in measures 69–72 (following a lead-in in m. 68). The second time, however, the ending of the phrase is elided with a suffix that begins in measure 72 and lasts for three measures. In this case, the elision also involves metric reinterpretation: measure 72 is reinterpreted from a weak position to a strong one. Try marking each alternate measure strong or weak in the example to confirm that this is so.

2.67   Listen to the conclusion of Mozart's first movement (shown in Example 20.7b), which is similar in construction. In this case, though, the phrase spills over beyond the four-bar norm, with an elision in measure 71. This five-measure phrase is an example of phrase expansion. Here, the expansion is accomplished by drawing out the cadential dominant for an entire measure (70) to lengthen the phrase internally (that is, not at the beginning or end). Such **internal expansions** result most frequently from immediate repetitions of material or a prolongation of one or more harmonies, but they may also be achieved by inserting new material within the phrase. Look for internal expansion when a phrase extends beyond the expected phrase length but has no prefix or suffix. The elision at the end of this five-measure phrase in measure 71 initiates a codetta (short coda) that brings the movement to a rousing close.

(b) Mm. 67–73

Baroque Melody

On your own instrument or on a keyboard, play through the beginning of the Prelude from Bach's Cello Suite No. 2, given in Example 20.8. Identify any important motives, determine how many phrases there are, and mark where these phrases begin and end.

EXAMPLE 20.8: Bach, Prelude, from Cello Suite No. 2 in D minor, mm. 1–13a

As you may have noticed, this melody does not conform to the principles of phrase and period structure that we considered earlier in this chapter. In fact, most Baroque melodies, other than those of dance movements, do not feature the four-measure phrases, antecedent-consequent pairs, and periodic structures we have examined so far. Much more common to the Baroque style is a melody that continuously "spins out" motives introduced in the first measures. This technique—which we call by its German name, ***Fortspinnung***—is found in Baroque preludes, fantasias, and fugues, as well as in choral works and larger instrumental forms.

Chorales often have clear phrases, but the phrases may be two, three, or five measures long rather than four, and typically do not pair with other phrases to form periods. Only if you look at movements derived from certain dance forms, like the sarabande or minuet, will you find regular, four-measure phrases and periodic structure in Baroque pieces.

Fortspinnung

In the Bach Cello Suite movement, the opening motive in measure 1—we'll call it **x**—expresses an ascending eighth-note D-minor triad. There are few other recurring motives, except perhaps a rhythmic motive, **y**—a long note (either a quarter tied across the beat or a dotted eighth) followed by descending sixteenths. The task of identifying phrases in solo music like this is challenging, in part because we must infer the harmonic structure from the melody. In addition, we cannot rely on pitches of longer duration or rests to identify phrase endings, since the rhythmic structure of this passage is mostly continuous sixteenth notes. Cadences often "rest" for only a sixteenth note—the end of one phrase is connected to the next through an elision—keeping the motion constant. Phrase elision is a common feature of Baroque melodies. In the Bach example, the cadence that ends the excerpt in measure 13 elides with the beginning of the next phrase. The **x** motive repeated here helps make the connection.

Where, then, are the cadences that define the phrases in this excerpt? Certainly there is a cadence at measure 13, but in F Major: the relative major. Are there any cadences in the tonic key? Perhaps you heard an imperfect authentic cadence from measure 3 to 4, where the implied harmony is V$_3^4$–i^6. If we judge phrases by the cadences, we find a four-measure phrase followed by a nine-measure phrase. Taking a little time at the downbeat of measure 4 will emphasize this intermediate arrival. The remainder of measure 4 serves as an anacrusis to the phrase that follows.

The nine-measure phrase is characterized by a falling-fifth sequence (see Chapter 18 for a review). The sequence pattern is two measures long, and features motive **y** in alternate measures (mm. 5, 7, 9). The sequence leads to the change of key to the relative major, F Major. Unequal phrase lengths are typical. If we were to look ahead in the score to the next cadence, we would find a twelve-measure phrase, also featuring sequential motion, that cadences in yet another key: A minor.

KEY CONCEPT _____

Continuous motion, unequal phrase lengths, melodic or harmonic sequences, change of key, and elided phrases are all characteristics of *Fortspinnung* passages. When you analyze such passages, focus on identifying cadential goals and sequence types. Don't expect balanced phrase lengths.

Fortspinnung passages can be quite beautiful; part of their excitement resides in their unpredictable harmonic language and their development of motivic material. In compositions after the Baroque era, *Fortspinnung* phrase structure does not disappear. Instead, its dramatic unpredictability and ability to connect key areas are found in the transition and development sections of sonata forms, and in improvisatory compositions such as fantasias.

Compound Melody and Step Progressions

In Baroque melodies like the passage in Example 20.9, also from the Bach Cello Suite Prelude, an instrument that plays one pitch at a time may create the effect of several melodic strands or even a four-part harmonic progression. We have seen this technique in previous chapters—for example, in an accompaniment's arpeggiated harmonies or in an Alberti bass pattern.

KEY CONCEPT

When two or more musical lines are expressed within a single melody, this technique is called **compound melody**.

The underlying melodic lines in a compound melody may be simple and obvious, as in an arpeggiated accompaniment, or very complex. Bach's solo violin and cello suites feature complex and artful compound melodies. Play through Example 20.9 on your instrument or a keyboard, noting the analytical marks.

EXAMPLE 20.9: Bach, Prelude, from Cello Suite No. 2 in D minor, mm. 40–48

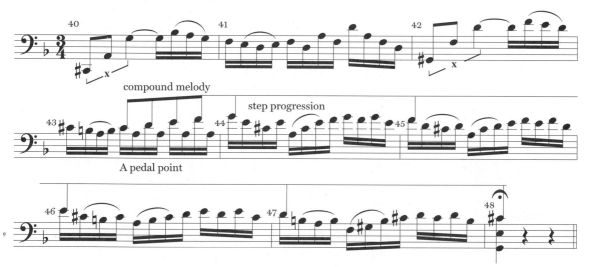

Most striking at the beginning of Example 20.9 is the development of motive **x**. Here, the initial span of a perfect fifth (D3–F3–A3) is transformed to a diminished twelfth (C♯2–A2–G3), while retaining the contour and rhythm of the original. One clear example of compound melody begins in measures 43–44, where the cello's repeated A3 (the dominant) becomes a "lower-voice" pedal point on the sixteenth-note offbeats, while the "upper voice" climbs by step from C♯4 to G4. The two voices are clearly audible, an effect created by leaping between two registers.

Another technique for writing compound melody is to connect nonadjacent pitches by stepwise motion, as in measures 44 and following: the first pitch of each measure creates a stepwise line: G4, F4, E4, D4, C♯4. This technique is sometimes called a **step progression** and can be marked on an analytical or performance

WF5

score by stems and beams as shown in the example. The entire passage between measures 43 and 48 prolongs the dominant harmony—notice how beat 2 of measures 44–46 touches on a lower-voice A3. Try playing the whole passage while singing an A pedal point. Cellists who can simultaneously convey the dominant prolongation and the different voices of the compound melody will create an exciting approach to the dominant ⁶₄ in measure 48, which leads to the closing section.

○ ○

Motivic Analysis

1.74

When we analyze musical phrases, there are many compositional aspects on which we can focus. We have looked at phrase structure and hypermeter; we turn now to an examination of motives. Listen once again to the opening of the Clementi sonatina, this time focusing on its motivic structure (Example 20.10).

EXAMPLE 20.10: Clementi, Sonatina in C Major, Op. 36, No. 1, first movement, mm. 1–11

The first period of the sonatina (mm. 1–8) is characterized by three motives: the arpeggiated-triad motive (mm. 1–2), the descending-scale motive (mm. 3–4), and the descending-third motive (m. 7). If we turn our attention to the phrase that begins in measure 8, we hear an ascending scale—surely derived from the descending-scale motive from measures 3–4. This type of transformation is called an **inversion**.

KEY CONCEPT

When you **invert** a motive, keep its succession of generic intervals the same, but reverse each one in direction—for example, an ascending third becomes a descending third, and a descending fifth becomes an ascending fifth.

This transformation has the effect of turning the melody upside down, like a reflection in a mirror. True mirror inversions retain all of the exact intervals, but reverse their direction. In tonal music, we invert generic intervals rather than exact intervals so that the inversion will stay diatonic within the key. This practice is sometimes called **tonal inversion**.

Sometimes motives are treated to rhythmic transformations that either lengthen or shorten them. Let's trace the motives in the sonatina's third period, given in Example 20.11. Identify any motives in this passage that are transformations of motives in measures 1–11. *(Try it #2)*

1.76

EXAMPLE 20.11: Clementi, Sonatina in C Major, Op. 36, No. 1, first movement, mm. 16–23a

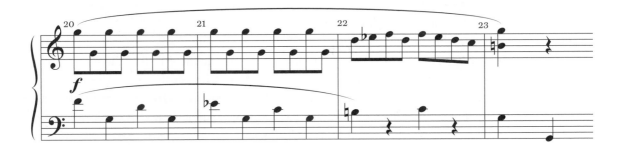

What is the motivic source of measure 18? It is a transposition of the descending-third motive we first heard in measure 7, but each of the note durations has been doubled: from eighth notes to quarter notes. This type of transformation is known as **augmentation**. What is the source of the right-hand octaves in measures 20–21? They are derived from the octave leaps in measures 9 and 11, now inverted, but each of these durations has been halved: from quarter notes to eighth notes. We call this kind of transformation **diminution**.

KEY CONCEPT

When you transform motives by augmentation or diminution, change each note duration proportionately to the original. For example, when you write an augmentation, exactly double or quadruple each duration. When you write a diminution, halve or quarter each duration. This will make the transformation easier to hear.

Another way to lengthen or shorten a motive is to extend, truncate, or fragment it. Consider the scale motive in Example 20.10. When first heard in measure 3, it is five notes long, but when it reappears (inverted) in measures 8 and 10, it is eight notes long. Clementi **extends** the motive in this passage, as well as inverting it. Look again at the octave-leap motive in measures 9 and 11. In its original context, it includes repeated notes: A4–A5–A5–A5 in measure 9 and C4–C5–C5–C5 in measure 10. When Clementi brings it back in measures 20–21, shown in Example 20.11, the repeated pitches at the end have been cut off, and only the octave leap remains—the motive has been **truncated**. The octave-leap motive is repeated, however, to last two measures instead of one. Finally, the falling-third motive in measures 6–7 (Example 20.10) includes five pairs of thirds; in measure 18 (Example 20.11), there are only two pairs of thirds—a small section of the original motive. The motive has been **fragmented** as well as augmented.

KEY CONCEPT

To write a motivic extension, repeat elements of the motive to make it longer. To truncate a motive, cut off the end to make it shorter. To fragment a motive, use only a small (but recognizable) piece of the original. (The term "fragmented" is usually employed instead of "truncated" when material has been removed from the beginning.)

Transformations in a Musical Context

Motivic transformation is an important element in many types of compositions from the Baroque and Classical eras, as well as more recent works. Among the Baroque masters of motivic development was J. S. Bach. We will look at several passages from his D♯-minor Fugue from *The Well-Tempered Clavier* (Book I) to identify such concepts as contour motives, transposition, inversion, and augmentation.

In fugal compositions, the theme—called the "subject"—can serve as the musical source for most of the melodic ideas in the entire piece. First play through Bach's subject, shown in Example 20.12a, then think about how this melody is divided into motives and how it is transformed when it is repeated in measure 3. Mark the motives in the example.

EXAMPLE 20.12: Bach, Fugue in D♯ minor, from *The Well-Tempered Clavier*, Book I

(a) Mm. 1–6a

The most memorable of the subject's motives is the ascending-fifth motive with which it begins. (This compact subject also includes the motive's inversion in m. 2.) Bach also employs a striking rhythmic motive: a quarter note tied across the beat into a group of stepwise descending eighths. This motive is stated in measure 1 (notated with a dot instead of a tie) and again, crossing the bar line, from measure 2 to 3. We'll call this the "cascade" motive, since the eighth notes cascade down in stepwise motion after the rhythmic impetus of the tie.

When the subject enters in imitation in measure 3, Bach transposes it, but he also alters the first and second intervals. This change makes the opening ascending-fifth motive a contour motive, since its distinctive interval changes in size.

Look now at the passage beginning in measure 27 (Example 20.12b).

(b) Mm. 27–34a

cascade motive

Here we see the subject appearing in the soprano and alto voices, transposed and in imitation as marked in the example. But what is happening in the left hand? Bach has truncated the cascade motive, separating the descending stepwise eighths from the tied-over quarter note of the original motive. We can recognize these eighths as related to the cascade motive because, in measures 27–28, they always begin their descent on the second eighth note of the beat, as shown. This rhythmic setting helps us hear the connection. Most important in this example is the reappearance of the subject in the top voice in measure 30—an inversion of the entire melody, with two interval changes (the opening fifth is exchanged for a fourth, and the last fourth for a fifth). The cascade motive also appears in this measure, in both its original form (left hand) and in inversion (right hand).

Now compare this passage with Example 20.12c. What further transformation does the subject undergo?

(c) Mm. 62–67a

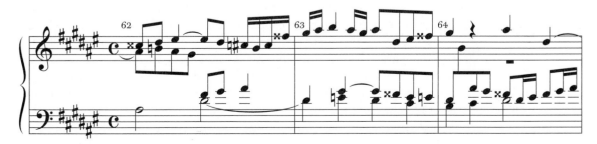

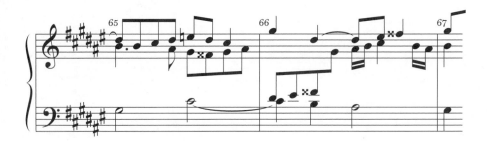

Compare the lowest voice in Example 20.12c with the highest. With great compositional skill, Bach combines an augmentation of the original subject in the bass (beginning in measure 62) with a statement of its inversion (beginning in measure 64), in the original rhythmic setting, in the soprano!

When studying fugues and other types of Baroque counterpoint, look for transformations of the entire subject (transposed, inverted, in augmentation, in diminution) and different types of motivic manipulations. The motivic references often become more complex or hidden as a fugue progresses. While this makes hearing the motivic connections a challenge to the listener, it also makes discovering them a musical joy.

TERMS YOU SHOULD KNOW

augmentation	*Fortspinnung*	phrase rhythm
cadential extension	fragmentation	rhythmic motive
coda	hypermeter	step progression
compound melody	inversion	subphrase
contour motive	lead-in	tonal inversion
diminution	link	truncate
elision	metric reinterpretation	
extension	overlap	

QUESTIONS FOR REVIEW

1. What type of information might we gain from phrase analysis? How might this information impact our performance interpretations?
2. How do Baroque *Fortspinnung* melodies differ from Classical melodies? What types of Baroque pieces contain melodies that are more like Classical melodies?
3. In what ways might a motive be transformed?
4. In music for your own instrument, find an example of (a) four-measure hypermeter, (b) phrase elision, (c) a *Fortspinnung* melody, (d) motivic transformations of your choice.
5. In performance, how might you articulate an elided phrase that is combined with metric reinterpretation?

PART IV

Further Expansion of the Harmonic Vocabulary

CHAPTER 21

Tonicizing Scale Degrees Other Than V

Outline of topics covered

Secondary-function chords within the basic phrase

- Which diatonic chords may be tonicized?
- Identifying secondary dominant and leading-tone chords

Secondary-function chords in musical contexts

- Tonicizing harmonies within a phrase
- Providing a temporary harmonic diversion
- Creating forward momentum
- Evading an expected resolution
- Text painting

Writing secondary dominant and leading-tone chords

- Spelling secondary dominant and leading-tone chords
- Resolving secondary dominant and leading-tone chords

  Embellished resolutions

  Irregular resolutions

Overview

In this chapter, we expand our understanding of secondary dominants and secondary leading-tone chords to include those tonicizing harmonies other than V. We also consider how these chords fit within the basic phrase model and how we may interpret them in performance.

Repertoire

Johann Sebastian Bach, Prelude in C Major, from *The Well-Tempered Clavier*, Book I (CD 1, track 17)

Bach, "Es ist gewisslich an der Zeit" (Chorale No. 260)

Ludwig van Beethoven, Piano Sonata in C minor, Op. 13 (*Pathétique*), second movement (CD 1, track 41)

Fanny Mendelssohn Hensel, "Neue Liebe, neues Leben" (CD 2, track 22)

Scott Joplin, "Solace" (CD 2, track 33)

Alan Menken and Tim Rice, "A Whole New World," from *Aladdin*

Wolfgang Amadeus Mozart, Variations on "Ah, vous dirai-je, Maman" (CD 2, track 86)

John Philip Sousa, "The Stars and Stripes Forever" (CD 3, track 41)

Secondary-Function Chords Within the Basic Phrase

In Chapter 19, we studied ways to use $V^{(7)}/V$ and $vii^{o(7)}/V$ to intensify the dominant. We called the resulting chords secondary dominants and secondary leading-tone chords; together, they are sometimes called applied chords (because they "apply" a dominant-function chord to a harmony other than tonic). In this chapter, we will consider their use in different positions within the basic phrase, when they tonicize harmonies other than V. Although our Roman numeral analyses will distinguish between secondary dominants and secondary leading-tone chords, remember that they serve the same purpose: to intensify the chords to which they resolve.

3.41 🎧
3.42 🎧

Begin by listening to Sousa's "The Stars and Stripes Forever," while following the score in your anthology. After listening, examine the harmonies in measures 5–8, which are reproduced in Example 21.1. Play through this short excerpt, or sing through the soprano and alto lines, while thinking about the function of each chromatic tone. Are the chromatic pitches merely embellishing tones, or do they change any chord qualities?

EXAMPLE 21.1: Sousa, "The Stars and Stripes Forever," mm. 5–8

Vertical:

Contextual:

You probably identified the E♮5 in measure 7 as a chromatic neighbor tone, which has no effect on chord quality or function. Likewise, you may have heard the B♮4 in the alto voice of measure 5 as a chromatic passing tone, but this inflection of B♭ to B♮ also changes the chord quality: it creates a Mm7 (dominant seventh), rather than the diatonic mm7. As we know from our study of V^7/V, dominant sevenths built on scale degrees other than $\hat{5}$ usually signal a secondary dominant function. Here the B♮ acts as a temporary leading tone to C ($\hat{6}$), and the harmony (G–B♮–D–F) functions as V^4_3/vi. Write a complete harmonic analysis of this passage below the example, using Roman numerals and figures. Provide a contextual analysis beneath, to show how the secondary dominants function within the basic phrase model. *(Try it #1)*

The secondary dominants in the Sousa example elaborate the basic progression I–vi–ii–V without changing the harmonic direction of the phrase: the V$^4_3$/vi in measure 5 provides a temporary tonicization of vi within the tonic area, and the V$^4_3$/V strengthens the half cadence by prolonging the dominant area in measures 7–8. The A♮3 in measure 7 serves as temporary leading tone to B♭ ($\hat{5}$); its voice-leading is like a chromatic lower neighbor tone to the repeated B♭3s in the tenor voice. The appearance of V$^4_2$ at the end of measure 8 prevents V from sounding too strong—confirming that V has been tonicized only temporarily. Both secondary dominants in this passage appear in second inversion, which allows a smooth descending bass line and stepwise connections in most voice parts. Stepwise voice-leading is typical of chromatic chords and, in particular, of inverted secondary dominants.

In the dominant area of the Sousa phrase, the V$^4_3$/V appears between two V chords, prolonging that harmony. We can use this technique to prolong other harmonies as well. Play through Example 21.2, the third phrase of Bach's "Es ist gewisslich an der Zeit" ("Indeed the Time Is Here"), or sing it with your class. Again, write a vertical analysis of each chord beneath the example, with Roman numerals and figured bass, then provide a contextual analysis underneath that shows how these chords function within the basic phrase model. *(Try it #2)*

EXAMPLE 21.2: Bach, "Es ist gewisslich an der Zeit," mm. 4b–6a

Vertical:

Contextual:

A secondary leading-tone chord appears on the last beat of measure 5. We know this is a secondary leading-tone chord because of its F♯, which functions as temporary leading tone to G, and because of its diminished-triad quality. Bach expressively embellishes the chord with a 7–6 suspension. What is the function of this chord within the basic phrase? The submediant harmony (a tonic substitute) is prolonged within the tonic area: vi–vii°⁶/vi–vi. In sum, the tonic area of the phrase moves from I to the prolonged vi and back to I⁶, before moving to the dominant area—a single V chord that ends the phrase with a half cadence.

For performers, this short phrase illustrates an important point: that two chords with identical vertical analyses may require strikingly different contextual analyses. The root-position V chord with which the phrase ends carries considerably more structural weight than the root-position V chord in measure 5, beat 2. The first V appears in the midst of the tonic area and passes between I⁶ and vi; it has very little harmonic function. Play the passage again, and listen to the different effects of the two V chords.

Which Diatonic Chords May Be Tonicized?

The most common role of secondary dominant and leading-tone chords is to highlight individual harmonies within a basic phrase progression. The applied chord intensifies or prolongs the chord it tonicizes, although the overall direction of the phrase remains unchanged.

KEY CONCEPT

Any major or minor triad other than tonic may be tonicized; we cannot tonicize diminished triads. Thus, in major keys, the diatonic triads that may be tonicized are ii, iii, IV, V, and vi. In minor keys, they are III, iv (or IV), V (or v), VI, and VII. The most common tonicizations other than V in major keys are ii, IV, and vi; and in minor keys, they are iv, VI, and III.

Chromatic harmonies may also be embellished by their own applied chords (as we will see in Chapters 25 and 29).

The presence of secondary dominant or leading-tone chords in a passage does not indicate a change of key (modulation), even though chromatically altered pitches derived from another key are used. This is because the music does not necessarily continue in the key of the tonicized chord. Rather, the applied chord creates a temporary sense of dominant-tonic motion in a different key, but that key disappears as soon as the two-chord connection is complete.

Identifying Secondary Dominant and Leading-Tone Chords

If you have memorized the sound of the various dominant-function harmonies moving to tonic, it should be easy to locate a secondary dominant or leading-tone chord by ear. It will simply sound like a dominant-function harmony moving to a temporary I or i. In particular, you will hear half-step voice-leading, as the temporary leading tone moves to its temporary tonic.

KEY CONCEPT

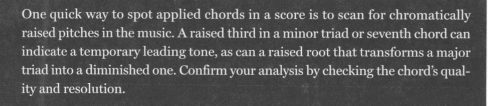

One quick way to spot applied chords in a score is to scan for chromatically raised pitches in the music. A raised third in a minor triad or seventh chord can indicate a temporary leading tone, as can a raised root that transforms a major triad into a diminished one. Confirm your analysis by checking the chord's quality and resolution.

As Example 21.3a shows, $\sharp\hat{1}$ can function as a leading tone to ii in major, $\sharp\hat{2}$ can function as a leading tone to iii in major, and so on. We use this altered tone as the third of a secondary dominant or dominant seventh (21.3b), or as the root of a secondary diminished triad or seventh chord (21.3c). Although the example shows only secondary dominant sevenths and fully diminished sevenths, remember that secondary dominant triads are possible as well, as are secondary leading-tone triads or (less commonly) half-diminished sevenths.

EXAMPLE 21.3: Secondary leading tones

Major:

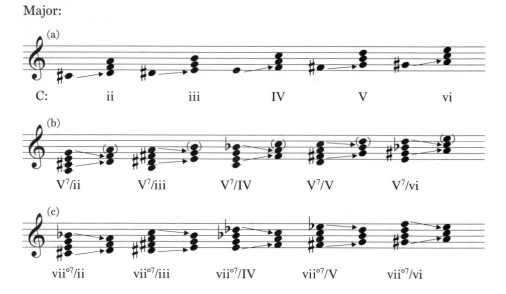

Minor:

In major keys (Examples 21.3a–c), all secondary-function chords except V/IV have at least one chromatically altered pitch, and most secondary leading-tone chords contain two. In fact, some fully diminished seventh chords may include two different types of chromatic alterations: a sharp or natural (usually on the root) and a flat (usually on the seventh). Only one secondary dominant in major keys has a chromatically lowered pitch—that is V^7/IV (Example 21.3b), which is spelled like a I^7 chord with a lowered $\hat{7}$. When you write a secondary dominant to IV, always use V^7/IV. Why? Because otherwise, V/IV–IV (which contains no chromatic alterations) will simply sound like I–IV. If there is no seventh in this progression, then the chord pair *should* be analyzed as I–IV, with no secondary dominant at all.

In minor keys (Examples 21.3d–f), several of the secondary dominants are diatonic in the key: V/III, V^7/III, and V/VI do not require any chromatically altered pitches. Follow the same guidelines for analysis of V/VI–VI as for the progression V/IV–IV. That is, if there is no seventh in the progression V/VI–VI, then the chord pair should be analyzed as III–VI. Likewise, the progression V/III–III should be analyzed as VII–III. We assume that a seventh added to the first chord in the pair (V^7/III) defines it as a secondary dominant.

Occasionally you will see a secondary leading-tone chord that is half-diminished. This chord imitates the type of leading-tone chord found in the diatonic progression $vii^{\varnothing7}$–I, and is only used to tonicize a major-quality triad. Since fully diminished seventh chords are more common, however, we will focus on them in this chapter.

KEY CONCEPT

To identify a secondary dominant or leading-tone chord:

1. Look for a chromatically altered pitch, and then determine whether it changes a chord's quality.
2. *If the altered chord is a major triad or major-minor seventh*, check the following chord in the progression. If the root of the following chord is a *perfect fifth below* (or a *perfect fourth above*) the root of the altered chord, you have identified a secondary dominant.
3. *If the altered chord is a diminished triad or fully diminished seventh* (or, less commonly, a half-diminished seventh), check the following chord in the progression. If the root of the following chord is a *half step above* the root of the altered chord, you have identified a secondary leading-tone chord.
4. Occasionally, an applied chord will not include a chromatically altered pitch. In that case, follow steps 2 and 3 to determine the chord's function.

Secondary-Function Chords in Musical Contexts

How do you know where to use secondary dominant and leading-tone chords? We will consider five possible contexts in which you may either write them or see them in music repertoire. When you prepare a piece for performance, you may want to identify which role each applied chord plays in order to help shape your performance.

Tonicizing Harmonies Within a Phrase

Within the basic phrase, applied chords may embellish any diatonic harmony that has a major or minor quality. Listen to the opening of the second movement of Beethoven's *Pathétique* Sonata while looking at the score in your anthology. Below the excerpt given in Example 21.4, there is a contextual analysis for measures 6–8. How would you explain the "unresolved" A♮ in measure 6? *(Try it #3)*

1.41

1.42

EXAMPLE 21.4: Beethoven, Piano Sonata in C minor, Op. 13 (*Pathétique*), second movement, mm. 5–8

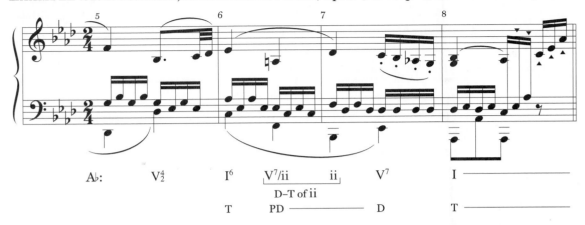

The analysis includes an extra layer to show how V^7/ii–ii functions as a dominant-tonic pair (labeled "D–T") within the supertonic harmonic area. In the contextual analysis beneath, both chords are part of the predominant area of the basic phrase.

Now listen to Variation VII of Mozart's Variations on "Ah, vous dirai-je, Maman" while following the score in your anthology. Mozart uses secondary dominants as harmonic embellishments in many of these variations, but we focus here on measures 172b–176, given in Example 21.5. Start by locating each accidental in these measures, and explain its function. (*Try it #4*)

EXAMPLE 21.5: Mozart, Variations on "Ah, vous dirai-je, Maman," Variation VII, mm. 169–176

Here, the predominant portion of the phrase features a falling-fifth sequence, alternating seventh chords and triads. The diatonic version of the sequence in root position is I–IV^7–vii°–iii^7–vi–ii^7–V–I (a sequence pattern we learned in Chapter

18). Although it is possible that multiple secondary dominants can embellish a sequence, only one of the chords here has been altered: the iii[7] in measure 174 has been converted to a V$^6_5$/vi by changing the chord quality to Mm7.

Providing a Temporary Harmonic Diversion

3.43 🎧

We now return to Sousa's "The Stars and Stripes Forever" to consider another use of applied chords. The second phrase of the strain that began in measure 5 (Example 21.1), shown in Example 21.6, begins by confirming I in E♭ Major with a I^6–V$^4_3$–I progression. Listen to the cadence in measure 12 to determine the role of the chords in measures 10–12. What type of cadence do you hear? *(Try it #5)*

EXAMPLE 21.6: Sousa, "The Stars and Stripes Forever," mm. 9–12

The progression in measures 10–12 is I V$^6_4$/vi | vi | V/vi. But this progression does not establish C minor (vi) as a new key; the only chords that sound like C minor are those we just heard, and the following measures immediately return to an emphasis on E♭ Major. Rather, the secondary dominant V$^4_3$/vi that we heard briefly in measure 5 returns here to add a bit of color and harmonic interest to this strain. But the B♮ that colored measure 5 is intensified here: it appears first as a chromatic passing tone, then as a chromatic neighboring tone, and finally as the melodic goal of the phrase.

In this passage, the secondary dominants do not elaborate a basic phrase progression—rather, they temporarily sidetrack the motion from tonic to dominant. After the digression, the following phrase immediately reestablishes the direction, leading to a third and fourth phrase, each ending on a half cadence on V of E♭ Major. Study the complete score in your anthology to see how this section of the march concludes. Are there any more secondary dominants? *(Try it #6)*

Creating Forward Momentum

2.33 🎧

2.36 🎧

Secondary dominants are a typical feature of Scott Joplin's ragtime piano pieces. Listen to "Solace" while following the score in your anthology. You will hear that the phrases in measures 53–56 and 61–64 are identical except for the final chord in measures 56 and 64. As you can see from comparing these phrases in Example 21.7a, both demonstrate the basic progression I–vi[7]–ii$^6_5$–V[7]–I, if we exclude the final chord under the fermata (m. 56). The contextual analysis for both phrases is T–Ts–PD–D–T (Ts stands for "tonic substitute").

EXAMPLE 21.7: Joplin, "Solace"

(a) Mm. 53–65

The chord at the end of measure 56 is a V^7 in the key of F Major. By its placement at the end of the measure, after the imperfect authentic cadence on the downbeat, it serves as a phrase anacrusis. The anacrusis creates harmonic tension and heightens anticipation, since it is sustained by a fermata before its tonic resolution at the beginning of the next phrase. Joplin then repeats this device in measure 60. In both cases, the V^7 emphasizes the tonic function of the chord that follows.

The last chord in measure 64 is likewise an anacrusis; the chord beginning the next phrase, however, is not tonic, but instead IV^6 (B♭-D-F). The preceding F-A-C-E♭ chord is thus a secondary dominant to IV. In this case, the V^7/IV is in third inversion ($^4_2$) and resolves in a typical fashion down to a first-inversion triad. From our previous study of seventh chords, can you explain why it resolves this way? *(Try it #7)* The resolution of the temporary leading tone (A4) upward, and the seventh of the chord (E♭3) downward, highlights the IV^6 that follows by intensifying motion toward this temporary goal.

A similar pattern is found throughout this rag. Look at the short excerpts given in Examples 21.7b and c. Circle the embellishing tones, then write a Roman numeral analysis in F Major beneath the excerpts. What secondary dominants do you find at the end of measures 72 and 80? Do the tendency tones resolve correctly? *(Try it #8)* In each case, the secondary dominant acts as an anacrusis to push forward toward the temporary tonic at the beginning of the next phrase.

(b) Mm. 72–73   2.37

(c) Mm. 80–81   2.38

How might such an analysis influence your interpretive decisions when performing Joplin's rag? Try harnessing the intensity of the dominant seventh and secondary dominant harmonies found at the end of many four-bar units. Be sure to follow Joplin's performance indications, lengthening the sonorities that are notated with fermatas, and observing the *a tempo* indications that usually follow. Continue *a tempo* after each fermata, even when it is not marked. This will propel each basic phrase unit forward to its cadence, preparing the listener for the next dominant seventh anacrusis. You may also want to experiment with "voicing out" the tendency tones. Try playing each anacrusis in such a way that you really hear the (temporary) leading tone resolving up and the chordal seventh resolving down.

Evading an Expected Resolution

We have already considered ways of evading or weakening a cadence after a strong V or V^7: for example, by using a deceptive cadence or resolving to an inverted tonic (or I^7) (see Chapter 17). Secondary-function chords may also be called on to evade an expected cadence or temporarily redirect a phrase. As an example, listen to Bach's C-Major Prelude. Write a Roman numeral analysis for measures 8–15, given in Example 21.8.

1.17
1.19

EXAMPLE 21.8: Bach, Prelude in C Major, mm. 8–15

In measure 11, there is a strong arrival on a G-Major chord (preceded by its own dominant): we would expect either (1) a continuation in the key of G Major or (2) the next chord to be a tonic. What happens instead? The chord that comes next shares two pitch classes with a tonic resolution—G and E—but it also has a C♯ and B♭! It is a fully diminished seventh chord. When you find a nondiatonic chord with that quality, look carefully at the following chord—does the fully diminished chord resolve as expected (leading tone up, seventh of the chord down)? Does the root of the following chord lie a half step away from the root of the diminished seventh? If so, the diminished seventh is a secondary leading-tone chord.

Here, the fully diminished seventh chord—vii°$_3^4$/ii—does resolve as expected, to a ii^6 chord in C Major. Although the V in measure 11 would not normally progress to the ii of measure 13, the progression Bach has written sounds smooth and logical, while providing a sense of surprise. How does Bach make this unexpected progression work? *(Try it #9)* The same progression appears in measures 14–15, transposed down a step (vii°$_3^4$ to I^6), creating a sequence that leads back to the tonic.

In performance, you need do nothing to bring out the harmonic surprise, but you might try focusing on the voice-leading aspects that make this progression work. In the upper voice, hear the connection between the pitches at the top of each arpeggio—they move in stepwise motion upward from measure 11 to 13: B4, C♯5, D5. The bass line of almost the entire composition to measure 19 is a slow stepwise descent from the initial C4 tonic down to C3. Think of the arrival in measure 19 as a large-scale goal, without getting too bogged down in small details.

Text Painting

In songs and choral works, the musical depiction of images found in the words is called **text painting**. Applied chords sometimes play a major role in this process. Play through the excerpt from Menken and Rice's "A Whole New World," given in Example 21.9. Here, the character Jasmine sings about the "whole new world" she is discovering. We considered the embellishing tones in this passage in Chapter 13, but now we look at the harmonic progression in more detail. Which words seem most important to the meaning of the text? Take a close look at the settings of "never knew" in measures 31–32 and "whole new world" in measure 36. Label the chords in measures 29–37 with Roman numerals and figures beneath the example. *(Try it #10)*

EXAMPLE 21.9: Menken and Rice, "A Whole New World," mm. 28b–37a

The words "never knew" are highlighted by secondary leading-tone and dominant seventh chords to vi, which arrives on "knew," making a deceptive cadence that brings out the foreignness of the world Jasmine is now seeing. The secondary dominant in measure 32 (on "But when I'm") combines with the rhythmic impetus of the quarter-note triplets to push forward harmonically, emphasizing that she's "way up here."

The final text-painting touch in this passage is the setting of "whole new world" in measure 36. The chord on the downbeat of the measure is preceded by a V^7/V, and followed by V^7 (with a 4–3 suspension)—a typical resolution for a V/V. But this first chord in measure 36 temporarily evades the expected dominant. We will learn more about this harmonic choice—a ♭VII chord—in Chapter 24. For now, observe how combining the V^7/V with the move to ♭VII before its resolution musically represents Jasmine's feeling that this is indeed a "whole new world."

Writing Secondary Dominant and Leading-Tone Chords

Spelling Secondary Dominant and Leading-Tone Chords

Now that you've seen and heard what secondary dominant and leading-tone chords can do, it is time to write some of your own.

KEY CONCEPT

To spell a secondary dominant seventh:

1. Begin by writing out the triad it tonicizes. For example, if you want to write a V^7/ii in the key of D Major, first write out the ii chord (E-G-B), leaving a space before it for the V^7/ii (Example 21.10a).
2. Imagine a box around the ii chord and the empty space before it. Pretend that the chords in that box are in the key of ii, or E minor, with one sharp (F♯) in the key signature (Example 21.10b).
3. Ask yourself: What chord is V^7 in E minor? Remember that in minor keys you need to raise scale-degree $\hat{7}$ to create a leading tone and give the dominant harmony its major quality: V^7 in E minor is B-D♯-F♯-A. Write this chord, remembering that the F♯ is already provided in the key signature of D Major, but the D♯ must be added as a chromatic alteration (Example 21.10c).
4. If you want to write a $vii^{\circ 7}/ii$ instead, follow the same procedure but write $vii^{\circ 7}$–i in the tonicized key instead (Examples 21.10d–f).

You may adapt these guidelines for triads, omitting the seventh, or for the vii°⁷ (presuming that the half-diminished leading-tone seventh precedes a major triad).

EXAMPLE 21.10: Procedure for writing secondary dominant and leading-tone chords

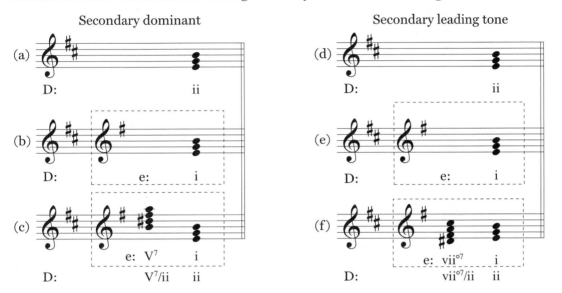

There are several other ways to spell applied chords. You may prefer the following method. First write the tonicized triad, as before (Example 21.11a). Then move up a P5 from the root of the tonicized chord (in this case, ii), and write the note heads for a seventh chord: B–D–F♯–A (Example 21.11b). Be sure to include any accidentals from the key signature: in this case, F♯. Now check the chord's quality—is it a dominant seventh chord (Mm7)? If not, correct the chord quality by altering the pitches with the necessary accidentals (Example 21.11c). In this case, change D to D♯ to get B–D♯–F♯–A.

For a fully diminished vii°⁷ chord, again begin by writing the tonicized triad (Example 21.11d). Then move down a half step from the root of the tonicized chord, and write the note heads for a seventh chord (retaining any accidentals from the key signature): D♯–F♯–A–C♯ (Example 21.11e). Now check the chord's quality—is it a fully diminished seventh chord? If not, correct the chord quality by adding the accidentals required (Example 21.11f). In this case, you would need to change C♯ to C♮. In D Major, vii°⁷/ii is D♯–F♯–A–C♮.

EXAMPLE 21.11: Alternate procedure for writing secondary dominant and leading-tone chords

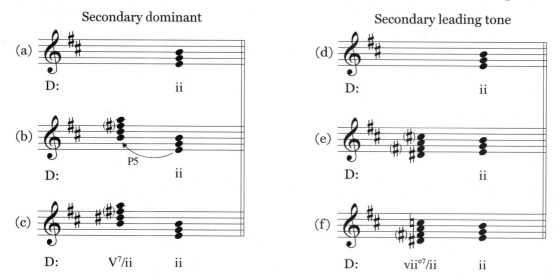

Another Way

Another way to spell secondary dominants quickly is to imagine them as "altered" diatonic chords, following the chart below for major-key secondary dominants. Add whatever accidentals are necessary to create a Mm7 quality from the diatonic triad given.

TO MAKE A...		START WITH...		ALTER QUALITY TO...
V⁷/IV	→	I	→	I⁷
V⁷/V	→	ii	→	II⁷
V⁷/vi	→	iii	→	III⁷
V⁷/ii	→	vi	→	VI⁷
V⁷/iii	→	vii°	→	VII⁷

Try it #11

For each key below, spell first the tonicized chord indicated by the Roman numeral, then the secondary dominant.

KEY	ROMAN NUMERAL	TONICIZED CHORD	SECONDARY DOMINANT
B♭ Major	V⁷/IV	E♭-G-B♭	B♭-D-F-A♭
F♯ minor	vii°⁷/III		
A Major	V⁷/ii		
G Major	vii°⁷/vi		
E♭ Major	V⁷/vi		
C minor	V⁷/V		
D Major	vii°⁷/IV		

Resolving Secondary Dominant and Leading-Tone Chords

As we learned in Chapter 19, secondary dominant and leading-tone chords normally resolve just like their diatonic counterparts: the leading tone of the temporary key moves up, and the chordal seventh resolves down. Secondary dominant and leading-tone chords usually appear with all four chord tones, but if you have a root-position secondary V or V⁷ chord, you may omit the fifth and double the root. Under no circumstances should you double the temporary leading tone or the seventh of the chord!

If the temporary leading tone is approached by a chord that contains the same scale degree in its unaltered (diatonic) form, you also need to conform to the guidelines for cross relations (familiar from Chapter 19), either by keeping the chromatic tone in the same voice as the altered version (for instance, $\hat{1}$–$\sharp\hat{1}$–$\hat{2}$; see Example 21.12b) or by using a chromatic voice exchange (Example 21.12c). When writing these

EXAMPLE 21.12: Avoiding cross relations

D: vi   V⁷/ii   ii   vi   V⁷/ii   ii   vi⁶   V⁷/ii   ii

progressions, aim for smooth voice-leading connections (by step or common tone), and follow the usual procedure of checking for parallel fifths and octaves.

Embellished Resolutions Because secondary dominant and leading-tone chords frequently appear in elaborate, highly chromatic Romantic-period music, you may encounter embellished resolutions of these harmonies. For example, listen to the passage from Hensel's "Neue Liebe, neues Leben" analyzed for you in Example 21.13a. The chords on the first three beats of measure 66 express I^6 in B♭ Major, and the last beat of the measure has D-B♮-A♭-F: vii°$^6_5$/ii. We expect this chord to resolve to a ii chord (C-E♭-G) in measure 67, and it does, but the resolution is delayed by suspensions in the soprano and alto voices and a retardation in the tenor. The ii^6 chord is also embellished by a voice exchange from the "and" of beat 1 to the "and" of beat 2.

2.25 🎧

EXAMPLE 21.13: Hensel, "Neue Liebe, neues Leben"

(a) Mm. 66–68a

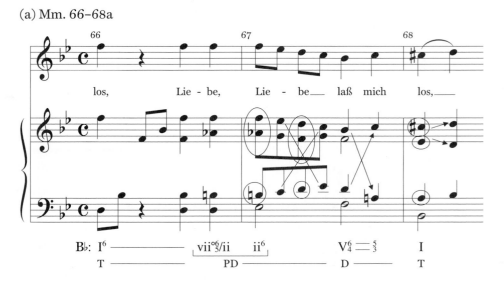

Translation: Love, love let me free.

The voice exchange in the ii^6 chord is followed by a similar exchange in beats 3 and 4 and another delayed resolution into measure 68. What chords are these? Is the voice-leading as you would expect? The chords are V$^{6-5}_{4-3}$ and I, but the ^{6} in the tenor resolves to ^{5} in the soprano, and the ^{4} of the soprano resolves to ^{3} in the tenor. This is thus not technically a voice exchange (where two members of the same chord exchange voices); rather, it is a transferred resolution (see Chapter 12).

The I chord in measure 68 is delayed in the three upper parts by embellishing tones on the downbeat: a retardation in the tenor, a passing tone in the alto, and a chromatic passing tone in the soprano. This accented dissonance comes at a particularly poignant moment in the text, when the singer asks a lover to "let me free!" Performers might want to emphasize this triple dissonance in some way, perhaps by a *tenuto* (slight hesitation) on the downbeat of measure 68.

2.27 🎧   Now consider another excerpt from the same song, shown in Example 21.13b. The vii°$^6_5$/ii in measure 75 also has an elaborated resolution. It resolves to a ii^6 chord as it should, but the tendency tones do not resolve in the correct octave until after a voice exchange in the soprano and tenor parts from beats 3 to 4.

(b) Mm. 75–77

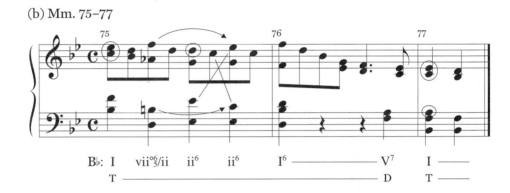

KEY CONCEPT

To recognize embellished resolutions:

1. Listen carefully for the point of resolution (this particularly helps when resolutions are delayed in multiple voices by suspensions, passing tones, or retardations).
2. Know what the expected resolution is, and look ahead a little if you do not find it where you expect it.

Irregular Resolutions   As we have seen, the quality of secondary dominant and secondary leading-tone chords makes their function aurally recognizable and strongly implies a particular resolution. But sometimes composers play tricks on our ears by not resolving these chords exactly as we expect. We call this type of resolution an **irregular resolution**. We will conclude by looking at an example of an irregular resolution in the Mozart Variations.

2.93 🎧   Listen to Variation X while following the score in your anthology. Then write in the Roman numerals and figures for each chord in measures 244b–248, reproduced as Example 21.14, and mark the resolution of all tendency tones. Add a contextual analysis beneath.

EXAMPLE 21.14: Mozart, Variations on "Ah, vous dirai-je, Maman," Variation X, mm. 241–248

Vertical:

Contextual:

The vii°⁷ and vii°⁷/V chords in measures 245 and 246 resolve as expected, to I and V respectively. What is unusual about the others? Why does this progression "work"? *(Try it #12)*

Passages like this one are fairly common in highly chromatic voice-leading. To analyze, carefully determine each chord's quality, then compare the actual resolution in the music with the expected one. With that information, you should be able to explain each chord's resolution. Your Roman numerals will show irregular resolutions automatically. For example, if you write V⁷/IV–ii⁶, it is clear that you expected a IV chord but found a ii⁶ instead.

TERMS YOU SHOULD KNOW

applied chord   secondary leading-tone chord
irregular resolution   temporary tonic
secondary dominant   tonicization

QUESTIONS FOR REVIEW

1. Which diatonic chords may be tonicized? What are the criteria for determining whether a chord may be tonicized by its own dominant or leading-tone chord?

2. What do we need to remember when spelling secondary dominant chords? secondary leading-tone chords? What voice-leading guidelines should we keep in mind when writing these chords?

3. What are some of the ways secondary dominant and leading-tone chords can be used in musical contexts?

4. In music for your own instrument, find two examples of secondary dominants other than V/V or V⁷/V (in two different keys). For each one, examine the context—does it fit within one of the uses of secondary-dominant-function chords we considered in this chapter? How might understanding the purpose of the secondary dominant influence your performance of that passage?

Modulation to Closely Related Keys

Overview

In this chapter, we expand our study of tonicization to include the concept of modulation. We will learn how to change keys by means of chords common to the original and new key. We will also consider a special relationship between keys that helps determine which keys are closely related. Finally, we will learn how to harmonize a melody that changes keys.

Repertoire

Anonymous, Minuet in D minor, from the *Anna Magdalena Bach Notebook* (CD 1, track 1)

Johann Sebastian Bach, Prelude in C Major, from *The Well-Tempered Clavier*, Book I (CD 1, track 17)

Bach, "O Haupt voll Blut und Wunden" (Chorale No. 74) (CD 1, track 7)

Muzio Clementi, Sonatina in C Major, Op. 36, No. 1, first movement (CD 1, track 74)

Wolfgang Amadeus Mozart, Piano Sonata in D Major, K. 284, third movement (CD 2, track 48)

Franz Schubert, "Nur wer die Sehnsucht kennt (Lied der Mignon)"

Common Pivot-Chord Modulations

Most tonal compositions of any length include passages that prolong a harmonic area other than the tonic. Many common-practice forms, such as binary and sonata forms, rely on these harmonic changes to help create contrast between sections (see Chapters 23 and 28). Indeed, composers show their ingenuity and artistry by how and where they move between key areas. Some analysts view these different harmonic areas as large-scale tonicizations of harmonies within a single key, the tonic. This approach emphasizes the overall harmonic coherence of the work.

WF1 Other analysts, however, view structurally significant tonicizations as **modulations**, or changes of key. This approach focuses on how chords function within the local context of a new key and how these new keys relate to the main tonic of the piece. For purposes of this chapter, we will take the latter approach so that we can consider specific ways composers move between harmonic areas.

2.48 Listen to the opening of the third movement of Mozart's Piano Sonata in D Major, K. 284, while examining the score in Example 22.1. In Chapters 15 and 16, we analyzed the basic phrase with which this piece begins (mm. 1–4). Now we look at the phrase that follows (mm. 5–8), to complete this first section. Pay particular attention to the two cadences in measures 4 and 8. How do they differ? *(Try it #1)*

EXAMPLE 22.1: Mozart, Piano Sonata in D Major, K. 284, third movement, mm. 1–8

While both cadences end on an A-Major triad, the second so strongly tonicizes A that we hear it as a PAC in A Major, as a modulation to the key of the dominant. The change is so smooth, you may not hear the shift of harmonic focus until the return to D Major when measures 1–8 are repeated. How does Mozart do this?

2.49 🎧

Look carefully at measures 5–6. Measure 5 begins with a I^6 in D Major—exactly what we would expect after the half cadence in measure 4. The I^6 is followed by vi^6, then in measure 6 a G♯ is introduced. This ♯4 could simply indicate a secondary dominant, V^7/V, except that the G♯ appears twice more in measure 6, and the remainder of the phrase functions according to the basic phrase model in the key of A Major. The key of V (A) is well established by the $I–ii^6–V^{8-7}_{4-3}–I$ progression in measures 7–8.

When a modulation is composed this smoothly, we can often find one or more transitional chords that function diatonically in both keys. The vi^6 (in D Major) on the second half of measure 5 is such a chord: it also functions as ii^6 in A Major, preparing the entrance of the V^7 in A in measure 6 and the subsequent cadence in that key. A chord like this one—which has "full membership" in both keys—is called a **pivot chord**, and this type of modulation is called a **pivot-chord,** or **common-chord, modulation.** It is the most common means of modulation between two keys that are closely related, a concept we will examine later in this chapter.

We notate this type of modulation by writing the key and Roman numerals for the first key in the normal way, then writing the key and Roman numerals for the second key underneath. The pivot chord (or chords) are labeled in both keys, with the two Roman numeral analyses (one for each key) right on top of each other, as shown in Example 22.2.

EXAMPLE 22.2: Mozart, Piano Sonata in D Major, K. 284, third movement, mm. 4b–8

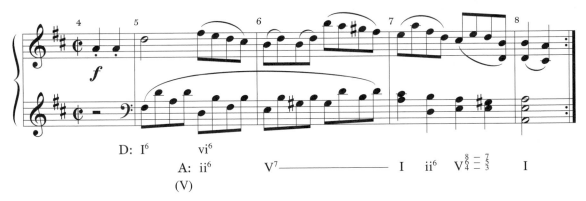

Some analysts draw a box or square bracket around the two Roman numerals for the pivot chord(s) to highlight their dual function. We also indicate the Roman numeral relationship between the primary key of the movement and the new harmonic area by writing a Roman numeral in parentheses beneath the new key label. In Example 22.2, the (V) beneath the A indicates that A Major is the dominant of the composition's overall key, D Major.

Modulation or Tonicization?

In Chapter 21, we learned how to create a temporary sense of tonic (tonicization) with a secondary dominant or leading-tone chord. We generally analyze tonicizations without leaving the primary key (for example, with secondary dominants). If we choose to analyze a passage as a modulation, on the other hand, we look for musical indications like a continuation of the new key following a secondary dominant, or a predominant harmony in the new key. The decision whether to analyze a passage as a tonicization or modulation is not always clear-cut, and different analysts may hear the passage in different ways. When making this decision, use the guidelines in the KEY CONCEPT box below to inform your choice, and be ready to defend it with concrete musical reasons.

KEY CONCEPT

If you analyze a passage as a modulation, you should have found at least one of the following:

- a PD–D–T progression in the new key;
- a firm cadence (usually a PAC or strong IAC) in the new key, preceded by a predominant-function harmony and/or followed by a continuation in the new key;
- an extended progression in the new key (not just V–I or i, or vii°⁷–I or i).

For our purposes, consider a progression a modulation if it meets one of the conditions listed above, but keep in mind that this "establishment of a new key" may only be a temporary emphasis on a harmonic area within the context of the larger harmonic structure. There is some latitude in what we call a key change; what may seem like a modulation on the small scale may be reinterpreted as a tonicization when we consider the entire composition. Further, in some Romantic-era music, you may come across extended progressions (several measures long) that focus on a temporary tonic without a cadence or clear PD–D–T motion. In such a case, ask yourself these questions: How long does the progression last? Does it seem to establish a new key because of its length, even without a cadence? If so, you may label it a modulation.

Modulation from a Major Key to Its Dominant

Let's return now to the Mozart phrase in Example 22.2. Does it fulfill one or more of our criteria, so that we might analyze it as a modulation? It does, because the progression in the new key, ii^6–V^7–I–ii^6–V$^{8-7}_{4-3}$–I, has two predominants preceding the cadential dominant-tonic (one of which also serves as the pivot). The pivot Mozart uses—vi in the primary key = ii in the key of the dominant—is one of the most common means of modulating from a tonic key to its dominant.

Pivot Chords Between Tonic and Dominant Keys in Major   Mozart's pivot chord is not the only possibility for moving between a tonic key and its dominant. Compare the chords in Figure 22.1 to find other pivot pairs.

FIGURE 22.1: Comparison of chords in D Major and A Major

D Major:	I	ii	iii	IV	V	vi	vii°
	D	e	f♯	G	A	b	c♯°
	D	E	f♯	g♯°	A	b	c♯
A Major:	IV	V	vi	vii°	I	ii	iii

All possible pivot chords are shown within the boxes. Pivot chords must have the same quality in both keys; thus, we cannot use ii in D Major as a pivot, since the chord built on E has a minor quality in the key of D Major but a major quality in the key of A Major. The pivot vi = ii makes a smooth progression because the triad has a predominant function in both keys, and both vi and ii are common triads in major-key progressions. The pivot I = IV is less effective because the chord tends to continue to sound like I in the tonic key. It is not easy to convince the ear that the tonic triad no longer has a tonic function, but instead is functioning as IV in the new key. For this reason, I^6 is not marked as a pivot chord (IV^6) in Example 22.2; it is unlikely that you heard the first chord in measure 5 functioning as IV^6 in A Major.

Although the chords V = I are boxed in Figure 22.1 as a possible pivot, this pairing is rarely found. The V chord tends to sound like V in the original key unless it is preceded by other chords in the second key—in which case *they* are the pivot chords. The other pivot-chord pair, iii = vi, is also less common, even though both chords can possess either predominant- or tonic-extension functions. Why? Simply because the mediant triad, iii, does not frequently appear in common-practice style. When you see a iii = vi pivot, you will often find that it is combined with other pivot chords into a pivot area several chords in length. Finally, chords that are not shared by the two keys also play an important role in establishing a modulation. Their appearance indicates that the key has changed from the initial key to the goal of the modulation.

When performing a phrase that contains a pivot-chord modulation, you might want to aid in the "deception" of the pivot chord's dual nature by playing or singing it as though nothing unusual has happened. Then once the new key has emerged, aim toward the cadence in the new key, attending to the resolution of the new leading tone, with expressive timing, to emphasize this intermediate tonal goal.

Modulation from a Minor Key to Its Relative Major

1.1 🎧
WF2

Listen now to the Minuet in D minor from the *Anna Magdalena Bach Notebook*, while looking at the score in your anthology. Then examine measures 1–8, shown in Example 22.3a (the staff below, part b, makes clear the implied harmonies in this two-voice texture). What type of cadence is found in measure 4? in measure 8? *(Try it #2)* By measure 8, the progression indicates a new harmonic area—a modulation to F Major, the relative major to D minor. What pivot chords would work for modulations between relative keys?

EXAMPLE 22.3: Anonymous, Minuet in D minor, from the *Anna Magdalena Bach Notebook*

(a) Mm. 1–8

(b) Implied harmonies in mm. 1–8

Pivot Chords Between Tonic and Mediant Keys in Minor Compare the chords in common between A minor and its relative major (or mediant), C Major, given in Figure 22.2. The figure shows all typical chords in A minor, including most of those built from the natural and harmonic minor versions of the scale. Many of them, as we can see, are potential pivots.

FIGURE 22.2: Comparison of chords in A minor and C Major

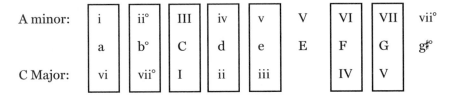

A minor:	i	ii°	III	iv	v	V	VI	VII	vii°
	a	b°	C	d	e	E	F	G	g#°
C Major:	vi	vii°	I	ii	iii		IV	V	

How can this chart help us plan a pivot-chord modulation? There are many common chords between the two keys; the most frequently used are i = vi, III = I, iv = ii, and VI = IV. As we observed when we modulated from I to V in a major key, pivot chords are most effective when they fall into the predominant-function area of the phrase; this remains true for modulation from minor keys to the relative major (for example, iv = ii). When we move from minor to relative major, though, chords that are tonic in one key and predominant in the other can also serve as pivot chords, particularly if paired with another predominant to form a pivot area.

The dominant-function chords that help establish the tonic in the minor key, V and vii°, are distinctive because of their altered leading tone—they do not appear as diatonic harmonies in C Major and therefore cannot function as pivot chords. However, the analogous dominant-function chords in the major key, V and vii°, *are* diatonic chords in the relative minor (VII and ii°) and can occasionally serve as pivots.

Now return to measures 5–7 of the Minuet, and write in the harmonic analysis as you proceed through the following discussion. When the phrase begins, the first chord is i in D minor, the tonic key, followed by v⁶ (decorated by an incomplete upper neighbor)—a typical use of minor v at the beginning of a phrase, where a dominant function is not desired. Although these chords function as vi and iii⁶ in F Major, it is unlikely that we would hear the first chord (the tonic triad in D minor) as vi in F Major. We choose instead v⁶ = iii⁶ as our pivot chord. Though the iii⁶ chord is not commonly used, here it is approached by "vi," one of the standard progressions that feature iii. From measure 6 to the end of the phrase, the harmonies are clearly in F Major: I⁶–V⁶₅–I–I⁶–V–I.

But what do we call the last chord in measure 5? If the D5 is part of the chord, it is VI in D minor and IV in F Major; if the C5 is the chord tone (decorated by an incomplete upper neighbor), the chord is V⁴₂ in F Major, which resolves as expected to a I⁶ in the next measure. In this two-part counterpoint, both harmonies are implied, but the V⁴₂ seems to capture better the impetus toward the new key, and in performance it makes sense to treat both the B♭4 and the D5 as incomplete upper neighbors (appoggiaturas) by stressing them slightly before sinking into the chord tone. This embellishing-tone pattern in Baroque music is sometimes referred to as a "sigh" motive and is typically performed with emphasis on the downbeat dissonance, pulling away dynamically from its resolution.

One more question before we leave this piece for now. Surely you noticed the luxuriant harmony in measure 3—what is it? (*Try it #3*)

What Are Closely Related Keys?

We have looked at the two most common harmonic goals for Classical-era modulations. What other modulations are possible with the pivot-chord technique? We can determine the possibilities with the help of the concept of closely related keys.

KEY CONCEPT _____

The most typical modulations in common-practice tonal music are from the primary key to a **closely related key**, effected by means of a pivot chord. Closely related keys are those whose tonic chords are diatonic in the primary key.

A closely related key to any given major key is represented by the triad on ii, iii, IV, V, or vi. As shown below, the closely related keys for D Major are E minor (key of the supertonic, ii), F♯ minor (mediant, iii), G Major (subdominant, IV), A Major (dominant, V), and b minor (submediant, vi, or the relative minor).

D Major:	I	ii	iii	IV	V	vi	vii°
	D	e	f♯	G	A	b	(c♯°)

WF3 Since the chord built on the leading tone is diminished, it cannot serve as a goal of modulation—tonics must be major or minor chords. Therefore, each key can claim five closely related keys. It is a good idea to practice naming closely related keys from any given tonic, so that you are aware of the possibilities for pivot-chord modulation when you compose.

Another Way

The closely related keys may also be identified by their key signatures: from the original key, those with the same key signature (relative major or minor) or with a signature containing one more or one fewer accidental are closely related. For example, closely related keys to D Major are B minor (relative minor, same key signature), A Major and F♯ minor (add one sharp), and G Major and E minor (remove one sharp). For E♭ Major, the closely related keys are C minor (relative minor, same key signature), B♭ Major and G minor (remove one flat), and A♭ Major and F minor (add one flat).

Try it #4

Name five keys that are closely related to each of the following major keys.

GIVEN KEY	CLOSELY RELATED KEYS
F Major	
E Major	
A Major	
G Major	
B♭ Major	

For a minor key, the process of determining closely related keys is the same, taking the triads built above scale degrees in the natural minor scale. A closely related key to any given minor key is represented by the triad on III, iv, v, VI, or VII. The closely related keys for A minor, shown below, are C Major (key of the mediant, III, or the relative major), D minor (subdominant, iv), E minor (minor dominant, v), F Major (submediant, VI), and G Major (subtonic, VII).

A minor:	i	ii°	III	iv	v	VI	VII
	a	(b°)	C	d	e	F	G

The major dominant key, E Major, is not considered a closely related key, and is not typically a goal of modulation from A minor.

Another Way

Relative major and minor keys share the same set of closely related keys. Another way to locate the closely related keys for A minor, therefore, is to consider those in C Major:

C Major:	I	ii	iii	IV	V	vi	vii°
	C	d	e	F	G	a	(b°)

Closely related keys for both C Major and A minor are D minor, E minor, F Major, and G Major; the fifth closely related key is the relative major or minor key, C Major or A minor.

Try it #5

Name five keys that are closely related to each of the following minor keys.

GIVEN KEY	CLOSELY RELATED KEYS
E minor	_____
G minor	_____
C♯ minor	_____
F minor	_____
B minor	_____

Other Pivot-Chord Modulations

From a Major Key to Its Submediant

We have already seen that in major-key compositions, modulation to the dominant is the most common tonal motion. Modulation to the submediant (or relative minor) is also a typical goal. Figure 22.3 shows the possible pivot chords.

FIGURE 22.3: Comparison of chords in D Major and B minor

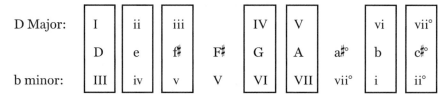

The modulation from a major key to its relative minor is relatively easy to write because of the large number of shared diatonic triads between these keys: I = III, ii = iv, iii = v, IV = VI, V = VII, vi = i, and vii° = ii°. As we have seen, typical pivot choices are those where both chords have a predominant function: in this case, ii = iv and IV = VI.

From a Minor Key to Its Minor Dominant

In minor keys, the only frequent destination of pivot-chord modulation other than the relative major is the minor dominant (v), a modulation especially common in Baroque-period compositions. The possible pivots for this modulation are shown in Figure 22.4.

FIGURE 22.4: Comparison of chords in A minor and E minor

A minor:	i	ii°		III	iv		v	V	VI	VII	vii°
	a	b°		C	d		e	E	F	G	g♯°
E minor:	a	b	B	C	D	d♯°	e		f♯°	G	
	iv	v	V	VI	VII	vii°	i		ii°	III	

This pairing of keys yields few workable pivot chords. The most typical is i = iv. The III = VI and VII = III pivots may look promising, but they are not as common. One possible reason is that they are associated with relative-major and relative-minor key relations, and therefore do not make as clean a modulation from a minor key to its dominant minor.

From a Major Key to Its Supertonic, Mediant, or Subdominant

While pivot modulations from a major key to its supertonic, mediant, or subdominant are possible, each of these pairings is problematic in ways we will see below. These key relations are therefore less common for pivot-chord modulations than those discussed thus far. But here is a good chance to practice identifying pivot chords. For each of these key relationships—I to ii, I to iii, and I to IV—draw a chart of pivot chords, using Figure 22.4 as a model and D Major as your initial key. Check your answers before reading further. *(Try it #6)*

The pivot choices from a major key to the key of its supertonic are limited: two of the pairings involve the tonic in one of the keys (I = VII and ii = i), one includes the mediant chord (IV = III), and one involves minor v (vi = v). Modulation to ii is often accomplished by tonicizing ii with V^7/ii or vii°⁷/ii, then continuing in the key of ii, or by sequence (see Chapter 29).

Modulation from a major key to its mediant is not a popular choice by Baroque or Classical composers, possibly because making vii° into V of the mediant means altering two chord members (the third and the fifth). The pivot choices are I = VI, iii = i, V = III, and vi = iv. Of these, I = VI and vi = iv work best.

The problem with modulating from a major key to its subdominant is that to be a convincing modulation, I of the original key has to stop sounding like tonic and take on the role of dominant. But if it starts sounding too convincingly like the dominant of IV, then we lose the sense of tonic as the home key. Modulations to IV in common-practice music are typically brief, or they occur well into a longer composition, so that the sense of home key is already well established. There are several good pivot chords, however, including I = V, ii = vi, IV = I, and vi = iii. The best of these is ii = vi, which often appears in a pivot area with vi = iii or IV = I.

SUMMARY

When planning modulations between closely related keys, you may want to make charts like those above to help you choose pivot chords. The smoothest pivots involve chords that occur in the predominant-function area in both keys. When you construct these charts, pay careful attention to the two key signatures in determining chord quality; don't try to use a "pivot" that has a different chord quality in the two keys.

Writing a Pivot-Chord Modulation

Now that we have looked at several pivot-chord modulations, identified which are the most typical tonal motions, and learned how to choose pivots, we will consider guidelines for writing these modulations.

KEY CONCEPT

To create a pivot-chord modulation:

1. Establish the first key. This may be done by writing one or more phrases in the initial key or by writing a progression that firmly establishes a sense of tonic.
2. Examine the possible pivot chords. Compare the diatonic chords in the two keys, and determine which chords can function in both.
3. Write a progression in the first key through the pivot chord(s).
4. Continue from the pivot chord with a normal progression in the new key.
5. Write a cadence in the new key.

The music that follows your modulation may continue in the new key or return to the old. All voice-leading guidelines that are relevant to the progressions in each key apply: follow normal guidelines for doubling and parallels, resolve leading tones according to the prevailing key at that moment, and don't forget to resolve sevenths and other tendency tones.

Direct Modulations

Not all modulations to closely related keys involve pivot chords. Sometimes a new phrase simply begins in the new key; or a new key may be introduced midphrase, without a pivot chord, by dominant-to-tonic motion in that key. These modulations are called **direct modulations** because the composer moves directly from one key to another, without pivot. Direct modulations are typical in chorale settings, but may also be found in other contexts. Depending on how sudden and unexpected the change of key is, some writers refer to direct modulations as **abrupt modulations**. Others may refer to phrases that begin in the new key without preparation or transition as **phrase modulations**.

1.7 🎧 Listen, for example, to the first two phrases from Bach's "O Haupt voll Blut und Wunden," shown in Example 22.4.

EXAMPLE 22.4: Bach, "O Haupt voll Blut und Wunden," mm. 1–4

Translation: O head, full of blood and wounds, full of sorrow and object of scorn.

The first phrase cadences in F Major, the primary key of this setting, with the progression (beginning in m. 1, beat 4) I–ii$^6_5$–V–I. The next phrase then starts right out in the new key of D minor, with V^6–i. If those two chords were immediately followed by chords in F Major, we would label them V^6/vi–vi and consider them a tonicization of vi. Instead, the phrase continues in D minor and cadences in that key, confirming a modulation to D minor. What aspect of the first phrase makes the direct modulation to D minor in the second phrase less jarring? *(Try it #7)*

Chorales Through the Ages

Why are there frequent modulations and tonicizations in many Bach chorale settings? Many of the chorale tunes that were popular in Bach's day were written in the 1500s (the late Renaissance), 150–200 years before Bach set them. They had been passed down from generation to generation as part of the Protestant religious tradition, but reflected the melodic style of a previous age, when composers were thinking in ecclesiastical modes rather than major and minor keys. When harmonized in major and minor keys, these chorale melodies often require frequent changes of key to accommodate their shape. Many of them, in Bach's settings, seem to waver between two or three different keys over the course of the chorale. This reflects their origin in a different melodic system, and Bach's struggle to make them fit into the harmonic system of his own day. Bach's harmonic solutions are even more remarkable for their sensitivity to the German text. Some key changes and harmonic choices are clearly examples of text painting.

You may find some of Bach's settings (now over 250 years old), or other settings of these tunes (some 400–450 years old), in Christian church hymnbooks still today, continuing the Protestant tradition of congregational singing. Bach's chorale settings can also be found in arrangements (without the words) for band or student orchestras. If you come across one of these arrangements, listen carefully for the twists and turns of key that are characteristic of these eighteenth-century tonal settings of sixteenth-century modal tunes.

Modulations Introduced by Secondary Dominants

You can introduce a direct modulation anywhere within a phrase with a secondary-dominant-function chord. Write the progression with a secondary dominant as though you planned a tonicization, then simply continue the progression in the new key. Be sure to include predominant-function chords and a cadence in the new key to confirm the modulation. While this type of modulation is not as seamless as a diatonic pivot-chord modulation, it does not have to sound abrupt. Because the modulation is to a closely related key, the listener, hearing the secondary dominant and its resolution, thinks it is a tonicization until the music continues in the new key.

For an example of this type of modulation, listen to the opening of Clementi's Sonatina in C Major, Op. 36, No. 1, shown in Example 22.5.

1.74

EXAMPLE 22.5: Clementi, Sonatina in C Major, Op. 36, No. 1, mm. 1–15

The first phrase establishes the main key of the piece, C Major. Measures 7–15, though, are in the secondary key of G Major. How does Clementi move from one key to the other? Measure 6 begins in C Major with a tonic triad, but the change of key is accomplished by what may seem at first to be a tonicization: a secondary leading-tone chord, vii°⁷/V, resolving to V in measure 7. This secondary dominant resolution is followed, however, by a typical phrase-model conclusion (T–PD–D–T) in G Major: I–ii⁶–V⁶₄–⁵₃–I. The G-Major key area then continues to measure 15.

Locating Modulations

The procedure for locating modulations is similar to the one we used in Chapters 19 and 21 to find secondary dominants. First, consider how the piece establishes the primary tonic. Then scan for accidentals to help locate a dominant-function chord that resolves to a tonic that is not the primary tonic. Remember that dominant-function chords may include both dominant sevenths (Mm7) and leading-tone seventh chords (usually fully diminished). You may also scan the score for the characteristic bass motion associated with dominant-to-tonic progressions. In many cases where there is a modulation, the dominant-to-tonic motion falls at the end of a phrase, making it easy to spot.

Next, back up from the point of the cadence or the first appearance of chromatic alterations. If there is a pivot chord, it will usually be located just before the entrance of the chromatic alteration that marks the new key. Keep in mind that there may be more than one chord that makes sense in both keys and acts as a pivot. In that case, choose one or label the whole pivot area in both keys.

If the modulation is made by a secondary dominant and continuation in the new key, the first accidental of the new key may be in the secondary-dominant-function harmony; look for a continuation in the new key, including a PD–D–T progression, before labeling the progression a modulation. If there is only a dominant-to-tonic cadence (without a predominant), check to see whether the next phrase continues in the new key. If so, the previous cadence may be interpreted as a modulation; if not, it should be labeled with a secondary dominant (a tonicization).

Modulations in Musical Contexts

1.17 🎧   Listen to the Bach C-Major Prelude, while following the score in your anthology. (This piece should be familiar from Chapters 8 and 21.) For measures 1–11, shown in Example 22.6, write a chordal reduction in the blank staves below the music, then label the chords with Roman numerals and figures. To make the reduction, simply ignore the keyboard-style figuration and write the pitch content of each measure as a single whole-note chord, as in measure 1. As you proceed, be sure to keep the chord members in the correct octave to maintain Bach's voice-leading.

EXAMPLE 22.6: Bach, Prelude in C Major, mm. 1–11

The chords in measures 1–4 establish the tonic and the style of the piece, following our phrase model (T–PD–D–T) exactly, though on a small scale: I–ii$^4_2$–V$^6_5$–I. The shared bass pitch between the I and ii$^4_2$ makes a smooth voice-leading connection, with the characteristic resolution of the $^4_2$ to a first-inversion chord (V$^6_5$). The chords in measures 2–3 are voiced so that they function like "neighbor chords" to the opening tonic triads; in a contextual analysis, we would label these entire four measures as a tonic expansion. The whole excerpt, in fact, could be analyzed in the tonic key of C Major, incorporating secondary dominants. The I–vi^6 progression in measures 4–5 is a typical instance of 5–6 tonic expansion (introduced in Chapter 16); you might have labeled these measures as I$^{5–6}$.

We turn now to the chords in measures 6 and 10, which are made up of the same pitch classes: D, F♯, A, and C. You may have labeled the chord in measure 6 as V$^4_2$/V and the chord in measure 10 as V^7/V. But are these chords only secondary dominants? Or do they indicate a modulation? Looking back at measure 5, we see that its vi^6 could also be considered a ii^6 in G Major, serving as a pivot chord for a modulation to the dominant. Likewise, the vi^7 in measure 9 could be interpreted as a ii^7 in the key of the dominant. Thus, since measures 5–11 meet the minimum criteria for a modulation—the presence of a PD–D–T progression in the new key—they may be analyzed in the key of the dominant.

The chord in measure 8 is a bit unusual in a Baroque-era composition, but you should have been able to identify it as a major-major seventh chord (MM7) in third inversion. What is it doing here? To answer that question, think carefully about the voice-leading connections between this chord and the chords on either side of it, considering both our initial reading of measures 5–11 in C Major and our revised labeling as a modulation to G Major. The chord in measure 7, if read in the primary key of the piece, is a V^6, whose expected resolution would be I. If the chord in measure 8 had been I, the T–PD–D progression in measures 4–7 would have ended in T, making a complete basic phrase, but it would also have stopped the forward motion with a cadence.

The chord Bach chooses instead has many elements of the expected resolution: the upper voices are C–E–G, but the bass line in measures 4–9 continues down by step, from $\hat{1}$ to $\hat{7}$, then from $\hat{7}$ to $\hat{6}$. The chord in measure 8 shares three pitches with the following vi⁷ (or ii⁷ if read in G Major), making a smooth voice-leading connection between the two chords. We could label the MM7 chord in measure 8 as a I$^4_2$ in C Major or a IV$^4_2$ in G Major, but neither label really captures its function here: a combination of the B bass note from the previous chord plus C–E–G, the expected resolution of the G–B–D harmony. We thus call this chord a **voice-leading chord**: it is created by the voice-leading motion of melodic lines between the two stable chords on either side. This particular voice-leading chord is a passing $^4_2$ chord.

| WF4 |

Harmonizing Modulating Melodies

The principles of pivot-chord and direct modulations may be applied to the harmonization of melodies as well.

KEY CONCEPT

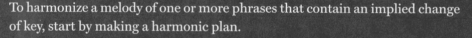

To harmonize a melody of one or more phrases that contain an implied change of key, start by making a harmonic plan.

1. Write in the scale degrees for the first few pitches at the beginning of the melody. Harmonize these pitches with chords that clearly establish the primary key. (If the melody has more than one phrase and the initial phrase is entirely in the tonic key, this key will be so firmly established that you may need as few as two chords in the original key at the beginning of the modulating phrase.)
2. Then examine the melodic cadence at the end of the modulating phrase. In what new key could the phrase end? Write in the melodic scale degrees in that key. Choose chords to make an effective cadence in the new key.
3. Now examine the middle of the modulating phrase. Are there accidentals related to the new key? Pick a location for the pivot chord or direct modulation before any accidentals in the new key, then write in the scale degrees for the entire melodic phrase, showing the change of key.
4. Choose remaining harmonies to make a good phrase progression. Remember to write in all the necessary accidentals for the new key.

If just the phrase ending indicates a cadence in a new key, you may be able to set the cadence either with a tonicization (V^7–I in the new key) or a full modulation. Think about how firmly you want the new key to be established, and choose progressions to make the effect you want. If the entire new phrase seems to be in a new key (most typical in chorales), you may use a direct or phrase modulation. These modulations are easy to write—simply think of the melody pitches for the whole second phrase in the new key, and set them in the normal fashion. Phrases with direct modulations often begin with a dominant-tonic anacrusis to start the phrase off in the new key.

We now apply these principles to a melody by Schubert, "Nur wer die Sehnsucht kennt" ("Only One Who Knows Longing"), shown in Example 22.7a.

EXAMPLE 22.7: Schubert, "Nur wer die Sehnsucht kennt (Lied der Mignon)"

(a) Mm. 7–14 (vocal line)

Nur   wer   die   Sehn - sucht   kennt,   weiß,   was   ich   lei - de

nur   wer   die   Sehn - sucht   kennt,_   weiß,   was   ich   lei - de!

Translation: Only one who knows longing knows what I suffer.

Begin by singing both phrases. The first begins and ends in the primary key of E minor, with $\hat{2}$ implying a half cadence at the end of the phrase. Although there are no accidentals to point toward a modulation, the second phrase ends on $\hat{3}$ of the original key, and seems to focus more on $\hat{3}$ than on $\hat{1}$. If you sing the second phrase by itself, it has a G-Major sound. We could set this second phrase in G Major by means of a phrase modulation. Schubert, however, provides a modulation in the midst of the phrase to make the transition more subtle.

Looking at measures 13 and 14, we see that the phrase ends with scale-degrees $\hat{1}$–$\hat{7}$–$\hat{6}$–$\hat{7}$–$\hat{2}$–$\hat{1}$ in G Major. In the 6/8 meter, we can set these measures with a cadential $^6_4$–V^7–I. Thus, if we begin with a tonic in E minor in measure 11a, we need to modulate between 11b and 12b. There are several ways to do this. Two are shown in Example 22.7b.

(b) Mm. 11–14 (vocal line)

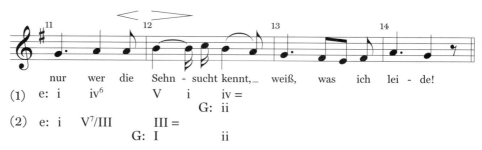

(1) e: i   iv⁶   V   i   iv =

                                       G: ii

(2) e: i   V⁷/III   III =

                        G: I   ii

Measures 11–12, beginning in E minor, could be set i iv⁶ | V i iv = ii (in G Major). Alternatively, i V⁷/III | III = I (in G Major) ii (with a suspension in the melody) would work. Schubert's setting is a little more complex than these. Write in the Roman numerals and figures under his setting, shown in Example 22.8. *(Try it #8)*

You may be able to think of other possibilities as well. To complete other settings, compose the bass line, using inversions where needed to make a good counterpoint with the melody, then part-write the inner voices as usual. When setting song melodies, you may want to give your piano accompaniment a keyboard figuration.

EXAMPLE 22.8: Schubert, "Nur wer die Sehnsucht kennt," mm. 7–15a

TERMS YOU SHOULD KNOW

closely related keys

modulation
- abrupt modulation
- direct modulation
- pivot-chord (common-chord) modulation

pivot chord

tonicization

QUESTIONS FOR REVIEW

1. What is a modulation?
2. What is the most common key to modulate to from a major key? from a minor key?
3. How do you locate the possible pivot chords between two keys?
4. What is the difference between a tonicization and a modulation? What criteria do you use to identify a modulation?
5. In music for your own instrument, find a modulation from a major key to its dominant. What clues did you look for to locate this modulation?
6. In music for your own instrument, find a modulation from a minor key to its relative major. What clues did you look for to locate this modulation?
7. What are the steps for setting a melody that modulates from one key to another?
8. How would identifying a modulation help you perform a passage? What might you think about in a different way?

CHAPTER 23

Binary and Ternary Forms

Outline of topics covered

Overview

In this chapter, we consider how the musical elements we have studied thus far contribute to the overall structure of musical compositions. Specifically, we will learn how to recognize two common forms: binary form and ternary form.

Repertoire

Anonymous, Minuet in D minor, from the *Anna Magdalena Bach Notebook* (CD 1, track 1)

Wolfgang Amadeus Mozart, Piano Sonata in D Major, K. 284, third movement (CD 2, track 48)

Robert Schumann, "Trällerliedchen," from *Album for the Young*, Op. 68, No. 3 (CD 3, track 40)

John Philip Sousa, "The Stars and Stripes Forever" (CD 3, track 41)

○ ○

Introduction to Binary Form

In earlier chapters, we focused on details of musical construction: intervals, chords, progressions, counterpoint, phrases, and cadences. While we have sometimes considered lengthy passages, we have not yet addressed the overall harmonic and thematic organization of compositions—which we call **musical form**. One of the most common musical forms, called **binary form**, is comprised of two sections, each of which is usually repeated. (*Bi-* means "two"—as in "bicycle" [two wheels] and "biped" [two feet].) To begin our study of binary form, we return to two pieces we considered in Chapter 22—Mozart's Piano Sonata in D Major, K. 284, and the Minuet in D minor from the *Anna Magdalena Bach Notebook*. They demonstrate two common ways binary form may be expressed in major and minor keys.

Binary Form in a Major-Key Piece

2.48   Listen first to the third movement of Mozart's Piano Sonata in D Major, K. 284 (a theme and variations movement), while following the score in your anthology. We previously examined the harmonic organization of measures 1–8, shown in Example 23.1a. We analyzed the modulation from the main key of D Major to the key of the dominant, A Major, by means of a pivot chord, as shown below.

EXAMPLE 23.1: Mozart, Piano Sonata in D Major, K. 284, third movement

(a) Mm. 1–8

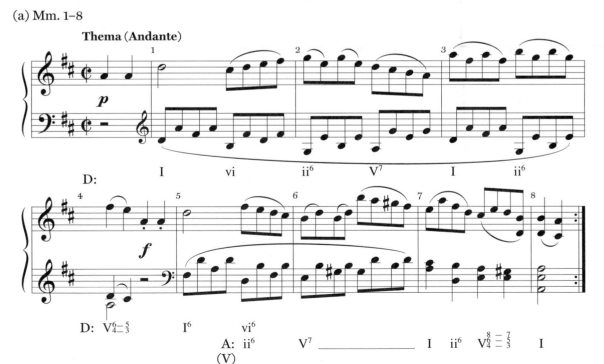

Now we consider these measures from the point of view of phrase organization. Drawing on the phrase-analysis terminology introduced in Chapter 20, identify the type of phrase structure Mozart builds here. *(Try it #1)*

Mozart's theme divides into two parts, each of which is repeated. The two phrases in measures 1–8 form the first part, or **section**, of the theme. When labeling phrases, we use lowercase letters from the beginning of the alphabet (**a**, **b**, **c**); for motives, lowercase letters from the end of the alphabet (**x**, **y**, **z**). Since it is customary to use capital letters to name sections, we will call this first section **A**.

KEY CONCEPT

When the first large section of a binary form ends with a cadence that is not on the tonic harmony, the form is called **continuous binary**, indicating that the harmonic motion of the piece must continue past the end of this section to a cadence on the tonic. When the first section ends with a cadence on the tonic, the form is called **sectional binary**, indicating that this section is tonally complete and could stand on its own.

Look again at the second half of Mozart's theme (mm. 9–17) in your anthology. What is its phrase structure? This second half also divides into two four-measure phrases. While listening to this piece, you may have noticed that measures 13–17, shown in Example 23.1b, are similar in motivic and harmonic design to the two phrases in section **A**. Compare these three phrases. How are they alike? How are they different? *(Try it #2)*

2.51

(b) Mm. 13–17

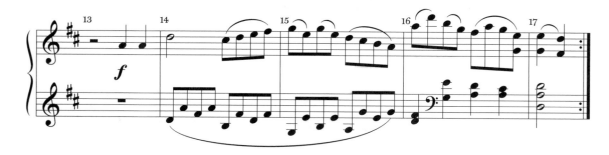

Although shorter in length than measures 1–8, the final phrase of the theme (mm. 13–17) encapsulates the melodic and harmonic ideas of the earlier **A**-section phrases, **a** and **a′**. We can label this phrase **a″** to indicate both the similarity to the first two phrases and the differences.

2.50 🎧

The third phrase of the theme (mm. 8b–12, shown in Example 23.1c) shares some motivic connections to the other phrases, but it sounds different and forms a contrast to what came before. We label it with a small **b** to show its contrasting role. What key or keys do you hear in this phrase? Remember that the first section ended in A Major—does that key continue here? The anacrusis emphasizes the pitch A5, which does suggest A Major. On the other hand, the first full measure features a short falling-fifth sequence, alternating dominant-seventh-quality chords and triads, so that it is hard to hear the tonic—and we already know that the section ends in D Major (Example 23.1b). Because of the sequential nature of measure 9, its underlying key is thus ambiguous. Measure 10 doesn't help us determine the key, either; these scalar motives do not imply a clear harmony.

(c) Mm. 8b–12

The tonal ambiguity here is intentional. This phrase ends in measure 12 with a half cadence in D Major, but Mozart interprets measures 11–13 quite differently in the various variations of this set. In some cases, the progression seems clearly in A Major; in others, D Major.

When there are strong melodic or motivic connections between the initial and concluding phrases of a binary piece, the form is called **rounded binary**: the return of material from the beginning "rounds out" the formal plan. The overall design of rounded binary is represented by ‖: **A** :‖ **B A** (or **A′**) :‖ to show the return of section **A** materials at the end. (The symbols ‖:   :‖ indicate that the music between them is to be repeated after it is played.) If the entire **A** section returns unchanged at the end, "**A**" is used; if the return of **A** material is shortened or substantially altered (changed to remain in the tonic key, for example), "**A′**" is used. (When you write a prime [′] with a letter designation in your analyses, be sure to indicate what is changed to merit the prime.)

KEY CONCEPT

The term "design" refers to the thematic form. "Structure" describes the harmonic scheme. Even though the thematic design of rounded binary suggests three sections (**A B A′**), its harmonic structure (and, usually, its framing repeat signs) defines a two-part form.

We diagram the form of Mozart's theme as shown below, with the thematic design elements on top and the harmonic structure, with Roman numerals, beneath. The form of this theme is rounded continuous binary: rounded because of its design (thematic elements at the beginning of the first phrase return in the final phrase), and continuous because of its structure (the first section does not cadence on the tonic).

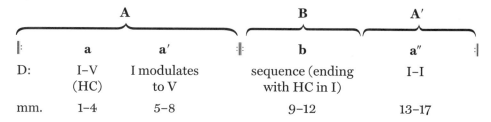

	A			**B**	**A′**	
‖:	**a**	**a′**	:‖:	**b**	**a″**	:‖
D:	I–V	I modulates		sequence (ending	I–I	
	(HC)	to V		with HC in I)		
mm.	1–4	5–8		9–12	13–17	

Binary Form in a Minor-Key Piece

In Chapter 22, we examined measures 1–8 of the Minuet in D minor from the *Anna Magdalena Notebook*, which modulate from the tonic key to F Major, the relative major. Listen to the Minuet again, then consider the phrase design of the opening section of this binary-form piece, shown as Example 23.2a.

1.1 🎧

EXAMPLE 23.2: Anonymous, Minuet in D minor, from the *Anna Magdalena Bach Notebook*

(a) Mm. 1–8

Unlike the Mozart example, the first eight measures of this Minuet (section **A**) consist of contrasting phrases, which we can label **a** (mm. 1–4) and **b** (mm. 5–8). The two phrases form a contrasting period. Because section **A** does not cadence in the tonic key, we also call this piece continuous binary.

What is the harmonic structure of the second half of the piece, shown in Example 23.2b? Start by analyzing the chords in measures 13–16. *(Try it #3)*

1.2

(b) Mm. 9–16

This last phrase is firmly in the key of the tonic, D minor, from beginning to end. Now what about measures 9–12? Listen to determine what is happening harmonically in these measures. *(Try it #4)* We can label these phrases, which are contrasting (with each other, as well as with those of the first section) **c** (mm. 9–12) and **d** (13–16).

While the phrases of this Minuet share enough motivic similarity to sound as though they are from the same composition, no two are similar enough to merit the same phrase label. The melodic or motivic materials from the opening section do not return at the end of the piece. This type of form is called **simple binary**, represented by the diagram ‖: **A** :‖: **B** :‖. A formal diagram of the piece is shown below, again with the tonal structure underneath and the section design letters above. We call the form of this Minuet simple continuous binary: simple because thematic elements of the first phrase do not return in the fourth, and continuous because the first section does not cadence in the tonic key.

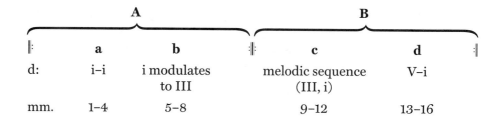

	A			B		
‖:	**a**	**b**	:‖:	**c**	**d**	:‖
d:	i–i	i modulates to III		melodic sequence (III, i)	V–i	
mm.	1–4	5–8		9–12	13–16	

Phrase Design in Binary Form

The Mozart theme and the D-minor Minuet are typical examples of binary form. As we consider the following characteristics of binary form, we will locate each characteristic in these two compositions and then outline other possibilities.

KEY CONCEPT

A binary form has two main sections, each of which is repeated. The repeats are customarily indicated by repeat signs ‖: :‖, but may also be written out.

Look back at the score for the Mozart theme in your anthology. You will see repeat signs in the middle of measure 8 and at the end of measure 17. The repeat signs are often the first clue that a piece is in binary form. The Minuet in D minor has first and second endings—which differ in the left-hand part—but it too includes the characteristic repeat signs. The first ending smooths the return to D minor as measures 1–8 are repeated, and the second allows for more finality at the cadence. In some editions of this piece, the repeats are written out, but the formal organization is unchanged.

KEY CONCEPT

The two sections of a binary form may be the same length, or the second may be somewhat longer than the first. The first section consists of at least one four- or eight-measure phrase; more commonly, it is a two-phrase parallel or contrasting period. Other typical lengths for the first section are sixteen or thirty-two measures, but it may be longer. Its length need not divide evenly into four-measure phrases.

Because binary form originated as a dance movement, individual phrases in binary-form pieces are usually four or eight measures long. In binary pieces written for concert performance (that is, not intended for dancing), there may be some variation in phrase lengths in the second section, often created by phrase extensions or elision.

WF1

As we have already observed, the first section of the Mozart theme is a parallel period made of two four-measure phrases. There is one unusual element, however, in the length of the second half of the theme: it is nine measures long rather than eight, the extra measure formed by the three-and-a-half-beat silence from 12b to 13a. When the theme is performed, this silence simply sounds as though the performer is taking some time between the third and fourth phrases for expressiveness and to heighten anticipation of the concluding phrase. In the other variations, however, Mozart fills this silent span in a variety of ways (see Chapter 27). Both sections of the Minuet in D minor, on the other hand, are eight measures long. You could dance to this Minuet!

Tonal Structures in Binary Form

KEY CONCEPT

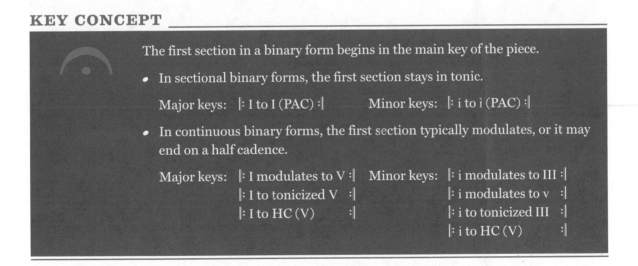

The first section in a binary form begins in the main key of the piece.

- In sectional binary forms, the first section stays in tonic.

  Major keys: ‖: I to I (PAC) :‖   Minor keys: ‖: i to i (PAC) :‖

- In continuous binary forms, the first section typically modulates, or it may end on a half cadence.

  Major keys: ‖: I modulates to V :‖   Minor keys: ‖: i modulates to III :‖
            ‖: I to tonicized V :‖   ‖: i modulates to v :‖
            ‖: I to HC (V)   :‖   ‖: i to tonicized III :‖
                                 ‖: i to HC (V)   :‖

The most common goal of the modulation in major-key pieces is the key of the dominant; most typical in minor-key pieces is the mediant (relative major) or the minor dominant (in Baroque-era works). In some brief and uncomplicated binary forms, a tonicization of V (major keys) or III (minor keys) may substitute for the full modulation, or the first section may remain in tonic and cadence there, with either a PAC (sectional) or a HC (continuous). In both pieces we have examined, the **A** sections follow the most common modulatory plan: for the major-key Mozart theme, a modulation from tonic to the dominant key area; for the D-minor Minuet, a modulation from tonic to the key of the relative major.

The second half in binary form also displays a typical harmonic structure, along with a dramatic scenario. After the first section's mild foray into new harmonic territory—with either a modulation to a (relatively safe) key like the dominant or relative major, or a (more cautious) tonicization—the second section begins with relative harmonic ambiguity or instability. This instability may be expressed by a sequential progression or a modulation to another key (usually one of the closely related keys). In the case of sectional binary forms, which do not modulate in the first section, the second half may begin with a prolongation of the dominant (major-key pieces) or a modulation to the relative major (minor-key pieces). The dramatic instability of the beginning of the second half is followed by a reassuring return to tonic, with a phrase (or at least a strong cadential pattern) reestablishing harmonic stability in the home key.

KEY CONCEPT

The organization of the second section of a binary form depends, in part, on the harmonic plan selected for the first section. Following are some typical harmonic plans for second sections in brief binary pieces.

	1st portion	2nd portion		1st portion	2nd portion
Major keys:	‖: sequence	I–I :‖	Minor keys:	‖: tonicized III	i–i :‖
	‖: tonicized V	I–I :‖		‖: tonicized iv	i–i :‖
	‖: tonicized ii	I–I :‖		‖: tonicized v	i–i :‖
	‖: tonicized vi	I–I :‖		‖: sequence	i–i :‖

In each case, the chart above shows the final portion of the second section entirely in the tonic key. While this is the most common ending of a binary-form piece, it is also possible for the last phrase or phrases to modulate back to the tonic from some previous "wandering." Occasionally, in slightly longer binary forms (those with a second section sixteen measures or longer), more than one sequence or tonicization may be completed before the main key is reestablished. As we have seen, the second sections of both the Mozart theme and the D-minor Minuet begin with relative harmonic instability and ambiguity, including a sequential passage, before the tonic key returns.

WF2

Types of Binary Form

The Minuet and the Mozart theme represent the two main types of binary form: simple and rounded binary. The simple design (as in the Minuet) is the most common binary plan in Baroque-era compositions: while the phrases in the two main sections are somewhat similar in motivic content, none of the material from the first section (**A**) returns identically in the second (**B**). Sometimes, however, the melodic motives of the two sections are *quite* similar. In these cases, a formal outline of ‖ **A** ‖ **A′** ‖ is more appropriate. Both of these thematic designs (‖ **A** ‖ **B** ‖ and ‖ **A** ‖ **A′** ‖) are simple binary forms.

The rounded binary design (as in the Mozart theme) is the most common in late eighteenth- and nineteenth-century compositions: material from the beginning of the **A** section returns at the end of the **B** section. This design (‖ **A** ‖ **B A′** ‖) is also the basis for sonata form, as we will see in Chapter 28.

You may come across another phrase design: material from only the end of the first section may return at the end of the second section. In this case, we call the sections **balanced**. We can diagram this design as ‖ **A** (**x**) ‖ **B** (**x**) ‖, where **x** represents the material that returns. In continuous binary movements, **x** appears in a nontonic key in the **A** section and then in the tonic key in the **B** section. In rounded binary forms, the return of **x** is not unexpected (since **x** may be part of the returning A material), but in simple binary forms the return of this material can be quite memorable.

SUMMARY

Binary forms are compositions in two parts. They are labeled according to their tonal structure and thematic design.

If the tonal structure of the first half
- ends on the tonic, the binary type is **sectional**;
- ends on a HC, modulates, or tonicizes a harmony other than tonic, the binary type is **continuous**.

If the thematic design of the second half
- contrasts with the first half, the binary type is **simple** (‖ **A** ‖ **B** ‖);
- varies or develops material from the first half, the binary type is also **simple** (‖ **A** ‖ **A′** ‖);
- brings back opening (phrase 1) melodic material from **A** in the final phrase, the binary type is **rounded** (‖ **A** ‖ **B A′** ‖);
- brings back material from the end of the first half, the two sections are **balanced** (‖ **A** (**x**) ‖ **B** (**x**) ‖).

Writing Binary-Form Pieces

We have already learned most of the techniques needed to compose short binary-form pieces: in Chapter 22, we practiced writing opening sections that modulate, and we are by now familiar with basic phrase progressions, which typically form the final phrase of the second section. All that's left to learn at this point is how to compose the beginning of the second section, which often features a sequence or some other sort of harmonic instability.

To help his students learn how to write this part of a short binary-form piece, Austrian theorist and composer Joseph Riepel (writing in 1755) suggested three progressions for the beginning of the second section, shown in the diagram below, and gave them rhyming Italian names to help his students remember them. These three are not the only possible progressions, but they suit our purposes nicely, as well as his.

1. *Ponte* (bridge): main key: V | V | V^{8-7} | I |
    Works well when the first section closes in the tonic key (sectional).

2. *Monte* (mountain): main key: V^7/IV | IV | V^7/V | V |
    Works well when the first section closes in the dominant key, on the tonicized dominant (continuous), or in the tonic key.

3. *Fonte* (fountain): main key: V^7/ii | ii | V^7 | I
    Works well when the first section closes in the dominant key, on the tonicized dominant, or in the tonic key.

The first progression is called *ponte*, the bridge, because it spans the measures with a prolonged dominant harmony. This progression is particularly useful in sectional binary designs, when the first section closes in the tonic key. Since it is not very interesting harmonically, you would need to revoice the chords or provide melodic interest. You would follow this phrase with a final phrase that begins and ends in the tonic.

The second progression is called *monte*, the mountain, because it sounds like a hiker gradually climbing a steep incline. This sequential progression works well when the first section closes in the key of the dominant, or on the tonicized dominant; it may also be used after a close in the tonic. In composing *monte* settings, include a melodic sequence to highlight the climbing effect. Here too, you would follow this phrase with a final phrase that begins and ends in the tonic. This progression does not work as well in minor keys, because of the two alternations needed to turn i into V^7/iv.

You can recognize *monte* by its two-chord pattern (a triad preceded by its own dominant) and the pattern's sequential repetition—up a step (from IV to V). It may also be transposed to other pitch levels within the key—for example, V/V–V–V/vi–vi, or V–I–V/ii–ii. The original *monte* is sometimes extended into the final phrase by the progression V^7/vi–vi, followed by a cadence on the tonic.

The third progression is called *fonte*, the fountain, because it sounds like water bubbling from one level of a fountain down to another. This sequential progression works well when the first section closes in the key of the dominant or on the tonicized dominant, and may also be used after a close in the tonic. In composing *ponte* settings, include a melodic sequence to highlight the bubbling effect. As in *ponte* and *monte*, you would follow this phrase with a final phrase that begins and ends in the tonic. You can recognize *fonte* by its two-chord pattern (a triad preceded by its own dominant) and the pattern's sequential repetition—down a step (from ii to I). This progression is not found in minor keys, because it tonicizes ii, but it may appear transposed to other pitch levels, such as V/iv–iv–V/III–III.

In minor-key pieces, the opening of the second section may be a phrase in the relative major or minor dominant key. The area of relative harmonic instability may end with a modulation back to tonic with a half cadence on V, or with a cadence in the temporary key followed by a direct modulation to tonic at the beginning of the next phrase.

Rolling for Binary Pieces

By the time Joseph Riepel was writing (1752–68), the components of binary form were so well established that binary pieces could be composed by throwing dice (or other random procedures) to select the phrase beginnings, cadences, and sequences to "plug in" to the formal model. Composing a variety of different pieces from a few stock segments was called *ars permutoria*—the art of combination and permutation. For example, to make an eight-measure parallel period, a two-measure phrase beginning could be selected, followed by one of several standard two-measure inconclusive and conclusive cadences. After choosing a four-measure sequence to begin the second section, a composer could arrange a four-measure concluding phrase from the components of the initial period—the phrase opening with the cadence—to make the second half of the rounded binary form.

○ ○

Introduction to Ternary Form

Simple Ternary

3.40 🎧

Another common musical form, composed in three sections, is called **ternary form**. Listen to "Trällerliedchen," by Robert Schumann, while following the score in your anthology. This little piece is part of a collection Schumann composed for his children to play, like the *Anna Magdalena Bach Notebook*. Brief ternary-form pieces like this one are sometimes called **simple ternary**.

In ternary form, the first large section, section **A**, usually begins and ends in the tonic, with a conclusive cadence at the end. In the Schumann piece, **A** comprises measures 1–8, a parallel period (**a** = mm. 1–4; **a´** = mm. 5–8) beginning and ending in C Major. The middle section, **B**, is normally in a contrasting key—usually selected from the closely related keys. Here, the **B** section, measures 9–16, is also a parallel period (**b** = mm. 9–12; **b´** = mm. 13–16), in the key of G Major. As with binary form, the most popular contrasting keys are the dominant in major-key pieces and the relative major in minor-key pieces.

The middle section in a ternary piece often contrasts with the **A** section in at least one way other than key change. Motives, texture, harmonic complexity, and other features may distinguish **A** from **B**. Here, the **B** section shares melodic and harmonic elements with the **A** section, but the roles of the two hands are reversed: in **A**, the right hand has the melody, while in **B** the left hand does. Sometimes the middle section ends with a conclusive cadence in the contrasting key, as the Schumann work does in measure 16. When this happens, the form is said to be sectional—both **A** and **B** are harmonically "closed" and complete in themselves.

When the **B** section ends inconclusively, on the other hand—either with some sort of inconclusive cadence or by connecting without a stop to the return of **A**—the form is said to be continuous: **B** cannot stand alone, and must continue into **A** to reach a harmonic conclusion. The **A** section may be repeated exactly as the third part of a ternary form (label it **A**), as it is in the Schumann piece, or it may be varied a little (label it **A´**). In all cases, the return of the **A** section begins and ends in the tonic key as before. The phrase design and tonal structure of "Trällerliedchen" are shown below.

	A			B			A		
‖	**a**	**a´**	‖	**b**	**b´**	‖	**a**	**a´**	‖
	C (I) ———————			G (V) ———————			C (I) ———————		
	mm. 1–4	5–8		9–16	13–16		17–20	21–24	

Sections in ternary form may be brief—as little as two phrases—or quite long. The three sections are usually balanced in length, as they are in the Schumann piece, but they don't have to be: sometimes the **A** sections are longer, sometimes the **B** sections. In ternary form, individual sections may be repeated (with or without first and second endings or written-out repeats), but often, as in the Schumann piece, they are not.

KEY CONCEPT

Simple ternary form may be distinguished from rounded binary by observing

- the repetition pattern: in ternary form, **B** and the return of **A** (or **A**´) are never repeated together, as a pair; if either section is repeated, it is repeated by itself.
- the character of the **B** section: the beginning of the **B** section in binary form is often unstable, sequential, or modulatory; in ternary form, **B** is usually more stable, in its own contrasting key.
- the length of the **B** section: **B** is often longer in ternary forms than in rounded binary.

Sometimes when the **A** section returns after **B**, unchanged from its original appearance, it is not written out but instead indicated by the words *Da capo al Fine*, written at the end of the **B** section. This marking tells the performer to play from the "head" (*capo*), or beginning of the piece, to the word *Fine* (end) at the end of the **A** section. Another indication, *Dal segno al Fine*, is written if there is an anacrusis or introduction at the beginning of the **A** section that should be skipped on the repeat (*segno* means "sign"). These indications were such a common way of saving paper in opera scores that ternary arias (solo songs within operas) are referred to as *da capo* arias.

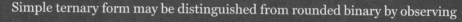

Binary Form as Part of a Larger Formal Scheme

Composite Ternary

Although a piece in binary form can be complete and freestanding, it can also function as part of a larger work. For example, themes for sets of "sectional variations" are often written in rounded binary form (see Chapter 27). Think back to previous chapters—what theme in rounded binary form have we studied in addition to the Mozart theme considered in this chapter? (*Try it #5*)

Sometimes two binary forms in contrasting keys are combined to make a large ternary design; examples are **minuet and trio** or **scherzo and trio** movements in sonatas and other multimovement works. This large formal design is called **composite ternary**: "ternary" indicating three independent sections, **A B A** (or **A B A´**), and "composite" referring to the joining together of smaller binary forms. A typical minuet or scherzo is in binary form (large section **A**), and is followed by a "trio," also in binary form, in a contrasting key or mode (large section **B**). In performance, the movement concludes with a repetition of the initial minuet or scherzo, either complete (**A** again) or without taking the repeats. In the diagram below, which summarizes a typical design, the highest-level letters are encased in boxes to distinguish them from the letters on the next level, the **A** and **B** sections of the binary form.

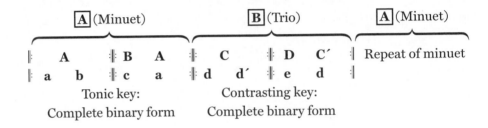

For an example of a composite ternary form, look at the third movement of Mozart's String Quartet in D minor, K. 421, in your anthology: the Menuetto (mm. 1–39a) is a rounded binary form, as is the Trio (mm. 39b–63a).

Marches and Ragtime

3.41 We can also find composite forms in marches, ragtime, and other types of pieces. Listen to Sousa's "The Stars and Stripes Forever," while following the score in your anthology. This work is typical of band marches, with an opening section in the tonic key (E♭), followed by a Trio in a contrasting key (A♭). You may want to follow the diagram below as you listen. As the diagram indicates, the March itself is a simple continuous binary form and could be played as a complete piece on its own; likewise, the Trio is a rounded sectional binary form and could stand on its own. In marches, the **A**, **B**, **C**, and **D** sections are sometimes called **strains**.

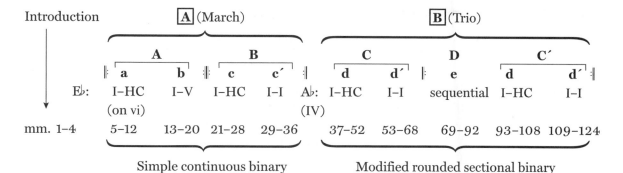

While Sousa's March is fairly standard in its tonal and thematic design, the lengthy and elaborate Trio presents some features worth noting. First, the "repeat" in the Trio's first section (**C**) is written out because of differences in ways the phrases end. Measures 37–40 and 53–56 are identical, but measures 41–52 are directed toward half cadences in measures 44 and 51, while measures 57–68 diverge to tonicize the submediant (F minor) before moving toward the tonic PAC in measure 68. Second, the Trio's second section (**D**) presents an energetic chromatic and sequential texture that is typical of the beginning of the second half of binary forms. In marches and rags, this section is sometimes called the "dogfight"—a term that aptly characterizes its nature!

The formal schemes for marches and rags are similar to composite ternary (for example, minuet and trio), except that they have two large sections instead of three—there is no final return to the first large section at the end—and within the large sections, the typical binary forms may be modified. Occasionally, you will find a rag or march in a composite form where one of the embedded smaller forms is ternary rather than binary. How would you describe the form of Joplin's "Solace" (in your anthology)? *(Try it # 6)*

TERMS YOU SHOULD KNOW

balanced sections	design	ternary form
binary form	minuet and trio	• composite ternary
• continuous binary	scherzo and trio	• simple ternary
• rounded binary	section	
• sectional binary	strain	
• simple binary	structure	

QUESTIONS FOR REVIEW

1. What is the basic principle of binary form?
2. What are the most common harmonic structures for first sections in a binary form in major keys? in minor keys?
3. What are the most common harmonic structures for second sections in a binary form in major keys? in minor keys?
4. Where are you most likely to find a sequence in a binary-form piece?
5. Where are you most likely to find a modulation in a binary-form piece?
6. What is the difference between simple binary and rounded binary?
7. What distinguishes simple ternary and rounded binary?
8. What is the difference between simple ternary and composite ternary?
9. How are binary forms used in composite ternary pieces?
10. In music for your own instrument, find one piece in simple binary form and one in rounded binary. How can you use the date of composition to help you locate a piece of each type?
11. What larger forms incorporate smaller binary forms within them?

Color and Drama in Composition:

Modal Mixture and Chromatic Mediants and Submediants

CHAPTER 24

Overview

In this chapter, we learn how to add harmonic color to compositions by borrowing chords from the parallel key. As we will see, these dramatic and unexpected chords are especially effective in music with texts, since the color change may highlight important words. We also consider the use and effect of chromatic mediants and submediants.

Repertoire

Johannes Brahms, Intermezzo in A Major, Op. 118, No. 2

Wolfgang Amadeus Mozart, Piano Sonata in D Major, K 284, first movement

Mozart, "Voi, che sapete," from *The Marriage of Figaro* (CD 2, track 82)

Franz Schubert, "Der Lindenbaum," from *Winterreise* (CD 3, track 16)

Schubert, "Du bist die Ruh" (CD 3, track 21)

Schubert, "Im Dorfe," from *Winterreise*

Schubert, *Moment musical* in A♭ Major, Op. 94, No. 6

o o o o o o o o o o o o o o o o o o o o o o o o o o o o o o o o o o o o o o o o o o o o o o o o o

Harmonic Color and Text Setting

2.82   We begin by listening to two contrasting vocal works: Mozart's "Voi, che sapete,"
3.21   from *The Marriage of Figaro*, and Schubert's "Du bist die Ruh" (both in your anthology). First read the text translations, given in Examples 24.1 and 24.2, and choose a few important words you would highlight musically if you were the composer. Then listen to the excerpts to see how Mozart and Schubert handle these words.

EXAMPLE 24.1: Mozart, "Voi, che sapete," from *The Marriage of Figaro*, mm. 29–36   2.85

Translation: I have a feeling, full of desire, which is by turns delightful and miserable.

EXAMPLE 24.2: Schubert, "Du bist die Ruh"

(a) Mm. 8–15   3.22

Translation: You are rest, the mild peace, you are longing, and what stills it.

(b) Mm. 54–65   3.24

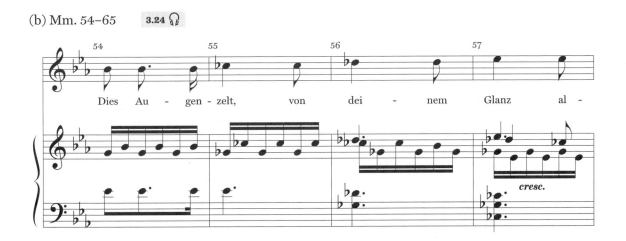

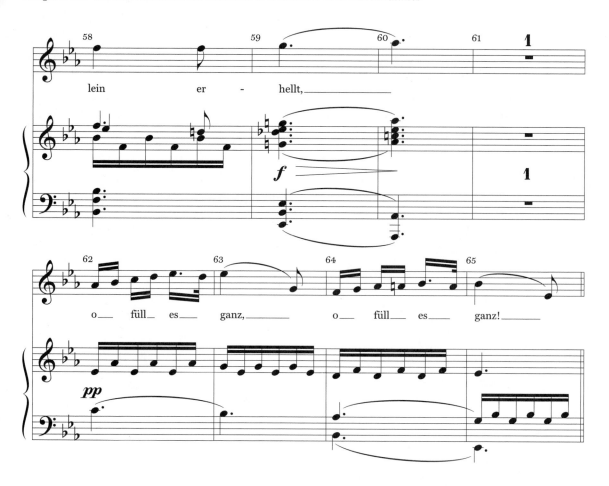

Translation: The tabernacle of my eyes by your radiance alone is illumined, oh fill it completely!

In Example 24.1, Mozart represents the conflicting emotions of the character Cherubino (see Chapter 4) by introducing chromatic alterations that change the chord quality. These unexpected changes make the chords stand out from their surroundings and illuminate the meaning of their text. The progression in measures 29–34 is a standard one in F Major—but the appearance of minor i instead of major I in measure 35 emphasizes Cherubino's state of simultaneous pleasure and pain. (The last chord in that measure combines a ♭6̂ and a ♯4̂ with the ♭3̂ to make a type of chord we will study in Chapter 25: an augmented-sixth chord.)

Now write in a Roman numeral analysis beneath the score of "Du bist die Ruh" given in Example 24.2a. The harmonic rhythm is one or two chords per measure. (*Try it #1*) In these eight measures, Schubert's harmonization is entirely diatonic. What accounts for the accidentals in Example 24.2b? Label these chords as well (the harmonic rhythm is one chord per measure), after reading the guidelines below. (*Try it #2*)

KEY CONCEPT

To analyze chords whose quality has been altered:

- Adjust the Roman numeral (uppercase or lowercase) to reflect whether the triad is major or minor.
- If the root of the chord has been altered, add a ♯ or ♭ before the Roman numeral to show that it is built on a raised or lowered scale degree (for example, ♭VI is built on ♭$\hat{6}$).
- If a chord has been altered to make it augmented or diminished, add a + to a capital Roman numeral for augmented, a ° to a lowercase Roman numeral for diminished.

In measures 54–55, the expected I–vi⁶ motion (alternatively labeled I⁵⁻⁶), which we heard in measures 8–9, is transformed into a I–♭VI⁶. This progression highlights the word "Augenzelt" (vision) and introduces the accidentals G♭ (scale-degree ♭$\hat{3}$) and C♭ (scale-degree ♭$\hat{6}$). Schubert includes chromatically altered chords in the next two measures (56–57) as well (♭III and ♭VI), leading to the song's climax in measure 60. Another possible analysis of these measures might interpret the ♭III chord as a secondary dominant to ♭VI (♭VI⁶–V/♭VI–♭VI): thus, the three measures 55–57 would form a temporary tonicization of the lowered submediant.

KEY CONCEPT

Secondary dominants may precede *any* chord with a major or minor quality. When you write them, follow the normal guidelines for writing secondary dominants, but be careful to include all the necessary chromatic alterations to achieve the correct chord quality.

Modal Mixture

The chromatic inflections of scale-degrees $\hat{3}$ and $\hat{6}$, like those we saw in the Schubert song, are not arbitrary but rather are a feature of **modal mixture,** or, more simply, **mixture**.

KEY CONCEPT

> Mixture, a "mixing" of parallel major and minor modes, is a technique composers employ to enrich their melodic and harmonic language. It is applied most often in major keys, where the modal scale-degrees ♭3̂, ♭6̂, and ♭7̂ are borrowed from the parallel natural minor. For this reason, mixture chords are sometimes called "borrowed chords."

Return to Example 24.2b, and list as many musical features as you can that help create the dramatic climax of this song (in m. 60). *(Try it #3)* How can our harmonic analysis help shape a performance of this passage? First, the introduction of C♭ in the vocal line at measure 55 is an unexpected and dramatic moment. One way to interpret this moment is to take your time here (pianist and singer alike) with an almost imperceptible hesitation between measures 54 and 55. Then continue in tempo—perhaps even pushing the tempo forward a bit until the climax of the phrase, where you might linger on the temporary tonicization of IV, setting the word "erhellt" (brightened).

This is not the end of the phrase, however: a phrase is defined by a cadence, which in this passage does not arrive until measures 64–65. The expectation and avoidance of a true cadence makes the silence in measure 61 even more tension-filled. You may want to lengthen this silence slightly, before continuing the phrase in measure 62 with a startling change of mood, dynamic, tessitura, and harmonic language. The phrase concludes with gentle motion toward the diatonic PD–D–T

WF1   cadence, and not a hint of the dissonance and chromaticism (suspensions, mixture chords, and secondary dominants) that shaped the first half of the phrase.

Mixture chords are typically found in pieces written in the Romantic era (around 1830–1910). During this time, the emotional content of a song or instrumental work was considered very important, and chromatic alterations of scale degrees and

WF2   chords were often used by composers to intensify a feeling. To see how a composer does this in a song, you first need to understand the meaning of the words. If the text is not in English, find a translation, and check especially any words set with chromatic inflection or mixture chords. Sometimes English "singing translations" provided with songs (in the music) move the words around or shift the meaning slightly; do not rely on this type of translation for your analytical investigation of text setting. Try to find a word-by-word translation; collections of these are available in most music libraries and on the Web.

Mixture Chords in Major

Example 24.3a shows triads built on each degree of an E♭-Major scale, labeled with Roman numerals. Example 24.3b shows triads built on an E♭-natural-minor scale, labeled as though the chords were to appear in E♭ Major as mixture chords. Circle any triad in part b that contains a modal scale degree (♭$\hat{3}$, ♭$\hat{6}$, or ♭$\hat{7}$). How many triads change quality between major and parallel minor keys? *(Try it #4)*

EXAMPLE 24.3:

(a) Triads built on the E♭-Major scale

E♭ Major:　　I　　　ii　　　iii　　　IV　　　V　　　vi　　　vii°　　　I

(b): Triads built on the E♭-natural-minor scale

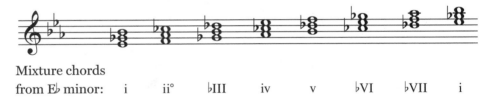

Mixture chords
from E♭ minor:　　i　　　ii°　　　♭III　　　iv　　　v　　　♭VI　　　♭VII　　　i

Try it #5

For each major key below, identify the key signature of the parallel minor (give the number of sharps or flats), and list the modal scale degrees.

KEY	PARALLEL MINOR SIGNATURE	♭3	♭6	♭7
C Major	_____	_____	_____	_____
E Major	_____	_____	_____	_____
B♭ Major	_____	_____	_____	_____
D Major	_____	_____	_____	_____
B Major	_____	_____	_____	_____

Intonation and Performance

If you are a singer or if you play an instrument (such as the violin) that requires careful attention to intonation, you may find that passages with mixture are difficult to sing or play in tune. If that is the case, you can draw on the skills you are practicing in aural skills or solfège classes for help.

KEY CONCEPT

When you sing or play passages that include mixture, use altered (movable *do*) solfège syllables.

Scale-degree $\hat{3} \rightarrow \flat\hat{3}$: *mi* becomes *me*
Scale-degree $\hat{6} \rightarrow \flat\hat{6}$: *la* becomes *le*
Scale-degree $\hat{7} \rightarrow \flat\hat{7}$: *ti* becomes *te*

Try singing the vocal line of Example 24.2b, measures 54–60, in solfège, paying careful attention to your intonation. *(Try it #6)*

The Spelling and Function of Mixture Chords

KEY CONCEPT

Among the most common mixture chords in major keys are those that contain $\flat\hat{6}$ and $\flat\hat{3}$, and that fall into the predominant and tonic-substitute categories: iv, ii°, $\flat$VI, and the minor tonic (i). These mixture chords are treated exactly like their diatonic counterparts: they have the same harmonic function and follow the same common-practice voice-leading guidelines as the diatonic chords they replace.

Spell mixture chords exactly as you would if they appeared in the parallel minor key. For example, to spell iv in C Major, imagine how you would spell iv in C minor: F-A♭-C. To spell $\flat$VI in F Major, imagine VI in F minor: D♭-F-A♭, and so on.

Try it #7

Try spelling some common mixture chords.

KEY	PARALLEL MINOR SIGNATURE	ii°	iv	♭III	♭VI
F Major					
A Major					
E♭ Major					
G Major					
C♯ Major					

When part-writing or composing, follow the same principles for doubling and voice-leading as if you were writing in the parallel minor: (1) double the root in a root-position chord, (2) double the soprano in a first-inversion chord, (3) double the bass in a second-inversion chord, and (4) double the third of a diminished chord. Don't worry about doubling an "altered tone" in the major key, but treat the chord exactly as though you had moved temporarily to the parallel minor key. Occasionally you will need to change these doubling rules to avoid parallels; see Example 24.4. When writing the progression V–♭VI or ♭VI–V, you will probably want to avoid doubling ♭6̂, since you may create parallel octaves moving 5̂–♭6̂ or ♭6̂–5̂ (*sol–le* or *le–sol*; Example 24.4a) or a melodic augmented second ♭6̂ to 7̂ (*le* to *ti*; Example 24.4c).

EXAMPLE 24.4: Doubling in V–♭VI and ♭VI–V

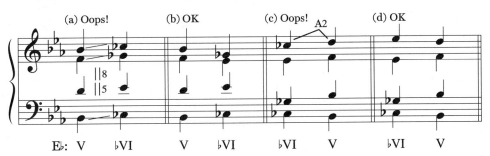

Eb: V   ♭VI   V   ♭VI   ♭VI   V   ♭VI   V

In choosing chords for your progression, follow the basic phrase model: T–PD–D–T. For example, write iv or ii° in the position where you would expect IV or ii, preceding V. You may use ♭VI to prolong the tonic, as in the Schubert example, or for a dramatic deceptive cadence: V–♭VI. Another common progression including ♭VI descends by thirds: I–♭VI–iv. You will often find ♭VII as a secondary dominant to ♭III.

KEY CONCEPT

> When part-writing, pay careful attention to the altered tones to avoid augmented seconds in any voice. Where possible, keep the chromatic motion (half-step voice-leading) in a single voice to avoid cross relations, especially between the outer voices. As a general rule, resolve chromatic tones that arise from mixture *down*, since they are derived from lowered scale degrees: for example, ♭6̂–5̂.

Mixture in the Cadential $^6_4$ Chord

Now consider a passage from Schubert's song "Im Dorfe" ("In the Village"), shown in Example 24.5. Try singing the melody on scale-degree numbers or solfège, paying careful attention to intonation. Write in the Roman numerals, and underline any mixture chords you find. *(Try it #8)*

EXAMPLE 24.5: Schubert, "Im Dorfe," from *Winterreise*, mm. 31b–50

Bellt mich nur fort, ihr wa - chen

Translation: Bark me away, you watchdogs, don't let me rest in the hour of slumber. I am finished with all dreams, why should I remain among sleepers?

This verse of the song includes many mixture chords. One spot that may have given you trouble is the cadential $^6_4$ chord in measure 45. As we have seen, we generally label cadential $^6_4$ chords as dominants to show their function: V$^{6-5}_{4-3}$. In the Schubert example, though, the pitches of the tonic triad change in quality from major to minor; how do we show that change and at the same time indicate the dominant function? The answer is to add an accidental to the figured-bass numbers to show that the sixth above the bass has been lowered: V$^{6-\flat6-5}_{4--3}$.

Measures 36–38 and 41–43 are also worthy of closer examination. The V$^6_5$/V in measure 36 moves to a i$^6_4$ (not the expected major quality) in measure 37 that does not proceed to V. It proceeds instead to an F-A-(C)-E♭ harmony—a secondary dominant of B♭—which resolves as expected to B♭ Major (♭VI in the key of D Major). Could the lack of resolution of the (minor-quality!) cadential $^6_4$ represent the wrenching "end of dreaming"? When this text returns, the progression is changed to I–♭VI–V$^6_5$/♭VI–♭VI, briefly tonicizing B♭ Major and representing a change in the character's feelings about the dream—perhaps a sense that the dreaming is really behind him.

As this passage shows, some seventh chords in major keys are also commonly altered by mixture. Possible mixture seventh chords include ii^7, which becomes ii^{ø7}, and vii^{ø7}, which becomes vii^{o7}.

Embellishing Tones

3.23 🎧

Mixture can occur in melodic lines as an expressive embellishment, without the composer's necessarily borrowing whole chords from the parallel key. Sometimes these melodic uses of mixture can foreshadow mixture chords or modulations that happen later in a work. Listen, for example, to the passage shown in Example 24.6, an interlude that falls between verses of "Du bist die Ruh." Up to this point, Schubert's setting has been mostly diatonic, except for a secondary diminished seventh chord that introduces the chromatic element ♭$\hat{3}$ (G♭), in measure 16. In the interlude, he introduces ♭$\hat{6}$ (C♭) as a passing tone and, in fact, emphasizes this chromatic embellishment by alternating between C♮ and C♭ in the following measures. These two chromatic elements prepare us for the mixture chords that arrive some twenty measures later.

EXAMPLE 24.6: Schubert, "Du bist die Ruh," mm. 26–30

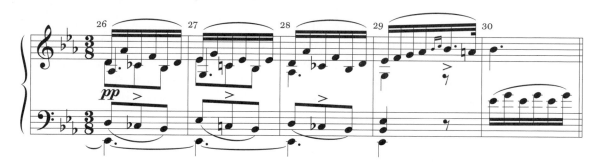

Mixture in Instrumental Music

In addition to highlighting important text in vocal music, mixture chords can create a similar dramatic effect in instrumental music. Consider measures 64–72 from the first movement of Mozart's Piano Sonata in D Major, K. 284, shown in Example 24.7. Here, the first chromatic element (in m. 64) is ♭$\hat{6}$ (B♭); two bars later, Mozart adds ♭$\hat{3}$ (F♮). Mixture appears throughout this passage, which ends with an authentic cadence in D Major and the beginning of the sonata's recapitulation (see Chapter 28). Provide an analysis beneath the score, then underline any Roman numeral that represents a mixture chord. *(Try it #9)*

EXAMPLE 24.7: Mozart, Piano Sonata in D Major, K. 284, first movement, mm. 64–72a

In this example, you may have noticed a new addition to our repertoire of mixture chords: ♭II⁶ (m. 69). Some theorists classify this chord as a mixture chord, even though one of its chromatic elements, ♭$\hat{2}$, does not come from the parallel minor scale. In passages that employ mixture for an extended period, you often find ♭II chords. We will study them in more detail in Chapter 25.

Mixture Chords in Minor

If we define mixture chords as borrowed elements from the parallel key, then some alterations we often make to chords in minor keys can be viewed as mixture. For example, in minor keys we almost always change the minor v chord to V, and the subtonic triad VII to the leading-tone vii°; both alterations arise from incorporating the leading tone, or borrowing scale-degree $\hat{7}$ from the parallel major key. Occasionally composers borrow other scale degrees from major—transforming the minor iv to IV, the major VI to vi, or the minor i to I (known as a Picardy third when placed at an authentic cadence)—but mixture (other than that involving the leading tone) is far less common in minor keys than in major.

○ ○

Chromatic Mediants and Submediants

Suppose you came across an E-Major or E♭-minor chord in the key of C Major. How might you explain it? Some theorists would call these chords mixture chords, even though there is no borrowing from C minor. The E-Major chord is a simple alteration of the chord quality from iii to III, or E minor to E Major. To achieve the E♭-minor chord, a kind of "double" mixture, first the ♭III chord is borrowed from the key of C minor, then its quality is altered to minor, to the ♭iii chord.

Such chords, known as **chromatic mediants**, provide even more unexpected color than the mixture chords we have seen thus far. They make possible a variety of harmonic colors in minor keys, which enjoy few mixture possibilities when limited to chords borrowed from the parallel major. Of the many possible chords of this type found in late Romantic-era music, the most common are alterations of the mediant triad—hence the name "chromatic mediant"—and alterations of the submediant triad. In major keys, you might encounter such chords as ♭iii and III (in addition to the ♭III of mode mixture) and VI and ♭vi (in addition to the mode mixture ♭VI). In music of the nineteenth and early twentieth centuries, you might also find chromatic chords that do not fall into the chromatic mediant or submediant category: for example, the D♭-minor chord in C Major, ♭ii. When analyzing such chords, first check to see whether the alterations in chord quality and resolution may be attributed to a temporary tonicization (or secondary-dominant function).

KEY CONCEPT

In writing Roman numerals for chords that have been chromatically altered:

- Use uppercase Roman numerals for major and augmented chords and lowercase for minor and diminished chords.
- Include + or ° for augmented and diminished chords.
- Check whether seventh chords need ⌀ or ° designations.
- Place an accidental before the Roman numeral only if the *root* has been altered. Remember: With Roman numerals or scale-degree numbers, we use flat for lowered and sharp for raised regardless of the key signature (for example, the lowered-submediant root in A Major is spelled with a natural sign, F♮, but the chord is still designated ♭VI).

Mixture and Modulation

There are a number of ways in which mixture can color longer spans of music. We will look at three here: the expansion of a mixture chord through extensive tonicization, direct modulation to a mixture-related key, and direct modulation to a chromatic-mediant-related key. In Chapter 29, we will explore chromatic modulations that feature mixture chords as pivots.

3.16

Listen to the first two verses of Schubert's song "Der Lindenbaum," then compare the opening of these verses, given in Examples 24.8a and b. (This song should be familiar to you from our discussion of parallel keys in Chapter 4.)

EXAMPLE 24.8: Schubert, "Der Lindenbaum," from *Winterreise*

(a) Mm. 8b–12a   3.17

Translation: By the fountain in front of the gate, there stands a linden tree.

(b) Mm. 28b–32a   3.20

Translation: I had to pass it again today in the dead of night.

A comparison of the texts shows sharp contrasts: the first is an objective, third-person statement of fact, while the second is written in the first person and conjures up the imagery of deep night and darkness. With this imagery, Schubert moves to the "darker," minor mode by shifting from E Major to E minor—an extended tonicization of the minor tonic mixture chord.

In your analyses, you may find tonicizations of other mixture chords too, as well as modulations to keys derived from mixture chords. Often composers introduce elements of mixture to prepare for a modulation. Look, for example, at the excerpt from Schubert's *Moment musical* in A♭ Major, Op. 94, No. 6, given in Example 24.9. After the repeat sign, Schubert introduces the modal scale-degrees ♭$\hat{3}$ (C♭) and ♭$\hat{6}$ (F♭) in a transitional chromatic section that leads to a new phrase clearly in E Major (complete with change of key signature). What is the relation of E Major to the tonic key of A♭ Major? It is an enharmonic respelling of ♭VI (F♭ Major). When you discover seemingly distant key relations, check to see whether the new tonic is an enharmonic respelling of a mixture chord. Such respellings are not unusual, since they allow the performer to read the score in a more comfortable key.

EXAMPLE 24.9: Schubert, *Moment musical* in A♭ Major, Op. 94, No. 6, mm. 1–39

We close with three brief snapshots from Brahms's Intermezzo in A Major, Op. 118, No. 2, to see how Brahms prepares our ears for the chromatic-mediant relation he explores later in the work. As shown in Example 24.10a, the Intermezzo begins in the key of A Major, with a phrase that ends in a half cadence preceded by a cadential $^6_4$. The melody of this phrase is repeated and varied in the opening section of this work. In contrast, a second large section begins with the music shown in part b; this passage is in F♯ minor, the relative minor of A Major. The excerpt in part c, which follows shortly after the F♯-minor passage, is in F♯ Major, a chromatic mediant. Brahms reached this relatively distant key by first "traveling" through a closely related key, then by modal coloration.

EXAMPLE 24.10: Brahms, Intermezzo in A Major, Op. 118, No. 2

(a) Mm. 1–4a

(b) Mm. 49–52

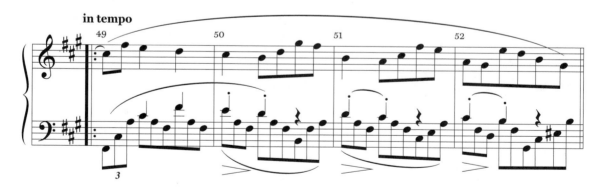

(c) Mm. 57–64a

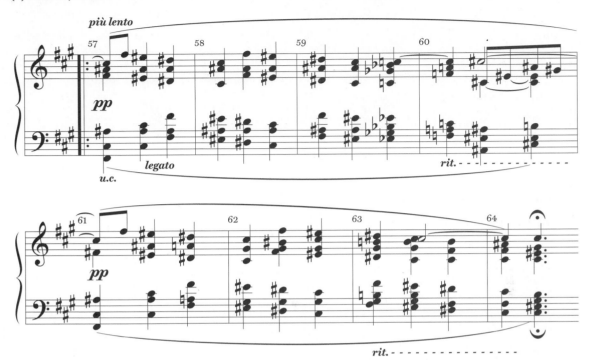

TERMS YOU SHOULD KNOW

borrowed chord	mixture	parallel key
chromatic mediant	modal scale degree	Picardy third

QUESTIONS FOR REVIEW

1. Why do we call mixture chords by that name? Why do some theorists call them "borrowed chords"?

2. What are the most common mixture chords in major keys? Where should they be used?

3. Explain how to label mixture chords with Roman numerals.

4. What alterations do we need to make in solfège syllables when singing mixture chords?

5. In a major-key composition for your own instrument, find a passage that includes mixture chords, and bring it to class. (Hint: The most likely places to look are in Romantic-period pieces. You can find these passages by imagining the parallel minor key, identifying which pitches would be ♭3 and ♭6, then hunting for these chromatic alterations.) Be ready to analyze the mixture chords with Roman numerals and sing the melodic line on solfège syllables.

CHAPTER 25

Chromatic Approaches to V:
The Neapolitan Sixth and Augmented Sixths

Outline of topics covered

Chromatic predominant chords

The Neapolitan sixth
- Voice-leading and resolution
- Writing Neapolitans: Spelling and voicing
- Intonation and performance
- Tonicizing the Neapolitan

Augmented-sixth chords
- Voice-leading and resolution
- Writing augmented sixths: Italian, French, German
- Identifying augmented-sixth chords
- Less common spellings and voicings
- Other uses of augmented-sixth chords

Overview

In this chapter, we consider two new ways in which chromatic voice-leading can intensify motion toward the dominant. The chords created by this voice-leading, the Neapolitan sixth and augmented-sixth chords, are among the most distinctive harmonies we have yet encountered. We will learn how to write them, recognize them in musical passages by ear and by eye, and interpret them in performance.

Repertoire

Ludwig van Beethoven, Piano Sonata in C♯ minor, Op. 27, No. 2 (*Moonlight*), first movement

Frédéric Chopin, Prelude in C minor, Op. 28, No. 20

Fanny Mendelssohn Hensel, "Nachtwanderer" (CD 2, track 19)

Jerome Kern and Oscar Hammerstein II, "Can't Help Lovin' Dat Man," from *Show Boat*

Wolfgang Amadeus Mozart, Dies Irae, from *Requiem*

Mozart, Piano Sonata in D Major, K. 284, third movement (CD 2, track 48)

Franz Schubert, "Der Doppelgänger"

Schubert, "Erlkönig" (CD 3, track 25)

John Philip Sousa, "The Stars and Stripes Forever" (CD 3, track 41)

Chromatic Predominant Chords

In Chapter 24, we learned about a type of chromaticism called mixture, in which diatonic scale degrees are temporarily replaced by chromatic variants taken from the parallel key. One characteristic example of mixture is the replacement of $\hat{6}$ with $\flat\hat{6}$ in major keys. This substitution creates a new tendency tone in the scale, one with a strong pull to resolve down by half step ($\flat\hat{6}$ to $\hat{5}$). In this chapter, we consider two new harmonies that share this chromatic voice-leading of $\flat\hat{6}$ to $\hat{5}$. They are generally found in minor keys (where $\flat\hat{6}$ is the "normal" sixth scale degree) or in passages in major keys that include elements of mixture. These harmonies, the Neapolitan sixth and a family of chords called augmented sixths, characteristically share the same position in the basic phrase: as chromatic predominant chords that intensify harmonic motion to V.

2.52 🎧   We begin by listening to Variation VII from the third movement of Mozart's Piano Sonata in D Major, K. 284. Follow the score in your anthology, and listen for chromatically altered chords that lead to V. Although the movement as a whole is in D Major, this variation is in D minor. Consider measures 1–4, shown in Example 25.1a. Write in the Roman numerals and figures for the chords that are familiar to you; write a question mark for any unfamiliar chord. *(Try it #1)*

EXAMPLE 25.1: Mozart, Piano Sonata in D Major, K. 284, third movement, Variation VII

(a) Mm. 1–4a

We have studied all the chords in this passage except the last chord in measure 3. This chord, spelled B♭-D-G♯, features the interval of an augmented sixth from B♭ (scale-degree $\hat{6}$ in D minor) to G♯ (scale-degree $\sharp\hat{4}$). The augmented sixth resolves outward to an octave: G♯5 moves up to A5 in the alto voice, while B♭2 (and B♭3, since it is doubled at the octave) resolves down to A2 (and A3) in the bass. The resolution, a half cadence on the dominant, is embellished by a cadential $\substack{6\\4}$.

2.55 🎧   Now consider a phrase from later in the variation, shown in Example 25.1b. These measures feature a variety of chromatic harmonies. Write in the Roman numerals and figures for the chords that are familiar to you. *(Try it #2)*

(b) Mm. 8b–12a

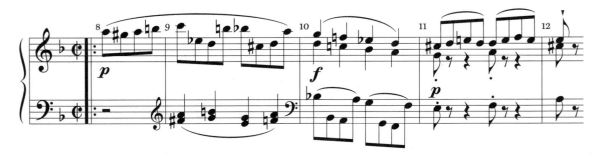

The third chord in measure 10 is part of a series of $^6_3$ chords, but it is not a harmony we have considered before. If stacked up in thirds, it is an E♭-Major chord: E♭-G-B♭. This triad, which includes both the lowered scale-degree $\hat{6}$ of D minor (that is, lowered when compared with major) and a lowered $\hat{2}$, is called a **Neapolitan sixth** chord (or ♭II⁶, in Roman numerals). If the diatonic scale-degree $\hat{2}$ (E♮) had been used in the chord instead, the harmony would be a typical predominant ii°⁶. The Neapolitan sixth substitutes in progressions like this one, where we normally find the diatonic predominants iv or ii°⁶.

We now examine each of these chord types in turn, beginning with the Neapolitan sixth.

o o o o o o o o o o o o o o o o o o o o o o o o o o o o o o o o o o o o o o o o o o o

The Neapolitan Sixth

Let's turn first to two compositions with greatly contrasting moods—the serene first movement of Beethoven's *Moonlight* Sonata and the frenetic Dies Irae from Mozart's *Requiem*—both of which feature the Neapolitan sixth. Play through the opening of the Beethoven, shown in Example 25.2a (slowly—the tempo is *Adagio sostenuto*!). Watch for accidentals that signal chromaticism. Which scale degrees are altered?

EXAMPLE 25.2: Beethoven, Piano Sonata in C♯ minor, Op. 27, No. 2 (*Moonlight*), first movement

(a) Mm. 1–5a

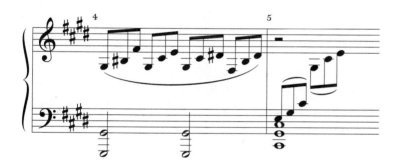

As we might expect, one of the scale degrees Beethoven alters is $\hat{7}$, which he raises in measure 4 to function as the leading tone (B♯) at the cadence. In measure 3, however, we see an unexpected accidental: D♮, the lowered supertonic. This pitch supports a major-quality triad (D♮-F♯-A), which appears in first inversion. This distinctive harmony is the chromatic predominant chord that we identified in Example 25.1b as a Neapolitan sixth chord, but which some analysts call the ♭II⁶ or Phrygian II chord. The Neapolitan is such a common chromatic harmony that analysts often designate it with N⁶ in place of a Roman numeral; ♭II⁶ is also correct, and you may use either label.

WF1

Another Way

There are a number of reasons why you might choose one label over another for Neapolitans. In sharp keys, like the Beethoven example, ♭II may seem misleading since the chord is built on D♮, not D♭; why not label the chord ♮II⁶? The answer is that ♭II generically stands for the lowered scale-degree ♭$\hat{2}$, regardless of spelling within a particular key, and it has now come into common usage. You may prefer to write N⁶

in sharp keys to avoid this problem. On the other hand, N⁶ provides no information about the scale degrees that make up the Neapolitan harmony; ♭II⁶ is more helpful in that respect, and it is consistent with our system for labeling mixture chords. Be careful not to confuse N⁶ with N for "neighbor"; usually the placement of these symbols on the score will distinguish the two.

Voice-Leading and Resolution

Example 25.2b reduces Beethoven's keyboard figuration to block chords, allowing us to examine the progression, voice-leading, and doubling more easily. Play through the example at the piano. The progression clearly follows our phrase model, T–PD–D–T, with the Neapolitan chord filling the predominant role and moving directly to V.

(b) Mm. 1–5 in block chords

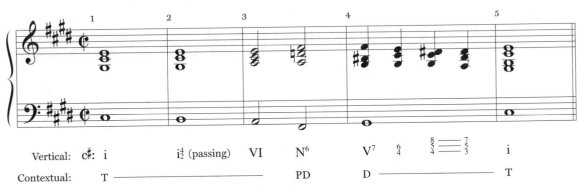

If you follow the alto voice of the block-chord reduction, you will see that it moves from ♭$\hat{2}$ directly to the leading tone in measures 3–4, spanning the interval of a diminished third. As we know from previous study, augmented or diminished melodic intervals are generally avoided in common-practice voice-leading, but in the case of the Neapolitan, composers considered the diminished third an acceptable interval (Example 25.3a). The voice-leading in the ♭II⁶–V progression acts like a "double leading tone" to the tonic: $\flat\hat{2}$ in the Neapolitan leads down to $\hat{1}$, while the leading tone in the dominant harmony tends to move up to $\hat{1}$. Some composers smooth the motion from $\flat\hat{2}$ to the leading tone by inserting a passing tone to soften the effect: $\flat\hat{2}-\hat{1}-(\sharp)\hat{7}$ (Example 25.3b). The passing tone might or might not be harmonized.

KEY CONCEPT

The N⁶ typically resolves

- directly to V (Examples 25.3a and b);
- through a cadential $^6_4$ (Example 25.3c); or
- through a vii°⁷/V (Example 25.3d), which may be followed by a cadential $^6_4$ (Example 25.3e).

EXAMPLE 25.3: Resolutions of the Neapolitan sixth

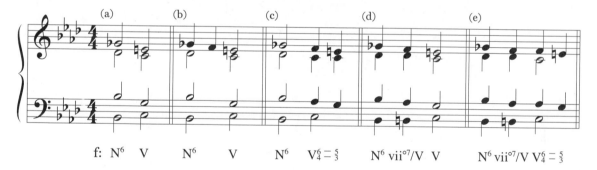

f: N⁶   V   N⁶   V   N⁶   V$^6_4$ − $^5_3$ N⁶ vii°⁷/V   V   N⁶ vii°⁷/V V$^6_4$ − $^5_3$

WF2   Now consider the dramatic excerpt from Mozart's Dies Irae shown in Example 25.4a. If possible, listen to a recording of this famous piece, or sing through the passage with your class. Although the movement is in D minor, this passage is in the minor dominant, A minor. Write in a Roman numeral analysis beneath the excerpt, then provide a contextual analysis underneath. Identify the Neapolitan sixth chord and cadential goal, paying close attention to how Mozart handles the diminished third. *(Try it #3)*

EXAMPLE 25.4: Mozart, Dies Irae, from *Requiem*

(a) Mm. 22–29

Translation: Day of wrath, that day shall dissolve the world into embers, as foretold by David with the Sibyl.

The text, taken from the Latin Requiem Mass (Mass for the Dead), depicts a wrathful Judgment Day when, according to Christian texts, sinners will be punished and the world destroyed. Mozart represents the day of wrath with agitated string arpeggiation, full chorus, a minor key, and colorful Neapolitan harmony—with ♭$\hat{2}$ prominently voiced in the soprano line, where it harmonizes the words "cum Sibylla." Here, Mozart avoids the diminished third in his voice-leading by choosing the harmonized passing-tone solution: ♭$\hat{2}$–$\hat{1}$–♯$\hat{7}$. In this case, he simply harmonizes $\hat{1}$ with a tonic harmony—a tonic with contrapuntal, not functional, importance—using the same series of first-inversion chords we heard in Example 25.1b. The sensitive conductor will realize that this tonic is not the goal of the phrase, nor a strong harmonic goal in any sense: the harmonic motion should be propelled forward, through this weakly positioned I, to V—the true goal of the phrase.

Now provide a vertical and contextual analysis for the Dies Irae passage in part b. You should find two Neapolitan sixth chords. *(Try it #4)* In what way, if any, does Mozart handle the ♭$\hat{2}$–♯$\hat{7}$ when resolving each of these chords?

(b) Mm. 34–40a

Translation: When the judge comes, the rigorous investigator of all things!

In this passage, Mozart prolongs the predominant area in measures 37–39 by means of descending parallel $\frac{6}{3}$ chords that extend from one Neapolitan chord to the other. Since the first Neapolitan does not move directly to V, there is no diminished third (although Mozart places an expressive augmented second in the soprano!). In the resolution of the second Neapolitan, Mozart harmonizes the passing tone $\hat{1}$ with a vii°⁷/V before the cadential V$^{6-5}_{4-3}$. This succession of harmonies—♭II⁶ vii°⁷/V | V$^{6-5}_{4-3}$—is one of the most common progressions associated with the Neapolitan's resolution.

SUMMARY

- We find the Neapolitan harmony most often in minor keys.
- Build it on ♭$\hat{2}$, with a major quality, and place it (usually) in first inversion (♭II⁶).
- When you write the Neapolitan in major keys, be sure to include ♭$\hat{6}$ (from mixture) to make the chord major.
- Place N⁶ in a predominant role and resolve it to V, with both its tendency tones moving down: (♭)$\hat{6}$ to $\hat{5}$, and ♭$\hat{2}$ (usually through passing tone $\hat{1}$) to ♯$\hat{7}$. Note: Do not resolve ♭$\hat{2}$ to ♮$\hat{2}$, since this voice-leading conflicts with the tendency of ♭$\hat{2}$ to move downward.
- If you harmonize the passing tone $\hat{1}$ when resolving N⁶, choose vii°⁷/V or V$^{6-5}_{4-3}$.

Writing Neapolitans: Spelling and Voicing

KEY CONCEPT

To spell Neapolitans, either

- find ♭$\hat{2}$, spell a major triad from this root, then place it in first inversion; or

- spell iv, then raise the fifth a minor second.

For example, to spell a Neapolitan in C minor, you could identify ♭$\hat{2}$ as D♭, spell a major triad (D♭-F-A♭), and then arrange it in first inversion: F-A♭-D♭. Alternatively, you could spell iv (F-A♭-C), then raise the fifth a minor second: F-A♭-D♭.

Try it #5

Spell N^6 chords in the following keys ($\hat{4}$-$\hat{6}$-♭$\hat{2}$). The first letter name should be scale-degree $\hat{4}$. Include a natural when needed to cancel an accidental from the key's signature.

KEY	NEAPOLITAN SIXTH
F♯ minor	_____
G minor	_____
A Major	_____
E minor	_____
F Major	_____
B minor	_____

As we have seen, Neapolitans characteristically appear in first inversion and often (though not always) with ♭$\hat{2}$ in the highest voice. One explanation for this voicing lies in the Neapolitan's possible origin as a chromatic embellishment of the iv chord. Look, for instance, at Example 25.5, which compares iv with ♭II^6 in D minor. The lowest two voices in these chords (scale-degrees $\hat{4}$-$\hat{6}$, or G-B♭) are identical; the Neapolitan's ♭$\hat{2}$ (E♭) is a simple half-step displacement of $\hat{1}$ (D). The ♭$\hat{2}$ not only changes the quality of the chord to major, it also adds an element of surprise to the harmony, since this chromatic tone lies outside the diatonic scale. The reason for placing ♭$\hat{2}$ in the soprano is to intensify this surprise effect, but $\hat{4}$ in the soprano is also a possibility.

KEY CONCEPT

When writing the N^6 chord, we usually place $\flat\hat{2}$ or $\hat{4}$ in the highest voice. Don't place $(\flat)\hat{6}$ in the highest voice if the N^6 moves through a tonic chord before progressing to V, because the resolution of $(\flat)\hat{6}-\hat{5}$ above $\flat\hat{2}-\hat{1}$ invariably leads to parallel fifths in the voice-leading.

EXAMPLE 25.5: Comparison of iv and N^6

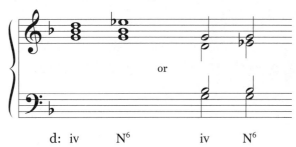

d: iv N^6 iv N^6

Let's return now to the Beethoven and Mozart examples to see how these composers handle the issues of progression, doubling, and resolution. In Example 25.2, the Neapolitan (in m. 3) is preceded by a VI (to create a tonic expansion), the third of the Neapolitan chord (scale-degree $\hat{4}$) is doubled, and $\flat\hat{2}$ resolves down to $\sharp\hat{7}$ in the dominant harmony. In Example 25.4a, the Neapolitan (in m. 28) is preceded by a descending string of $\substack{6\\3}$ chords, the third of the Neapolitan chord (scale-degree $\hat{4}$) is doubled in the choral parts, and $\flat\hat{2}$ resolves down, through a harmonized passing tone $\hat{1}$, to $\sharp\hat{7}$ in the dominant harmony. From these examples, we can add the following to our list of guidelines.

KEY CONCEPT

When writing N^6 chords:

1. Precede the Neapolitan with any harmony that would normally precede a predominant-function harmony. This may include another predominant harmony, a tonic harmony, tonic substitute, or tonic expansion; another possibility is a string of parallel $\substack{6\\3}$ chords.
2. Double $\hat{4}$ (the bass note, when the harmony appears in its characteristic first inversion). If necessary, you may try another doubling; but if $\flat\hat{2}$ is doubled, it moves to $\natural\hat{2}$ in an inner voice only—never in the soprano.

Mozart's treatment of the Neapolitan in Example 25.4b differs somewhat from our guidelines, however. Look first at the final Neapolitan of this example (mm. 39–40). Again Mozart precedes the N^6 with a descending string of $\frac{6}{3}$ chords, but here the fifth of the chord (scale-degree $\hat{6}$) is doubled in the choral parts. The $\flat\hat{2}$ resolves normally, down through a harmonized passing-tone $\hat{1}$ to $\sharp\hat{7}$ in the dominant harmony, but because of the doubled scale-degree $\hat{6}$, the composer must resolve one of them irregularly in order to avoid parallel octaves. The $\hat{6}$ in the tenor thus leaps upward by a perfect fifth. Mozart chooses an unconventional doubling in the first Neapolitan of this passage as well, doubling $\flat\hat{2}$ in the choral parts. This results in unusual voice-leading in the soprano, which moves upward by an augmented second (E♭ to F♯).

Why might Mozart have decided on these unconventional doublings? Perhaps he felt that the augmented second in measure 37 and the tenor leap to a high F4 in measure 39 would contribute to the overall sense of despair and frenzy that the text portrays. In your own writing, conform to the guidelines for doubling and voice-leading unless you have an equally good reason for doing otherwise.

Intonation and Performance

What performance issues might we keep in mind when performing the Mozart *Requiem* excerpt given in Example 25.4b and, by extension, other passages with Neapolitan sixth chords? Since $\flat\hat{2}$ lies outside the diatonic scale and since the Neapolitan relies on its major quality for its identity, correct tuning should be a primary concern. Try singing the soprano line of Example 25.4b with solfège syllables. You will need to use three inflected syllables: *ti* for $\sharp\hat{7}$, *ra* for $\flat\hat{2}$ (*re* lowered a half step), and *mi* for $\sharp\hat{3}$. Keep in mind that the excerpt begins with a prolonged leading-tone harmony before the first tonic triad in measure 36. (Surely Mozart chose this fully diminished quality to portray the fear in the text!) *(Try it #6)*

You may have found the diminished fifth (*ti–fa*) with which the excerpt begins somewhat difficult to tune, but probably more challenging was the augmented second in measure 37: *ra–mi*. It is sometimes helpful to exaggerate the altered scale degrees to tune them correctly: think $\flat\hat{2}$ (*ra*) very low, and think $\sharp\hat{3}$ (*mi*) very high. You may even wish to color your tone a bit darker for the lowered pitches and brighter for the raised pitches. The same advice applies in measure 39: try to make the interval between $\flat\hat{2}$ and $\hat{1}$ (*ra–do*) an especially narrow half step. Such exaggerations hold true especially in ensemble singing and playing, where your line is crucial in tuning the chord qualities correctly.

Tonicizing the Neapolitan

3.30

The Neapolitan harmony can be tonicized, either by its own secondary dominant or by a more extended progression in the ♭II key area. Listen to the passage from Schubert's famous song "Erlkönig" given in Example 25.6, and write a Roman numeral analysis beneath the score (this passage is in D minor). What is unusual about Schubert's voicing of the Neapolitan? Where is the Neapolitan tonicized? How do the harmonies in this passage correspond with the meaning of the text? (*Try it #7*)

EXAMPLE 25.6: Schubert, "Erlkönig," mm. 115–123a

Translation (sung by the Erlking): "I love you, I'm aroused by your beautiful form; and if you are not willing, I'll take you by force."

KEY CONCEPT

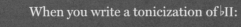

When you write a tonicization of ♭II:

1. Think temporarily in the ♭II key area in order to help yourself remember the correct accidentals (♭II is typically in root position when tonicized, and ♭$\hat{2}$ may be doubled).
2. Double-check that your secondary dominant or secondary leading-tone chord has the correct quality (Mm7 or fully diminished seventh).
3. Follow the regular guidelines for resolution that should be familiar to you from Chapters 19 and 21.

Augmented-Sixth Chords

Voice-Leading and Resolution

2.52 🎧

2.53 🎧

Listen again to Variation VII from Mozart's Piano Sonata in D Major, with which we began the chapter. As you follow the score in your anthology, pay special attention to the cadence in measures 3–4, shown in Example 25.7a.

EXAMPLE 25.7: Mozart, Piano Sonata in D Major, K. 284, third movement, Variation VII

(a) Mm. 3–4a

With the predominant IV⁶ chord on the third beat of measure 3, we expect motion from IV⁶ to V—a typical half cadence. At the last moment, though, Mozart raises scale-degree $\hat{4}$ to #$\hat{4}$, resolving in the next measure to $\hat{5}$. This chromatic alteration (#$\hat{4}$–$\hat{5}$) is already familiar to us, from our study of the V⁽⁷⁾/V and vii°⁽⁷⁾/V chords. Mozart also lowers scale-degree 6 to ♭6—a familiar technique from modal mixture—then moves down by half step to $\hat{5}$.

These chromatic alterations are what define the predominant family of chords called **augmented-sixth chords**, so called because the interval from (♭)$\hat{6}$ to $\sharp\hat{4}$ is an augmented sixth (A⁶). The particular chromatic predominant in the Mozart example—built of scale-degrees (♭)$\hat{6}$, $\sharp\hat{4}$, and $\hat{1}$ (or, in solfège, *le, fi,* and *do*) and featuring a resolution to V by half-step motion outward ($\sharp\hat{4}$–$\hat{5}$ in an upper voice and ♭$\hat{6}$–5 in the bass)—is called an **Italian augmented-sixth chord** and is labeled It⁶.

2.54

Now listen to the Mozart variation to hear another type of augmented-sixth chord. In measures 5–8, shown in Example 25.7b, the key has changed to A minor (the minor dominant of D minor). The chord in measure 6 contains the notes F, A, C♮, and D♯. In addition to the *le, do,* and *fi* (scale-degrees $\hat{6}$, $\hat{1}$, and $\sharp\hat{4}$) of the Italian sixth, this chord includes *me* (the minor $\hat{3}$). This sonority is known as the **German augmented-sixth chord**, labeled Gr⁶. As expected, D♯5 resolves up to E5 in measure 7, and F3 resolves down to E3. As the Mozart example shows, it is common for a Gr⁶ to resolve to an embellished V⁶₄–₃, rather than directly to V: the left-hand triad (F-A-C) would produce audible parallel fifths if it were to move directly to V (E-G♯-B).

(b) Mm. 5–8

Sometimes $\hat{2}$ (*re*) is added instead of $\hat{3}$ to scale-degrees $\hat{6}$, $\hat{1}$, and $\sharp\hat{4}$ of the Italian sixth, making a sonority known as the **French augmented-sixth chord** (Fr⁶). All three types are shown in Example 25.8.

EXAMPLE 25.8: Three common types of augmented-sixth chords

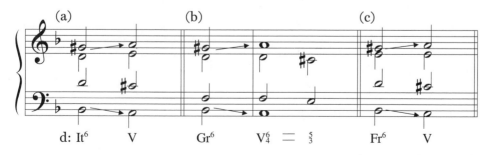

KEY CONCEPT

Although there are several varieties of augmented-sixth chords, they all share the same pattern of voice-leading to V: #4̂ up to 5̂ in an upper voice, and (♭)6̂ down to 5̂ in the bass. In addition, augmented-sixth chords typically include scale-degree 1̂, which usually resolves down to the leading tone.

Example 25.9 summarizes this voice-leading principle. Think of the two tendency tones of the augmented-sixth chord as derived from two ideas we have already studied: #4̂ up to 5̂ captures the temporary leading tone of secondary dominants to V, while (♭)6̂ down to 5̂ derives from mixture. Because of these two chromatic elements, augmented-sixth chords have the strongest tendency to move to V. They usually go directly to V, without intervening chords (as we have seen, the Gr⁶ is an exception).

EXAMPLE 25.9: Voice-leading diagram for augmented-sixth chords

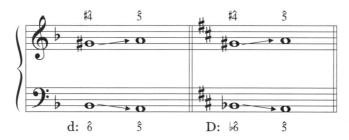

Although augmented-sixth chords more naturally arise in minor keys, they are not uncommon in major keys. It is for this reason that we write the bass-line resolution pattern as (♭)6̂ to 5̂—to indicate that in major keys, scale-degree 6̂ must be lowered. One familiar example of an augmented-sixth chord in a major key is the introduction to "The Stars and Stripes Forever." Listen to Example 25.10 to hear how Sousa prepares for the #4̂ and ♭6̂.

3.41

EXAMPLE 25.10: Sousa, "The Stars and Stripes Forever," mm. 1–4a

Sousa expands the tonic area with a vi chord, then introduces an element of mixture by transforming the submediant harmony to ♭VI; this prepares the bass motion of the augmented sixth. Then in the soprano, Sousa introduces a chromatic ascent that naturally leads through ♯4̂ to 5̂.

The augmented-sixth sonority is not often heard in pre-Classical-era compositions, and does not appear frequently in figured basses. In Classical style, augmented-sixth chords are typically placed to emphasize the arrival of a particularly significant dominant harmony. The dramatic sound of the augmented-sixth chord is more freely employed in Romantic-era compositions, but even then the sound is saved for dramatic points in the piece.

While these sonorities are not common in twentieth-century popular music, they can be found. Look, for example, at the approach to the cadence in measure 33 of Example 25.11, an excerpt from Kern and Hammerstein's "Can't Help Lovin' Dat Man." In measure 32, we see the now-familiar tendency tones of the German augmented sixth: the C♭ (♭6̂) in the bass, resolving down to B♭ (5̂), and the A♮ (♯4̂) in the alto voice. In this freer style, the ♯4̂ does not resolve up to 5̂, but the sound of the augmented-sixth chord is still a distinctive intensification of the motion to V. Interestingly, the popular-music symbol given above the staff is B♭7, an enharmonic respelling of the augmented-sixth chord. We will learn more about this enharmonic relationship in Chapter 29.

EXAMPLE 25.11: Kern and Hammerstein, "Can't Help Lovin' Dat Man," mm. 27–33a

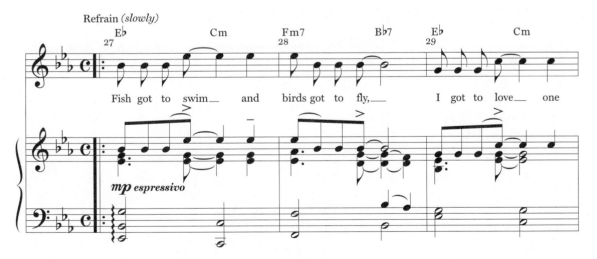

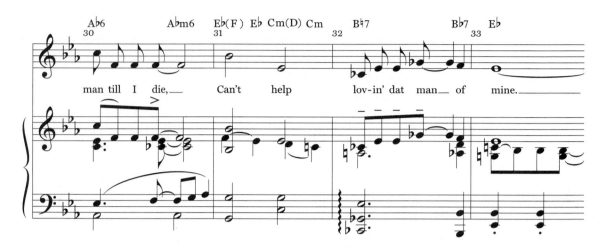

Writing Augmented Sixths: Italian, French, German

Consider the $\sharp\hat{4}$–$\hat{5}$ / $\flat\hat{6}$–$\hat{5}$ outer-voice pattern as the scaffold upon which to build each of the three types of augmented-sixth chords: Italian, French, or German.

KEY CONCEPT

To write an A^6–V progression in four voices:

1. Place scale-degree $\hat{5}$ in the bass and an upper voice (the soprano is a characteristic but not required voicing), leaving an empty space before it for the augmented sixth (Example 25.12a).
2. In the empty space, write in the two tendency tones leading to $\hat{5}$: $(\flat)\hat{6}$–$\hat{5}$ in the bass and $\sharp\hat{4}$–$\hat{5}$ in the upper voice. If you are writing in a major key, don't forget to add the correct accidental to lower scale-degree $\hat{6}$ (Example 25.12b).
3. Add scale-degree $\hat{1}$ in one of the inner voices (Example 25.12c).
4. Add a fourth note, following these guidelines (Example 25.12d).
   - If you are writing an Italian sixth (It^6), double scale-degree $\hat{1}$.
   - If you are writing a French sixth (Fr^6), add scale-degree $\hat{2}$ (an augmented fourth above the bass note).
   - If you are writing a German sixth (Gr^6), add scale-degree $\hat{3}$ from the minor mode (a perfect fifth above the bass note; in major keys, you will need to add an accidental).

5. Resolve the tendency tones by half step to $\hat{5}$, and move the remaining tones to the closest possible chord tone in the dominant harmony.

6. Resolve an It^6 or Fr^6 directly to V; Gr^6 chords often resolve to V$_{4-3}^{6-5}$ in order to avoid parallel fifths.

EXAMPLE 25.12: Spelling augmented-sixth chords

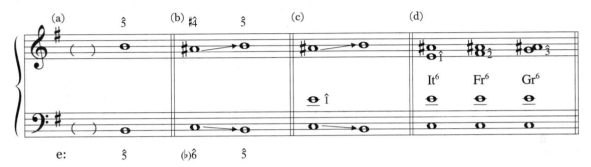

Try it #8

Follow the procedure in the KEY CONCEPT box above to spell augmented-sixth chords in the keys and chord types below.

KEY	A^6 TYPE	($\flat$)$\hat{6}$	$\sharp\hat{4}$	$\hat{1}$	REMAINING PITCH
G minor	Gr^6	_____	_____	_____	_____
A Major	It^6	_____	_____	_____	_____
C Major	Fr^6	_____	_____	_____	_____
D minor	It^6	_____	_____	_____	_____
F$\sharp$ minor	Gr^6	_____	_____	_____	_____

In keyboard pieces, augmented sixths are often voiced within an octave, resolving in the outer voices to the octave $\hat{5}$ in the V chord. They are generally preceded by harmonies from the tonic or predominant area of the phrase, as shown in Example 25.13. A common approach is one that features $(\flat)\hat{6}$—either iv⁶ (part a) or $(\flat)$VI (part b)—followed by an alteration of scale-degree $\hat{4}$ to $\sharp\hat{4}$. (The iv⁶–V motion is familiar to us from the Phrygian cadence.) Another, elegant way to introduce these pitches is by means of a chromatic voice exchange, where $\hat{6}$ and $\hat{4}$ exchange with $\sharp\hat{4}$ and $\flat\hat{6}$ (part c). This voice exchange also works if one of the chromatic elements is present in the first chord through mode mixture (part d) or the use of a secondary dominant (part e).

EXAMPLE 25.13: Approaches to augmented-sixth chords

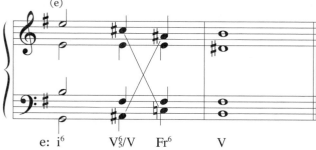

Another Way

You may want to invent your own ways of remembering which chord is which. You might, for example, think of the geography of these countries in relation to the scale degrees added: moving from the south to the north, you have Italy ($\hat{1}$), France ($\hat{2}$), Germany ($\hat{3}$). Another way is to visualize each chord as a sandwich: $\flat\hat{6}$ and $\sharp\hat{4}$ are the two pieces of bread, which stay the same for each chord. The Italian sandwich is rather plain: just bread and meat ($\hat{1}$). The French sandwich adds Dijon mustard—this piquant flavor reminds us of the augmented fourth above the bass. The German sandwich has no mustard, but instead adds hearty sauerkraut—the hearty perfect fifth above the bass. Use your imagination!

WF3

We will generally refer to augmented-sixth chords by their "geographic" abbreviations—It^6, Fr^6, and Gr^6—though you may see alternate labeling systems in other texts. One way to remember which chord is which is to memorize the figured bass associated with each chord: It^6, Fr$^4_3$, and Gr$^6_5$. (Keep in mind that these numbers represent figured bass, *not* inversion symbols. Augmented-sixth chords function as voice-leading chords, not as inversions of some "altered chord." Don't attempt to stack the thirds to find a "root"!) These figures should remind you that for the Fr$^4_3$, for example, in addition to the augmented sixth above the bass, you must also write a third (scale-degree $\hat{1}$) and a fourth (scale-degree $\hat{2}$).

You will also want to refer to the geographic names as you develop strategies for identifying these chords aurally. Probably the easiest to identify by ear is the Fr^6, since, in addition to the augmented sixth (between $\flat\hat{6}$ and $\sharp\hat{4}$) and the augmented fourth (or diminished fifth, between $\hat{1}$ and $\sharp\hat{4}$), you can listen for the augmented fourth between $\flat\hat{6}$ and $\hat{2}$. Some listeners may also be able to identify the Fr^6 from the whole step (or minor seventh in some voicings) between $\hat{1}$ and $\hat{2}$. In all, the Fr^6 typically sounds the most dissonant.

The It^6 and Gr^6 are easier to confuse with each other: listen carefully for scale-degree $\hat{3}$ (the perfect fifth above the bass), which distinguishes the Gr^6. The Gr^6 may also be recognized by its similarity in sound to a dominant seventh chord (with which it is enharmonic). But although the sound is similar, the characteristic pattern of resolution for the $\sharp\hat{4}$ and $\flat\hat{6}$ in the augmented sixth is quite different from the dominant seventh resolution, making their functions easy to distinguish.

Chords as National Character?

The geographical names for augmented-sixth chords are used widely today, but until recently their origin was shrouded in mystery. Theorist Robert Gauldin has identified the source of the terms as an 1806 treatise by John Calcott called *A Musical Grammar* (London). The chords were named according to Calcott's perception of the national character of the Italians ("elegance"), French ("feebleness"??!), and Germans ("strength"). Most treatises from that time, however, do not refer to these terms when they describe augmented-sixth sonorities and explain how to resolve them.

Identifying Augmented-Sixth Chords

Listen one more time to Variation VII from Mozart's Piano Sonata in D Major, while following the score in your anthology. This time we examine measures 13–17, given in Example 25.14. Find an augmented-sixth chord, identify its type, then examine how it is approached and resolved.

EXAMPLE 25.14: Mozart, Piano Sonata in D Major, K. 284, third movement, Variation VII, mm. 13b–17

KEY CONCEPT

To identify an augmented-sixth chord quickly, look for $\flat\hat{6}$ to $\hat{5}$ in the bass, then confirm by checking for $\sharp\hat{4}$ moving to $\hat{5}$ in an upper voice.

WF4   The augmented-sixth chord, an It^6, appears at the beginning of measure 16. The chord that precedes it is the predominant IV^6. The resolution to the dominant is normal: G♯5 resolves up to A5, and B♭3 resolves down to A3. The only unusual feature is the embellishment of the dominant by $\hat{6}\text{-}\hat{5}$.

Look now at an excerpt from Chopin's Prelude in C minor, Op. 28, No. 20, shown in Example 25.15. As before, identify the augmented-sixth chord, then examine its voice-leading and resolution.

EXAMPLE 25.15: Chopin, Prelude in C minor, Op. 28, No. 20, mm. 5–6

This augmented sixth, on beat 2 of measure 6, is the French type. Like the augmented sixth in Example 25.1, this one is approached by a descending chromatic bass line, doubled in octaves. The chord immediately preceding the Fr^6 is a tonic triad (with chromatic passing tone in the bass). The Fr^6 resolves as expected to V, with F♯ in the alto moving up to G, and A♭ in the bass resolving down to G.

When you perform an augmented sixth, try to make the resolution of these tendency tones clear—bring out the voices that carry the ♯$\hat{4}$–$\hat{5}$ and ♭$\hat{6}$–$\hat{5}$ voice-leading. You may find that singing solfège syllables helps you identify and tune these altered pitches: *fi–sol* for ♯$\hat{4}$ to $\hat{5}$, and *le–sol* for ♭$\hat{6}$ to $\hat{5}$. Again, think high in tuning the ♯$\hat{4}$ and low when tuning the ♭$\hat{6}$ on a nonkeyboard instrument, so that the interval is absolutely clear.

Less Common Spellings and Voicings

Occasionally you might see an augmented-sixth chord in a less characteristic voicing—with ♭$\hat{6}$ above ♯$\hat{4}$, creating a diminished third rather than an augmented sixth. Listen, for example, to the final cadence of Fanny Mendelssohn Hensel's "Nachtwanderer," given in Example 25.16.

2.21

EXAMPLE 25.16: Hensel, "Nachtwanderer," mm. 34–39

Translation: My singing is a cry, a cry only from my dreams.

Since the chord in question (in m. 37) appears on the word "Träumen" (dreams), its dissonant ambiguity may be an element of text painting. The analyst who tries to stack this chord in thirds gets B♮-D♭-F-A♭—not a type of seventh chord with which we are familiar, given its diminished third from B♮ to D♭. Instead, we need to recognize the familiar elements of the augmented sixth in this F-Major context: B♮ is ♯$\hat{4}$, and D♭ is ♭$\hat{6}$. Since the chord also includes scale-degrees $\hat{1}$ and ♭$\hat{3}$, we would call this a Gr°³ (German diminished-third) chord. It is approached by a chromatic voice exchange, as marked in the example. In measure 35, Hensel elegantly prepares all the chromatic elements of the diminished-third chord by introducing D♭ as a chromatic passing tone in the bass, and B♮ and A♭ as the root and seventh of a vii°⁷/V; she then maintains ♭$\hat{6}$ as an element of mixture in the word "Rufen" (cry) in measure 36.

One other less common spelling of the augmented sixth is a variant of the Gr⁶ chord. Occasionally, for voice-leading purposes, composers spell the German sixth in major keys with a doubly augmented fourth above the bass, rather than a perfect fifth (that is, with ♯$\hat{2}$ instead of ♭$\hat{3}$), as shown in Example 25.17a. In analysis, it's easier simply to call this chord a Gr⁶ rather than create a new name and symbol.

There are other chords possible in the "augmented-sixth family"—for example, ♭$\hat{6}$-$\hat{7}$-$\hat{2}$-♯$\hat{4}$, the so-called half-diminished augmented-sixth chord, where $\hat{7}$ substitutes for $\hat{1}$ of a Fr⁶ (Example 25.17b). In this and related chords, the augmented sixth usually resolves as expected, and the other voices move by step to members of the next chord.

EXAMPLE 25.17: Other types of augmented-sixth chords

Other Uses of Augmented-Sixth Chords

For special effect, composers sometimes apply the voice-leading principles of the augmented-sixth chord to scale-degree $\hat{1}$ and the tonic triad, lending the augmented-sixth chord a kind of dominant function. We label this type of A⁶ as though it were a secondary dominant: for example, Gr⁶/I (German sixth of I). Here, the characteristic voice-leading is ♭$\hat{2}$–$\hat{1}$ in the bass and (♯)$\hat{7}$–$\hat{1}$ in an upper voice. All varieties (It, Fr, Gr) include scale-degree $\hat{4}$; the French adds $\hat{5}$, and the German adds (♭)$\hat{6}$.

Look at Example 25.18, drawn from Schubert's song "Der Doppelgänger" ("The Ghostly Double"), and identify an example of this secondary-dominant kind of augmented-sixth chord. Which type is it? *(Try it #9)*

EXAMPLE 25.18: Schubert, "Der Doppelgänger," mm. 36–46a

Translation: [I shudder] when I see his face—the moon shows me my own form. You ghostly double, you pale companion!

TERMS YOU SHOULD KNOW

augmented-sixth chord Fr^6 Neapolitan $\frac{5}{3}$

diminished-third chord Gr^6 Neapolitan sixth

It^6

QUESTIONS FOR REVIEW

1. Where are Neapolitan sixth chords typically found in a phrase? What is their function?
2. What chords may precede a Neapolitan? Which chords usually follow it?
3. Where are augmented-sixth chords typically found in a phrase? What is their function?
4. What chords may precede an augmented-sixth chord? Which chords usually follow it?
5. Why are N^6 and A^6 chords often found in minor-key pieces or major-key pieces that employ mixture?
6. Under what special conditions may the Neapolitan appear in root position? What is doubled if it is in root position?
7. Which elements of the A^6 chords are shared with secondary-dominant-function chords to V? In major keys, which elements are shared with mixture chords?
8. In music for your own instrument, find one Neapolitan sixth chord and at least two different types of augmented-sixth chords (solo-line instrumentalists will need to consider both melody and accompaniment). If in a piece for voice, how does the N^6 or A^6 reflect the text? If for another instrument, how does the chord color the passage in question? How might you play the passage to bring out this unusual chord color?

PART V

Musical Form and Interpretation

CHAPTER 26

Popular Song and Art Song

Outline of topics covered

Overview

Having studied chromatic harmony and modulation, we now turn to short, complete compositions in which these musical elements come into play: songs. Because the repertoire is vast, we will limit ourselves to two types, early twentieth-century American popular song and the nineteenth-century German Lied. We will consider standard song forms, musical interpretation of the text, and new harmonic features typical of popular songs.

Repertoire

Johannes Brahms, "Die Mainacht" (CD 1, track 63)

George Gershwin, "I Got Rhythm," from *Girl Crazy* (CD 1, track 87)

John Lennon and Paul McCartney, "Eleanor Rigby," from *Revolver*

James Myers and Max Freedman, "Rock Around the Clock"

Franz Schubert, "Erlkönig" (CD 3, track 25)

Clara Schumann, "Liebst du um Schönheit" (CD 3, track 34)

Robert Schumann, "Im wunderschönen Monat Mai," from *Dichterliebe* (CD 3, track 38)

Meredith Willson, "Till There Was You," from *The Music Man* (CD 3, track 63)

○ ○

The Musical Language of the Popular Song

3.63 We begin by listening to Meredith Willson's "Till There Was You," familiar from our analysis in Chapter 17. As you listen to the entire song, mark in your anthology score where each phrase ends and with which type of cadence, then identify similar and contrasting phrases with lowercase alphabet letters.

3.65 We know from Chapter 17 that "Till There Was You" begins with a parallel period, with the antecedent phrase (**a**) ending on a half cadence in measure 8, and the consequent phrase (**a´**) ending on an authentic cadence in measures 15–16. You probably labeled the following phrase, shown in Example 26.1, as contrasting (**b**): here, the harmonic rhythm speeds up, and the melody soars into a higher register, to its climax on the words "music" and "wonderful," then slowly descends to a half cadence on "dew" in measure 24. Finally, you probably noticed that the opening melody returns with the upbeat to measure 25, rounding out a four-part **a a b a** formal scheme—or, more precisely, **a a´ b a´**, since the concluding phrase repeats the initial consequent phrase (**a´**), to end the song on the tonic harmony.

EXAMPLE 26.1: Willson, "Till There Was You," mm. 16b–24a

Quaternary and Verse-Refrain Forms

In a four-part song form with an **a a b a** design—sometimes called a **quaternary,** or **thirty-two-bar, song form**—the first two phrases begin the same (they may be identical or may differ at the cadence). They are followed by a contrasting section, then a return to the opening material.

KEY CONCEPT

In quaternary (**a a b a**) song form, the opening (**a**) sections are called **chorus 1**. The contrasting section (**b**) is known as the **bridge**, and the final return to the opening material (**a**) is called **chorus 2**. The bridge section may temporarily tonicize another key.

Mark each section with the correct term in your anthology score of "Till There Was You." *(Try it #1)* Quaternary song forms may also be written with other designs, most commonly **a b a c**.

1.87 Listen now to another familiar song, George Gershwin's "I Got Rhythm," while following the score in your anthology. One of the first things you may have noticed is that the familiar part, "I got rhythm," doesn't appear until measure 29. This portion of the song is known as the **refrain**. Often the most memorable part of a song, the refrain may be performed without its accompanying verse or verses. What is the form of the refrain in this song? *(Try it #2)*

The opening twenty-eight measures are known as the **verse**, and the song form as a whole as **verse-refrain**. The verse of a song plays a similar role to the recitative in an opera's recitative-aria pairing: it sets the scene and tells a story. The verse may display a less predictable harmonic structure than the refrain, and may modulate. Is this the case in Gershwin's song? *(Try it #3)*

KEY CONCEPT

The design of a verse-refrain song generally follows this model:

Verse	Refrain
Like recitative	Like aria
(may modulate)	Chorus 1–bridge–chorus 2
	a a b a

Chord Extensions: Added-Sixth and Ninth Chords

1.88 Let's turn now to a more detailed harmonic analysis of Gershwin's verse. Listen again to measures 3–10 of the verse (the initial vocal phrase that follows the two-bar introduction), while marking Roman numerals in Example 26.2a.

EXAMPLE 26.2: Gershwin, "I Got Rhythm"

(a) Mm. 3–10

The first three measures of this vocal phrase seem to express a typical harmonic phrase opening, with a neighboring $^6_4$ chord prolonging the tonic harmony: i $^5_3$ $^6_4$ $^5_3$. Yet the tonic harmony of measure 5 is "clouded" by an additional pitch, E♭3. How are we to analyze this chord? It has a tonic function, but includes an extra pitch a major sixth above the bass note. Pitches added to triads or seventh chords are sometimes called **extensions**—and this added sixth is an example. We call this sonority an **added-sixth chord** (written i^{add6}).

WF1

KEY CONCEPT

An added sixth may color a triad or seventh chord. It is generally a major sixth, whether the triad to which it is added is major or minor. We analyze an added-sixth chord with its regular Roman numeral plus the label ^{add6} or $^{+6}$.

The next chord in the Gershwin song (m. 6) consists of the pitches E♭-G-B♭-D♭-F. These pitches create a **ninth chord**, a seventh chord plus a major ninth (F) above the E♭ root.

KEY CONCEPT

In popular styles, major or minor sevenths may be added to chords on almost any degree of the diatonic scale. In addition, composers sometimes add ninths above the root. No matter what the quality of the underlying harmony, the added ninth is usually a major ninth—except in the case of the dominant seventh chord, where minor ninths are typically added.

The added sixth and the ninth are the two most common extensions to any triad or seventh chord. When analyzing ninth chords, use the traditional figured-bass method of labeling intervals above the bass note.

Mark as many sevenths and ninths as you can in Example 26.2b, measures 15–18 of the Gershwin verse.

(b) Mm. 15–18

You should have found seventh chords in every measure of this example. Measure 15 begins with a tonic triad that shifts to i⁷ on the third beat; measure 16 begins with a iv⁹₇ (C-E♭-G-B♭-D) and concludes with an F⁷ᵃᵈᵈ⁶ sonority that functions as V⁷/III. Indeed, the tonicization of III in the last three measures of this excerpt hint at the modulation to B♭ Major with which the verse ends.

Pentatonic and Blues Scales

Many popular songs are based on pentatonic scales—both the major pentatonic (*do-re-mi-sol-la*) and minor pentatonic (*do-me-fa-sol-te*; see Chapters 3 and 4 for a review). Art songs also sometimes draw on these scales to evoke a folk style.

Another scale resource associated with popular styles is the **blues scale**. Sing through example Example 26.3, the vocal line from the 1950s song "Rock Around the Clock." What scale underlies this melody? The melody begins firmly in C Major, but includes both a lowered seventh and a lowered third scale degree—two of three possible **blue notes** found in popular songs.

EXAMPLE 26.3: Myers and Freedman, "Rock Around the Clock" (refrain melody)

Example 26.4 gives an example of the blues scale. You may find blue notes within the context of a complete blues scale or, more commonly, as isolated pitches within a primarily diatonic passage. You may also see them in passages that feature mixture, where $\hat{6}$ and $\flat\hat{6}$ are heard as well.

EXAMPLE 26.4: Blues scale

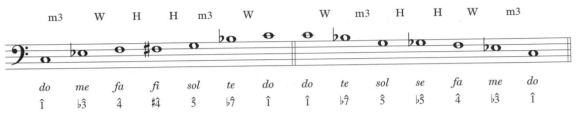

do	*me*	*fa*	*fi*	*sol*	*te*	*do*	*do*	*te*	*sol*	*se*	*fa*	*me*	*do*
$\hat{1}$	$\flat\hat{3}$	$\hat{4}$	$\sharp\hat{4}$	$\hat{5}$	$\flat\hat{7}$	$\hat{1}$	$\hat{1}$	$\flat\hat{7}$	$\hat{5}$	$\flat\hat{5}$	$\hat{4}$	$\flat\hat{3}$	$\hat{1}$

KEY CONCEPT

In the blues style, the distinction between major and minor is blurred by permitting both $\hat{3}$ and $\flat\hat{3}$ and both $\hat{7}$ and $\flat\hat{7}$. It also allows $\sharp\hat{4}$ and $\hat{4}$ and $\flat\hat{5}$ and $\hat{5}$.

The Twelve-Bar Blues   One of the most striking aspects of blues compositions is a characteristic harmonic progression known as the **twelve-bar blues**. This progression, shown in the diagram below, begins with four measures of tonic harmony, followed by two measures of IV and two of I. The last four bars feature V–IV–I and end with a final tonic measure. The last measure may serve as a "turnaround" measure, leading back to the beginning of the progression for a repetition.

I | I | I | I or V⁷/IV | IV | IV | I | I | V | IV | I | I |

The twelve-bar blues progression was adopted by rock musicians in the 1950s, and appears in songs of many styles after that time. While the blues progression is solidly in the major mode, except for possible limited mixture or chromaticism, the vocal parts or other solo lines typically augment it with the minor pentatonic (*do-me-fa-sol-te*). This juxtaposition of major-key harmonies with a minor pentachord in the solo parts accounts for two of the blue notes within the blues scale, $\flat3$ and $\flat7$. For an example of the twelve-bar blues progression, look back at Example 26.3, "Rock Around the Clock." Play through the progression, represented by the chord symbols, in block chords while singing the melody. This progression provides a good harmonic basis for composing or improvising your own song.

Mixture Chords

Some show tunes, such as "I Got Rhythm," also include ♭5̂ in a type of extended mixture, prominently featured in Example 26.2a on the word "sigh." This note is accentuated by its position at the top of the musical phrase and the end of a vocal subphrase, as well as by its coloring of "sigh." Listen now to Example 26.5, drawn from the major-key refrain of the song. Provide a Roman numeral analysis of the example, circling any mixture notes you hear. What effect do these mixture notes have on the harmonies? *(Try it #4)*

1.89 🎧

EXAMPLE 26.5: Gershwin, "I Got Rhythm," mm. 37–44

Mixture notes appear in measures 39 (D♭, or ♭3̂), 42 (G♭, or ♭6̂), and 44 (A♭, or ♭7̂). We might also consider the E♮ in measure 39 to be a ♯4̂. The two altered pitches in measure 39 create a fully diminished seventh chord built on E♮. In common-practice style, fully diminished seventh chords on scale degrees other than $\hat{7}$ usually function as secondary diminished sevenths. In this case, we might expect a vii°⁷/V, where the E♮ would resolve up to F and the D♭ would resolve down to C. But the chord does not resolve this way, and should therefore be considered a voice-leading chord without Roman numeral.

KEY CONCEPT

> In popular styles, fully diminished and half-diminished seventh sonorities may appear on any scale degree, and need not function as secondary diminished seventh chords.

The A♭ in measure 44 is a brief chordal embellishment ($♭\hat{7}$) that initiates a lead-in to the bridge.

Suspensions and Rhythmic Displacement

Suspensions that conform to common-practice voice-leading may also be found in popular styles. Look, for example, at the 4–3 suspensions (B♭ to A) in measures 40 and 43 of Example 26.5. But in popular styles, we sometimes find "4–3 suspensions" with no resolution—that is, an added fourth above the bass that displaces the third. Such harmonies are sometimes known as **sus chords** and might be labeled F^{sus} or F$^{\text{sus4}}$.

Other sonorities may be the result of a rhythmic displacement of pitches—for example, pitches that are "held over" like suspensions from one chord to the next, or pitches that "arrive early" before the rest of a harmony. Look, for instance, at the first harmony of measure 39 in Example 26.5. Here, the chord symbol implies a B♭ root, yet no B♭ is notated in this score. Instead, the C from the previous chord is held over across the bar, displacing the B♭, which returns at the end of measure 39. Jazz musicians intuit these "missing" pitches; they know the notes will be supplied by the rhythm section.

We analyze chords with rhythmic displacement as though the chord tone were present, rather than the displaced pitch. In this case, the harmony would be I$^{\text{add6}}$, as the chord symbol implies. Alternatively, you may hear the C as creating a ninth chord above the missing pitch—this implies an analysis of I$^{\text{add}^9_6}$. You may also find in some textbooks and lead sheets symbols for eleventh or thirteenth chords, extensions to the basic triad or seventh beyond the added sixth or ninth discussed here. To interpret these chord symbols, simply continue to add the specified interval above the bass.

Chords with Altered Fifths

1.90 Listen now to a final excerpt from "I Got Rhythm," this one drawn from the bridge (Example 26.6). Listen especially to the chromatic voice-leading in the tenor and alto voices in the right hand. Analyze the harmonies in these measures for chord quality rather than with Roman numerals.

EXAMPLE 26.6: Gershwin, "I Got Rhythm," mm. 45–52a (bridge)

The bridge begins with a D dominant seventh chord. Then the tenor and alto voices begin to rise chromatically in parallel thirds for two measures, through the end of the word "Trouble," prolonging this sonority through the ninth chord at the end of measure 46. In measure 47, the parallel thirds reach their high point and begin to descend chromatically. You can see one harmonic by-product of Gershwin's voice-leading technique by looking at the chord symbols: the Dm7 chord of measure

46 has its fifth lowered by a half step (shown as "Dm7-5"), and the last sonority of measure 47 has its fifth raised by a half step ("D aug 5"). Triads and seventh chords with **altered fifths** are a common harmonic feature of American popular song, and may also be found in common-practice music of the nineteenth century.

KEY CONCEPT

Triads or seventh chords may be colored and intensified by lowering or raising the fifth of the chord by a half step, thereby altering the quality of the interval between the root and fifth.

Can you find additional triads or seventh chords with altered fifths in the remainder of this passage? *(Try it #5)*

When analyzing harmonies with altered fifths, add traditional symbols (°7 or ⌀7) to Roman numerals for those that create diminished or diminished seventh sonorities. Major triads or sevenths with raised fifths are labeled with the Roman numeral plus either +5 or ♯5, and lowered fifths with either −5 or ♭5. (You may see "aug 5" or "dim 5" in popular music, but not with a Roman numeral.) What Roman numeral [WF2] would we give the harmony on the downbeat of measure 51, assuming a B♭ tonic key? *(Try it #6)*

o o o o o o o o o o o o o o o o o o o o o o o o o o o o o o o o o o o o o o o o o o o o o o

Analysis of Songs

The Relation Between Text and Song Structure

Unlike other types of music analysis, the study of song involves text as well as music, and when we analyze songs, we try to find relationships between them. The words can add complexity and nuance to our analysis and to our musical interpretation. When analyzing songs, then, we must always look at the text: at its rhyme scheme, imagery, story, and structure. We can try to determine from the words alone what type of musical structure might have suggested itself to the composer, and then see whether our intuitions are borne out in the musical realization.

Let's begin with the verse to "I Got Rhythm," whose lyrics were written by Gershwin's brother Ira. The text follows, with a simple analysis of the rhyme scheme.

Days can be sunny,	a
With never a sigh;	b
Don't need what money	a
Can buy.	b
Birds in the tree sing	c
Their dayful of song.	d
Why shouldn't we sing	c
Along?	d
I'm chipper all the day,	e
Happy with my lot.	f
How do I get that way?	e
Look at what I've got:	f
(refrain follows)	

Gershwin's text consists of three four-line **strophes** (sometimes called "stanzas" or "verses" in their musical realizations). Each four lines pair into two **couplets** (two lines each), which share the same rhyme scheme (represented by the alphabet letters to the right). Each strophe has an abab rhyme scheme, but because the rhymes differ in subsequent verses, we represent them with new letters: cdcd and efef.

Look now at the imagery and story these lines convey. The first two strophes are almost entirely objective—lines written in the third person that simply describe a spring or summer day. The third strophe focuses on the subjective point of view, when the protagonist describes how he or she feels: "I'm chipper all the day . . . " Listen again, while following the score in your anthology, to see how the structure of the lyrics is portrayed musically.

Gershwin parallels the structure of the rhyming words by creating musical rhymes: compare his settings of "Days can be sunny" and "Don't need what money," for example. In addition, he reflects the objective-subjective structure by composing the whole verse in an **a a b** form, with the repeated **a** sections representing the two objective stanzas and the contrasting **b** section the subjective. The turn to the subjective text is marked by a wider vocal range, and accents and rests within the line.

Let's look now for similarities between Gershwin's setting and Robert Schumann's setting of poetry by Heinrich Heine. Listen to Schumann's "Im wunderschönen Monat Mai" while following the text below. Use alphabet letters to analyze the rhyme scheme of the German text, and think about whether the objective-subjective distinction might apply here as well. (*Try it #7*)

Im wunderschönen Monat Mai,	In the lovely month of May,
Als alle Knospen sprangen,	when all the buds were bursting,
Da ist in meinem Herzen	then within my heart
Die Liebe aufgegangen.	love broke forth.
Im wunderschönen Monat Mai,	In the lovely month of May,
Als alle Vögel sangen,	when all the birds were singing,
Da hab' ich ihr gestanden	then I confessed to her
Mein Sehnen und Verlangen.	my longing and desire.

Each phrase of text corresponds with a musical phrase. Listen again to determine whether Schumann uses "musical rhyme" as Gershwin does. The melodies of phrases 1 and 2 are nearly identical, while phrases 3 and 4 are related by transposition. The musical rhyme of Schumann's setting (**a a b b´**) therefore differs from the rhyme scheme of the text (abcb). Why might this be the case?

Like Gershwin's text, Heine's poem is full of the imagery of spring: buds bursting and birds singing. In each strophe, the first couplet describes the setting objectively, while the second couplet turns to the subjective feelings of the protagonist: of love, longing, and desire. In Schumann's setting, the two objective phrases are set in parallel structure (**a a**), as are the two subjective phrases (**b b´**). Thus, the musical setting parallels the meaning of the text rather than the rhyme scheme.

Text Painting

Common in Romantic poetry are references to nature, wandering, unattainable or lost love, and eventual death. Sometimes several poems linked by a narrative, characters, and imagery are grouped in a cycle. **Song cycles** are groups of songs, generally performed as a unit, that are either set to a single poet's cycle of poetry or set to poems that have been grouped by the composer into a cycle. "Im wunderschönen Monat Mai" is the first song of Schumann's cycle *Dichterliebe*. Let's look at this song again to see how the composer takes ideas from the poetry and represents them in music—a concept generally known as text painting.

WF3

On first reading, Heine's poem seems to express the joys of spring and first love. We might therefore expect an exuberant major-key setting. Yet the song instead seems uneasy and restless. In fact, Schumann's musical treatment suggests that all is not well with this relationship, perhaps that the love is not returned. In this way, the composer foreshadows the disappointments that are to come as the song cycle progresses. Listen to the song again to identify ways in which this uneasiness is expressed; mark in your anthology any change of key, plus any distinctive harmonies or embellishing tones that help establish the mood.

Consider first the role of the piano introduction, given in Example 26.7. While some piano introductions and accompaniments may simply support a song's harmonic structure, others may be filled with text painting that depicts images from the poem: the rustling of trees, the babbling of a brook, the thunder of horse hooves, or the cooing of a dove. You may come across similar effects in Romantic-era instrumental compositions without text, when these works are based on a "program"— a story line, characters, or a specific location or setting.

EXAMPLE 26.7: Schumann, "Im wunderschönen Monat Mai," from *Dichterliebe*, mm. 1–6a

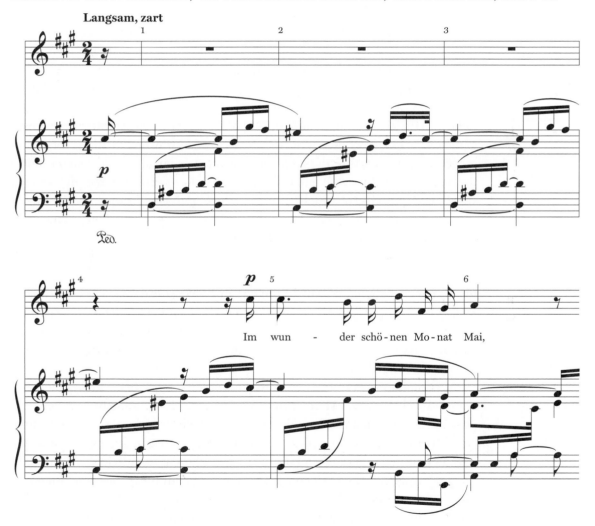

In Schumann's song, the piano first establishes the uneasiness that is a hall-mark of this setting. In what key does the introduction begin? It begins ambiguously by implying F♯ minor, but only through a series of Phrygian cadences (see Chapter 17), without ever expressing any tonic harmony at all. Further clouding the tonality is the initial C♯5, which is part of a dissonant 7–6 suspension. That same C♯5 emerges in measures 4–5 as the first pitch of the vocal line, which finally leads unambiguously into A Major for the objective first phrase of text. But we might well ask, in what key is this song written? The tonality continues to be unstable throughout, alternating between A Major and F♯ minor at the beginning and end of each stanza.

In what other ways do we see text painting in the song? Look again at the complete score in your anthology. In his setting of the subjective couplets, Schumann brings the singer into his highest vocal range for the crucial words "Herzen" and "aufgegangen," and even more importantly for "Verlangen" (desire). The rising lines of measures 9–12 and 20–23 express the heightened emotion of these subjective lines, and the accented dissonant incomplete neighbor tone (G) on the downbeat of measures 12 and 23 highlights the words that portray love breaking forth, and especially desire. Further, the subjective lines are less tonally stable than the objective ones, moving through B minor and D Major before the piano interlude (between verses) and postlude (at the end) return to the F♯ minor of the opening. This tonal instability raises the question "Does she love him?" Does the postlude bring resolution—does it answer this crucial question? *(Try it #8)*

In performance, pianist and singer alike might try to bring out the ambiguities of the setting, as preparation for the story of love and loss to come. For example, the pianist could hesitate on the opening C♯5, whose role is unclear, before adding the supporting harmony that explains its dissonant function. The perpetual arpeggiated texture of the piano part—perhaps representing wind through the trees or some other image of nature—might be played with the rhythmic freedom of nature, especially where the voice is not present.

Also important for the pianist is the close of the song, with its unresolved dominant seventh harmony. Here Schumann notates a ritard at the beginning of the postlude and a fermata both on the downbeat of the last measure and on the final chord. The most active tones of the chord are left exposed in the upper voices: the leading tone in the soprano and the unresolved chordal seventh in the top voice of the final arpeggio. The performance should bring out these tones and linger on them before the next song, which returns us to A Major.

The singer's role is, in part, to portray the objective-subjective duality of the poem. When he enters with the first line, again the C♯5 is a dissonant suspension against the harmony that supports it. (As throughout in this discussion, the C♯5 is the notated pitch, although a male singer's pitch would sound an octave lower.) The singer can linger on this beautiful dissonance, which highlights the descriptive word "wunderschönen," before proceeding. The objective lines might be sung with a vocal tone that supports the joy and beauty of the spring day, without a hint of the tragedy that follows. But with the subjective lines, the singer may wish to change to a tone that expresses love, longing, and uncertainty of what is to come. As he climbs to the higher tessitura, he may also want to *crescendo* and linger on the accented dissonances that climax on "aufgegangen" and "Verlangen." Indeed, he will want to find a special interpretation for the final word, which will surely involve a *ritard* and a *tenuto* on the high G5. The singer's face and body should then maintain the sense of longing throughout the postlude, as the piano reinforces the mood of the text so effectively.

Motivic Analysis

We turn now to another famous German Lied for motivic analysis: Schubert's "Erlkönig." We have listened to portions of this work in recent chapters, as we studied secondary dominants, modulation, and the Neapolitan sixth chord. We now consider the song as a whole, to see how its text, harmony, and motivic structure work together to create a powerful musical drama. Read through the poem's translation in your anthology, and decide which of the four characters—the narrator, the father, the son, or the Erlking—is speaking at any given moment. In your score, mark the beginning and end of each stanza, as well as your decisions about who is speaking. *(Try it #9)*

3.25 🎧 While you listen again, try to associate musical motives with each of the four characters; mark these in your score as well. One of the most striking motives in the song appears in the piano (Example 26.8a). This triplet motive, in the left hand (mm. 2–3), accompanies the narrator and is heard in the introduction and interludes. Meanwhile the triplet octaves in the right hand evoke the thundering of horse hooves through the night as the boy and his father travel toward their destination. The motive most associated with the boy is the half-step neighbor tone,

3.28 🎧 often sung to the text "Mein Vater, mein Vater," as shown in Example 26.8b. Each time the son sings this plaintive plea to his father, the motive appears higher in his tessitura: compare measures 72–74 (D5–E♭–D) with 97–99 (E5–F–E) and 123–125 (F5–G♭–F). Even before the "Mein Vater" pleas, the son uses the half-step motive in his first exclamation (mm. 42–43, D5–E♭; mm. 46–47 and 48–49, C5–D♭).

EXAMPLE 26.8: Schubert, "Erlkönig"

(a) Mm. 1–5 (piano motive)

(b) Mm. 72b–76a (son's motive)

Translation: My father, my father, do you not hear?

What motive represents the father? His reassurances to the son often feature perfect intervals of the fourth or fifth—to the text "Mein Sohn," in staunch denial of any danger—and his tessitura lies consistently lower than the boy's. Example 26.8c gives the father's first rising P4 motive, which also climbs higher and higher as the song progresses, from measures 36–37 (D4–G) to 80–81 (F♯4–B) and 105–106 (G♯4–C♯5).

3.26 🎧

(c) Mm. 36–40 (father's motive)

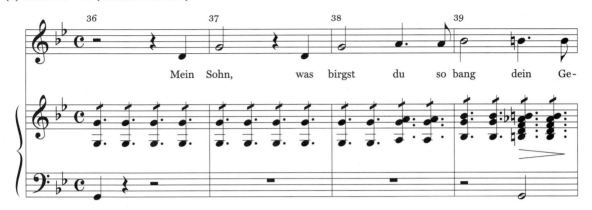

Translation: My son, why do you hide, so fearfully, your face?

Both of these motives, while associated with son and father, appear in the music of the narrator and—more chillingly—the Erlking. Where does the narrator introduce the half-step son's motive and P4 father's motive? *(Try it #10)* The Erlking attempts to coax the son rather than frighten him; his music is almost always in a major key, for example. In measures 69–70, he appropriates the rising P4 from the father and sings it to the text "meine Mutter" (my mother). In measures 116–117, in his final appeal before snatching the boy away, the Erlking uses both the son's neighbor-tone motive and the father's perfect fourth, now descending, as he sings 3.30 🎧 "Ich liebe dich" (I love you). Example 26.8d shows this climactic moment, tonicizing the Neapolitan of the local D-minor tonic.

(d) Mm. 115–117 (son and father motives sung by Erlking)

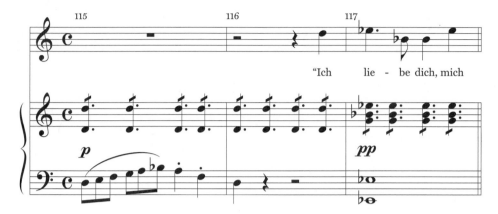

Sometimes composers embed motives in their works at different hierarchical levels. That is, a motive that originally appears within a single measure of the melody may be drawn out to span many measures, in a new rhythmic and tonal context—a practice called **motivic parallelism**. We can see a few instances of the left-hand G-minor "rider" motive from the song's introduction drawn out into larger statements. The motive is characterized by two parts. The first is a rising scale with half-step neighbor tone at the top, perhaps the source of the son's half-step motive: G–A–B♭–C–D–E♭–D. The second part is a descending minor triad: D–B♭–G. The first part of the motive, the rising scale, helps structure the narrator's final speech, shown in Example 26.8e.

3.32

(e) Mm. 135–141a

Translation: [The father] rides swiftly, he holds in his arms the groaning child.

Here, the narrator's melody climbs the G-minor scale to place the neighbor E♭–D on the word "Armen"—a large-scale replication of the rider motive in the vocal part, which is accompanied by the original version simultaneously in the piano. This subphrase ends by combining the P4 and neighbor-tone motives to the text "ächzende Kind." An even more striking motivic parallelism has been pointed out by several music theorists. The large-scale succession of keys in the song also "spells out" most of this motive: G minor (beginning in m. 1), B♭ Major (m. 58), C Major (m. 87), D minor (m. 112), E♭ (briefly tonicized as a Neapolitan, m. 117), D minor (m. 123), tonicized V/B♭ (m. 124), to G minor (m. 131).

WF4

○ ○

Other Song Forms

In "Erlkönig," the music for each stanza is different: the composition continues to develop in new, though related, ways as the story unfolds. This type of song form is sometimes known as **through-composed**. In contrast to through-composed songs are those, like "Im wunderschönen Monat Mai," that rely on the repetition of music.

KEY CONCEPT

Songs in which more than one strophe of text is sung to the same music are called **strophic** songs.

In a strophic song, multiple strophes of text may be aligned beneath a single line of music, as shown in Example 26.9—with repeat or *da capo* signs to bring the performers back to the beginning of each new stanza—or each stanza may be written out separately, as is the case in Schumann's song. Stanzas may also be set apart by instrumental interludes.

EXAMPLE 26.9: Lennon and McCartney, "Eleanor Rigby," mm. 9–12

Sometimes you will encounter songs where the basic outline seems strophic, but each stanza is somehow varied. The stanzas may each begin the same way but end differently. Listen, for example, to Clara Schumann's song "Liebst du um Schönheit" while following the score in your anthology. The poem is structured in a way that suggests a strophic setting. Each strophe begins with the same formula: the first says, "Liebst du um Schönheit, O nicht mich liebe!" (If you love for beauty, oh do not love me!), and subsequent stanzas substitute another word at the end of the first line (youth, treasure, love). Schumann begins her setting of each stanza identically, but adds subtle differences in the continuations. (We look at this song in more depth in the workbook exercises for this chapter.) The form of this type of setting is generally called **modified strophic**.

Some songs are in ternary form. We have already seen instrumental examples of ternary form in Chapter 23. The principles we learned there hold as well for songs in ternary form, except that the three parts may be arranged with the contrasting section either in the middle or at the end—that is, **A B A** or **A A B**. In Chapters 24 and 25 of the workbook, we analyzed harmony and text painting in Brahms's "Die Mainacht." Listen to the Brahms now for form, while following the score in your anthology. Does this ternary song fall into an **A B A** or **A A B** design? In some ways, it might be termed "modified ternary." Why? *(Try it #11)*

Determining the form of a song, or any composition, is an important first step to its effective performance. In strophic settings, the performers need to consider how to create a sense of the story's development despite the literal repetition of music. They might do this by inflecting the text, contrasting the dynamics, making subtle changes in tempo, or through other expressive means. In ternary songs, the same strategy applies for the repeated **A** sections, while the **B** sections need to be set apart from the rest of the song more dramatically. In verse-refrain forms, the verse is often performed with more rhythmic freedom than the refrain in order to convey the story effectively.

In any form, consider the distinction between textual phrase and musical phrase (look for the cadence!) when determining timing of the phrases and where to take a breath. Think about the effect of unexpected harmonies or mixture chords and how these relate to crucial words of the text. Above all, the singer and accompanist should study the text and music together to make collaborative decisions in service of the poetry and song.

TERMS YOU SHOULD KNOW

added-sixth chord
altered fifth
blue notes
blues scale
bridge
chorus 1 and 2
couplet
extensions
modified strophic
motivic parallelism
ninth chord
quaternary (thirty-two-bar) song form
refrain

rhyme scheme
rhythmic displacement
song cycle
strophe
strophic
sus chord
ternary form
through-composed
twelve-bar blues
verse
verse-refrain song form
voice-leading chord

QUESTIONS FOR REVIEW

1. What are some phrase designs typical of early twentieth-century American popular songs?
2. What added notes might you find in the chords used to harmonize popular songs? Which scale degrees may be altered to create blue notes?
3. What other formal designs are commonly found in song settings?
4. In music for your own instrument, find a piece with added notes in chords or blue-note alterations. (Hint: Look in music of the twentieth century, especially by jazz composers or those who have been influenced by jazz.)
5. In music for your own instrument, find a piece that uses text painting. (Instrumentalists: Examine pieces with titles that imply a story line or other programmatic elements; consider ensemble works as well.) What types of motives represent the ideas in the text or program? How might you perform those motives to express the meaning of the text or program?

CHAPTER 27

Variation and Rondo

Outline of topics covered

Sectional variations
- Variation themes
- Organization in variation sets
- Figural variations
- Chromatic variations
- Character variations
- Textural and timbral variations

Continuous variations
- Formal organization

Performing variations

Rondo
- Five-part rondo
- Refrains and episodes
- Transitions and retransitions
- Seven-part rondo

Overview

In Chapter 23, we considered how phrases may be combined to make movements with either a binary or ternary design. Here, we look at other formal designs from the Baroque and Classical eras, including continuous variation, sectional variation, and rondo.

Repertoire

Johann Sebastian Bach, Chaconne, from Violin Partita No. 2 in D minor (CD 1, track 23)

Ludwig van Beethoven, Variations on "God Save the King"

Beethoven, Piano Sonata in C minor, Op. 13 (*Pathétique*), second movement (CD 1, track 41)

John Barnes Chance, Variations on a Korean Folk Song (CD 1, track 66)

Wolfgang Amadeus Mozart, Piano Sonata in C Major, K. 545, third movement (CD 2, track 71)

Mozart, Variations on "Ah, vous dirai-je, Maman" (CD 2, track 86)

Henry Purcell, "Music for a While" (CD 3, track 5)

Sectional Variations

When we think of variations, what probably comes to mind first is the Classical theme-and-variations movement or piece. We considered several compositions of this type in previous chapters, including Mozart's Variations on "Ah, vous dirai-je, Maman" and a more recent contribution, Chance's Variations on a Korean Folk Song. We now return to these pieces to consider in more detail how their melodies are varied and how they are organized formally. Listen to the Mozart and Chance variations while following the scores in your anthology; what characteristics do they share?

Among other features, these variations share a sectional design. That is, each variant is clearly articulated from the next by a strong conclusive cadence (and even by double bars) or by a striking change in style or timbre. Since each variant could be played as a brief but complete stand-alone section, these sets are called **sectional variations**. We have seen the term "sectional" before, to distinguish between continuous and sectional binary; in a variation form, it refers primarily to the authentic cadence that separates one variation from the next.

Variation Themes

Each of these sets of variations is based on a melody that serves as a **theme**—the main idea to unify the set. How many measures long is each theme? *(Try it #1)* While the length may vary, melodies for sectional variations are typically sixteen measures or more. Like the two themes here, the melodies typically show a clear phrase structure and end with a definitive cadence.

Sectional variation themes also often articulate a complete formal unit, such as the rounded binary of the Mozart. They are long enough that a single setting of the theme can make a complete short piece in itself. Many sectional variations are based on a preexisting melody—such as "God Save the King" or "Twinkle, Twinkle, Little Star." Folk songs, patriotic songs, and other types of familiar melodies work particularly well for this type of piece: when the melody is familiar, listeners can more easily follow its outline even when it is transformed as a part of the variation process. Variations, however, may also be based on a newly composed melody.

Organization in Variation Sets

We considered musical details in Mozart's variations—on a melody he knew as a French folk song, "Ah, vous dirai-je, Maman"—in earlier chapters. We now consider the piece's overall organization. Begin by listening to the theme while following the score in your anthology, to review its phrase structure and overall formal organization. Label each phrase (**a**, **b**, etc.); with what kind of cadence does each one end? *(Try it #2)*

In this piece, the variations are labeled in the score—a convention that is fairly typical of sectional variations. If they were not indicated, as in the Chance set, our next step would be to locate the starting and ending points for each variation. Now glance through the rest of Mozart's score; does each variation follow the formal organization of the theme? *(Try it #3)*

Take a close look at the last variation: the first section is eight measures long as before, and the first ending of the second section cadences as expected, but the second ending adds eleven measures beyond the typical length for the second section. These added measures, which help bring the piece to a close, constitute a coda. Like the codettas and suffixes we saw in Chapter 20, codas usually follow a conclusive cadence in the tonic key. They are generally longer and more substantive than codettas ("little codas"). While codas are not common in shorter pieces in binary and ternary form, they are very common in longer pieces, such as sets of variations, rondos, and sonata-form movements.

Now listen to the entire piece. As you listen, consider what has been changed in each variation when compared with the theme and also how the variations work together as a set.

KEY CONCEPT

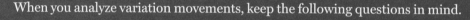

When you analyze variation movements, keep the following questions in mind.

- Does the variation you are analyzing differ in key, mode, meter, phrase structure, length, or character from the theme?
- Is a melodic or rhythmic figure or a specific embellishment pattern featured? If so, what is it?
- Does the variation form a pair with another, or a unit with several others?
- Is chromaticism used? If so, is the chromaticism surface embellishment, or does it change the harmonic function?
- Are the harmonies more complex than the theme or previous variation? Are they simplified?

You may want to collect your answers to these questions in a chart or graph. We will learn several possible formats for recording and presenting such analyses in the workbook exercises for this chapter.

A cursory examination of the sections in Mozart's variations reveals that the key and mode (C Major) are consistent in every variation except the eighth, which is in C minor. In addition, the meter is $\frac{2}{4}$ in most variations. Which ones are notated in a different meter, or have other rhythmic elements that make the meter sound different from $\frac{2}{4}$? *(Try it #4)* Each variation conforms to the phrase and formal structure of the theme, with the exception of the last variation, to which a coda has been added.

Figural Variations

Now look closely at the first variation in Mozart's set. Most of the variations in this piece are **figural variations**: they feature a specific embellishment pattern or figure throughout. Figural variations are often grouped in pairs. In the Mozart set, for example, the first and second variations share sixteenth-note motion in one hand against quarter-note motion in the other; this rhythmic relationship reverses hands from Variation I to II. The third and fourth variations then share triplet motion in one hand against primarily quarter-note motion in the other, with the rhythmic relationship again reversing hands from Variation III to IV. This movement of the figuration from one hand to the other is sometimes known as *Stimmtausch*, a German word for another type of "voice exchange." Variations VIII and IX both feature imitative textures and suspensions in the upper voices (these first appeared in Variation II). Rounding out the piece is a return in Variation XII of the sixteenth-note accompanimental pattern we heard in Variation II, now adapted for triple meter.

In Chapter 9, we considered the relationship between the right-hand parts of Variation I and the original melody. If you have not already circled the melody's embellishing pitches in your score for this variation, do so now. Look at Example 27.1a to see how the melody is embellished in this variation. The embellishment figure consists first of a step above the melody pitch (upper neighbor, or UN), then the melody pitch, a lower neighbor (LN), melody pitch, LN, melody pitch, UN, and melody pitch. This type of pattern, with slight alterations, appears many places in this variation. Can you find a second figure featured in measures 28–30 (Example 27.1b)? *(Try it #5)*

EXAMPLE 27.1: Mozart, Variations on "Ah, vous dirai-je, Maman," Variation I

(a) Mm. 33–36

(b) Mm. 28–30

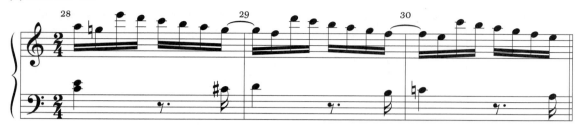

2.89

Variation V is built on a rhythmic figure—eighth rest, eighth note, quarter note—that is applied to both the melody and accompaniment, as shown in Example 27.2. In other variations, such as Variation VI (Example 27.3), each hand is characterized by a different figure. Some figures embellish and disguise the melody, while others appear in the accompanimental voice, with the melody floating above the figuration.

EXAMPLE 27.2: Mozart, Variations, Variation V, mm. 121–124

EXAMPLE 27.3: Mozart, Variations, Variation VI, mm. 145–148

Chromatic Variations

Several of Mozart's variations feature chromaticism. When you find chromaticism, check to see whether it is embellishing a melodic line or whether it represents a change in harmony. Which type of chromaticism does Mozart use back in Example 27.1a? The F♯5, D♯5, and C♯5 are all chromatic neighbors—the chromaticism is thus embellishing the melodic figure, and does not represent a change of harmony.

For an instance of chromaticism that does change the harmonic progression, look at Example 27.4. In measure 68, the C♯3, C♯4, and B♭4 on beat 2 transform the original C-Major tonic into a fully diminished seventh chord that resolves in the next measure. The addition of A♭4 on beat 2 of measure 69 has the same effect. The chromaticism here stems from the insertion of chromatic harmonies: secondary leading-tone chords. The C♯4 and A♯3 in measure 69, in contrast, are simply chromatic neighbors.

2.87

EXAMPLE 27.4: Mozart, Variations, Variation II, mm. 68–69

In variation sets built on a major-key theme, you may also find chromaticism in passages that include modal mixture or a complete change of mode. Look, for instance, at measures 197–198 of Variation VIII, shown in Example 27.5. Minor-mode variations, like this one, are normally in the parallel minor rather than the relative minor, to retain the same key center as the rest of the variations. This gives the effect of modal mixture and the opportunity for expressive chromaticism. Here, the accidentals indicate inflections of the melodic minor. Elsewhere in minor-mode variations, composers often substitute dramatic chromatic harmonies such as the Neapolitan and augmented-sixth chords.

2.91

EXAMPLE 27.5: Mozart, Variations, Variation VIII, mm. 193–200

Character Variations

Some variations are designed to represent a particular style or "character." Play through Variation VI from Beethoven's "God Save the King" Variations (an excerpt is shown in Example 27.6). This variation is styled after a march: the tempo, meter, and rhythmic patterns are all typical of march style. There are even "trumpet flourishes," shown in the last measure of this excerpt. The march strongly contrasts with the previous variation, a lyrical, minor-mode serenade. Although a character variation may feature a repeated melodic or rhythmic figure, the figure is not itself the driving impetus of the variation. Many of the variations in Beethoven's set are intended to represent a particular type of musical character.

EXAMPLE 27.6: Beethoven, Variations on "God Save the King," Variation VI, mm. 1–6

Textural and Timbral Variations

In most variation sets, one of the elements that is varied is **texture**. When we speak of a musical passage's texture, we are referring to how many separate and independent voice-leading strands are active there. In a general sense, we might refer to a "thin" texture when there are only a few voices and/or simple rhythmic patterns—such as in the theme for the Mozart variations—and a "thick" texture when there are many voices and/or a lot of rhythmic activity.

We can also use more precise language: a single-line melody is a **monophonic** texture, while the interplay of two or more fairly independent lines is a **polyphonic**, or **contrapuntal**, texture. Chordal passages are **homophonic**. Another common texture, particularly in sectional variation sets, is a **melody plus accompaniment**. Remember that lines may be doubled in octaves, doubled by other instruments, or sometimes doubled in thirds or sixths; but while this may create a somewhat thicker texture, doubling does not create additional independent lines.

In general, variations tend to be organized texturally from the simplest to the most complex, but sometimes composers include a variation with a thin texture or reduced harmonic palette in the middle of a set for contrast. Variation VII from the Mozart variations is an example (an excerpt is shown in Example 27.7); this type is sometimes called a **simplifying variation**. Another relatively common textural variant, a **polyphonic variation**, may include imitative entries, as several of the Mozart variations do, or a change from a harmonically based setting to one with more independent voices. Refer back to Example 27.5 for an example of imitative entries.

2.90

EXAMPLE 27.7: Mozart, Variations, Variation VII, mm. 169–172

The Mozart and Beethoven variation sets call for the same instrumentation, a keyboard instrument, throughout. The Chance variations, on the other hand, offer a wide range of possible timbral combinations. Listen to the opening theme, given in Example 28.8. This statement of the theme sounds quite different in the rich, low range of the clarinets than it does when it returns in the saxophones and baritone (mm. 17–24) and in the horns and clarinets (mm. 25–32).

1.66

EXAMPLE 27.8: Chance, Variations on a Korean Folk Song, mm. 1–8

1.68 🎧 Perhaps the most unusual variation is at the "Con Islancio" marking, beginning in measure 199, where the percussion section begins the variation. Look at this passage in your anthology score. The snare drum starts a rhythmic pattern, soon joined by cymbal and gong. Then in measure 208, the temple blocks layer on a figure that was introduced in a previous figural variation (beginning at m. 128). Three measures later (m. 211), the vibraphone enters with the theme's melody, answered in imitation by the flutes and piccolos. In the rest of the variation, Chance passes the melody to every section of the band. This variation thus explores both timbre and texture by changing timbral colors and building up layers.

As in the "Con Islancio" variation, which combines textural, timbral, figural, and contrapuntal elements, composers may freely combine types of variation procedures that we have looked at in isolation—and usually this is the case! When analyzing variations, feel free to combine the labels as needed. If none of the labels fits, come up with your own to describe what you are hearing.

Continuous Variations

While sectional variations were the standard type of variation movement in the Classical era, when clear phrase and sectional organization was prized, some variations from the Baroque era show a different design. Rather than strong sectional divisions articulated by authentic cadences and double bar lines, some Baroque variations feature a continuous flow of musical ideas and *Fortspinnung* phrase structure. These are called **continuous variations**. We begin our study of continuous variations by reviewing two pieces we considered previously: Bach's Chaconne in D minor and Purcell's "Music for a While."

1.23 🎧
3.5 🎧

Listen to both of these pieces again to refresh your memory, while following the scores in your anthology. Examples 27.9 and 27.10 reproduce the opening two statements of the theme for each work. How long are these themes? How do they differ from themes in the sectional variations we previously considered? (*Try it #6*)

EXAMPLE 27.9: Bach, Chaconne in D minor, mm. 1–9a

EXAMPLE 27.10: Purcell, "Music for a While," mm. 1–7a

A primary difference is that the repeated element—the basis for the variations—in continuous sets is typically a bass line or a chord progression, rather than
a melody with accompaniment. In addition, these themes are usually shorter than
those in sectional variations, and the repetitions of the theme tend to be elided at
the cadence to maintain the continuous structure. The rhythmic flow throughout
the variations is likewise continuous. Where phrases are not connected by elision,
a lead-in (or connecting idea) typically links one variation with the next.

Some of the names associated with Baroque continuous variations are "passacaglia," "chaconne," and "ground bass." As you study compositions in this genre,
you will discover some inconsistency in how the terms are applied; this is because
the musical characteristics associated with each term (especially "chaconne" and
"passacaglia") varied depending on the time and place of composition.

KEY CONCEPT _____

For our purposes, we define a **ground bass** or **passacaglia** as a continuous variation in which a repeated bass line remains constant while the upper voices are varied. The variations in a passacaglia may reharmonize the bass line and may include phrase lengths that differ from, and overlap with, the statements of the ground bass. A **chaconne** is a set of continuous variations in which the entire harmonic texture, not just the bass line, is repeated and varied. While the bass line in a chaconne may remain unchanged for several successive variations, it is usually altered as the composition progresses—rhythmically, harmonically, or through inversion.

It is helpful to differentiate between these two types of compositional method— repeated ground bass versus repeated harmonic progression—even if, historically, their labels may have varied. Look through the Bach and Purcell scores in your anthology. Which technique is used in each? (*Try it #7*)

Formal Organization

Chaconnes and passacaglias may include as many as sixty or more variations. Chaconne variations are typically grouped into pairs or sets that are linked by a common figure or other musical characteristic; for example, the first and second variations might form a pair, as well as the third and fourth, fifth and sixth, and so on. Paired variations help keep the movement from sounding choppy or heavily segmented.

1.23 🎧

Listen now to the first forty-one measures of the Bach Chaconne, and number each repetition of the chaconne theme in your anthology score. Are there any pairings in the first six variations? If so, what musical elements link the pairs? (*Try it #8*) These forty-one measures also illustrate a large-scale rhythmic process that often structures portions of variation movements. The work begins with predominantly quarter-note motion, then moves gradually through shorter note values to sixteenth-note motion in measures 28 and following. This is known as **rhythmic acceleration**, or **rhythmic *crescendo***. Another rhythmic acceleration begins in measure 57 with mostly eighth-note motion, gradually moving to sixteenth notes and culminating in thirty-second-note motion in measures 65 and following.

In addition to the variation process, most continuous variations also exhibit a large-scale structure, often some type of **A B A´**. How can the composer create a "contrasting" section within a form that is so highly unified by its theme? In many cases, this contrast is achieved by motion to the parallel key. Bach's Chaconne is no exception: measures 133–208 are in D Major. Example 27.11 gives the opening of the D-Major section. The passage is not a simple transcription of the beginning measures into the parallel major key, but it does share some features with the opening, including the initial rhythmic motives and a similar (though not identical) harmonic progression.

EXAMPLE 27.11: Bach, Chaconne in D minor, mm. 133–137a

Another way to create contrast, in passacaglias, is to move the repeated bass-line theme out of the bass voice temporarily, into an upper voice. This practice can be particularly effective in an organ passacaglia, since it means moving the theme out of the distinctive pedal register and timbre.

Purcell's "Music for a While" illustrates yet another way to help keep a continuous variation set from sounding too sectional and repetitive. We already saw two presentations of the ground bass in Example 27.10. Listen to the entire song now, while following the score in your anthology. As you listen, focus on the bass line. Number each complete presentation of the ground bass in the tonic key (A minor); make a notation in your score if you hear the bass line change. How many exact statements of the ground bass did you count? *(Try it #9)*

You should have noticed that the bass line is first repeated exactly, note for note, three times in measures 1–12, but then is altered to modulate to new keys. It passes briefly through E minor (m. 15, with the ground bass now shifted to begin mid-measure), G Major (m. 18), and C Major (m. 22). The ground bass returns to A minor briefly in measure 23, and passes once more through E minor (m. 28) before settling in the tonic key for the remainder of the piece. Throughout these tonal changes, the bass line never loses its characteristic rhythm, contour, or prominence as the organizing principle behind the musical structure, even when transposed or extended.

Listen to the entire song one last time, now focusing on the vocal melody and large-scale design. Purcell's song has an **A B A′** structure superimposed on the continuous variation. This large-scale organization is most clear when the **A** section returns in measure 29. At this point, the text and a substantial part of the melody from the song's opening return (nearly six measures of the opening melody are repeated exactly), and the ground bass returns to its downbeat metrical position. The beginning of the **B** section (shown in Example 27.12) is more difficult to determine, but it surely includes the modulatory statements of the ground bass and introduction of new text. We can therefore begin the **B** section in measure 10, with the new text.

EXAMPLE 27.12: Purcell, "Music for a While," mm. 9–15a

How does the phrase structure of the vocal line interact with the statements of the ground bass? The beginnings of the ground bass theme often correspond to a strong arrival in the vocal line, yet the continuous nature of the vocal melody often results in phrase boundaries that don't quite align with the bass-line repetitions. Example 27.12 provides an illustration of this technique. Here, the ending of one vocal phrase aligns with the completion of one ground bass pattern and the beginning of the next (on the word "beguile"), but the next vocal phrase begins on the third beat of the ground bass theme. Further, the vocal phrase continues ("were eas'd") right through the partial ground bass repetition in measure 13. The two are then back in alignment at the cadence in E minor in measure 15. Places where the vocal melody and ground bass pattern do not align help create a more seamless (and more interesting) piece than complete alignment of the two would provide.

Performing Variations

In the centuries before recorded music, variation movements were an ideal format for listeners who might hear a piece of music only one time. They would listen to the initial idea—perhaps a typical chord progression or a familiar tune—at the beginning of the piece, then follow the transformation of the idea through a series of variations without having to hear the work several times to perceive its organization. When performing variations, however, you need not "bring out" the subject or theme each time you play it. Instead, shape the music in a way that is appropriate to the style, being aware of the repeated theme but not overemphasizing it.

A first step in preparing a variation set for performance might be to locate each presentation of the theme to make sure you can find it in the midst of the embellishment, transposition, or other type of technique present. In the case of continuous variations, you may want to choose an articulation for the bass line that remains consistent so that the beginning of each repetition is clear without being emphasized. In sectional variations, be careful that you don't "miss the forest for the trees"—that is, that you don't overemphasize the embellishments and lose the theme. It is then the listener's task to discern the increasingly disguised melody, the repeated bass line, or the varied harmonic progression as the set progresses—if he or she wishes to listen that way.

To further prepare for performance, identify the phrase and sectional form, the type of melodic or harmonic embellishment, and the elements of continuity (to help with memorization), and determine the style or character of individual variations. Understanding the role of overall form—especially paired or grouped variations, rhythmic acceleration, contrasting sections, and the dramatic shaping of the set—will help you achieve the sweep and grace of a well-designed variation movement in performance.

Rondo

Five-Part Rondo

1.41 We begin our consideration of rondo form with the beautiful, lyrical second movement of Beethoven's *Pathétique* Sonata. Listen first without the score to get an idea of how this movement is organized, then listen again while following along in your anthology. The opening may be familiar from earlier chapters, in which we considered its outer-voice counterpoint and how its phrases are changed when they recur later in the piece. In your anthology, label the first sixteen measures **A** to indicate that they constitute the first large section. Find and label each cadence in measures 1–8, given in Example 27.13, then use this information to determine the phrase organization of the entire sixteen-measure **A** section.

EXAMPLE 27.13: Beethoven, Piano Sonata in C minor, Op. 13 (*Pathétique*), second movement, mm. 1–8a

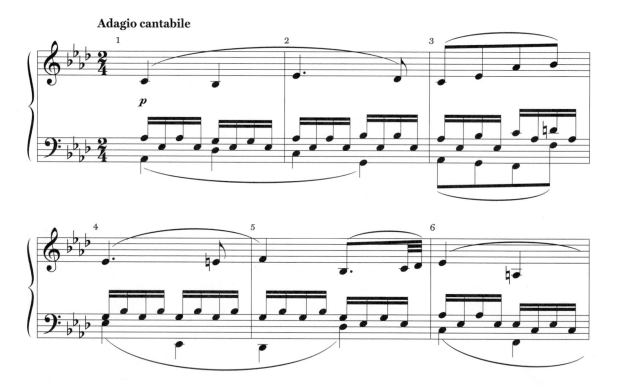

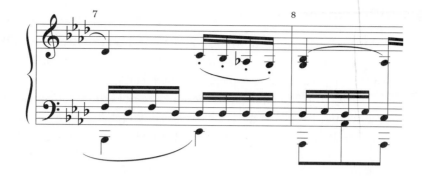

The **A** section is divided into two periods—measures 1–8 and 9–16—each of which is made up of two phrases; the second period is a varied repetition of the first. The first phrase ends with a tonicized half cadence, the second with a PAC. You may have thought that the first eight measures were a single phrase, since the inner-voice accompaniment does not pause and the melody and bass lines are elided over the phrase break. If so, try listening to the first four measures again and stopping before beat 2 in measure 4, to hear the resolution of the V$_3^4$/V to V. You should hear a clear point of repose at the half cadence.

As a first step in charting the form of this movement, listen again and mark any return of the **A** material in your score. If the section is altered when it returns, add prime marks (**A′** or **A″**). Does the **A** section return in the same key or a contrasting key? Mark any changes of key you hear. Label the measures between the **A** sections with other alphabet letters, as shown on the chart below. This formal design is called a five-part rondo. (The arrows indicate tonal instability.)

A	**B**	**A′**	**C**	**A″**	Coda
mm. 1–16	16b–28	29–36	37–50	51–66	67–73
A♭	f–E♭→	A♭	a♭ → E →	A♭	A♭

KEY CONCEPT

Rondo form is characterized by a repeated section (called a **refrain**, or **ritornello**) alternating with sections that contrast in key, mode, texture, harmonic complexity, thematic content, and/or style. The contrasting sections are called **episodes**. Although other designs are possible, the two most common are

five-part rondo: **A B A C A** (plus optional coda) and

seven-part rondo: **A B A C A B** (or **D**) **A** (plus optional coda).

After their initial presentation, the restatements of **A** and **B** may be varied.

Refrains and Episodes

As the Beethoven example shows, the rondo's refrain is usually harmonically closed—it ends with a conclusive cadence—and it returns each time in the tonic key. Its phrase structure is typically balanced and symmetrical. How are the episodes characterized? Beethoven's **B** section does not exhibit four-measure phrase lengths or regular hypermeter. It is harmonically unstable: the section begins by touching on F minor (vi of A♭), then drifts to E♭ Major (V of A♭, m. 23). The cadence at the end of the section elides with the beginning of the **A′** section. The melody of the **B** section, with its leaps, contrasts with the more lyrical **A** melody.

Section **C** likewise does not have regular four-measure phrase lengths or regular hypermeter. This section is chromatic and dramatic. The initial key is A♭ minor, followed by a modulation to E Major (we will learn more about that chromatic relation in Chapter 29). The **C** section introduces triplet sixteenth notes, which will reappear in the **A″** section. It also elides with the refrain's return in measure 51.

The episodes in the Beethoven movement are typical of episodes in general: they present contrasting keys and are often harmonically open. Episodes may include modulations or end in a key different from that in which they began, and they may elide with the refrain that follows without achieving harmonic closure. While the refrain often consists of four- or eight-measure phrases organized in period structure with a regular hypermeter, the episodes tend to fall into irregular phrases with irregular hypermeter. The diagram below is a typical design for five-part rondos.

Refrain	Episode	Refrain	Episode	Refrain
A	**B**	**A**	**C**	**A** (optional coda)
I–I	V* →	I–I	i* →	I–I
i–i	III or v* →	i–i	I* →	i–i

*or other contrasting key

Finally, consider the music that concludes the Beethoven movement. A perfect authentic cadence elides the conclusion of the **A″** section with the beginning of the final section—a coda. The remaining music has the character of an extended cadence with repeated dominant-tonic chord successions. Do you hear any familiar-sounding motives in those measures? *(Try it #10)* This coda has multiple formal functions: it reminds listeners of the motives of the piece, "closes out" each of the registers (in mm. 66–68 and 68–70), and slows down the action by shortening the length of melodic ideas (in mm. 70–73a) until all that remains is a repeated chord (m. 73) to end the movement.

Transitions and Retransitions

The end of a rondo's episodes typically provides cues for the listener that the **A** section is about to return. For example, both contrasting sections in the Beethoven movement end with a modulation back to the **A** section's key. In addition, the **B** section also ends with a short dominant pedal (mm. 27–28), while the **C** section closes with an acceleration of the harmonic rhythm.

KEY CONCEPT _____

The end of an episode, where the music audibly begins to turn back toward the **A** section's return, is called a **retransition**. Most retransitions prolong the dominant harmony, in preparation for the return of the refrain's tonic key. Refrains in turn may be linked to episodes by **transitions**, modulatory passages that move toward the key of the new section.

Both transitions and retransitions usually consist of repetitions of short motives (possibly transposed) and irregular hypermeters, rather than balanced four- or eight-measure phrases.

2.71 🎧 Listen now to the final movement of Mozart's Piano Sonata in C Major, K. 545, while following the score in your anthology. The refrain is given in Example 27.14a. As you listen, mark the large formal sections with alphabet letters; mark any change of key in the score as well. Do you hear a transition between the refrain and first episode? Do you hear a retransition after the first episode to prepare for the return of the refrain?

EXAMPLE 27.14: Mozart, Piano Sonata in C Major, K. 545, third movement

(a) Mm. 1–8

The **A** section, repeated, is an antecedent-consequent period with a half cadence in measure 4 and PAC in measure 8. After the double bar, the **B** section begins immediately in a new key, G Major, without a transition. The eight-measure **B** section stays in G throughout, again with antecedent-consequent phrases. Interestingly, the consequent phrase takes motives from the **A** section and states them in the new key. In cases like this, think of the key (rather than theme) as the stronger identifier of the formal section—don't be fooled into thinking that the refrain has returned!

2.73 🎧   Look now at the passage given in Example 27.14b, drawn from the end of the **B** section. What is the musical and harmonic function of measures 16b–20a?

(b) Mm. 15–24a

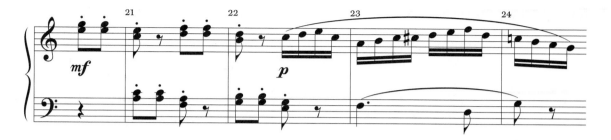

This passage provides a clear example of a retransition. As the key moves away from the G Major of the **B** section, Mozart prolongs the G chord, transforming it via the F♮ into a dominant seventh of the tonic key, C Major. The entire four bars prolong V^7 of C, in preparation for the refrain's return.

The chart below is a partial summary of the form of the Mozart rondo. Listen to the movement again, and then complete the chart. Be sure to include any transitions or retransitions. Use the "Comments" section to note cadence types, motivic recurrences, unusual key relationships, or any other musical feature you find striking. (When a theme begins on an upbeat, like Mozart's, start counting measures with the first downbeat of the phrase.) What is unusual about the **C** section? Are there any unexpected tonal areas, based on what we've learned about rondos thus far? *(Try it #11)*

SECTION	PHRASES	MEASURES	KEY/MODE	COMMENTS
A		1–8	C Major	Section repeated.
	a	1–4		Ends with an HC.
	a′	5–8		Ends with a PAC.
B		9–16	G Major	No transition.
	b	9–12		HC.
	a″	13–16		PAC; motives from A!
Retransition		17–20		Prolongs V^7 of C.
A		21–28	C Major	Same as 1–8.
	a	21–24		Same as 1–4.
	a′	25–28		Same as 5–8.
C		_____	_____	_____
	_____	_____		_____
	_____	_____		_____
Retransition?		_____		_____
		_____		_____
A′		_____	_____	
	_____	_____		_____
	_____	_____		_____
Coda?		_____		_____

Seven-Part Rondo

Seven-part rondos are generally extended movements, with longer refrains and episodes. A typical design for a seven-part rondo is shown below. The **C** section is typically much longer than the other sections; it may be developmental or exhibit a small, self-contained binary or ternary form. The transitions and retransitions (not shown on the chart) are also generally more extended in a seven-part rondo.

A	B	A	C	A	B′ (or D)	A
I–I	V* →	I–I	i* →	I–I	I (or i) →	I
i–i	III or v* →	i–i	I* →	i–i	i (or I) →	i

*or other contrasting key

The seven sections may group into a larger ternary design: the initial **A B A** might express the tonal areas I–V–I (or i–III–i), with the **C** section providing large-scale contrast in the parallel key and the final **A B′ A** returning all in the tonic key.

TERMS YOU SHOULD KNOW

chaconne

character variation

chromatic variation

coda

continuous variation

episode

figural variation

five-part rondo

ground bass

passacaglia

polyphonic variation

refrain

retransition

rhythmic acceleration

rondo

sectional variation

seven-part rondo

textural variation

timbral variation

transition

QUESTIONS FOR REVIEW

1. What characteristics distinguish continuous and sectional variations?
2. In what ways may a theme be varied?
3. What are typical types of larger structural organization in variation movements?
4. In a rondo, how do the nonrefrain sections typically contrast with the refrain?
5. In music for your own instrument, find an example of (a) a continuous variation movement, (b) a sectional variation movement, (c) a rondo.
6. In what ways may analysis inform a performance of variations? of a rondo?

Sonata-Form Movements

CHAPTER 28

Outline of topics covered

Basic sonata form
- The first large section
  - Minor-key expositions
- The second large section
  - The return of opening material
  - Harmonic instability
  - The retransition

Sonata form in the Romantic era
- Increasing length and complexity
- Key areas and the organization of the exposition
- The development section
- The recapitulation and coda

Sonatas, sonatinas, concertos, and sonata-form movements
- Sonata form and concerto form

Performing and listening to sonata-form movements

Overview

In this chapter, we will learn about a form whose roots are in binary design: sonata form. We consider the roles of melody and harmony in shaping a sonata-form movement, and observe how sonata form changed from the Classical to the Romantic era.

Repertoire

Ludwig van Beethoven, Piano Sonata in C Major, Op. 53 (*Waldstein*), first movement (CD 1, track 51)

Wolfgang Amadeus Mozart, Piano Sonata in G Major, K. 283, first movement (CD 2, track 40)

o o o o o o o o o o o o o o o o o o o o o o o o o o o o o o o o o o o o o o o o o o o o o o o o o o

Basic Sonata Form

2.40 🎧

We begin by listening to the first movement (*Allegro*) of Mozart's three-movement Piano Sonata in G Major, K. 283. Listen to the movement in its entirety while following the score in your anthology. Think about the overall formal organization, and mark in your score where you hear sections beginning or ending. Label any familiar musical material that appears later in the movement, and write in measure numbers to indicate where you first heard these themes or motives. (As you read this chapter, keep your anthology score and CD at hand to see and listen to each new element under discussion.)

WF1

While you were listening, you may have noticed some musical hints indicating the form. One obvious cue is the repeat signs—at measure 53 to indicate a repeat of measures 1–53a and at the end to indicate a repeat of measures 53b–120. Based on our study of binary form in Chapter 23, this movement seems to be organized like a large-scale continuous rounded binary form. What, other than the repetition, would you expect to happen in a continuous rounded binary movement in G Major? (*Try it #1*)

The First Large Section

How many features of binary form can you locate in this movement? Let's begin by looking at the opening. The first section is fifty-three measures long, longer than the first section in a typical binary movement. The first two phrases (mm. 1–4 and 5–10, shown in Example 28.1) establish the key of G Major and form a contrasting period (IAC, PAC) in the tonic key. Why do you think the second phrase is six measures long instead of the typical four? (*Try it #2*) The second phrase is then repeated with slight variations to make a sixteen-measure opening idea in the tonic key.

WF2

In sonata form, this opening musical idea in the tonic is sometimes called the **first theme**, or **primary theme**. Because there may be more than one melodic idea expressed in this tonic-key opening, however, some musicians instead call it the "first tonal area" or "first theme group." We will generally speak of the **first theme group** (your teacher may prefer another term), understanding that it may consist of more than one thematic idea but expresses the tonic key throughout.

EXAMPLE 28.1: Mozart, Piano Sonata in G Major, K. 283, first movement

(a) Mm. 1–10a (first theme group)

Scanning ahead, we locate the next significant cadence in measure 22. This cadence could be interpreted as a half cadence preceded by a secondary-dominant-function chord, but the music continues in the new key of D Major, as shown by the consistent presence of C♯ in the following measures and by cadences up through measure 53. Measures 16b–22, shown in Example 28.1b, thus have a transitional function: they lead from the first theme group to a cadence that prepares a second key area. For this reason, we call measures 16b–22 the **transition**.

2.41

(b) Mm. 16b–22 (transition)

Transition sections are typically sequential and modulatory. This transition consists of two short melodic sequences—measures 16b–19a and 19–21—with a modulation at the end of the second sequence. (We consider these melodic sequences because there is only one real "line" here: the upper parts essentially double the bass line in octaves and add embellishing tones.) Transitions that incorporate motives from the first theme are sometimes called "dependent transitions," while those that introduce new material are called "independent transitions." Which type is this transition? *(Try it #3)*

When you see a dependent transition, you may have difficulty deciding where the first theme group ends and where the transition begins—after all, they use the same thematic material. The key is to listen for tonal function: if the passage sounds like it is leaving the tonic key, then it is transitional. Independent transitions, like this one, can be identified by the change in melodic material and by sequential activity, even when the modulation is delayed until the very end.

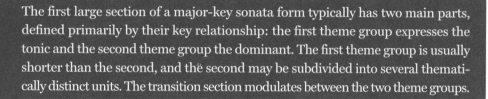

Measures 23–53 are in the key of D Major. We call this section the "second tonal area," or **second theme group**. (Other possible terms include "secondary theme" or "subordinate theme.") The word "group" is especially apt here because the second theme group typically divides up into a number of themes that may seem unrelated, except for the fact that they are united by a single key area: usually the dominant. Perhaps the best way to explore the organization of measures 23–53 is to look at how the section divides into motives, sequences, and phrases.

KEY CONCEPT

The first large section of a major-key sonata form typically has two main parts, defined primarily by their key relationship: the first theme group expresses the tonic and the second theme group the dominant. The first theme group is usually shorter than the second, and the second may be subdivided into several thematically distinct units. The transition section modulates between the two theme groups.

Mozart's second theme group shows how many short thematic ideas—some stable melodies, others more transitional in nature—can work together in a single unified key area. How does this section subdivide? Measures 23–31a present a syncopated melody that is clearly in D Major, the second key area. The first phrase of this theme, measures 23–26 (shown in Example 28.1c), ends with a half cadence; then the phrase is repeated and varied in measures 27–30, with an added ending that cadences on D Major in measure 31.

(c) Mm. 23–26 (second theme group)

2.43 🎧   Measures 31–34 (Example 28.1d) have a transitional character, because of the repeated motive and secondary leading-tone chords, but they do not modulate. They are followed by a harmonically stable progression in D Major in measures 35–38a. Measures 38–43a are then a varied repetition of 33–38a.

(d) Mm. 31–38a (second theme group)

Measures 43–44, based on a motive from the transition (mm. 16–18), connect to a final theme in measures 45–51a (Example 28.1e). Some analysts call this third theme another secondary theme; others refer to it as a closing theme, since it comes just before the close of the section. We will use the latter term, but with the understanding that the closing theme is really part of the second theme group when it expresses the same harmonic area (in this case, the dominant).

In sonata-form movements of the Romantic era, the closing theme group may appear in a distinct third key area, and it may include more than one distinct melody. In that case, we may call it the "third theme group," "closing theme group," or simply "closing group." The closing theme often contrasts in its motives or character with the previous musical materials of the second theme group. In this movement, however, the theme in measures 45–47 and 48–51a is reminiscent of the syncopated melody of measures 23–31, making a connection back to the beginning of the D-Major key area (compare Examples 28.1c and e).

2.44

(e) Mm. 45–51a (closing theme)

2.45

Finally, what is the function of measures 51–53 (Example 28.1f)? There is a strong PAC on D in measure 51, but stopping the section there would have seemed abrupt. Measures 51–53 form a codetta that ends the section by extending and repeating the cadence in D Major.

(f) Mm. 51–53 (codetta)

As we have observed, this first large section is similar to a binary-form first section in its key areas, but is much longer and includes transitional passages and a codetta. In addition, it features three harmonically stable melodies (mm. 1–16a, 23–31a, and 45–51a), one in the tonic key and two in the dominant key. This organization is typical of a sonata-form movement's first large section, a section called the **exposition** (in which the themes and motives for the entire movement are "exposed" for the first time).

SUMMARY

Typical Classical-era sonata-form expositions in major keys consist of the following sections:

First theme group	Transition	Second theme group (optional codetta)
Key: I	Modulates to V	V (may include a closing theme, still in V)

The exposition is usually repeated. The first and second theme groups always contrast in key, and may present themes with contrasting moods. In some early sonata-form movements, particularly those of Haydn, the first and second themes are quite similar, differing primarily in their keys.

Minor-Key Expositions   Sonata-form movements in minor keys follow a similar course, except that the second key area is usually the relative major (III) or, less often, the minor dominant (v).

KEY CONCEPT

Typical Classical-era sonata-form expositions in minor keys consist of the following sections:

First theme group	Transition	Second theme group (optional codetta)
Key: i	Modulates to III (or v)	III (or v) (may include a closing theme in the same key)

The Second Large Section

2.40

Before we continue with the second large section of Mozart's sonata, you may want to listen again to the entire movement, while following the score in your anthology. Did you hear the first and second theme groups (including the closing theme) come back in the second section? (If not, listen again, and pay close attention to measures 71b–120!) This return of earlier material is another similarity between sonata form and rounded binary form, but the way the two forms treat the returning material is not identical: in rounded binary, sometimes only a part of the music from the first section returns; in sonata form, the entire contents of the first section usually reappear, but with some alterations.

The Return of Opening Material   Compare measures 1–53 with 71b–120: what is alike and what is different? The return of the exposition in the second large section of a sonata form is called the **recapitulation** (a word that means "return to the head," or beginning). When the exposition's material returns, however, some changes are customary. Since the beginning of the recapitulation initiates a final return to the tonic key, it traditionally presents *all* of the exposition materials in the tonic. The first theme, already in the tonic key in the exposition, can usually be restated in the recapitulation with little or no alteration. What about this sonata? Compare the first theme group, measures 1–16, with the corresponding passage,

2.47

shown in Example 28.2a. *(Try it #4)*

EXAMPLE 28.2: Mozart, Piano Sonata in G Major, K. 283, first movement

(a) Mm. 71b–83a (recapitulation)

The first phrase of the first theme group returns unchanged in the recapitulation, but the second phrase (which was repeated in the exposition) has been replaced with a variation of the first phrase, which tonicizes A minor (ii) by means of its secondary dominant (represented by the G♯s). The only part of the original second phrase that remains here is the rhythm of measures 79b–80, which corresponds to that of measures 12b–13.

The transition from the first to the second theme group modulates in the exposition; that transition is usually modified in the recapitulation to stay in the original key. Is that the case in this movement? Compare measures 16–22 with 83–89. (*Try it #5*) Recall that in the exposition, the end of the transition could have been analyzed as a half cadence with V tonicized, except that the movement continued in the key of D. Here the cadence *is* treated as a half cadence—there is no modulation—and the movement continues in the tonic key, G. Perhaps, in retrospect, the changes to the second phrase of the first theme were intended to balance the reappearance of the transition exactly as before.

In a typical sonata-form movement, the second theme group and codetta (if any) are transposed from the key of the dominant (in the exposition) to the original tonic for the recapitulation. We would therefore expect measures 90–120 to appear in G Major, a transposition of the corresponding measures (23–53)—and they do.

Composers also generally make some slight changes in the second theme group when transposing it to the tonic key for the recapitulation. For example, the registral placement of musical elements—a melody and its accompaniment, two contiguous phrases, or even repetitions of sequence patterns—may be altered; elements may be transposed up a fourth or down a fifth. Where does that happen in this sonata form? *(Try it #6)* The second large section may close with a coda, sometimes added after the second section is repeated, but this movement simply ends with the codetta from the exposition, transposed into the tonic.

Harmonic Instability   The only measures we have not yet considered are 54–71a. Do you anticipate that these measures will present yet another tonally stable theme or perhaps less stable developmental material? In a rounded binary form, we would expect the beginning of the second large section to display harmonic instability through a modulation or through sequences that touch on different keys; the same is true for Classical-era sonata-form movements. A quick glance at the score for these measures reveals several chromatically inflected pitches. Listen carefully to the passage again, and consider these three questions. Are there any places that seem to establish a temporary key? Do you hear a sequence or modulation or both? Is the musical material similar to anything you heard in the exposition? *(Try it #7)*

2.46

WF4

The beginning of the second large section in a sonata-form movement is often called the **development**, because in sonatas by Beethoven and later Romantic-era composers, this section was devoted to the development and exploration of motives and themes from the exposition. A close examination of measures 54–62, though, shown in Example 28.2b, reveals few connections to the motives of the exposition. Instead, the dominant is prolonged through its own dominant (hence the C♯s). Mozart's treatment of the "development" is typical for sonata-form movements of his time. In essence, this section is simply an expanded version of the same type of harmonic instability and sequential material that would be found here in a rounded binary form. Mozart's development does not systematically explore the motivic potential of the exposition, as occurs in the sonatas of Beethoven and other later composers.

(b) Mm. 54–62a (development)

The Retransition   After the harmonic instability that is typical of most development sections, there are a few measures that have a special task: preparing for the return of music from the opening of the piece. This part of the development, called the **retransition**, serves as a connector between the development and recapitulation sections. The retransition sets up the return of the first theme harmonically—by establishing and often prolonging the V⁷ chord of the tonic key. The retransition also sets the mood for the first theme's return. In some sonata-form movements, the retransition builds tension, making the listener anticipate the first theme's triumphant return; in others, it brings back the first theme almost as a surprise—the listener does not even hear it coming. Many other dramatic roles for the retransition are possible, but the harmonic function of this passage is consistent: to return to the dominant seventh chord of the tonic key.

In Mozart's sonata, the retransition features a long dominant pedal, extending from measure 62 to 68 (Example 28.2c). This rearticulated pedal point, with a melodic sequence above it, builds tension, but does not immediately connect into the return of the first theme. Instead, Mozart inserts two ascending pentachords (mm. 68–70a), each ending with a brief rest, as if to say, "Not yet, not yet." Then, in measures 70–71, a descending scalar pattern brings back the first theme.

(c) Mm. 62–73a (retransition)

Listen to this retransition in several different performances: in some, the pianist will slow measures 68 and 69 dramatically, perhaps extending the rests, to heighten anticipation of the resolution in measure 72; in others, the performer maintains a consistent tempo throughout. How would you perform this passage?

SUMMARY

The second large section of Classical-era sonata-form movements includes the development and recapitulation sections. This section is usually repeated, and may end with a coda.

Development sections may explore thematic material from the exposition or may simply represent an area of modulatory activity or harmonic instability. In early sonata forms, the development section is usually brief compared with the exposition and recapitulation.

Typical Classical-era sonata-form recapitulations consist of the following sections:

First theme group	Transition	Second theme group (optional codetta and/or coda)
Key: I (or i)	Altered to stay in tonic	I (or i) (may include a closing theme, still in tonic)

○ ○

Sonata Form in the Romantic Era

The rise of the Romantic style brought changes and new developments to sonata form. We will consider some of these changes as they appear in a sonata-form movement by Beethoven: the first movement of his Piano Sonata in C Major, Op. 53 (known as the *Waldstein* Sonata, after the patron to whom it was dedicated). Listen to the entire movement while following the score in your anthology. While listening, mark in your score any formal elements you notice—themes, transitions, phrases, cadences, key areas, and so on—and try to identify the main parts of the sonata form. Some Romantic-era sonata forms also add a slow introduction and lengthy coda—does this one?

Increasing Length and Complexity

Some differences between the Mozart and Beethoven movements that are immediately apparent are the length—302 measures for the Beethoven, 120 for the Mozart—and the later sonata's tumultuous, chromatic, and exuberant Romantic character. Scan through the score to find the repeat signs marking the end of the exposition (with a first and second ending, mm. 86 and 87). After you have identified the first theme as beginning in measure 1 (there is no slow introduction), locate and mark the beginning of the recapitulation (m. 156). In the Romantic era, both the development and recapitulation gradually grew to balance the exposition in length and complexity, overlaying a ternary element—exposition (**A**), development (**B**), recapitulation (**A′**)—on the sonata form's formerly binary-based organization.

WF5

On hearing this work for the first time, you may have noticed the complexity of the harmonic choices, particularly as compared with the Mozart movement: mode mixture, embellishing and harmonically functional chromaticism, and sequential progressions associated with Romantic-era harmony are all present. We will consider some of these interesting details in this chapter; others we will visit in Chapter 29.

Key Areas and the Organization of the Exposition

1.51

Listen again to the exposition of the *Waldstein's* first movement, and consider these questions: Are the themes and transitions located where you would expect, based on the model we saw in the Mozart sonata? Are the key areas what you would expect?

The first idea of the first theme group is four measures long (like Mozart's first phrase), ending on a half cadence. In an earlier Classical-era sonata, the initial idea would probably have been followed by a phrase of similar length and character that ended with a conclusive cadence, making a period structure. This opening period would firmly establish the tonic key. What does Beethoven do instead? (*Try it #8*) The expected PAC in C Major does not arrive—instead, there is a half cadence (m. 13) in C minor (through mode mixture). Where, then, is the movement's first strong cadence in C Major? (*Try it #9*)

Measures 14–17 sound like a rhythmic variation of m. 1–4, but then the passage begins to veer in a new harmonic direction. What happens in measure 18?

1.52

How do measures 18–21 compare with 5–8? (*Try it #10*) Because the passage beginning in measure 14 initiates a sequential and modulatory section, we identify it as the beginning of the transition. In addition, since this sounds so much like a variant of the opening phrase, we call it a "dependent transition." Measures 23–30 continue the transition section with a prolonged B Major (and B dominant seventh) chord expanded by an E minor $^6_4$, chromatically embellished. Perhaps this harmonic motion implies a move to E minor (iii in C Major). It does not lead directly to the second theme group, however—it dissipates into a B-Major arpeggiation in measures 29–30, then connects to an ascending scale fragment (doubled in octaves) in measures 31–34, which leads to the E-Major arrival on the downbeat of measure 35.

1.53 🎧   What are we to make of the E-Major passage that follows? The theme that begins in measure 35 initiates the second theme group of the movement, identified by its harmonic stability, regular phrase lengths, and chorale-style voicing. The key here is indeed E Major, the chromatic mediant, not the expected G Major (the dominant) of the Classical-era sonata-form movement. This type of harmonic innovation is a hallmark of Romantic-era sonatas. The eight-measure second

1.54 🎧   theme is then followed immediately by a variation (mm. 43–50a), with the harmonic chorale decorated by a triplet melody in the highest part.

The rest of the exposition may be divided into a number of distinct subsections, all of which are part of the second theme group. In larger sonata forms, like this Beethoven movement, it is sometimes helpful to label the subsections of the second theme group with alphabet letters: 2a, 2b, 2c, and so on. If we call the "chorale" melody (mm. 35–42) and its embellished restatement (mm. 43–50a) 2a, how should we label measures 50 and following? Here, a syncopated rhythmic idea joins the continuing triplets of the second-theme restatement. Is this a theme?

We hear this passage as a new subsection (2b), but not as a true theme. Measures 50–53 state transitional material based on the alternation of an E-Major $^6_4$ chord and a B dominant seventh, prolonging V^7 in E Major (as mm. 23–30 prolong V in E minor); they are followed by a similar passage, beginning in measure 54, that prolongs I. The triplets soon accelerate to sixteenth notes, and the introduction of a D6 in the upper voice (m. 60) turns the tonic function into an applied chord to IV, which then resolves to IV in measures 62–63. A V^6_5/V in measures 64–65 introduces a new arpeggiating motive in measure 66, when the progression reaches a climactic cadential $^6_4$ chord, increasing in tension as the $^6_4$ resolves into a V^9_7 in measure 70. This harmony is prolonged for four drawn-out measures, making us wait and wait for its resolution, before the most dramatic point of arrival of the entire exposition in measure 74—a PAC in E Major.

1.55 🎧   The cadence initiates a new subsection in measure 74, which we could call 2c. This passage might be labeled the closing theme (still part of the E-Major second theme group), but a better term would be codetta, since it follows harmonic closure in E Major and since this section serves a dual role—as preparation for the return to the beginning of the exposition and for the sequence that connects to the development section. There are many motivic links between themes in this movement—where, for example, have you heard the upper part of measures 74–76a before? What is the origin of the left-hand material here? (*Try it #11*)

The Development Section

One interesting question to ask about the development section is "Where does it begin?" The answer would affect how you perform the passage. In a typical Classical-era sonata-form movement, the answer is clear-cut: the development section begins after the repeat markings, usually following the exposition's definitive final cadence.

Listen again to this movement up to about measure 90 to identify the beginning of the development. The sequence in measures 80b–89 is what makes locating it difficult. This sequence, the first time through, modulates from E minor back to C Major for the repeat of the exposition; yet the second time through, the same music keeps spinning on past C to cadence in measure 90 (on F Major), with a motion so smooth that you probably didn't notice that the music passed the point where it had turned back to the beginning before.

To consider this question more broadly, let's look at developmental aspects of the exposition: what are measures 5–8 and especially 14–22 if not a "development" of the primary theme (mm. 1–4)? Consider also the "variation" of the second theme in measures 43–50a; that activity is developmental in nature as well. And if we look back at the first four measures, even there a developmental principle is at play: the basic idea (mm. 2–3) is only two measures long, with a rumbling extension at the beginning and a varied repetition of the half cadence of measure 3 transposed up an octave in measure 4. One of Beethoven's innovations in writing sonata-form movements was the incorporation of the principle of development into all aspects of the movement, not just the development section. Other Romantic-era composers to a greater or lesser extent followed his lead. Which of the materials in the exposition does Beethoven explore in the development "proper" (mm. 90–156a)? *(Try it #12)*

Before we look into Beethoven's treatment of motivic material in the development, we need to locate the harmonic goal of the section: the retransition. Recall that the function of the retransition is to prolong the dominant harmony in preparation for the return of the primary key and first theme group in the recapitulation. We should look, then, for a prolonged G dominant seventh. The first inkling of a prolonged G7 is in measure 136, but the texture and rhythm of this passage unites it to the sequential passage that came before. The retransition seems more likely to begin at measure 142, where the texture and rhythm change and a new section clearly begins. This retransition is quite long and dramatic, beginning with the introduction of a "rumbling motive" and G pedal point in the bass. The development process continues through the retransition, with the continued exploration of the sixteenth motive that originated from measure 3 of the first theme.

Of the many motives developed in measures 90–156, we will focus on two especially prominent ones, shown in Example 28.3: the skip up a third with stepwise return (the "skip motive"), and the descending five-note scale (the "scale motive"). The derivation of these motives from the first theme should be obvious; the variants and repetitions in measures 94–111 are numerous and also fairly obvious. But what about measures 142–156a? Do these motives also play a role in the retransition? Take a look at the "rumble" in the left hand in measure 142, and listen carefully to that pattern—can you hear it as the combination of the skip motive and the scale motive? Are there other motives in the retransition that are variants of the skip and scale motives? *(Try it #13)*

EXAMPLE 28.3: Two motives from Beethoven's *Waldstein* Sonata, mm. 92 and 93

"skip motive"   "scale motive"

The harmonic activity in the development is interesting as well. While listening to this section, you may have noticed that most of the development is made from falling-fifth sequence patterns. A glance at the accidentals indicates that the mode mixture we heard in the exposition is featured here as well. Some of the tonal areas briefly tonicized include G minor (v in C Major; mm. 96–99a), C minor (i; mm. 100–103), F minor (iv; m. 104)—a pattern of falling fifths. Then beginning in measure 112, Beethoven initiates another extended falling-fifth sequence, including tonicizations of C Major (I; mm. 112–113), F Major (IV; mm. 116–117), B♭ Major (♭VII; mm. 120–121), E♭ minor (♭iii; mm. 124–125), and B minor (vii; mm. 128–129). While these tonicizations are brief, each may be identified by the presence of at least a dominant seventh chord and its resolution to the temporary tonic. In addition, some of these falling-fifth sequences include a chain of secondary dominants, a particularly common type of chromatic sequence. We will consider this type of sequence in more detail in Chapter 29.

The Recapitulation and Coda

We turn now to the last large section of the piece, the recapitulation. In this section of a sonata-form movement, we expect each of the main parts of the exposition to return in order, all in the tonic key. Let's examine the reappearance of each element briefly in turn. The first twelve measures of the first theme return essentially unchanged, as measures 156–167. In measure 168, however, we hear something unusual and strikingly different from the exposition: the arpeggiated C-minor triad ends not on the expected G, but with a deceptive move to A♭. Another arpeggiation in measure 169 spans a D♭-Major chord, then ends on B♭ (and to think that all of this was supposed to return in C Major!). Measures 167–173 explore more deeply the modal mixture only hinted at in the first theme of the exposition. What would the Roman numeral analysis be for these seven measures? *(Try it #14)*

After three measures (171–173) of new material, we return to C Major, to the first-theme variant that begins the transition: measures 14–21 return as 174–181, measure 22 is expanded and altered as measures 182–183, and measures 23–34 reappear as measures 184–195. The transition section in a recapitulation plays a different role from the one it plays in an exposition—if in the recapitulation the first and second theme groups appear in the same (tonic) key, then the transition no longer needs to serve a modulatory function. It is usually altered, often extended, so that its sequential motion will return to the tonic key. Is that the case here? In what key does the chorale theme (the first part of the second theme group) return? This theme (originally mm. 35–50a, including the triplet variation) extends from measure 196 to 211a in A Major, the chromatic submediant—or is it A minor (look at mm. 200–203)? The transition in measures 184–195 was altered not to stay in C Major but instead to move toward A Major.

After stating the chorale theme in A Major, Beethoven shifts to A minor, in part to bring back the expected key of C Major for the triplet variation (mm. 204–211a). We also hear a return of measures 50–74a, now in C Major (mm. 211–235a). The codetta starts off in measure 235 in C Major, incorporating elements of mixture even more—look at all the flats! Measures 241b–249a present the sequence that connected the exposition and the development. Compare measures 245–249 with the earlier spot (the second ending of the exposition): both times Beethoven suggests motion toward F Major, by transforming the C-Major tonic to a C^7: V^7/IV. The second time, however, he colors the passage—through mixture—to F minor and resolves the V^7 deceptively, to $\flat$VI (or D$\flat$ Major), in measure 249. Has Beethoven prepared us at all for this D$\flat$ arrival? *(Try it #15)* We are suddenly quite far afield from C Major, and the composer seizes this opportunity to begin the coda on D$\flat$.

At this point, you are probably wondering what is going on here formally and tonally—and rightly so. There are several pages of music left, implying that this coda is far longer than any we have heard previously. Uncharacteristically, we heard no perfect authentic cadence in C Major before it began. Further, the second theme has yet to reappear in the tonic key. In all, this coda seems to have the character and structure of another development section. Well, it *is* another development section—a Beethovian innovation, the "developmental coda." Measures 249–277 are essentially another development section, preceding another retransition in measures 278–283 that ends on a strong and convincing V^7 in the key of C Major. Finally, we hear strong tonal closure with a perfect authentic cadence that overlaps in measure 284 with the "missing" second theme in C Major. At the cadence in measure 295, all of the tasks of the recapitulation are completed. A brief codetta based on the main theme finally brings the sonata movement to an end.

1.59

SUMMARY

The exposition section of Romantic-era sonata forms usually includes several distinct contrasting themes. The two key areas are typically tonic and dominant (for major-key sonatas) and tonic and relative major (for minor-key sonatas), but contrasting keys other than the dominant and relative major (including distant keys) may also be explored. In late Romantic sonata-form movements, a third key is sometimes introduced in the closing theme. The exposition in Romantic (and some Classical) movements may be preceded by an introduction, possibly in a contrasting tempo and/or key area. The exposition may be repeated.

The development and recapitulation of Romantic-era sonata forms are sometimes paired as a section and repeated, as in Classical sonatas, but often constitute separate sections that are near-equal in length. The Romantic sonata form may end with a substantial coda, which includes additional development of the themes.

Typical Romantic-era development sections explore thematic material or motives from the exposition and may feature sequences, modulation to distant keys, harmonic instability, or even a new theme. The retransition normally follows the pattern of Classical sonatas by prolonging V^7.

○ ○

Sonatas, Sonatinas, Concertos, and Sonata-Form Movements

The term "sonata" technically refers to a multimovement composition for piano or a solo-line instrument (such as the violin) and keyboard accompaniment. Sonatas typically have three or four movements. The first is almost always in sonata form, which is sometimes called "sonata-allegro form," after the typical tempo marking for such movements. Mozart's Piano Sonata in C Major, K. 545, which we have studied in previous chapters, is an example of a three-movement sonata (it is included in its entirety in your anthology): the first movement is sonata-allegro, the second a slow movement (*Andante*), and the third a rousing rondo. The first and/or last movement of a sonata, symphony, or string quartet may be in sonata form.

A **sonatina** is simply what it sounds like—a little sonata. The first movement of a sonatina is usually in an abbreviated sonata form. Sonatinas may have a very short development section (about the same scope as the **B** section in a rounded binary) or no actual development at all. Their first and second themes are also

WF6

typically compact (often four to eight measures), without lengthy transitions. Sonatina form is distinguished from rounded binary by the presence of themes, transitions, development, and other elements of sonata form—only on a reduced scale. Sonatinas are associated with Classical-era composers, but these "little sonatas" were written in the Romantic era as well, usually composed for children or beginning players.

Sonata Form and Concerto Form

Concertos—compositions for a solo instrument and orchestra—often consist of three movements, arranged fast-slow-fast, that follow a formal pattern similar to the three-movement sonata. Concerto first movements are usually based on sonata form, but alternate sections featuring the orchestra and the soloist. In early Classical-era concertos, sometimes the first movement is written with a "double exposition." That is, the orchestra begins the movement by playing both the first and/or second theme group in the tonic key, without the soloist. Then the ensemble plays material from the exposition a second time, this time featuring the solo instrument (with the orchestra playing an accompanimental role) and with the standard modulation to the dominant or relative-major key. The double-exposition format is not maintained in the recapitulation, however, where the orchestra and soloist share thematic material more equally. In later Romantic-era concertos, the double exposition was less favored; indeed, some concertos begin with the solo performer.

Concertos are showcases for virtuosic performers. Nowhere are their talents more evident than in the **cadenza**, a solo passage that features rapid passagework and technical challenges. It is generally positioned between the end of the recapitulation and the beginning of the coda, and is prepared harmonically by a cadential $^6_4$ chord played by the orchestra, which the soloist expands. The cadenza's end is signaled in the solo instrument by a prominent scale-degree $\hat{2}$ (often with trill or other ornamentation) over a dominant-function harmony, which resolves to tonic with the beginning of the coda (and entrance once again of the orchestra).

In Classical concertos, it was expected that the soloist would improvise the cadenza (or prepare it in advance). Performers could thus showcase both their technical and their compositional skills in the cadenzas. In later concertos, cadenzas were more often composed. Today, most concerto editions include a cadenza written out by the composer, a different composer, a reputable soloist, or the editor after the style of a particular performer.

○ ○

Performing and Listening to Sonata-Form Movements

When you perform or listen to a movement in sonata form, your familiarity with its expected structure should help you to understand, convey, and remember the movement better. Here are some questions you might ask to gain insight into a sonata-form movement.

Which passages exhibit a stable key area? Where are there clear phrases? What is the character of each theme—is it stolid, humorous, energetic, lyrical? What musical clues help you decide? Which passages are transitional? What is the intended effect of a transition—do the harmonies and melodic patterns indicate increasing tension that is released with the arrival of the new key, or is the section designed to flow to the new key area without the listener even noticing?

Consider the development section carefully. Are there motives that should be brought out by the performer? What is the affect of the development: mysterious, agitated, seemingly aimless, joyous? Which keys are visited and where? At what point do the harmonies begin to turn toward the home key by reestablishing the dominant? Is the retransition intended to build tension, which is released as the first theme reappears? Or does the return come as a surprise?

When the music from the exposition returns in the recapitulation, what has changed? Are there coda and codetta passages? Do these closing sections bring the piece to a gentle end, or do they end with a flourish?

Finally, consider the date of composition and the style of the movement carefully; that information will provide important clues to the form and an appropriate interpretation. Classical-era pieces need to be played cleanly, with lightness, precision, and expressiveness. In the Romantic era, on the other hand, the overt expression of emotion was valued and encouraged, and your performance can bring such emotions to the fore.

Think also about the drama that unfolds in the sonata you are playing. If you are a listener, ask what the performer is trying to convey. Music is about so much more than simply "music"—it expresses the emotion and the flow of life. A performer who merely plays the correct notes and the durations is like an actor who reads a text accurately, but without feeling. Enjoy the dramatic aspects of this extended form, and your audience will, too.

TERMS YOU SHOULD KNOW

cadenza
closing theme
coda
   • developmental coda
codetta
concerto

development
exposition
   • double exposition
first theme
first theme group
recapitulation

retransition
second theme group
sonata
sonata form
sonatina
transition

QUESTIONS FOR REVIEW

1. What key areas are expected in the exposition of a sonata-form movement in a major key? in a minor key?
2. What characteristics distinguish the first theme group from the second theme group?
3. Where are we likely to find a codetta? What are the characteristics of a codetta?
4. What are some typical elements of a development? How do we identify where a development section starts? How do we locate the retransition?
5. How is the material from the exposition typically changed when it reappears in the recapitulation? Where are changes expected? Why?
6. How is Classical-era sonata form like a continuous rounded binary form? How are the two forms different?
7. What are some differences between the Romantic-era and Classical-era sonata form?
8. In music for your own instrument, find an example of sonata form. How does that example correspond to the models presented in this chapter?
9. How do we identify themes? transitional passages? In performance, how might you differentiate between themes and transitional passages?
10. How might knowing that a piece is in sonata form save you time in preparing and memorizing the music? Which sections might you compare as you prepare the work for performance?
11. In music for your own instrument, find an example of a concerto first movement in sonata form. How does the movement correspond to the description presented in this chapter?

CHAPTER 29 Chromaticism

Overview

In this chapter, we learn how to write chromatic progressions by embellishing familiar diatonic ones, and discover new ways to modulate to close and distant keys. We also consider harmonies and voice-leading characteristic of late Romantic-era chromaticism.

Repertoire

Ludwig van Beethoven, Piano Sonata in C minor, Op. 13 (*Pathétique*), first and second movements (CD 1, track 41)

Beethoven, Piano Sonata in C Major, Op. 53 (*Waldstein*), first movement (CD 1, track 51)

Frédéric Chopin, Prelude in E minor, Op. 28, No. 4

George Frideric Handel, Chaconne in G Major, from *Trois Leçons* (CD 2, track 1)

Fanny Mendelssohn Hensel, "Neue Liebe, neues Leben" (CD 2, track 22)

Scott Joplin, "Pine Apple Rag" (CD 2, track 28)

Jerome Kern and Otto Harbach, "Smoke Gets in Your Eyes," from *Roberta*

Wolfgang Amadeus Mozart, Piano Sonata in D Major, K. 284, third movement (CD 2, track 48)

Mozart, String Quartet in D minor, K. 421, first movement

Franz Schubert, "Der Wegweiser," from *Winterreise*

Robert Schumann, "Ich grolle nicht," from *Dichterliebe* (CD 3, track 35)

John Philip Sousa, "The Washington Post March"

Richard Wagner, Prelude to *Tristan und Isolde*

The Chromatic Elaboration of Diatonic Frameworks

Diatonic Sequence Patterns

2.9 We begin by listening to Variation 16 of Handel's Chaconne in G Major, shown in Example 29.1. As you listen, try to identify any sequential passage(s) in this variation (see Chapter 18 for a review of sequences). Write in the Roman numerals and figures for the relatively straightforward opening and closing measures, then consider the chromatic harmonies of the middle section.

EXAMPLE 29.1: Handel, Chaconne in G Major, Variation 16, mm. 129–136

This variation, like Variations 9, 10, and 14, opens with a 5–6 intervallic gesture in the left hand, setting up an expressive chain of 7–6 suspensions in the bass and tenor voices of the opening measures. In your anthology, compare this opening with that of Variation 14 to see how Handel has turned a diatonic progression into a chromatic one. Here, the stepwise bass line has been elaborated to create a chromatic descent from $\hat{1}$ to $\hat{5}$.

We begin our Roman numeral analysis with the diatonic portions: measure 1 begins with i–VI⁶ (or i⁵⁻⁶) in G minor, a standard tonic prolongation. Likewise, the final measures (134b–136) make the typical cadential gesture i⁶–ii°⁶₅–V⁸₄⁻₃⁷–i. Now, how would you analyze measures 132–134a? Begin by considering the chord qualities. How do these chords connect? Does each resolve as expected? *(Try it #1)*

The progression is based on a falling-fifth sequence, but each triad has been made into a dominant seventh chord—the V⁷ of the chord that comes next in the sequence. The voice-leading here is typical of a falling-fifth sequence with root-position dominant seventh chords: the chordal sevenths all resolve down by step as expected, but the leading tones also resolve down—pulled downward in a stepwise descending chromatic line. This is the most common type of chromatic sequence, in which dominant-seventh-quality chords are substituted for all or some (usually every other chord) of the chords in a falling-fifth sequence. The falling-fifth chromatic sequence is quite typical with root-position chords, as in the Handel example; it may also include inversions.

KEY CONCEPT

You may transform many diatonic sequences into chromatic sequences by substituting chromatic harmonies for similar diatonic ones or by chromatically embellishing the diatonic framework.

Listen again to this variation, or play through it at the keyboard. What is the chord quality of the harmony on the downbeats of measures 130 and 131? To what harmonies would you expect these chords to resolve? *(Try it #2)* In Handel's variation, neither chord resolves as we would expect. The chordal sevenths of these diminished seventh chords do resolve downward, following the 7–6 linear pattern we saw in previous variations. However, the roots F♯3 and E3 move downward by half step as a part of the chromatically embellished bass line that created these diminished seventh chords in the first place. These chords are best analyzed as voice-leading chords (VL).

On the second beat of measure 131, we see a diminished triad that is produced by a chromatic embellishment—the step between the Ds in the first chord and the

Cs in the iv⁶ chord that ends the measure. How might we analyze that sonority? If we gave the C♯-E-G chord a Roman numeral, it would be a viiº⁶/V that resolves irregularly; but this "chord" is best labeled simply by identifying the C♯s as chromatic passing tones.

Descending Chromatic Bass Lines

2.23 🎧

As mentioned earlier, we can also use a falling-fifth sequence with chords in inversion. If we choose the correct inversions, we can write a descending chromatic bass line. Listen to the excerpt from Hensel's "Neue Liebe, neues Leben" shown in Example 29.2. After a repetition of the opening parallel period (mm. 1–8) in measures 17–24, and a two-measure extension that cadences in B♭, the character of the song begins to change—with a new vocal line and accompanimental texture, and a chromatic descent in the bass line. Undoubtedly, this change in character is sparked by the unrest of the text, which speaks of quickly fleeing away. Determine the quality and inversion of each chord in measures 26–30, then assign Roman numerals in the key of B♭. Write your analysis beneath the example.

EXAMPLE 29.2: Hensel, "Neue Liebe, neues Leben," mm. 26–34a

Translation: If I rush to escape her, to take heart and flee her, in a moment, ah, my way leads back to her.

After the cadential tonic in the first half of measure 26, we hear a new phrase beginning with vi in B♭ Major, followed by its own dominant (V⁶₅/vi). But instead of resolving upward, as we expect, the leading-tone F♯ is pulled down by the chromatic bass motion to F♮. This resolution, combined with a B♮, turns the expected vi into a V⁴₂/ii. The seventh of the ⁴₂ then resolves down, but to E♮ rather than E♭ as expected, making the chord of resolution not ii⁶ but V⁶₅/V. What is the root progression of these measures? What is unusual about the connection of V⁶₅/V in measure 28 to the second chord in that measure? *(Try it #3)* The chromatic sequence is followed by a modulation to G minor in measures 29–30.

In the Handel and Hensel examples, we have seen how familiar diatonic sequences may be embellished chromatically by substituting secondary dominant and leading-tone chords for diatonic ones. We have also seen how chromatic pitches can be inserted between whole steps in the basic framework.

KEY CONCEPT

Any sequence that features stepwise voice-leading is a candidate for chromatic embellishment. The embellishment can be as simple as filling in whole steps chromatically in one voice (usually the bass), or it may involve elaborate chromaticism in several voices. In falling-fifth sequences, some or all of the seventh chords may be replaced with chromatic secondary-dominant-function chords in root position or inversions.

Voice Exchanges

Play through the music shown in Example 29.3, a chromatic introduction. In this progression, the inner voices (D4 and F4) stay the same, while the outer voices move in contrary motion from G2 (bass) and B4 (soprano) to B2 and G4 and back again—making a voice exchange, filled in with half steps. As is typical with a voice exchange, the chord with the interval that is exchanged is prolonged; in this case, it is a V⁷ chord. The "chords" in between are not strong functional harmonies, but rather are by-products of voice-leading.

EXAMPLE 29.3: Chromatic introduction

In Chapters 15, 16, and 19, we learned about prolongations that include voice exchanges filled in with a passing chord—usually a second-inversion triad or seventh chord, as shown in Example 29.4a. We also considered the chromatic voice exchange; for example, a progression between ii⁷ and V⁶₅/V where scale-degrees $\hat{2}$ and $\hat{4}$ in the ii⁷ chord exchange places with $\hat{2}$ and ♯$\hat{4}$ in the V⁶₅/V (Example 29.4b). In Romantic-era compositions, voice exchanges provide a framework for some elaborate chromatic progressions. For example, we could make a relatively simple elaboration of the basic voice exchange shown in Example 29.4a by filling in the half steps between the scale degrees that are exchanged, as shown in part c. This sequence of pitches may be immediately reversed to return chromatically to the beginning points, like the chromatic introduction in Example 29.3.

If we chromaticize the voice exchange of Example 29.4b, we will need to repeat a pitch (or use a longer note value) in the upper part to match the lower (Example 29.4d). There are many possible variants of the chromatically filled voice exchange: try inverting so that you begin with outer voices spanning a sixth rather than a third (part e), staggering the chromatic motions (compare part f with c), and so on. While it is sometimes possible to analyze the chords between the "ends" of the voice exchange with Roman numerals and figures, these labels do not make sense functionally; such a chromatic succession of sonorities merely prolongs the chords at either end of the voice exchange.

EXAMPLE 29.4: Voice exchanges and their chromatic elaborations

Now play through the piano accompaniment of Example 29.5a, an excerpt from Schubert's song "Der Wegweiser" ("The Sign Post"), from the song cycle *Winterreise*. Where do you hear chromatic motion in this excerpt? In measures 68b–75, two voices move in contrary motion by half step. The upper voice spans G4 (supplied by the vocal anacrusis to m. 69 and continuing in the piano part) down to B♭3 (beat 2 of m. 75), while the bass line spans B♮1 to G2—a chromaticized voice exchange. Example 29.5b shows how each part progresses chromatically, with the held root of the G chord filling in an inner voice.

EXAMPLE 29.5: Schubert, "Die Wegweiser," from *Winterreise*

(a) Mm. 68b–77a

Translation: One sign I see standing, unmoving before my gaze; one street must I go down, from which no one has come back.

(b) Reduction of mm. 68b–75

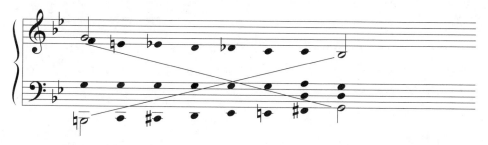

How would we analyze these sonorities with Roman numerals? While we might be able to come up with a series of secondary dominants and augmented-sixth chords (even a diminished third chord!), the resolutions implied by these Roman numerals are not fulfilled. Better to simply label the chord that is prolonged, and

WF1

not worry about a vertical analysis of the simultaneities in between.

Play through the excerpt again, while following the text, to see how Schubert interprets the words "unverrückt" (unmoving) and "keiner" (no one) musically. His phrase begins with the vocal line literally unmoving, with a repeated G4 unremitting above the accompaniment's chromatic lines. These repeated notes might be sung with a fairly uninflected "straight" interpretation to portray the unmoving sign. The high point of the line in terms of tessitura, duration, and emotional content falls on the word "keiner," and Schubert's use of the lowered scale-degree $\hat{2}$ and Neapolitan harmony on the last syllable all work to create a sense that this is a road from which no one returns. Singer and pianist alike can intensify this foreboding through tone color and timing decisions.

Common-Tone Diminished Seventh and Augmented-Sixth Chords

3.35 🎧

3.37 🎧

We turn now to two contrasting songs to learn about additional ways we can embellish harmonies chromatically. Listen first to Schumann's poignant "Ich grolle nicht," from the *Dichterliebe* cycle, while following the score in your anthology. Write in a harmonic analysis in the key of C Major underneath Example 29.6. How do you analyze the fully diminished seventh chord in the first half of measure 18? Does it function as we would expect—as a leading-tone or secondary leading-tone chord? (*Try it #4*)

EXAMPLE 29.6: Schumann, "Ich grolle nicht," from *Dichterliebe*, mm. 16b–19a

Translation: I have known that for a long time.

WF2   Look now at another fully diminished seventh chord, from Kern and Harbach's famous song "Smoke Gets in Your Eyes" (Example 29.7). Play and sing through the passage, concentrating on the diminished seventh chord (D♯-F♯-A♮-B♯ [C♮], with the chord symbol F♯ dim) at the cadence. What is this chord's function? The diminished seventh embellishes the dominant harmony, and it holds a common tone with the prominent melody pitch, F♯ (on "doubt my love"). This type of sonority is sometimes called a **common-tone diminished seventh chord** (abbreviated CT°7), or **embellishing diminished seventh chord**. These diminished sevenths do not resolve as dominant-function chords. They are, in essence, collections of chromatic and diatonic neighbor or passing tones that happen to make a fully diminished seventh sonority; and they always share one pitch with the chord that precedes or follows them. In the Schumann and Kern examples, the common tone is in the uppermost voice.

EXAMPLE 29.7: Kern and Harbach, "Smoke Gets in Your Eyes," mm. 21–24

KEY CONCEPT

To write common-tone diminished seventh chords:

1. Find a position for the chord between two harmonies that share one or more common tones (it may be the same harmony, possibly with change of voicing).
2. Write the first and third chords, leaving a space in the middle for the CT°7 chord.
3. Choose a common tone to share with the first or third harmony; build a diminished seventh chord with that common tone as one element and stepwise motion in the other voices.
4. Remember that CT°7 chords generally have a neighboring function (Example 29.8a) or passing function (Example 29.8b).
5. Because the $\frac{4}{2}$ inversion is typical for CT°7 chords, you may keep the common tone in the bass and build a °7 chord in $\frac{4}{2}$ position above this pitch by raising the fourth and second above the bass (Example 29.8c).

It is also possible to find similar collections of chromatic neighbors that make a so-called **common-tone German augmented-sixth chord**, shown in Example 29.8d. The CT A⁶ chord typically prolongs the tonic harmony, since its distinctive interval of the augmented sixth still resolves outward to $\hat{5}$ (though in this context, to the fifth of the tonic harmony).

EXAMPLE 29.8: Common-tone embellishing chords

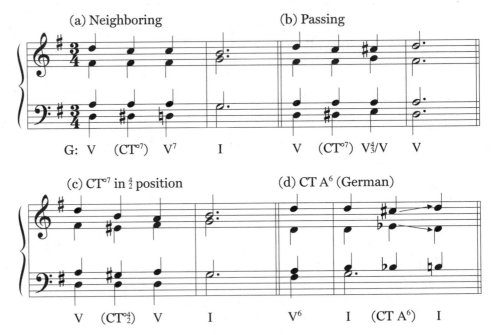

(a) Neighboring

G: V   (CT°7)   V⁷   I

(b) Passing

V   (CT°7)   V$\frac{4}{3}$/V   V

(c) CT°7 in $\frac{4}{2}$ position

V   (CT°$\frac{4}{2}$)   V   I

(d) CT A⁶ (German)

V⁶   I   (CT A⁶)   I

KEY CONCEPT

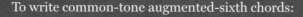

To write common-tone augmented-sixth chords:

1. Write the tonic chord of resolution, with a doubled fifth.
2. Before this chord, write the pitches of the augmented-sixth interval and its half-step resolutions, $\sharp\hat{4}$ and $\flat\hat{6}$ resolving outward to $\hat{5}$.
3. Fill in the remaining pitches of the A^6 chord. The common tone ($\hat{1}$) is usually maintained in the bass. The missing element is $(\flat)\hat{3}$ for a German A^6 (the most frequently used CT A^6).

Some Additional Chromatic Embellishments

Many of the other types of passing and neighboring voice-leading chords we have examined in previous chapters may be elaborated chromatically. For example, you can embellish neighboring $\substack{6\\4}$ chords by filling in whole-step voice-leading with chromatic half steps. You can also create passing motion by using chromatic rather than diatonic passing tones in some or all of the parts. Although these chromaticized voice-leading chords may sound more exotic, they have the same function as the diatonic voice-leading paradigms they replace: to decorate and prolong chords of the basic phrase.

Listen to, or play through, the introductions to Sousa's "The Washington Post March" and Joplin's "Pine Apple Rag," given in Examples 29.9 and 29.10. Both introductions pick up a chromatic flavor—the implication of chromatic harmonies without the complexity—by doubling a chromatic line in octaves. A chromatic melodic line may be doubled in parallel triads or even seventh chords to make a thicker texture; as such chord successions are nonfunctional, they may be considered doublings. Chromatic melodic and harmonic embellishments are a typical feature of rags and marches—as shown in Examples 29.11 and 29.12, from the same two pieces—sometimes creating functional chromatic harmonies, such as secondary dominants, but sometimes simply providing decoration and conforming to late nineteenth-century style.

EXAMPLE 29.9: Sousa, "The Washington Post March," mm. 1–7

EXAMPLE 29.10: Joplin, "Pine Apple Rag," mm. 1–4   2.28 🎧

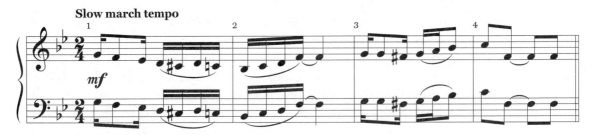

EXAMPLE 29.11: Sousa, "The Washington Post March," mm. 8–17

EXAMPLE 29.12: Joplin, "Pine Apple Rag," mm. 5–12 2.29

Another typical alteration of a diatonic harmony is the chromatic inflection of a fifth up a half step to create an augmented triad. This occurs most frequently in the tonic harmony (sometimes as a variant of $^{5-6}$ motion, to $^{5-\sharp5-6}$), in the dominant or dominant seventh harmony, and in secondary dominants. We may analyze these chords simply by identifying the embellishing tone that creates the augmented triad; alternatively, we may analyze them with Roman numerals and figures, as I^{+5}, V^{+5} or V$^{+\frac{6}{3}}$. Because of the association of $^{+5}$ with the dominant harmony, this augmented triad can create a secondary-dominant effect in the progression I–IV: when the tonic harmony has a raised fifth, the effect is like V^{+5}/IV to IV, as Example 29.13 (from "Smoke Gets in Your Eyes") shows. The V^{+5}/IV to IV appears in measures 15–16, notated with the popular-music symbols E♭, E♭+, and A♭.

EXAMPLE 29.13: Kern and Harbach, "Smoke Gets in Your Eyes," mm. 13–16a

○ ○

Chromatic Modulation

In Chapter 22, we learned how use pivot chords to modulate to a closely related key—a key whose tonic chord is diatonic in the original key. In the Romantic era, composers became increasingly interested in modulating to keys that are more distantly related. For example, instead of modulating to V, vi, IV, or ii from C Major, they might modulate to ♭VI, VI, ♭III, or III (to A♭ Major, A Major, E♭ Major, or E Major—chromatic mediant- and submediant-related keys), to the Neapolitan ♭II (D♭ Major), or even to such distant keys as ♯i, ♯IV, or ♭VII (C♯ minor, F♯ Major, or B♭ Major). While diatonic pivot-chord modulations may also be used when moving between keys that are not closely related, fewer pivot choices are available.

We also learned about direct modulations, sudden changes of key effected by means of a secondary dominant or simply by starting a phrase in a new key. Both of these modulation types may be used to move between keys that are not closely related, but the change may sound quite abrupt if it occurs suddenly within a phrase.

KEY CONCEPT

There are several techniques for writing a seamless modulation between two distantly related keys: modulation by

- sequence,
- common tone,
- chromatic inflection,
- mixture, or
- enharmonic reinterpretation.

Each is discussed below.

By Falling-Fifth Sequence

2.48

2.50

Listen now to the theme from the third movement of Mozart's Piano Sonata in D Major; measures 8b–10 are shown in Example 29.14. Observe in measure 9 the brief falling-fifth sequence with secondary dominants (B⁷–E–A⁷–D). This progression, arising from A Major at the end of the previous section, could be labeled in A as V⁷/V–V–V⁷/IV–IV; or the last three chords could be interpreted in D Major as V/V–V⁷–I. This chromatic falling-fifth sequence is ambiguous without further consideration of its context: it can serve equally well to connect the two keys or to stay in either. (Measure 10 does not clarify the situation—it is also sequential, but the underlying chord progression is less clear.) Sequences like that in measure 9 may thus function like pivot chords, in that they are at home in two or more keys. The multiple possibilities mask the point of modulation until after arrival in the new key.

EXAMPLE 29.14: Mozart, Piano Sonata in D Major, K. 284, third movement, mm. 8b–10

While any type of sequence may be used to modulate—you simply "get off" the sequence when you've arrived at a new tonic, and establish this tonic with a cadence—falling-fifth sequences containing secondary dominants work particularly well. A dominant seventh chord at any point in a falling-fifth sequence may resolve to a triad, which can then be established as a new key by a cadence, a continuation in the new key, or both.

In the Mozart example, each pattern of the sequence lasted only one beat. We also find this type of sequence with a much longer pattern. Listen to measures 112–125 from the development section of the first movement of Beethoven's *Waldstein* Sonata. Example 29.15 shows the initial pattern for this falling-fifth sequence (the entire movement is in your anthology). The four-measure unit begins with an arpeggiated C-Major triad and ends (in m. 115) with a C dominant seventh chord (with an added flatted ninth, D♭). What other chords appear as part of the prolongation of the C-Major chord? *(Try it #5)*

1.56 🎧

EXAMPLE 29.15: Beethoven, Piano Sonata in C Major, Op. 53 (*Waldstein*), first movement, mm. 112–116

The V$^{7\flat9}$ of measure 115 resolves down by fifth as expected, to an F-Major triad in measure 116, then the entire four-measure pattern is repeated in measures 116–119, transposed to F Major (with a very slight alteration in the arpeggiation in m. 118). The third statement of the sequential pattern—again transposed down a fifth, this time to B♭—begins in measure 120 and ends in measures 124–125 with the resolution of the B♭ dominant seventh/flatted ninth chord to E♭ minor, where the falling-fifth sequence ends.

The distance traveled by this sequence is thus from C Major to E♭ minor, a chromatic mediant not closely related to C Major. Since these measures are drawn from the middle of a development section, the goal of this lengthy modulatory passage is not further developed as a new key; E♭ minor is tonicized for only two measures (124–125) before moving on.

Other Chromatic Sequences   Listen to the opening of Beethoven's *Waldstein* Sonata to hear how the sequential transposition of a phrase or longer pattern can bring about a juxtaposition of passages in distantly related keys that does not sound jarring. For example, the phrase in the opening four measures (shown in Example 29.16) is transposed down a whole step, creating a "distantly related" phrase in B♭ Major. This type of modulation by sequential transposition is like a direct modulation, yet the repetition of the pattern makes the effect seem less abrupt. Such modulations often function as tonicizations when considered in the larger musical context. In this case, the B♭ might be heard on a larger scale as a passing tonicization on the way to the dominant G.

EXAMPLE 29.16: Beethoven, *Waldstein* Sonata, first movement, mm. 1–8

3.36 🎧

Many passages in Romantic-era music make use of sequences to introduce striking chromaticism. Listen again to measures 12–19a of Schumann's "Ich grolle nicht," shown in Example 29.17. In this passage, measures 12b–14a are repeated in sequence, transposed up a whole step to make measures 14b–16a. The chord progression in this sequence pattern is quite simple (v–i–v–i in A minor), yet the effect is dramatic with the shift from A minor to B minor in a song whose primary key is C Major. How is the transition made from C Major at the beginning of the passage (m. 12)? How does this sequence then connect back to C Major? *(Try it #6)*

EXAMPLE 29.17: Schumann, "Ich grolle nicht," from *Dichterliebe,* mm. 12–19a

Translation: Although you shine in diamond splendor, no beam falls into the night of your heart. I have known that for a long time.

By Common Tone

As modulations to increasingly distant keys became common in the Romantic era, composers devised a wide range of methods to facilitate these modulations. They continued to use the pivot- (or common-) chord modulation where the two keys were closely related, but variants were also developed for two keys that did not share an entire triad but did contain triads or seventh chords with one, two, or three pitches in common. The common tones in such variants are held, and the other pitches of the modulating chord are shifted up or down, usually by half step. This type of modulation is called a **common-tone**, or **pivot-tone**, **modulation** if only a single pitch is held in common between the two keys, and **common-dyad**, or **pivot-dyad**, **modulation** if two pitches are common to both keys.

1.43 🎧   A single shared pitch is enough to make a smooth modulation, to either a closely related or a more distant key. Listen to the short passage from the second movement of Beethoven's *Pathétique* Sonata shown in Example 29.18. Here, the C4 from the cadence in A♭ Major in measure 16 becomes an anacrusis for the melody in measure 17, accompanied by a repeated C in the left hand. This isolation of a single pitch smooths the transition to F minor (vi in A♭), tonicized in measures 18–19.

EXAMPLE 29.18: Beethoven, Piano Sonata in C minor, Op. 13 (*Pathétique*), second movement, mm. 16–19

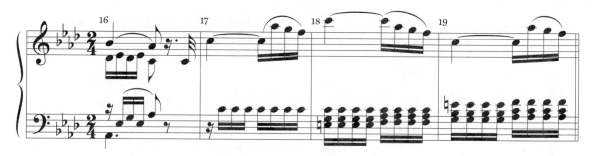

While common-tone modulations may appear between closely related keys, they are particularly helpful in modulations involving distantly related keys. For an example, look at the excerpt from "Smoke Gets in Your Eyes" shown in Example 29.19. The first verse of the song is in E♭ Major, where it cadences in measures 19–20. What is the key of the following phrase? The new key is B Major (the excerpt ends with a half cadence in m. 24); as spelled, this new key is a "sharped V." However, this is an enharmonic spelling of a more traditional chromatic submediant-related key to E♭ Major: ♭VI, or C♭ Major. The connection is made by the melody pitch E♭4 of measures 19–20, which seamlessly becomes D♯4 in the following measure. Kern makes this move to a distant key sound not-so-distant by its chromatic submediant relation, by its pivot tone, and by the fact that pitch-class B (the new tonic) was introduced as a prominent embellishing tone in measures 15–16.

EXAMPLE 29.19: Kern and Harbach, "Smoke Gets in Your Eyes," mm. 16b–24

By Chromatic Inflection

1.52 Listen again to measures 18–30 of Beethoven's *Waldstein* Sonata, following the score in your anthology. As you may recall from Chapter 28, this passage includes part of the transition from the first key area, C Major, to the second key area, E Major. We will focus on measures 20–23, shown in Example 29.20. In these measures, the harmonic reference point moves from C Major to establish V in E Major—quite a distant tonal area from C Major.

The A-minor first-inversion chord in measures 20–21 can be analyzed as a vi⁶ chord in C Major, although in its immediate context—the sequential repetition of measures 14–17 up a whole step in 18–21—it could also be considered v⁶ in D minor. How do the chords in measures 21 and 22 move smoothly to the new key area? The chord in measure 22 is a C-E-A♯ chord—an Italian augmented sixth, which resolves normally to the B-D♯-F♯ chord in measure 23. The A-minor triad and the augmented-sixth chord share two pitch classes in common, C and E, which connect the two harmonies while the A moves to A♯.

Because the modulation is activated by the shift of one pitch by a half step, this type is sometimes called **modulation by chromatic inflection**. The chromatic motion does not sound abrupt; rather, it seems an intensification of the drama already unfolding. The blurring of the key by the sequence in measures 14–21 helps make this striking modulation work.

EXAMPLE 29.20: Beethoven, *Waldstein* Sonata, mm. 20–23

Through Mixture

Sometimes it is easier to modulate to a distantly related key by shifting to the parallel major or minor key through mode mixture. Look back at Example 29.20. In retrospect, we can understand the A-minor chord in measures 20–21 as a pivot, if we consider the palette of mixture chords available in the new key: the vi⁶ chord in C Major could be heard as iv⁶, a mixture chord in E Major that leads to the augmented sixth discussed above.

KEY CONCEPT

When a mixture chord acts as a pivot between two distantly related keys, one of the two keys will be closely related to the key of the pivot chord.

In the Beethoven example, although the original key, C Major, is distantly related to E Major, the ultimate goal of the modulation, it is closely related to E minor, from which the minor iv chord comes. Modulations that include such a chromatic pivot chord—typically a mixture chord such as i, ♭III, Neapolitan, or ♭VI, or possibly a secondary dominant or leading-tone chord—are sometimes called **altered common-chord,** or **altered pivot-chord, modulations**.

In the second movement of the *Pathétique* Sonata, Beethoven moves to the same enharmonically respelled ♭VI as in the Kern song, but he gets there by a different route. This route uses mixture, but not as a pivot. Look at measures 37–44, shown in Example 29.21. At this point, the previous section has just ended in A♭ Major, the key of the movement, with a firm PAC. This section begins in A♭ minor, a direct shift through mixture to the parallel minor. A two-measure motive in A♭ minor appears in measures 37–38 and 39–40. Then, on its third repetition, something unusual happens—look at all the sharps in measure 42! The chord on the downbeat of measure 42 is a B-D♯-F♯-A chord, a V⁴₂ in E Major, which resolves to a first-inversion E-Major chord. Glancing ahead to measures 43–44, we can see that the phrase will cadence in E Major. How did the music get from A♭ minor to E Major? *(Try it #7)* The move first to the parallel minor, through mixture, made the common-dyad (enharmonically respelled: A♭-C♭-E♭ and B-D♯-F♯-A) modulation possible, thereby making the distance between A♭ Major and its chromatic submediant, E Major (enharmonically F♭ Major), much easier to negotiate.

EXAMPLE 29.21: Beethoven, *Pathétique* Sonata, second movement, mm. 37–44

Enharmonic Modulation with Augmented-Sixth Chords

Throughout our studies of chromatic harmony, we have been careful to spell chromatic chords to represent their function and resolution. The spelling a composer chooses is also a cue to the performer as to how to expect the chord to resolve. One chord that has a distinct enharmonic equivalent is the German augmented-sixth chord, which sounds exactly like a dominant seventh chord when played without its chord of resolution. The ambiguity between the chord functions is especially valuable in modulations, because the "major-minor seventh" sonority can be resolved two or more ways depending on how it is spelled. It may be approached with one spelling, yet resolve as though spelled another way, and that "deceptive" resolution will suddenly introduce a new key area. The effect is like an aural sleight of hand—it plays tricks on our ears!

Look back at Example 29.20, from the *Waldstein* Sonata. Another way to hear the modulation from C Major to E Major in this passage is to think of the harmony in measure 22 through the lens of the old key (C Major). If you weren't looking at the spelling of the chord but merely listening to the passage, you might expect the chord to resolve as V^7/IV in C, as though spelled C-E-(G)-B♭. But the spelling, C-E-A♯, and the resolution move toward the new tonal area of E Major.

Look now at the passage given in Example 29.22a, an excerpt from the development section of the first movement of Mozart's String Quartet in D minor, K. 421. The key in measure 42 is E♭ Major, the Neapolitan of D minor. The passage is heavily colored by mixture chords, including the minor tonic and minor subdominant (see the reduction and analysis in Example 29.22b). In measure 45, we see and hear a V^7/V in E♭ Major, which we expect to resolve to a B♭ dominant harmony. Yet it resolves instead to a cadential $^6_4$ in the key of A minor.

Although the resolution sounds a bit surprising, it makes sense in retrospect. Example 29.22c shows the chords from measures 44b and 45 with the resolution we expect, then with the measure 45 chord respelled to indicate its augmented-sixth function—with a D♯ instead of an E♭. The resolution to a cadential $^6_4$ instead of directly to V (E Major, V of A minor) is customary with any German A^6 chord. The modulation to A minor is then confirmed when the passage continues in that key through measure 53.

EXAMPLE 29.22: Mozart, String Quartet in D minor, K. 421, first movement

(a) Mm. 42–46

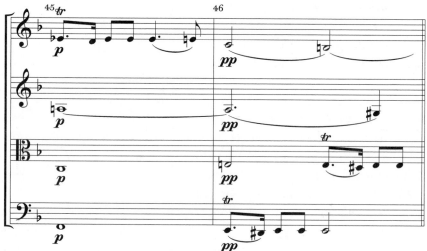

(b) Reduction of mm. 42–46

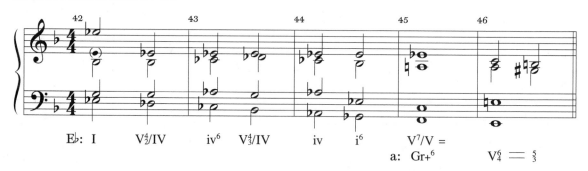

(c) Expected and respelled resolutions of mm. 44b–45

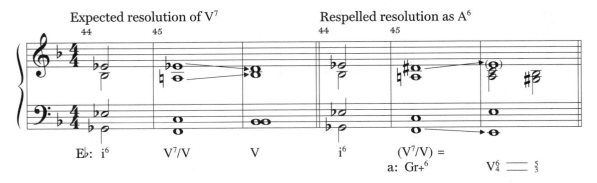

This type of modulation is called an **enharmonic modulation**. Because the harmonies resolve in ways that require us to reinterpret them (whether the resolutions are respelled or not), we sometimes call such progressions **modulation through enharmonic reinterpretation**.

The Mozart modulation connects two distant keys a tritone apart—E♭ Major and A minor—and involves the enharmonic reinterpretation of a secondary dominant as an augmented-sixth chord. More common is the enharmonic respelling of the diatonic dominant seventh.

KEY CONCEPT

Enharmonic reinterpretation with German augmented-sixth chords and dominant sevenths is an effective way to modulate to a new key a half step higher or lower than the original.

- If an augmented sixth is reinterpreted as a dominant seventh, the resulting modulation is a half step up (Example 29.23a).
- If a dominant seventh is reinterpreted as an augmented sixth, the resulting modulation is a half step down (Example 29.23b).

EXAMPLE 29.23:

(a) Enharmonic modulation up by half step

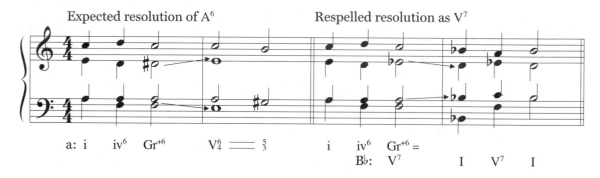

(b) Enharmonic modulation down by half step

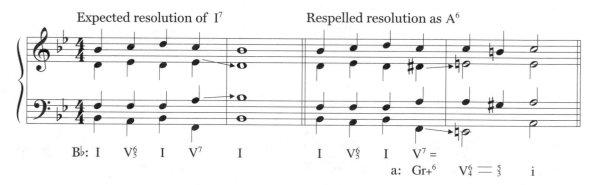

When you write modulations that require enharmonic reinterpretation, pay careful attention to accidentals in the new key, since the half-step tonal relation requires many chromatic alterations to establish the new tonic. Play these examples to hear how the harmonic "deception" sets up the new tonic.

Enharmonic Modulation with Diminished Seventh Chords

The fully diminished seventh chord is an even more flexible means of enharmonic modulation. It may potentially resolve in four different ways depending on how it is spelled, since the spelling determines both the root and resolution of the chord. In each case, the diminished seventh chord may resolve to either a major or minor "temporary tonic," as shown in Example 29.24. Look at the B diminished seventh, for example. If spelled with B as the root (Example 29.24a, first line), it can resolve either to C Major or C minor; if spelled with D as the root (part b), it resolves either to E♭ Major or E♭ minor, and so on. In addition, in music of the Romantic era, you may see a voice-leading shift from one fully diminished seventh chord up or down a half step to a second fully diminished seventh chord before the chord resolves to a new key.

EXAMPLE 29.24: Fully diminished seventh chords and their possible resolutions

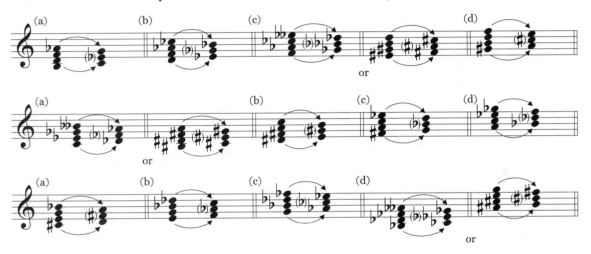

You may modulate to any of the major or minor keys by using the diminished seventh chord as a secondary leading-tone chord. For an example of such an enharmonic modulation, look at Example 29.25a, a passage from the beginning of the development section of the first movement of Beethoven's *Pathétique* Sonata, with a reduction underneath (b). In measure 134, an F♯-A-C-E♭ diminished seventh chord resolves to G-B♭-D after a voice exchange involving C and E♭ in the highest and lowest parts, filled in with passing-tone Ds. The motive is repeated in measure 135, but the F♯-A-C-E♭ is respelled D♯-F♯-A-C on the third beat, and resolves instead to a cadential ⁶₄ in the key of E minor—the chromatic submediant of G minor, the key of measures 133–134. This resolution sets up a development of the first theme in E minor (the chromatic mediant of C minor, the main key of the movement). Play through Example 29.25b several times to hear the effect of the different resolutions of the diminished seventh chord.

EXAMPLE 29.25: Beethoven, *Pathétique* Sonata, first movement

(a) Mm. 133–136

(b) Reduction of mm. 134–136a

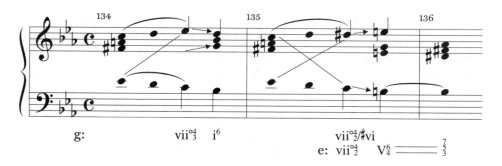

KEY CONCEPT

An enharmonic pivot chord can be spelled as it functions in the first key or as it functions in the second key. It may also appear twice, spelled once each way (Example 29.25).

1.45 🎧

Sometimes modulations involve a combination of techniques we have considered in this chapter. Listen to the modulation in measures 49–50 of the second movement of the *Pathétique* Sonata. The passage shown in Example 29.26 is the transition back from E Major (enharmonically F♭ Major) to A♭ Major for the return of the **A** section of the rondo in measure 51. The chord in measure 47, an E-Major triad, is followed by a fully diminished seventh chord (D-F-A♭-C♭) in measures 48–49. What is the chord on the downbeat of measure 50? How are we to interpret these seventh chords? What type of voice-leading connects them? *(Try it #8)*

EXAMPLE 29.26: Beethoven, *Pathétique* Sonata, second movement, mm. 47–51

As you have probably observed, there are many ways to modulate, especially between distant keys, as was customary in the Romantic era. When you come across a modulation in music you are analyzing or performing, listen carefully to the passage, then examine the evidence with the techniques you have learned. With patience, you should be able to solve the puzzle.

Linear Chromaticism

Chromaticism and Voice-Leading Chords

In previous chapters, we considered a number of chords whose primary role is to connect harmonies that have a strong function within the basic phrase. We used both vertical analysis (Roman numerals and figures) and contextual analysis (their function in the overall progression) to understand the musical contexts for these sonorities, which we have called voice-leading chords, or linear chords. In the Romantic era, some composers took the voice-leading idea even further, writing pieces where long spans of music consist of linear chords held together by their smooth, chromatic voice-leading without much, if any, sense of progression or root motion. For a famous example, play through Chopin's Prelude in E minor, Op. 28, No. 4. The opening phrase is shown in Example 29.27. Start your analysis by labeling the harmonies at the beginning and end with Roman numerals and figures. *(Try it #9)*

EXAMPLE 29.27: Chopin, Prelude in E minor, Op. 28, No. 4, mm. 1–12

In this example, the beginning and end of the phrase are the only places where we hear clearly functional harmonic progressions. What about the harmonies in the middle? Write out the chords in measures 1–12 beneath the example, using simple triads and sevenths in stacked thirds, then determine their quality and inversion. Include pitches from the right-hand melody only where it seems to fit in the chord (the others will be considered embellishing tones). What chord qualities can you identify? Do any resolve correctly? (*Try it #10*)

While providing a vertical analysis (with Roman numerals) is good practice for identifying chord types, such an analysis does not explain much about this passage other than the general qualities of the sounds. Here, we need to concentrate instead on the linear motion. The melody in the right hand prolongs a B4 with a neighboring C5 in measures 1–4, then it descends via a passing-tone B♭4 to prolong A4 in measures 5–8 with a neighboring B4. A skip from A4 in measure 8 to F♯4 in measure 10 is embellished in measures 8–9 and reiterated in 10–11. The basic strategy for both the melody and accompanying harmonies seems to be a gradual descent from the i⁶ chord at the beginning to the V⁷ in measure 12. The descent in the melody is primarily diatonic; the descent in the harmonies is primarily chromatic, with voices taking turns moving chromatically downward.

This book has tried to draw a balance between discussing "strength of progression" (that is, passages with strong root-movement-based chord progressions) and "strength of line" (passages with less strong root movement, but very smooth linear connections between chords). The chord patterns in the Chopin prelude do not make much sense from a root-progression standpoint, yet the chords connect easily because of extremely smooth voice-leading—in particular, voice-leading based on chromatic half-step motion. The strength of line in the harmonies makes this phrase work musically.

Intentional Harmonic Ambiguity

Pieces like the Chopin prelude demonstrate intentional harmonic ambiguity. Although the prelude is written for piano and is not associated with a specific programmatic idea, harmonic ambiguity is often called on in songs to express multiple meanings of the text, and it is an important element in Romantic-era opera. Perhaps the most famous intentionally ambiguous passage in Romantic-era music is the opening of the Prelude to Richard Wagner's great love story, the opera *Tristan und Isolde*, shown in a piano reduction in Example 29.28. In what key does this passage begin?

WF3

EXAMPLE 29.28: Wagner, Prelude to *Tristan und Isolde*, mm. 1–17a

Here are some basics to help you decide. Measures 1–3 and 4–7 form a sequence, with the entire texture transposed up a minor third (except for the anacrusis—perhaps to make the first two pitches in mm. 4–5 match the B-G♯ in m. 3). Since the work begins with A3 and measure 3 ends with an E dominant seventh chord, the opening could imply A minor, with a $\hat{6}$–$\hat{5}$–$\sharp\hat{4}$ encircling $\hat{5}$ (but continuing chromatically downward to introduce $\hat{4}$ of the V^7). As sequences often function as "traveling music," this opening is quite ambiguous—by measure 7, no key has yet been established as a point of departure!

The third presentation of the sequence pattern, in measures 8–11, is not an exact transposition. It begins with the anacrusis transposed up a minor third from the previous pattern, again matching pitch classes in the last chord of measure 7. But the next portion is expanded, with notes added as it strives forward and upward. Measures 12–15 simply reiterate 10–11 in a truncated form. In measures 16–17, the first standard type of cadence, an E dominant seventh resolves deceptively to an F-Major triad. Does that mean the piece is in A minor? Clearly the ambiguity of harmony and key is a musical depiction of unfulfilled desire or longing, and it prepares the listener beautifully for the drama between two lovers that is to follow.

○ ○

Analyzing and Performing Chromatic Passages

When you find chromaticism in pieces you are analyzing or performing, first try to determine what type it represents. Can the chromatic pitches be attributed to embellishing tones, mixture, sequential transpositions, applied chords? Getting your bearings in this way can be very helpful. If you identify chromatic embellishments (passing tones and neighbor tones), remember that this type of chromaticism is basically a surface event—a flourish or decoration within a diatonic context. The chromatic "additions" do not usually imply harmonic function or need resolution beyond the completion of the embellishment pattern. These chromatic pitches may often be circled and labeled N or P. Even if they make "chords," sonorities may not need a Roman numeral if their origin in voice-leading is clear.

In performance, however, chromatic embellishments need to be considered carefully; they often give a line a sense of direction or help to establish the music's character. It is vitally important to this sense of direction and character that chromatic alterations be performed in tune! Simple chromatic embellishments are a typical element of Baroque and Classical compositions; more elaborate embellishments, such as the chromatic voice exchanges and sequences of this chapter, are a hallmark of the Romantic repertoire.

You might also identify chromatic chords that serve within the basic phrase as substitutes for diatonic chords with a similar function. These include secondary dominant and leading-tone chords, mixture chords, and the Neapolitan and augmented-sixth chords. Chromatic falling-fifth sequences fall within this category as well. Substituting a chromatic chord for a diatonic often intensifies the sense of forward motion in a progression; for this reason, resolutions of chromatic tendency tones need to be considered carefully in performance, as do changes of tone color that might highlight the composer's use of mixture.

Passages that are in their very essence chromatic and linear, where chords resolve linearly or deceptively rather than according to their function, can present quite a challenge to the analyst and performer. You may come across passages whose beginning and end are firmly functional, or passages where voice-leading chords permeate the harmonic language throughout. When you study a chromatic passage, try to determine the harmonic "goalposts," and make sure that your performance makes these goalposts clear. Carefully consider each embellishment to establish which ones affect the underlying harmonic progression and which are ornamental. Identify the quality of each sonority, and ask yourself whether dominant-function seventh chords or A6 chords resolve as expected. Do they resolve deceptively, tonicize scale degrees, or initiate new keys? Is there a sequence at work? These questions will help you create a hierarchy of musical function in your mind. Remember that not all sonorities carry equal weight, and only after you have determined the musical function of each can you convey your vision effectively to an audience.

Finally, when analyzing pieces that include chromatic voice-leading, don't forget to use your ears. In pieces like the Chopin prelude, you will find progressions that sound (and are) functional—label those first, then listen attentively to the rest. Careful analysis of some chromatic musical surfaces may reveal a relatively simple underlying diatonic progression, which you can convey through performance; other passages may rely almost entirely on harmonic ambiguity. It is your job as musical interpreter to determine which passages are which.

TERMS YOU SHOULD KNOW

altered common chord
altered pivot chord
chromatic inflection
chromaticized sequence
chromaticized voice exchange
common-dyad modulation
common-tone augmented sixth
common-tone diminished seventh

common-tone modulation
embellishing diminished seventh
enharmonic modulation
enharmonic reinterpretation
harmonic ambiguity
pivot-dyad modulation
pivot-tone modulation

QUESTIONS FOR REVIEW

1. What are some ways that diatonic frameworks may be embellished chromatically?
2. How may a chromatic falling-fifth sequence be used to modulate?
3. How may mixture make modulation to a distant key smoother?
4. How may the principle of diatonic pivot-chord modulations be expanded for use in modulation to more distantly related keys?
5. Which qualities of chords are suitable for enharmonic reinterpretation?
6. How many ways is it possible to modulate from C Major to A♭ Major? List as many possibilities as you can.
7. In music for your own instrument, find examples of (a) a chromaticized voice exchange, (b) a chromaticized sequence, (c) a common-tone or -dyad modulation, (d) a modulation with an altered pivot chord, (e) enharmonic reinterpretation. (Hint: To save time, think first about the time period when each technique was common.)
8. How does the function of chromaticism affect the way it should be interpreted in performance?

PART VI

Into the Twentieth Century

Modes, Scales, and Sets

Overview

In this chapter, we consider scales and pitch-class collections other than major and minor. We will also learn the terminology musicians have developed to discuss the motives, chords, and compositional techniques we hear in this music.

Repertoire

Béla Bartók, "Five-Tone Scale," from *Mikrokosmos* (No. 78)

Bartók, "Song of the Harvest," for two violins (CD 1, track 37)

Claude Debussy, "Voiles," from *Preludes*, Book I

Igor Stravinsky, "Lento," from *For the Five Fingers* (CD 3, track 47)

Anton Webern, String Quartet, Op. 5, third movement (CD 3, track 54)

Listening to Twentieth-Century Compositions

In this chapter, we will listen to works by four prominent composers of the early twentieth century: Béla Bartók, Claude Debussy, Igor Stravinsky, and Anton Webern. Although their works are very different, these composers employ some of the same compositional techniques. None of them follow the conventions of functional tonality we have studied thus far. Here and in the following chapters, we will learn new ways composers might organize musical ideas in the absence of functional tonality.

1.37

3.54

We begin with two works for strings: Bartók's "Song of the Harvest" and the third movement of Webern's String Quartet, Op. 5. Both are quite short. Try listening first without the scores, then listen again following your anthology scores. As you listen, open your mind to these works, and compare them with others we have studied. For each piece, ask yourself the following questions, and be ready to discuss your responses in class:

- Can you hum a tonic at any point in the piece?
- What makes the piece work formally? (Can you identify phrases or formal sections, changes in motive, texture, or mood?)
- Can you hear familiar compositional techniques (transposition, imitation, inversion)?
- What musical features contribute to your emotional reaction to the piece? Make notes on your anthology score of any of these aspects you noticed. Some of these questions we will revisit later in the chapter.

When you analyze music of the twentieth or twenty-first century, don't make the mistake of working solely from the score, without fully involving your ears. Always take time to listen, preferably several times through, then use your musical intuitions to make basic observations about form, phrase, imitation, variation, contrast, and other elements. Such observations will inform your more detailed analysis and give you a deeper appreciation for the music.

Pitch-Class Collections and Scales Revisited

Many stylistic features make these two pieces sound different from each other. Webern's composition features shorter motives and fuller instrumentation than Bartók's; it also covers a wider range and calls for numerous string effects—for example, *pizzicato* (plucking rather than bowing the strings) and *col legno* (playing with the wood, rather than the hair, of the bow). Bartók employs longer

WF1

melodic lines and easily perceived patterns of imitation between the two violin parts. He incorporates tempo and meter changes, as well as the transposed repetition of melodies, to distinguish between musical sections. The collections of pitch classes (or pcs) these composers choose also give the works their distinct sounds.

Remember that a pitch class represents all the pitches that sound exactly one or more octaves apart—for example, C4, C6, C3, B♯2, and D♭♭5 are all members of the same pitch class. When using the term, we invoke both enharmonic equivalence (grouping C and B♯ in the same pitch class) and octave equivalence (grouping C4 and C6 in the same pitch class).

KEY CONCEPT

The word "collection" refers to a group of pitch classes that serves as a source of musical materials for a work or a section of a work. We examine the pitch-class materials of a piece by "collecting" them and writing them in ascending order, without repetitions.

Listen to the two excerpts below. Beneath each example, write out a list of the pitch classes included in the excerpt. How do the collections differ? In each example, is there one pitch class that seems more important than the others?

3.55   **EXAMPLE 30.1:** Webern, String Quartet, Op. 5, third movement, mm. 6–7

EXAMPLE 30.2: Bartók, "Song of the Harvest," mm. 30–33 1.40 🎧

Were you able to hum a tonic while listening to the Webern movement? Probably not, since Webern features all twelve pcs in this composition—a complete chromatic collection—without strongly emphasizing any pc over the others. In fact, we can find all twelve pcs in just the two measures of Example 30.1. Music that

WF2

does not establish a tonic or tonal hierarchy is sometimes called **nontonal** music to distinguish it from music that does.

KEY CONCEPT

Recall that tonal music is characterized by

- melodies built from major and minor scales, whose scale-degree functions point toward the tonic (for example, scale-degree $\hat{7}$ resolves to $\hat{1}$);
- harmonies that relate to each other in functional progressions leading toward a tonic harmony;
- identifiable embellishing tones (dissonant suspensions, neighbors, passing tones) that resolve, or imply a resolution.

Music lacking one or more of these organizational conventions is nontonal music.

In nontonal music, the pervasive chromaticism, symmetry, and absence of consistent whole- and half-step scale patterns make it more difficult to identify aurally a "tonic" pitch class.

In contrast with pitches in the Webern movement, Bartók's E♭4 (the first and last pitch of Example 30.2) does seem to provide a strong starting and ending point for the excerpt. This E♭ serves a similar function to the tonic in a tonal piece, even though the Bartók work is not built on functional harmonies. The other pitches of the phrase seem to expand outward from the E♭4 and converge back to it to form a cadence. We will thus use the terms "phrase" and "cadence" even in nontonal contexts when they seem musically appropriate. When you apply these terms, be sure to indicate what musical features lead you to hear a nontonal passage as a complete musical thought, or phrase, with a close at the end.

KEY CONCEPT

If a pitch or pc appears pervasively in a work (or section of a work) and establishes a sense of hierarchy, we call this pitch or pc a **center**, and music that features it **centric** music. While traditional tonal music technically falls within the centric category, the term customarily refers to nontonal music.

When we can determine a center and there is a sense of hierarchy—in other words, when not all the pcs are treated equally—we can list the pitch-class collection as a scale, starting and ending with the center.

Even in fully chromatic nontonal works such as the Webern movement, some pitch classes may be more prominent than others in a portion of the piece because of repetition, registral placement, duration, or other means. All pitch classes do not have to be treated equally in nontonal music. Look, for example, at the complete score of the Webern movement in your anthology. Consider the pitch-class C♯, which begins and ends the movement in the cello, and functions as a repeated ostinato in the bass. This C♯ helps provide cohesiveness to the opening section of the movement and some measure of "closure" when it returns at the end; but it is emphasized only through repetition. It does not function as a pitch-class center here because there is no sense of hierarchy between the C♯ and the other pcs.

KEY CONCEPT

We call pitches or pcs that are emphasized through repetition or motivic use, but that do not establish a functional hierarchy, **focal pitches** or **pcs**. Focal pitches or pcs are not tonics because they do not imply a functional system of scale degrees in any key or mode. And they are not centers because they do not imply any hierarchy among the remaining pitches of the collection.

Analyzing Mode and Scale Types

Look back now at Example 30.2, the end of "Song of the Harvest," and the list of pitch classes you compiled previously. What scale is used in this excerpt? If we begin on E♭ (the cadential resting point) and list all the pitch classes, we get the following scale: E♭ F G♭ A♭ B♭ C♭ D♭ E♭. This familiar arrangement of whole and half steps is E♭ natural minor. But because the piece does not speak the familiar melodic and harmonic functional language of tonal music, the modal name is more fitting for this pitch-class collection: E♭ Aeolian.

KEY CONCEPT

To determine the scale or mode of a musical passage, first list the pitch classes in ascending order without repetitions. Listen carefully for the pitch or pc center, then rewrite the pitch classes in ascending order beginning with the center.

SUMMARY

1. When analyzing a piece of nontonal music, first identify the collection of pitch classes from which it is composed, by listing each pc in ascending order, without repetitions.
2. If the pitches or pcs relate hierarchically to a stable pitch or pitch-class center, then rewrite your list in ascending order beginning with that centric pc.
3. A nontonal piece may have no pitch or pc center: all pcs may be treated equally, or one or more may be emphasized as focal pitches or pcs (but without a sense of centric hierarchy).

Sets and Subsets

As we continue our study of nontonal compositions, we will need additional terminology for identifying meaningful musical relationships.

KEY CONCEPT

The term **set** refers to a group of pitches (pset) or pitch classes (pcset). While the terms "set" and "collection" may be used interchangeably, collections are generally considered to be larger sets of five elements or more.

The pitches or pcs in a set are called its **elements**. We list elements of a set only once. When we discuss only selected elements, we call this subgroup a **subset** and the larger set from which it comes a **superset**.

The Bartók excerpt in Example 30.2 includes only seven pitches of the chromatic scale; they make up a subset of the chromatic collection. This seven-element set is divided between the two violin parts so that each part consists of a four-element subset (a tetrachord) of the larger seven-element collection.

KEY CONCEPT

We often refer to a group of pitches or pcs by a single word that specifies its number of elements, or **cardinality**. Among the terms you should know:

two elements—interval, or dyad	six elements—hexachord
three elements—trichord	seven elements—heptachord, or heptad
four elements—tetrachord	eight elements—octachord, or octad
five elements—pentachord	nine elements—nonachord, or nonad

A trichord has a cardinality of 3, a hexachord has a cardinality of 6, and so on.

Composing with Diatonic Modes

In the twentieth and twenty-first centuries, composers have discovered new possibilities for the diatonic modes. For one thing, with modern equal temperament, composers and jazz musicians are able to transpose modal materials more freely than their predecessors, so that any mode can begin on any pitch class; the Aeolian mode, for instance, need not begin and end on A. The E♭ Aeolian of Example 30.2 is a good example, and its unconventional key signature is also characteristic of Bartók's musical notation. Contemporary composers are more likely to draw on all possible modal rotations of the diatonic scale, including the Locrian mode (the B-to-B rotation of the C-Major scale), which was avoided in Renaissance works because of its prominent tritone. Some composers create mixed modes by combining a distinctive portion of one diatonic mode with another. For example, the Lydian-Mixolydian mode (C D E F♯ G A B♭ C) is derived from the lower tetrachord of the

Lydian mode and the upper tetrachord of the Mixolydian. Jazz musicians also call this mode the "Lydian-dominant," or "overtone scale." The Lydian-Mixolydian mode is not a diatonic mode, however, since it is not a rotation of the major scale.

KEY CONCEPT

When you analyze modal passages, use your ear to decide whether the third scale degree is major or minor. Then refer to this chart to determine which mode you hear.

Modes with a major scale-degree $\hat{3}$:

- Ionian   —identical to major
- Mixolydian   —like major, but with a lowered $\hat{7}$
- Lydian   —like major, but with a raised $\hat{4}$
- Lydian-Mixolydian   —like major, but with a raised $\hat{4}$ and lowered $\hat{7}$

Modes with a minor scale-degree $\hat{3}$:

- Aeolian   —identical to natural minor
- Dorian   —like natural minor, but with a raised $\hat{6}$
- Phrygian   —like natural minor, but with a lowered $\hat{2}$
- Locrian   —like natural minor, but with a lowered $\hat{2}$ and lowered $\hat{5}$

Try it #1

Spell each of the following modes, starting with the given pc center.

MODE	PC CENTER	LETTER NAMES
Mixolydian	F	_____
Dorian	C♯	_____
Lydian	B♭	_____
Aeolian	F♯	_____
Phrygian	G	_____
Locrian	E	_____
Ionian	A♭	_____
Lydian-Mixolydian	A	_____

As in tonal repertoire, it is common in twentieth-century music for a mode, scale, or collection to be represented by only some of its members. Listen now to Stravinsky's short piano piece "Lento," from *For the Five Fingers*, while following the score in your anthology. What is the form? Which musical elements distinguish one section from another? (*Try it #2*)

Example 30.3a reproduces the opening measures. How do we determine the key or mode here? The key signature suggests D minor (or F Major), and the pc center is clearly D. But a list of the pitch classes in the opening measures produces no scale or mode that we know of: D E F F♯ G A. This collection corresponds to the combined lower pentachords of the D Ionian (D E F♯ G A) and Aeolian (D E F G A) modes—one mode in each hand. (Stravinsky's emphasis on pentachords is surely a reference to the *Five Fingers* of the title.)

EXAMPLE 30.3: Stravinsky, "Lento," from *For the Five Fingers*

(a) Mm. 1–4a

Different analysts may focus on different aspects of Stravinsky's compositional language. Some might examine the harmony created by the two simultaneous modes: the arpeggiated four-note chord (D-F-F♯-A) that spans these measures. Because this sonority sounds like a "triad" with both a major and a minor third above the root, it is sometimes called a **split-third chord**, or a **major-minor tetrachord**. Other analysts might focus on the linear aspects of the two contrapuntal melodies (in the right and left hand), and on the subsets in each. They would label this composition **bimodal**, or **polymodal**, with one musical stream (or layer, or stratum) based on one mode and another stream based on another. You may also see the terms "bitonal" and "polytonal" applied to this technique.

Indeed, one hallmark of Stravinsky's musical style is a **stratification** of musical materials. This piece shows linear, or horizontal, stratification, while others (such as *The Rite of Spring*) show vertical stratification—sudden short juxtapositions of register, rhythm, texture, timbre, and/or pc collection. Stravinsky's use of bimodality is even more prominent in the **B** section of this piece, shown in Example 30.3b, where the right hand expresses F Ionian while the left continues in D Aeolian.

(b) Mm. 9–13

SUMMARY

When you analyze modal compositions of the twentieth or twenty-first century, you may find that

- the entire composition expresses a single mode;
- the composer articulates new formal sections by changing the pc center and/or mode;
- the composer presents two modes (bimodality) or more than two modes (polymodality) simultaneously in different musical layers, or strata (stratification).

Pentatonic Scales

WF3

We turn now to a second short composition for piano—this one again by Bartók, "Five-Tone Scale" (from *Mikrokosmos*). Play through measures 1–8, given in Example 30.4a. In this excerpt, we consider E to be the pc center, since the passage ends on an octave doubling, E3 and E4, and since the melody begins with a characteristic skip up a fourth to E5. List the pcs beneath the example.

EXAMPLE 30.4: Bartók, "Five-Tone Scale," from *Mikrokosmos* (No. 78)

(a) Mm. 1–8

You should have found only five distinct pitch classes (as Bartók's title implies): E G A B D. This collection is a minor pentatonic scale, familiar to us as the *do-me-fa-sol-te* pentachord from Chapter 4. The major pentatonic scale, known to us as the *do-re-mi-sol-la* pentachord, is actually a rotation of the minor pentatonic: that is, E G A B D can be rotated to G A B D E. We can therefore think of both scales as representing the pentatonic collection. You will sometimes see pentatonic collections written as scales, with the first pitch class repeated at the end: E G A B D (E) (parentheses denote the pc repetition).

SUMMARY

> The pentatonic collection is a subset of the diatonic collection. For example, the major pentatonic scales C D E G A, F G A C D, and G A B D E are subsets of the major scale C D E F G A B. The minor pentatonic scale E G A B D is also a subset of C D E F G A B, and is the same pitch-class set as G A B D E.

One easy way to remember the interval pattern that makes up the pentatonic collection is to think of the black keys on the piano: C♯ D♯ F♯ G♯ A♯ (C♯). These pitch classes are also a subset of the C♯-Major scale, missing E♯ and B♯. The black-key pentatonic collection combined with the white-key diatonic collection make a chromatic collection.

KEY CONCEPT

> The white-key diatonic collection and the black-key pentatonic collection are considered **literal complements**, because they share no common elements and combine to make a complete chromatic collection. When literal complements appear together—for example, with each set in a different hand or layer—they make an **aggregate**, a collection with all twelve pitch classes.

The pentatonic collection is **symmetrical**, because its pitch classes can be ordered so that the intervals between adjacent scale steps—m3, M2, M2, m3 in our E G A B D collection—are the same going forward as backward. While we do not often think of it this way, the diatonic collection is also symmetrical in one of its rotations (Dorian): the intervals in D E F G A B C D (W H W W W H W) read the same way forward and backward. Some twentieth-century composers explore this symmetrical property in their works.

Because of the symmetry of the pentatonic scale, and its lack of the major scale's $\hat{4}$ and $\hat{7}$ tendency tones, you may find it difficult to decide which pitch class is functioning as center in a pentatonic passage. It often doesn't matter, since any of the pitch classes in the set can be made to sound stable by the musical context. Bartók's pentatonic collection, for example, might be realized in another composition as D E G A B (D), with D as its center, or in the major pentatonic ordering G A B D E (G), with G as its center.

Now look at Example 30.4b, the next section of Bartók's piece. Play through the excerpt, then list the pcs in this collection beneath the example. Here the composer introduces a new pitch class. Does this signal a change of scale type? The new pc appears in the left hand only, and a pitch-class list reveals another pentatonic collection: A B D E F♯. If we compare the first pentatonic set (E G A B D) with this one, we can see and hear that the two share a four-note subset, A B D E. (This set is sometimes called the "I Got Rhythm" tetrachord, after George Gershwin's famous song.) The change from G in the opening section to F♯ in the second creates an effective contrast, while maintaining the pentatonicism that characterizes the work. In the final section, Bartók returns to the opening collection to end the piece.

(b) Mm. 9–19

Other Types of Scales

Whole-Tone Scales

Whole-tone scales are made up of six distinct pitch classes that, when listed in scale order, are a whole step apart. Consider the excerpt shown in Example 30.5, from Debussy's prelude "Voiles." List the pitch classes in measures 33–40 as a scale, beginning with B♭, which is emphasized by its constant presence as a pedal tone.

EXAMPLE 30.5: Debussy, "Voiles," from *Preludes*, Book I, mm. 33–40

You should have found B♭ C D E F♯ A♭. Each element of the scale is a whole step from the next, but some whole steps are obscured by their spellings (for example, F♯ and A♭). Music theorists have devised an analytical tool to reveal such relationships more clearly: they translate the pitch classes to numbers, with enharmonic pcs receiving the same number. This technique is called **integer notation**. For uniformity, most theorists adopt C as the reference pitch class for integer notation: C = 0, C♯ or D♭ = 1, D = 2, D♯ or E♭ = 3, and so on. To avoid confusing 1 and 0 with the two-digit 10 and 11, we substitute the letters t for ten and e for eleven.

KEY CONCEPT

It is sometimes helpful to think of the pitch classes around a clock face, with 0 (C) at the top and (F♯/G♭) at the bottom.

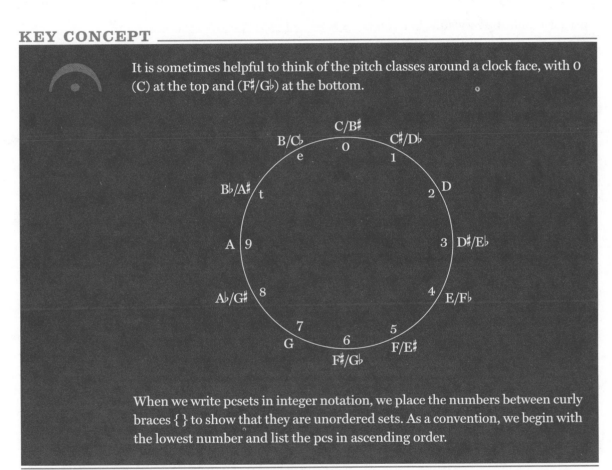

When we write pcsets in integer notation, we place the numbers between curly braces { } to show that they are unordered sets. As a convention, we begin with the lowest number and list the pcs in ascending order.

To help with pitch-class set analyses, try to memorize the number that goes with each pitch class, and practice until this notation becomes second nature. Remember that the integer notation system applies only to pitch classes; there is no distinction between octave-related pitches.

Try it #3

Write each of the sonorities below in integer notation. Maintain the ordering of the original; the lowest number need not be listed first. Then rewrite each answer as an unordered set in ascending order. The first one has been completed for you.

SONORITY	INTEGER NOTATION	UNORDERED SET
Dominant seventh chord on A	9 1 4 7	{1 4 7 9}
Half-diminished seventh chord on D		
Do-re-mi-fa-sol on E		
Augmented triad on F♯		
Fully diminished seventh chord on C♯		
Major-major seventh chord on A♭		

Using integer notation, we can identify the collection B♭ C D E F♯ A♭ from Example 30.5 as t 0 2 4 6 8, or {0 2 4 6 8 t}. Such notation makes the whole steps between the pcs readily apparent: from each pc integer to the next is two half steps. It thus gives us a handy way to identify whole-tone collections.

KEY CONCEPT

There are only two possible whole-tone collections, {0 2 4 6 8 t} and {1 3 5 7 9 e}; they are literal complements of each other. We sometimes refer to them as the "even" and "odd" whole-tone collections. Whole-tone collections may be written as a scale, starting with any of their pitch classes.

In major and minor scales, diatonic modes, and even pentatonic scales, there are at least two types of intervals between adjacent scale members: half steps, whole steps, or minor thirds. In a whole-tone scale, however, there are only whole steps (or their enharmonic equivalents) between adjacent scale members—it is not possible to discern any aural landmarks from the scale itself. This scale is completely symmetrical: from any starting pitch class, the intervals between scale members read the same forward and backward (M2 M2 M2 M2 M2).

If we examine Example 30.5 more closely, we can see that within the whole-tone texture of measures 33–40 there are several layers of activity. For example, we observed earlier that there is a pedal point: B♭1. There are also triads in measures 33–36 (voiced with the bass note doubled at the octave and double octave) that connect in parallel motion in an inner part. If we write out those triads as stacks of pitch-class integers, as in the diagram below, we can quickly determine their qualities—all are augmented triads {0, 4, 8} or {2, 6, t}, two subsets of the even whole-tone collection—and we can see how they connect. Play these chords (leaving out the octave doublings) to hear how the passage works.

m. 33			m. 34	m. 35				m. 36		
4	6	8	t	0	t	8	6	4	6	4
0	2	4	6	8	6	4	2	0	2	0
8	t	0	2	4	2	0	t	8	t	8

KEY CONCEPT

The type of chord connection where a line is doubled in several voices, resulting in parallel motion, is called **planing** and is associated particularly with Debussy's style.

We also hear an ostinato—D5 E5 D6 E5—in an upper voice, based on the dyad {2 4}, which repeats throughout this passage. Debussy's texture is clearly stratified in three layers (both rhythmically and registrally), with the bass pedal point, the sixteenth-note treble ostinato, and the inner-voice planed augmented triads moving in eighth, quarter, and sixteenth notes.

Octatonic (Diminished) Scales

1.37 🎧 Let's return now to Bartók's "Song of the Harvest," the beginning of which is shown in Example 30.6a. What is the scale or mode of this example? A pitch-class list yields the collection D♯ E♯ F♯ G♯ A B C D, with A D C B in the first violin and G♯ F♯ E♯ D♯ in the second. The pc content in integer notation, beginning with 0, is {0 2 3 5 6 8 9 e}, revealing a clear pattern of alternating whole and half steps. This type of symmetric scale in called an **octatonic scale**.

EXAMPLE 30.6: Bartók, "Song of the Harvest"

(a) Mm. 1–5

KEY CONCEPT

The octatonic collection consists of eight pitch classes that alternate whole step and half step. There are three possible octatonic collections: {0 1 3 4 6 7 9 t}, {0 2 3 5 6 8 9 e}, and {1 2 4 5 7 8 t e}. We refer to them by their initial two pcs: OCT 01, OCT 02, and OCT 12. These can be arranged into scales beginning with any pc and with either a half or whole step first.

Try it #4

Spell each of the following scales, starting with the given pitch class. Then rewrite each answer in integer notation. (The first one has been completed for you.)

SCALE TYPE	STARTING PC	LETTER NAMES	INTEGER NOTATION
Octatonic 01	F♯	F♯ G A B♭ C D♭ E♭ E♮ (F♯)	6 7 9 t 0 1 3 4 (6)
Whole tone	E♭	_____	_____
Minor pentatonic	D	_____	_____
Octatonic 02	E♭	_____	_____
Major pentatonic	B	_____	_____
Whole tone	B♭	_____	_____

The pitch-class center in the opening measures of the Bartók is more ambiguous than in the last phrase of the piece, which we considered in Example 30.2. Either the first violin's focal pitch, A4, or the second violin's repeated lowest pitch, D♯4, could be interpreted as the beginning pitch class of the scale or mode. Example 30.6b gives the second phrase of the work; write out its pitch-class collection, and compare the sets in sections **A** (mm. 1–5) and **B** (mm. 6–15).

1.38 🎧

(b) Mm. 6–15

The collection in the second section is {1 2 4 5 7 8 t e} (OCT 12). How does it compare with the first—{0 2 3 5 6 8 9 e} (OCT 02)? While both sets are octatonic, they are not the same set. Neither are they are complementary sets (like the two whole-tone collections), since they have four pcs in common: {2 5 8 e}. This common subset is a familiar chord type—the fully diminished seventh chord B-D-F-A♭. Each octatonic collection shares one diminished seventh subset with each of the other two collections. Further, any two different fully diminished seventh chords may be combined to make an octatonic collection (for example, {0 3 6 9} plus {1 4 7 t} equals {0 1 3 4 6 7 9 t}), and the literal complement of that collection will always be the third fully diminished seventh chord (in this case, {2 5 8 e}). In fact, octatonic scales are saturated with diminished seventh chords—you can build one on every degree of the scale. This is why jazz musicians, in particular, call the octatonic the **diminished scale**.

Try it #5

In the two examples below, spell each fully diminished seventh chord with integer notation. Then combine the diminished sevenths into an octatonic scale (also in integers).

1. Diminished seventh on C: _____

   Diminished seventh on G: _____

   Combine to form which octatonic scale? _____

2. Diminished seventh on D♭: _____

   Diminished seventh on E♭: _____

   Combine to form which octatonic scale? _____

   How are the two octatonic scales related? _____

Scale Analysis and Formal Design

1.37 Listen once again to "Song of the Harvest" while following the score in your anthology. Listen for changes indicating formal divisions; make a notation when you hear motivic, rhythmic, dynamic, tempo, and other changes that distinguish one section from the next. What features recur from section to section? In each section, identify one or more focal pcs, and write the pcs in scale order beneath the staff. When you are finished, complete the chart below. (*Try it #6*)

Section:	A	B			Coda
Measures:	1–5				
Scale type:	OCT 02				
Focal pcs:	A/D♯				

One thing that makes this short piece so interesting is that although its motivic and rhythmic structure divides into a clear **A B A′ B′** form, plus coda, the changes in scale type and focal pcs do not coincide with this form. The pitch-class structure instead is rounded, with OCT 02 in the beginning and ending sections (excluding the coda) and the contrasting OCT 12 in the middle two sections. The focal pitch classes in each section are tritone-related between the two violins, but the **B′** section brings back the initial pair {D♯ A} as a kind of tonal closure, though respelled enharmonically and reversed between the two instruments. What else reverses between the two instruments? In the first two sections, violin 1 is the leader while violin 2 follows in imitation, but in the second half of the piece, violin 2 becomes the leader and violin 1 follows (until the coda).

As for the motivic structure, the two **B** sections are simply transpositions of each other, up a half step, but the relationship between **A** and **A′** is more complex. **A′** not only swaps the melodic lines between violins 1 and 2, it also inverts each of these lines. The opening violin melody begins with an upward leap of a P4, followed by a descending whole-step, half-step, whole-step sequence. Violin 2 in measure 16 does the opposite: it makes a downward leap of a P4, followed by an ascending whole step, half step, and whole step. The other part is inverted as well.

Finally, how do we account for the pitch structure of the coda, the only non-octatonic measures of the duet? Although we have focused on octatonicism in this piece, the individual melodies for each instrument are tetrachords *shared* by the diatonic and octatonic collections. In the opening measures, for example, violin 1 has the diatonic tetrachord A B C D, while violin 2 has the diatonic tetrachord D♯ E♯ F♯ G♯. Only when the tetrachords are combined do we hear the full octatonic collection. The coda takes one tetrachord from each octatonic collection—E♭ F G♭ A♭ from the OCT 02 collection, and A♭ B♭ C♭ D♭ from the OCT 12 collection. Together they make the E♭ Aeolian collection.

How might an understanding of the octatonic structure help in performing the duet? Knowing that the octatonic collections will change from section to section may help the violinists prepare for key signature changes and avoid playing incorrect accidentals. Assuming that they practice their parts alone first, they will probably be surprised to hear how the two parts sound together. In particular, they may find it difficult to tune the focal pitches, which are a tritone apart. Hearing the underlying octatonic scale in advance (perhaps playing or singing the full scale in preparation for the duo rehearsal), and learning to expect its characteristic diminished sonorities, should help the violinists stay in tune.

TERMS YOU SHOULD KNOW

aggregate	integer notation	polymodal
bimodal	literal complement	segment
cardinality	Locrian mode	set
center	Lydian-Mixolydian	• subset
centric	major-minor tetrachord	• superset
collection	nontonal	• symmetrical set
diminished scale	octatonic	split-third chord
element	pentatonic	whole-tone scale
focal pitch	planing	

QUESTIONS FOR REVIEW

1. What is the difference between the adjacent-interval structure in a diatonic mode and in a symmetrical scale? How does this difference impact our ability to hear a tonic pitch class?
2. Name three symmetrical scales, and describe how they are constructed.
3. Name the diatonic modes. For each, explain how to spell it as an alteration of major or minor, using the signatures we know. Which scale degree(s) must be altered?
4. Why do we use integer notation?
5. Trichords have three elements, tetrachords have four. What word best describes a set with five elements? with six? with seven? with eight?
6. In music for your own instrument, find an example written by Debussy, Ravel, Stravinsky, or Bartók in any diatonic mode or symmetrical scale. Identify the mode or scale. (Consult with your teacher, if necessary.)
7. How can analysis of modes or scales in a piece you are performing help you to learn, interpret, and/or memorize the work?

Music Analysis with Sets

CHAPTER 31

Overview

In this chapter, we focus on a work by Bartók in order to learn how to transpose and invert pitch sets and pitch-class sets. We will also learn how to label sets related by transposition and inversion.

Repertoire

Béla Bartók, "Bulgarian Rhythm," from *Mikrokosmos* (No. 115) (CD 1, track 33)

o o o o o o o o o o o o o o o o o o o o o o o o o o o o o o o o o o o o o o o o o o o o o o o o o

Relationships Between Sets

1.33 🎧 　First, listen to Bartók's "Bulgarian Rhythm" while following the score in your anthology. Do you hear a pitch-class center? As you listen, mark phrase endings and formal divisions in your score. Write alphabet letters to show which sections you hear as contrasting or similar. In music without common-practice functional harmony, terms like "cadence" and "phrase" still seem to make musical sense, but we must broaden their definitions if we are to fit these terms in nontonal contexts. (For this reason, some musicians prefer words like "unit" or "gesture" to designate what we call phrases.) In this part of the book, we will use the term "phrase" as before, to indicate a complete musical thought that ends with a cadence—but our definition of cadence is no longer limited to authentic, half, or other familiar types.

KEY CONCEPT

A "cadence" in nontonal music is a point of musical repose, which may be designated by a longer pitch or sonority, phrase markings, the return to a pitch or pitch-class center, or the completion of a musical process.

"Bulgarian Rhythm" divides primarily into four-bar phrases (usually with two-bar subphrases) that articulate a large-scale ternary form, **A B A′**, as shown in the diagram below. The **B** section is distinguished from **A** by its change of texture (from two-part counterpoint to a single motive spread between the two hands), its new melodic material, and the move away from G and D as centric pitch classes.

A		**B**		**A′** (extended)	
a	**a′**	**b**	**b′**	**a″**	**a‴**
mm. 1–4	5–8 (melodic inversion of **a**)	9–12	13–16 (melodic inversion of **b**)	17–24 (canonic and transposed to D)	25–32 (imitation ends)

As we learned in Chapter 30, we call compositions like "Bulgarian Rhythm" centric music. In this case, the primary center is G—the soprano and bass lines begin and end the work on G, and many of the melodic phrases and subphrases end on G (for example, mm. 6, 8, 26, 28, 30, and 32). We also hear a secondary emphasis on D, with many phrases and subphrases beginning on D (mm. 5, 7, 17, 19, 22, and 25). In addition, a cadential gesture at the end of the piece evokes dominant-tonic motion from D to G in the bass. But this is not a work built on common-practice tonality, and for that reason we call it a centric nontonal composition.

If we make a list of the pitch classes in this piece, we find that all twelve are included, though some phrases draw on only part of the chromatic collection. Simply analyzing the collection, however, does not capture the many interesting features of the piece. We also need to consider other musical details—such as chords, motives, and melodic ideas—to get a more complete sense of how the piece is structured. We begin by looking at some characteristic motives. Listen again to measures 5–8 (Example 31.1), or play through them at a keyboard. Make a list of all the pitch classes in the melodies of each hand. (*Try it #1*)

EXAMPLE 31.1: Bartók, "Bulgarian Rhythm," mm. 5–8

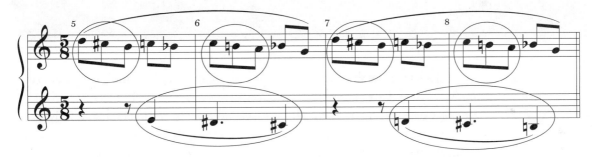

Now look at the circled pitches. This basic first step, choosing groups of pitches to analyze, is called **segmentation**. Thoughtful and musical segmentation is crucial for the success of your analysis. The sets circled in the Bartók example were chosen because they are clearly defined as units by such features as slurring, rests before or after the grouping, beams, and changes of contour in a melodic line. Other segmentation factors might include repetition, articulation as a chord, or the grouping of a melody note together with the chord that harmonizes it. While your segmentation will normally focus on pitches that are temporally adjacent, we can also group nonadjacent pitches if some feature such as similar register, timbre, or articulation groups them aurally. When in doubt, trust your ears!

Listing the Elements of a Pitch-Class Set

Now play or sing the circled pitch sets in Example 31.1; you will find that they sound very similar. When we listen to these measures, we hear relationships for which we do not yet have precise terminology. How can we label and discuss these relations? Our first step is to write out the pitch classes of the sets—in a uniform order, so that we may compare the sets more easily. You may remember that when we first began studying tonal triads—which were voiced across several octaves in SATB textures, in inversions, or in figuration patterns like Alberti bass—our first step was to take out octave doublings and pitch duplications, and then rewrite the triad in its simplest form: root-third-fifth. We then read the triad in ascending order, as in C-E-G, and gave it a name: C Major. Our reordering of pcs in a set serves a similar function: to make the set easier to recognize and compare with others. We will learn in Chapter 32 how to give sets their names.

KEY CONCEPT _____

The elements of a pitch-class set are listed as integers in ascending order. Arrange the ascending elements as though around a clock face, with the smallest possible gaps between pcs.

A clock face like the one in Figure 31.1 can help us find the most compact ordering with the smallest gaps. As an example, look at the first three pitches in the Bartók excerpt and find them on the clock face: pcs 2, 1, and e. We might list them in ascending order as {1 2 e}, but when we locate these pcs on the clock, we see a large gap (clockwise) between 2 and e. Much more compact is the ordering {e 1 2}, which wraps around the top of the clock with no large gap at all.

FIGURE 31.1: Clock-face diagram

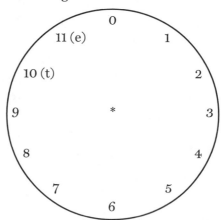

Try it #2

For each set below, write out the pcs in ascending order (as though around a clock face), in the most compact form with fewest gaps.

B E♭ C♯ A   {9 e 1 3}   E C♯ A   { _____ }

F♯ D B   { _____ }   F A♭ D A { _____ }

D A E♭ C♯ E { _____ }   D C F♯ A { _____ }

Now write the appropriate integer under each circled pitch in Example 31.1. Place the pcs of each set in ascending order, referring to the clock face to find the most compact arrangement. You should have written {e 1 2} under the identical sets in the right hand in measures 5 and 7, and in the left hand spanning measures 7–8. In addition, you should have written {9 e 0} under the sets in the right hand in measures 6 and 8, and {1 3 4} under the set spanning measures 5–6 in the left hand. You probably noticed that the left-hand set in measures 7–8 is an octave transposition of the first set in the right hand—both are {e 1 2}. The other pcsets are related by transposition as well. For small sets like these, the transpositions are easy to hear and identify; for larger sets, we need a procedure to ensure that we identify transpositions accurately.

Pitch-Class Set Transposition and mod12 Arithmetic

To transpose pcsets, we need to use pitch-class intervals. Each interval (and its enharmonic equivalents) can be represented by a single integer: for example, a m7 and an A6 are both pitch-class interval (pci) 10. You will find it helpful to memorize the pci integers in the chart below.

INTERVAL	PCI INTEGER	INTERVAL	PCI INTEGER
unison	0	tritone	6
unison	1	P5	7
m2	2	m6	8
m3	3	M6	9
M3	4	m7	10 (t)
P4	5	M7	11 (e)

When pcsets are represented in integer notation, we transpose them by adding to each pc of the set one of the pitch-class intervals given above. For example, we can transpose {3 5 7} by a minor third, or pci 3, by adding 3 to each element. We get {6 8 t}; that is, {E♭ F G} becomes {G♭ A♭ B♭}. Sometimes it is helpful to refer to the clock face when we transpose. For example, what if we want to transpose {e 1 2} by pci 2? Imagine the clock face again, or refer to Figure 31.1. Think of the original set circled on a transparent overlay, fastened with a thumbtack in the middle of the clock, so that the overlay can spin around. Then spin the overlay clockwise the number of "clicks" you want to transpose the set. For example, we transpose the set {e 1 2} up two semitones by circling e, 1, and 2 on the overlay, then rotating it two positions to the right, so that the circle that was around e is now over 1. The other circles will be over 3 and 4, yielding the transposition of {e 1 2} by pci 2: {1 3 4}.

We can get the same result with what we call **mod12 arithmetic**. Mod12 arithmetic helps us convert a number greater than 11 to an integer between 0 and 11. We rely on this system when reading twenty-four-hour clocks (in the military or overseas): when we see a time like 16:00, we must convert it to find out that the time is 4:00 p.m.

KEY CONCEPT

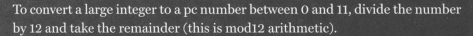

To convert a large integer to a pc number between 0 and 11, divide the number by 12 and take the remainder (this is mod12 arithmetic).

Shortcut: for integers between 12 and 23, simply subtract 12 (you get the same result).

To continue with our military clock, showing 16:00: $16 \div 12 = 1$, remainder 4; therefore 16 mod12 = 4. Taking the shortcut, we get the same result (16 −12 = 4); thus, 16:00 is the same as 4:00 p.m. Integers that differ by a multiple of 12 are "equivalent mod12"; you can add 12 to any integer and get its mod12 equivalent. For example, 7 = 19 mod12, and 11 = 23 mod 12.

If we add 2 to each element of {e 1 2} using mod12 arithmetic rather than the clock face, we also get {1 3 4}. This is because 11 + 2 = 13, which we convert to pc 1 by mod12 arithmetic (shortcut: 13 − 12 = 1). To take another example, what if we wanted to transpose the same set by pci 7? We would add 7 to each element of {e 1 2}, and get {6 8 9}.

Transposition by 7:

$$\begin{array}{rccc}
 & 11 & 1 & 2 \\
+ & 7 & 7 & 7 \\
\hline
 & 18 & 8 & 9, \text{ which converts mod12 to \{6 8 9\}.}
\end{array}$$

Some advantages of integer notation and arithmetic are precision, speed, the elimination of enharmonic spelling problems and octave placement questions, and the ability to do transpositions quickly in your head. Some advantages of the keyboard realization are the connection with your ear (the ear can detect mistakes!) and the kinesthetic reinforcement of the process in your fingers. Try all of these methods, and tailor an approach that works best for you.

Another Way

We can transpose pitch-class sets without resorting to clock faces, arithmetic, or integer numbers simply by working at the keyboard or other instrument. Try transposing pcset {2 4 8} by a tritone, or pci 6: (1) play the set in any pitch realization—for example, {D4 E4 G♯4}; (2) listen for the succession of intervals (up a M2, up a M3); (3) find the first note of the transposed set, a tritone away (A♭); then, (4) play the same succession of intervals beginning on that pitch: {A♭ B♭ D}. The same transposition in mod12 arithmetic is: {2 4 8} + 6 = {8 t 2}.

Try it #3

Translate each trichord on the left into integer notation, then transpose it by the designated interval. The first one has been completed for you.

TRICHORD	INTEGER NOTATION	TRANSPOSED BY WHAT INTERVAL?	TRANSPOSED SET IN INTEGER NOTATION
{D F A}	{2 5 9}	minor third	{5 8 0}
{B C C♯}		minor second	
{C♯ D F♯}		minor second	
{E F♯ A♯}		pci 5	
{C E G♯}		pci 7	
{G♭ A♭ B♭}		pci 4	
{C D F}		pci 6	

Pitch-Class Intervals

We know from Chapter 6 that there are many ways to analyze intervals—as generic intervals, pitch intervals, melodic or harmonic intervals, as well as compound intervals. Here, we focus on ordered and unordered pitch-class intervals and pitch intervals.

1.33 Listen again to the Bartók passage in Example 31.1, or play through it at the piano. Another way to compare sets in a piece of music is to examine their intervals: we can look at the intervals between pcs within each set, and then compare the results. For now, we will analyze pitch classes rather than pitches, and so will use ordered **pitch-class intervals** and subtraction mod12 to discover the intervals of a pcset.

KEY CONCEPT

To find the ordered pitch-class interval between two pitch classes, a and b, subtract (b − a) mod12. For example, the ordered pci between pc 2 and pc 7 is (7 − 2), or 5.

To practice subtraction mod12, find the ordered pcis for the dyads D–F♯ and F♯–D. Will they be the same or different? For the first dyad, we subtract 2 from 6 and get 4. But for the second dyad, where we must subtract 6 from 2, we need to use mod12 arithmetic: add 12 to the smaller number so that 2 becomes 14, then subtract: 14 − 6 = 8. The ordered pci from D to F♯ is 4, while the ordered pci from F♯ to D is 8. These intervals, 4 and 8, are in a complementary relationship—together they span the entire octave (twelve half steps).

KEY CONCEPT

If you compare the ordered pitch-class intervals (a − b) and (b − a), they will always sum to 12. Pcis in this relationship are called **inverses**, or complementary intervals. Inverses appear directly across the clock face from each other (for example, 3 and 9, 2 and 10).

To compute ordered pcis on a clock face, count the number of moves around the clock (clockwise) from the first integer to the second. If we take the dyad D to F♯, we count each move from 2 to 6: 2 to 3, 3 to 4, 4 to 5, and 5 to 6—four moves, so the ordered pci is 4. If we are looking for the ordered pci between 6 and 2, we still proceed in a clockwise direction: 6 to 7, 7 to 8, and so on. The ordered pci is therefore 8. Incidentally, when we speak of pitch-class intervals, there is no "up" or "down"—these intervals have size but not direction, since pcs belong to no particular octave. If you want to talk about interval direction, you must analyze pitch intervals, which show direction up and down by means of positive and negative integers.

Pitch Intervals

To measure the distance between pitches (not pitch classes), we simply count semitones; for example, the interval from D4 to F♯5 is sixteen semitones. If the two pitches occur simultaneously, or if we do not care to specify an order or direction (up or down), we call this an unordered pitch interval. For example, if D4–F♯5 were set in a chord, where order didn't matter, we would label the **unordered pitch interval** ± 16.

We can also analyze the interval between ordered pitches, like D4 up to F♯5, with a plus or minus sign to show direction: D4 up to F♯5 is +16, F♯5 down to D4 is –16. The distance between two ordered pitches is called an **ordered pitch interval**. Ordered pitch intervals represent both direction (plus or minus sign) and size (integer). Pitch intervals can thus accurately represent compound intervals; pitch-class intervals cannot, because octaves are equivalent. We will calculate both pitch and pitch-class intervals in analyzing music of the twentieth and twenty-first centuries.

Interval Classes and the Interval-Class Vector

How can intervals help us explain why some pcsets sound similar to each other and others sound different? We can see how if we make a list of all the intervals in one set and compare it with a list of intervals in another set. This method also gives us a rough idea of the sound of a pcset, since a set with many minor seconds, for example, will sound different from one with many perfect fourths. To make our lists really general, so that they can apply to any musical realization of the set, we need to find **unordered pitch-class intervals**.

KEY CONCEPT _____

We find unordered pitch-class intervals by subtracting both (b – a) and (a – b) and taking the smaller of the two differences.

If we return to the dyads D–F♯ and F♯–D, we calculate both (2 – 6) = 8 and (6 – 2) = 4. The lower number, 4, is the unordered pci between pcs 6 and 2. We may also compute unordered pcis on a clock face: we mark the two pc integers, 2 and 6, then move the shortest distance (*not* always clockwise) between them and count the number of moves. The distance from pc 2 to pc 6 is four moves clockwise, but eight moves counterclockwise. The unordered pci is therefore 4, the shortest distance.

KEY CONCEPT

Another name for an unordered pitch-class interval is an **interval class** (ic). Each interval class contains one ordered pc interval and its inverse. There are six interval classes.

INTERVAL CLASS	PCIS	SOME TONAL INTERVAL NAMES
ic 1	1, e	m2, M7, d8
ic 2	2, t	M2, m7, A6
ic 3	3, 9	m3, M6, A2
ic 4	4, 8	M3, m6, d4
ic 5	5, 7	P4, P5
ic 6	6	A4, d5

It may help you to memorize ic numbers if you remember that a pc interval and its inverse always sum to 12 (so ic 3 consists of pci 3 plus its inverse, 9). Interval class 6 is its own inverse. Even pc 0 fits this guideline, since pc 0 is equivalent to 12 mod12.

Now let's construct a list of intervals in a set, so that we can compare sets and get an idea of their sound. Look back at the Bartók passage in Example 31.1. What are the interval classes of the trichord (three-note set) with which the passage begins, {e 1 2}? We see ic 2 between the elements in {e 1}, ic 1 between those in {1 2}, and ic 3 between those in {e 2}. There is thus one instance each of ic 1, 2, and 3, but no instances of ic 4, 5, or 6. We can summarize our analysis easily by representing each interval class with a box, and writing in each box the number of times we found that particular ic in our set.

1	2	3	4	5	6	= interval classes
1	1	1	0	0	0	

We call this tally an **interval-class vector** (or **ic vector**) and write it within square brackets without commas or spaces: [111000]. The ic vector shows at a glance that pcs in this trichord can be paired to make one half step, one whole step, and one minor third (or compounds or inverses of these)—but no other intervals. What are the ic vectors of the other two pcsets we identified in the Bartók, {1 3 4} and {9 e 0}? How do these vectors compare with that of {e 1 2}? (*Try it #4*)

Let's try calculating the ic vector for a larger pcset: {0 1 2 4 8}. First, we need to find the interval class from every pc to every other pc. You could realize the set as pitches at the keyboard or on staff paper, then make a hand tally of the interval classes you find. But a quicker method involves subtraction and a triangular chart of ordered pc intervals, as shown below.

```
0   1   2   4   8
    1   2   4   8 (subtract 0 from each pc after the first: 1 – 0, 2 – 0, 4 – 0, 8 – 0)
        1   3   7 (subtract 1 from each pc after the second: 2 – 1, 4 – 1, 8 – 1)
            2   6 (subtract 2 from each pc after the third: 4 – 2, 8 – 2)
                4 (subtract 4 from the remaining pc: 8 – 4)
```

Next, convert each pci above 6 into an interval class (for example, 8 becomes 4), and count how many of each interval class appears in the triangle.

```
1   2   4   4
    1   3   5
        2   6
            4
```

We have two ic 1s, two ic 2s, one ic 3, three ic 4s, one ic 5, and one ic 6. The ic vector is [221311]. As you may have noticed, larger pcsets have higher numbers in the ic vector.

WF1

Now try calculating the ic vector for the following two sets: {0 2 4 6 9} and {0 1 3 5 7 8}. (*Try it #5*)

SUMMARY

We measure the intervals between pitches and pitch classes in the following ways.

1. Pitches: Count the semitones between pitches; show direction with + or −.
   - Ordered pitch interval: B♭3 to C5 = +14

     C5 to B♭3 = −14
   - Unordered pitch interval: B♭3 and C5 = ± 14

2. Pitch classes: For two pitch classes, a and b, subtract (b − a) mod12; if order is unimportant, subtract both (a − b) and (b − a) and take the lower number.
   - Ordered pci: t to 0 =2

     0 to t = t
   - Unordered pci: t and 0 = 2 (also called interval class)

○ ○

The Inversion of Pitch Sets and Pitch-Class Sets

Passages of music saturated with repetitions of the same type of sets create a different effect from passages that feature diverse or contrasting sets. One of our tasks, when we analyze music, is to point out similarities and differences between sets and relate these to observations about form, motive, text, or other musical features. But how do we define which sets are "the same"? Some early theories of nontonal music considered any two sets that shared the same ic vector to be equivalent. For example, {C E G} and {A C♯ E} would be equivalent because their pcs span the same three interval classes: one ic 3 (E–G, C♯–E), one ic 4 (C–E, A–C♯), and one ic 5 (C–G, A–E; pci 7 becomes 5), for an ic vector of [001110]. As we will see, two sets sharing the same ic vector are usually related by transposition (as are {C E G} and {A C♯ E}) or by inversion. But because music theorists have found that certain sets share an ic vector but are not related by transposition or inversion, we now define set equivalence in terms of transposition and inversion instead of interval-class content.

The Inversion of Pitch Sets

We know how to invert pitch intervals and how to invert triads and seventh chords, but what is **inversion** in relation to pitch sets? It is not so different from the melodic inversion of motives. Let's begin, then, by looking at pitch sets and ordered pitch intervals to see, play, and hear inversionally related sets as motives.

1.33 🎧

Listen again to the opening of "Bulgarian Rhythm," shown in Example 31.2. We will call the right-hand motives in measures 1 and 2 pentachords A and B. (Remember, a pentachord is any five-note set.) How are these motives related? Play or sing them, then write the ordered pitch intervals for each pentachord beneath the staff, with positive and negative integers to show direction up and down.

EXAMPLE 31.2: Bartók, "Bulgarian Rhythm," mm. 1–2 (pentachords A and B)

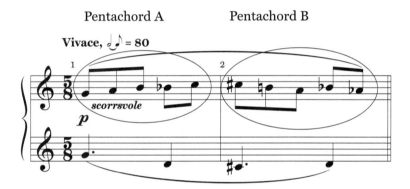

The ordered pitch-interval sequence for pentachord A is +2, +2, –1, +2. The sequence for pentachord B is –2, –2, +1, –2. Pentachords A and B are inversions of each other because they share the same ordered sequence of pitch intervals, with the directions reversed. At the keyboard, try playing additional transpositions and inversions of the motive by beginning on different random pitches and following the ordered pitch-interval sequence to determine the remaining pitches. Listen carefully to hear the aural links between the inversionally related sets.

KEY CONCEPT

To write or play the inversion of an ordered pitch set:

1. Analyze its ordered pitch intervals.
2. Choose a beginning pitch for your inverted set.
3. Write or play the remaining pitches from the ordered pitch-interval sequence, but with the direction of each sign reversed.

Now sing or play the motive from "Bulgarian Rhythm" given in Example 31.3. At the keyboard or on paper, analyze the ordered pitch intervals. Then write or play an inverted set for this motive, beginning on E4, in the empty measure. Where does this set appear later in the composition? (*Try it #6*) At the keyboard, play additional transpositions and inversions of the set.

EXAMPLE 31.3: Bartók, "Bulgarian Rhythm," m. 9

The Inversion of Pitch-Class Sets

One way we can recognize inversionally related pitch-class sets is by comparing their ordered pcis. In the diagram below, the motives from Example 31.2 are written in integer notation. The numbers below are the ordered pc intervals, determined by subtracting (b – a) mod12. What is the relationship between the two interval sequences?

$$A = \quad 7 \ 9 \ e \ t \ 0 \qquad B = 1 \ e \ 9 \ t \ 8$$
$$\text{pc intervals:} \quad 2 \ \ 2 \ \ e \ \ 2 \qquad \qquad t \ \ t \ 1 \ t$$

Each pc interval in set A is replaced by its inverse in set B: pci e becomes 1, and pci 2 becomes t. (Remember: An ordered pci and its inverse always sum to 12.) What does this relationship indicate about the ic vectors of the two sets? (*Try it #7*)

We can write the inversion of a given pcset, however, without first calculating the pcis.

KEY CONCEPT _____

To find the inversion of a pcset, replace each pc of the set with its inverse. To find the transposed inversion of a pcset, always *invert* first, then transpose.

Let's use integer notation to find the precise relationship between Bartók's pentachords A and B. (We will list these pcs in the order they appear in Bartók's melody, rather than in the most compact order.) First we find the inversion of pentachord A: 7 9 e t 0. If we replace each pc with its inverse, we get 5 3 1 2 0. We then need to transpose by eight semitones to get pentachord B: 1 e 9 t 8.

Another way to invert pcsets is to represent them on a clock face, as shown in Figure 31.2. This time, instead of spinning the overlay around a thumbtack in the middle, flip it on the 0–6 axis, like a revolving door turning on its vertical axis. On the overlay, circle the pcs of the set you want to invert, then flip it, keeping 0 and 6 in the same place. Try it with set A: 7 9 e t 0. First circle each of the pc integers, then flip the imaginary overlay on the 0–6 axis: 7 flips over the axis to 5, 9 flips to 3, 11 flips to 1, 10 flips to 2, and 0 stays 0. That yields set 5 3 1 2 0. If we then transpose this set by eight semitones (by spinning the transparency eight clicks clockwise or four counterclockwise), we get Bartók's set B: 1 e 9 t 8. (You might want to construct a pitch-class clock face at home so that you see these relations more easily yourself.)

FIGURE 31.2: Clock-face diagram (pcset inversion)

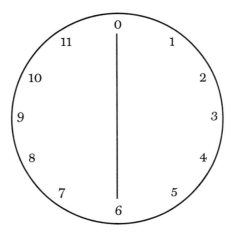

Try it #8

For each pcset below, write out the inversion by substituting for each pc its inverse.

{e 1 4}   { _____ }   {3 6 8 9}   { _____ }

{9 t 2 3}   { _____ }   {e 1 2 3 5}   { _____ }

{e 2 5}   { _____ }   {6 9 0 1}   { _____ }

Pitch-class transpositions and inversions may not be as easily recognized by the ear as pitch transpositions and inversions. Composers can place pcs from a pcset into any octave as pitches, without disturbing the transpositional or inversional relationship between pcsets; this means that the musical contour and effect may differ greatly between equivalent sets. However, the interval classes in transpositionally or inversionally related pcsets (as summarized in the ic vector) are an audible feature of nontonal music. This feature is analogous to our aural recognition of chord quality in tonal music. We can hear this quality whether or not the chords share the same inversion or spacing in their musical setting.

Identifying Transposition and Inversion

We have discovered that some of the pcsets in "Bulgarian Rhythm" are transpositions and/or inversions of each other. How can we express these relationships accurately and succinctly? Let's start with transpositions: compare pentachord B (Example 31.2) with pentachord D, shown in Example 31.4. First we place the pentachords in their most compact ascending order (around the clock) and line them up, one beneath the other, for comparison. We can show their transpositional relationship by subtracting the pc integers of one set from the other, mod12:

$$
\begin{array}{r}
\text{B}\,\{8\ 9\ t\ e\ 1\} \\
-\ \text{D}\,\{3\ 4\ 5\ 6\ 8\} \\
\hline
5\ 5\ 5\ 5\ 5
\end{array}
$$

EXAMPLE 31.4: Bartok, "Bulgarian Rhythm," mm. 17–18 (pentachords C and D)

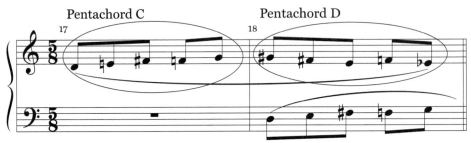

We express this relationship as follows: $\text{B} = \text{T}_5\text{D}$ (where T stands for "transposition" and the subscript 5 represents the pci 5 between the two pcsets). Now look at pentachord C in Example 31.4. We can compare pentachords A and C, with similar results: $\text{A} = \text{T}_5\text{C}$.

$$
\begin{array}{r}
\text{A}\,\{7\ 9\ t\ e\ 0\} \\
-\ \text{C}\,\{2\ 4\ 5\ 6\ 7\} \\
\hline
5\ 5\ 5\ 5\ 5
\end{array}
$$

Recall that we are working with ordered pc intervals. If we subtract A from C, we get the inverse: $C = T_7A$.

$$
\begin{array}{r}
C\{2\ 4\ 5\ 6\ 7\} \\
-A\{7\ 9\ t\ e\ 0\} \\
\hline
7\ 7\ 7\ 7\ 7
\end{array}
$$

How do we express the "distance" between inversionally related sets? Let's look at pentachords C and D, which are inversionally related (as are A and B). First we list the pcs of each in ascending and most compact order: C is {2 4 5 6 7}, and D is {3 4 5 6 8}. To compare inversionally related pcsets, we must reverse the order of one of them. We will take pentachord D and list it as {8 6 5 4 3} beneath C. What is the mathematical relationship between C and D?

$$
\begin{array}{l}
C\{2\ 4\ 5\ 6\ 7\} \\
D\{8\ 6\ 5\ 4\ 3\}
\end{array}
$$

Did you discover that if you *add* (mod12) the pcs that are vertically aligned, you consistently get 10 (t)? We call 10 the **index number** between the two inversionally related sets, and we represent their relationship as follows: $C = T_tI\ D$, and also $D = T_tI\ C$ (where I stands for "inversion" and the subscript t stands for the index number 10). What is the index number between pentachords B and C? Don't forget to put the pcs of B and C in ascending order, then reverse the order of either B or C. (*Try it #9*)

In "Bulgarian Rhythm," we can observe fairly easily that some of the pentachords are transpositionally or inversionally related because of their musical context: the way Bartók uses specific pitches, contours, and rhythms to make the relationships stand out. Further, if we calculate the ic vectors for pentachords A, B, C, and D, we find that they have the exact same interval classes between pcs, which gives them a similar sound. As with other musical details we have identified in previous chapters, we may not choose to bring out these relationships when we play the piece, but knowing about them helps us understand why and how the music sounds the way it does, and what factors make the piece cohesive. We will learn more about relationships between sets in Chapter 32.

TERMS YOU SHOULD KNOW

interval class	mod12	pitch-class interval
interval-class vector	pentachord	segmentation
inversion	pitch interval	trichord

QUESTIONS FOR REVIEW

1. How are the terms "cadence" and "phrase" adapted in this chapter for non-tonal music?
2. What musical factors do we focus on when choosing pitch or pitch-class sets for analysis?
3. How do we transpose pcsets? pitch sets?
4. How do we invert pcsets? pitch sets?
5. How do we construct ic vectors, and how can they be helpful in analysis?
6. How do we find the transpositional relatonship between two pcsets? the inversional relationship?

Sets and Set Classes

CHAPTER 32

Overview

In this chapter, we will group sets into set classes. We will also learn how to recognize some of the most distinctive set classes in twentieth-century compositions, as found in works by Bartók, Debussy, Messiaen, and Webern.

Repertoire

Béla Bartók, "Bulgarian Rhythm," from *Mikrokosmos* (No. 115) (CD 1, track 33)

Bartók, "Whole-Tone Scales," from *Mikrokosmos* (No. 136)

Bartók, *Sonata for Two Pianos and Percussion*

Claude Debussy, "La cathédral engloutie," from *Préludes*

Olivier Messiaen, "Liturgie de crystal," from *Quartet for the End of Time*

Anton Webern, String Quartet, Op. 5, third movement (CD 3, track 54)

Set-Class Membership

1.33 🎧 Listen once again to Bartók's "Bulgarian Rhythm," while following the score in your anthology. As you listen, keep in mind the form, centricity, and transpositionally and inversionally related sets we identified in Chapter 31. Now look at the left-hand melody in measures 1–2, labeled in Example 32.1 as trichord x. This set is the trichord {1 2 7}. (When a segment repeats a pitch, as with D4 in this motive, we list it only once in the pcset.) Compare trichord x with trichord y in measure 9, shown in Example 32.2. What are the elements in trichord y, and what is the relationship between the two sets? (*Try it #1*)

EXAMPLE 32.1: Bartók, "Bulgarian Rhythm," mm. 1–2 (pentachords A and B)

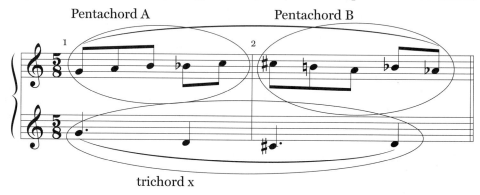

trichord x

EXAMPLE 32.2: Bartók, "Bulgarian Rhythm," m. 9

trichord y

Within the work's first few measures, you may have identified (by ear or eye) other sets that are transpositionally or inversionally related. For example, look at the left-hand parts in measures 5–6 and 7–8 in your anthology. These sets, {1 3 4} and {e 1 2}, are related by T_t. You may also have heard pcsets that are simply repeated. Pentachord A is an example: it appears in the right hand in measures 3, 6, 8, 24, 26, and 27. Sets that are repeated, that are related by some operation, or that share identical interval classes help lend coherence to nontonal works. Sets that differ may help provide contrast, just as motion to a new key may help to provide contrast in tonal music. If we did a thorough analysis of this piece, we could identify many different sets to discuss. To keep this number of sets a manageable size, we consider transpositionally and inversionally related sets to be equivalent, and group them together into **set classes**.

KEY CONCEPT

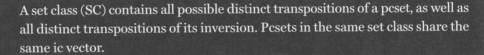

A set class (SC) contains all possible distinct transpositions of a pcset, as well as all distinct transpositions of its inversion. Pcsets in the same set class share the same ic vector.

Look at pentachord B from Example 32.1: {8 9 t e 1}. To find all members of the set class for pentachord B, begin by writing B with its eleven transpositions— {8 9 t e 1}, {9 t e 0 2}, {t e 0 1 3}, and so on. Next, find the inversion of {8 9 t e 1} by replacing each pc with its inverse: {4 3 2 1 e}. Rearrange the pcs into the most compact ascending order around the clock face: {e 1 2 3 4}. Finally, write out this inversion's eleven transpositions as well. How many distinct forms of pentachord B do you find? (*Try it #2*)

Most set classes, like pentachord B's, have twenty-four distinct members, representing each transposition and each (transposed) inversion. However, there are some SCs with fewer members. Why? Because when you transpose or invert some pcsets, they "reproduce themselves." (For an example, try transposing the augmented triad, {0 4 8}, by T_4 or T_8: you get {4 8 0} and 8 0 4}.) The number of operations that will reproduce the elements of the original set is called the set's "degree of symmetry." For {0 4 8}, the degree of symmetry is 6; the set reproduces itself when transposed by pci 0, 4, or 8, or when it is inverted and then transposed by 0, 4, or 8. The augmented triad's set class consists of only four distinct members; other common sets with fewer than twenty-four members include the diminished seventh chord (three members), the octatonic collection (three members), and the whole-tone collection (only two members!). We will return to this property later in the chapter.

WF1

Set Classes and Their Prime Forms

Once we have grouped pcsets into set classes, how do we refer to the set class? One way is by designating a single pcset to represent the entire group. We write this representative pcset in an ordering and transposition called **prime form**. Pcsets in prime form always begin with a zero and are written between square brackets [ ].

Remember that a pcset in prime form is a "token" that represents all the transpositions and inversions that belong to that single set class. In music analysis, finding the prime form of pcsets allows us to compare two pcsets that may look rather different in the musical score (different contour, timbre, pitch classes, rhythm) and discover that they are actually members of the same set class.

To find the prime form for a given pcset, we manipulate the order and transposition of the set in the following two steps: (1) we find the best **normal order** (the order of consecutive pcs that spans the smallest overall interval) for the pcset, and possibly for its inversion as well; and (2) we transpose so that the prime form begins on 0. Then we list the pcs of prime form in square brackets.

SUMMARY

In set analysis, brackets and braces have specific purposes.

[ ]: Square brackets are used for the prime form of set classes and the interval-class vector.
{ }: Curly braces are used for the normal order (when not transposed to 0), or for unordered pitches or pcs drawn from a musical passage.

Finding Prime Form from Pitches on the Keyboard or Staff Playing pitches at the keyboard and writing them on a staff can help us get to know the prime-form process informally, so we can see and hear how it works.

KEY CONCEPT

To find a pitch set's prime form:

1. Reorder the pitches, substituting octave displacements as needed, so that they all fall within a single octave (for example, between C4 and C5). Play or write them like a scale.
2. Now play or write each rotation of the scale by moving the lowest pitch to the top (like playing successive inversions of a triad). Look for the most compact rotation—the one that spans the smallest interval from the lowest to highest note.
3. We call this most compact rotation the normal order. (See also the "tie-breaker" rule below.)
4. If your set in normal order has smaller intervals (half and whole steps) near the bottom and wider intervals near the top, you are nearly finished. Transpose your set so that the first pitch is C. (Just move your hand to C and play the same succession of intervals.)

5. If your set in normal order has larger intervals near the bottom and smaller intervals near the top (for example, {F4 G4 A4 B♭4 B♮4}), you'll need to invert it. Beginning on any pitch, simply play the set's ordered pitch-interval sequence going "down" instead of "up" (for example, {A4 G4 F4 E4 E♭4}). Reverse the order of pitches so they ascend {E♭4 E4 F4 G4 A4}, then transpose to C [C4 C♯4 D4 E4 F♯4].

What happens if you find a "tie" between two compact rotations of the set, with equally small spans? Tie-breaker rule: Look for the "best" normal order—the one with the smallest intervals toward the bottom. Compare the interval between the first and second pcs in both rotations, and choose the one with the smaller interval. If that also results in a tie, then compare the interval between the first and third pcs, and so on, until you break the tie. (This method is based on that of music theorist Allen Forte, from *The Structure of Atonal Music*; other methods are possible.)

WF2

Let's return now to the opening of "Bulgarian Rhythm" (Example 32.1) to find the prime form of the work's opening pitch sets. Sing or play each of the pentachords several times to get their sound in your ears, beginning with pentachord B.

Example 32.3 shows the pitches of pentachord B written in ascending order: {A♭4 A♮4 B♭4 B♮4 C♯5}. What pitch interval does this pentachord span? A♭4 to C♯5 is pitch-interval 5. Now play or write the rotations. The first two, {A♮4 B♭4 B♮4 C♯5 A♭5} and {B♭4 B♮4 C♯5 A♭5 A♮5}, are also given in Example 32.3. Complete the rest on the blank staff below. Which rotation is the most compact? That is, which spans the smallest interval from bottom to top? Once you have chosen this as the pentachord's normal order, transpose it down to begin on middle C. Convert to pc integer notation, and you have the prime form for the pcset. (*Try it #3*)

EXAMPLE 32.3: Bartók, "Bulgarian Rhythm," m. 2 (pentachord B)

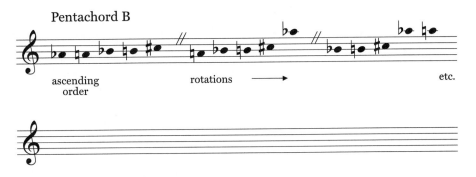

Pentachord B

ascending order   rotations ⟶   etc.

Now try the same procedure for pentachord A (Example 32.1). Play or write out the rotations, and choose the normal order. (*Try it #4*) What do you notice about the normal order that makes it different from pentachord B's? The normal order for pentachord A (Example 32.4a) has the larger interval near the bottom and smaller intervals near the top; we therefore need to invert it. Say we choose G4 (arbitrarily) as our beginning pitch for the inverted pitch set. First play (or write) the pitch-interval sequence: +2 +1 +1 +1. Then reverse the direction of each interval, beginning on G4 (–2 –1 –1 –1). Compare your solution with Example 32.4b. Now find the normal order and prime form for the inverted set. How do they compare with pentachord B's? (*Try it #5*)

EXAMPLE 32.4: Bartók, "Bulgarian Rhythm," m. 1 (pentachord A)

(a) Normal order

Pentachord A

(b) Inversion on G4

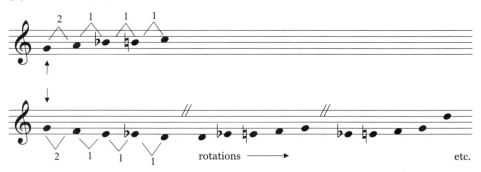

Finding Prime Form from pcs in Integer Notation We can calculate prime form more quickly when we use integer notation. We order the pcs simply by placing the integers in ascending order, and we calculate interval distance with subtraction mod12. Taking pentachord A as our example, {9 t e 0 7}, we write out each rotation and then calculate the interval spanned by subtracting the first pc from the last, as shown below:

{9 t e 0 7} ⟶ {9 t e 0 7} interval spanned = t   (7 – 9) = (19 – 9) = t
                  {t e 0 7 9} interval spanned = e   (9 – t) = (21 – t) = e
                  {e 0 7 9 t} interval spanned = e   (t – e) = (22 – e) = e
                  {0 7 9 t e} interval spanned = e   (e – 0) = e
                  {7 9 t e 0} interval spanned = 5   (0 – 7) = (12 – 7) = 5

The best normal order of these is {7 9 t e 0}, since it spans the smallest "outside" interval: pci 5. Does our set in normal order need to be inverted? Yes, we see that a larger interval is at the bottom (to the left). We replace each pc with its inverse: {7 9 t e 0} becomes {5 3 2 1 0}. Then we reverse the order of the pcs so they ascend, and we have the prime form: [0 1 2 3 5].

Try it #6

For each set of pcsets below, find the prime form.

{E A♭ A}   [_____]   {D C F♯ A}   [_____]

{G C♯ D}   [_____]   {F♯ D B C E}   [_____]

{F A♭ D A}   [_____]   {D A E♭ C♯ E}   [_____]

{B E♭ C♯ A}   [_____]

Finding Prime Form on a Clock Face   The now-familiar clock face can help us find this shortest span and normal order without writing out all the rotations. Take the pcset {9 t e 0 7} and imagine it around a clock face (see Figure 32.1). Determine the interval between each pair of adjacent pcs. Look for the *largest* interval: 0 to 7. The second pc of the largest interval will be the first pc of the set in normal order: {7 9 t e 0}. To find the prime form, we must invert. Flip these pcs around the central axis (e becomes 1, t becomes 2, and so on). Place in ascending order, then transpose to 0.

FIGURE 32.1: Clock-face diagram (prime form)

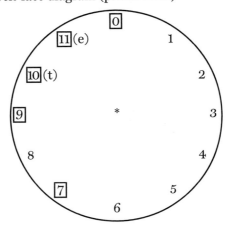

1.35 Return now to "Bulgarian Rhythm," and listen to the **A′** section, measures 17 to the end. We will use integer notation to practice finding the prime form of pcsets in this passage, to discover whether they belong to the same set class as penta- chords A and B or to a different one. Begin by placing pentachord C, shown in Example 32.5, in integer notation in ascending order: {2 4 5 6 7}. If you imagine each of the rotations, you will see that this ordering spans the smallest interval. Since the larger interval is to the left and semitones are to the right, we must replace each pc with its inverse, {t 8 7 6 5}, and reverse the order so that the integers ascend: {5 6 7 8 t}. Transpose to the 0 level to find the prime form: [0 1 2 3 5]. Pentachord C has the same prime form as A and B; the three pentachords are equivalent, and are members of the same set class.

Further, we know from Chapter 31 that pentachords C and D are inversion- ally related ($C = T_t I\ D$). Pentachord D thus belongs to the same set class as A, B, and C. Practice working with the pcs of pentachord D to find its prime form [0 1 2 3 5].

EXAMPLE 32.5: Bartók, "Bulgarian Rhythm," mm. 17–18 (pentachords C and D)

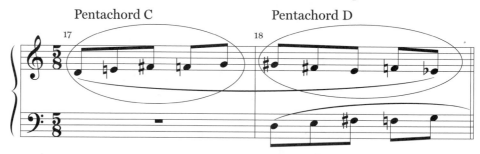

Now find the prime form for the two pentachords in Example 32.6. One of them is not equivalent to the rest. Which one? (*Try it #7*)

EXAMPLE 32.6: Bartók, "Bulgarian Rhythm," mm. 25–26 (pentachords E and F)

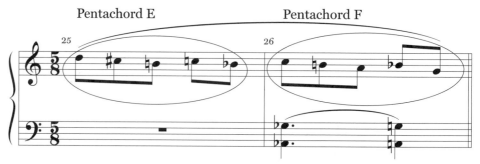

Finally, we look at one last "Bulgarian Rhythm" pentachord, shown in Example 32.7; for this one, we need to apply the tie-breaker rule to find the prime form. The pcs in ascending order are {1 4 6 9 t}. If we look for the rotation with the smallest span, we get a three-way tie: {9 t 1 4 6}, {1 4 6 9 t}, and {4 6 9 t 1}. All span pci 9. Which is the best normal order? Check the interval between the first and second pcs (or, in case the pcset needs to be inverted, the next-to-last and last pcs). This eliminates {4 6 9 t 1}, which has gaps at both ends. Pcset {9 t 1 4 6} transposed to 0 produces {0 1 4 7 9}. The other choice, {1 4 6 9 t}, needs to be inverted: we get {e 8 6 3 2}. Reorder so that the integers are in ascending order, {2 3 6 8 e}, and transpose to 0: {0 1 4 6 9}. Of these two choices—{0 1 4 7 9} and {0 1 4 6 9}—the prime form is the latter. If we compare the intervals between each pc and the first, we get a smaller interval in the second pcset when we come to the {0 7} versus {0 6} comparison.

EXAMPLE 32.7: Bartók, "Bulgarian Rhythm," m. 9 (pentachord G)

Pentachord G

SUMMARY

To find a pcset's prime form:

1. Reorder the pcs so that they ascend numerically, and consider each rotation.
2. Look at the intervallic span from first to last pc in each rotation, and choose the rotation with the smallest possible span. This is the normal order. (Remember also the tie-breaker rule described above.)
3. If the rotation with the smallest span results in a pc order with larger intervals toward the left and consecutive numbers toward the right, invert the set (replace each pc with its inverse, or subtract each pc from 12) and look for the normal order of this inverted form (repeat steps 1 and 2).
4. Once the normal order is found, transpose so that the first pc is 0. That is prime form.

Set-Class Labels Each set class can be identified with a label, just as the labels "augmented triad," "Mm7," and "fully diminished seventh" identify three- and four-note sets in tonal music. We will borrow labels derived from Allen Forte's complete set-class list. Forte grouped together pcsets with the same number of elements (or cardinality) and then ordered them by ic vector. To each set class, he gave a hyphenated number (for example, 5-35). The number before the hyphen represents the cardinality of the pcset, and the number after represents the pcset's position on the list; thus, 5-35 is a pcset of five elements that appears thirty-fifth on the list. These numbers are sometimes called "Forte numbers." Forte's complete set-class table, helpful for set-class analysis, is given in Appendix 5. When analyzing a nontonal work, first identify musical segments of interest, find the prime form, and then look up the set-class label. The labels help us discuss sets without having to write out and compare all the pcs each time.

Characteristic Trichords of Familiar Scales and Modes

You will find it easier to analyze nontonal music as well as understand it aurally if you learn to recognize the trichords by eye and ear. One effective way to do this is to associate them with the collections we studied in Chapter 30: whole-tone, diatonic, pentatonic, octatonic, and chromatic. Try to learn them all; if you look at the set-class table in Appendix 5, you will see that there are only twelve three-element set classes. Many of these you already know—for example, triad types. Spend some time at the piano, playing through the pieces cited below; identify as many trichords as you can. Sing them back after playing them; try to find and play their inversions as well. Once you learn to recognize the twelve trichord types, you will have a strong foundation upon which to build your appreciation of and skill in performing nontonal repertoire.

Whole Tone

Play through Example 32.8, drawn from Bartók's "Whole-Tone Scales." Find at least one of each of the following set classes: [0 2 4], [0 2 6], and [0 4 8]. (Remember, these are prime forms; you are looking for pcsets that may be transpositions or inversions of the prime form.) Circle them in the example. These are the only trichords closely associated with the whole-tone collection; identify them by their whole steps, major thirds, and tritones. (*Try it #8*)

EXAMPLE 32.8: Bartók, "Whole-Tone Scales," mm. 1–3

Pentatonic

The most characteristic trichords of the pentatonic collection are [0 2 5] and [0 2 7], but pentatonic compositions also share [0 2 4] with the whole-tone and diatonic collections, and [0 3 7] with the diatonic collection. Example 32.9, from the Debussy piano prelude "La cathédral engloutie," includes all of these. For each trichord circled in the example, provide the prime form. (*Try it #9*)

EXAMPLE 32.9: Debussy, "La cathédral engloutie," mm. 72–75

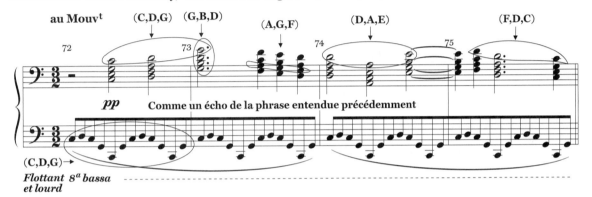

Each pc in Debussy's melody is harmonized by a major or minor triad. Find the prime form for each triad in measure 73—what can you say about their set-class membership? (*Try it #10*)

Octatonic

We turn now to the octatonic collection to discover its characteristic trichords. Look first at one form of the scale in pc integer notation—{0 1 3 4 6 7 9 t}—to see how diminished, major, and minor triads are embedded in it. The diminished triad [0 3 6] can be built on any degree of the scale: {0 3 6}, {1 4 7}, {3 6 9}, and so on. Pcs 0, 3, 6, or 9 can support either a major or minor triad: {0 3 7} and {0 4 7}, {3 6 t} and {3 7 t}, {6 9 1} and {6 t 1}, and so on. (These scale degrees can also support the "split-third" chord we identified in Chapter 30: [0 3 4 7].)

Just as characteristic to the octatonic scale, but new to our study, are the subsets that begin with a semitone: [0 1 3], [0 1 4], and [0 1 6]. Examples 32.10a and b show two primary themes of Bartók's *Sonata for Two Pianos and Percussion.* Sing or play the melody line (top voice) in each, then identify the set class that each group of circled pitches (labeled x, y, or z) belongs to. Try to find other instances of [0 1 3], [0 1 4], and [0 1 6] as well. (*Try it #11*)

EXAMPLE 32.10: Bartók, *Sonata for Two Pianos and Percussion*

(a) Mm. 1–2 (piano 1)

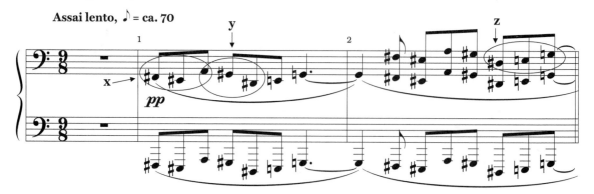

(b) Mm. 33–34 (pianos 1 and 2)

Chromatic

3.54   We complete our trichord study by looking at a passage from the third movement of Webern's String Quartet, Op. 5. This passage includes almost the entire chromatic collection and is saturated with SCs [0 1 2], [0 1 4], and [0 1 5]. Listen to the passage, then write the prime form for each of the trichords circled in Example 32.11. You may find it helpful to play individual lines slowly at the keyboard to help you identify the sound of these trichords. (*Try it #12*)

EXAMPLE 32.11: Webern, String Quartet, Op. 5, third movement, mm. 8–10

SUMMARY

There are only twelve distinct trichords. Learn them as characteristic subsets of familiar collections.

- Subsets of the whole-tone collection: [0 2 4], [0 2 6], [0 4 8].
- Subsets of the pentatonic and diatonic collections: [0 2 4], [0 2 5], [0 2 7], [0 3 7].
- Subsets of the octatonic and diatonic collections: [0 3 6], [0 3 7].
- Subsets of the octatonic and chromatic collections: [0 1 3], [0 1 4], [0 1 6].
- Subsets of the chromatic collection: [0 1 2], [0 1 5], and others.

(All trichords can be considered subsets of the chromatic collection.)

Your teacher may ask you to memorize the Forte set-class numbers for the trichords, listed below for quick reference. In practice, it is helpful to list both the Forte number and prime form for each set class. Thus, we would write SC 3-3 [0 1 4], or SC 5-35 [0 2 4 7 9].

SUMMARY

The twelve trichords with their Forte numbers, prime forms, and interval-class vectors:

3-1 [0 1 2]	icv [210000]	3-7 [0 2 5]	icv [011010]
3-2 [0 1 3]	icv [111000]	3-8 [0 2 6]	icv [010101]
3-3 [0 1 4]	icv [101100]	3-9 [0 2 7]	icv [010020]
3-4 [0 1 5]	icv [100110]	3-10 [0 3 6]	icv [002001]
3-5 [0 1 6]	icv [100011]	3-11 [0 3 7]	icv [001110]
3-6 [0 2 4]	icv [020100]	3-12 [0 4 8]	icv [000300]

∘ ∘

Reading Set-Class Tables

Look for a moment at the table in Appendix 5. The first column gives Forte's set-class number. The number in parentheses shows how how many distinct sets belong to that set class, if other than twenty-four. (The set class for the augmented triad, for example, 3-12, gives the number 4 in parentheses to show that there are only four distinct augmented triads.) The second column lists the pcs for the prime form of that set class, and the third column lists the interval-class vector. (For visual clarity, all brackets are omitted in the table.)

The remainder of this chapter discusses further properties of sets and set classes that can be learned from reading the set-class table, once you know what to look for. In particular, we focus on properties of set classes that can be revealed by studying the interval-class vector.

Complementary Sets

Sets listed directly across from each other on Forte's list are **complements**.

KEY CONCEPT

Complementary sets, when combined in the proper transposition, form an **aggregate** (one set completes the aggregate of all twelve tones begun by the other). Complementary sets have parallel set-class numbers: 3-12 and 9-12 are complements, as are 4-28 and 8-28, 5-35 and 7-35, and so on.

As an example of complementation, look at one pair of set classes: SC 4-28 [0 3 6 9] and SC 8-28 [0 1 3 4 6 7 9 t]. (These should be familiar to you as the fully diminished seventh chord and the octatonic scale.) In their prime forms, the sets don't necessarily show their complementary relation, since {0 3 6 9} is actually a literal subset of {0 1 3 4 6 7 9 t}. But if we transpose 4-28 by T_2 to {2 5 8 e}, we find the literal complement of {0 1 3 4 6 7 9 t}. When two set classes—such as [0 3 6 9] and [0 1 3 4 6 7 9 t]—are related by complementation in some transposition, though not necessarily the transposition we see in the music, we call them **abstract complements**.

The ic vectors of complementary set classes are related in a particular way: the difference between entries is the same as the difference in cardinality between the two sets. The only exception is in the last ic position, 6 (because 6 is its own complement). For example, the ic vector of 4-28 is [004002] and that of 8-28 is [448444]: each entry in the 8-28 vector (except the last) is four more than the corresponding entry in the 4-28 vector; the last entry is only two more. While the larger set may create many more intervals, the two complementary set classes share a similar distribution of interval classes, which is part of the reason they tend to sound like each other. Because a pcset's interval-class content (as represented in the ic vector) does not change as it is transposed, any representatives of 4-28 and 8-28 have this relationship.

WF3

KEY CONCEPT

When you analyze nontonal music, make note of repeated set classes, subset/superset relationships, and complementary sets. These set relationships often correspond to a consistent sound within a section of music.

Using ic Vectors

We can get a quick profile of the sound of a set class by examining its ic vector. For example, the ic vector of SC 6-35 [0 2 4 6 8 t], the whole-tone scale, is [060603]. This vector clearly gives us the picture of a set class completely saturated with major seconds (6 in the ic 2 position), major thirds (6 in the ic 4 position), and tritones (3 in the ic 6 position). Similarly, the ic vector of SC 7-35 [0 1 3 5 6 8 t], the diatonic collection, is distinctive for the fact that no two entries in its vector are the same: [254361]. Another ic vector of interest is that for 4-15 [0 1 4 6] and 4-29 [0 1 3 7]: [111111]. These two tetrachords are often called the "all-interval" tetrachords, since their pcs span one each of every interval class. They also share a special relationship: although they have the same ic vector, they are not related by transposition or inversion (such set classes are said to be Z-related). Forte lists these as 4-Z15 and 4-Z29 in his table.

Composer Olivier Messiaen was fascinated by what he called the "charm of impossibilities" in various musical dimensions. For example, some modes and scales can be transposed only a limited number of times before they repeat the same pcs again. Messiaen called set classes with this property "modes of limited transposition." We can use ic vectors to help us predict which set classes have this limited-transposition property.

KEY CONCEPT

The number in each position of the ic vector also tells how many common tones will be generated between a pcset and its transposition by that interval class. For example, a 1 in the ic 3 position means that when the set is transposed by 3, there will be one common tone. This property is sometimes called the **common-tone theorem**. The only exception is that the number in the ic 6 position must be doubled.

Let's look at a mode of limited transposition and its ic vector to see how the common-tone theorem works. The whole-tone set class, 6-35, exists in only two distinct forms: {0 2 4 6 8 t} and {1 3 5 7 9 e}. Any transposition (or inversion) reproduces one of these two collections. In its ic vector, [060603], we see two entries with a 6. What do these 6s tell us? That when we transpose either of these pcsets by ic 2, the transposition will yield six common tones with the original pcset—because there is a 6 in the ic 2 position of the vector. Similarly, when we transpose either pcset by ic 4, we will also find six common tones—because there is a 6 in the ic 4 position.

The common-tone theorem also means that when we transpose the whole-tone scale by ic 1, 3, or 5, these transpositions will yield no common tones with the original pcset (because there are zeros in the 1, 3, and 5 vector positions). What about the 3 in the ic 6 position? We double this entry and get another 6; therefore, transposition by ic 6 also yields six common tones. (Why do we double the 3? Because while each other interval class represents two intervals—for example, ic 3 represents both pci 3 and 9—ic 6 is its own inverse; we need to "count" it twice.) To sum up, transposition of {0 2 4 6 8 t} by ic 2, 4, or 6 yields exactly the same pcset back again (try this in your head!). On the other hand, transposition by ic 1, **WF4** 3, or 5 produces no common tones; it yields the other pcset: {1 3 5 7 9 e}. This is an example of Messiaen's "charm of impossibilities"—that all possible transpositions produce only two distinct forms of the set.

Messiaen identified seven modes of limited transposition. Three of them we already know: his mode 1 is SC 6-35 (the whole-tone collection); mode 2 is SC 8-28 (the octatonic collection); and mode 3 is SC 9-12 (the complement of the augmented triad). Now look at a passage from a composition by Messiaen—the "Liturgie de cristal," from *Quartet for the End of Time* (Example 32.12). Find Messiaen's modes 1, 2, or 3 in the two circled portions of the score. (*Try it #13*)

WF5

EXAMPLE 32.12: Messiaen, "Liturgie de crystal," from *Quartet for the End of Time*, mm. 5–9

TERMS YOU SHOULD KNOW

aggregate

common-tone theorem

complement

Forte number

inverse

mode of limited transposition

normal order

prime form

set class

trichord

QUESTIONS FOR REVIEW

1. What properties do pcsets belonging to the same set class share?
2. What purpose does prime form serve in music analysis? Describe the process for finding prime form.
3. In twentieth-century music for your own instrument, or a piece specified by your teacher, find a passage that seems to fall naturally into pc groupings of threes (in chords, motives, and so on). Analyze the trichords; find their prime forms. If applicable, show transposition or inversion levels of sets belonging to the same set class.

Ordered Segments and Serialism

Overview

In this chapter, we will learn how composers use ordered pitch and pitch-class segments in their works. We will also consider strategies for listening to serial music.

Repertoire

Luigi Dallapiccola, "Die Sonne kommt!" from *Goethe-lieder* (CD 1, track 85)

John Tavener, "The Lamb" (CD 3, track 49)

○ ○

Serial Composition

3.49 Listen to the opening verse of John Tavener's 1982 composition "The Lamb" without a score. Would you call this work nontonal, centric, tonal? You might decide on more than one answer. Tavener beautifully contrasts tonal passages in this work with centric passages that feature transformations of ordered pitch segments. Since medieval times, musicians have experimented with ordered pitch and rhythmic segments in their works. In the twentieth and twenty-first centuries, such a method of composition has reached its pinnacle.

KEY CONCEPT

> **Serial** music is composed with ordered segments of musical elements—typically pitch or pitch-class segments. Other elements, such as durations, dynamics, and articulations, may also be ordered in the serial design.

Ordered Pitch Segments

Look at the first phrase of "The Lamb," given in Example 33.1a. The tender opening melody sung by the sopranos sounds at first like G Major. When the altos join them in measure 2, however, their melodic line creates dissonant intervals with the sopranos in ways we would not expect in a major key. Sing each line, then calculate the ordered sequence of pitch intervals in the soprano melody (using pluses and minuses). Compare this sequence with that of the alto melody to discover their relationship.

EXAMPLE 33.1: Tavener, "The Lamb"

(a) Mm. 1–2

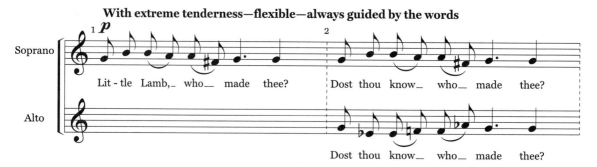

KEY CONCEPT

The distinction between sets and segments is an important one in nontonal and serial-music analysis.

The term "set" refers to *unordered* collections.
- We write the elements of sets in curly braces: {0 5 6}.
- We write the prime form of sets and set classes in square brackets: [0 1 6].

The term "segment" refers to *ordered* collections.
- We write the elements of segments in angle brackets: <7 e 9 6>.

We specify the number of elements in a set or segment with terms like "trichord" (three elements), "tetrachord" (four elements), "pentachord" (five elements), "hexachord" (six elements), and so on.
- The term "element" may refer to pitches, pitch classes, intervals, interval classes, durations, dynamics, or other musical features.

(See Chapter 30 for a review of these terms.)

3.50 🎧 Write the ordered pitch intervals for the soprano and alto lines in angle brackets beneath the music in Example 33.1a. Did you find that <+4 −2 −3 +1> in the soprano line becomes <−4 +2 +3 −1> in the alto? The two melodies are pitch **inversions (I)** of each other—that is, they share the same ordered sequence of pitch intervals, but the direction (+ or −) is reversed. How are the melodic segments of the next two measures, given in Example 33.1b, related to each other? Begin by singing the passage or listening again on your CD.

(b) Mm. 3–4

The soprano melody in measure 4 is identical to that of measure 3, only it appears in reverse order. This relationship, called **retrograde (R)**, is easiest to see and hear if you attend to the pcs (rather than the intervals). But what happens to the ordered sequence of pitch intervals when two phrases are retrograde related? Any time you retrograde a pitch segment, its intervals will reverse order and change direction (up or down) as well. For example, sing the beginning of measure 3, <G4 B4 A4 F♯4>, and then its retrograde, <F♯4 A4 B4 G4>. The first segment's intervals are <+4 −2 −3> and the second's are <+3 +2 −4>. Now compare the complete pitch-interval sequence of measure 3 with that of measure 4. (*Try it #1*)

Finally, look at Example 33.1c, the third phrase of this piece. The soprano's melody in measure 5 is the same as in measure 3. We will take this soprano segment (m. 3 or 5) as our standard—what we call the "prime" segment (P). Why did we not take the melody of measure 1 as our standard? Because as the work continues, we discover that the measure 1 melody is only a fragment drawn from the work's prime segment. The complete segment—repeated numerous times in the piece—is the one in measure 3.

(c) Mm. 5–6

KEY CONCEPT

We usually designate the first complete ordered segment in a piece the prime (P) and compare later segments with it, using one of four transformations: T (transposition), R (retrograde), I (inversion), or RI (retrograde inversion).

In Example 33.1c, the sopranos sing P followed by R. The altos sing I, followed by a transformation we have not yet seen: the retrograde of the inversion. We call this segment the **retrograde inversion (RI)** of P. How does the alto's pitch-interval sequence in measure 6 compare with P? (*Try it #2*)

3.49 Listen again to "The Lamb," while following the score in your anthology. Try to hear the relationships between P and each of its transformations (I, R, and RI) in measures 1–6 by listening for the relations between the pitch-interval sequences. Listen also to identify where the music is composed by serial procedures and where it is not. (*Try it #3*)

SUMMARY

One way to begin training our ears to hear relationships between ordered pitch segments is to listen for transformations of their pitch-interval sequences. (Later we will adapt this strategy to handle pitch classes and pc intervals.)

Transpositions (T): The pitch-interval sequences are identical.

Inversions (I): The direction of each pitch interval reverses (+ becomes −, and vice versa).

Retrograde (R): The pitch-interval sequence is in reverse order and inverted.

Retrograde inversion (RI): The pitch-interval sequence is in reverse order.

Labeling Pitch-Class Segments

Let's turn now to a pitch-class analysis of Example 33.1c to see how segments are labeled. We can represent relationships between segments in a precise way with labels based on the first pc integer of the segment's P (or I) form. For example, the P segment (m. 5, soprano) begins with pc 7; we therefore call the segment T_7P. We add an R to the prime label to show the retrograde form (m. 6, soprano): RT_7P. The inversion of P (m. 5, alto) also begins with pc 7; we call it T_7IP. We add an R to the inverted segment's label to show retrograde inversion (m. 6, alto): RT_7IP. Write these labels in Example 33.1c.

While the labels are accurate and precise, some people prefer a shorthand notation: P_7 (or T_7) instead of T_7P, R_7 instead of RT_7P, and so on. We will use the shorthand labels here, but be aware of one common source of confusion: while P and I labels match the first pc integer of the segment, R and RI labels do not. For example, R_7 does not begin with pc 7. Its more precise label makes this clear: RT_7P is the retrograde of T_7P. Since P_7 starts with pc 7, R_7 *ends* with pc 7. The same principle holds for RI_7, which also ends with pc 7 (check the alto line in m. 6 of Example 33.1c to confirm that this is so).

SUMMARY

P_7: a segment P that begins with pc 7

R_7: a retrograde form of P that *ends* with pc 7

I_7 : an inverted form of P that begins with pc 7

RI_7: a retrograde of P's inversion that *ends* with pc 7

Another Way

There are two main systems for labeling segments. The first system (P_7, R_7, and so on) you have just read about. But some analysts label the first appearance of the segment as T_0P, or P_0, to show that it is the first and "original" form, on which others are based. Each subsequent transposition is then calculated from this original. (That is, transposition up a whole step would be labeled P_2.) The two systems are akin to fixed *do* and movable *do*. The system that labels each segment by the number of its first pc is a fixed-*do* system; the system that labels the original P_0 is a movable-*do* system. Because the fixed-*do* system is becoming more common, we will follow it here.

Operations on Pitch Classes

Given a pitch-class segment, P, how do we calculate its R, I, and RI forms? Look again at Example 33.1c, which shows all four forms. The integer notation for P_7, in the soprano's measure 5, is <7 e 9 6 3 5 8>. The R_7 form, which follows in measure 6, is the same sequence in reverse order: <8 5 3 6 9 e 7>. To find the inversion of <7 e 9 6 3 5 8>, substitute for each pc its inverse: <5 1 3 6 9 7 4>. Then, since Tavener chose the form beginning on pc 7 for the alto line of measure 5, we need to transpose this segment by adding 2 to each element: <7 3 5 8 e 9 6>.

KEY CONCEPT

Always invert *first* before transposing pcs or retrograding the order of pcs. Performing these operations in the opposite order will result in a different set of pcs.

Finally, find the retrograde inversion by running the pcs of the inverted form backward: we get <6 9 e 8 5 3 7>, the same as the alto melody of measure 6.

SUMMARY

Following are the four classic operations for pitch classes in a prime segment (P).

Transposition (T): To each pc in P is added a constant integer (mod12).
Retrograde (R): The pc order of P is reversed (so the pcs run backward).
Inversion (I): Each pc in P is replaced with its inverse (mod12).
Retrograde inversion (RI): The pc order of I is reversed.

When these operations are combined, always invert first, then transpose, then retrograde.

○ ○

Twelve-Tone Rows

Serial music composed with twelve-pc segments is called **twelve-tone,** or **dodecaphonic**, music (from the Greek for "twelve sounds").

KEY CONCEPT

When an ordered segment consists of twelve distinct pcs, one from each pitch class, we call it a **twelve-tone row.**

WF1

Dodecaphonic composition originated with Arnold Schoenberg and his students Anton Webern and Alban Berg in Vienna in the 1920s. Later, many other composers—even Igor Stravinsky and Aaron Copland, whose nonserial music may be more familiar to you—wrote some twelve-tone works. Elsewhere in Europe, composers such as Pierre Boulez and Luigi Dallapiccola wrote music with twelve-tone rows, as did Milton Babbitt and Elliott Carter in the United States. We begin our study of twelve-tone composition with a song from 1953 by Dallapiccola.

1.85 🎧

Listen to "Die Sonne kommt!" for soprano and E-flat clarinet (the second in a set of songs), while following the translation below. Watch for text painting around the words "comes up," "crescent," "such a pair," and "riddle." Can you find other associations between text and music?

Die Sonne kommt! Ein Prachter scheinen!	The sun comes up! A glorious sight!
Der Sichelmond umklammert sie.	The crescent moon embraces her.
Wer konnte solch ein Paar vereinen?	Who could unite such a pair?
Dies Rätsel, wie erklärt sich's? wie?	This riddle, how to solve it? How?

Probably most obvious are the ways the melody's contour fits the words: for example, the broad ascending intervals to which the composer sets "sun comes up!" and the twisting of the musical line around "crescent." "Moon" is set to broad descending intervals, perhaps to contrast with the sun's ascent. "Such a pair" refers to the sun and moon, but Dallapiccola provides additional associations by scoring the piece for voice and clarinet duo, and by basing the primary pitch material on two transpositions of a twelve-tone row. We will return to the question of the riddle!

Let's begin by looking at the vocal line alone, measures 1–9a, given in Example 33.2a. Listen to these measures again. Identify the first row in the example, and label it as the prime. This row divides, by means of rests and changes in register, into three-note segments, or trichords. Identify the pcs in each trichord, then label each trichord with a prime form and set-class number.

EXAMPLE 33.2: Dallapiccola, "Die Sonne kommt!"

(a) Mm. 1–9a (voice)

The first row in the song (mm. 1–5) is the prime row. We label it P$_8$, since it begins with pc 8. The row divides into set classes 3-1 [0 1 2], 3-5 [0 1 6], 3-4 [0 1 5], and a repetition of 3-5 [0 1 6]. Set-class identification remains an important tool for the analysis of serial music; if you had any difficulty identifying the set-class labels for these trichords, work through the review that follows (otherwise, you may skip ahead to "Labeling Rows").

REVIEW

When we list the pcs in the order they appear in the musical score, we enclose them in angle brackets to show that they are *ordered* segments: <8 9 7>, <5 e 4>, <2 3 t>, <1 0 6>. In order to find the set-class labels for these segments, we must rearrange the pcs (in ascending order, around the clock face) into a normal order that no longer represents their order in the composition. They are now considered *unordered* sets, and for these we use curly braces. The normal order for each of the trichords in the Dallapiccola row (not yet transposed to prime form) is {7 8 9}, {e 4 5}, {t 2 3}, and {0 1 6}.

Two steps remain to find prime form and the set-class label: first we determine whether any trichord needs to be inverted (because the larger intervals lie to the left rather than to the right), and then we transpose so that the first pc is 0. The first trichord of the row, {7 8 9}, can be transposed by T$_5$ to begin on 0; it belongs to SC 3-1 [0 1 2]. The second trichord, {e 4 5}, must be inverted to {1 8 7}, reordered around the clock to {7 8 1}, and transposed (also by T$_5$); it belongs to SC 3-5 [0 1 6], as does the last trichord. The third trichord, {t 2 3}, must also be inverted, to {2 t 9}, then reordered to {9 t 2} and transposed by T$_3$. It belongs to SC 3-4 [0 1 5]. How are the two 3-5 trichords—{e 4 5} and {0 1 6}—related? They are T$_5$I related, because the pcs when aligned properly (when one trichord is reversed) sum to 5.

Labeling Rows

How are we to determine the row label for the next phrase of "Die Sonne kommt!" beginning "Der Sichelmond" (mm. 6–9a)? You might initially be confused by the fact that Dallapiccola repeats pitches here: <9 8 t 9 8>. While a twelve-tone row itself does not repeat pcs, composers may repeat one or more pcs when they set the row in a piece of music, just as a motive might be repeated. When this happens, we simply disregard the repetition to label rows.

Compare the ordered pc intervals of the "Sichelmond" phrase with those of the original row. The ordered pci succession will help us determine the row form. (Remember that ordered pcis need to be measured *clockwise* around the clock face, or subtracted [b – a] mod12.)

	"Die Sonne kommt! ..."	"Der Sichelmond ..."
pcs	<8 9 7 5 e 4 2 3 t 1 0 6>	<9 8 t 0 6 1 3 2 7 4 5 e>
ordered pcis	1 t t 6 5 t 1 7 3 e 6	e 2 2 6 7 2 e 5 9 1 6

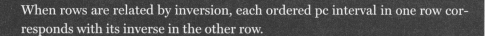

KEY CONCEPT

> When rows are related by inversion, each ordered pc interval in one row corresponds with its inverse in the other row.

The two rows are inversionally related, because each ordered pc interval of the first row is replaced by its inverse in the second. We can label the "Sichelmond" row I_9—because it begins with pc 9.

Another Way

If you were using the movable-*do* system of row labeling, you would have labeled the initial row P_0. How would you determine the form of the row beginning in measure 6?

Since the original row began on G♯ as P_0, the I form beginning on A would be labeled a half step above that: I_1.

1.86 🎧   Example 33.2b gives phrases 2 and 3, including the entrance of the clarinet. Label the rows in this next portion of the song; listen, and let your ears help you. Does the clarinet line sound familiar? It should, since the melody is an exact repetition of the opening vocal line (mm. 1–5). It is unusual—and not characteristic of most twelve-tone music—that Dallapiccola repeats not just the original row's pcs, but its exact original pitches, with the same contour and rhythm.

(b) Mm. 6–12

KEY CONCEPT

Sometimes composers make a row's construction or relationships between row forms obvious by the way the row is set in the musical context: by the rhythm, contour, register, or correspondence to motives or phrases. They may also obscure rows in various ways, such as setting them as chords where the ordering may be difficult to discern.

Listen now to the vocal line the clarinet accompanies, beginning with "Wer konnte." Does it sound familiar? The vocal line is the retrograde of the preceding vocal phrase. What would its label be? (*Try it #4*) Just as the clarinet melody does, the vocal line takes the exact contour and rhythm of the line it is modeled on, but now in retrograde.

The rest of the song continues in the same vein, with exact repetitions of previous row forms and exact retrogrades, including contour and rhythm. When a segment of music is followed by a repetition entirely in retrograde (pitch, rhythm, and so on), the two segments together are called a **palindrome**. Perhaps the palindrome represents the poem's "riddle." Dallapiccola builds an entire work out of simple repetition and transformation, in the same way that Renaissance and Baroque composers wrote "riddle" canons whose solutions involved performing the canonic melody backward or upside-down.

WF2

Choosing Row Forms

The internal structure of a row has a great deal to do with larger decisions composers make about their twelve-tone pieces, just as a small-scale motive in a tonal work might foreshadow a change of key or large-scale tonal design. Let's look, for example, at Dallapiccola's row choices in light of the T_5I relationship we found between the two statements of SC 3-5 [0 1 6] in the row. Because these two trichords are related by index number 5, any two inversionally related rows whose T_n numbers sum to 5 will reproduce the pcs of these two trichords adjacent to each other. More advanced study of twelve-tone theory can explain why this is so. For our purposes, we can simply observe that Dallapiccola has chosen row pairs—P_8 and I_9, plus their retrogrades—that sum to 5. We will also find pc duplications, called **invariant pcs**, or **invariant sets**, between pairs of rows.

KEY CONCEPT

Invariance means "kept the same," or "does not vary." Composers use pitch, pitch-class, or segment invariance to make connections between rows, sets, or segments. These invariant elements are often audible features of a work, and may contribute to its musical coherence.

To see invariance at work, let's review the rows found at the beginning of "Die Sonne kommt!" in the vocal line (Example 32.2a), P_8 in measures 1–5 and I_9 in measures 6–9. (The statements of SC 3-5 [0 1 6] are underlined.)

P_8: <8 9 7 5 e 4 2 3 t 1 0 6> I_9: <9 8 t 0 6 1 3 2 7 4 5 e>

When looking at the score, remember that Dallapiccola repeats pitches at the beginning of the I₉ statement to create text painting for "Sichelmond" ("crescent moon"). Don't let this confuse you when you identify the rows in measures 8–12 (Example 33.2b). (We hear pcs that seem out of order, since the composer is running the melody from m. 6, which contains pc repetitions, backward.) The two rows in measures 8–12 are P₈ (clarinet, beginning in m. 8) and RI₉ (voice, m. 9b). Their transposition levels, 8 and 9, again sum to index number 5 (mod12). Study the rows below to see how trichords {e 4 5} and {0 1 6} reappear (though their order varies):

$$P_8: \quad <8\ 9\ \underline{7\ 5\ e\ 4}\ 2\ 3\ \underline{t\ 1\ 0}\ 6> \qquad RI_9: \quad <\underline{e\ 5\ 4}\ 7\ 2\ 3\ \underline{1\ 6\ 0}\ t\ 8\ 9>$$

WF3 Pcs {8 9} and {2 3} also appear consecutively in the two rows. (This too is a predictable feature, since 8 + 9 and also 2 + 3 sum to 5.)

Now look at Example 33.2c (mm. 6–12 again) to see how Dallapiccola features some of these pc recurrences in his musical setting. The circles mark instances where the composer has placed these invariant pcs in close proximity. His choice to realize many of them in the same pitch register helps us to hear the pc correspondences between rows, and to hear the text "such a pair" played out musically by repetitions of {e 4 5} and {2 3}.

(c) Mm. 6–12 (showing invariant pcs)

Hearing Row Relationships

You need no special abilities, other than patience and practice, to hear how rows are related. The first step is to analyze aurally the ordered pci sequence of a row. Write down this sequence as you hear it: often it will contain distinctive intervals or trichords at the beginning and end that will help you determine which row form is being used. Take, once again, Dallapiccola's row. It begins with the [0 1 2] trichord, so we can listen for opening chromaticism or leaps of major sevenths. It ends with a distinctive interval: a tritone. Thus, if we hear a row beginning with chromaticism, it must be a P or I form. If we hear a row beginning with a tritone, it must be an R or RI form.

If the beginning and end of the row are highly similar, then you will want to write down the entire sequence of intervals as you hear them. It is often easier to take ordered pitch intervals in dictation than it is to take pc intervals. Write down these pitch intervals, and then convert them to pc intervals. When you hear the next row, compare its pci sequence with the one you have written down. With time and practice, you can learn to do this. But while such dictation helps you appreciate one dimension of the composition, don't forget to listen for other musical aspects: form, phrase, harmony or distinctive set classes, motivic repetition, and so on. The early twelve-tone composers saw their innovation as an outgrowth of motivic devel-

WF4   opment and variation technique in Western music—not as a rejection of the earlier tradition but as a continuation and enrichment of that tradition.

Realizing Twelve-Tone Rows

A row is a precompositional idea—a sequence of pitch classes that composers then realize musically in various ways (just as Baroque composers could realize figured bass in different ways). The repetitions of a row might involve an entirely different contour and sequence of pitches (the same pitch classes, but different pitches), or a different rhythm or tempo. Some pcs may be repeated before proceeding to the next pcs of the row, and the row may be presented linearly (in a melody or voice-leading strand), harmonically, or with melody and harmony together. The row may be performed by one instrument or shared among a group of instruments. More than one form of the row (or even two or more different rows) may be heard at the same time.

The row, or a segment of it, may be rotated—with elements of the ordered segment moved from the end to the beginning, or vice versa. This allows composers great flexibility in creating contrasting musical sections, by any number of musical means, while still maintaining the order of intervals in the row. Schoenberg was convinced that a composer's craft included the ability to work with material from a row. In fact, he wrote: "The time will come when the ability to draw thematic material from a basic set of twelve tones will be an unconditional prerequisite for obtaining admission into the composition class of a conservatory" (*Style and Idea*, 1948). Musical unity in a serial composition is created both by the row and by its realization through the compositional process.

TERMS YOU SHOULD KNOW

dodecaphonic

invariance

inversion (I)

palindrome

prime (P)

retrograde (R)

retrograde inversion (RI)

row

serial

twelve tone

QUESTIONS FOR REVIEW

1. What is serialism? Can elements other than pitches be ordered?
2. What are some characteristics to look for in studying a row for a serial piece? How can properties of the row be brought out (or not) in its musical realization?
3. Are all serial works twelve tone? Explain, citing examples from this chapter.

Twelve-Tone Rows and the Row Matrix

CHAPTER 34

Outline of topics covered

The row matrix
- Hexachordal combinatoriality
- Finding combinatorial row pairs

Serialism and compositional style

Overview

In this chapter, we will learn advanced twelve-tone techniques, including how composers choose which row forms to combine. We will see and hear how twelve-tone compositions may differ in style by contrasting two piano works, by Schoenberg and Webern.

Repertoire

Arnold Schoenberg, *Klavierstück*, Op. 33a (CD 3, track 12)

Anton Webern, Variations for Piano, Op. 27, second movement (CD 3, track 62)

○ ○

The Row Matrix

3.12 🎧

To see how a composer might create contrasting material from a single row, we turn now to a more extended work: Schoenberg's *Klavierstück*, Op. 33a. Begin by listening to the piece while following the score in your anthology. It is sometimes called a twelve-tone sonata form, following the nineteenth-century sonata model. As you listen, try to identify an expository first theme and more lyrical second theme; then try to find where those two themes return in the "recapitulation." Mark these spots in your score. (*Try it #1*) Of course, without tonality we cannot have a true sonata, since the form by definition hinges on the tension between contrasting keys. Nevertheless, Schoenberg's composition does seem to allude to sonata form, even in this nontonal context. In fact, his pupil Webern once said in a lecture (later published as *The Path to the New Music*), "we too are writing in classical forms, which haven't vanished."

Example 34.1a gives the opening of the work. How are we to find a row in this chordal setting? We can't, because we are unable to determine the row's order from the chordal texture. We need to look for a melodic statement of the row, where the ordering is clearer. One possibility is to look at the return of this first theme in the "recapitulation," shown in Example 34.1b. Here, the right hand brings back the chordal opening in measures 32–33, after the fermata, but now in arpeggiated form. When we have determined the order of the row pcs, we can label their placement in the chords by giving them **order numbers**—counting out the elements of the row from 1 to 12. Write out the pcs in Schoenberg's row above the

WF1

right-hand pitches in Example 34.1b. Write order numbers next to each pc. Then use this information to write the order numbers in part a of the example.

EXAMPLE 34.1: Schoenberg, *Klavierstück*, Op. 33a

(a) Mm. 1–2

(b) Mm. 32–34

KEY CONCEPT

When the first row in a piece is presented chordally, we need to look for a later appearance of the row as a melody to determine the pc order. We label individual row elements in the score with order numbers from 1 to 12, to show where they appear in the musical context.

What distinctive set classes or intervals lie at either end of this row (<t 5 0 e 9 6 1 3 7 8 2 4>) that might help you to hear row relationships? P and I forms begin with an ic 5, and the first trichord is the pentatonic subset 3-9 [0 2 7]. The R and RI forms begin with an ic 2, and the whole-tone subset 3-8 [0 2 6].

We will now take Schoenberg's row and build a **row matrix**. A row matrix is a 12 x 12 chart that displays all possible P, I, R, and RI forms of a row, a convenient aid to musical analysis. We can calculate the matrix with either letter names or pc integers; because integer notation allows us to add and subtract mod12 to calculate the transpositions and inversions, we choose integers for our matrix.

If we transpose the initial row to begin on 0, then the main diagonal from the upper left- to lower right-hand corner will contain all zeros. This is a helpful property, since we can judge from the diagonal of zeros whether we've calculated correctly. What would the transposition of Schoenberg's row to pc 0 be? (*Try it #2*)

WF2

KEY CONCEPT

To build a row matrix:

1. Write the P form of the row across the top, transposed to begin on 0.
2. Write the I form of the row—found by taking the inverse of each pc in the row—down the left-hand column.
3. Consider each pc in the left-hand column as the first pc in each P form (transpose the original P row to begin on this pc).

The matrix on the opposite page is partially completed. Read P forms left to right; in this matrix, the first row is P_0, the second is P_5, the third is P_t, and so on. To find R forms, read the rows backward, right to left. The first row is R_0, the second is R_5, the third is R_t, and so on. (Remember, R forms are named by the first pc of their related P form.) We read the I forms top to bottom as columns. The first column is I_0, the second is I_7, the third is I_2, and so on. Finally, we read the RI forms as columns bottom to top: the first column is RI_0, the second is RI_7, the third is RI_2, and so on. (Remember, RI forms are named by the first pc of their related I form.) Now fill in the remaining positions in the matrix on your own. (You may find the task easier if you complete the matrix in this order: P_0, P_1, P_2, P_3, and so on. This way you only have to add 1 each time.) (*Try it #3*)

P ⟶   ⟵ R

I ↓											
0	7	2	1	e	8	3	5	9	t	4	6
5	0	7	6	4	1	8	t	2	3	9	e
t	5	0	e	9	6	1	3	7	8	2	4
e	6		0			2					
1	8			0		4					
4	e				0	7					
9	4					0					
7	2					t	0				
3	t					6		0			
2	9					5			0		
8	3					e				0	
6	1	8	7	5	2	9	e	3	4	t	0

RI ↑ (bottom-left label)   R ← (top-right label)

When you have completed the matrix, refer to it as you label the remaining rows in the Schoenberg examples. In Example 34.1a, one P form appears in the first measure and one I form in the second. What are the correct labels? What row forms do you find in the separate hands in part b of the example? (*Try it #4*)

Hexachordal Combinatoriality

3.13 🎧   Listen again to the second theme of Schoenberg's piece, given in Example 34.1c. This theme has a slower "harmonic rhythm"—that is, it takes longer for each row to be completed. Label the row forms, one in the right hand and one in the left. (*Try it #5*) Interestingly, Schoenberg uses the same transpositions of the row as earlier in the composition, but to very different musical effect.

(c) Mm. 14–18

Had you not been tipped off to look for one row in each hand, you might have had difficulty identifying rows in this passage. Why? Because Schoenberg completes an aggregate in measures 14–16, before either row concludes. To understand this concept, let's look at the passage in pc integer notation. We divide the row in each hand into two hexachords, just as Schoenberg does in measure 16, by means of rests and changes in register.

		mm. 14–16a	mm. 16b–18
right hand:	P_t	<t 5 0 e 9 6	1 3 7 8 2 4>
left hand:	I_3	<3 8 1 2 4 7	0 t 6 5 e 9>
		aggregate	aggregate

Look at the first hexachord of each row. When they are performed in combination, we hear all twelve pcs—an aggregate. Likewise, the second hexachords of each row, when combined, make a complete aggregate.

KEY CONCEPT

Hexachordal combinatoriality occurs when two forms of the same row are paired so that the rows' initial hexachords, when combined, complete an aggregate. Similarly, the rows' second hexachords, when combined, complete an aggregate.

When aggregates are created by pcs from more than one row form, they are sometimes called **secondary sets** (from the old naming of rows as "sets"). Hexachordal combinatoriality may help create variety in the pcs and intervals in the counterpoint between voices. It can also contribute to a faster "harmonic rhythm"—that is, the frequency with which one aggregate is completed and the next one begins.

We can diagram the combinatorial relationship as follows, where A represents the unordered pc content of one hexachord, and B the content of the other.

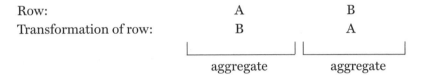

In the Schoenberg example, hexachord A is {5 6 9 t e 0} and hexachord B is {1 2 3 4 7 8}.

There are four types of combinatoriality: P-combinatoriality, I-combinatoriality, R-combinatoriality, and RI-combinatoriality. We have already seen an example of I-combinatoriality (in the Schoenberg example), where a row is paired with its inversion. In P-combinatoriality, a row is paired with another P form (a transposition of the original). In R- or RI-combinatoriality, a row is paired with a retrograde or retrograde-inversion form. A hexachord that can generate all four types of combinatoriality is called an **all-combinatorial hexachord**.

Finding Combinatorial Row Pairs

If you wanted to compose a twelve-tone work that featured combinatorial row pairs, you would need to know how to "find" pairs that work. Your teacher may decide that this is an advanced topic and ask that you skip to the next section on compositional style. But if you'd like to learn learn more about serial composition, read on.

The easiest way to determine whether a row is combinatorial is by examining its row matrix. As an example, consider the row matrix for Webern's Variations for Piano, since this row happens to feature an all-combinatorial hexachord (although, as we will see, the movement we will analyze does not employ combinatoriality at all). To find a combinatorial pair of rows, first divide the matrix into four quadrants, as shown below. This isolates the hexachords for comparison. If we wanted to find a P-combinatorial pair for P_5, whose first hexachord is <5 1 0 4 3 2>, we would mark this collection on the left side of the matrix and hunt for the same unordered collection, {0 1 2 3 4 5}, on the right side of the matrix. Why on the right side? Because we want the content of the A hexachord to appear in the second (B) hexachord of the new row. Once we have found it, we see that P_5 and P_e are P-combinatorial.

0	8	7	e	t	9	3	1	4	2	6	5
4	0	e	3	2	1	7	5	8	6	t	9
5	1	0	4	3	2	8	6	9	7	e	t
1	9	8	0	e	t	4	2	5	3	7	6
2	t	9	1	0	e	5	3	6	4	8	7
3	e	t	2	1	0	6	4	7	5	9	8
9	5	4	8	7	6	0	t	1	e	3	2
e	7	6	t	9	8	2	0	3	1	5	4
8	4	3	7	6	5	e	9	0	t	2	1
t	6	5	9	8	7	1	e	2	0	4	3
6	2	1	5	4	3	9	7	t	8	0	e
7	3	2	6	5	4	t	8	e	9	1	0

P_5:   <5 1 0 4 3 2   8 6 9 7 e t>
P_e: <e 7 6 t 9 8   2 0 3 1 5 4>

           aggregate   aggregate

Now follow the same procedure to find another pair of P-combinatorial rows. Circle your answer.

To find an I-combinatorial pair, we again begin by circling the first hexachord of the P form on the left side of the matrix, as shown. This time, we hunt for the equivalent content of this unordered hexachord as a column in the bottom half of the quadrant. Why? We are looking at columns rather than rows, because we are looking for I forms; and we are looking in the bottom half because we want to find an I row whose second (B) hexachord is equivalent in content to hexachord A.

0	8	7	e	t	9	3	1	4	2	6	5
4	0	e	3	2	1	7	5	8	6	t	9
5	1	0	4	3	2	8	6	9	7	e	t
1	9	8	0	e	t	4	2	5	3	7	6
2	t	9	1	0	e	5	3	6	4	8	7
3	e	t	2	1	0	6	4	7	5	9	8
9	5	4	8	7	6	0	t	1	e	3	2
e	7	6	t	9	8	2	0	3	1	5	4
8	4	3	7	6	5	e	9	0	t	2	1
t	6	5	9	8	7	1	e	2	0	4	3
6	2	1	5	4	3	9	7	t	8	0	e
7	3	2	6	5	4	t	8	e	9	1	0

Again, once you have found it, simply read the row forms from the matrix: P_5 and I_6 are I-combinatorial.

P_5:   <5 1 0 4 3 2   8 6 9 7 e t>
I_6:   <6 t e 7 8 9   3 5 2 4 0 1>

          aggregate   aggregate

Follow the same procedure to find another pair of I-combinatorial rows. Circle your answer.

WF5

We can use an analogous procedure to find RI-combinatoriality. If you'd like to try it, you can check your answer in WebFact 5. The R-combinatorial pair in this row is P₅ and R₅. Of course, any row paired with its own retrograde will produce R-combinatoriality.

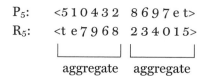

WF6
$$P_5: \quad <5\ 1\ 0\ 4\ 3\ 2 \quad 8\ 6\ 9\ 7\ e\ t>$$
$$R_5: \quad <t\ e\ 7\ 9\ 6\ 8 \quad 2\ 3\ 4\ 0\ 1\ 5>$$
aggregate   aggregate

o o o o o o o o o o o o o o o o o o o o o o o o o o o o o o o o o o o o o o o o o o o o o o o o o

Serialism and Compositional Style

Together, the centric serialism of Tavener's "The Lamb," the riddle canons of the Dallapiccola song, and the sonata-like Schoenberg piano work demonstrate that not all serial music sounds alike. Indeed, there is a greater resemblance between Schoenberg's later twelve-tone works and his early, "free" (nonserial) compositions than there is between the twelve-tone music of Schoenberg and Webern, or Webern and Berg. Twelve-tone compositional technique is independent of musical style and genre, and it can be difficult to determine by ear whether a work is serial or more freely nontonal. We close the chapter with Webern's Variations for Piano, which demonstrates a few musical features that are typical of this composer.

3.62 🎧

Listen to the second movement of this piece, at first without a score, as an introduction to the composer's style. Webern is much less likely than his teacher, Schoenberg, to write long, lyrical melodies. Instead, he opts for short movements with a succession of brief melodies, creating a tapestry of sound. One thing that stands out on a first hearing is that the movement sounds repetitive in ways that extend beyond the repeat signs of the binary form. Why, for instance, do we keep hearing the A4—a repeated pitch in the midst of so much dissonance? Other pitches stand out because of their extreme high register: the same high notes, G6 and E6, appear here and there. Listen again while following the score in your anthology, then we will begin a row analysis to see if we can find the answers to these questions.

Webern's row for the entire three-movement composition is the same, and we have already seen the row matrix in the discussion of combinatoriality above. Refer to the matrix to analyze the row forms in Example 34.2. Here are some guidelines. First, there is one row in each hand. Second, the row placement switches from one hand to the other midway through the phrase. Third, Webern employs a technique similar to phrase overlap, or elision, in this composition—that is, he chooses row forms where the last pc in one row is the same as the first pc in the next. These shared pcs he states only once, so you'll need to "count" them twice. This technique is sometimes called **row elision** (or "row linkage"). Mark the rows in the example, and number the pcs by their order number. For a retrograde row, number backward, starting with 12.

EXAMPLE 34.2: Webern, Variations for Piano, Op. 27, second movement, mm. 1–11

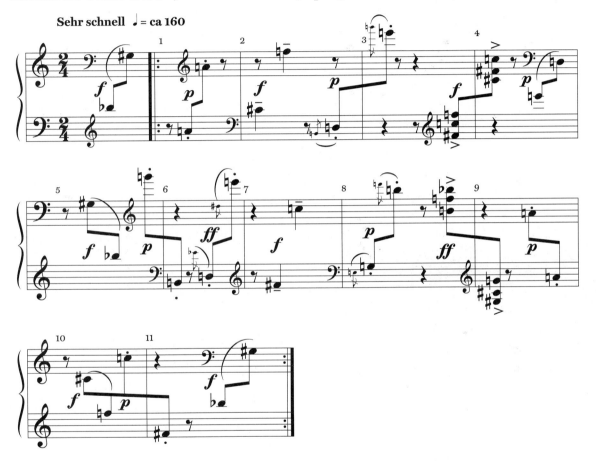

We can think of the texture as a canon between hands. The rhythms, articulations, and dynamics are identical from the left hand (the **dux**, or leader) to the right (the **comes**, or follower). This relationship swaps midway through the row (m. 5), which helps identify the point at which the rows switch from one hand to the other. The dux/comes relationship continues to swap throughout the piece, and can help you locate the rows.

It is sometimes helpful to write out the row pairs in integer notation to consider relationships of interest (just as we did for the combinatorial pairs). The rows in the first half of the movement are listed below (the pcs that are elided are given in parentheses):

R₃: <8 **9** 5 7 4 6 0 1 2 t e 3>   <(3) 4 0 2 e 1 7 8 **9** 5 6 t> Rₜ

RI₃: <t **9** 1 e 2 0 6 5 4 8 7 3>   <(3) 2 6 4 7 5 e t **9** 1 0 8> RI₈

Let's begin by exploring why we heard those repeated A4s. Webern specifically chose row forms where pc 9 appears in the same position (the same holds true for pc 3, which makes the elisions possible). In his realization of the rows, the composer highlights this relationship by writing pc 9 always in the same register, rhythm, and dynamic level, to make the repetition stand out aurally. Just as striking is the fact that every dyad (or pair of pcs) found "harmonically" between the rows is maintained as a dyad throughout the movement, and the pitches of these dyads are symmetrical around A4. Take, for instance, the dyad {8 t} with which the first

WF7

row pair begins. Search for any other pc 8 or t in the movement, and you will see that almost every pc 8 is paired with pc t. Now refer again to the score to see how Webern emphasizes this relationship: each pair is set in the same register, with the same rhythm and dynamic marking.

Another aspect of Webern's row realization may contribute to the repetitive sound of this movement: a technique called **registral invariance** (also sometimes called "frozen register" or "pitch fixation"). Over half of the pcs in Webern's row appear in one and only one register. Example 34.3 gives these pitches in their frozen, or fixed, position.

EXAMPLE 34.3: Seven pitches from Webern, Variations for Piano, Op. 27, second movement

To hear how registral invariance works, play the pitches in Example 34.3 on a piano (all together or as a rolled chord) while listening to the movement; these pitches will stand out from the rest of the texture because of their repetition as pitches (rather than pitch classes).

In *The Path to the New Music,* Webern hints at the fact that he composed rows according to certain guiding principles he was reluctant to share: "Now I'm asked, 'How did I arrive at this row?' Not arbitrarily, but according to certain secret laws." Perhaps he is referring to a system for predicting which row forms will produce the types of relationships discussed in this chapter. On the other hand, later in the same passage, Webern attributes his row composition to "inspiration."

TERMS YOU SHOULD KNOW

aggregate   hexachordal combinatoriality   row elision
all-combinatorial hexachord   order number   row matrix
dux   registral invariance   secondary set
comes   rotation

QUESTIONS FOR REVIEW

1. What is combinatoriality? What does this feature allow the composer to do in the music?
2. Is it always possible to tell if a work is serial or freely nontonal by listening?
3. After consulting your teacher, find one twelve-tone work for your own instrument. Try to identify the row and at least one transformation. Does the composer choose to align phrase structure with row forms?
4. What are some ways different composers use rows to make their compositions sound distinctive in style? (Hint: Compare the pieces by Webern, Schoenberg, Dallapiccola, and Tavener in this chapter and the previous one.)

CHAPTER 35

New Ways to Organize Rhythm, Meter, and Duration

Outline of topics covered

Rhythm and meter in early twentieth-century music
- Perceived and notated meter
- Changing meter and polymeter
- Asymmetrical meter
- Ametric music
- Additive rhythm

Rhythm and meter in post-1945 music
- Nontraditional rhythmic notation
- Serialized durations
- The Fibonacci series
- Metric modulation

Analyzing and performing contemporary rhythm and meter

Overview

In the twentieth and twenty-first centuries, composers have explored new kinds of rhythms and metrical frameworks, some of which we will consider in this chapter. We will learn how to distinguish between perceived and notated meter, and will look at new methods of notation.

Repertoire

Béla Bartók, from *Mikrokosmos*
   No. 115, "Bulgarian Rhythm" (CD 1, track 33)
   No. 133, "Syncopation"
   No. 148, "Six Dances in Bulgarian Rhythm," No. 1
Bartók, "Song of the Harvest," for two violins (CD 1, track 37)
Luciano Berio, *Sequenza III*, for voice
Pierre Boulez, *Structures Ia,* for two pianos
John Cage, *4'33"*
Elliott Carter, String Quartet No. 2
John Corigliano, "Come now, my darling," from *The Ghosts of Versailles* (CD 1, track 82)
György Ligeti, *Continuum*
Ligeti, *Hungarian Etudes*, third movement
Olivier Messiaen, "Danse de la fureur," from *Quartet for the End of Time*
Luigi Nono, *Il canto sospeso*
Igor Stravinsky, "Bransle Gay," from *Agon* (CD 3, track 46)
Stravinsky, *Les noces,* Tableau II
Edgard Varèse, *Density 21.5,* for solo flute (CD 3, track 52)
Anton Webern, Variations for Piano, Op. 27, second movement (CD 3, track 62)
La Monte Young, *Composition 1960*, No. 5

Rhythm and Meter in Early Twentieth-Century Music

In common-practice style, rhythmic patterns and notated meter reinforce each other—with a few notable exceptions, such as syncopations and hemiola, which must contrast with the regular beat to achieve their intended effect. In common-practice style, we also recognize hierarchical levels of meter, including hypermeter, that work together to reinforce the measurement of time into regular units. In the twentieth century, however, while many pieces of music conform to common-practice rhythmic and metrical conventions, others explore new ways of organizing durations, as we will see.

Perceived and Notated Meter

3.62 To begin our study of twentieth-century rhythm and meter, listen once again to the second movement of Webern's Variations for Piano, whose serial pitch and pitch-class organization we considered in Chapter 34. Listen without reference to the score, and conduct along with the music. Which conducting pattern did you select? Now look at measures 1–4, shown in Example 35.1. Although this movement is notated in $\frac{2}{4}$, most listeners would not select that pattern to conduct. What they tend to hear is a series of evenly spaced beats, with downbeats on the second note of each group of two (the G♯3 of the anacrusis, the second A4 of m. 1, the F5 of m. 2, and so on). Some listeners group these stronger pulses into measures of $\frac{3}{8}$; others may choose $\frac{6}{8}$ or another meter—but rarely $\frac{2}{4}$ as notated! This piece thus illustrates a distinction between the notated meter, $\frac{2}{4}$, and the perceived meter.

EXAMPLE 35.1: Webern, Variations for Piano, Op. 27, second movement, mm. 1–4

In common-practice compositions, the notated meter and the perceived meter are usually one and the same (with brief exceptions). If a listener perceives units other than measure units, they tend to be combinations of two or more measure units—as in hypermeter—or subdivisions when the tempo is very slow. In twentieth-century music, on the other hand, the notated meter and the perceived meter may not correspond at all. In some cases, pieces carefully notated in traditional ways may not convey a meter of any sort, while other pieces that are not notated in a traditional meter may have a clear and regular perceptible beat or meter created by the rhythmic patterns. With twentieth-century scores, what you see is not always what you hear. While the performer must attend to the music as notated, the primary metrical framework of the piece is the one perceived by the listener.

Changing Meter and Polymeter

WF1

3.46 🎧

Now we turn to Stravinsky's "Bransle Gay," from the ballet *Agon*. Many sections of the ballet, including this one, are based on old dance patterns. Listen to "Bransle Gay" twice without looking at the score: the first time, conduct along with the castanet; the second time, with the wind parts (flutes, clarinet, and bassoons). Is there always a clear meter? What conducting patterns did you choose? Did you pick the same pattern for the castanet as for the winds? (*Try it #1*)

Now look at measures 1–6, shown in Example 35.2. Stravinsky notates the first measure in ⅜, matching the castanet at the beginning. The castanet part provides a rhythmic ostinato (a repeated pattern), which continues to sound in three-beat groups throughout the passage. Then, beginning in measure 2, Stravinsky notates measures of $\frac{7}{16}$, $\frac{5}{16}$, and $\frac{7}{16}$ to match the rhythmic patterns of the wind parts. Why do you think the example is notated this way? (*Try it #2*)

EXAMPLE 35.2: Stravinsky, "Bransle Gay," from *Agon*, mm. 1–6

KEY CONCEPT

Switching between different notated meters is called **changing meter**.

Listeners can hear changing meters if the rhythms clearly articulate the metrical organization. On the other hand, the meter changes may simply be a notational feature for the convenience of the players and conductor, and may be difficult for listeners to perceive. Other terms for this kind of notation include "mixed meter," "variable meter," and "multimeter."

In Example 35.2, the castanet and wind parts imply at least two different meters: the continuing $\frac{3}{8}$ in the castanet and the changing asymmetrical patterns in the winds. When we hear two or more different meters at once, we call it **polymeter**.

KEY CONCEPT

Polymeter occurs when two or more different metric streams are heard at the same time.

The Stravinsky example illustrates both changing meter in the wind parts and polymeter in the relation between the castanet and the winds. Polymetrical passages are easiest to identify when the music is notated in two or more meters, but they may be perceived even when notated in one meter throughout all the parts. We see an example of this in Example 35.3, from Stravinsky's *Les noces*. All of the parts are notated in $\frac{2}{4}$, but the strongly accented entrances of the ostinato pattern in pianos 2 and 4 and the percussion sound like downbeats in $\frac{3}{4}$. This type of polymeter occurs when the metrical accent patterns in different lines of a composition are not aligned.

EXAMPLE 35.3: Stravinsky, *Les noces*, Tableau II, mm. 54–59

Translation: And to whom do you belong now, beautiful round curls? To the girl with red cheeks, with a name like [Nastasia].

Example 35.4 summarizes four different types of polymeter: (a) same beat unit but different measure lengths; (b) same beat unit but nonaligned measures; (c) same beat unit but different beat divisions; and (d) same beat division but different beat units. In Example 35.5, from Bartók's "Song of the Harvest," we see the possibilities of 35.4a and b combined. In measures 11–12, one part is notated in $\frac{3}{4}$ followed by $\frac{2}{4}$, while the other part has the reverse. The different metrical strands in measure 11 lead to offset measures of $\frac{3}{4}$, when the lower part begins a new measure on beat 3 of the upper part's measure. Bartók helps us perceive this polymeter by placing accents on the downbeats of many measures. These should be carefully articulated when performing the piece.

EXAMPLE 35.4: Four types of polymeter

(a)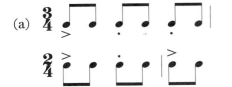

Same beat unit but different measure lengths

(c)

Same beat unit but different beat divisions

(b)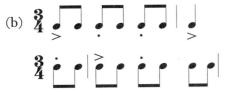

Same beat unit but nonaligned measures

(d)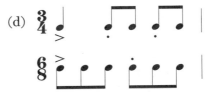

Same beat division but different beat unit

EXAMPLE 35.5: Bartók, "Song of the Harvest," mm. 11–15

In Example 35.4c, the beat divides in twos (simple meter) in one line and divides in threes (compound meter) in the other; this polymeter may be a notated or implied $\frac{2}{4}$ against $\frac{6}{8}$, for example. In Example 35.4d, the polymetric structure results in a different number of beats: three beats in simple meter against two beats in compound meter. Here, $\frac{3}{4}$ is placed against $\frac{6}{8}$, with the eighths the same duration in each meter. There are six eighth notes in each measure, but the grouping of eighths and the accent patterns differ (2 + 2 + 2 vs. 3 + 3). (In contrast, the eighths in 35.4c have different durations.)

Finally, polymeter may also be created by assigning different tempi to individual parts, as in the third movement of Ligeti's *Hungarian Etudes*. In this composition, all five choir parts are notated in $\frac{4}{4}$, but in five different tempi—quarter note equals 90, 110, 140, 160, and 190! Example 35.6 is drawn from the opening of this movement, with the entrances of the choir 1 bass section at quarter = 90 and the altos at quarter = 160. (Your class may want to discuss strategies a conductor might consider to keep the choir together!)

EXAMPLE 35.6: Ligeti, *Hungarian Etudes*, third movement, mm. 1–7

Translation

Bass: Cheap apples! Here they are in a heap. Who buys them, eats them. Cheap apples!

Alto: The dog sled runs, it races truly, truly. I am the sled master.

Asymmetrical Meter

All of the common-practice meters we have studied feature beats grouped into twos, threes, or fours; beats divided into two or three parts; and beats subdivided into four or six parts. These meters are considered **symmetrical** because the primary beats within each measure are equally spaced and each beat has a consistent number of divisions.

1.33

Listen to the opening of Bartók's "Bulgarian Rhythm" (Example 35.7a), which should be familiar to you from our discussion in Chapter 31. Try to conduct the meter as you listen. Is this a symmetrical meter? Do you conduct in equally spaced beat units? The meter signature is $\frac{5}{8}$ and a measure lasts for five eighth notes, but the primary beat unit is not the eighth note. This meter divides into two unequal "halves": the first half has three eighths, the second half only two. Thus, the beat unit is not consistent; as the left-hand part shows, the beat unit shifts between a dotted quarter and quarter note. Later in the same piece, the division reverses, as

1.34

seen in Example 35.7b: $\frac{5}{8}$ is grouped into two eighths, then three.

EXAMPLE 35.7: Bartók, "Bulgarian Rhythm," from *Mikrokosmos*

(a) Mm. 1–4

(b) Mm. 9–12

KEY CONCEPT

Asymmetrical meters are compound meters that have beat units of unequal duration. These "irregular" beat lengths are typically created by a measure with five or seven eighth notes or quarter notes at the beat-division level, which cannot group into evenly spaced beats.

For example, the five eighths of $\frac{5}{8}$ may be divided 3 + 2, 2 + 3, or even 2 + 2 + 1 (or some other combination of 2 and 1) to make beat-level durations of a quarter note and a dotted-quarter note or two quarter notes and an eighth note. The meter $\frac{5}{4}$ works the same way, creating beats of a half note and dotted-half note or two half notes and one quarter note. Like other compound meters, these meters are typically conducted at the beat level, or possibly at the beat-division level if the tempo is slow. Other common asymmetrical meter signatures are $\frac{7}{4}$ and $\frac{7}{8}$, which may divide 2 + 2 + 3, 3 + 2 + 2, 2 + 2 + 2 + 1, and so on. Less common signatures include $\frac{11}{8}$, $\frac{13}{8}$, $\frac{5}{16}$, and $\frac{7}{16}$.

Sometimes, when the same division groupings run through several measures, the composer will indicate the subdivisions in the meter signature, as shown in Example 35.8. Play these measures at the keyboard to hear the grouping. In this meter signature, the upper numbers indicate the subdivisions within the measure, such as $\frac{4 + 2 + 3}{8}$. The signature could have read $\frac{9}{8}$ (the sum of 4 + 2 + 3), but that would have not shown the groupings and subdivisions, which differ from the expected 3 + 3 + 3.

EXAMPLE 35.8: Bartók, "Six Dances in Bulgarian Rhythm," from *Mikrokosmos*, No. 1, mm. 1–2

Asymmetrical meters can be heard as transformations of symmetrical meters—that is, listeners may interpret $\frac{5}{8}$ as a $\frac{6}{8}$ that is missing an eighth, or as a $\frac{2}{4}$ with a "hiccup." When performing these meters, observe the groupings carefully and make slight accents at the beginning of groups. When meters include an upper number of 5 or 7, avoid holding the last note in the measure too long, making $\frac{5}{8}$

sound like $\frac{6}{8}$, or $\frac{7}{8}$ like $\frac{4}{4}$. You may need to practice counting the beat divisions in groups, beginning each group with an accented number 1 ("$\overset{>}{1}$-2-3, $\overset{>}{1}$-2" or "$\overset{>}{1}$-2, $\overset{>}{1}$-2, $\overset{>}{1}$-2-3") until the patterns are familiar and you can feel the proper accentuation of the unequal beat units.

Meters that are usually considered symmetrical may be divided asymmetrically, as we saw in Example 35.8, where "$\frac{9}{8}$" was divided $\frac{4 + 2 + 3}{8}$. Example 35.9 shows several measures of another Bartók piece from *Mikrokosmos*, "Syncopation." This passage features a changing meter pattern alternating $\frac{5}{4}$, an asymmetrical meter, with $\frac{4}{4}$, usually a symmetrical meter. Play the excerpt at the piano. How are the beats divided in each measure? (*Try it #3*) In this example, the $\frac{4}{4}$ meter is treated like the $\frac{5}{4}$, with asymmetrical groupings in each. In some pieces with such rhythms, you see a signature of $\frac{8}{8}$ instead of $\frac{4}{4}$. Other meters, such as $\frac{3}{4}$, $\frac{9}{8}$, and $\frac{12}{8}$, may also be treated like asymmetrical meters.

EXAMPLE 35.9: Bartók, "Syncopation," from *Mikrokosmos*, mm. 1–4

Ametric Music

3.52 | WF2

Listen now to Varèse's *Density 21.5* without the score, and conduct along. What do you observe about the meter in this piece? Is there a clear, even beat? (*Try it #4*) Look at measures 1–17, shown in Example 35.10. The score is notated in a regular common-time (**c**) meter. Although the piece sounds as if it is played with a lot of rubato, or flexibility in the tempo, the performer is given the following instructions: "Always [play] strictly in time—follow metronomic indications."

How do the rhythms in this piece avoid articulating a clear, consistent meter? And how does Varèse achieve the sense of tempo variation through a score that is so precisely notated? Explore these questions by marking the example with the location of each beat, then conducting in a quadruple meter while listening to the music again, this time following the score. Circle the places where the beginning of a rhythmic idea lines up with a notated beat.

EXAMPLE 35.10: Varèse, *Density 21.5*, mm. 1–17

Several prominent rhythms do line up with beats; for example, the initial motive (F4–E4–F♯4) and its repetition in measure 3 fall on notated beats. That motive and its repetition do not reinforce a sense of meter, however, since the first presentation begins on beat 1 and the repetition starts on beat 4. Two related motives, in measures 9 and 15, do appear on beat 1, like the original motive.

While common-practice composers tend to limit the number of different rhythmic patterns in a piece, we see no such limitation here. How many different rhythmic patterns do you find in this piece? Locate rhythms that imply a duple (or quadruple) subdivision of the quarter-note beat, and others that imply a triple subdivision. (*Try it #5*)

As you have probably discovered, many of the rhythms in this piece do not line up neatly with the notated beats. Some notes are tied over to the following beat, or through several beats, with a new pitch entering in the middle of a beat unit. If there were a strong sense of beat in an accompaniment or other instrumental part, or if the solo flute had established a clear, regular pulse, these tied-over notes would sound syncopated against the established beat. But because there is no regular pulse in this music—or perhaps because there are too many implied meters not corresponding to a consistent beat unit, each lasting only a brief time—the effect is one of no perceived meter.

WF3

KEY CONCEPT

In some twentieth-century music notated in the traditional manner, rhythmic patterns may conflict with the notated meter and resist alignment into regular beat and accent patterns. If there is no meter perceived, the music is said to be **ametric**. Ametric music may also be notated in nontraditional ways.

Additive Rhythm

One method of generating a series of durations that sounds ametrical is known as **additive rhythm**. That is, instead of conceiving of rhythm in terms of a beat unit with divisions and subdivisions, we instead begin with a small unit (often a sixteenth note or smaller) and add these small durations together to create larger, ametric rhythm patterns. This type of rhythm is typically notated without a meter.

One composer who is well known for his additive rhythms is Olivier Messiaen. Look now at the rhythm in Example 35.11, drawn from "Danse de la fureur" ("Dance of Fury"), a movement scored for piano, cello, B♭ clarinet, and violin from the *Quartet for the End of Time*. Most obvious are the absence of a meter signature and the irregular durations of the melody notes (doubled in octaves). Among the elements that help Messiaen to achieve this rhythmic structure are ties and what the composer calls "dots of addition." For example, in measure 27, the durations are dotted eighth, quarter tied to a sixteenth, half note, quarter tied to a sixteenth, and dotted eighth. The dotted eighths and the ties keep the rhythm from falling into metric regularity. Try tapping the rhythm of this passage, or chanting the rhythm on a neutral syllable like "tah." When you first read it through, you may need to count in sixteenth notes: for measure 27, 1-2-3, 1-2-3-4-5, 1-2-3-4-5-6-7-8, and so on. After it becomes familiar, you should be able to feel the durations in larger note values.

EXAMPLE 35.11: Messiaen, "Danse de la fureur," from *Quartet for the End of Time*, mm. 27–31

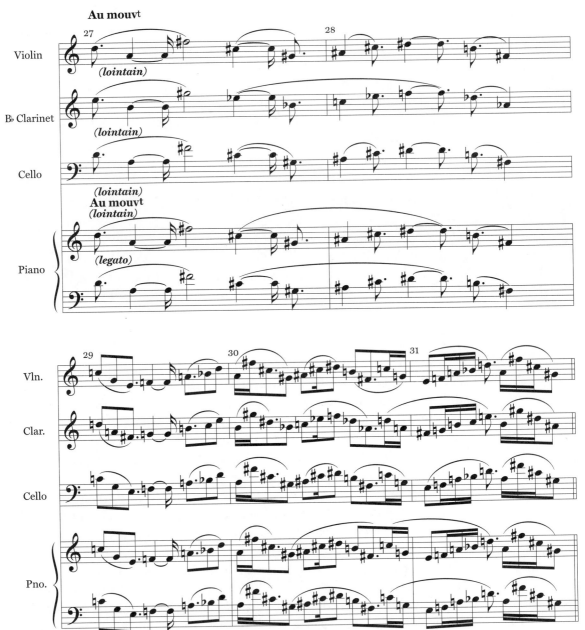

Another interesting rhythmic technique is at work in this excerpt as well. Consider each measure a one-bar unit. Compare the first duration of the measure with the last, then the second with the next-to-last, until you reach a single duration that stands at the center. Every measure of this excerpt is a palindrome—the same going backward and forward. Rhythms like these are another example of Messiaen's delight in the "charm of impossibilities"—it is impossible to run this

`WF4` rhythm in reverse order, since the result is the same as the original rhythm.

○ ○

Rhythm and Meter in Post-1945 Music

In the early twentieth century, there was a tendency toward precise and careful notation of every musical parameter: durations were indicated exactly, with as many ties or dots as needed, dynamic markings were abundant (in some cases provided for individual notes), articulations were carefully specified. While conveying the composer's intention, however, these practices when taken to an extreme made scores difficult to perform because of the need to pay attention to so many details.

Nontraditional Rhythmic Notation

The two decades after World War II were marked by an intense exploration of compositional methods, including new approaches to rhythm, meter, durations, and their notation. Example 35.12, a score for solo voice by Luciano Berio, is an example of **time-line notation**. In this system, the passing of time is measured out in the number of seconds elapsed between markers (10 seconds, 20 seconds, and so on), and the musical events take place between the markers, resulting in ametrical rhythms. This piece, *Sequenza III* (1966), illustrates an innovative notation of pitch as well. This type of score, where both pitch and duration are indicated with nonstandard symbols, is called **graphic notation**. It may seem to be an imprecise method of communicating musical information to the performer, but a comparison of performances of the Berio score reveals remarkable consistencies—results almost as similar as performances generated by scores with highly detailed traditional notation.

EXAMPLE 35.12: Berio, *Sequenza III*, for voice, first staff

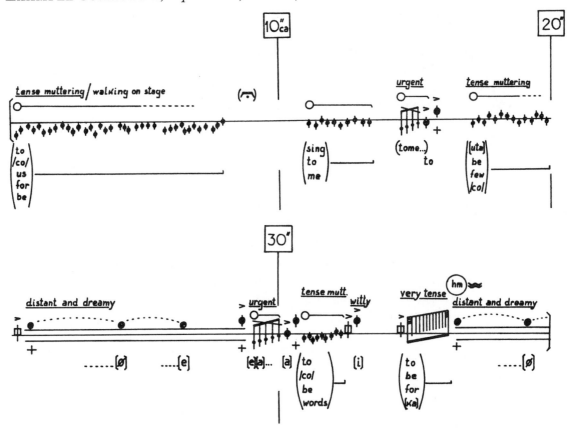

In other works, you may see pitches specified exactly, but without precise durations. For example, a group of pitches may be notated in a box, with instructions to play them in any order and as fast as possible or with durations of the performer's choosing. Another variation of this idea is Witold Lutosławski's aleatoric counterpoint, which gives the ordering of pitches but leaves the durations of individual pitches to the performer. Other scores, including works by Morton Feldman, show note heads with horizontal lines extending from them to indicate that the pitch is held for a long time.

Some pieces composed during the second half of the twentieth century are characterized by **text notation** (or "text scores"): instructions for performing the piece are written out in prose or poetry, without any traditional musical notation. Some of these pieces explore the edges of musical performance—extremes of dynamics or instrument ranges, elements of noise, or even dance or drama. Some works indicate that a passage or a rhythmic pattern is to be played "as fast as possible" or a pitch is to be sustained "as long as possible." Sometimes the sounds produced in such compositions are very soft, like the sounds butterflies make in La Monte Young's *Composition 1960*, No. 5, shown in Example 35.13.

EXAMPLE 35.13: Young, *Composition 1960*, No. 5

Turn a butterfly (or any number of butterflies) loose in the performance area.

When the composition is over, be sure to allow the butterfly to fly away outside.

The composition may be any length, but if an unlimited amount of time is available, the doors and windows may be opened before the butterfly is turned loose and the composition may be considered finished when the butterfly flies away.

The entire score of John Cage's *4'33"* is shown in Example 35.14; in this composition, no sounds at all are notated for the performer (the durations for the three movements are to total four minutes and thirty-three seconds, but the performer's part is marked "Tacet"). This work raised awareness of, and appreciation for, the role of silence in music, as well as appreciation for the role of environmental sounds as music.

EXAMPLE 35.14: Cage, *4'33"*

I
Tacet

II
Tacet

III
Tacet

You may also encounter variants on traditional rhythmic notation—for example, meter signatures with a duration symbol rather than a lower number (such as 4 over a dotted quarter instead of $\frac{12}{8}$). Other pieces, such as György Ligeti's *Continuum* (1967), stick with simple and traditional notation but create new effects nevertheless. Look at the opening of *Continuum* in Example 35.15. Here, all durations are eighth notes, but they combine to produce complex and detailed rhythmic interactions, which gradually change as the piece progresses. There are no traditional bar lines, but Ligeti does provide dotted lines as a visual reference. We will consider these "measures" in order to pinpoint particular moments in the score.

Play through this passage slowly at the keyboard (Ligeti's tempo is "extremely fast, so that individual tones can hardly be perceived, but rather merge into a continuum"). You will hear that the work opens with a two-note minor-third pattern in both hands. In measure 10, the pattern changes in the right hand; it is enlarged to a three-note set spanning a perfect fourth. The interplay of a three-note pattern against a two-note creates an unsettling rhythmic effect. The next change comes in measure 15: now each hand plays a three-note pattern, but the patterns are offset by one eighth note. Play the rest of the passage again, and use your ears to find the remaining pattern changes. Mark these in your score. (*Try it #6*)

As the work proceeds, the length and starting point of patterns continue to change and occasionally become aligned again. In measures 21–22, for example, the patterns are realigned—now in five-note sets in contrary motion. Where patterns align like this, we hear clear accents.

EXAMPLE 35.15: Ligeti, *Continuum*, "measures" 1–22

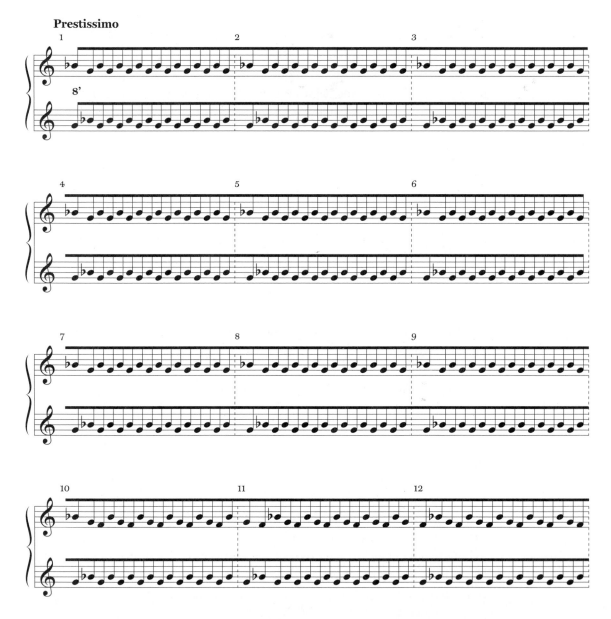

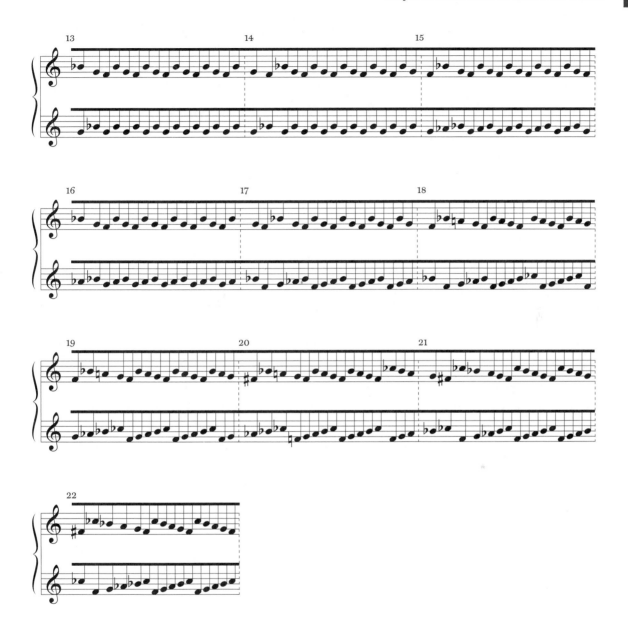

Serialized Durations

At the same time that graphic notation and text scores were being explored by some composers—as a way to make rhythmic notation more flexible or to reduce the composer's control over the durations of sounds—other composers who wanted precise control of durations, articulations, and dynamics continued the trend toward extreme detail in traditional notation. One significant development in the

1950s and early 1960s was the extension of serial procedures to dimensions other than pitch—a procedure referred to as **total serialism**, or **integral serialism**. In a groundbreaking experimental piece from the 1950s, *Structures 1a* (for two pianos), Pierre Boulez serialized not only pitch classes, but also durations, articulation, and dynamics. Pitch-class rows were paired with duration rows, and each section of the work was assigned a dynamic level and articulation type from an ordered series of dynamics and articulations.

EXAMPLE 35.16: Boulez, *Structures Ia*

(a) Mm. 24–31 (piano 2)

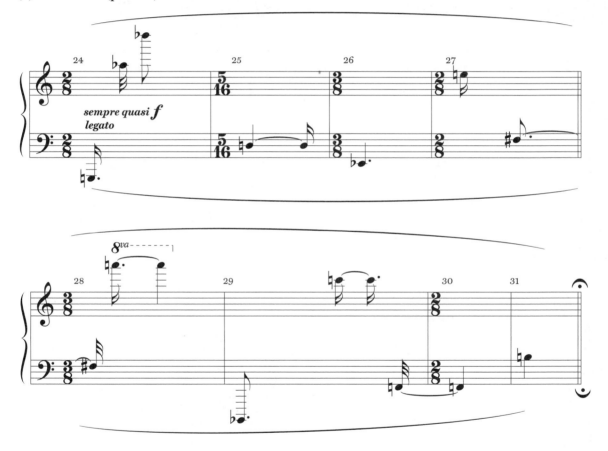

(b) Pitch-class series

Duration series (each number represents the duration in thirty-second notes)

(c) Articulation sequence

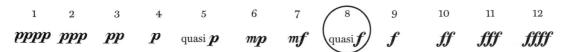

Dynamic sequence

1	2	3	4	5	6	7	8	9	10	11	12
pppp	*ppp*	*pp*	*p*	quasi *p*	*mp*	*mf*	(quasi *f*)	*f*	*ff*	*fff*	*ffff*

(d) Articulations (one level per section)

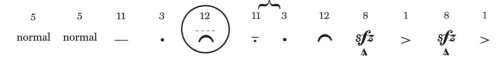

Dynamics (one level per section)

5	2	2	8	8	12	12	8	8	2	2	5
quasi *p*	*ppp*	*ppp*	quasi *f*	(quasi *f*)	*ffff**	*ffff**	quasi *f*	quasi *f*	*ppp*	*ppp*	quasi *p*

Look at the score excerpt in Example 35.16a, drawn from the fourth section of the work. Only piano 2 is playing here, from the pitch-class and duration series shown in part b. In the score, the pitch-class series appears as shown in part b, and the duration series is in retrograde form. How are the articulations and dynamics of this passage related to Boulez's serial design? First the composer created ordered sequences of these elements (for example, from very soft to very loud) and numbered each from 1 to 12. These are shown in part c; part d shows the serial ordering Boulez chose for the entire work (derived from the diagonals in his row matrices). Now refer back to the piano score in part a. This section is notated *legato* and *quasi forte*, corresponding to the fifth position in the articulation and dynamic series (circled in part d). The articulation number 12 and dynamic number 8 refer to their place in the sequence of twelve possible articulations and dynamics. The next section of the work uses the sixth position (11 and 12) in these series.

The Fibonacci Series

Boulez's duration series (Example 35.16b) shows one way composers can create ametric rhythms: by "adding up" small durations, like thirty-second notes or sixteenths, into a series of longer note values. Composers generally make a precompositional decision to determine how to structure such rhythms.

In *Structures Ia*, Boulez's durations were achieved by serial principles. Other types of manipulations of durations are possible as well. In *Il canto sospeso*, Luigi Nono selected durations for the eight choral parts based on the **Fibonacci series**—an infinite series of numbers in which each new member of the series is the sum of the previous two. (If we begin the series with 1, it runs 1 1 2 3 5 8 13 21 34, and so on.) Look at Example 35.17 to see how this works in a short passage for sopranos and altos. Nono assigned each part a basic duration; these are shown to the right of the example. All durations in the passage were then determined by multiplying the basic duration by one of the Fibonacci numbers: 1, 2, 3, 5, 8, or 13. In the first soprano line, for example, the first duration (a dotted eighth) is a sixteenth multiplied by 3; the second duration is a sixteenth multiplied by 13. Follow each of the other lines to verify the duration.

EXAMPLE 35.17: Nono, *Il canto sospeso*, mm. 108–109 (soprano and alto parts)

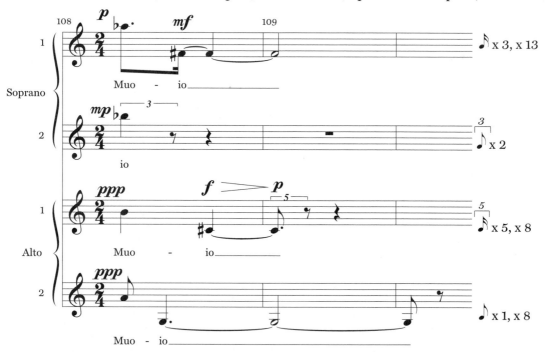

Translation: I am dying.

Musical applications of the Fibonacci series are not limited to the post–1945 time period—Bartók drew on the series to locate significant events in several pieces (see, for example, the first movement of *Music for Strings, Percussion, and Celeste*, where important events enter in measures that match Fibonacci numbers). He was also fond of using asymmetrical meters with Fibonacci numbers as the upper value, such as $\frac{5}{8}$, $\frac{8}{8}$, and $\frac{13}{8}$. The Fibonacci series may determine the length of phrases or sections or the placement of climactic moments in a piece. There is a connection to music of even earlier eras as well. Pairs of adjacent Fibonacci numbers converge (as the infinite series continues) toward a proportion associated with balance in artworks since Greek antiquity, known as the **golden section**. This proportion, about 62 percent (.618) of the total length of a piece or section, has been shown to be significant in music of previous centuries. For example, in many Classical sonatas, the recapitulation begins about 62 percent of the way through the movement.

Metric Modulation

1.82 🎧

We turn now to a recent composition, John Corigliano's 1991 opera *The Ghosts of Versailles*. Listen to the duet "Come now, my darling," sung by mezzo-soprano Cherubino and soprano Rosina—characters borrowed from Mozart's *The Marriage of Figaro*. (Corigliano's work features an "opera within an opera.") While this duet draws its inspiration from Mozart, its tonal and rhythmic language are decidedly of our own time. In the opening section, beginning at measure 19, we see and hear changing meters and find that Cherubino is characterized by primarily stolid eighth-note motion in simple meters. Rosina (whom he is trying to seduce) sings of her fear and anger in contrasting broad quarter-note triplets. Once she gives in to the seduction (m. 50), however, the meter stabilizes in simple-quadruple meter and the two sing without rhythmic conflict.

Example 35.18 shows measures 58–66, near the close of the duet. Listen to the passage again, focusing on the effect of the small rhythmic notations above the staff at the end of measures 60 and 61. This first notation, triplet quarter note = triplet eighth note, changes nothing in the rhythm except for the notation of the beat unit. The duration that was once notated as a quarter is simply renotated as an eighth. But what of the next notation, triplet eighth note = "regular" eighth note? In this instance, the triplet subdivision is reinterpreted (like a "pivot" duration) as an eighth note, which speeds up the beat unit and tempo. (In measures 60–62, try tapping the piano right-hand rhythm with your right hand and the beat unit with your left, to feel the tempo change.) This type of rhythmic change is called a **metric modulation**. Metric modulation is more accurately a tempo modulation—a means of smoothing what would otherwise be abrupt changes of tempo by introducing subdivisions or groups of beats in the first tempo that match durations in the new one. The new tempo is recognized in retrospect, much like a modulation by pivot chord.

EXAMPLE 35.18: Corigliano, "Come now, my darling," from *The Ghosts of Versailles*, mm. 58–66

The composer most often associated with metric modulation is Elliott Carter. Example 35.19, from his String Quartet No. 2, illustrates the technique in a characteristic way. The quartet begins with a tempo of quarter = 105. In measure 9, performers need to think about the cello's sixteenth-note subdivisions of the beat as though they are grouped into threes, to make accurate dotted-eighth durations (violin 2) in measure 10. This dotted-eighth pulse is then renotated in the next section at a tempo of quarter = 140. Between measures 9 and 10, we see sixteenth = sixteenth, which tells us that the dotted eighths in measure 10 should be equal in duration to three sixteenths with no change (yet) in the duration of those sixteenths or, by extension, of the tempo. But the notation between measures 10 and 11, dotted eighth = quarter, tells us that the duration that was formerly notated as a dotted eighth is now to be represented as a quarter note, thus speeding up the tempo. This makes the quarter note = 140 tempo in measure 11 faster by one-third than the quarter note = 105 in measure 9, but smooths the change from one to the other.

EXAMPLE 35.19: Carter, String Quartet No. 2, mm. 7–13

The pieces presented above represent only a small sampling of the variety of treatments of rhythm, meter, and duration in post–1945 avant-garde composition. Tape-recording equipment, synthesizers, computers, and MIDI sequencers have made it possible for composers to execute levels of rhythmic complexity and exact control over durations, articulations, and dynamics that would not be possible with human performers. On the other hand, performances of **indeterminate pieces**—compositions including graphic notation, text notation, and other methods that rely on the performer's choices—may vary substantially in their rhythmic and durational details from performance to performance. Interestingly, to the listener who does not know what the scores look like, the pieces with extremely detailed traditional notation or precise electronic control of pitch, durations, articulation, and dynamics often sound similar in their rhythm to those with indeterminate notation.

Analyzing and Performing Contemporary Rhythm and Meter

When considering rhythm and meter in an unfamiliar piece of contemporary music, begin by doing a "beat check": while listening, tap your foot along with the music to determine whether there is a regular underlying pulse. If you perceive one, consider whether the beats fall into any sort of regular groupings. Listen to determine whether individual strata of the music have different metrical implications. Remember that the notated meter may not correspond to the perceived meter.

An important way that listeners relate to music is to move to it: tap their feet, clap their hands, conduct along, dance, or otherwise feel the beat of the music in their bodies. Listeners new to contemporary music may be frustrated by the lack of a regular beat and metrical organization, perhaps even more than by the lack of functional tonality. But if you listen to an ametrical piece until it becomes familiar, you may learn to feel more comfortable with the treatment of time in absence of a continuous beat or regular metrical organization.

When you perform contemporary music that uses traditional notation, you should execute the rhythms as precisely as possible. You may have to work carefully with a sequence of durations to get the timing exactly right, and also with the meter (if present) to get the metric accents correct. Familiarity and careful practice are key. Passages in a piece without a clear metrical framework may have to be practiced longer than a similarly difficult passage in a metrical piece before it feels secure. For post–1945 pieces with unusual notation, composers often provide an explanation of the notation in "Notes for Performance" either in the individual parts or in the score. As with any piece of music you are preparing for performance, it is essential to understand all of the score notation to realize the piece correctly. These pieces can be very interesting to play—don't let unfamiliar notation keep you from learning a new work!

TERMS YOU SHOULD KNOW

additive rhythm	graphic notation	symmetrical meter
ametric	indeterminate	text notation
asymmetrical meter	integral serialism	time-line notation
changing meter	metric modulation	total serialism
Fibonacci series	polymeter	

QUESTIONS FOR REVIEW

1. What are typical characteristics of common-practice meters?
2. How do rhythmic patterns reinforce the perception of a meter? What is the role of metrical accent in the perception of a meter?
3. Is it possible to have changing meter and polymeter at the same time?
4. How are asymmetrical meters similar to traditional compound meters? How are they different?
5. How do durations, rhythm, and notated meter interact to make a piece that sounds ametric?
6. How would you recognize a passage that features additive rhythms? Which composer is this technique associated with?
7. How does metric modulation work? Which composer is this technique associated with?
8. In music for your own instrument, find one piece with changing meter, one with an asymmetrical meter, and one with polymeter. How can the date of composition help you locate a piece of each type?
9. In music for your own instrument, find one piece with graphic notation or text notation. How can the date of composition help you locate a piece of each type? (Ask your teacher for help with questions 8 and 9 if necessary.)

New Ways to Articulate Musical Form

CHAPTER 36

Outline of topics covered

Form in post-common-practice music

- Sectional forms
- Form and register
- Substitutes for tonal function

New approaches to traditional musical forms

- Repetition forms in nontonal music
- Canon and imitation

New developments in musical form

- Form as process
- Moment form and mobile form
- Indeterminacy and chance

Analyzing form in recent music

Overview

In this chapter, we examine new approaches to musical form in compositions written after the common-practice era. We will learn to listen for phrases and sections in pieces that lack functional tonality, and discover how to represent new types of form in our analyses.

Repertoire

Béla Bartók, *Bagatelle*, Op. 6, No. 2 (CD 1, track 26)

György Ligeti, *Ten Pieces for Wind Quintet*, ninth movement

Ligeti, "Wenn aus die Ferne," from *Three Fantasies on Texts by Friedrich Hölderlin*

Kenneth Maue, *In the Woods*

Krzysztof Penderecki, *Threnody for the Victims of Hiroshima* (CD 3, track 1)

Steve Reich, *Piano Phase* (CD 3, track 11)

Terry Riley, *In C*

Karlheinz Stockhausen, *Klavierstück XI*

Anton Webern, String Quartet, Op. 5, fourth movement (CD 3, track 57)

o o o o o o o o o o o o o o o o o o o o o o o o o o o o o o o o o o o o o o o o o o o o o o o o o o

Form in Post-Common-Practice Music

Musical form in many compositions written after the common-practice era can be thought of as an adaptation of the traditional ideas of form we studied in Chapters 23, 26, 27, and 28. Indeed, the skills you have developed for hearing form in tonal music should help you listen for form in the nontonal compositions we consider in this chapter. Here, we will learn how musical elements that play supporting roles in defining form in tonal pieces—contrasts in range, register, timbre, dynamics, motivic content, articulation, and durations—may work together to create form in pieces without tonal cadences. Collections, sets, rows, and nontriadic chords may also take the place of tonal keys, modulation, and triads to help define formal sections. In recent works, older compositional methods like canon and imitation are finding a place, and new structural elements, such as symmetry, are helping to articulate form.

We will examine formal processes on several levels, from the organization of materials into phrases and sections to the overall structure of a work. While most common-practice works have a hierarchical formal organization, not all later works do. Each piece you study will have to be approached on its own terms.

Sectional Forms

3.1 🎧

We begin by listening to the first large section (up to rehearsal number 25) of a piece by Krzysztof Penderecki, originally called simply *Piece for 52 Strings* but best known as *Threnody for the Victims of Hiroshima*. Listen to this excerpt several times without reference to the score, and think about where you hear formal divisions. Do you hear distinct subsections? How are they articulated? How does Penderecki create closure at the end of the excerpt?

Now look at the score in your anthology from the beginning to rehearsal number 10. This piece is written with graphic notation developed by Penderecki (similar to the time-line notation described in Chapter 35). The number of seconds between rehearsal numbers (the dotted vertical lines, like bar lines) is provided at the bottom of the score. The string parts are notated with symbols explained in a key on the first page: the little triangles pointing up mean to play the highest note possible on the instrument, and the wavy lines indicate the presence and intensity of vibrato. The other symbols seen after rehearsal number 6 indicate sound effects, as listed on the first page. After the imitative entrances at the beginning of the piece, the effect is of one large mass of sound, rather than of individual instruments. The sound quality up to rehearsal 10 changes smoothly, with one type of sound eliding to the next.

Listen to the whole excerpt again. How does the music up to rehearsal number 10 connect to the music that follows? Where do you hear the next division? (*Try it #1*)

3.3 Now look at the score for rehearsal numbers 10–18. The graphic notation here depicts what the music sounds like, with the black pitch clusters expanding and then contracting. The outer boundaries of the clusters are notated exactly, but the players must listen carefully to fill in their portion of the space in between and to coordinate the creation of the musical shape. In rehearsal numbers 15–16, the score specifies the pitches for each player within the cluster. Many listeners will hear each of these clusters as an individual phrase—with a starting point, midpoint, and close—even though each cluster is elided with the entry of the next. The subsection is unified and characterized by these elisions and by the sonic similarity of the pitch clusters. Closure at the end of the section is achieved by the *glissandi* in opposing directions, which make a cadential gesture, and by the entrance of the next contrasting subsection.

The third subsection begins with individual, pointillistic entrances at rehearsal number 18. The score indicates the exact pitches and order of entry for each instru-

3.4 ment with an "arrowhead" notation. Listen again to 18–25. How does Penderecki create a sense of an ending in rehearsal 25? (*Try it #2*)

The close of this first large section draws on elements that, in tonal music, would typically support a tonal cadence: a closing of range, a thinner texture, softer dynamics, arrival on a point of rest, and silence. When these elements are combined in contemporary pieces, they can create closure as definitive as any in tonal music, even without functional harmony. The end of this section is also confirmed by the entrance of contrasting music at rehearsal number 26 (not shown), the beginning of the second large section.

The problem with identifying formal divisions in nontonal music is that we have no standard system of "markers" (such as tonal cadences) used by all composers in the time period. The key to identifying phrases and sectional design in unfamiliar nontonal pieces is listening. We need to listen to become familiar with the piece, and then decide whether it has some sort of sectional structure. If you followed the instructions above carefully, you should have listened to the first section of *Threnody* five or more times, enough to begin hearing its sectional form. If, after repeated listening to a nontonal composition that is new to you, you hear a musical gesture that creates for you the same effect as a phrase, cadence, or sectional division would in tonal music—trust your ears! Then take the next step: try to explain how and why the gesture conveys that musical function.

Form and Register

1.26 🎧

In *Threnody*, range and register play important roles in creating form: sections open with an expansion of range, while phrases and sectional closure are created when that range shrinks to a unison or when string clusters *glissando* in opposing directions. Composers writing in a variety of styles use similar techniques to create formal divisions. Listen now to Bartók's *Bagatelle*, Op. 6, No. 2, while following the score in your anthology. Mark in the score where you hear sectional divisions, and consider why you hear a division there.

This little *Bagatelle* begins with an ostinato Ab4-Bb4 in the right hand, as shown in Example 36.1a. The left hand moves outward by half steps from the pitches of the ostinato, making a wedge shape. Most listeners hear this first section as ending on the downbeat of measure 7—why? (*Try it #3*) Using traditional labeling, we will call measures 1–7a section **A**. This section consists of a single long phrase.

EXAMPLE 36.1: Bartók, *Bagatelle*, Op. 6, No. 2

(a) Mm. 1–7

You may have found the wedge and the relationship between the hands easier to hear than to see; the traditional notation disguises the hands' overlapping range and half-step voice-leading. In contrast, Penderecki's graphic score for *Threnody* clearly shows the expansions and contractions in range and register. It is sometimes helpful when analyzing pieces in traditional notation to transcribe the work into a graph, to help show how range and texture work together to shape musical form.

One example is a **pitch-time graph**. This is easy to construct, either by using the piano-roll notation on a MIDI sequencing program or by hand on graph paper. On a piece of graph paper, plot pitches on the y-axis (vertically, to show the pitch range from high to low) and the passage of time on the x-axis (horizontally). Example 36.1b shows a sample analytical graph of measures 1–7a of the *Bagatelle*. Each square on the vertical axis represents one pitch of the equally tempered chromatic scale; each square on the horizontal axis represents one eighth note duration (the smallest duration in this passage). The shading represents the "voices": the right-hand ostinato is lighter, while the pitches of the left-hand wedge are darker. The **pitch symmetry** around the silent A4 (the note in between the A♭4 and B♭4 of the ostinato) and the interaction of the hand parts are clearly visible in the graph.

(b) Pitch/time graph of mm. 1–7a

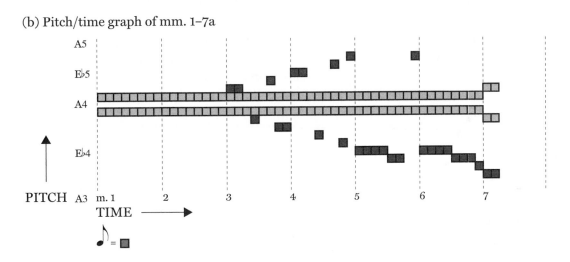

Substitutes for Tonal Function

The section **A** material returns later in the *Bagatelle*. Check your anthology score and listen to the piece again—where does it return? (*Try it #4*) What is different? You may have noticed in measures 18–20 that the repeated dyad is D4-E4 (with E♭4 as its center), and that the wedge is centered on a silent E♭5: the ostinato has moved down a tritone, while the wedge has moved up a tritone. We can refer to measures 18–23 as **A′** to show its relation to the opening section.

1.32 🎧

In measures 24–30, **A** returns as the center of the symmetries, but now in three octaves. We hear the wedge in the left hand, symmetrical around A3, and we hear the A♭–B♭ dyad with A5 as its center. The center of these two symmetries is A4. Because of the octave duplications, we might consider this a pitch-class center. We label measures 24–30 **A″**; they feature a return of the original pitch-class center, but the range has expanded outward a tritone from the E♭4/E♭5 of the previous section.

The overall form of this *Bagatelle* is thus **A B A′ A″**. In some ways, however, it also resembles a ternary form: the first section (mm. 1–7) and the last (18–30) are similar in material, while the middle section (mm. 7–18) is contrasting. What is the function of measures 15–18? (*Try it #5*)

1.28 🎧
1.30 🎧

In some nontonal music, composers use the tritone interval in a way analogous to the tonic-dominant perfect fifth of tonal pieces. In the *Bagatelle*, the motion from A4 as a center of symmetry to pitch-class E♭ and back to pitch-class A can be thought of as replacing the traditional motion from tonic to the key of the dominant and back to tonic. This use of the tritone is called a **tritone axis** (as the traditional motion is called the "tonic-dominant axis"). In Bartók's music, a primary tritone axis (such as A–E♭ here) may be supplemented by a secondary axis. For an A–E♭ primary axis, the secondary axis would be C–F♯, so that the octave is divided into four equal parts by minor thirds: C–A–F♯–E♭. The relationships between this type of axis and other materials in his music, such as the octatonic collection, should be readily apparent. For good examples of a tritone axis in a larger work, see Bartók's *Music for Strings, Percussion, and Celeste* or Sonata for Two Pianos and Percussion. Music analyst Erno Lendvai has written extensively on these two pieces and developed an entire system of analysis for Bartók's "axis tonality."

○ ○

New Approaches to Traditional Musical Forms

Repetition Forms in Nontonal Music

In earlier chapters, we learned that form in tonal music is defined by contrasting key areas and by the repetition of motives, phrases, and sections. In music without tonality, some composers have devised nontonal materials that substitute for familiar elements of functional tonal form. The tritone axis substituting for the tonic-dominant axis (a technique primarily associated with Bartók) is one example. In addition, some composers use contrasting sets or collections—or contrasting transpositions of scales—to carry out the formal function that contrasting keys would perform in a tonal piece.

3.57 🎧

An example of this technique is found in the fourth movement of Webern's String Quartet, Op. 5. Listen to this movement at least twice, and take note of the form. As you listen, keep in mind the ways we have seen pieces structured by other composers in the twentieth century. In particular, try to hear how Webern creates a contrasting section by means of timbre and texture, and also by means of contrasting set classes.

The movement opens with two shimmering *am Steg* (on the bridge) *tremolo* chords played by the violins (set classes 4-8 [0 1 5 6] and 4-9 [0 1 6 7]), set off by a cello "foghorn," as shown in Example 36.2a. The *pizzicato* chord in measure 2, which has the same pitch content as the first "shimmer" chord, also belongs to SC 4-8. The second shimmer chord is arpeggiated into a melody in measure 3, which is passed in canonic fashion first to the second violin (transposed down a perfect fifth), then to the cello (down three octaves) in measure 4. The cello then continues in measures 5–6 with a canonic imitation of the first violin. Listen again to hear these features.

EXAMPLE 36.2: Webern, String Quartet, Op. 5, fourth movement

(a) Mm. 1–6

3.61 The texture of the opening returns in measures 11–13, as do many of the pitch-class sets (see Example 36.2b) and even a melody. The first violin's ordered pcset <0 5 1 0> of measures 4–5 also returns in measures 11–12, transposed up an octave in the viola and violin 2 parts. Thus, if we label the opening section (mm. 1–6) **A**, we could label measures 11–13 **A′**. The entire texture in measures 11–12 (through the *pizzicato* chord) forms SC 8-8 [0 1 2 3 4 7 8 9], the abstract complement of the **A** section's SC 4-8. (Remember, "abstract" complements are those that demonstrate literal complementation only after they are transposed: SC 4-8 when transposed to [5 6 t e] is the complement of SC 8-8 [0 1 2 3 4 7 8 9].) The *pizzicato* chord in measure 12 itself belongs to SC 4-9, circled and labeled in the example. These set classes—4-8, 4-9, 8-8, and others of the opening and closing measures— are rich in tritones and semitones, creating a dissonant tapestry of sound typical of Webern's compositions. If you were to undertake a thorough analysis of these two passages, you would find that the pitch-class sets marked in Examples 36.2a and b represent only a few of the sets shared by the **A** and **A′** sections.

(b) Mm. 7–13

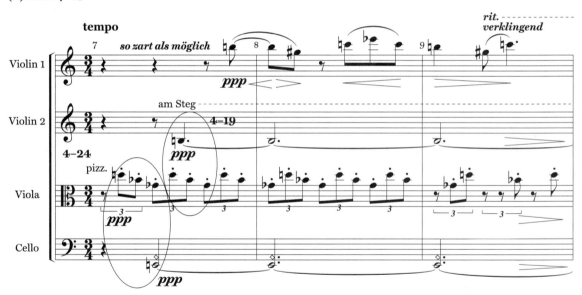

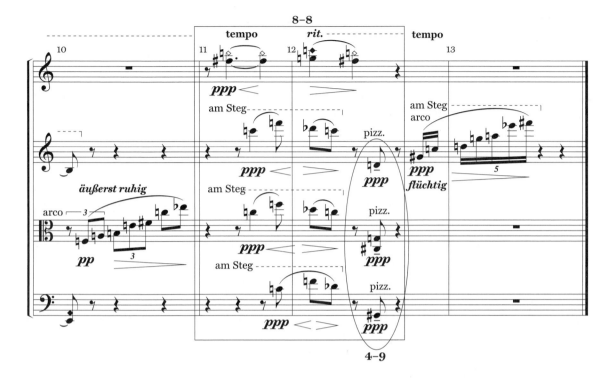

3.60 ⟨⟩ In contrast, the middle section—measures 7–10, shown at the beginning of Example 36.2b—features completely different sets. You should recognize the chord made by the viola *pizzicato* notes: D–B♭–G♭, an augmented triad (SC 3-12 [0 4 8]). When combined with the pc 4 in the cello, the resulting pcset {2 4 6 t} is the whole-tone subset 4-24 [0 2 4 8]. This whole-tone sound is disrupted by the second violin's pc e, which combines with the *pizzicato* notes to make {t e 2 6}: a statement of SC 4-19 [0 1 4 8], the augmented triad plus a semitone. The overall effect, represented by the collection of all the pcs in measures 7–10, SC 8-24 [0 2 3 4 6 8 t e], includes a strong whole-tone component, in contrast to the sets of the opening.

In this movement, the sectional divisions shown in the set analysis above are reinforced by the contrasting texture of the middle section, melody over ostinato accompaniment, and by the return of melodic and textural elements in measures 11–12. We would label the movement a ternary form: **A B A′**. What is the relationship of the ascending seven-tone figures (in mm. 6, 10, and 12–13) that mark the end of each section? (*Try it #6*)

We can find additional examples of pitch-class relationships, rather than tonal keys, helping to define form in previous chapters. In Bartók's "Song of the Harvest" (Chapter 30), we saw how different versions of the octatonic collection help establish the form. In Webern's Piano Variations (Chapter 34), we identified aspects of rows and repetition patterns that articulate a simple binary form. In both works, range and register also play a key role in defining form.

Canon and Imitation

Many twentieth-century and contemporary composers draw on pre-twentieth-century counterpoint as a compositional resource. For example, Webern is well known for using canonic procedures in his nontonal and serial works, and we have considered several pieces by Bartók with imitative entrances between the voices—yet the sounds of the two composers' works are quite distinct.

For a different type of counterpoint, from the 1960s, consider the ninth movement of Ligeti's *Ten Pieces for Wind Quintet*, shown in Example 36.3a. In this little piece, all three instruments play the same melodic line, but with slightly different durations assigned to the pitches (the pitch sequence is shown in Example 36.3b). The form of this piece is represented in the pitch-time graph in part c. Its beginning and end are similar to a description in one of the earliest written sources of information about counterpoint, the *Musica enchiriadis* from around 900: it opens with a unison and ends with a gradual close to an octave.

EXAMPLE 36.3: Ligeti, *Ten Pieces for Wind Quintet*

(a) Ninth movement

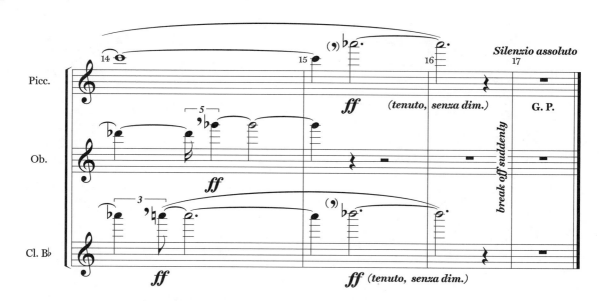

(b) Pitch sequence for ninth movement

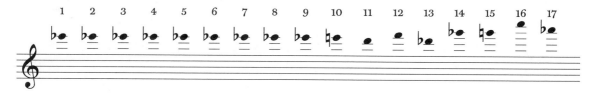

(c) Pitch/time graph for ninth movement

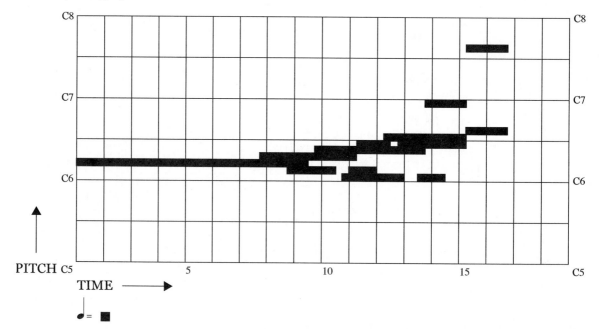

Ligeti employs other types of imitation in his compositions as well. Look at Example 36.4, measures 19–23 of the second song from *Three Fantasies on Texts by Friedrich Hölderlin* (composed in the 1980s). This passage, the alto parts, shows a typical imitative entry at the unison. Try singing the passage with your class. (The downward-pointing arrows on the B♭s mean to sing a quarter tone flat!)

EXAMPLE 36.4: Ligeti, "Wenn aus die Ferne," from *Three Fantasies on Texts by Friedrich Hölderlin*, mm. 19–23 (alto parts)

Translation: How flowed the lost hours, how calm was my soul.

3.1 🎧 For another example of imitation, listen again to the beginning of Penderecki's *Threnody* while following the score: how are the entrances of sound effects organized? Example 36.5 shows the patterns for the four entrances in the cellos at rehearsal number 6, labeled A, B, C, and D. How do these entrances compare with those in the violas, violins, and basses (from there to rehearsal 10)? Mark those entrances in your anthology score with the same labels. The individual parts enter in a kind of imitation. Although this portion of the *Threnody* follows strict contrapuntal procedures, you probably did not hear it this way; instead, it sounds like a swirling insect ostinato! The choice of imitative entries is significant to the sound of this passage, however: it allows Penderecki to balance the diverse string effects and thus achieve an even blending.

EXAMPLE 36.5: Penderecki, *Threnody for the Victims of Hiroshima*, cello entrances at rehearsal number 6

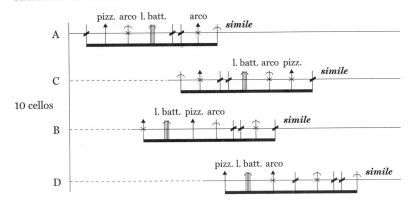

New Developments in Musical Form

Form as Process

Beginning in the 1960s, some composers reacted to the extremes of integral serialism by composing pieces in a style known as **minimalism**, in which each piece was created from a "minimum" of musical materials. Some minimalist pieces are notated in text scores, like La Monte Young's *Composition 1960*, No. 5, which we considered in Chapter 35. Other minimalist pieces feature the incessant repetition of a series of pitches (usually drawn from a diatonic collection) that change gradually over time. In the pattern-repetition pieces—preferred in the 1960s by composers Terry Riley, Philip Glass, and Steve Reich—the gradual change of pitches involves a process that, once started, must run to completion. For example, Riley's *In C* requires a group of players to move through a set of fifty-three melodic patterns, repeating each one for a while before proceeding to the next. (The first four patterns are shown in Example 36.6.) Each player chooses when to start a new pattern and how long to repeat the old one, but must stay with the group, so that all players move through the score within a few patterns of each other, making a gradually changing musical kaleidoscope.

EXAMPLE 36.6: Riley, *In C*, first four patterns

Several of Steve Reich's compositions from the 1960s draw on the idea of **phasing**: patterns moving in and out of alignment, creating additional sounds and patterns not visually present in the score. Reich discovered this effect by accident, when trying to get two reel-to-reel tape players to play copies of the same tape in synchronization (nearly impossible with the equipment he had). His composition *Piano Phase*, an excerpt of which is shown in Example 34.7, begins with one pianist playing a repeated melodic pattern. A second pianist joins with the same pattern, in synchronization, then gradually accelerates until his or her part is one pitch off from the original aligned pairing. The process of pattern repetition, acceleration, and realignment one pitch off continues until the two parts are once more aligned, as at the beginning.

3.11 🎧   Listen now to the first section of *Piano Phase*. While listening, concentrate on the rhythmic and pitch patterns that emerge from the pairings of the two parts. Can you hear the approach of the alignment at the end of the section? In a piece like this one, when the process is complete, the section (or whole composition) is also complete—the process defines the overall form.

EXAMPLE 36.7: Reich, *Piano Phase*, first three patterns

Moment Form and Mobile Form

One of the new developments in form in the second half of the twentieth century was the idea that formal sections of a piece did not have to connect in some logical way or in a predetermined order. Compositions featured abrupt changes from one style of music to another, without any attempt at (or interest in making) a logical connection. Rather than hearing the piece as a structured and unified whole, listeners were to hear and enjoy whatever music was sounding at a particular time "in the moment"; hence the term **moment form**. This type of piece is said to have a **nonteleological form** (as opposed to the **teleological**, or goal-directed, forms of traditional tonal music).

A famous example of nonteleological form is Stockhausen's *Klavierstück XI*, which consists of nineteen different independent musical fragments in (for the most part) traditional music notation. Two of the fragments are shown in Example 36.8. Tempo, dynamics, and articulation for any given segment are specified at the end of the previous segment. (For example, the end of the first segment in Example 36.8 specifies Tempo 2, *forte*, and a sustained articulation [—].) In performance, any one of the fragments may follow any other; the pianist chooses the order according to where his or her eye falls next on the score. (This is Stockhausen's instruction. However, many pianists select their order of segments initially at random, but then practice the segments in that same order to prepare the performance. The piece is just too difficult to make formal decisions at sight!)

EXAMPLE 36.8: Stockhausen, *Klavierstück XI*, two segments

Pieces like *Klavierstück XI*, where segments, sections, or movements may be played in varying orders, have what we call a **mobile form**, after artist Alexander Calder's mobile sculptures, whose parts may move into different positions relative to each other, perhaps as a result of the wind or a mechanical action. In analyzing a piece with a mobile form, we must keep in mind the possible permutations of sections or segments. While the contents of segments may remain consistent from one performance to another, the overall organization of the piece will not.

Indeterminacy and Chance

Indeterminate pieces, composed primarily after 1950, incorporate some elements that are either not specified by the composer, selected by a random procedure (such as throwing dice or flipping coins), or selected by chance (such as turning on a radio and including whatever sounds it happens to be making at the time, whether tuned to a station or not). Mobile form compositions also typically include some degree of indeterminacy. Indeterminacy is not really new in the twentieth century—in Mozart's time, musicians played dice games in which music was composed by a random selection of phrase beginnings and endings (indeterminacy of composition). Further, any realization of a figured bass required choices on the part of the performer that could result in different voicings of chords (indeterminacy of performance). Indeed, all music has an element of indeterminacy: performers must make many choices as they bring the notated music to life! We can think of indeterminacy on a continuum, with indeterminate compositions from the post–World War II era actually focusing on relinquishing control as an organizing feature.

Compositions in graphic scores or text notation often have a degree of indeterminacy in their performance. Some graphic scores, like Penderecki's *Threnody*, represent the tasks of the performer as accurately as (or even more accurately than) a traditionally notated piece; others leave much room for interpretation. Consider the piece *In the Woods*, by Kenneth Maue, reproduced in Example 36.9. What elements of the piece are indeterminate? Which would be the same in every performance that follows the score closely? (*Try it #7*)

EXAMPLE 36.9: Maue, *In the Woods*

Begin in the morning. Bring some lunch, four large discs of day-glo paper, some thumb-tacks, and some tape. Choose a roughly rectangular or circular area of solid woods.

Enter the woods at different locations along the periphery. Start walking in any direction. Sometimes move toward specific locations; sometimes just wander here and there; sometimes follow streams or paths, sometimes bushwhack; sometimes just sit.

As you walk around, find places to tack or tape your day-glo discs, in such a way that they can be seen by other players as they walk by. And be on the look-out for other players' discs. When you come across one, take it down, carry it for a while, then put it in a new location for someone else to find.

In the middle of the day, find each other by making noises. Make noise by any available means. Make sounds and listen. Move toward sounds you hear. When everyone has gathered together, have lunch. Then set out again, each in a different direction. This time, when you find a disc, take it down and keep it. After the day seems to be ending, make your way to the periphery, and wait to be picked up by a car.

What is the form of *In the Woods*? Is it consistent in every accurate performance? The piece, surprisingly enough, does have a consistent form that is comparable to traditional forms. There is a setting out (the first section), which lasts all morning; a span of time where performers are making noises to assemble for lunch (the middle section), which concludes with the eating of lunch together; and a returning to the periphery (a final section), which takes all afternoon and is similar to the beginning section in many respects. The piece thus has an overall ternary form, **A B A'**. *In the Woods* reminds us that each piece must be approached on its own terms. A score's appearance does not always indicate the presence or absence of form.

Surely by this point some of you are arguing, "This isn't music!" A definition of music contemporaneous with this piece is "Music is organized sound." Indeed, there are sounds in this piece, and they are organized in such a way that any accurate performance should be recognizable as *In the Woods*. But musicians must choose for themselves how to define "music." You will have an opportunity to make that decision in the workbook exercises for this chapter.

○ ○

Analyzing Form in Recent Music

The basic form-defining element in the musics we have studied is contrast. In common-practice-era music, the contrast might involve key areas, motives, themes, or even types of musical activity (exposition, transition, or development). In more recent music, the contrast may be found in timbre, texture, dynamics, collections or rows or sets, or other features. As we have seen in this chapter, it is possible to create formal closure in music without functional tonality by drawing on other elements that help make a point of repose. These include a slowing of musical activity, a stop on a longer duration than normal, a rest that breaks the musical flow, and a contrapuntal close to a unison or octave or some other stable interval or harmony.

One of the problems with analyzing form in recent music is that we have such a wide range of possibilities. If you were examining the first movement of a Beethoven sonata, you should have a good idea of what form to expect. On the other hand, music of the twentieth and twenty-first centuries tends to be less predictable. The starting point for any formal analysis is listening to the piece enough times that you can clearly hear it in your head—then attempting to explain what you hear. As you study and perform more repertoire from the twentieth and twenty-first centuries, you will become better able to predict which elements of style and form a composer will choose. While comparing form in nontonal pieces to tonal conventions is sometimes useful, be cautious in making these comparisons. Consider carefully which elements of the piece are traditional in some way, but also consider the effect of nontraditional elements. Treat the examples in this chapter as an introduction, then move on to discover the formal processes in the contemporary pieces that you play or study.

TERMS YOU SHOULD KNOW

chance	nonteleological form	teleological form
indeterminate	ostinato	time-line notation
minimalism	phasing	tritone axis
mobile form	pitch symmetry	
moment form	pitch-time graph	

QUESTIONS FOR REVIEW

1. What are typical characteristics of common-practice forms?
2. How have composers adapted common-practice forms in the posttonal era? What are some substitutes for the tonal relationship of tonic and dominant in nontonal works?
3. How are formal units defined without tonal cadences? What features may create closure without functional harmony?
4. What are some elements that help articulate sections in nontonal works?
5. How is closure achieved in pattern-repetition pieces?
6. If a piece contains indeterminate elements, is its form also indeterminate? Explain.
7. In music for your own instrument, find one piece that does not use functional tonality but has clearly audible formal divisions.
8. In music for your own instrument, find one piece that incorporates indeterminacy. (Ask your teacher for assistance, if needed, with questions 7 and 8.)

The Composer's Materials Today

CHAPTER 37

Overview

At the threshold of the twenty-first century, composers have many materials and compositional methods at their disposal. In this chapter, we consider works (from five composers) that illustrate materials in use at the end of the twentieth century; we also look ahead to compositions of the twenty-first.

Repertoire

John Corigliano, "Come now, my darling," from *The Ghosts of Versailles* (CD 1, track 82)

György Ligeti, "Désordre," from *Piano Etudes*, Book I

Arvo Pärt, *Magnificat*

Steve Reich, *City Life*

Reich, *Proverb*

John Williams, "Imperial March," from *The Empire Strikes Back*

o o o o o o o o o o o o o o o o o o o o o o o o o o o o o o o o o o o o o o o o o o o o

Contemporary Composers and Techniques of the Past

For most of the recorded history of Western music (or any musics, for that matter), there were, at any particular location and time, specific styles associated with composers of that place and time. The styles typically included (1) slightly older compositional methods (practiced by traditionalists and the somewhat old-fashioned composers) that formed the bulk of what composers were taught; (2) the current style, practiced by those in vogue; and (3) the beginnings of a new style—whatever came next. For example, when J. S. Bach (1685–1750) was young, he was trained in the old-fashioned styles of the late seventeenth century, including modal counterpoint and traditional church music styles. As his career progressed, he incorporated newer ideas and developed his mature style, which included complex tonal counterpoint and pieces written in all twelve keys. Late in his life, his compositions were considered old-fashioned by his sons and others writing in the new "galant" style.

From the early twentieth century through the 1970s, it was typical in art-music circles for particular styles to be in vogue and other styles (such as functional tonality) to be rejected, even though some composers still wrote in these older styles. The conflict of the **modernist** aesthetic—espoused by twentieth-century composers such as Schoenberg, Stravinsky, Bartók, and later Stockhausen and Babbitt—was to reject the past while at the same time venerating it. Modernist composers adopted the novel, scientific, mathematical, and revolutionary, yet wished to be considered the successors to the great musical masters of the past.

In the last fifteen years of the twentieth century, this tendency changed. Both popular and art music began to draw more freely on earlier musical languages, making a new style from the combination of materials originating from different times. This style is sometimes referred to as **postmodernism**, a term borrowed from literary and art criticism. At the end of the twentieth century and today, the composer's materials include everything that we know from previous musical eras. In the 1970s, art-music composers began to rediscover tonal materials: triads, melody and melodic development, regular beat and meter, consonant sonorities, diatonic scales and resources. Of course, those materials were present through the entire century in a wide variety of popular and folk musics, and in the works of some art-music composers, but they had been out of fashion in the mainstream modernist art-music community since the early part of the century. The resurgence of interest in older materials did not mean a wholesale return to writing music that could be mistaken for an earlier century. The music produced at the end of the twentieth century is, for the most part, obviously "contemporary"—

bearing the mark of the experimentation of the previous fifty years even when it draws on materials from earlier eras.

Our fast-paced, information-age society is reflected in **style juxtaposition**: elements strongly associated with one style or musical culture appear side by side with another type of music without a transition between the two, or any attempt to reconcile the musical differences. Some compositions include literal quotations or **stylistic allusions** to works of other composers (both contemporaneous and from previous centuries) that are intended to be recognized by the listener; others employ **parody** (where previous ideas are distorted or reshaped to emphasize particular aspects). Quotation, allusion, and parody are not new techniques in the twentieth century, but recent compositions take them to extremes, juxtaposing radically different musical styles.

In this chapter, we will examine excerpts from works inspired by compositional styles of the past. The examples illustrate how musical borrowings and allusions were used at the end of the last millennium and are still being practiced today. The chapter is too brief to be more than an overview; consider it an introduction and a stimulus to further study. After all, the meaning and significance of many of the techniques we consider here, especially those of the past quarter century, will not be fully understood until more time has passed and historical distance clarifies them.

Materials from the Pretonal Era

Among the composer's materials today are an increasing number of influences from music written before 1650. In the medieval and Renaissance eras, limited communications, a lack of printing facilities, and difficult travel conditions restricted musicians' knowledge of music to what was available in their native locales. Musicians today are not so restricted; in fact, by the end of the twentieth century, more was known about Western music composed before 1650 than at any previous time, including the time when the music was originally composed! Partly as a result, the last century saw an upsurge of interest in historically accurate performance practice. This interest was backed by detailed research into traditions of composition and performance, the restoration of old instruments and the production of new "historical" instruments, as well as the publication of editions, translations, and treatises that describe "how it was done at the time." New recording technology has made it possible for pieces preserved in centuries-old manuscripts to be performed and distributed worldwide, and for today's listeners to appreciate their beauty. Who would have thought that one of the best-selling CDs of art music in the 1990s would be a recording of monks singing medieval chant? Yet that was the case.

We now consider two works that draw on pretonal compositional ideas. First is Steve Reich's *Proverb*, a work from 1995 for three sopranos, two tenors, two vibraphones, and two samplers or electronic organs, based on a text from the twentieth-century philosopher Ludwig Wittgenstein. The piece begins with a single *a cappella* soprano voice singing, "How small a thought it takes to fill a whole life . . . how small a thought," shown in Example 37.1. This melody, in a modal-sounding B minor, captures the haunting spirit of plainchant. The soprano is soon joined by a second soprano, singing the same melody in canon with a delay of only one beat. Try performing the passage with your class.

WF1

Although the spirit of medieval chant continues to be present in the counterpoint, the clashing half-step harmonic intervals, produced by the time-delayed canonic voice, clearly mark this piece as a product of the twentieth century. The entire piece combines contrapuntal techniques and an *a cappella* singing style that are almost a thousand years old with a text that is not much more than fifty years old, electronic organs (a typical sound of the 1960s), and vibraphones (a percussion instrument invented in the first quarter of the twentieth century).

EXAMPLE 37.1: Reich, *Proverb*, mm. 1–22a (sopranos 1 and 2)

A second piece that evokes the sounds of an earlier era is Arvo Pärt's *Magnificat*, written in 1989. The opening of this work is shown in Example 37.2. First listen to or sing each of the two phrases in class, then answer the following questions: Where are the phrase divisions? What marks the end of each phrase? What determines the placement of the dashed measure divisions? Are there tonal centers or scales or triads that you recognize? How is the ametric rhythm structured? (*Try it #1*)

EXAMPLE 37.2: Pärt, *Magnificat*, opening two phrases

Translation: My soul doth magnify the Lord, and my spirit hath rejoiced in God my savior.

WF2

This composition is intended as contemplative religious music—a type of sounding icon. It is written in Pärt's *tintinnabuli* style, which he developed in the late 1970s: that is, it is built on a modal scale, is homophonic, does not modulate, and does not feature functional harmony. Instead, the piece draws on the resonance available in the triad. The primary melodic line is diatonic and generally stepwise, with occasional skips emphasizing accented words; the accompanying lines fill in the chord members of the primary triad of the work, F minor (F-Ab-C), or provide stepwise motion between members of the triad. The only dissonances are those occasionally created between a melody pitch and the triad, and they are not "resolved" in a traditional fashion, but dissipate as the melody moves to a chord tone.

Both of these pieces call for the "pure," no-vibrato singing style revived in the twentieth century for the performance of early music. In the *Magnificat*, the singers are to listen carefully, blending to make pure triadic intervals—the resonant triads of the overtone series—not the slightly adjusted intervals of the equal-tempered chromatic scale. This blending gives Pärt's works their characteristic bell-like sound. Both the Reich and Pärt selections are "minimalist" in their use of a limited palette of compositional materials, but are very different in sound from the pattern-repetition minimalist compositions we considered in previous chapters.

Elements of pretonal styles that recent composers have adopted include modal scales and counterpoint from the Renaissance (see Chapters 8 and 9) and the oldest types of contrapuntal cadences, such as closing in to a unison or expanding out to an octave (as in the ninth movement from Ligeti's *Ten Pieces for Wind Quintet*, discussed in Chapter 36). Chant and monophonic techniques have also been borrowed in recent compositions. In addition, compositional details like **isorhythm** (a repeated series of durations combined with a repeated melodic idea, usually of a different length; see Nono's *Il canto sospeso* in Chapter 35) and **quodlibet** (multiple texts, usually not all in the same language) appear in some compositions as early as the 1960s. The idea of writing a piece without specifying the precise instrumentation (for example, Riley's *In C*, from Chapter 36) has also been adapted from earlier practice. Tunings other than equal temperament found their way into pieces from mid-century on, influenced by both non-Western and Western sources. At first these works were performed with handmade instruments or with altered fingerings or performance techniques on traditional instruments, but later synthesizers and electronic means were used to create variant divisions of the pitch spectrum.

Materials from the Baroque, Classical, and Romantic Periods

In the last few decades, some composers have incorporated quotations of older pieces or even newly composed fragments intended to capture the style of an older composer into a larger work. One example is John Corigliano's opera *The Ghosts of Versailles*, which blends newly composed "faux Mozart" with characters and plot elements drawn from operas by Mozart and Rossini (and references to quite a few other styles) into a work that clearly sounds like the late twentieth century. Listen to measures 1–72 of the duet "Come now, my darling," while following the score in your anthology.

If you know Mozart's *The Marriage of Figaro*, to which this scene refers, the characters will be familiar to you. The setting is a flashback to the seduction of Rosina by Cherubino. As we saw in Chapter 35, Cherubino, a young man of the Count's household (actually the singer is a mezzo-soprano; this is a "pants" role), is seducing Rosina, the Count's wife. How does the tonal language express Rosina's reluctance? To answer this question, we will focus on the interaction between the characters in measures 10–13, shown as Example 37.3a. Begin by identifying the keys implied in this passage. (*Try it #2*) What other aspects of Rosina's music indicate her internal conflict? (*Try it #3*)

EXAMPLE 37.3: Corigliano, "Come now, my darling," from *The Ghosts of Versailles*

(a) Mm. 10–13

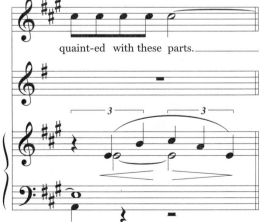

1.84 🎧 Listen to a second excerpt from later in the duet (mm. 38–41), shown as Example 37.3b. This passage has many features that are associated with Mozart's music, including the two-measure symmetrical phrases, the melodic style, the chord choices, and the Alberti bass accompaniment; in fact, the melody bears a striking resemblance to the beginning of Mozart's "Voi, che sapete," also sung by Cherubino. Yet this duet could not be mistaken for one from Mozart's time. The changes of key and meter that come later in the passage are too extreme.

(b) Mm. 38–41

In addition to references to Mozart's operas, *The Ghosts of Versailles* includes "ghost music" reminiscent of Penderecki, an aria with Middle Eastern influences, and elements of musical stage productions from Rossini to Wagner to Broadway. In many ways, the scope and scale of this contemporary work resembles the grand operas of the Romantic period more than those of Mozart.

Elements of Romantic style—from lush orchestration to the use of recurring motives like Wagner's leitmotivs (to represent a person, action, idea, or place)—have appeared throughout the twentieth century in pieces that are not in a Romantic style overall. For example, Berg, in his nontonal opera *Wozzeck* (from the first half of the twentieth century), includes leitmotivs made from pitch-class sets, much in the same way they appear in Wagner's operas, but without the tonal harmonies. In addition to extended chromatic harmony and the adaptation of traditional forms, the Romantic period was a time of expanded orchestral resources and colorful orchestration. Art song, opera, and programmatic orchestral works flourished in the expression of the Romantic ideal: love and loss on an epic scale.

The influence of Romantic-period compositional techniques is clearly audible in much twentieth-century film music dealing with similar themes. For example, John Williams's music for the epic films of the *Star Wars* series, such as the "Imperial March" from *The Empire Strikes Back* (the beginning is shown in Example 37.4), draws on accepted prototypes of heroic music. Williams's scores are predominantly tonal (with functional tonality), yet contain elements that mark them as twentieth-century compositions. In addition, musical themes and motives are associated with particular characters and places, just as Wagner's leitmotivs are.

EXAMPLE 37.4: Williams, "Imperial March," from *The Empire Strikes Back*, mm. 1–7

In the last quarter century, art-music composers have shown a resurgence of interest in incorporating elements from Baroque, Classical, and Romantic styles into their own works. Among the materials they have borrowed are traditional forms (binary, ternary, and sonata) and genres (concertos, sonatas, symphonies, and variation sets); traditional phrase structure and cadences; tonal counterpoint, including fugue and canon; symmetrical meters and rhythms that reinforce them; motivic development and melodic embellishment; and functional tonal harmony and dissonance treatment.

Today's composers will usually pick and choose among the older elements. For example, in Chapter 36 we considered pieces with traditional formal structures but no tonal harmony or phrase structure. We also studied minimalist pieces that draw on a diatonic collection, repeated motives, and motivic development, but lack scale-degree function. In some compositions, functionally tonal passages combine with other sections employing newer techniques. For example, in Tavener's "The Lamb," considered in Chapter 33, serial techniques are juxtaposed with functional tonal sections.

Materials from the Twentieth Century

The composer's materials from the first half of the twentieth century include many of the techniques we considered in Chapters 30–36: octatonic, pentatonic, whole-tone, and other nondiatonic scale materials; nonfunctional harmonies built on intervals other than thirds; pitch-class sets and serialism; and rhythmic innovations such as changing meter, asymmetrical meters, and ametrical music. In contrast, they also include the innovations of early jazz, the song forms of the Broadway musical, and some world music resources.

In the second half of the century, there was an increasing emphasis on timbre and rhythm as compositional materials—some pieces require a stage full of percussion instruments. Such timbres as environmental noises, speech, and electronically produced sounds were considered fair game. World music influences have brought new ways of considering time and rhythm, from the patterns of the Balinese gamelan to those of West African drumming. After their absence in avant-garde music for much of the century, a regular beat and traditional meter found their way back into art music in the 1980s and 1990s, along with metrical and rhythmic practices of the earlier twentieth century.

"Désordre," from György Ligeti's *Piano Etudes*, is an example of this rhythmic eclecticism (Example 37.5). At the time the piece was written, Ligeti was very interested in the cross rhythms created in various styles of African drumming. His music also draws on the rhythmic and metrical practices of Bartók and on mimimalist pattern repetition from the 1960s.

WF4

EXAMPLE 37.5: Ligeti, "Désordre," from *Piano Etudes,* Book I, mm. 1–8

Minimalism continued as an active style to the end of the twentieth century, but with some changes; this style, once associated with highly restricted materials, became more "maximal," with larger ensembles and increased levels of activity. A recent piece by Steve Reich, *City Life,* illustrates this change. In the first movement—scored for two flutes, two oboes, two clarinets, two pianos, two samplers (which play digitized snippets of recorded sounds), percussion, string quartet, and string bass—a recording of a New York street vender saying "Check it out" provides the primary rhythmic idea. Other movements bring in car horns, sirens, door slams, heartbeats, a pile driver, and speech samples from the New York City Fire Department's field communications on February 26, 1993, the day the World Trade Center was bombed—all treated as musical sounds and incorporated into the texture. Pattern repetition is a significant element in this piece, as in Reich's pieces from the 1970s, but the texture is much thicker, with a variety of event layers combining to make a wall of sound. The excerpt shown in Example 37.6 includes "Check it out" and some of the instrumental motives derived from that spoken rhythm.

EXAMPLE 37.6: Reich, *City Life*, first movement, mm. 30–35

In many pieces written at the end of the century, the materials are so well integrated that their origin is not easy to determine. One composer who successfully crosses stylistic boundaries is the Japanese composer Toru Takemitsu. While primarily trained in Western compositional techniques, Takemitsu incorporates some elements of Japanese aesthetics. His works are often evocative of Debussy, Ravel, and Messiaen, yet bring to mind images of a Japanese garden—nature, balance, and calmness. His music is nontonal but also motivic, with repetition at times reminiscent of the minimalists, though his materials are not minimal. Like many end-of-century works, his resist labeling as belonging to any one compositional practice.

A Look Ahead into the Twenty-first Century

It is impossible for us to know what changes will take place in music composition, performance, recording, and score production in the current century. One thing that seems clear is that performers, composers, conductors, and music teachers in the twenty-first century will be expected to know more than ever about music of the past. That includes music of the common-practice era—our primary focus in this book—and of the twentieth century. All of the styles of music discussed in this book are continuing to be studied and performed, a state of affairs that is unlikely to change. Musicians are expected to know the conventions of each period represented in their repertoire, and to apply these conventions in a stylistic and musical performance.

Your studies have just begun. The process of becoming a musician is a life's task, not something accomplished in one semester, or year, or even an undergraduate course of study. What you should have now, though, is a firm foundation for continuing your studies. Be curious, take more courses, and above all, perform and investigate music of many styles and periods. We are lucky to live, and to be able to make music, in the twenty-first century—everything is open to us. Enjoy and explore!

TERMS YOU SHOULD KNOW

modernism	postmodernism	stylistic allusion
parody	style juxtaposition	

QUESTIONS FOR REVIEW

1. For each of the pieces discussed in this chapter, make a list of the elements in the music that are based on older styles. Which elements indicate that the piece is contemporary?
2. What aspects of counterpoint do you find in the compositions included in this chapter?
3. How would you determine if a piece that features triads has functional tonality?
4. What characteristics of rhythm and meter mark pieces as twentieth-century?
5. What elements of minimalism are found in pieces in this chapter?
6. Find a piece of contemporary music for your own instrument that draws on stylistic elements of an earlier era. (Confer with your instrumental teacher for ideas!)

Appendixes

Try it Answers

Chapter 1

Try it #1 7 above G: F; 6 above F: D; 2 above D: E; 4 below B: F; 5 below A: D; 3 above E: G; 8 below C: C; 1 below A: G.

Try it #2 G♭ enharmonic: F♯; B♯ = C; A♯ = B♭; D♭ = C♯; B = C♭; A♭ = G♯; E♯ = F

Try it #3 Half step above G♭: G; below C♯: C (or B♯); below B: B♭ (or A♯); above E: F (or E♯); above D: D♯ (or E♭); below B♭: A; above B♯: C♯ (or D♭).

F♯ to E: whole step; C♯ to D: half step; B♭ to A♭: whole step; C to B♭: whole step; E to F: half step; F to G: whole step; B♯ to C: enharmonic!

Try it #4 The letter names for "Eleanor Rigby" (*a*) are A, A, B, G, (G), E | G, A, B, D, (D), C♯, B, C♯ | (C♯) B, A, B, (B), A, G, A. We will learn about ties in Chapter 2 (for now, letter names representing tied notes are repeated in parentheses). The letter names for (*b*) are F, D, E♭, B, G♯, A♭, D, C♯, G.

Try it #5 The letter names for the Bach (*a*) are D, C, B, C♯, A | D, C♯, D, E, F♮ D | G♯, E, A. The letter names for (*b*) are F♯, G, D♭, B, F♯, A♭, C, G.

Try it #6 The pitches of the Bach (*a*) are E, C♯, F♯ | F♯, F♯, A | D, B, G | C♯, B. (If you said F instead of F♯, don't worry; we will learn about the effect of "key signatures" in Chapter 3.) The pitches of (*b*) are: alto clef, A, F♯, E, E♭, C; tenor clef, B♭, D, F♯, G, C.

Try it #7 (*a*) The two circled pitches in measure 4 of "On Top of Old Smoky" (Example 1.5) are B and A. The three circled pitches between the staves in measure 7 are E, G, and C. The answers to (*b*) are: treble—C, D, G, A; bass—D, E, F, A; alto—D, C, F; tenor—A, G, F.

Try it #8 (*a*) The solo violin, flute 1, and violin 1 read the most ledger lines.
(*b*) Answer to flute line is: B, C, B, C | A, G, A, C, B, A | G, B, C, B, C | A, G, A, C, B, A | G.

Try it #9 Pitches in the final chord of the Bach (*a*), from lowest staff to highest are: strings and continuo B2 (played by several instruments), F♯4, D♯5, B5; flutes D♯5, B5; and solo violin B5. The pitches given in (*b*) are: treble clef—G4, B5, A3, E5; bass clef—D3, F2, E4, B2; alto clef—D4, C5, F3, G4; and tenor clef—E4, C3, B4, B3.

Chapter 2

Try it #1 The Hensel is in compound meter.

Try it #2 The meter type for the Gershwin is simple duple; for the Bach chorale, simple quadruple; for the Mozart, simple triple; for the Joplin, simple duple; for the *Brandenburg Concerto*, simple triple.

Try it #3:
$\frac{2}{2}$: simple duple (meter), half note (beat unit)
$\frac{3}{16}$: simple triple, sixteenth note
$\frac{4}{8}$: simple quadruple, eighth note
$\frac{3}{4}$: simple triple, quarter note

Try it #4 Handel's beat divisions and subdivisions include the following:

Other possible beat divisions and subdivisions include the following:

Try it #5

(*a*)

(*b*)

(*c*)

Try it #6

(*a*) Bach, *Brandenburg Concerto* No. 4, second movement, mm. 13–18 (solo violin)

(*b*) Gershwin, "'S Wonderful!" mm. 29–36 (vocal line)

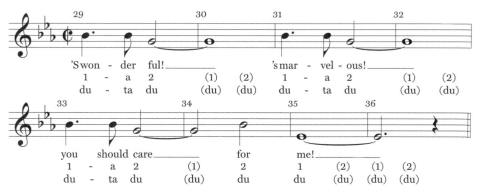

(*c*) Joplin, "Pine Apple Rag," mm. 1–4 (right hand)

(*d*) There are ties in the cello in measures 1-2 and in the violin in measures 3-4, where quarter notes are tied across the bar. Compare these with the five slurs in the first two measures of the violin part.

Try it #7 The first and second notes have the stem on the wrong side of the note head. The fourth note has the flag on the wrong side of the stem.

Try it #8

(*a*)

(*b*)

(*c*)

Chapter 3

Try it #1 The pitch-class collections for the Mozart and the Sherman and Sherman are identical.

Try it #2 The chromatic scale segments appear in measures 77–80 and again in measures 81–84; each chromatic scale contains nine pitches (followed by a whole step).

Try it #3 The Mozart sonata and "Feed the Birds" share many of the same pitch classes in the same order, as the example below shows.

Sherman and Sherman

Mozart

Try it #4 "Frère Jacques" is $\hat{1}\,\hat{2}\,\hat{3}\,\hat{1}\mid\hat{1}\,\hat{2}\,\hat{3}\,\hat{1}\mid\hat{3}\,\hat{4}\,\hat{5},\mid\hat{3}\,\hat{4}\,\hat{5},\mid\hat{5}\,\hat{6}\,\hat{5}\,\hat{4}\,\hat{3}\,\hat{1}\mid\hat{5}\,\hat{6}\,\hat{5}\,\hat{4}\,\hat{3}\,\hat{1}$ $\mid\hat{1}\,\hat{5}\,\hat{1},\mid\hat{1}\,\hat{5}\,\hat{1}.$ "Happy Birthday" is *sol sol | la sol do | ti, sol sol | la sol re | do, sol sol | sol mi do | ti la, fa fa | mi do re | do.*

Try it #5 At the beginning of the Sousa march, you see the key signature for E♭ Major (and many accidentals as well). Then the key signature changes for the Trio to four flats, or A♭ Major.

Try it #6

Try it #7 $\hat{4}$ in F Major: B♭; leading tone in G Major: F♯; $\hat{5}$ in A♭ Major: E♭; mediant in E Major: G♯; supertonic in B Major: C♯; $\hat{6}$ in D♭ Major: B♭.

Chapter 4

Try it #1 B Major: 5♯, B minor: 2♯; F Major: 1♭, F minor: 4♭; C Major: 0♭, C minor: 3♭; F♯ Major: 6♯, F♯ minor: 3♯; A Major: 3♯, A minor: 0♯.

Try it #2 G–A–B♭–C–D (minor pentachord); G–A–B♭–C–D–E–F♯–G (ascending melodic minor); G–A–B♭–C–D–E♭–F–G (natural minor); G–A–B♭–C–D–E♭–F♯–G (harmonic minor).

Try it #3 E Major: C♯ minor; four flats: F minor; D Major: B minor; E♭ Major: C minor; five sharps: G♯ minor; one flat: D minor.

Try it #4 A minor: C Major; G♯ minor: B Major; C minor: E♭ Major; D minor: F Major; C♯ minor: E Major; F minor: A♭ Major.

Try it #5 Joplin—F Major; Purcell—A minor; Handel—G minor; Gershwin—E♭ Major. (Note: The Handel is primarily in G Major, but Variations 15–16 are in G minor.)

Try it #6 E Dorian: E–F♯–G–A–B–C♯–D–E; B♭ Lydian: B♭–C–D–E–F–G–A–B♭; B Aeolian: B–C♯–D–E–F♯–G–A–B; A Mixolydian: A–B–C♯–D–E–F♯–G–A; F♯ Phrygian: F♯–G–A–B–C♯–D–E–F♯; E♭ Ionian: E♭–F–G–A♭–B♭–C–D–E♭

Chapter 5

Try it #1 In "Norwegian Wood," the top number tells us that there are four beats per measure (12 ÷ 3 = 4). To find the beat unit, add up three eighth notes to get a dotted quarter. You can see and hear this beat unit in the vocal phrase: for example, in measures 13 and 14, each of the dotted-quarter-note words "I," "rug," "time," and "wine" lasts one beat.

The ⁶⁄₄ meter of the *St. Anne* Fugue is compound duple, with two beats per measure (6 ÷ 3 = 2). For the beat unit, add together three quarter notes (from the bottom number of the signature): the beat unit is a dotted half.

Try it #2 "Down in the Valley":

"Norwegian Wood" (new units not found in "Down in the Valley"):

Try it #3 Units found in neither "Down in the Valley" nor "Norgwegian Wood":

Try it #4 You should have found the following beat units in the Bach example:

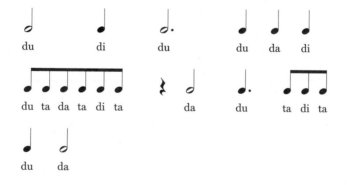

Chapter 6

Try it #1 Intervals in measure 60: third, second, second, third, third, fourth, fourth, fifth, fifth, sixth, sixth.

Try it #2 A5 down to G5: second; G5 up to A5: second; A5 down to F♯5: third; F♯5 up to A5: third; A5 down to E5: fourth; E5 up to A5: fourth; A5 down to D5: fifth; D5 up to A5: fifth; A5 down to C5: sixth; C5 up to A5: sixth.

Try it #3   The bass-clef pitches in measure 58 are F♯3, A3, and D4. The intervals are:

> F♯3 to A3: third
> A3 to D4: fourth
> F♯3 to D4: sixth

The bass-clef pitches in measure 60, beat 1, are D3, A3, and D4. The intervals are:

> D3 to A3: fifth
> D3 to D4: octave
> A3 to D4: fourth

The interval F♯3 to A3 in beat 3 makes a third.

Try it #4   The only intervals included are seconds, thirds, and fourths. Each two-measure unit begins with repeated pitches and ends with a third down. The two-measure units are connect by fourths upward in measures 5–13, and by seconds upward in measures 14–20. Interestingly, Gershwin uses the same pattern of intervals for the beginning of the refrain ("'S wonderful! 'S marvelous!") as he does for the beginning of the verse (repeated pitches followed by a third down).

Try it #5   m6 above D: B♭; M7 above A: G♯; P5 above B♭: F; m3 above F: A♭; M2 above E♭: F; m7 above C: B♭.

Try it #6   G up to F♯: M7; C up to A♭: m6; B♭ up to D: M3; A up to C: m3; C♯ up to G♯: P5; B up to E: P4.

Try it #7   m6 below D: F♯; M7 below A: B♭; P5 below B♭: E♭; m3 below F: D; M2 below E♭: D♭; m7 below C: D.

Try it #8   The intervals in measure 58 include m2, P4, P5, m6, m7, P8 in the melody. All of these intervals are consonant except the m2 and m7. (The P4 is consonant in this context.)

Try it #9

A up to G♯:	M7	G♯ up to A:	m2
G up to D♭:	d5	D♭ up to G:	A4
E♭ up to B♭:	P5	B♭ up to E♭:	P4
C♯ up to A:	m6	A up to C♯:	M3
B up to D:	m3	D up to B:	M6

Chapter 7

Try it #1 Handel's chords are built on scale-degrees $\hat{1}$ (mm. 9 and 13), $\hat{6}$ (m. 11), $\hat{5}$ (m. 12), and $\hat{4}$ (m. 14).

Try it #2 To spell an E-Major triad, first place three note heads on the staff: E-G-B. Next, ask: What is the key signature of E Major? E Major has four sharps, one of which is G, so an E-Major triad is E-G♯-B. To spell C minor, we place the note heads C-E-G on the staff, then take the C-minor key signature of three flats: C-E♭-G.

Try it #3 Minor triad above B♭: B♭-D♭-F; major triad above F: F-A-C; minor triad above G: G-B♭-D; minor triad above G♯: G♯-B-D♯; augmented triad above E♭: E♭-G-B; minor triad above D: D-F-A; diminished triad above B♭: B♭-D♭-F♭; major triad above D: D-F♯-A; major triad above A: A-C♯-E.

Try it #4 We can find other triads in inversion in measures 10, 13 (second and third beats), and 14 (second and third beats).

Try it #5 The first chord is C-E-A, a first-inversion A-minor triad (A-C-E; Roman numeral ii in the key).

Try it #6

B♭ Major: ii⁶₅	E♭-G-B♭-C	mm7
D Major: V⁴₂	G-A-C♯-E	Mm7
E♭ Major: IV⁶₅	C-E♭-G-A♭	MM7
E Major: V⁴₃	F♯-A-B-D♯	Mm7
G major: ii⁶₅	C-E-G-A	mm7

Try it #7 (*a*) G-B-D-F; (*b*) C-E♭-G-B♭; (*c*) F♯-A-C-E; (*d*) B-D-F-A♭; (*e*) F-A-C-E; (*f*) G-B♭-D♭-F; (*g*) E-G♯-B-D; (*h*) C♯-E-G-B♭.

Chapter 8

Try it #1 The intervals (from the beginning) are:
8 8 | 3 5 | 3 6 | 3 5 | 3 5* | 3 5 | 6 5-6 | 8
The fifth marked with an asterisk is a diminished fifth, which was avoided in strict modal practice, but was more common in eighteenth-century practice.

Try it #2 The tritone is on the second beat of measure 5—a diminished fifth between B4 (scale-degree $\hat{7}$) and F5 (scale-degree $\hat{4}$). It moves to a third—C4 to E5.

Try it #3 The melody has one sharp in the key signature, and the phrase begins and ends on G4. It is in the key of G Major.

Try it #4 Oblique motion (O) connects measures 1–2, 2–3, 4–5, 5–6, 7–8, 8–9, 9–10. Contrary motion (C) connects measures 3–4, 6–7, 10–11. Parallel motion (P) and similar motion (S) are not used in this excerpt.

Try it #5 Some of them are dissonant passing tones. Measure 1, beats 3 and 4, form the intervals 3–4–6, with 4 a dissonant passing tone. You should also have found dissonant passing tones in measure 2, beat 1, and measure 3, beat 4.

Try it #6 Yes, it mostly follows the guidelines, except that the bass line has less stepwise motion and more chordal skips than we have seen previously. Also, the composer is freer with the approach to perfect intervals (e.g., m. 35, octave Gs; m. 37, beat 3, the skip to P5) and with resolutions of sevenths (e.g., m. 37, last beat).

Try it #7 Yes, it follows all the guidelines.

Chapter 9

Try it #1 Variations VI, X, and XII also feature this rhythmic combination. In Variation VI, the quarter note in the upper part is replaced by an eighth note and an eighth rest, but it still falls within 4:1.

Try it #2 In Variation III, you should have found arpeggiation in measures 73, 76 (beat 2), 77 (beat 2), 78 (beat 2), and 80. Beat 1 in measures 77–78 shows a consonant skip from a chord member to the main melody pitches F5 and E5.

The first beats in measures 75 and 81 feature unaccented chromatic lower neighbor tones.

Try it #3

Try it #4 The upper part in Example 9.12b has the same pitches as Example 9.12c, but most are shifted later in time by a half measure and tied or repeated over the bar line.

Try it #5 To solve this question, think about the note-to-note framework that is displaced to make the suspensions. If 4–3 suspensions are made from a 3–3–3, then 9–8 and 2–1 would be made from 8–8–8 and 1–1–1, which are not allowed in note-to-note counterpoint. The same problem arises with the consonant suspensions 6–5 and 5–6.

Chapter 10

Try it #1 The beat is not beamed together in measure 6 for the words "all your" and "cares be-."

Try it #2 "My Country" conforms to these vocal ranges precisely. In "Wachet auf," only the bass extends beyond these guidelines (by a half step), with several E♭4s.

Try it #3 Both "My Country" and "Wachet auf" conform to the spacing guidelines.

Try it #4 Bach's "Wachet auf" setting includes voice crossing in measure 35 to give the tenor a smooth melodic line.

Chapter 11

Try it #1 Yes, these voices follow our species guidelines. The alto and bass are set in parallel thirds in measures 32b–33 as if they were in 1:1 counterpoint at the quarter note. In the first half of measure 34, they are 2:1, with a passing tone in the bass. For the rest of the phrase, they are 1:1 in half notes, with the chordal dissonance 7 resolving as expected in measure 36. The tenor-bass counterpoint is predominantly 2:1, with passing tones, a neighbor, and a chordal skip.

Try it #2 In the triads of "My Country," the doubling departs from these guidelines in only two places. In measure 4, on the syllable "-ty" (of "liberty") the D-minor triad doubles the third, F. The reason for this compositional choice is that scale-degree $\hat{7}$, E, typically resolves up to $\hat{1}$. This voice-leading tendency overrides the doubling guideline. The same voice-leading concept is at play in the final resolution of "freedom ring." Here the setting of "ring" has three roots and a third. This doubling is common at the cadence to allow the resolutions of both $\hat{7}$–$\hat{1}$ and $\hat{4}$–$\hat{3}$. Scale-degree $\hat{7}$ in an inner voice may also skip away to complete the triad to which it resolves.

Try it #3 In the piano score to "My Funny Valentine," the Cm+7 chord in measure 2 is missing its fifth (G) and includes a D (a ninth!); the Cm7 in measure 3 is also missing the fifth and has a doubled root. In measures 7–8, the G7 chord is missing its fifth (D). Here, however, the seventh (!) is doubled.

Try it #4 There are three distinct key signatures in the Brahms score: three flats, one flat, and no flats.

Try it #5

Try it #6 Key of transposed part for B♭ instrument (concert key in E♭): F; for F instrument (C): G; for E♭ instrument (B♭): G; for A instrument (G): B♭; for F instrument (F): C; for B♭ instrument (C): D; for F instrument (E♭): B♭; for E♭ instrument (C): A.

Try it #7 The scale degrees are $\hat{3}$ $\hat{3}$ $\hat{4}$ $\hat{2}$ $\hat{2}$ $\hat{5}$; the solfège is *mi-mi-fa-re-re-sol*.

Try it #8 Compare your horn part with the one given here.

Try it #9: If we transposed "My Country" to the concert key of B♭ Major, the B♭ trumpet parts would have the key signature of C Major (no flats or sharps); the horn would be in F Major; and the trombone would be in B♭ Major, the concert key.

Try it #10 The "8—" beside the flute and piccolo parts (Fl., Picc.) indicates that they double the clarinets (Cls.), soprano saxophone, and first and second B♭ cornets up an octave. The "8 bassa" shows that the baritone saxophone (Bar. Sax.) and basses (tuba and possibly bass trombone) double the bass line down an octave. Elsewhere, there are also doublings of inner parts not present in the piano score.

There are quite a few changes between the two scores. Here are two: the bass-line ornaments (sixteenth notes) are added in the short score, and the rhythm of the harmonies in the inner voices is changed quite a bit. Compare the changes you found with those your classmates located—how many differences can you find?

Chapter 12

Try it #1 In the first phrase of the Haydn, the tonic area extends through measures 1 and 2, the dominant is in measure 3, and tonic closure follows in measure 4. In the second phrase, the tonic area extends through measures 5 and 6, the dominant is in measure 7, and tonic closure concludes the phrase in measure 8.

Try it #2 As shown on the reduction below, the C♯4 does resolve up to D4 as expected. The G5 in the uppermost strand resolves down, as it should, to F5 at the change of chord in measure 8 (with a metrically weak chordal skip to E5 in between).

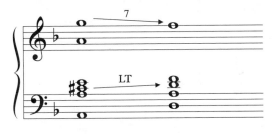

mm. 4–7   m. 8

Try it #3   The V$^4_2$ is found in measure 3 (beat 2) and measure 5 (beat 1); both progress to I^6, with the seventh resolving down to $\hat{3}$ as expected.

Try it #4   The Handel IAC is in measures 6–7, where the V^7–I cadence ends with $\hat{4}$ to $\hat{3}$ in the soprano. The PAC is at the end of the excerpt in measures 8–9, with $\hat{7}$ to $\hat{1}$ in the soprano.

Try it #5   "Clementine" is in F Major, and has two phrases that are then repeated (with different words) in the chorus. The first phrase ends inconclusively with scale-degree $\hat{2}$ (on the word "mine"); this implies a half cadence, ending on V. The second phrase ends conclusively with $\hat{7}$–$\hat{2}$–$\hat{1}$ (on "Clementine") and would be harmonized with a PAC. The harmonies for the eight measures are I, I, I, V || V, I, V, I.

Chapter 13

Try it #1   The accompaniment provides several examples of consonant skips without passing tones: for example, in measure 6, where the right hand leaps from C5 to E4. The bass line has many consonant skips, starting with the one that begins the excerpt in measure 4: A2–E3. In the second half of that measure, the harmony is G-B-D, and beat 4 has a consonant skip from G3 to B2. This type of skip continues in each measure (e.g., m. 5, beats 3–4, leaps within the B-D-F triad, and so on).

Try it #2   Purcell sets the word "eas'd" with repeated suspensions in the vocal line, doubled an octave below in the accompaniment: a 4–3 suspension, followed by a 9–8 and 7–6. The harmonic rhythm is two chord changes per bar, and chromatic incomplete neighbors also embellish the bass line. All of the suspensions resolve to first-inversion chords and conform to our guidelines for resolution. The 4–3 suspension resolves over a first-inversion F-Major seventh chord, the 9–8 over a first-inversion G-Major triad, and the 7–6 over a first-inversion A-minor triad. Each suspension has a consonant preparation, though they are somewhat obscured by rests in the vocal line.

Try it #3 The suspension is in the tenor voice, measure 3, on beat 3: a 4–3 suspension (D4–C♯4).

Try it #4 The suspension in measure 2 is a 7–6; measure 4 features two simultaneous suspensions (a 9–8 and 4–3). Other embellishing tones include passing tones A♭4 and F4 in measure 1 (upper part), bass-line consonant skips and a lower neighbor G3 in measure 2, and additional passing tones in measure 3 (upper part): E♭5 and C5.

Try it #5 No. Although the D4 occurs in the correct rhythmic and melodic context, it does not function as an anticipation because it is part of the B♭ dominant seventh harmony on this beat.

Try it #6 The 4–3 suspension in measure 35 follows most of the common-practice guidelines. The A3 in the alto line of the piano accompaniment (beat 3 of m. 35) is prepared by a chord tone in the previous beat, and it resolves down by step to G♯3 in the following chord. The main difference between this 4–3 suspension and a common-practice one is that the dissonant fourth is "prepared" by a chord tone that in itself could be considered dissonant: the seventh of the Bm7. The 4–3 suspension in measure 36 is not prepared, but it resolves correctly.

Try it #7   The Lloyd Webber and Rice cadence is an ornamented 4–3 suspension. (Although the piano left hand is arpeggiated, we still hear C as the bass above which the 4–3 suspension operates.)

Chapter 14

Try it #1   The melody shows a key signature of one flat and ends with $\hat{2}$–$\hat{1}$ in D minor. Because it concludes with scale-degree $\hat{1}$, it has a conclusive cadence that would probably be harmonized with a PAC.

Try it #2   If we double the third (F4) in the tenor, we create parallel octaves with the soprano. If we double the fifth (A3) in the tenor, this less common doubling gives the tenors a difficult leap to sing and creates potential spacing and voice-leading problems for the connection to i^6.

Try it #3   Our setting differs from Bach's in only a few respects.

    1. You may have noticed that our alto and tenor parts were not very interesting as melodic lines. Bach solves this problem by embellishing the tenor line twice with suspensions, on beats 1 and 3 of measure 3.

    2. Bach adds rhythmic interest to the alto line by treating the seventh in the final V^7 as a passing tone, on the offbeat.

    3. Bach prefers a complete triad on the final chord: he resolves the leading tone down to the fifth of the tonic triad. Either voice-leading choice is acceptable at the cadence in this style.

Try it #4

At (a): Leading tone not raised; incorrect doubling; incorrect resolution of leading tone; parallel octaves.

At (b): Contrary fifths; no third in final chord; seventh resolves incorrectly.

With corrections:

c: i   V⁶   i———— 6   V———— 7   i

Try it #5 In measure 2, the ♮7 implies a B♮ above the bass. The slash through the ⁶ in measure 4 implies an F♯ above the bass (which occurs in the tenor's line as well). Finally, the sharp in measure 5 applies to the third above the bass: it requires F♯ in the realization.

Try it #6 For now, we label every beat with a Roman numeral, but in Chapter 15 we will learn a system of contextual analysis that will help us convey the relative strength of each harmony. Our analysis of this chorale phrase includes a "passing $\frac{6}{4}$ chord," which has less structural weight in this progression.

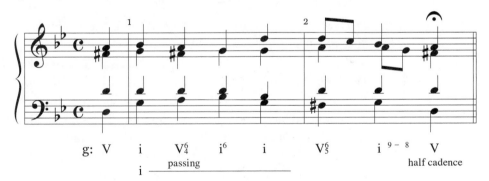

g: V   i   V$^6_4$ i⁶   i   V$^6_5$ i $^{9-8}$ V
           i ————— passing ——————   half cadence

Chapter 15

Try it #1 The Roman numeral analysis for each "vertical" chord is:

D: I I V⁶ V | I $^6_4$ $^5_3$ vii°⁶ | I⁶ vii°⁶ I I⁶ | V $^6_4$ $^5_3$ $^4_2$.

Later in the chapter, we will learn more about how to interpret the strength and function of these chords in a musical context.

Try it #2   The doublings in the Clarke are correct.

Try it #3

KEY	SPELLING	CHORD TYPE
G minor	F♯-A-C-E♭	vii°⁷
B Major	A♯-C♯-E-G♯	vii°⁷
D minor	C♯-E-G-B♭	vii°⁷
F♯ minor	E♯-G♯-B-D	vii°⁷
E♭ Major	D-F-A♭-C	vii°⁷

Try it #4

KEY	$\hat{7}$-$\hat{1}$	$\hat{4}$-$\hat{3}$
C minor	B♮-C	F-E♭
A Major	G♯-A	D-C♯
B minor	A♯-B	E-D
E minor	D♯-E	A-G
A♭ Major	G-A♭	D♭-C

Try it #5   If scale-degree $\hat{2}$ resolved down to $\hat{1}$ in Example 15.6a, it would produce parallel fifths between the soprano and alto voices.

Try it #6   In measure 8, Bach doubles the fifth ($\hat{4}$) of the vii°⁶—probably to create smoother voice-leading in the tenor line and contrary motion between the tenor and bass, and tenor and soprano. (The soprano line cannot be changed, incidentally, since it is a preexisting chorale melody that Bach harmonized.) In the same measure, the E4 on beat 2 creates a ii chord just before the vii°⁶. We will learn more about this progression in Chapter 16.

Try it #7   Some of the diatonic chords we have not yet considered are ii, iii, IV, and vi in major and ii°, III, iv, and VI in minor.

Try it #8   The supertonic triad in minor is diminished—and diminished triads are usually written in first inversion to avoid the strong sound of the diminished fifth between the bass and an upper voice when the triad is in root position. The seventh chord ii°⁷ is also inverted most of the time, but occasionally will be found in root position.

Chapter 16

Try it #1 To answer this question, listen carefully to the right-hand piano part—does it come to a rest on the downbeat of measure 3? No; the melody is continuous until the half cadence in measure 4. We sometimes refer to this type of progression as an evaded resolution: the left-hand harmonic progression sets up a cadential progression, but the right-hand part refuses to cooperate. Remember: Not every V^7–I harmonic progression makes a final cadence. All of the musical elements—melody, rhythm, and harmony—must cooperate to create a sense of finality.

Try it #2 The V^4_3 of Example 16.5a could have been a V^4_2 (change the alto G4 to E4) or a vii^{o6} (change the tenor A3 to G3). A $vii^{ø6}_5$ would result in bad voice-leading in this example, since the tenor substitution of B3 for the A3 would produce parallel fifths with the bass.

In Example 16.5b, the vii^{o6} could have been a V^4_2 (change the tenor G3 to A3) or a V^4_3 (change the tenor G3 to A3 and the alto E4 to G4). We also could have used a vii^{o6}_5 (change the tenor G3 to B♭3 and the alto E4 to G4). This choice produces unequal fifths between the bass and tenor, which is permissible since the leading-tone chord is inverted.

Try it #3

KEY	SOPRANO	BASS	HARMONIZATION 1	HARMONIZATION 2
Major	$\hat{3}$–$\hat{2}$–$\hat{1}$	$\hat{1}$–$\hat{2}$–$\hat{3}$	I–V^6_4–I^6	I–V^4_3–I^6
Major	$\hat{1}$–$\hat{2}$–$\hat{1}$	$\hat{1}$–$\hat{7}$–$\hat{1}$	I–V^6–I	I–V^6_5–I
minor	$\hat{1}$–$\hat{7}$–$\hat{1}$	$\hat{1}$–$\hat{4}$–$\hat{3}$	i–V^4_2–i^6	i–vii^{o4}_3–i^6
Major	$\hat{3}$–$\hat{4}$–$\hat{5}$	$\hat{1}$–$\hat{2}$–$\hat{3}$	I–V^4_3–I^6	I–vii^{o6}–I^6
minor	$\hat{3}$–$\hat{4}$–$\hat{3}$	$\hat{1}$–$\hat{7}$–$\hat{1}$	i–V^6_5–i	i–vii^{o7}–i

Try it #4 In major keys, the fifth between scale-degrees $\hat{7}$ and $\hat{4}$ is diminished; thus, the root progression between IV and vii° (or iv and vii° in minor) is a diminished fifth. In minor keys, there is a tritone between $\hat{6}$ and $\hat{2}$; thus, the root progression between VI and ii is also a diminished fifth.

Try it #5 The chords are

d: i | $ii^{ø4}_2$ V^6_5 | i VI | iv III(??) vii° (??) | i | $ii^{ø4}_2$ V^6_5 | i VI | iv V^7.

All of the chords are normal root progressions except those marked by (??): the I–$ii^{ø4}_2$ and iv–V^7 progressions are by ascending second, crossing functional areas as expected. The $ii^{ø4}_2$–V^6_5–i progressions are by falling fifth; and i–VI–iv is by falling third. The vii° is a little odd—that triad is not found often in root position—and III follows iv in an unusual descending-step pattern. Return to the main text for another interpretation that "explains" these unusual harmonies.

Try it #6 The III, VI, and VII chords in a minor key are the same as I, IV, and V in the relative-major key. They are sometimes used to evoke major keys temporarily in a minor-key context by imitating V–I falling-fifth progressions: VII–III or III–VI.

Chapter 17

Try it #1 Bach treats the repeated B♭4 in the soprano (scale-degree $\hat{5}$) differently in the two phrases: as V–I in the first phrase, but as I–V in the second. In addition, the second phrase is ornamented with a suspension and has a predominant area before the cadence.

Try it #2 The rising stepwise three-note pattern with which the Willson song begins (set to the text "There were bells") could be identified as a motive—let's call it **x**. Motive **x** is repeated twice more in measures 1–3. The second subphrase begins with a variation of motive **x** (mm. 4–5), transposed down and embellished. Both of these motives recur in the second phrase, which begins identically with the first. We might also identify a rhythmic motive, **y**, as the quarter-note triplet, which appears in measures 5–6 and 13–14. In fact, the quarter-note triplet of measures 6 and 14 combines the two motives: the melodic pattern of **x** and the rhythmic pattern of **y**.

Try it #3 A few American folk songs with this melodic structure are "Home on the Range," "Clementine," and "Red River Valley."

Try it #4 Both periods are parallel.

Try it #5 The pattern of the sequence in Example 17.13b is also one measure long. The left-hand part suggests a half-measure pattern, but it is the full measure that is consistently transposed down by step.

Chapter 18

Try it #1 You should have bracketed the left-hand part in measures 3–4 (an octave transposition down of mm. 1–2), the right-hand part of measures 5–6 (an octave transposition up of mm. 1–2), the right-hand part in measures 7–8 (opening pitch of the motive altered, transposed down a step) and 9–10 (mm. 7–8 transposed down a step), and the left-hand part in measures 11–12 (the motive from mm. 7–8 transposed down a fourth from the 9–10 version), 13–14, and 15–16 (each time down a step from the previous iteration).

Try it #2 The chromatic sequence is in measures 22–27. In the first two iterations of this sequence (mm. 22–23, 24–25), the main motive has been inverted: it moves downward, then upward (the opposite of the original motive). The third appearance (mm. 26–27) has it in the original position. These sequence iterations include accidentals that are not a part of either D minor or F Major, the two harmonic areas that have been previously established in this invention.

Try it #3 Look first at the left hand of the Handel. The first triad is arpeggiated (G3–B♭3–D4), divided between the bass and tenor parts (the voicing is shown by the stems—bass down, tenor up). Then a passing tone (F3) connects the bass line G3 to E♭3. The C4 at the end of the measure is the tenor part in the iv^6 chord.

Now for the right-hand part. The B♭4 in measure 89 is decorated first by a consonant skip to D5, then passing tones are added to make B♭4–C5–D5–C5–B♭4. The B♭4 is then ornamented with a double neighbor. The G4 on the third beat is a chord tone in an inner voice, and the chord tone E♭5 is decorated by a lower neighbor.

Try it #4 The sequence extends from measure 5 to 9, with the two-measure pattern in measures 5–6 and 7–8. The Roman numerals in D minor are VI^7–$ii^{\varnothing 7}$–v^7–i^7–iv^7. It differs from Handel's falling-fifth sequences in that Bach's incorporates seventh chords in each measure.

Try it #5 In measure 10 of the Kern song, the expected gm7 (ii^7) is replaced with G7 (a dominant seventh chord on G), and the expected C7 (the C dominant seventh that is V^7 in F minor) in measure 11 is replaced with Cmaj7 (a major seventh chord on C). These replacements set up a cadence in measure 11 on the word "long." After the cadence, Kern returns to Cmin7 and begins another falling-fifth sequence from measure 13 to 19. Although this sequence is not diatonic in its entirety and includes seventh chords, a basic understanding of falling-fifth sequences will help you figure it out. Incidentally, the G7 in measure 10 is a "secondary dominant" to C (marked V^7/V). We will learn about these chords in Chapter 19.

Try it #6 The Roman numerals in measures 5–9 are vi I$^4_3$ | IV^7 vi$^4_3$ | ii^7 IV$^4_3$ | vii^{ø7} ii$^4_3$ | V^7. It is a falling-third sequence (alternating $^4_3$ and ^{7}) with stepwise bass.

Chapter 19

Try it #1 From your study of previous chapters, you should be able to provide Roman numerals and figures for all the chords in measures 6b–16 except those in measures 9 and 10, the subject of this chapter. These are marked with ?? below, then discussed in the text.

E♭ Major: V($^4_2$) | I^6 | I | V^6 ?? | V ?? | V | I | IV^6 I | IV vi | ii^7 V^7 | I |

Try it #2 Yes, the F dominant seventh chord on beat 4 in measure 9, in first inversion, resolves as expected to a B♭-Major triad. The dominant triad at the end of measure 10, in root position, resolves to a B♭-Major triad as well.

Try it #3 In minor keys, we must raise both $\hat{4}$ and $\hat{6}$ of the primary key to write V^7/V. Imagine C minor (three flats); the temporary dominant key is G minor (two flats). The change in key signatures gives us the raised $\hat{6}$ (A♮), but we must also raise the seventh scale degree (F♯) to create a leading tone and to get the major-minor seventh quality. In sum, V^7/V in C minor is spelled D-F♯-A♮-C.

Try it #4

KEY	DOMINANT KEY AREA	V^7/V CHORD
B♭ Major	F Major	C-E♮-G-B♭
E minor	B minor	F♯-A♯-C♯-E
A Major	E Major	B-D♯-F♯-A
D Major	A Major	E-G♯-B-D
G minor	D minor	A-C♯-E♮-G

Try it #5 The chord in both spots is E♭-G-B♭-D♭, which has a dominant seventh quality that undermines the tonic function of the E♭-Major triad. As we know, Mm7 chords imply dominant function. The temporary tonic of the E♭7 chord is A♭ (IV). The Roman numeral label would be V^7/IV. (We will learn more about these chords in Chapter 21.)

Try it #6   In the freer texture of "Pine Apple Rag," Joplin doubles the temporary leading tone (E♮). In the left hand, the normal resolution of E♮4 upward is clouded by the leap downward to the octave F2 and F3. In the right hand, the texture changes from three to two voices, but the E♮5 could be viewed as resolving upward to F5. The chordal seventh (B♭) is also doubled; it resolves down by step as we would expect in the right hand, but does not resolve by stepwise motion in the left.

Try it #7

KEY	DOMINANT KEY AREA	vii°⁷/V CHORD
E♭ Major	B♭ Major	A♮-C-E♭-G♭
A minor	E minor	D♯-F♯-A-C
E Major	B Major	A♯-C♯-E-G♮
F Major	C Major	B♮-D-F-A♭
G minor	D minor	C♯-E♮-G-B♭

Chapter 20

Try it #1   The **A** section returns at measure 49 almost exactly as it was in measures 1–16. You may verify this in your anthology score by comparing measures 49–64 with the opening of the movement. The one measure that is a little different is measure 64, which does not have the weak-beat ending with suspensions of measure 16.

Try it #2   The first two measures of this period are based on the arpeggiated motive, now featuring minor thirds rather than major ones. Measure 18 also has a motive related to the descending-third motive from measure 7.

Chapter 21

Try it #1   Vertical: E♭:   I V⁴₃/vi | vi ii | V⁶ V⁴₃/V | V V⁴₂

(Ts ——)

Contextual: T —— PD D —————

The secondary-dominant-function chords are a V⁴₃/vi (G-B♮-D-F) in measure 5, beat 2, and a V⁴₃/V (F-A♮-C-E♭) in measure 7, beat 2. The B♮ and A♮ are the first clues that these are secondary dominants; after you spot them, check the quality and resolution to confirm their function. Remember that vi is a tonic substitute (Ts) that prolongs the tonic area.

Try it #2 Vertical: B♭: I | I⁶ V vi vii°⁶/vi | vi I⁶ V

(Ts ———)

Contextual: T ——————————— D (HC)

Try it #3 While it may at first appear that the A♮ is left hanging without proper resolution, we need to consider Beethoven's melody as an example of compound melody. Think of the lower line of the compound melody beginning with B♭3 in measure 5, moving to A♮3 in measure 6, and back to B♭3 in measure 7.

Try it #4 The first accidental, F♮5 in measure 173, cancels an F♯ from the previous measure. The second, the left-hand G♯s in measure 174, is a temporary leading tone in V⁶₅/vi—a secondary dominant harmony. The final accidental, the G♮s in measure 175, cancels the G♯s of the previous measure. Two of the three accidentals here are thus "courtesy" accidentals: they do not indicate secondary dominant-function chords.

Try it #5 You should be hearing a half cadence, but if you look in the score, you will notice that the half cadence is not in the main key.

Try it #6 The third and fourth phrases, measures 13–16 and 17–20, follow a similar harmonic design to the measures we have already analyzed. Alterations in measures 18 and 19 (as compared with 14 and 15) make the second HC sound more definitive. Once again, the element that adds emphasis is a secondary dominant (V⁷/V in m. 19).

Try it #7 The seventh is in the bass. The seventh should resolve down, and does, creating a first inversion in the chord of resolution.

Try it #8 The chord in measure 72 is a V⁶₅/ii. The temporary leading tone, this time in the bass, resolves up; the seventh, introduced by a 6–5 motion in the upper voice, resolves down as expected, but after being suspended to the downbeat of the next measure. The secondary dominant in measure 80 is a V⁶₅/IV.

Try it #9 Here are three possible reasons why this works; you may think of others. (1) As already mentioned, the vii°⁴₃/ii shares two pitch classes with the anticipated C-Major harmony—E and G. (2) The inversion, keeping the G in the bass following the V of measure 11, also creates a pedal point effect, strengthening the connection between the chords in measures 11–12. (3) The voice-leading in measures 11–13 is very smooth: common tones are held, and all other parts move by step.

Try it #10   The chords in measures 29–37 are

D: V | I | V vii°⁷/vi V$^6_5$/vi | vi V⁷/IV | IV I⁶ | IV I⁶ | vi⁷ V⁷/V | ?? V⁷ | I

Think about the role of the chord marked "??"—it is not a standard chord here.

Try it #11

KEY	ROMAN NUMERAL	TONICIZED CHORD	SECONDARY DOMINANT
B♭ Major	V⁷/IV	E♭–G–B♭	B♭–D–F–A♭
F♯ minor	vii°⁷/III	A–C♯–E	G♯–B–D–F♮
A Major	V⁷/ii	B–D–F♯	F♯–A♯–C♯–E
G Major	vii°⁷/vi	E–G–B	D♯–F♯–A–C
E♭ Major	V⁷/vi	C–E♭–G	G–B♭–D–F
C minor	V⁷/V	G–B–D	D–F♯–A–C
D Major	vii°⁷/IV	G–B–D	F♯–A–C–E♭

Try it #12   The analysis, beginning with measure 244, follows.

Vertical: C: I⁶ vii°⁷/ii | V/V (or II?) vii°⁷ | I vii°⁷/V | V$^{8-7}_{4-3}$ | I ‖

(Ts ———)

Contextual: T ——————————————— D ——————— T

In each case, the tendency tones all resolve, but the expected ii in measure 245, beat 1, is replaced with V/V (a triad with the correct root but a surprising chord quality), and the expected V in measure 245, beat 2, is replaced by vii°⁷ (a chord with the same function that shares three common tones with V⁷, but not the expected root). The F♯5 in the V/V resolves down, pulled down by the descending chromatic line in the piano melody.

Chapter 22

Try it #1 Both phrases end on an A-Major chord, but the cadence in measure 4 is a half cadence in the tonic key (D Major); the second cadence sounds more like a move to the key of A Major because of the measures that precede the final chord.

Try it #2 The cadence in measure 4 is an authentic cadence: V^7–i in D minor. The cadence in measure 8 is likewise an authentic cadence: this time a PAC in F Major, the relative major of D minor.

Try it #3 The arpeggiated chord sounds like a combination of V^7 (A-C♯-E-G) and vii°⁷ (C♯-E-G-B♭). This dominant-function harmony, which may be labeled V^9_7, represents a typical "ninth chord" in Baroque writing. The B♭4, the ninth above the bass A3, though approached by arpeggiation as a chord tone, immediately resolves linearly to the octave (A4), then passes through the seventh of the chord (G4) as the chord resolves to tonic.

Another way to interpret this ninth is as part of a 9–8 suspension. Where was the suspension prepared? If we hear the top note of the arpeggio as the "soprano voice," then it connects back to the B♭4 of measure 2 as the suspension's consonant preparation. The suspended tone then resolves down by step (B♭–A) as expected. The rich sound of this rising arpeggiation makes a truly magical moment in this brief, deceptively simple-looking composition.

Try it #4

GIVEN KEY	CLOSELY RELATED KEYS
F Major	g, a, B♭, C, d
E♭ Major	f♯, g♯, A, B, c♯
A Major	b, c♯, D, E, f♯
G Major	a, b, C, D, e
B♭ Major	c, d, E♭, F, g

Try it #5

GIVEN KEY	CLOSELY RELATED KEYS
E minor	G, a, b, C, D
G minor	B♭, c, d, E♭, F
C♯ minor	E, f♯, g♯, A, B
F minor	A♭, b♭, c, D♭, E♭
B minor	D, e, f♯, G, A

Try it #6 Pivot chords from a major key to its supertonic (I–ii):

D Major:	I		ii	iii	IV	V	vi		vii°
	D		e	f♯	G	A	b		c♯°
e minor:	D	d♯°	e	f♯°	G	a	b	B	C
	VII	vii°	i	ii°	III	iv	v	V	VI

Pivot chords from a major key to its mediant (I–iii):

D Major:	I		ii	iii	IV	V	vi		vii°
	D		e	f♯	G	A	b		c♯°
F♯ minor:	D	E	e♯°	f♯	g♯°	A	b	c♯	C♯
	VI	VII	vii°	i	ii°	III	iv	v	V

Pivot chords from a major key to its subdominant (I–IV):

D Major:	I	ii	iii	IV	V	vi	vii°
	D	e	f♯	G	A	b	c♯°
G Major:	D	e	f♯°	G	a	b	C
	V	vi	vii°	I	ii	iii	IV

Try it #7 The direct modulation in this chorale setting is less abrupt than it could be because the arrival of D minor is prepared by the beginning of the first phrase. The first two chords of this phrase could be labeled i–VI in D minor instead of vi–IV in F Major, although the rest of the first phrase confirms that the F-Major analysis is the preferred one. Still, without this opening emphasizing a D-minor triad, the shift to D minor at the beginning of the second phrase would seem more sudden.

Try it #8 The progression is:

$$\text{e:} \quad \text{i V}^7 \text{ (tonic ped)} \mid \text{i} \mid \text{V}^7 \text{ i} \mid \text{V}^{8-7} \mid \text{i iv}^6 \mid \text{V} \boxed{\text{iv}^6}$$

$$\text{(HC)} \qquad \text{G:} \boxed{\text{ii}^6} \; \text{V}^6\text{/V} \mid \text{V}^{6-7}_{4-3} \mid \text{I}$$

$$\text{(III)}$$

Chapter 23

Try it #1 The two phrases form a parallel period. The first phrase (antecedent) ends with an inconclusive HC; the second (consequent), with a PAC. Both phrases begin similarly, with a perfect fourth A4–D5 followed by a scale fragment, and the cadential patterns at the end of the phrases are also similar. The phrases can be labeled **a** and **a´**, reflecting their relationship in the parallel period.

Try it #2 Measures 13b–15 are identical to measures 0b–2 of the first phrase; measures 16–17 are a transposition of measures 7–8 into the key of D Major.

Try it #3 The chords in measures 13–16 are

$$\text{d:} \; \text{V}^6_5 \mid \text{V}^7 \mid \text{i ii}^{\circ 6} \text{ V} \mid \text{i} \parallel.$$

The dominant harmony in measure 13 is arpeggiated $\frac{4}{2}$, $\frac{4}{3}$, then $\frac{6}{5}$; in cases like this, we generally label the lowest-sounding bass note in the measure. The V^7 in measure 14 has a minor 9th to 8 motion, as in measure 3, but the bass moves to the third of the chord, making a 9–6 (like the change of bass suspensions we have seen previously).

Try it #4 The phrase features a melodic sequence. The harmonies are similar on each iteration of the sequence, but do not follow the same pattern exactly:

$$\text{F:} \; \text{I I}^6 \text{ IV}^* \mid \text{V} \mid \text{d: i (passing } \tfrac{4}{2}\text{) VI}^* \mid \text{V}$$

The harmonies marked with an asterisk will vary in their analysis, depending on how you read the embellishing tones. This analysis considers them accented passing tones. At the first asterisk, you might have analyzed a ii^6, and in the second case a ii$^{\circ 6}_4$—in either case, their function is PD.

Try it #5 The theme of Mozart's Variations on "Ah, vous dirai-je, Maman," which we considered in some detail in Chapters 8 and 9, is in rounded binary form.

Try it #6 Like the Sousa march, "Solace" is a composite form, with the first large section, **A** (mm. 5–52), in the tonic key (C) and the second section, **B** (mm. 53–84), in the subdominant (F). The piece opens with a four-bar introduction. The **A** section is a simple sectional binary with both halves repeated. Surprisingly, the **A** section returns in measures 37–52; we hesitate to call this a ternary form, however, because **A**, **B**, and **A** all stay in the tonic key. The subdominant-key **B** section is in simple sectional binary form.

Chapter 24

Try it #1 Roman numerals for measures 8–15:

> E♭: I^{5-} |$^{-6}$ | I^6 V^7 | I | I^{5-} |$^{-6}$ | I^6 V^7 | I
>   ↑   ↑
>   (or vi^6)   (vi^6)

Try it #2 Roman numerals for measures 54–65:

> E♭: I | ♭VI^6 | ♭III | ♭VI | V | V^7/IV | IV || IV^6 | V$^8_4$$^{=}$ |$^{=}$$^7_3$ | I
>   ↑   ↑
>   (or V/♭VI)

Try it #3 Many musical features contribute to the climax of this passage. Schubert's vocal line ascends by step to its highest point in the song, A♭5, while the piano accompaniment reaches its lowest pitch, A♭1. Meanwhile, rhythmic durations are lengthened, and the performers *crescendo* to the loudest dynamic of the song. We feel the harmonic tension heightened by the mixture chords, but also by the dissonant suspensions in measures 56–58: 4–3, then 9–8, and then 4–3. These lead to a secondary dominant of IV (m. 59), then IV, followed by a dramatic measure of silence before the phrase concludes.

Try it #4 Every triad of the scale contains a modal scale degree that changes its quality in the parallel minor (you should have circled all the triads).

Try it #5

KEY	PARALLEL MINOR SIGNATURE	♭3	♭6	♭7
C Major	3 flats	E♭	A♭	B♭
E Major	1 sharp	G♮	C♮	D♮
B♭ Major	5 flats	D♭	G♭	A♭
D Major	1 flat	F♮	B♭	C♮
B Major	2 sharps	D♮	G♮	A♮

Try it #6 The solfège for this passage, measures 54–60, is *sol-sol-sol, le-le, te-te, do-do, re-re, mi, fa.*

Try it #7

KEY	PARALLEL MINOR SIGNATURE	ii°	iv	♭III	♭VI
F Major	4 flats	G-B♭-D♭	B♭-D♭-F	A♭-C-E♭	D♭-F-A♭
A Major	0 accidentals	B-D♮-F♮	D-F♮-A	C♮-E-G♮	F♮-A-C♮
E♭ Major	6 flats	F-A♭-C♭	A♭-C♭-E♭	G♭-B♭-D♭	C♭-E♭-G♭
G Major	2 flats	A-C-E♭	C-E♭-G	B♭-D-F	E♭-G-B♭
C♯ Major	4 sharps	D♯-F♯-A	F♯-A-C♯	E-G♯-B	A-C♯-E

Try it #8 The mixture chords are boldface.

D: V⁷ | I I⁶ | I I⁶ | **ii°⁶₅ ii°⁴₃** | **ii°⁶₅ ii°⁴₃** | V⁶₅/V V⁴₃/V | I⁶₄ **V⁶₅/♭VI** | **♭VI iv⁶** | I⁶₄ IV | I⁶₄ (passing) IV⁶ V⁴⁻³ | I I⁶ | **♭VI V⁶₅/♭VI** | **♭VI** ?? | I⁶₄ IV | I⁶₄ IV⁶ V⁶₄₋⁵♭₃ | ₄₋³⁵ | I | I (arp. ⁶₄) I⁶ | I | I ‖

The ?? is an augmented-sixth chord, the subject of Chapter 25. This chord combines the quality of the iv in the analagous spot in measure 38 with a ♯4, which pushes more strongly toward the dominant.

Try it #9 The mixture chords are underlined.

D: ii^6 <u>ii^{o6} $^{-\,\varnothing 6}_{5}$</u> | <u>vii$^{o4}_{3}$</u> | i^6 vii^{o6} i^6 V^6 | <u>♭VI^6</u> V^6 <u>♭VI^6</u> vii^{o6}/iv | <u>iv^6</u> vii^{o6}/iv <u>iv^6</u> <u>♭III^6</u> | <u>♭II^6</u> I^6 <u>♭II^6</u> vii^o/V | V | (V) | I

Chapter 25

Try it #1 The analysis, beginning with the first complete measure, is

d: i | ii^{o6} V^7 | i V$^4_2$/iv IV^6 ?? | V$^{6-5}_{4-3}$

Try it #2 The analysis is

d: vii^{o7}/iv IV vii$^{o6}_{5}$ i^6 | iv^6 III^6 ??^{6} i^6 | vii^{o6} i^6 | V

Try it #3 The Roman numerals for measures 22–29 of the Mozart are

a: i | V$^6_5$ (bass suspension) | V$^6_5$ | i | iv i | V$^4_3$ i v^6 | iv^6 III^6 ♭II^6 i | V$^{6-5}_{4-3}$ (HC)

   T ———————————————————— parallel $^6_3$ PD   D ———

Try it #4 The Roman numerals for measures 34–40 of the Mozart are

d: vii$^{o4}_{2}$ | vii$^{o4}_{2}$ V^7 V$^4_2$ | V$^4_2$ i^6 | ♭II^6 vii$^{o6}_{5}$/iv | iv^6 III^6 | ♭II^6 vii^{o7}/V | V$^{6-5}_{4-3}$ (HC)

Dominant   T PD ——————————— D ———————
preparation

Try it #5

KEY	NEAPOLITAN SIXTH
F♯ minor	B–D–G♮
G minor	C–E♭–A♭
A Major	D–F♮–B♭
E minor	A–C–F♮
F Major	B♭–D♭–G♭
B minor	E–G–C♮

Try it #6 The soprano line on solfège would be *ti–fa | re–ti–sol–ti | ti–do–do | ra–mi | fa–me | ra–do | do–ti ‖* (half cadence).

Try it #7 The Neapolitan is in root position and tonicized by a secondary leading-tone chord in measure 118. The Roman numeral analysis for the excerpt is

$$\text{d: i } | \text{ i } | \text{ ♭II } | \text{ vii}^{\circ 6}_{3}/\text{♭II } | \text{ ♭II } | \text{ vii}^{\circ 4}_{3} | \text{ vii}^{\circ 7}/\text{V } | \text{ V}^{6\text{–}5}_{4\text{–}3} | \text{ i ‖}.$$

↑

(over E♭ pedal)

The Erlking is a sinister creature who tries to entice a young boy to his death, while the boy and his father ride on horseback through a dark storm. In this excerpt, Schubert's tonicization of the Neapolitan coincides with the other-worldly character and falsely affectionate words of the Erlking ("I love you . . . "), while the return to tonic signals a return to the reality of the situation: if the boy will not go willingly, the Erlking will take him by force.

Try it #8

KEY	A⁶TYPE	(♭)$\hat{6}$	#$\hat{4}$	$\hat{1}$	REMAINING PITCH
G minor	Gr⁶	E♭	C♯	G	B♭
A Major	It⁶	F♮	D♯	A	A (doubled)
C Major	Fr⁶	A♭	F♯	C	D
D minor	It⁶	B♭	G♯	D	D (doubled)
F♯ minor	Gr⁶	D	B♯	F♯	A

Try it #9 Schubert uses a Gr⁶/I in measure 41, but changes it on the last beat of measure 42 to a Fr⁶/I, before resolving it to I in the following measure.

Chapter 26

Try it #1 Chorus 1 of "Till There Was You" extends from measure 1 to 16a, the bridge from 16b to 24a, and chorus 2 from the last beat of measure 24 to measure 32.

Try it #2 The refrain has a quaternary **a a b a´** design. The bridge section briefly tonicizes other scale degrees in a circle-of-fifths progression: D⁷–G⁽⁷⁾–C⁷–F⁷.

Try it #3 Yes, the verse modulates in Gershwin's song from an opening in G minor to a cadence in B♭ Major, the key of the refrain.

Try it #4 Roman numeral analysis:

m. 37	38	39	40
I I^{+6}	ii^7 V^7	??	ii^7 V^7

41	42	43	44
I I^{+6}	ii^7 V^7 ii^{ø7}	V$^{8-7}_{4-3}$	I

Measure 39 presents the greatest challenge. The chord symbol for the first beat is B♭6, yet the chord has no B♭ at all, unless we consider the C5 a rhythmic displacement of the B♭ chord tone that follows. If we assume the B♭4, then the chord becomes a tonic harmony with added sixth (and perhaps an added ninth, if we "count" the C), a chord that does make harmonic sense as the resolution of the previous dominant seventh. The E°7 that follows does not resolve as we might expect (as a secondary diminished seventh chord); it should be considered a voice-leading chord without Roman numeral, since its D♭4 and E♮4 could be analyzed as nonchord tones. If you like, you may label such spots VL for "voice-leading chord."

Try it #5 There are two additional chords with altered fifths in this passage: in measures 50 (Cm$^{7-5}$) and 51 (C$^{7-5}$).

Try it #6 In measure 51, the chord symbols above the melody line indicate a dominant seventh sonority with lowered fifth, V$^{7}_{♭5}$/V, but it is voiced in the accompaniment with the ♭5 in the bass, which means it is voiced as a Fr^6. This chord leads to F^7, the dominant of the B♭ tonic of chorus 2, which follows.

Try it #7 The rhyme scheme for each verse is abcb. Each verse has an objective couplet followed by a subjective one.

Try it #8 The postlude does not answer the question (or perhaps answers it in the negative), since the final cadence ends with an unresolved dominant seventh chord, which heightens the sense of tonal ambiguity and its associated image of unrequited love. In fact, in Schumann's cycle, the girl marries another man and the protagonist weeps over the loss, finally symbolically burying his grief in a coffin sunk deep into the sea.

Try it #9 Stanza 1 (narrator) begins in measure 15, stanza 2 (father, son, father) in m. 36, stanza 3 (Erlking) in m. 57, stanza 4 (son and father) in m. 72, stanza 5 (Erlking) in m. 86, stanza 6 (son and father) in m. 97, stanza 7 (Erlking and son) in m. 116, and stanza 8 (narrator) in m. 132.

Try it #10 The narrator introduces the half-step neighbor motive with the first pitches of his line: "Wer reitet so spät" in measures 15–17 is sung to A4–B♭–A. He introduces the rising P4 of the father in measures 20–21, appropriately to the text "Es ist der Vater."

Try it #11 The song is in **A B A** form. The "modified ternary" label might be more appropriate, however, since elements of both the **A** (mm. 1–14) and **B** (mm. 15–32) sections find their way into the concluding section (an **A B A/B** form!). The **B** section closes with an expressive climb to its highest point: "und die einsame Träne rinnt" in measures 27–31. The final **A** section picks up this material again to set the parallel text: "Und die einsame Träne bebt" (mm. 39–43).

Chapter 27

Try it #1 The melody for the Chance variations is sixteen measures long, and the theme for the Mozart variations is twenty-four measures without repeats.

Try it #2 The first phrase, **a**, spans measures 1–8 and ends with a PAC in the main key, C Major. The second, contrasting phrase, **b**, extends from measure 9 to 16, ending with a half cadence delayed by a typical Mozartean cadential $^6_4$ progression, with the arrival of the V on the weak part of the measure. The last phrase, measures 17–24, is identical to the first, so we also label it **a**. The repetitions and the arrangements of phrases identify this little piece as being in rounded binary form, ‖ **a** ‖ **b a** ‖, with the harmonic motion away from tonic in the first half of the second part represented by a dominant pedal.

Try it #3 Each of the variations is in rounded binary form. Some have slight changes in the third phrase. In those variations, we might alter our description of the formal design to ‖ **a** ‖ **b a′** ‖.

Try it #4 Variation XII is notated in $^3_4$. Variations III and IV feature triplets throughout, which makes them sound as though they are in $^6_8$ meter. The *adagio* tempo of Variation XI may make it sound like $^4_4$, with quarter notes instead of the notated eighth-note beat subdivisions in $^2_4$.

Try it #5 The melody pitch is preceded by an upper neighbor, then there is a skip up a sixth (to a pitch that would normally be in an inner voice-leading strand if the texture of the theme were thicker), followed by a scale down to the melody pitch. We also find this figure in measures 44–46.

Try it #6 The Bach theme extends to the downbeat of measure 5. The bass-line theme in the Purcell extends to the downbeat of measure 4 (eliding with the beginning of its first repetition). Themes for continuous variations are usually shorter than those for sectional variations.

Try it #7 The Bach composition does indeed begin by repeating its entire harmonic texture for several variations, consistent with its title "chaconne." The bass line begins to change as early as the third variation, and is less consistent than the Purcell bass line. The Purcell is much more clearly a ground-bass variation, or passacaglia, with a bass line that is unchanging (save for transposed statements of the theme).

Try it #8 There are ten variations in the first forty-one measures. Each variation is five measures long, with the final bar of one variation elided with the first bar of the next. Variations 1 and 2 (mm. 1–9) are linked by the homophonic texture, with double- and triple-stop chords (where the violin plays two or three notes at once, using several strings) in a Sarabande-like rhythm (quarter, dotted-quarter, eighth). Variations 3 and 4 (mm. 9–17) are nearly identical for their first three measures, and feature the rhythmic figure dotted-eighth plus sixteenth. Variations 5 and 6 (mm. 17–25) are likewise nearly identical for their first three measures; they include the dotted-eighth-and-sixteenth rhythms of the previous pair, but add more chromatic motion in the lower line. The remaining variations (7 to 10) are not paired.

Try it #9 There are seven complete presentations of the ground bass in the tonic key, four statements in measures 1–12 and three statements in measures 29–38.

Try it #10 The E♭–E♮–F motive in the right hand is derived from the melody in measure 4. The motive in measures 70–71 is not a direct repetition of any earlier melodic material, but may be considered a transposed and compressed version of the opening of the refrain theme: the C–B♭–E♭–D♭–C of measures 1–3a transformed into the D♭–C–D♭–F–E♭–D♭ pattern of measure 70 .

Try it #11 The remainder of the diagram follows. The **C** section includes motives from the refrain and treats them developmentally. This section is longer, proportionally, than the rest and includes more chromatic harmonies (including Neapolitans in mm. 33 and 47). The first half of the **C** section ends with a four-bar suffix that extends the dominant. The key area (relative minor) is a closely related key, and thus not unexpected.

SECTION	PHRASES	MEASURES	KEY/MODE	COMMENTS
		(see text for opening of movement)		
C		29–48	A minor	Relative minor; no transition; longer section; developmental.
	a´´´	29–40		HC; 4-bar suffix (mm. 36–40) prolongs V.
	a´´´´	41–48		PAC; *Stimmtausch* of mm. 29 ff.
Retransition		49–51		Stays in A minor until last bar.
		52		Ends with dramatic fermata to meet 4-bar hypermeter expectation.
A´		53–60	C Major	
	a	53–56		Like mm. 1–4.
	a´	57–60		Like mm. 5–8.
Coda		61–73		Cadential flourishes.

Chapter 28

Try it #1 In a rounded binary movement, the music from the beginning of the first section, or even the entire first section, should return at the end. In any continuous binary form in a major key, you would probably find a modulation to the dominant (as a second key area) partway through the first section. For a movement in G Major, you would expect D Major, and that is what happens here. The second section should start off with an area of harmonic instability, then establish the V^7 chord in G Major to return to the tonic area for the second half of this section. The Mozart movement also follows this pattern.

Try it #2   The phrase could have ended with the G-Major chord on the downbeat of measure 8, but that would not have made a very firm cadence (another IAC). Instead, there is cadential extension in measures 8–10 that leads to a perfect authentic cadence.

Try it #3   This is an independent transition, since the scale patterns ornamented with skipping thirds and incomplete neighbors are new ideas.

Try it #4   Measures 1–4 are identical to measures 71b–75a, but the rest of the passage (mm. 75–83a) is different from the exposition.

Try it #5   The transition passages here are identical!

Try it #6   The second-theme phrase from measures 23–26 is transposed down a perfect fifth in 90–93, while the following phrase, measures 27–31, is transposed up a perfect fourth in 94–98, altering the registral relationship between the phrases. The same transposition pattern is followed for the two phrases of measures 45–51 (and 112–118).

Try it #7   This section does establish a temporary key, the dominant—similar to the beginning of the second large section in some binary-form movements; and there are sequences, especially in measures 62–70. However, the motivic materials are not immediately recognizable as related to the exposition's themes.

Try it #8   The first idea is abruptly transposed down a whole step to B♭ Major—not a closely related key to C Major, but it is VII in C minor. What an unusual way to start a sonata! The dramatic shift in harmony brings in elements of mixture, E♭ and B♭, which are present through the C-minor half cadence in measures 11–13.

Try it #9   As amazing as it may seem, it is in the first ending, measures 85–86, at the end of the exposition. There is no C-Major PAC before then.

Try it #10   Instead of being transposed abruptly down a step, the music from measures 14–17 is transposed up a step to D, and the mode changes to minor.

Try it #11   The right hand is reminiscent of the upper line in measures 9–10, which are themselves an expansion of the melodic upper part in measure 4. Compare also measure 23, and the contour (although it is much slower-moving) of the second theme. The left hand is drawn from the chorale theme.

Try it #12   Some of the elements of the exposition explored in the development section include the main theme from measures 1–4 (see mm. 90–95 especially, though motives from the main theme persist through measure 111); the accompaniment pattern from 14–22 (in mm. 96–103); the arpeggiation accompaniment from 23–28 (in mm. 104–110); subsection 2b, with its syncopation and triplets, from measures 50–56a (in mm. 112–141).

Try it #13   Consider the ascending fragments in the right hand in measures 146–156a. Some of the rhythms are reminiscent of the skip motive without the opening dotted-quarter note, and the contour of those fragments is that of the skip motive inverted; other fragments seem related to the scale motive, again ascending instead of descending. The real test of these connections is whether the motives sound like each other—what do you think? How might the identification of these motives influence performance choices?

Try it #14   Assuming that the measures with only a single octave-doubled (or -tripled) pitch represent root-position triads, the analysis for measures 167–173 is

$$i \mid \flat VI \mid \flat II \text{ (Neapolitan)} \mid \flat VII \mid \flat III \mid iv^7 \text{ } vii^{\circ 4}_{2} \text{ } vii^{\circ 7}/V \mid V^{8-7} \text{ prolonged.}$$

Try it #15   Beethoven introduces the $\flat$II (Neapolitan) in the recapitulation, in the extension to the first theme, measure 169. The Neapolitan is also touched upon in the development section, measure 134.

Chapter 29

Try it #1   The pattern in measures 132–134a is a sequence of root-position secondary dominants: D^7–G^7–C^7–F^7–$B\flat^7$. This progression may be thought of as V^7/G to $G \rightarrow V^7/C$ to $C \rightarrow V^7/F$ to $F \rightarrow V^7/B\flat$ to $B\flat \rightarrow V^7/E\flat$. In G minor, we can interpret it as V^7–V^7/iv–V^7/VII–V^7/III–V^7/VI, a variant of the descending-fifth sequence. The initial V^7 is preceded by iv^6, a normal progression in G minor, but the sequence ends with a 7–6 deceptive resolution of the final V^7/VI to i^6.

Try it #2   On beat 1 of measures 130 and 131, we see diminished seventh chords. The first is F♯-A-(C)-E♭, or $vii^{\circ 7}$ in G minor, which would normally resolve to i; the second is E-G-(B♭)-D, or $vii^{\varnothing 7}/VII$, which would normally resolve to VII.

Try it #3 These measures make a falling-fifth root progression of D to G to C. The second chord in measure 28 is not V—but IV! Hensel holds two common tones, B♭3 and G4, and moves the other two voices by step—E3 to E♭3 and C5 to B♭4. The text of this phrase is "If I rush to escape her, to take heart and flee her, in a moment, ah, my way leads back to her." Perhaps Hensel chose to reflect the indecisiveness expressed by the text in the harmonic progressions.

Try it #4 For measures 16b–19a, you should have written

C: V^7 | V^7 IV^6 (under a G inverted pedal) | ?? V$^6_5$ | I.

The fully diminished seventh chord does not have a dominant function; it is a voice-leading chord. The A♯ and C♯ result from filling in the A–B and C–D whole steps. You may have wondered about the V^7–IV^6 progression—that chord succession is also motivated by passing motion.

Try it #5 The chords are (in C Major): I V^7 | I vii°$^4_3$ | V$^{7♭9}$/IV | V$^{7♭9}$/IV. Then this sequence of chords is repeated on F. The chord in the first half of measure 114 shows a G bass dropping to C in the second half of the measure, which strongly implies a dominant function, and it has some elements of a cadential $^6_4$, but no B♮ or D or F of the normal V^7 in C Major.

Try it #6 In measure 12, the bass line arpeggiates from C to E—ostensibly a change of inversion in a C-Major chord—but an inner voice also moves from C4 down a half step to B3, creating an E-minor triad from the C-Major cadence of the previous phrase.

In measure 16b, the bass line seems to be continuing the sequence when it moves to G. The chord there, however, is V^7 in the key of C Major; the sudden return to C is fairly smooth because this V^7 is an enharmonic respelling of the German augmented sixth in B minor (the F would have been spelled E♯). We will learn more about this relationship later in the chapter. The V^7 in C is prolonged for two measures (17–18, including a common-tone diminished seventh chord) before resolving to C in measure 19.

Try it #7 Look carefully at the connection from measure 41 to 42. The chords A♭-C♭-E♭ and B-D♯ -F♯-A do share some common pitches: E♭ sounds the same as D♯, and C♭ sounds the same as B. Although enharmonically respelled, the common dyad helps make the connection between i in A♭ minor and V^7 of E Major.

Try it #8 The F-A♭-C♭-D chord in measures 48–49 might be heard as vii°⁷/ii in the old key of E Major (enharmonically respelled from E♯-G♯-B-D) or as vii°₅⁶/V in the new key of A♭. The chord that begins measure 50 is a half-diminished (B♭-D♭-F♭-A♭) seventh chord. It is approached from the D-F-A♭-C♭ chord that precedes it by holding the common tone, A♭, and moving the other voices by half step: D to D♭, C♭ to B♭, and F to F♭. The B♭ half-diminished chord typically functions as vii°⁷ in C♭ Major or minor. Enharmonically, it may be respelled A♯-C♯-E-G♯, or vii°⁷ in B Major or minor. Here it does not resolve in either of those ways; instead, the B♭ and D♭ are held as a common dyad, and F♭ and A♭ both move down a half step, forming an E♭-G-B♭-D♭ chord (V⁷ of A♭ Major).

Try it #9 The piece begins with a repeated E-minor first-inversion triad, which establishes the tonic. In measures 10–11, there is an alternation of V and iv⁶, which ends in a half cadence in measure 12, concluding the first phrase.

Try it #10 The chords stacked in thirds (including the right-hand part in parentheses where it stacks in thirds) include the following.

None of these chords resolve exactly as expected.

Chapter 30

Try it #1

MODE	PC CENTER	LETTER NAMES
Mixolydian	F	F G A B♭ C D E♭ F
Dorian	C♯	C♯ D♯ E F♯ G♯ A♯ B C♯
Lydian	B♭	B♭ C D E F G A B♭
Aeolian	F♯	F♯ G♯ A B C♯ D E F♯
Phrygian	G	G A♭ B♭ C D E♭ F G
Locrian	E	E F G A B♭ C D E
Ionian	A♭	A♭ B♭ C D♭ E♭ F G A♭
Lydian-Mixolydian	A	A B C♯ D♯ E F♯ G A

Try it #2   This short composition falls into a ternary form: **A** (mm. 1–8), **B** (mm. 9–13), and **A′** (mm. 14–19). The **A** section juxtaposes the major triad in the right hand with the minor triad in the left. The **A**-section melody is accompanied by descending arpeggios in the left hand. The melody of the **B** section contrasts with **A**'s in pitch and motives, while the left hand plays an ostinato that features a prominent tritone. The **A′** section is an almost literal repeat of the opening.

Try it #3

SONORITY	INTEGER NOTATION	UNORDERED SET
Dominant seventh chord on A	9 1 4 7	{1 4 7 9}
Half-diminished seventh chord on D	2 5 8 0	{0 2 5 8}
Do-re-mi-fa-sol on E	4 6 8 9 e	{4 6 8 9 e}
Augmented triad on F♯	6 t 2	{2 6 t}
Fully diminished seventh chord on C♯	1 4 7 t	{1 4 7 t}
Major-major seventh chord on A♭	8 0 3 7	{0 3 7 8}

Try it #4

SCALE TYPE	STARTING PC	LETTER NAMES	INTEGER NOTATION
Octatonic 01	F♯	F♯ G A B♭ C D♭ E♭ E♮ (F♯)	6 7 9 t 0 1 3 4 (6)
Whole tone	E♭	E♭ F G A B D♭ (E♭)	3 5 7 9 e 1 (3)
Minor pentatonic	D	D F G A C (D)	2 5 7 9 0 (2)
Octatonic 02	E♭	E♭ F F♯ G♯ A♮ B C D (E♭)	3 5 6 8 9 e 0 2 (3)
Major pentatonic	B	B C♯ D♯ F♯ G♯ (B)	e 1 3 6 8 (e)
Whole tone	B♭	B♭ C D E F♯ G♯ (B♭)	t 0 2 4 6 8 (t)

Try it #5

1. Diminished seventh on C: 0 3 6 9
   Diminished seventh on G: 7 t 1 4
   Octatonic scale: 0 1 3 4 6 7 9 t
2. Diminished seventh on D♭: 1 4 7 t
   Diminished seventh on E♭: 3 6 9 0
   Octatonic scale: 0 1 3 4 6 7 9 t
The two octatonic scales are the same.

Try it #6

Section:	A	B	A′	B′	Coda
Measures:	1–5	6–15	16–20	21–29	30–33
Scale type:	OCT 02	OCT 12	OCT 12	OCT 02	Aeolian
Focal pcs:	A/D♯	D/G♯	B♭/E	E♭/A	E♭

Chapter 31

Try it #1 The right hand has a chromatic collection spanning A4 to D5, plus G4. The left hand also has a chromatic collection, C♯4 to E4, plus B3.

Try it #2

B E♭ C♯ A	{9 e 1 3}
F♯ D B	{e 2 6}
D A E♭ C♯ E	{9 1 2 3 4}
E C♯ A	{9 1 4}
F A♭ D A	{2 5 8 9}
D C F♯ A	{6 9 0 2}

Try it #3

TRICHORD	INTEGER NOTATION	TRANSPOSED BY WHAT INTERVAL?	TRANSPOSED SET IN INTEGER NOTATION
{D F A}	{2 5 9}	minor third	{5 8 0}
{B C C♯}	{e 0 1}	minor second	{0 1 2}
{C♯ D F♯}	{1 2 6}	major second	{3 4 8}
{E F♯ A♯}	{4 6 t}	pci 5	{9 e 3}
{C E G♯}	{0 4 8}	pci 7	{7 e 3}
{G♭ A♭ B♭}	{6 8 t}	pci 4	{t 0 2}
{C D F}	{0 2 5}	pci 6	{6 8 e}

Try it #4 All three sets share the same ic vector.

Try it #5 The ic vectors for {0 2 4 6 9} and {0 1 3 5 7 8} are as follows.

0   2   4   6   9
    2   4   6   9   (subtract 0 from each pc after the first)
         2   4   7   (subtract 2 from each pc after the second)
              2   5   (subtract 4 from each pc after the third)
                  3   (subtract 6 from the remaining pc)

1	2	3	4	5	6	= interval classes
0	3	2	2	2	1	

0   1   3   5   7   8
    1   3   5   7   8   (subtract 0 from each pc after the first)
         2   4   6   7   (subtract 1 from each pc after the second)
              2   4   5   (subtract 3 from each pc after the third)
                  2   3   (subtract 5 from each pc after the fourth)
                       1   (subtract 7 from the remaining pc)

1	2	3	4	5	6	= interval classes
2	3	2	3	4	1	

Try it #6 The ordered pitch-interval sequence is −5 +3 +5 +1. If we begin on E4, taking the sequence +5 −3 −5 −1, we get the set that appears in measure 13: E A F♯ C♯ B♯.

Try it #7 The ic vectors will be the same: [332110].

A

7   9   e   t   0
    2   4   3   5
         2   1   3
              e   1
                  2

B

1   e   9   t   8
    t   8   9   7
         t   e   9
              1   e
                  t

1	2	3	4	5	6	= interval classes
3	3	2	1	1	0	

Try it #8

{e 1 4}	{1 e 8}
{9 t 2 3}	{3 2 t 9}
{e 2 5}	{1 t 7}
{3 6 8 9}	{9 6 4 3}
{e 1 2 3 5}	{1 e t 9 7}
{6 9 0 1}	{6 3 0 e}

Try it #9 C = T_3IB and B = T_3IC. The index number is 3.

$$
\begin{array}{r}
B\,\{1\ e\ t\ 9\ 8\} \\
+\quad C\,\{2\ 4\ 5\ 6\ 7\} \\
\hline
3\ 3\ 3\ 3\ 3
\end{array}
$$

Chapter 32

Try it #1 The elements in trichord y are {4 9 t}. As we learned in Chapter 31, we can compare the ordered intervals: –5, –1 for trichord x in measures 1–2, and +5, +1 for trichord y. The sets are inversionally related. To express the relation precisely, reverse the order of one set, and add. The two sets are related by T_eI.

$$
\begin{array}{r}
1\ 2\ 7 \\
+\quad t\ 9\ 4 \\
\hline
e\ e\ e
\end{array}
$$

Try it #2 There are twenty-four members of the set class for pentachord B. They include the set plus its eleven transpositions—{8 9 t e 1}, {9 t e 0 2}, {t e 0 1 3}, {e 0 1 2 4}, {0 1 2 3 5}, {1 2 3 4 6}, {2 3 4 5 7}, {3 4 5 6 8}, {4 5 6 7 9}, {5 6 7 8 t}, {6 7 8 9 e}, and {7 8 9 t 0}—and the inversion plus its eleven transpositions: {e 1 2 3 4}, {0 2 3 4 5}, {1 3 4 5 6}, {2 4 5 6 7}, {3 5 6 7 8}, {4 6 7 8 9}, {5 7 8 9 t}, {6 8 9 t e}, {7 9 t e 0}, {8 t e 0 1}, {9 e 0 1 2}, and {t 0 1 2 3}. Note that pentachord A is included in the latter group: {7 9 t e 0}.

Try it #3 The original pentachord, {A♭4 A♮4 B♭4 B♮4 C♯5}, spans the smallest interval. The rotations given in Example 32.3 span pitch-intervals 5, e, and e, respectively. (Remember, with pitch intervals, we simply count the semitones.) The remaining rotations with pitch-interval spans calculated are:

The transposition to C yields [C4 C♯4 D4 E♭4 F4], for a prime form of [0 1 2 3 5].

Try it #4 The pitch-interval spanned by pentachord A is 5. The remaining rotations with interval spans calculated are:

The normal order is therefore {G4 A4 B♭4 B♮4 C5}.

Try it #5 The normal order is {D4 E♭4 E♮4 F4 G4}; transposed to C, we get [C4 C♯4 D4 E♭4 F4], for a prime form of [0 1 2 3 5]. This is the same prime form we found for pentachord B; pentachords A and B thus belong to the same set class.

Try it #6

{E A♭ A}	[0 1 5]*
{G C♯ D}	[0 1 6]
{F A♭ D A}	[0 1 4 7]*
{B E♭ C♯ A}	[0 2 4 6]
{D C F♯ A}	[0 2 5 8]*
{F♯ D B C E}	[0 1 3 5 7]
{D A E♭ C♯ E}	[0 1 2 3 7]

(*An asterisk indicates that it was necessary to invert the pcset to find prime form.)

Try it #7 Pentachord E is a chromatic pentachord with a normal order of {t e 0 1 2} and a prime form of [0 1 2 3 4]. Pentachord F is equivalent to penta-chords A, B, C, and D.

Try it #8 The pc content of measure 1 is [0 2 6]. The first three pitches of measure 2 (including the sustained C) are [0 4 8]. If we exclude the "pedal point" C, the melody pitches of measure 2 are [0 2 4] (transposed to 0, the prime form). In addition, the ascending scale that ends measure 3 is another statement of [0 2 4], as are the first three pcs of that measure (including C4).

Try it #9 The circled trichords are: measure 72 (bass)—[0 2 7]; measures 72–73 (soprano)—[0 2 7]; measure 73—downbeat [0 3 7], and end of measure [0 2 4]; measure 74—[0 2 7]; and measure 75—[0 2 5].

Try it #10 The prime form for every triad in measure 73 is [0 3 7]. This is because all major and minor triads belong to SC [0 3 7]; they are inversionally related. To test whether this is so, try inverting {0 3 7} by replacing each pc with its inverse: {0 9 5}. If we reorder as {5 9 0} and transpose to 0, we get the major triad {0 4 7}.

Try it #11 Sets x and z, {5 6 9} and {3 4 7}, are both members of SC [0 1 4], as we can see by transposing them to 0. In addition, the second three pcs {5 8 9} (not circled) also belong to [0 1 4]; first invert to {7 4 3}, then reorder and trans-pose to 0. Set y, {3 8 9}, must also be inverted, to {9 4 3}. We reorder and trans-pose to find its prime form: [0 1 6]. The trichord {3 4 8}, on beat 2 of measure 1, is a member of SC [0 1 5]. Finally, the melody of the passage at measure 33 con-sists of {9 t 0}. It is a member of SC [0 1 3].

Try it #12 Trichords a and b in measure 8 are instances of SC [0 1 4]. The first chord's pcs are {9 0 1} and the second chord's are {8 e 0}; both need to be inverted to find prime form, because the larger interval is found on the left and the chromatic interval on the right. The inverted forms are {3 0 e} and {4 1 0}, respectively. Reorder and transpose to 0 to find their prime form.

The cello melody, set c ({4 5 9}), belongs to SC [0 1 5]. Violin 1 in measure 9, set d ({t 1 2}), also needs to be inverted ({2 e t}) in order to find its prime form, [0 1 4]. Trichord e, {t e 0}, belongs to SC [0 1 2]. The other two accompanying instruments in measure 9 state [0 1 4] (both sets g and h need to be inverted to find this prime form). The descending violin motive, set f, in measure 10 is SC [0 1 5]. The melody in violin 2, set i, is SC [0 1 2]. If you have trouble finding these prime forms, check carefully to determine whether you need to invert the pcset.

Try it #13 Messiaen uses mode 3 in measures 5–7a, {0 1 2 4 5 6 8 9 t}, and mode 2 in portions of measures 7–8 {1 2 4 5 7 8 t e}.

Chapter 33

Try it #1 The pitch-interval sequence of measure 3 is <+4 −2 −3 −3 +2 +3>. Its retrograde, in measure 4, is <−3 −2 +3 +3 +2 −4>. The pitch-interval sequences are reversed in order, with interval direction inverted as well (each + changed to −, and vice versa).

Try it #2 The pitch-interval sequence of our prime is <+4 −2 −3 −3 +2 +3>. The RI in measure 6 (altos) is <+3 +2 −3 −3 −2 +4>. As this example shows, when two segments are related by retrograde inversion, their ordered pitch-interval sequences are in reverse order (but the pitch-interval direction is the same).

Try it #3 The serial passages of "The Lamb" are found in measures 1–6 and 11–16. The more tonal passages are in measures 7–10 and 17–20.

Try it #4 The row label would be RI_9. It is I_9 backward and ends with pc 9.

Chapter 34

Try it #1 You may want to compare your impressions of the "sonata" form with the following. The exposition's first theme begins in measure 1; its more lyrical second theme begins in measure 14, marked by *a tempo* and *cantabile*, and preceded by a *molto ritard*. (It is unclear which measures form the transition between the two themes, possibly 10–13.) The development begins with the *a tempo* of measure 25, and the recapitulation begins after the fermata in measure 32. The recapitulation is more compressed; each theme is only a few measures long. A final coda extends from the upbeat to measure 39 to the end.

Try it #2 To calculate the transposition of Schoenberg's row to begin on zero, we must subtract 10 from each pc integer as follows:

<t 5 0 e 9 6 1 3 7 8 2 4>
−t t t t t t t t t t t t
<0 7 2 1 e 8 3 5 9 t 4 6>

Try it #3 The completed matrix:

0	7	2	1	e	8	3	5	9	t	4	6
5	0	7	6	4	1	8	t	2	3	9	e
t	5	0	e	9	6	1	3	7	8	2	4
e	6	1	0	t	7	2	4	8	9	3	5
1	8	3	2	0	9	4	6	t	e	5	7
4	e	6	5	3	0	7	9	1	2	8	t
9	4	e	t	8	5	0	2	6	7	1	3
7	2	9	8	6	3	t	0	4	5	e	1
3	t	5	4	2	e	6	8	0	1	7	9
2	9	4	3	1	t	5	7	e	0	6	8
8	3	t	9	7	4	e	1	5	6	0	2
6	1	8	7	5	2	9	e	3	4	t	0

Try it #4 In the opening of the movement, P_t appears in measure 1 and RI_3 in measure 2. In measures 32–33, P_t appears again in the right hand and I_3 in the left hand. Beginning midway through measure 33, new rows begin: RI_3 in the right hand and R_t in the left hand.

Try it #5 The row in the right hand is P_t, and the row in the left is I_3.

Chapter 35

Try it #1 There is a clear and regular beat throughout this example. Following the castanet part, you likely conducted in a regular three-beat pattern. The wind parts, while coordinating with the beats in the castanet part, usually do not group neatly into a three-beat pattern. While it is possible to conduct the winds in three, their rhythmic patterns correspond better to Stravinsky's notation (as you will see when you examine the score).

Try it #2 Though the rhythmic patterns in the wind parts could be notated in other meters, Stravinsky's choice indicates how we should place metrical accents in performance to give these parts their characteristic sound. The conducted changes of meter help to keep the winds together and to give them a uniform pattern of metrical accent. The castanet player simply has to continue articulating a regular $\frac{3}{8}$ throughout the meter changes.

Try it #3 The division in measure 1 is not a usual one for $\frac{5}{4}$. The eighth notes group into a 3 + 3 + 2 + 2 pattern, or two dotted quarters followed by two quarters. In the second measure, the $\frac{4}{4}$ meter is grouped in eighths, 3 + 3 + 2—not the usual division of $\frac{4}{4}$, but a truncated version of the previous measure. Measure 3 yields too little information to determine definitive groups. In measure 4, the $\frac{4}{4}$ grouping is the retrograde of measure 2: 2 + 3 + 3.

Try it #4 It is likely that you found this task frustrating! In careful, accurate performances of this piece, it should be hard to determine a regular beat or meter. You may be able to distinguish a regular pattern for several beats, but the music does not continue with the pattern you are conducting.

Try it #5 There are perceivable triple divisions of the quarter-note beat in measure 4, beat 2, and measure 12, beat 1, and two-beat triplets in the second half of measures 5 and 7. Other notated triplets are less easy to hear because of ties extending over the beat. Duple divisions of the quarter-note beat are found in measure 13, beat 1, with several other spots (such as measure 8, beat 1) likely to be heard as a duple division even though one of the notes is tied over.

Try it #6 The pattern changes again in measures 17, 18 (in both hands), and 20.

Chapter 36

Try it #1 We have seen that there is a sectional division at rehearsal 10, as the "insect sounds" stop to reveal an underlying cluster of pitches expanding, then shrinking in range. But because this connection is elided, not all listeners will hear a sectional division here. The next subsection (10–18) is marked by clusters that are sustained, then *glissando* up or down, sounding like fireworks rockets taking off. The division is reinforced by a change in texture to individual, pointillistic, imitative entries. You may have heard internal ideas within this section, made by individual pitch clusters expanding and then shrinking in range, similar to the way the subsection opened (at rehearsal 10).

Try it #2 The end of this section is made by a combination of a thinning texture (cellos and basses, to cellos, to a solo cello), clusters that *glissando* outward, convergence on a single pitch, decreasing dynamic levels, the ceasing of vibrato, and five seconds of silence.

Try it #3 Several elements contribute to the creation of a sectional division here: the "resolution" of the A♭4-B♭4 dyad outward to G4-B4; the expansion of the wedge figure downward to C4 then B3 (joining the chord in the right hand); the slowing of tempo; the decreasing dynamics; and the change of tempo, dynamic level, and motive that follows in the rest of measure 7.

Try it #4 Measure 17 serves a transitional function, leading to the return of material similar to section **A** in measures 18–23. Material in measures 24–30 is also derived from the original **A**.

Try it #5 These measures serve as a retransition from the **B** section materials back to prepare for the return of **A**-related materials in measure 18b. The sharps at the end of the **B** section gradually give way to the D-E dyad (represented in several octaves) of the **A′** section.

Try it #6 Perhaps the easiest way to determine their relationship is to write them as pc integers:

m. 6	<0 4 6 e 1 7 t>
m. 10	<5 9 e 4 6 0 3>
mm. 12–13	<8 0 2 7 9 3 6>

They are transpositions of each other: the first one is transposed by T_5 (in pitch intervals down seven semitones) to make the second, which is transposed by T_3 (up fifteen semitones) to make the third.

Try it #7 Here are a few to get you started: The length of the piece and the range of sounds available from materials in the woods would depend on the location and time of year; but it takes all day to perform, and the resources and sounds available in a section of woods are predictable. The tasks undertaken by the performers are specified, but the details are left to each individual.

Chapter 37

Try it #1 Each phrase division follows a unit of text and is marked by a change in which vocal parts are singing. The dashed lines indicate the ends of words. The first phrase centers on C5, which is repeated in the soprano 1 part; the phrase spans a third above and below the center. The second phrase, with its repeated F-minor triads, centers on F3. The bass part carries the main melody, and the tenor parts support it with F-minor chord members. The ametric rhythm is structured to emphasize, by increased duration, the accented syllable of each word.

Try it #2 The passage opens with Cherubino singing in G Major. In measure 11, Rosina's entry (with a change of key signature to A Major) disturbs an impending half cadence in G by introducing a B-minor $^6_4$ followed by a E dominant seventh chord, which progresses to an A-Major chord in measure 13—a harmonic destination quite distant from Cherubino's key.

Try it #3 As noted in Chapter 35, Rosina's accompaniment includes two-beat triplets, a striking contrast to Cherubino's even quarters and eighths. The chords in her section are also inverted, which weakens the harmonic strength of the progression. Later in the passage, her melodies feature some dramatic wide intervals, as opposed to Cherubino's lyrical melody.

Glossary

1:1 (one-to-one): Counterpoint written so that each note in one voice is paired with a single note in the other voice, using only consonant intervals. Another name for *first-species* counterpoint.

2:1 (two-to-one): Counterpoint written so that one voice has two notes for every single note in the other voice. Permits consonances and passing tones, according to strict rules of voice-leading; in eighteenth-century style, also allows neighbor tones. Another name for *second-species* counterpoint.

3:1 (three-to-one): Counterpoint written so that one voice has three notes for every single note in the other voice. Considered a type of second species according to Fux, but in eighteenth-century practice it is more closely related to third-species counterpoint in its use of dissonance.

4:1 (four-to-one): Counterpoint written so that one voice has four notes for every single note in the other voice; permits consonances, passing tones, and neighboring tones, according to strict rules of voice-leading. Another name for *third-species* counterpoint.

A

a a b a: The formal design associated with quaternary song form.

A B A: The formal design associated with ternary form.

abrupt modulation: Another term for *direct modulation*.

abstract complement: Two set classes where one representative of each, when combined, make a lit-eral complement. This relationship is shown in the Forte numbers: the numbers before the hyphen sum to 12; the numbers after the hyphen are the same (e.g., 4-Z15, 8-Z15).

accent: Stress given to a note or other musical element that brings it to the listener's attention—by playing louder or softer, using a different timbre or articulation, slightly changing rhythmic durations.

accidental: A musical symbol (sharp, flat, natural, double sharp, or double flat) that appears before a note to raise or lower its pitch chromatically.

added-sixth chord: A triad that contains an extra pitch a major sixth above the bass note.

additive rhythm: An ametric rhythm created when a brief duration (often a sixteenth or smaller) is chosen as a base element, and then several brief durations are added together to form larger durations.

Aeolian mode: An ordered collection with the pattern of whole and half steps corresponding to the diatonic collection starting and ending on A; the same collection as the natural minor scale.

aggregate: A collection of all twelve pitch classes. The term generally refers to the combination of two or more twelve-tone rows so that, together, new twelve-note collections are generated. Aggregates may also appear in non-twelve-tone music.

Alberti bass: A common Classical-period accompaniment formed by arpeggiating triads in repeated patterns, such as root-fifth-third-fifth.

all-combinatorial hexachord: A hexachord capable of all four types of combinatoriality (P-, I-, R-, and RI-combinatoriality).

altered common-chord modulation: A type of modulation whose pivot chord is a chromatic chord in one or both keys (e.g., mixture chord, secondary dominant, secondary leading-tone chord).

altered-fifth chord: A triad or seventh chord that has been colored and intensified by raising or lowering the fifth by a half step.

altered pivot-chord modulation: Another term for *altered common-chord modulation*.

alto: The second-highest voice in four-part SATB writing, usually directly below the soprano.

alto clef: A C-clef positioned on a staff so that the middle line indicates middle C (C4); typically read by violas.

ametric: Music for which no regular meter is perceived; may be notated in nontraditional ways.

anacrusis: Occurs when a melody starts just before the first downbeat in a meter; also called an *upbeat*, or pick-up.

anhemitonic pentatonic: A pentatonic scale with no half steps.

antecedent phrase: The first phrase of a period; ends with an inconclusive cadence (usually a half cadence).

anticipation: An embellishing tone whose pitch of resolution arrives "early." An anticipation is unaccented, and almost always a dissonance. It does not resolve by step—rather, it is repeated as a consonance on the next beat, where it "belongs."

applied chord: A dominant-function harmony (V or vii°, with or without the chordal seventh) "applied" to a chord other than tonic. An applied chord typically includes chromatic alterations (relative to the tonic key). Also called a *secondary dominant*.

appoggiatura: A dissonance that occurs on a strong beat and usually resolves down by step. Some theorists restrict this term to an accented dissonance approached by skip or leap; others consider appoggiaturas accented incomplete neighbors (or complete if approached by step).

arpeggiated $\hat{6}$: A $\hat{6}$ created when the bass line sounds each note of a triad in turn (root, third, fifth), or alternates between the root and the fifth.

arpeggio, arpeggiated: A chord played one pitch at a time.

articulation: The different ways a note can be attacked and connected to other notes. It might be played very short (*staccato*), held (*tenuto*), or played suddenly and loudly (*sfzorzando*). The notes of a melody may be highly connected (*legato*) or separated.

art song: A song, usually featuring a literary poetic text, written for performance outside the popular- and folk-music traditions.

asymmetrical meter: A compound meter with beat units of unequal duration. These "irregular" beat lengths are typically (though not always) created by five or seven beat divisions, grouped into beat lengths such as $2 + 3$ or $2 + 3 + 2$.

atonal: Another term for *nontonal*.

augmentation: The process of systematically lengthening the duration of pitches in a musical line. There is usually a consistent proportion in relation to the original melody (e.g., each original duration may be doubled).

augmented interval: An interval one half step larger than a major or perfect interval.

augmented-sixth chord: A chord featuring (♭)$\hat{6}$ in the bass and $\sharp\hat{4}$ in an upper voice, creating the interval of an augmented sixth. Such chords usually resolve to V: (♭)$\hat{6}$ and $\sharp\hat{4}$ resolve outward by half step to $\hat{5}$.

augmented triad: A triad with major thirds between the root and third and between the third and fifth. The interval between the root and fifth is an augmented fifth.

B

B♭ instrument: An instrument whose sounding pitch is a whole step lower than the notated pitch. The most common B♭ instruments are the trumpet, clarinet, bass clarinet, and tenor saxophone (the last two sound a whole step plus an octave lower than the notated pitch).

balanced sections: A feature of binary forms in which material from the end of the first section returns at the end of the second section.

bar line: A vertical line that indicates the end of a measure.

Baroque era: The period in Western music history dating roughly from 1600 until 1750. Some Baroque composers are Johann Sebastian Bach, George Frideric Handel, François Couperin, Antonio Vivaldi, and Henry Purcell. Genres associated with this era are the concerto grosso, oratorio, keyboard suite, and cantata.

basic phrase: A conclusive phrase that consists of an opening tonic area (T), an optional predominant area (PD), a dominant area (D), and tonic closure

(T, a cadence on I). Written in contextual analysis as T–PD–D–T, beneath Roman numerals (vertical analysis).

bass: The lowest voice in four-part (SATB) writing. The bass pitch does not always represent the root of a chord.

bass clef: On a staff, the bass clef (also known as the F-clef) rests on the line that represents F3; its two dots surround the F3 line; typically read by bassoons, cellos, basses, and piano left hand.

beat: The primary pulse in musical meter.

beat division: The secondary pulse in musical meter; the first level of faster-moving pulses beneath the primary beat.

bimodality: The simultaneous use of two modes in two different layers of music.

binary form: The formal design of a composition organized into two sections. Usually each section is repeated.

bitonality: The simultaneous use of two keys in two different layers of music.

blue note: One of three possible pitches, derived from the blues scale, that can be altered in popular music for expressive effect: $\flat\hat{3}$, $\sharp\hat{4}$ (or $\flat\hat{5}$), and $\flat\hat{7}$.

blues scale: This scale blurs the distinction between major and minor by permitting both $\hat{3}$ and $\flat\hat{3}$ and both $\hat{7}$ and $\flat\hat{7}$. It also allows $\sharp\hat{4}$ and $\hat{4}$, and $\flat\hat{5}$ and $\hat{5}$.

borrowed chord: A harmony whose spelling and chord quality are derived from the parallel mode. Most often, chords from the parallel minor mode appear in a major key. Another name for *mixture* chord.

bridge: The contrasting **b** section in an **a a b a** thirty-two-bar song form.

C

C-clef: A movable clef that may be placed on a staff to identify any one of the five lines as middle C (C4).

C instrument: An instrument whose sounding pitch is the same as the notated pitch. Common C instruments include the piano, flute, oboe, bassoon, trombone, tuba, harp, and most of the string family.

C score: A nontransposed score that shows all the parts in the concert key—i.e., all the pitches in the score are the pitches that the instruments sound. Also known as *concert-pitch* score.

cadence: The end of a phrase, where harmonic, melodic, and rhythmic features articulate a complete musical thought.

cadential extension: A type of extension occurring at the end of a phrase. Typically, the cadence is repeated with little new or elaborative melodic material.

cadential $^6_4$: A $^6_4$ chord that embellishes the V chord. The cadential $^6_4$ is spelled like a second-inversion tonic chord, but it has no tonic function. Instead, it displaces the V chord with simultaneous 6–5 and 4–3 suspension-like motions above the sustained bass note $\hat{5}$. Usually occurs on a strong beat.

cadenza: A solo portion at the end of a concerto movement that features rapid passagework and other technical challenges. Can appear in any concerto movement, but is generally found in the first movement after a prominent cadential $^6_4$ harmony in the orchestra, before the beginning of the coda.

cantus firmus: The given melody against which a counterpoint is written.

cardinality: The number of elements in a collection.

center: A pitch or pitch class pervasively heard in a work or section of a work. A center does not imply a functional system of scale degrees in any key or mode (as does traditional functional tonality), but it can establish a sense of hierarchy.

centric: Music that focuses on a pitch or pitch-class center, but not in the sense of a conventional tonal hierarchy.

chaconne: A set of continuous variations in which the entire harmonic texture, not just the bass line, is repeated and varied. While the bass line may remain unchanged for several successive variations, it is usually altered as the chaconne progresses—through rhythmic variation, changes in inversion, or substitute harmonies.

chance: A method of composition or performance that is determined by a random or unpredictable procedure, such as the toss of coins, dice, or the *I-Ching*.

change of bass suspension: A type of suspension in which the bass changes when the suspension resolves; e.g., a 9–8 suspension that becomes a 9–6 because the bass skips up a third.

changing meter: In contemporary pieces, meter that changes from measure to measure.

character variation: A variation intended to reproduce a particular musical style or evoke a certain genre.

chorale: A hymn set for four voices. The voices tend to move together, creating a chordal texture. Often, the melody is given to the soprano.

chord: A group of pitches sounded together. In common-practice harmony, chords are generally built in thirds.

chord members: The pitches that make up a chord. In tonal music, each chord member is described by the interval it forms with the lowest (or bass) pitch of the chord.

chordal skip: A melodic embellishment made by skipping from one chord member to another.

choruses 1 and 2: The outer sections of an **a a b a** quaternary song form. They share the same or similar musical material.

chromatic: Chromatic music includes pitches from outside the diatonic collection. The chromatic collection consists of all twelve pitch classes.

chromatic half step: A semitone spelling in which both pitches have the same letter name (e.g., D and D♯).

chromatic inflection: A method of modulation effected by shifting one pitch by a half step.

chromatic neighbor tone: A nondiatonic half-step neighbor that embellishes a chord tone.

chromatic passing tone: A passing tone that divides a diatonic whole step into two half steps.

chromatic variation: A variation that contrasts with the original theme through increased chromaticism. The chromaticism can embellish the melodic line or elaborate the chord progressions.

chromatic voice exchange: The chromatic alteration of one of the pitches in a voice exchange (e.g., scale-degrees $\hat{2}$ and $\hat{4}$ in a ii$^{(7)}$ might exchange places to become ♯$\hat{4}$ and $\hat{2}$ in a V^7/V).

chromaticized sequence: A diatonic sequence transformed by substituting chromatic harmonies for diatonic ones, or by chromatically embellishing the sequence.

circle of fifths: A circular diagram showing the relationships between keys when sharps or flats are added to the key signature. The sharp keys appear around the right side of the circle, with each key a fifth higher. The flat keys appear around the left side of the circle, with each key a fifth lower.

Classical era: The period in Western music history dating roughly from 1750 until 1830. Some Classical composers are Wolfgang Amadeus Mozart, Franz Joseph Haydn, and Ludwig van Beethoven. Genres most associated with this era are the string quartet, the sonata, the symphony, and opera.

clef: A symbol that appears on the far left of every staff to designate which line or space represents which pitch (in which octave).

closed: Term referring to a melody or formal section that ends with a conclusive cadence on the tonic.

closely related key: Any key whose tonic is a diatonic triad (major or minor) in the original key. The key signatures of closely related keys differ at most by one accidental.

closing theme: A "third theme" that might be found near the end of a sonata-form exposition; part of the second theme group if it shares the same key.

coda: A section of music at the end of a piece, generally following a strong cadence in the tonic. Serves to extend the tonic area and bring the work to a close.

codetta: A "little coda" at the end of a section or piece.

coda/codetta theme: A distinctive, identifiable melody introduced in a coda or codetta.

collection: A group of unordered pitches or pitch classes that serve as a source of musical materials for a work or a section of a work; a large set.

common-chord modulation: Modulation from one key to another by means of a harmony (the pivot chord) that functions diatonically in both keys.

common-dyad modulation: A type of modulation in which two pitches of a chord in the initial key function as a "pivot" between the two keys. Other pitches of this modulating chord may shift up or down a half step, making a chromatic connection.

common practice: The compositional techniques and harmonic language of the Baroque, Classical, and Romantic eras.

common-tone modulation: A type of modulation in which only a single pitch of a chord or melodic line in the initial key functions as a "pivot" between the two keys. Other pitches of this modulating chord may shift up or down a half step, making a chromatic connection.

common-tone theorem: The number in each position of a pcset's ic vector tells two things: (1) the number of times a particular interval class occurs between elements of the set, and (2) the number of common tones that will result when that particular interval class is used to transpose the pcset. The latter principle is called the common-tone theorem.

composite ternary: A formal scheme created by joining smaller, complete forms into an **A B A** form (such as a minuet and trio, or scherzo and trio). The **A** and **B** sections themselves may have their own formal type (such as rounded binary).

compound duple: Any meter with two beats in a measure, with each beat divided into three (e.g., $\frac{6}{8}$ or $\frac{6}{4}$).

compound interval: An interval larger than an octave.

compound melody: A melody created by the interaction of two or three voices, usually separated by register. Often features large leaps.

compound meter: Any meter in which the beat divides into threes and subdivides into sixes. The top number of the meter signature will be 6, 9, or 12 (e.g., $\frac{9}{4}$ or $\frac{6}{8}$).

compound quadruple: Any meter with four beats in a measure, with each beat divided into three (e.g., $\frac{12}{8}$ or $\frac{12}{4}$).

compound triple: Any meter with three beats in a measure, with each beat divided into three (e.g., $\frac{9}{8}$ or $\frac{9}{4}$).

concert pitch: The sounding pitch of an instrument. For transposing instruments, this differs from notated pitch.

concerto: A composition for a solo instrument and orchestra. Concertos often consist of three movements, arranged fast-slow-fast (following a formal pattern similar to the three-movement sonata).

conclusive cadence: A cadence that makes a phrase sound finished and complete. Generally the harmonic progression is V–I, with both soprano and bass ending on scale-degree $\hat{1}$.

conjunct motion: Melodic motion by step.

consequent phrase: The second phrase of a period. The consequent phrase ends with a strong harmonic conclusion, usually an authentic cadence.

consonance, imperfect: The intervals of a third and sixth.

consonance, perfect: The intervals of a unison, fourth, fifth, and octave. The harmonic interval of a fourth is treated as a dissonance in common-practice style.

consonant: A relative term based on acoustic properties of sound and on the norms of compositional practice. A consonant harmonic interval—unison, third, fifth, sixth, or octave—is considered pleasing to hear.

consonant skip: Another term for *chordal skip*.

contextual analysis: A second level of harmonic analysis, showing how passing chords (and other voice-leading chords) function to expand the basic phrase model (T–PD–D–T).

continuo: An instrumental accompaniment that is read from only a given bass line (often with figures). The continuo typically consists of a low bass instrument (cello, bass viol, or bassoon) that plays a single-voice bass line, and an instrument capable of producing chordal harmonies (harpsichord, organ, guitar, or lute). The chordal instrument must realize the bass line harmonically—from figures if given, or following principles of harmonic progression and voice-leading.

continuous: Term referring to a section of a piece that has a tonally open ending and must therefore continue into the following section for tonal completion.

continuous binary: A binary form in which the first large section ends with a cadence that is not in the tonic key. The harmonic motion of the piece must continue into the following section to a conclusion in the tonic key.

continuous variation: A variation form characterized by a continuous flow of musical ideas—as opposed to strong, section-defining cadences—and *Fortspinnung* phrase structure. Continuous variations usually feature a short bass line or harmonic progression that remains constant through repeated variations.

contour motive: A motive that maintains its contour, or musical shape, but changes its intervals; its rhythm may or may not be altered.

contrapuntal: (1) A composition based on the principles of counterpoint. (2) A musical texture in which the interaction of several lines creates harmonies. "Contrapuntal chord" is another name for *linear* or *voice-leading chord*.

contrary fifths or octaves: Motion from one perfect interval to another of the same type, in which the voices move in opposite directions. One of the perfect intervals will be a compound interval.

contrary motion: Contrapuntal, or voice-leading, motion in which two voices move in opposite directions.

contrasting period: A period in which the two phrases do not share the same initial melodic material.

counterpoint: A musical texture that sets two or more lines of music together so that the independent lines together create acceptable harmony; or harmonies set one after another so that the individual voices make good, independent melodic lines.

couplet: Two successive lines of poetic text that rhyme or establish a rhyme scheme.

cross relation: The sudden chromatic alteration of a pitch in one voice part, immediately after the diatonic version has sounded in another voice.

D

deceptive cadence: The cadence $V^{(7)}$–vi in major, or $V^{(7)}$–VI in minor. Generally, any nontonic resolution from V at a cadence.

deceptive resolution: A midphrase resolution to the submediant from V.

design: In discussions of musical form, the melodic or thematic aspects, as distinct from the harmonic structure.

development: The section of a sonata form devoted to the exploration and variation of motives and themes from the exposition. Generally features sequential and modulatory passages.

developmental coda: A coda having the character and structure of a sonata-form development; sometimes called a "second development."

diatonic: (1) The collection of seven pitch classes that, in some rotation, conforms to the pattern of the whole and half steps of the major scale (a subset of the chromatic collection). (2) Made up of pitches belonging to a given diatonic collection.

diatonic half step: A semitone spelled with different letter names for the two pitches (e.g., D and E♭).

diatonic sequence: A sequence made up of pitches belonging to the diatonic collection. When the sequence pattern is transposed, generic melodic intervals stay the same, but interval qualities change (e.g., major to minor, or perfect to diminished).

diminished interval: An interval one half step smaller than a minor or perfect interval.

diminished scale: Another name for *octatonic scale*, so called because of the fully diminished seventh chords that are subsets of any octatonic scale.

diminished seventh chord: A seventh chord consisting of a diminished triad and a diminished seventh. Sometimes called a *fully diminished seventh chord* to distinguish it from the *half-diminished seventh chord.*

diminished-third chord: A version of the augmented-sixth chord, with (♭)$\hat{6}$ in an upper voice and ♯$\hat{4}$ in the bass, creating the interval of a diminished third.

diminished triad: A triad with minor thirds between the root and third and between the third and fifth. The interval between the root and fifth is a diminished fifth.

diminution: The process of systematically shortening the duration of pitches in a melodic line. There is usually a consistent proportion in relation to the original melody (e.g., all note values may be reduced by a half).

direct fifths or octaves: Similar motion into a perfect interval, permitted only in inner voices or if the soprano moves by step.

direct modulation: Modulation accomplished without the use of a pivot chord or pitch.

disjunct motion: Melodic motion by skip or leap.

displacement: (1) The rhythmic offsetting of a pitch so that it is "held over" like a suspension from one sonority to the next, or "arrives early" before the rest of a harmony. (2) The offsetting of a triadic pitch in a harmony by another pitch, as in a sus chord.

dissonant: A relative term based on acoustic properties of sound and on the norms of compositional practice. A dissonant harmonic interval—second, fourth (in common-practice harmony, as in a 4–3 suspension), tritone, or seventh—is considered unpleasant or jarring to hear.

dodecaphonic: See *twelve-tone.*

dominant: (1) Scale-degree $\hat{5}$. (2) The triad built on $\hat{5}$.

dominant area: One of the harmonic areas in a basic phrase. In a conclusive phrase, the dominant area precedes the final tonic close.

dominant seventh chord: A seventh chord consisting of a major triad and a minor seventh. Occurs diatonically on $\hat{5}$.

dominant substitute: The harmony vii°, vii°⁷, or vii°⁷ (built on the leading tone), which may function as a substitute for the dominant. Because they lack the harmonically strong scale-degree $\hat{5}$, dominant substitutes are weaker in dominant function than $V^{(7)}$.

Dorian mode: An ordered collection with the pattern of whole and half steps corresponding to the white-key diatonic collection starting and ending on D. Equivalent to a natural minor scale with scale-degree $\hat{6}$ raised by a half step.

dot: Rhythmic notation that adds to a note half again its own value (e.g., a dotted half equals a half note plus a quarter note).

double exposition: A feature of sonata form in some Classical-era concertos, where material in the exposition is heard twice: once played by the orchestra without modulation to the secondary key, and then by the soloist following the standard tonal scheme (and with the orchestra playing an accompanimental role).

double flat: An accidental (♭♭) that lowers a pitch two half steps (or one whole step) below its letter name.

double neighbor: The combination of successive upper and lower neighbors (in either order) around the same pitch.

double passing tones: Passing tones that occur simultaneously in two or more voices, usually creating parallel thirds or sixths.

double sharp: An accidental (𝄪) that raises a pitch two half steps (or one whole step) above its letter name.

doubling: In four-part writing, a triad pitch represented in two different voices.

downbeat: Beat 1 of a metrical pattern.

duple meter: Meter in which beats group into units of two (e.g., $\frac{2}{4}$, $\frac{2}{2}$, or $\frac{6}{8}$).

duplet: In compound meters, a division of the beat into two equal parts (borrowed from simple meters) instead of the expected three parts.

dyad: A collection of two distinct pitches or pitch classes.

dynamics: The degree of loudness or softness in playing. Common terms (from soft to loud) are *pianissimo, piano, mezzo piano, mezzo forte, forte,* and *fortissimo.*

E

E♭ instrument: An instrument whose sounding pitch is a major sixth lower (or minor third higher) than the notated pitch. The most common E♭ instruments are the alto and baritone saxophone and E♭ clarinet.

eighth note: A stemmed black note head with one flag. In duple beat divisions, two eighth notes divide a quarter-note beat; in triple beat divisions, three eighth notes divide a dotted-quarter-note beat.

element: Most commonly, each single pitch class in a set, segment, or collection. The elements of a set or segment may also be dynamics, durations, articulations, or other musical features.

elision: The simultaneous ending of one phrase and beginning of another, articulated by the same pitches.

enharmonic: Different letter names for the same pitch or pitch class (e.g., E♭ and D♯).

enharmonic equivalence: The idea that two or more possible names for a single pitch (e.g., C♯, D♭, B𝄪) are musically and functionally the same.

enharmonic modulation: A type of modulation in which a chord resolves according to the function of its enharmonic equivalent to establish a new key. Chords that can be spelled (and therefore resolved) enharmonically include fully diminished sevenths, dominant sevenths, and German augmented sixths.

episode: (1) A contrasting section in a rondo; generally less tonally stable than the rondo's refrain. (2) A modulating passage in a fugue.

exposition: In a sonata form, the first large section (often repeated), where the themes and motives for the entire movement are "exposed" for the first time. The typical Classical-era exposition features two primary key areas with a modulatory transition between them.

extension: (1) The lengthening of a motive, melody, or phrase. (2) A pitch added to a triad or seventh chord (e.g., an added sixth, ninth, or eleventh).

F

falling-fifth chain: Root motion by a series of descending fifths (or ascending fourths), creating a segment (or the entirety) of the chain I–IV–vii°–iii–vi–ii–V–I in major, or i–iv–VII (or vii°)–III–VI–ii°–V–i in minor.

falling-third chain: Root motion by a series of descending thirds, creating a segment (or the entirety) of the chain I–vi–IV–ii–vii°–V–iii–I in major, or i–VI–iv–ii°–vii° (or VII)–V–III–i in minor.

Fibonacci series: An infinite series in which each new member is the sum of the previous two (e.g., 1, 1, 2, 3, 5, 8, 13, etc.). Associated with compositions by Bartók and others, and sometimes used in conjunction with time points.

fifth: (1) The distance spanned by five consecutive letter names. (2) The pitch in a triad that is five scale steps above the root.

fifth species: Counterpoint that combines the patterns of each of the other species. Sometimes known as "free composition."

figuration prelude: A prelude featuring a rhythm based on a consistent arpeggiation scheme. In a sense, the prelude could be notated as a series of chords, with each harmony unfolding according to the arpeggiation pattern.

figured bass: The combination of a bass line and Arabic numbers (figures), indicating chords without notating them fully; the numbers represent some of the intervals to be played above the bass line. Typically found in continuo parts.

first inversion: A triad or seventh chord voiced so that the chordal third is in the bass.

first species: Counterpoint written so that each note in one voice is paired with a single note in the other voice, using only consonant intervals. Also called 1:1 counterpoint.

first theme (group): The tonic-key melody (or melodies) with which a sonata form begins.

five-part rondo: A rondo with the form **A B A C A** or **A B A B´ A**, plus optional coda.

flat: An accidental (♭) that lowers a pitch by one half step.

focal pitch: A pitch or pitch class that is emphasized in a piece through repetition or other means, but does not establish a hierarchy with other pitches in the piece's collection.

Forte number: A set-class-labeling system developed by Allen Forte, in which set classes are ordered by size (or cardinality) and then by ic vector. To each set class, Forte gave a hyphenated number (e.g., 5-35). The number before the hyphen represents the *cardinality* of the pcset, and the number after it represents the pcset's ordinal position on the list; thus, 5-35 is a pcset of five elements that appears

thirty-fifth on the list. Each pcset belongs to one of the set classes, and can be identified by its Forte number. (See Appendix 5.)

Fortspinnung: A feature of Baroque-era works in which a melody is "spun out" in uninterrupted fashion. Continuous motion, uneven phrase lengths, melodic or harmonic sequences, changes of key, and elided phrases are all characteristics of *Fortspinnung* passages.

fourth species: A variant of second-species counterpoint in which one voice is rhythmically displaced by ties across the bar. Characterized by its use of suspensions.

fragmentation: The isolation and/or development of a small but recognizable part of a motive.

French augmented-sixth chord (Fr⁶ or Fr$\frac{4}{3}$): An augmented-sixth chord with $\hat{1}$ and $\hat{2}$ in the upper voices. The distinctive sound of this chord is created by two dissonances above the bass: the augmented sixth and the augmented fourth.

fugue: A composition or part of a composition that features a number of voices (usually three or four) entering one after another in imitation, after which each continues independently but in accordance with the rules of counterpoint.

full score: A score showing each instrumental part in the piece on a separate staff (or staves).

fully diminished seventh chord: A seventh chord consisting of a diminished triad and a diminished seventh. Because its thirds are all minor, it has no audible root; it often appears in enharmonic spellings that indicate different chord members as the root. May be used as a means to modulate to distantly related keys.

fundamental bass: An analytical bass line consisting of the *roots* of a chord progression, as opposed to the sounding bass line.

G

generic interval: The distance between two pitches as measured by the number of steps between their letter names (e.g., C up to E is a third, D up to C is a seventh).

German augmented-sixth chord (Gr⁶ or Gr$\frac{6}{5}$): An augmented-sixth chord with $\hat{1}$ and $(♭)\hat{3}$ in the upper voices. This chord, characterized by its perfect fifth above the bass, is an enharmonic respelling of a major-minor seventh chord.

grand staff: Two staves, one in the treble clef and one in the bass clef, connected by a curly brace; typically found in piano music.

graphic notation: The nonstandard symbols used to indicate pitch, duration, articulation, etc., in some nontonal scores.

ground bass: The repeated bass line in a set of continuous variations. It remains constant while the upper voices are varied.

H

half cadence: An inconclusive cadence on the dominant.

half-diminished seventh chord: A seventh chord consisting of a diminished triad and a minor seventh.

half note: A stemmed white note head; its duration is equivalent to two quarter notes.

half step: The musical space between a pitch and its next-closest pitch on the keyboard.

harmonic ambiguity: Characteristic of highly chromatic passages in late Romantic music. The musical coherence comes not through "strength of progression" (strong root-movement-based chord progressions) but rather through "strength of line": smooth linear connections between chords.

harmonic interval: The span between two notes played simultaneously.

harmonic minor: The natural minor scale with raised scale-degree $\hat{7}$.

harmonic rhythm: The rate at which harmonies change in a piece (e.g., one chord per measure or one chord per beat).

harmonic sequence: A succession of harmonies based on a root-progression chain and with repeated intervallic patterning in an upper voice.

harmony: (1) Another name for a chord. (2) A progression of chords, usually implying common-practice principles of voice-leading.

hemiola: A special type of syncopation in compound meters, in which the normal three-part division of the beat is temporarily regrouped (over two beats) into twos. Also possible in simple-triple meters, using ties across the bar lines.

heptad: A collection of seven distinct pitches or pitch classes.

hexachord: A collection of six distinct pitches or pitch classes.

hexachordal combinatoriality: A compositional technique in which two forms of the same row are paired so that the rows' initial hexachords, when combined, complete an aggregate. Similarly, the rows' second hexachords, when combined, complete an aggregate. There are four kinds of hexachordal combinatoriality, based on the transformational relationships between the row forms: P, I, R, and RI.

hypermeter: A high-level metric grouping that interprets groups of measures as though they were groups of beats within a single measure. Hypermetric analyses may label entire bars of music as metrically strong or weak.

I

I-combinatoriality: Hexachordal combinatoriality achieved by pairing a row and its appropriate inversion form(s) to create aggregates.

imitation: The contrapuntal "echoing" of a voice in another part.

imperfect authentic cadence: An authentic cadence weakened by (1) placing the I or V harmony in inversion, or (2) ending the soprano on a scale degree other than $\hat{1}$.

imperfect consonance: The intervals of a third and sixth.

incomplete neighbor: A neighbor tone minus either (1) the initial motion from the main pitch to the neighbor, or (2) the returning motion of the neighbor to the main pitch.

inconclusive cadence: A cadence that makes a phrase sound incomplete, as though the music needs to continue further. Generally, either the soprano or the bass ends on a scale degree other than $\hat{1}$.

indeterminate: Some musical element or event in a score that is left to chance (either in performance or during composition).

index number: The value that measures the "distance" between two inversionally related pcsets. If pcsets A and B are inversionally related by the index number n, then $A = T_n I\ B$, and $B = T_n I\ A$. When paired correctly, every pc in one set added to the corresponding pc in the other set will sum uniformly to the index number.

insertion: See *internal expansion*.

integer notation: The system of labeling pcs by number instead of letter name: C = 0, C♯ or D♭ = 1, D = 2, D♯ or E♭ = 3, and so on. We substitute the letters t for 10 (B♭ or A♯) and e for 11 (B).

integral serialism: The extension of serial procedures to musical elements other than pitch. Also called *total serialism*.

internal expansion: The lengthening of a phrase between its beginning and end. Results from immediate repetitions of material, an elongation of one or more harmonies, or the addition of new material within the phrase.

interval: The musical space between two pitches or pitch classes.

interval class (ic): All pitch intervals that can be made from one pair of pitch classes (or transpositions of these pitch classes by the same distance) belong to a single interval class (e.g., M3, m6, or M10). Also called "unordered pitch-class interval."

interval-class vector (ic vector): Six numbers within square brackets, without commas, that describe the interval-class content of a given pcset. For example, the ic vector for the trichord {0 4 6}, [010101], shows that pcs in this trichord can be paired to make one whole step, one major third, and one tritone—no other intervals.

invariance: The duplication of pitch-class groups in two serial rows or two pcsets; also, anything unchanged after inversion or some other transformation.

inverse: Given a pc or pc interval, the inverse is the corresponding pc or pc interval such that the two sum to 0 (mod12). For example, the inverse of pc 5 is pc 7.

inversion (chordal): A voicing in which a chord member other than the root is the lowest-sounding pitch.

inversion (motivic): A melodic or motivic transformation in which successive generic intervals reverse direction (e.g., an ascending third becomes a descending third).

inversion (pitch): A melodic or motivic transformation in which successive ordered pitch intervals reverse direction (e.g., a +2 becomes a –2).

inversion (pitch class): A transformation in which each pc in a pcset is replaced by its inverse (e.g., the inversion of {0 1 6 7} is {0 e 6 5}). To find the transposed inversion of a pcset, always invert first, then transpose.

inversion (row): The form of a twelve-tone row in which each pc is replaced by its inverse. Abbreviated I_n, where n is the pc integer of the row's first element.

inversionally related intervals (tonal): Two intervals that, when combined, span an octave (e.g., E3-G♯3, a major third, plus G♯3-E4, a minor sixth). When inverted, major intervals become minor (and vice versa), diminished become augmented (and vice versa), and perfect stay perfect. The generic interval numbers of inversionally related intervals sum to 9 (third and sixth, second and seventh, etc.).

Ionian mode: An ordered collection with the pattern of whole and half steps corresponding to the diatonic white-note collection starting and ending on C; the same collection as the major scale.

isorhythm: A repeating series of durations (that may be associated with repeating pitch materials); used in various style periods throughout history, but most prominently in the medieval and twentieth-century periods.

Italian augmented-sixth chord (It⁶): An augmented-sixth chord with (doubled) 1̂ in the upper voices.

K

key: (1) The key of a tonal piece takes its name from the first scale degree of the major or minor tonality in which that piece is written; this pitch class is the primary scale degree around which all other pitches in the piece relate hierarchically. (2) A lever on an instrument that can be depressed with a finger (like a piano key).

key signature: Located at the beginning of each line of a musical score after the clef, a key signature shows which pitches are to be sharped or flatted consistently throughout the piece or movement. Helps determine the key of the piece.

L

lead-in: A musical passage that connects the end of one melodic phrase with the beginning of the next.

leading tone: Scale-degree $\hat{7}$ of the major scale and harmonic or ascending-melodic minor scale; a half step below the tonic.

leading-tone chord: Harmonies built on the leading tone: vii°, vii°⁷, or vii°⁷.

leap: A melodic interval larger than a fourth (larger than a chordal skip).

ledger line: Extra lines drawn through the stems and/or note heads to designate a pitch when the notation extends above or below a staff.

Lied: German art song of the Romantic era (plural is "Lieder").

linear chord: A "chord" resulting from voice-leading motions. See *voice-leading chord*.

linear-intervallic pattern (LIP): The intervallic framework between outer voices. LIPs underlie all sequences, although sometimes they are hidden behind complicated surface elaborations.

link: Same as *lead-in*.

literal complement: The pcset that, when combined with a given pcset, produces the complete aggregate.

Locrian mode: An ordered collection with the pattern of whole and half steps corresponding to the diatonic white-note collection starting and ending on B. Sounds like a natural minor scale with scale-degrees $\hat{2}$ and $\hat{5}$ lowered by one half step.

Lydian mode: An ordered collection with the pattern of whole and half steps corresponding to the diatonic white-note collection starting and ending on F. Equivalent to a major scale with scale-degree $\hat{4}$ raised by one half step.

M

major interval: The quality of the intervals second, third, sixth, and seventh from scale-degree $\hat{1}$ in the major scale.

major-minor seventh chord: A seventh chord consisting of a major triad and a minor seventh (abbreviated Mm7). Another name for *dominant seventh chord*.

major pentatonic: A five-note subset of the diatonic collection that features scale-degrees $\hat{1}$, $\hat{2}$, $\hat{3}$, $\hat{5}$, and $\hat{6}$ (*do, re, mi, sol, la*).

major scale: An ordered collection of pitches arranged according to the following pattern of whole and half steps: W-W-H-W-W-W-H.

major seventh chord: A seventh chord consisting of a major triad and a major seventh.

major triad: A triad with a major third between the root and third and a minor third between the third and fifth. The interval between the root and fifth is a perfect fifth. Corresponds to scale-degrees $\hat{1}$, $\hat{3}$, and $\hat{5}$ of a major scale.

measure: A unit of grouped beats; generally, a measure begins and ends with notated bar lines.

mediant: (1) Scale-degree $\hat{3}$. (2) The triad built on $\hat{3}$.

medieval era: The period in Western music history dating roughly from 800 to 1430. Some medieval composers are Hildegard of Bingen, Pérotin, and Guillaume de Machaut. Genres associated with this era are Gregorian chants, motets, chansons, and organum.

melisma: A vocal passage that sets one syllable of text to many notes.

melodic interval: The span between two notes played one after another.

melodic minor: The natural minor scale that includes the raised $\hat{6}$ and $\hat{7}$ as it ascends, but reverts to the natural minor form of $\hat{6}$ and $\hat{7}$ as it descends.

melodic sequence: A motive repeated several times in successive transpositions (often up or down by step).

melody: A sequence of pitches with a particular rhythm and contour; a tune.

meter: The grouping and divisions of beats in regular, recurring patterns.

meter signature: Located at the beginning of the first line of a musical score, after the clef and key signature, the meter signature indicates the beat unit and grouping of beats in the piece or movement; also called a "time signature."

metric modulation: A means of smoothing what would otherwise be abrupt changes of tempo by introducing subdivisions or groups of beats in the first tempo that match durations in the new tempo. The new tempo is recognized in retrospect, much like a modulation by pivot chord.

metric reinterpretation: A disruption in the established regular hypermetric pattern at the cadence. This can occur when a weak measure simultaneously functions as a strong measure in the case of a phrase elision.

metrical accent: The pattern of strong and weak beats based on the "weight" of the downbeat and the "lift" of the upbeat.

Middle Ages: Same as *medieval era*.

middle C: Designated C4 by Acoustical Society of America standards, the C located at the center of the piano keyboard.

minor interval: The quality of the intervals third, sixth, and seventh from scale-degree $\hat{1}$ in the minor scale. A minor second (diatonic half step) is formed between $\hat{7}$ and $\hat{1}$ in a major, harmonic minor, or ascending melodic minor scale.

minor pentatonic: A five-note subset of the diatonic collection that features the minor-key scale-degrees $\hat{1}, \hat{3}, \hat{4}, \hat{5},$ and $\hat{7}$ (*do, me, fa, sol, te*).

minor scale: There are three kinds: The natural minor scale is an ordered collection of pitches arranged according to the pattern of whole and half steps W-H-W-W-H-W-W; it shares the same key signature of its relative major. The harmonic minor scale raises scale-degree $\hat{7}$. The melodic minor raises $\hat{6}$ and $\hat{7}$ ascending, but takes the natural minor form descending.

minor seventh chord: A seventh chord consisting of a minor triad and a minor seventh.

minor triad: A triad with a minor third between the root and third and a major third between the third and fifth. The interval between the root and fifth is a perfect fifth. Corresponds to scale-degrees $\hat{1}, \hat{3},$ and $\hat{5}$ of a minor scale.

minuet and trio: The most common type of composite ternary form, generally written in triple meter. Typically the third (dance-like) movement of a Classical-era sonata, string quartet, or symphony.

Mixolydian mode: An ordered collection with the pattern of whole and half steps corresponding to the diatonic white-note collection starting and ending on G. Equivalent to a major scale with scale-degree $\hat{7}$ lowered by one half step.

mixture (or **modal mixture**): (1) Harmonic technique of shifting temporarily from a major key to the parallel minor (or vice versa) in a musical passage. (2) A technique of "mixing" the parallel major and minor modes, used most often in major keys, where the modal scale-degrees $\flat\hat{3}, \flat\hat{6},$ and $\flat\hat{7}$ are borrowed from the parallel natural minor.

mixture chord: A chord resulting from the mixing of major and minor parallel keys; also known as a *borrowed chord*.

mobile form: The form of compositions with segments, sections, or movements that may be played in varying orders. While the contents of segments may remain consistent from one performance to another, the overall form of the piece will not.

mod12 arithmetic: An arithmetic that keeps integers in the range 0 to 11. To convert a number greater than 11, divide by 12 and take the remainder. For example, $14 \div 12 = 1$, remainder 2; therefore, 14 mod12 = 2. Used to label pcs in integer notation and perform operations such as transposition or inversion.

modal scale degrees: The scale degrees that differ between major and natural minor scales: $\hat{3}, \hat{6},$ and $\hat{7}$.

mode: (1) Rotations of the major (or natural minor) scale (e.g., the Dorian mode is a rotation of the C-Major scale beginning and ending on D). (2) Term used to distinguish between major and minor keys (e.g., a piece in "the minor mode").

mode of limited transposition: Composer Olivier Messiaen's term for pc collections that can be transposed by only a few intervals; other transpositions replicate the original collection. The whole-tone and octatonic collections are examples.

modified strophic: A variation of strophic form. Rather than repeating the melody exactly, the music may be slightly altered from verse to verse.

modulation: A change of key, usually confirmed by a (perfect) authentic cadence.

moment form: The concept that sections of a piece do not have to connect in some logical way or in a predetermined order, but can change abruptly from one style of music to another.

motet: A polyphonic choral work.

motive: The smallest recognizable musical idea. Motives may be characterized by their pitches, contour, and/or rhythm, but rarely contain a cadence. To qualify as a motive, an idea generally has to be repeated (exactly or varied).

musical form: The overall organization of a composition into sections, defined by harmonic structure—change of key, mode, pcset, collection, or row form—as well as by changes in (or a return to) a theme, texture, instrumentation, rhythm, or other feature.

N

natural minor: The major scale with lowered $\hat{3}, \hat{6},$ and $\hat{7}$, arranged according to the pattern of whole and half steps W-H-W-W-H-W-W. Natural minor shares the same key signature as the relative major key.

natural sign: An accidental (♮) that cancels a sharp or flat.

Neapolitan: The major triad built on ♭II; typically occurs in first inversion (Neapolitan sixth), with $\hat{4}$ in the bass and ♭$\hat{2}$ and (♭)$\hat{6}$ in the upper voices. May also appear in root position, with ♭$\hat{2}$ in the bass.

neighbor tone: An embellishment that decorates a melody pitch by moving to a pitch a step above or below it, then returning to the original pitch. Neighbor tones are approached and left by step, in opposite directions.

neighboring ⁴₃: A ⁴₃ chord arising from neighbor tones in all three of the upper parts (e.g., in the tonic expansion I–ii⁴₃–I).

neighboring ⁶₄: A ⁶₄ chord that embellishes and prolongs whichever chord it neighbors—whether a tonic, dominant, or predominant chord—and is usually metrically unaccented. It shares its bass note with the harmony it embellishes, while two upper voices move in stepwise upper-neighbor motion above that bass. Sometimes called a "pedal ⁶₄."

ninth chord: A triad or seventh chord with a ninth added above the bass.

nonad: A collection of nine distinct pitches or pitch classes.

nonmetric: Another word for *ametric*; having no meter.

nonteleological form: Form in which the music lacks a sense of a goal or direction. Moment form and mobile form are examples.

nontonal: Music that freely employs all twelve pitch classes. The pervasive chromaticism and absence of whole- and half-step scale patterns make a true "tonic" pitch class impossible to discern in nontonal music.

normal order: The order of consecutive pcs in a pcset that (1) spans the smallest interval and (2) places the smallest intervals toward the left.

notated meter: The way in which rhythms are notated in a score. In common-practice music, notated meter and perceived meter are usually the same. In music of the twentieth century and later, they may not be.

note-to-note: Another name for *first species*, or *1:1*, counterpoint.

O

oblique motion: Contrapuntal, or voice-leading, motion in which one part repeats the same pitch while the other moves by leap, skip, or step.

octad: A collection of eight distinct pitches or pitch classes.

octatonic scale: A scale composed of eight (*octa-*) distinct pcs in alternating whole and half steps.

octave: The distance of eight musical steps.

octave equivalence: The concept that two pitches an octave apart are functionally equivalent.

offbeat: A weak beat or weak portion of a beat.

omnibus: A special chromaticized voice exchange, usually prolonging the dominant. The exchanged pitches form the interval of a tritone, which enables the voice exchange to continue chromatically until the exchanged voices arrive where they began (but up or down an octave). All the resulting chromatic simultaneities are nonfunctional (*voice-leading chords*).

open: A harmonic feature of a phrase or section of a piece in which the end is inconclusive, or in a different key from the beginning.

open score: A score with a staff for every part, unlike a piano score; for example, an SATB choral score on four staves.

orchestration: Music set or composed for a large ensemble.

ostinato: A repeated rhythmic and/or pitch pattern.

overlap: (1) A means of phrase connection in which one phrase ends simultaneously with the beginning of the next. May involve more than one musical layer: while one or more voice parts finish the first phrase, one or more other voice parts simultaneously begin the next. (2) A voice-leading error in which one voice overlaps into the register of an adjacent voice on an adjacent beat.

P

P-combinatoriality: Hexachordal combinatoriality achieved by pairing a row and its appropriate transposed form(s) to make aggregates.

palindrome: A segment (of pitches, pcs, intervals, and/or rhythms) that reads the same backward and forward.

parallel keys: Keys in different modes that share the same letter name and tonic, such as F Major and F minor.

parallel major: The major key that shares the same tonic as a given minor key. The parallel major raises $\hat{3}$, $\hat{6}$, and $\hat{7}$ of the minor key.

parallel minor: The minor key that shares the same tonic as a given major key. The parallel minor lowers $\hat{3}$, $\hat{6}$, and $\hat{7}$ of the major key.

parallel motion: Contrapuntal, or voice-leading, motion in which both parts move in the same direction by the same generic interval.

parallel period: A period in which the two phrases share the same beginning melodic material.

parody: The compositional borrowing or reshaping of another composer's materials to emphasize particular aspects.

passacaglia: Continuous variations with a repeated bass line. The bass melody (or ground bass) remains constant, while the upper voices are varied.

passing chord: A linear "chord" arising from passing motion.

passing $\frac{6}{4}$: A $\frac{6}{4}$ chord created by passing motion in the bass (e.g., in the progression I–I$\frac{6}{4}$–IV^6).

passing $\frac{6}{4}$: A voice-leading $\frac{6}{4}$ chord, usually connecting root-position and first-inversion chords of the same harmony. We call it "passing" because the $\frac{6}{4}$ harmonizes a bass-line passing tone.

passing tone: A melodic embellishment that fills in the space between chord members by stepwise motion. It is approached by step and left by step in the same direction.

pcset: Abbreviation of "pitch-class set."

pedal point: A note held for several measures while harmonies change above it. Chords above a pedal point do not participate in the harmonic framework.

pentachord: A collection of five distinct pitches or pitch classes.

pentatonic scale: A scale with five pcs. In Western music, the pentatonic scale is a subset of the diatonic collection. The two most common are the minor pentatonic (*do, me, fa, sol, te*) and the major pentatonic (*do, re, mi, sol, la*)

perfect authentic cadence: A strong conclusive cadence in which a root-position V$^{(7)}$ progresses to a root-position I, and the soprano moves from scale-degree $\hat{2}$ or $\hat{7}$ to $\hat{1}$.

perfect consonance: The intervals of a unison, fourth, fifth, and octave. The harmonic interval of a fourth is treated as a dissonance in common-practice style.

period: A musical unit consisting (usually) of two phrases. Generally, the first phrase ends with a weak cadence (typically a half cadence), answered by a more conclusive cadence (usually a PAC) at the end of the second phrase.

phasing: The compositional technique of moving musical patterns in and out of alignment, creating additional sounds and patterns that are not present in the original materials.

phrase: A basic unit of musical thought, similar to a sentence in language, with a beginning, a middle, and an end. In tonal music, a phrase must end with a cadence; in nontonal music, other musical features provide closure.

phrase group: Three or more phrases with tonal and/or thematic design elements that group them together as a unit.

phrase modulation: Modulation accomplished directly, without the use of a pivot chord (e.g., the new phrase simply begins in the new key). Another name for *direct modulation*.

phrase rhythm: The interaction of hypermeter and phrase structure.

phrase structure: The melodic and harmonic characteristics of a phrase or group of phrases, identified by cadence type, harmonic motion, number of measures, and melodic or motivic repetition or contrast.

Phrygian cadence: The half cadence iv^6–V in minor keys, so called because of the half-step descent in the bass.

Phrygian mode: An ordered collection with the pattern of whole and half steps corresponding to the diatonic white-note collection starting and ending on E. Equivalent to a natural minor scale with scale-degree $\hat{2}$ lowered by a half step.

Phrygian II: Another name for the *Neapolitan*.

Picardy third: In a minor key, the raised third of a tonic chord (making the harmony major), typically at an authentic cadence at the end of a piece.

pitch: A tone sounding in a particular octave.

pitch class (pc): Notes an octave (or several octaves) apart that share the same name (e.g., F3, F5, and F2 all belong to pc F). Pitch-class names assume octave and enharmonic equivalence.

pitch-class interval (pci): The interval spanned by two pcs. (1) Ordered pitch-class intervals measure the distance from pc a to b by subtracting (b – a) mod12; the distance can range from 0 to 11. (2) Unordered pitch-class intervals measure the shortest distance between two pcs, either from the first to the second or vice versa; the distance ranges from 0 to 6. "Unordered pitch-class interval" is another name for *interval class*.

pitch interval: The musical space between two pitches, described either with tonal labels (e.g., minor second, augmented sixth, perfect fifth) or by the number of half steps from one pitch to the other. Unordered pitch intervals measure distance; ordered pitch intervals measure distance and direction (shown by preceding the interval number with a + or –).

pitch symmetry: The spacing of pitches at equal distances above and below a central pitch.

pitch-time graph: A graph that plots pitch (the vertical axis) against time (the horizontal axis).

pivot chord: In a common-chord modulation, a harmony that functions diatonically in both the old key and the new key.

pivot-chord modulation: See *common-chord modulation*.

pivot-dyad modulation: See *common-dyad modulation*.

pivot-tone modulation: See *common-tone modulation*.

plagal cadence: The cadence IV–I (iv–i in minor), sometimes called the "Amen cadence." Because the IV–I motion can be viewed as a tonic expansion, and because the plagal cadence often follows an authentic cadence, some use the term "plagal resolution" or "plagal expansion of tonic."

polymeter: Music with two or more different simultaneous metric streams.

polymodality: Music with several modes sounding in different layers of music simultaneously.

polytonality: Music with several keys sounding in different layers of music simultaneously.

postmodernism: A style in which materials originating from different times and styles are combined. The term is borrowed from literary and art criticism.

posttonal music: Music that is not restricted to compositional principles of the common-practice era.

predominant: (1) The triad or seventh chord built on scale-degrees $\hat{2}$, $\hat{4}$, or $\hat{6}$. (2) A category of harmonic function that includes chords that precede the dominant, typically ii and IV (ii° and iv in minor keys), but also the Neapolitan sixth and augmented-sixth chords.

predominant area: A harmonic area in the basic phrase model that precedes the dominant area (T–PD–D–T). Predominant harmonies include ii and IV (ii° and iv in minor keys) plus their inversions and seventh chords. Chromatic predominant harmonies include the Neapolitan sixth and augmented-sixth chords.

primary theme (group): Another name for *first theme (group)*, or first tonal area, in a sonata-form movement.

prime (row): The row in a twelve-tone composition that the analyst considers a starting point, usually the first appearance of the row; labeled P_n, where n is the first pc of the row.

prime form: The representative pcset for a set class, beginning with 0 and enclosed in square brackets. To find the prime form of a set, determine the set's best normal order (which may include finding the normal order for its inversion), and transpose to begin with 0.

prolong: To expand the function of a harmony by means of contrapuntal motion and contrapuntal or linear chords.

pset: Abbreviation of "pitch set."

Q

quadruple meter: Meter in which beats group into units of four (e.g., $\frac{4}{4}$ or $\frac{12}{8}$).

quadruplet: In compound time, a subdivision group borrowed from simple time.

quarter note: A stemmed black note head, equivalent in duration to two eighth notes.

quaternary song form: A song form consisting of four (usually eight-bar) phrases. The first two phrases (chorus 1) begin the same (they may be identical or may differ at the cadence). They are followed by a contrasting section (bridge) and then a return to the opening material (chorus 2), making the overall form **a a b a**. Also known as "thirty-two-bar song form."

quodlibet: A medley, or amalgamated borrowing, of songs; may feature multiple texts, sometimes in different languages.

R

R-combinatoriality: Hexachordal combinatoriality achieved by pairing a row and its appropriate retrograde form(s) to make aggregates.

raised submediant: Raised scale-degree $\hat{6}$ in melodic minor.

realization: (1) A full musical texture created from a figured (or unfigured) bass. (2) In pieces composed with pcsets or rows, pitch classes in a specific register and rhythm. (3) Performance of a work from a text or graphic score.

rearticulated suspension: A suspension in which the suspended voice sounds again (instead of being held over) at the moment of dissonance.

recapitulation: The final section of a sonata form (or penultimate section, if the movement ends with a coda), in which the music from the exposition is heard again, this time with the theme groups usually in the tonic key.

reduction: (1) A score transcribed so that it can be performed by fewer instrumental forces (usually by piano). (2) The underlying harmonic framework and linear counterpoint of a passage of music, revealed after embellishing tones or harmonies have been eliminated.

refrain: (1) The section of a song that recurs with the same music and text. (2) In popular-music verse-refrain form, the second portion of the song; generally in **a a b a**, or quaternary, song form. (3) In rondo form (usually **A B A C A** or **A B A C A B (D) A**), the refrain is the **A** section, which returns with opening thematic material in the tonic key. Another word for *ritornello*.

register: The particular octave in which a pitch sounds.

registral invariance: A compositional technique in which certain pcs are realized as pitches only in one specific register. Also known as "frozen register" and "pitch fixation."

relative keys: Major and minor keys that share the same key signature (e.g., C Major and A minor).

relative major: The major key that shares the same key signature as a given minor key. The relative major is made from the same pitch-class collection as its relative minor, but begins on scale-degree $\hat{3}$ of the minor key.

relative minor: The minor key that shares the same key signature as a given major key. The relative minor is made from the same pitch-class collection as its relative major, but begins on scale-degree $\hat{6}$ of the major key.

Renaissance era: The period in Western music history dating roughly from 1430 until 1600. Some Renaissance composers are Josquin des Prez, Palestrina, Guillaume Dufay, and Carlo Gesualdo. Genres most associated with the era are the mass, madrigal, masque, and instrumental dances.

resolution: The way a harmony or scale step progresses to the next harmony or pitch. The term usually refers to the manner in which a dissonant interval moves to a consonant one.

rest: A duration of silence.

retardation: A rhythmic embellishment where a consonance is held over to the next beat, creating a dissonance with the new harmony. The dissonance is resolved upward by step, creating another consonant interval.

retransition: A musical passage that harmonically prepares for the return of previously heard material. In sonata form, it appears at the end of the development section and prolongs the dominant harmony in preparation for the tonic return of the recapitulation's first theme group. In rondo form, a retransition may appear before any recurrence of the refrain (**A** section).

retrograde: The form of a twelve-tone row in which the pcs are in the reverse order of the prime. Abbreviated R_n, where n refers to the *last* pc of the row, i.e., the first pc of the original, prime row.

retrograde inversion: The form of a twelve-tone row in which the pcs are in the reverse order of the inversion. Abbreviated RI_n, where n refers to the *last* pc of the row, i.e., the first pc of the inverted row.

retrogression: "Backward" progressions that reverse typical common-practice harmonic norms; common in other musical idioms (e.g., V–IV in blues and rock music).

rhyme scheme: The pattern of rhyming in a poetic verse or stanza, generally designated with lowercase alphabet letters. Repeated letters indicate lines that end with rhyming words.

rhythm: The patterns made by the durations of pitch and silence (notes and rests) in a piece.

rhythmic acceleration: The gradual move from long note values to shorter note values in a passage of music; also called a "rhythmic *crescendo.*"

rhythmic motive: A motive that maintains its rhythm but changes its contour and interval structure.

RI-combinatoriality: Hexachordal combinatoriality achieved by pairing a row and its appropriate retrograde-inversional form(s) to create aggregates.

ritornello: An instrumental section of a piece that returns. Another word for *refrain.*

Romantic era: The period in Western music history dating roughly from 1830 until 1910. Some Romantic composers are Robert Schumann, Frédéric Chopin, Giuseppe Verdi, and Richard Wagner. Genres most associated with this era are the art song, program symphony, character piece, tone poem, and grand opera.

rondo: A musical form characterized by a repeated section (refrain, or ritornello) alternating with sections that contrast in key, mode, texture, harmonic complexity, thematic content, and/or style (usually **A B A C A** or **A B A C A B (D) A**). The contrasting sections are called episodes.

root: The lowest pitch of a triad or seventh chord when the chord is spelled in thirds.

root position: A chord voiced so that the root is in the bass.

rounded binary: A binary form in which melodic or motivic features in the initial phrase return at the end of the piece, "rounding out" the formal plan.

row: A specific ordering of all twelve pitch classes.

row elision: One way of connecting rows in a twelve-tone piece: the same pc or pcs are shared at the end of one row and the beginning of the next. Also called "row linkage."

row matrix: A twelve-by-twelve array that displays all possible P, I, R, and RI forms of a row.

S

SATB: An abbreviation for the four main voice ranges: soprano, alto, tenor, and bass. Also indicates a particular musical style or texture: chorale style.

scale: A collection of pitch classes arranged in a particular order of whole and half steps.

scale degree: A name for each pitch class of the scale, showing its relationship to the tonic pitch (for which the key is named). Scale-degree names may be numbers ($\hat{1}$, $\hat{2}$, $\hat{3}$), words (tonic, supertonic, mediant), or solfège syllables (*do, re, mi*).

scale step: Same as *scale degree.*

scherzo and trio: A composite ternary form in a fast tempo, usually in triple meter. Typically the third movement of a Romantic-era sonata, quartet, or symphony.

second inversion: A triad or seventh chord voiced so that the chordal fifth is in the bass.

second species: Counterpoint written so that one voice has two notes for every single note in the other voice. Permits consonances and passing tones, according to specific rules of voice-leading; eighteenth-century style also allows neighbor tones. Another name for *2:1* counterpoint.

second theme (group): The melody (or melodies) heard at the start of the new key area in a sonata form.

secondary dominant: A dominant-function harmony (V or vii°, with or without the chordal seventh) "applied" to a chord other than tonic (may also refer only to a secondary V chord). A secondary dominant typically includes chromatic alterations (relative to the tonic key). Also called an "applied dominant," or *applied chord.*

secondary leading-tone chord: A leading-tone chord that functions as an applied, or secondary, dominant; usually a fully diminished seventh chord.

secondary set: An aggregate formed by combining segments belonging to more than one row form.

section: A large division within a composition, usually set off by a cadence (or other elements denoting closure). May be delineated by repeat signs or a double bar.

sectional: A harmonic feature of tonal forms, in which a section is tonally closed (with an authentic cadence in the tonic key); the section could stand on its own.

sectional binary: A binary form in which the first section ends with a cadence on the tonic. The section is tonally complete and could stand on its own.

sectional variation: A variation form in which each variation is clearly distinguished from the next by a strong conclusive cadence (and often by double bars). Each variation could be played as a complete stand-alone section.

segment: An ordered sequence of pitches or pcs.

sentence: A phrase design with a 1 + 1 + 2 (or 2 + 2 + 4) motivic structure.

sequence: A musical pattern that is restated successively at different pitch levels. See *harmonic sequence* and *melodic sequence*.

sequence pattern: The arrangement of intervals that underlies a sequence.

serial music: Music composed with (ordered) pitch-class segments and ordered transformations of these segments; may also feature ordered durations, dynamics, and articulations.

set: A group of unordered pitches or pitch classes. See *collection*.

set class: The collection of pcsets that contains all possible distinct transpositions of the pcset, as well as all distinct transpositions of its inversion. Pcsets in the same set class also share the same ic vector.

seven-part rondo: A rondo whose form is **A B A C A B (D) A**, plus optional coda.

seventh chord: A chord that can be arranged as a root-position triad with another third stacked on top. This third forms a seventh with the root. There are five types of seventh chords in common-practice tonal music: major seventh, minor seventh, major-minor seventh (dominant seventh), half-diminished seventh, and fully diminished seventh.

sharp: An accidental (♯) that raises a pitch a half step.

short score: A score that shows several parts combined on each staff.

similar motion: Contrapuntal, or voice-leading, motion in which both parts move in the same direction, but not by the same generic interval.

simple binary: A binary form that generally has an ||: **A** :||: **B** :|| or ||: **A** :||: **A′** :|| design.

simple duple: Any meter with two beats in a measure, with each beat divided into two (e.g., $\frac{2}{4}$).

simple meter: Meter in which the beat divides into twos and subdivides into fours. The top number of the meter signature will be 2, 3, or 4 (e.g., $\frac{4}{8}$ or $\frac{3}{2}$).

simple quadruple: Any meter with four beats in a measure, with each beat divided into two (e.g., $\frac{4}{4}$).

simple ternary: A ternary form that is relatively brief (as opposed to composite ternary), with three distinct sections, usually in the form **A B A**. The **B** section generally expresses both a contrasting key and contrasting thematic material.

simple triple: Any meter with three beats in a measure, with each beat divided into two (e.g., $\frac{3}{4}$ or $\frac{3}{2}$).

sixteenth note: A stemmed black note head with two flags. In duple beat divisions, two sixteenths divide an eighth-note beat; in triple beat divisions, three sixteenths divide a dotted-eighth-note beat.

skip: A melodic interval of a third or fourth.

slur: An arc that connects two or more different pitches. Slurs affect articulation but not duration.

solfège, fixed-*do*: A singing system in which a particular syllable is associated with a particular pitch class; e.g., *do* is always C, *re* is always D, etc., no matter what the key.

solfège, movable-*do*: A singing system in which a particular syllable is associated with a particular scale step; e.g., *do* is always $\hat{1}$, *re* is always $\hat{2}$, etc., no matter what the key.

sonata: A multimovement composition for piano or a solo-line instrument (usually with keyboard accompaniment), typically in three or four movements. The first movement is almost always in sonata form.

sonata form: A formal plan with a three-part design (exposition, development, recapitulation) and a two-part harmonic structure (the most common is ||: I–V :||: → I :|| for major keys, with motion to III instead of V in minor keys). Sonata form can be thought of as an expanded continuous rounded binary form.

sonatina: A "little sonata." The first movement of a sonatina is usually a reduced sonata form, with compact first and second themes and a very short development section or no development at all.

song cycle: A group of songs, generally performed as a unit, either set to a single poet's cycle of poetry or set to poems that have been grouped by the composer into a cycle.

soprano: The highest voice in four-part (SATB) writing.

sounding pitch: The pitch that is heard when a performer plays a note on an instrument. For transposing instruments, this differs from notated pitch. Also called *concert pitch*.

spacing: The arrangement of adjacent parts in four-part writing, in which vocal range and the intervals between voices are considered.

species: A particular type of counterpoint, used as a tool for teaching composition. The various species (types) of counterpoint differ by the embellishments permitted and the rhythmic relationship between the voices. See *first species (1:1)*, *second species (2:1)*, *third species (4:1)*, *fourth species*, and *fifth species*.

spelling: The letter names and accidentals of the pitches in a scale, chord, or other musical sonority.

split-third chord: A four-note "triad" with both a major and a minor third above the root.

staff: The five parallel lines on which we write music.

step: The melodic interval of a half or whole step.

step progression: A technique for writing compound melody, in which nonadjacent pitches are connected by an overall stepwise motion.

strain: In marches, the sections corresponding to the **A** and **B** portions of binary (or ternary) forms.

strophe: A stanza, or verse, in a song.

strophic: A song form in which more than one strophe (verse) of text is sung to the same music.

style juxtaposition: A method of composing in which elements strongly associated with one musical style are placed side-by-side with another style without a transition between the two.

stylistic allusion: A musical passage that either literally quotes another composition, or is written in imitation of a previous style, intended to be recognized by the listener as belonging to another time or piece.

subdivision: The third level of pulse in musical meter: beat → division → subdivision.

subdominant: (1) Scale-degree $\hat{4}$. (2) The triad built on $\hat{4}$.

submediant: (1) Scale degree $\hat{6}$. (2) The triad built on $\hat{6}$.

subordinate theme (group): Another name for *second theme (group)*.

subphrase: A melodic and harmonic unit smaller than a phrase. Subphrases complete only a portion of the basic phrase progression and do not conclude with a cadence.

subset: A subgroup of a given set.

substitute chord: A harmony that can stand for another. The most common are vi for I, ii for IV, and vii° for V.

subtonic: (1) Scale-degree $\hat{7}$ of the natural minor scale, so called because it is a whole step below tonic. (2) The triad built on $\hat{7}$ of natural minor.

superset: The larger set from which a subset is derived.

supertonic: (1) Scale-degree $\hat{2}$. (2) The triad built on $\hat{2}$.

sus chord: In popular music, a chord with a fourth above the bass instead of a third. The fourth does not necessarily resolve, as in a typical 4–3 suspension.

suspension: A rhythmic embellishment where a consonance is held over to the next beat, creating a dissonance with the new harmony. The dissonance is resolved downward by step, creating another consonant interval. Suspensions are designated by intervals above the bass; the most common are 7–6, 4–3, and 9–8.

suspension chain: A combined succession of suspensions, sometimes of a single type (e.g., 4–3, 4–3) or alternations of two kinds (e.g., 7–6, 4–3, 7–6, 4–3); the resolution of each suspension prepares the next.

symmetrical meter: A meter with equally spaced primary beats within each measure, each beat having the same number of divisions.

symmetrical phrase: A phrase with an even number of measures.

symmetrical set: A set whose pcs can be ordered so that the intervals between adjacent elements are the same when read left to right or right to left. The pentatonic scale, whole-tone scale, octatonic scale, and chromatic collection are all symmetrical sets.

symmetry: Having the same pattern from start to middle as end to middle.

syncopation: Off-beat rhythmic accents created by dots, ties, rests, dynamic markings, or accent marks.

T

teleological form: Form that gives the listener a sense that the music moves toward a goal; usually associated with common-practice forms.

tempo: How fast or slow music is played. Examples of tempo markings include *adagio* (slow), *andante* (medium speed), and *allegro* (fast).

temporary tonic: The chord to which a secondary dominant or secondary leading-tone harmony is applied; also known as a "tonicized harmony."

tendency tone: A chord member or scale degree whose dissonant relation to the surrounding tones requires a particular resolution in common-practice style (i.e., chordal sevenths resolve down, and leading tones resolve up).

tenor: The second-lowest voice in four-part (SATB) writing. Usually directly above the bass.

tenor clef: A C-clef positioned on a staff so that the fourth line from the bottom indicates middle C (C4); typically read by bassoons, cellos, and tenor trombones in their higher registers.

ternary form: A composition divided into three sections. The outer sections usually consist of the same musical material, while the inner section features contrasting musical qualities (including key), creating an overall **A B A** form. In some song forms, the contrasting section may occur last (**A A B**).

tessitura: The vocal or instrumental range most used by a singer or instrumentalist.

tetrachord: (1) A collection of four distinct pitches or pitch classes. (2) A segment of four consecutive members of a scale.

text notation: A musical score with instructions written in prose or poetry, without any traditional musical notation.

textural variation: A variation written in a texture that contrasts with that of surrounding variations or the original theme. Two possibilities are (1) the simplifying variation, which features only a few voices, resulting in a thin texture; and (2) the contrapuntal variation, which features imitative entries of the voices.

theme and variations: A variation set based on a given theme, in which each variation differs in melody, rhythm, key, mode, length, texture, timbre, character, style, or motive. Theme and variation sets after the Baroque era are usually sectional variations, in which each variation could be considered a brief, stand-alone piece. See also *continuous variation*.

third inversion: A seventh chord voiced so that the chordal seventh is in the bass.

third species: Counterpoint written so that one voice has four notes for every single note in the other voice; allows consonances, passing tones, and neighboring tones, according to strict rules of voice-leading. Another name for *4:1 counterpoint*.

thirty-second note: A stemmed black note head with three flags; equal in duration to two sixty-fourth notes.

thirty-two-bar song form: Another term for *quaternary song form*.

through composed: A composition organized so that each section (e.g., each verse in a song) consists of different music, with little or no previous material recurring as the work progresses.

tie: A small arc connecting the note heads of two (or more) identical pitches, adding the durations of the notes together.

timbral variation: A variation that exploits instrumentation and/or sound color different from previous variations.

time-line notation: Music written so that the passing of time is measured out in the number of seconds elapsed between markers.

time points: Locations in a score indicating a musical event; determined by a duration series, a numerical pattern, chance, or a series of proportions.

time signature: Another term for *meter signature*.

tonal music: Music based on the following organizational conventions: (1) melodies built from major and minor scales using scale-degree function, in relation to a tonic scale degree (e.g., $\hat{7}$ resolving to $\hat{1}$); (2) harmonies that relate to each other in functional progressions leading toward a tonic harmony; (3) identifiable embellishing tones (dissonant suspensions, neighbors, passing tones) that resolve (or imply a resolution).

tonal plan: The progression of keys in a composition.

tonic: (1) Scale-degree $\hat{1}$. (2) The triad built on $\hat{1}$.

tonic area: Usually the opening and closing area in a basic phrase (T–PD–D–T).

tonic closure: A conclusive ending that confirms the key of a musical passage, usually accomplished by means of an authentic cadence.

tonic expansion: An extension of tonic function effected by means of contrapuntal motion and voice-leading chords.

tonic substitute: A chord other than tonic (most often the submediant) that fulfills tonic function in the basic phrase model.

tonicization: The result when a chord becomes a temporary tonic by means of a secondary, or applied, dominant. The key of the passage does not really change, and the temporary tonic soon returns to its normal functional role in the primary key.

total serialism: The extension of serial procedures to musical elements other than pitch. Also called *integral serialism.*

transferred resolution: The movement of a tendency tone from one voice part to another prior to resolution.

transition: A musical passage that modulates from one key and establishes another, often by means of sequential treatment. In sonata form, the transition links the first and second theme groups.

transpose: (1) To notate a score for transposing instruments so that pitches will sound correctly in the concert key. (2) To rewrite a section of music at a different pitch level. (3) To add or subtract a constant to pitches or pitch classes in integer notation.

transposed score: A score that shows the pitches as notated in the performers' parts (which may be transposed for certain instruments), rather than the sounding pitches.

transposing instrument: An instrument (e.g., clarinet, saxophone, or horn) whose notated pitches are not the same as the pitches that sound when played.

transposition (row): The form of a twelve-tone row derived by transposing the prime. Abbreviated P_n, where n is the pc integer of the row's first element.

transpositional equivalence: The relationship between two sets such that each one can be transposed into the other.

treble clef: On a staff, the treble clef (also known as G-clef) denotes the line for G4, by means of the end of its curving line; typically read by flutes, clarinets, oboes, horns, sopranos, altos, and piano right hand.

triad: A chord made from two stacked thirds.

triad quality: The description of a triad according to the quality of its stacked thirds and fifth: major, minor, diminished, or augmented.

trichord: A collection of three distinct pitches or pitch classes.

triple meter: Meter in which beats group into units of three (e.g., $\frac{3}{2}$ or $\frac{9}{8}$).

triplet: In simple meters, a division group borrowed from compound meters.

tritone: An interval made up of three whole tones or six semitones: an augmented fourth or diminished fifth. By some definitions, only an augmented fourth is a tritone, since in this spelling the interval spans three whole steps.

tritone axis: Music (in nontonal pieces) that moves from a first pitch center to a second pitch center a tritone away, and then returns; analogous to the tonic-dominant axis in tonal music.

truncate: To cut off a melody or motive before it ends.

twelve-tone: Music with a specific ordering of all twelve pitch classes, called a row. The row is musically realized by means of transformations (transposition, inversion, retrograde, or retrograde inversion) throughout a composition.

U

unequal fifths: Similar motion from a d5 to P5. Prohibited in strict counterpoint, but allowable in some situations in four-part writing if not placed in the outer voices.

unison: The interval size 1, or the distance from a pitch to itself; interval 0 if measured in semitones.

upbeat: Occurs when a melody starts just before the first strong beat in a meter; named for the upward lift of the conductor's hand. Another word for *anacrusis.*

V

verse: (1) The section of a song that returns with the same music but different text. (2) In popular song forms, the first section of verse-refrain form; the verse is usually not repeated, and it may be tonally less stable than the refrain.

verse-refrain form: A typical form of popular songs and show tunes: an introductory verse, possibly modulatory, precedes a chorus that is often in quaternary song form (**a a b a**).

vertical analysis: A first level of analysis, assigning a Roman numeral label to each chord and inversion; in contrast to contextual analysis, which interprets function within the basic phrase model.

vocal range: The range of pitches (high and low) that may be sung comfortably by singers of a particular voice type (e.g., alto or tenor).

voice crossing: In four-part writing, one voice written higher than the part above it or lower than the part below it; considered poor voice-leading in common-practice style.

voice exchange: The expansion of a functional area in which two voices exchange chord members (e.g., $\hat{1}$ moves to $\hat{3}$ in the bass, and $\hat{3}$ moves to $\hat{1}$ in the soprano). This skip is often filled in with a passing tone or passing chord.

voice-leading: The combination of melodic lines to create harmonies according to principles of common-practice harmony and counterpoint.

voice-leading chord: A "chord" created by combining embellishing tones in the expansion of a structural harmony. In analysis, we label the individual embellishments rather than the chord, or we label the chord as "voice-leading" (VL) or as a passing or neighboring chord.

W

whole note: A stemless white note head; equal in duration to two half notes.

whole step: The combination of two adjacent half steps.

whole-tone scale: An ordered collection of pcs arranged so that each scale step lies a whole step away from the next. A whole-tone scale consists of six elements and exists in two distinct forms: pcs {0 2 4 6 8 t} and {1 3 5 7 9 e}.

Guidelines for Part-Writing

Contents

I. Vocal Ranges

Typical ranges for common-practice SATB writing:

- Soprano: C4 to G5
- Alto: G3 to D5
- Tenor: C3 to G4
- Bass: E2 to D4

II. Doubling Guidelines

- If the triad is in *root position* (and major or minor quality), double the root. Sometimes we double the third or fifth, but these doublings are much less common.
- If the triad is in *first inversion*, double any chord member that is not a tendency tone or other altered tone. Doubling the soprano is a common strategy (for major or minor triads only).
- If the triad is in *second inversion*, double the fifth (the bass).
- Never double a tendency tone. This guideline applies most frequently to the leading tone (7̂) and to the seventh of the dominant seventh chord (4̂), but includes any tone that must be resolved, such as a chromatic passing tone or altered tone.
- For *diminished triads* (which typically appear in first inversion), double the third. Doubling the root emphasizes the dissonance and causes voice-leading problems. Occasionally, the fifth may be doubled.
- For *N⁶ chords*, double the bass (the third of the chord).
- For *It⁶ chords*, double scale-degree 1̂.

III. Spacing Guidelines

When writing SATB parts, check to see that

- the interval between soprano and alto, and the interval between alto and tenor, is an octave or less;
- the interval between the tenor and bass line usually remains within a tenth;
- no alto pitch is higher than soprano or lower than tenor;
- no tenor pitch is higher than alto or lower than bass.

IV. General Voice-Leading Guidelines

A. Work to achieve smooth voice-leading:

- Resolve tendency tones correctly, and never double them.

- Move each voice to the closest possible member of the following chord (without creating parallel perfect intervals or errors in doubling or spacing).
- Avoid skipping down to a chordal seventh.
- If two chords share a common tone, keep the common tone in the same voice.

B. Aim for independence of the four voices based on principles of good counterpoint:

- Keep each voice within its own characteristic range.
- Write the soprano-bass counterpoint first before filling in the inner voices.
- Avoid moving all four voices in the same direction.
- Avoid placing a pitch in one voice part so that it crosses above or below the pitch sung by an adjacent voice part—either within a single chord (voice crossing) or between two consecutive chords (overlapping).
- Avoid prolonged parallel or similar motion; balance with contrary and oblique motion.

C. Make each voice a "singable" melody:

- Avoid large leaps (except bass leaps between chord members).
- Avoid melodic motion by augmented or diminished intervals (e.g., the augmented second between scale-degrees $\hat{6}$ and $\hat{7}$ in harmonic minor).
- Use passing or neighboring tones to create a smooth line or add melodic interest.

D. Pay careful attention to voice-leading to and from perfect intervals:

- Choose contrary or oblique motion when you approach and leave any perfect interval (unison, octave, fifth), since parallel perfect intervals are prohibited in this style.
- Do not use
  (1) direct octaves or fifths (similar motion into a perfect interval in the soprano-bass pair)—these are permitted only in inner voices or if the soprano moves by step;
  (2) contrary octaves or fifths (contrary motion from one perfect interval to another of the same size);

(3) unequal fifths (motion from a diminished fifth to a perfect fifth, especially in the soprano-bass pair), since they interfere with proper resolution of the tendency tones ($\hat{7}$ resolving up to $\hat{1}$ and $\hat{4}$ resolving down to $\hat{3}$); motion from a perfect fifth to a diminished fifth is acceptable.

E. Keep in mind typical voice-leading based on root progressions:

- Roots a fifth apart: hold the common tone in the same voice, and move all the other parts to the closest possible chord member.
- Roots a third apart: hold the common tones, and move the other parts to the closest possible chord member.
- Roots a second apart: move the upper parts in contrary motion to the bass line.

F. Remember to write musically:

- When a harmony is repeated, create some variety by changing the soprano pitch, the inversion, and/or the spacing of the chord.
- Where possible, avoid static or repetitive melodic lines.

V. Realizing Figured Bass

- Sing the given line(s) to help orient yourself tonally.
- Place pitches above the bass in an appropriate octave according to the generic intervals written in the figured bass.
- Use pitches diatonic in the key.
- An accidental next to a number means to raise or lower the pitch associated with that number by one half step.
- An accidental by itself means to raise or lower the third *above the bass* (not necessarily the third of the chord).
- A slash through a number means to raise the pitch associated with that number.
- Accidentals in the figure apply only to that single chord.
- A figured bass does not list all intervals above the bass; some, like octaves and thirds, may be implied by the figures.

- Follow all doubling and voice-leading guidelines when voicing or connecting chords.
- A dash between two numbers means that those intervals belong in the same voice-leading strand (like a suspension: 4–3).
- Melodic embellishing tones (other than suspensions) are not shown in the figures because they are not a part of the main harmonic framework.

VI. Voice-Leading Considerations for Specific Harmonies

A. When resolving V^7 to I:

- Two tendency tones resolve at once.
- The chordal seventh moves down (scale-degree $\hat{4}$ moves to $\hat{3}$), and
- the leading tone resolves up by half step (scale-degree $\hat{7}$ resolves to $\hat{1}$).
- Typically, either the V^7 or I will be incomplete (lacking the fifth) for smooth voice-leading.
- At a cadence, scale-degree $\hat{7}$ may leap to $\hat{5}$ to complete the tonic triad.
- The same rules apply when resolving secondary dominant chords, except that scale-degree numbers refer to the "temporary" tonic.

B. When resolving the leading-tone triad or seventh chord:

- If the tritone is spelled as a diminished fifth ($\hat{7}$ below $\hat{4}$), it normally resolves inward to a third: $\hat{1}$–$\hat{3}$.
- If the tritone is spelled as an augmented fourth ($\hat{4}$ below $\hat{7}$), it may follow the voice-leading of the tendency tones and resolve outward to a sixth, or
- it may move in similar motion to a perfect fourth ($\hat{5}$–$\hat{1}$).
- When the tritone is spelled as a diminished fifth, resolve scale-degree $\hat{4}$ up to $\hat{5}$ in only one context: when the soprano-bass counterpoint moves upward in parallel tenths ($\hat{2}$ to $\hat{3}$ in the bass, $\hat{4}$ to $\hat{5}$ in the soprano). The strength of the parallel motion in this contra-

puntal pattern overrides the voice-leading tendency of $\hat{4}$ to resolve down.
- We normally resolve the tendency tones of vii°⁷ and vii°⁷ like V^7: resolve $\hat{7}$ up to $\hat{1}$, resolve $\hat{4}$ down to $\hat{3}$, and resolve the chordal seventh down ($\hat{6}$ to $\hat{5}$).
- The same rules apply when resolving secondary leading-tone chords, except that scale-degree numbers refer to the "temporary" tonic.

C. When writing a cadential $^6_4$:

Always double the bass (the fifth of the chord).
- Hold the common tones between the chord of approach and the $^6_4$, and move other voices the shortest distance.
- Write the cadential $^6_4$ on a strong beat in the measure; it displaces the V or V^7 to a weaker beat.
- Resolve the "suspended" tones of the $^6_4$ downward: the sixth above the bass moves to a fifth, and the fourth above the bass moves to a third.
- If there is a seventh in the dominant harmony that follows the cadential $^6_4$, the doubled bass note (an octave above the bass) usually moves to the seventh of the dominant seventh chord.

D. When writing other types of $^6_4$s:

- Each second-inversion triad will be one of the following types: cadential $^6_4$, passing $^6_4$, neighboring $^6_4$, or arpeggiating $^6_4$.
- Always double the bass (fifth) of the chord.
- In all $^6_4$s except arpeggiating (which are consonant), all voices should approach and leave chord members by step (forming neighbor or passing tones) or by common tone.
- Arpeggiating $^6_4$s may include skips within members of the chord that is arpeggiated, but must resolve correctly to the next harmony.

E. When writing N⁶ chords:

- Use the Neapolitan harmony most often in minor keys. Build it on $\flat\hat{2}$, with a major quality, and (usually) in first inversion ($\flat$II⁶). In major keys, be sure to include $\flat\hat{6}$ (from mixture) to ensure the chord's major quality.

- Precede the Neapolitan with any harmony that would normally precede a predominant-function harmony: e.g., I, VI, iv⁶, a string of parallel $\frac{6}{3}$ chords.
- Double $\hat{4}$ (the bass note, when the harmony appears in its characteristic first inversion). If necessary, you may try another doubling: if $\flat\hat{2}$ is doubled, it may move to $\natural\hat{2}$ in an inner voice only—never in the soprano.
- Place the N⁶ in a predominant role and resolve it to V, with both its tendency tones moving down: ($\flat$)$\hat{6}$ to $\hat{5}$, and $\flat\hat{2}$ (usually through the passing-tone $\hat{1}$) to $\hat{7}$. Note: Don't resolve $\flat\hat{2}$ to $\natural\hat{2}$, since this voice-leading conflicts with the tendency of $\flat\hat{2}$ to move downward.
- If you harmonize the passing-tone $\hat{1}$ when resolving the N⁶, choose vii°⁷/V or V$^{6-5}_{4-3}$.
- Typically, $\flat\hat{2}$ or $\hat{4}$ appears in the highest voice. Don't place ($\flat$)$\hat{6}$ in the highest voice if the N⁶ moves through a tonic chord before progressing to V, because the resolution of ($\flat$)$\hat{6}$–$\hat{5}$ above $\flat\hat{2}$–$\hat{1}$ invariably leads to parallel fifths in the voice-leading.

F. When writing augmented-sixth chords:

- Place scale-degree $\hat{5}$ of the V chord (the chord of resolution) in the bass and an upper voice (the soprano is a characteristic but not required voicing), leaving an empty space before it for the augmented sixth.
- In the empty space, write in the two tendency tones leading by half step to $\hat{5}$: ($\flat$)$\hat{6}$–$\hat{5}$ in the bass, and ($\sharp$)$\hat{4}$–$\hat{5}$ in the upper voice. In major keys, don't forget to add the correct accidental to lower scale-degree $\hat{6}$.
- Add scale-degree $\hat{1}$ in one of the inner voices.
- Add a fourth note, following these guidelines.
  (1) Italian 6 (It⁶): double scale-degree $\hat{1}$;
  (2) French 6 (Fr⁶): add scale-degree $\hat{2}$ (an augmented fourth above the bass note);
  (3) German 6 (Gr⁶): add scale-degree $\hat{3}$ from the minor mode (a perfect fifth above the bass note—in major keys, you will need to add an accidental).
- Resolve the tendency tones by half step to $\hat{5}$, and move the remaining tones to the closest possible chord tone in the dominant harmony.
- Resolve an It⁶ or a Fr⁶ directly to V; Gr⁶ chords often resolve to V$^{6-5}_{4-3}$ to avoid parallel fifths.

Ranges of Orchestral Instruments

INSTRUMENT	WRITTEN RANGE	SOUNDING RANGE
Strings		
Violin		as written
Viola		as written
Cello		as written
Bass		octave lower
Harp		as written
Guitar		octave lower
Banjo		as written, but tenor banjo sounds an octave lower

SOURCE: Samuel Adler, *The Study of Orchestration*, 3rd ed. (New York: Norton, 2002)

INSTRUMENT	WRITTEN RANGE	SOUNDING RANGE

Woodwinds

Piccolo — octave higher

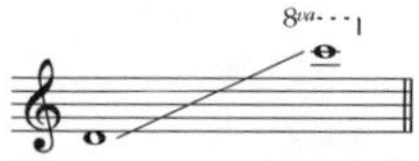

Flute — as written

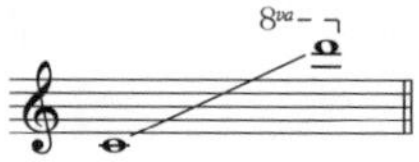

Oboe — as written

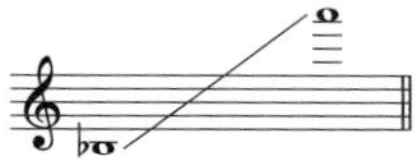

English horn — perfect fifth lower

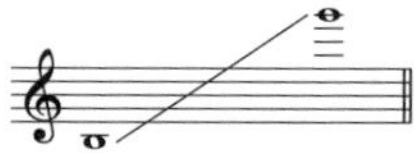

All clarinets except bass

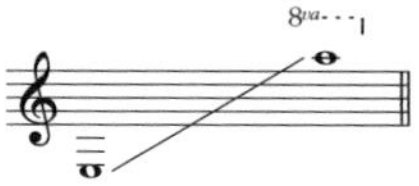

Bb: major second lower
A: minor third lower
D: major second higher
Eb: minor third higher
Eb alto: major sixth lower

Bass clarinet

major ninth lower;
if written in bass clef,
major second lower

Bassoon — as written

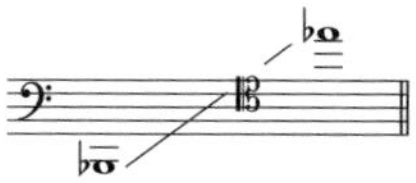

Contrabassoon — octave lower

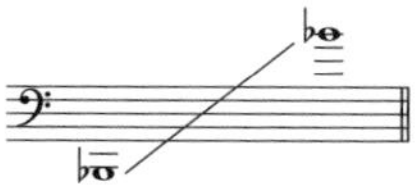

All saxophones

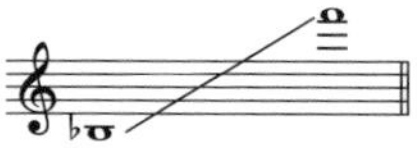

Bb soprano: major second lower
Eb alto: major sixth lower
Bb tenor: major ninth lower
Eb baritone: octave plus
    major sixth lower
Bb bass: two octaves plus a
    major second lower

INSTRUMENT	WRITTEN RANGE	SOUNDING RANGE

Brass

Horn (plus pedal notes)		perfect fifth lower
All trumpets except E♭ and D bass		C: as written B♭: major second lower D: major second higher E♭: minor third higher B♭ cornet: major second lower C bass: octave lower B♭ bass: major ninth lower
E♭ and D bass trumpets		E♭: major sixth lower D: minor seventh lower
Tenor trombone		as written
Bass trombone		as written
Alto trombone		as written
Tuba		as written
Euphonium		as written; if notated in treble clef, major ninth lower
Baritone		as written; if notated in treble clef, major ninth lower

Percussion

Timpani		as written

INSTRUMENT	WRITTEN RANGE	SOUNDING RANGE
Xylophone		octave higher
Marimba		as written
Vibraphone		as written
Glockenspiel		two octaves higher
Chimes		as written

Keyboard

Piano		as written
Celesta		octave higher
Harpsichord		as written
Organ	Manuals / Pedal	as written

Set-Class Table

NAME	PCS	IC VECTOR	NAME	PCS	IC VECTOR
3-1(12)	0,1,2	210000	9-1	0,1,2,3,4,5,6,7,8	876663
3-2	0,1,3	111000	9-2	0,1,2,3,4,5,6,7,9	777663
3-3	0,1,4	101100	9-3	0,1,2,3,4,5,6,8,9	767763
3-4	0,1,5	100110	9-4	0,1,2,3,4,5,7,8,9	766773
3-5	0,1,6	100011	9-5	0,1,2,3,4,6,7,8,9	766674
3-6(12)	0,2,4	020100	9-6	0,1,2,3,4,5,6,8,t	686763
3-7	0,2,5	011010	9-7	0,1,2,3,4,5,7,8,t	677673
3-8	0,2,6	010101	9-8	0,1,2,3,4,6,7,8,t	676764
3-9(12)	0,2,7	010020	9-9	0,1,2,3,5,6,7,8,t	676683
3-10(12)	0,3,6	002001	9-10	0,1,2,3,4,6,7,9,t	668664
3-11	0,3,7	001110	9-11	0,1,2,3,5,6,7,9,t	667773
3-12(4)	0,4,8	000300	9-12	0,1,2,4,5,6,8,9,t	666963
4-1(12)	0,1,2,3	321000	8-1	0,1,2,3,4,5,6,7	765442
4-2	0,1,2,4	221100	8-2	0,1,2,3,4,5,6,8	665542
4-3(12)	0,1,3,4	212100	8-3	0,1,2,3,4,5,6,9	656542
4-4	0,1,2,5	211110	8-4	0,1,2,3,4,5,7,8	655552
4-5	0,1,2,6	210111	8-5	0,1,2,3,4,6,7,8	654553
4-6(12)	0,1,2,7	210021	8-6	0,1,2,3,5,6,7,8	654463
4-7(12)	0,1,4,5	201210	8-7	0,1,2,3,4,5,8,9	645652
4-8(12)	0,1,5,6	200121	8-8	0,1,2,3,4,7,8,9	644563
4-9(6)	0,1,6,7	200022	8-9	0,1,2,3,6,7,8,9	644464
4-10(12)	0,2,3,5	122010	8-10	0,2,3,4,5,6,7,9	566452
4-11	0,1,3,5	121110	8-11	0,1,2,3,4,5,7,9	565552
4-12	0,2,3,6	112101	8-12	0,1,3,4,5,6,7,9	556543
4-13	0,1,3,6	112011	8-13	0,1,2,3,4,6,7,9	556453
4-14	0,2,3,7	111120	8-14	0,1,2,4,5,6,7,9	555562
4-Z15	0,1,4,6	111111	8-Z15	0,1,2,3,4,6,8,9	555553
4-16	0,1,5,7	110121	8-16	0,1,2,3,5,7,8,9	554563
4-17(12)	0,3,4,7	102210	8-17	0,1,3,4,5,6,8,9	546652
4-18	0,1,4,7	102111	8-18	0,1,2,3,5,6,8,9	546553
4-19	0,1,4,8	101310	8-19	0,1,2,4,5,6,8,9	545752

NOTE: Numbers in parentheses show the number of distinct sets in the set class if other than 48. All brackets are eliminated here for ease of reading.

NAME	PCS	IC VECTOR	NAME	PCS	IC VECTOR
4-20(12)	0,1,5,8	101220	8-20	0,1,2,4,5,7,8,9	545662
4-21(12)	0,2,4,6	030201	8-21	0,1,2,3,4,6,8,t	474643
4-22	0,2,4,7	021120	8-22	0,1,2,3,5,6,8,t	465562
4-23(12)	0,2,5,7	021030	8-23	0,1,2,3,5,7,8,t	465472
4-24(12)	0,2,4,8	020301	8-24	0,1,2,4,5,6,8,t	464743
4-25(6)	0,2,6,8	020202	8-25	0,1,2,4,6,7,8,t	464644
4-26(12)	0,3,5,8	012120	8-26	0,1,2,4,5,7,9,t	456562
4-27	0,2,5,8	012111	8-27	0,1,2,4,5,7,8,t	456553
4-28(3)	0,3,6,9	004002	8-28	0,1,3,4,6,7,9,t	448444
4-Z29	0,1,3,7	111111	8-Z29	0,1,2,3,5,6,7,9	555553
5-1(12)	0,1,2,3,4	432100	7-1	0,1,2,3,4,5,6	654321
5-2	0,1,2,3,5	332110	7-2	0,1,2,3,4,5,7	554331
5-3	0,1,2,4,5	322210	7-3	0,1,2,3,4,5,8	544431
5-4	0,1,2,3,6	322111	7-4	0,1,2,3,4,6,7	544332
5-5	0,1,2,3,7	321121	7-5	0,1,2,3,5,6,7	543342
5-6	0,1,2,5,6	311221	7-6	0,1,2,3,4,7,8	533442
5-7	0,1,2,6,7	310132	7-7	0,1,2,3,6,7,8	532353
5-8(12)	0,2,3,4,6	232201	7-8	0,2,3,4,5,6,8	454422
5-9	0,1,2,4,6	231211	7-9	0,1,2,3,4,6,8	453432
5-10	0,1,3,4,6	223111	7-10	0,1,2,3,4,6,9	445332
5-11	0,2,3,4,7	222220	7-11	0,1,3,4,5,6,8	444441
5-Z12(12)	0,1,3,5,6	222121	7-Z12	0,1,2,3,4,7,9	444342
5-13	0,1,2,4,8	221311	7-13	0,1,2,4,5,6,8	443532
5-14	0,1,2,5,7	221131	7-14	0,1,2,3,5,7,8	443352
5-15(12)	0,1,2,6,8	220222	7-15	0,1,2,4,6,7,8	442443
5-16	0,1,3,4,7	213211	7-16	0,1,2,3,5,6,9	435432
5-Z17(12)	0,1,3,4,8	212320	7-Z17	0,1,2,4,5,6,9	434541
5-Z18	0,1,4,5,7	212221	7-Z18	0,1,2,3,5,8,9	434442
5-19	0,1,3,6,7	212122	7-19	0,1,2,3,6,7,9	434343
5-20	0,1,3,7,8	211231	7-20	0,1,2,4,7,8,9	433452
5-21	0,1,4,5,8	202420	7-21	0,1,2,4,5,8,9	424641
5-22(12)	0,1,4,7,8	202321	7-22	0,1,2,5,6,8,9	424542
5-23	0,2,3,5,7	132130	7-23	0,2,3,4,5,7,9	354351
5-24	0,1,3,5,7	131221	7-24	0,1,2,3,5,7,9	353442
5-25	0,2,3,5,8	123121	7-25	0,2,3,4,6,7,9	345342
5-26	0,2,4,5,8	122311	7-26	0,1,3,4,5,7,9	344532
5-27	0,1,3,5,8	122230	7-27	0,1,2,4,5,7,9	344451
5-28	0,2,3,6,8	122212	7-28	0,1,3,5,6,7,9	344433
5-29	0,1,3,6,8	122131	7-29	0,1,2,4,6,7,9	344352
5-30	0,1,4,6,8	121321	7-30	0,1,2,4,6,8,9	343542
5-31	0,1,3,6,9	114112	7-31	0,1,3,4,6,7,9	336333
5-32	0,1,4,6,9	113221	7-32	0,1,3,4,6,8,9	335442
5-33(12)	0,2,4,6,8	040402	7-33	0,1,2,4,6,8,t	262623
5-34(12)	0,2,4,6,9	032221	7-34	0,1,3,4,6,8,t	254442
5-35(12)	0,2,4,7,9	032140	7-35	0,1,3,5,6,8,t	254361

NAME	PCS	IC VECTOR	NAME	PCS	IC VECTOR
5-Z36	0,1,2,4,7	222121	7-Z36	0,1,2,3,5,6,8	444342
5-Z37(12)	0,3,4,5,8	212320	7-Z37	0,1,3,4,5,7,8	434541
5-Z38	0,1,2,5,8	212221	7-Z38	0,1,2,4,5,7,8	434442
6-1(12)	0,1,2,3,4,5	543210			
6-2	0,1,2,3,4,6	443211			
6-Z3	0,1,2,3,5,6	433221	6-Z36	0,1,2,3,4,7	*
6-Z4(12)	0,1,2,4,5,6	432321	6-Z37(12)	0,1,2,3,4,8	
6-5	0,1,2,3,6,7	422232			
6-Z6(12)	0,1,2,5,6,7	421242	6-Z38(12)	0,1,2,3,7,8	
6-7(6)	0,1,2,6,7,8	420243			
6-8(12)	0,2,3,4,5,7	343230			
6-9	0,1,2,3,5,7	342231			
6-Z10	0,1,3,4,5,7	333321	6-Z39	0,2,3,4,5,8	
6-Z11	0,1,2,4,5,7	333231	6-Z40	0,1,2,3,5,8	
6-Z12	0,1,2,4,6,7	332232	6-Z41	0,1,2,3,6,8	
6-Z13(12)	0,1,3,4,6,7	324222	6-Z42(12)	0,1,2,3,6,9	
6-14	0,1,3,4,5,8	323430			
6-15	0,1,2,4,5,8	323421			
6-16	0,1,4,5,6,8	322431			
6-Z17	0,1,2,4,7,8	322332	6-Z43	0,1,2,5,6,8	
6-18	0,1,2,5,7,8	322242			
6-Z19	0,1,3,4,7,8	313431	6-Z44	0,1,2,5,6,9	
6-20(4)	0,1,4,5,8,9	303630			
6-21	0,2,3,4,6,8	242412			
6-22	0,1,2,4,6,8	241422			
6-Z23(12)	0,2,3,5,6,8	234222	6-Z45(12)	0,2,3,4,6,9	
6-Z24	0,1,3,4,6,8	233331	6-Z46	0,1,2,4,6,9	
6-Z25	0,1,3,5,6,8	233241	6-Z47	0,1,2,4,7,9	
6-Z26(12)	0,1,3,5,7,8	232341	6-Z48(12)	0,1,2,5,7,9	
6-27	0,1,3,4,6,9	225222			
6-Z28(12)	0,1,3,5,6,9	224322	6-Z49(12)	0,1,3,4,7,9	
6-Z29(12)	0,1,3,6,8,9	224232	6-Z50(12)	0,1,4,6,7,9	
6-30(12)	0,1,3,6,7,9	224223			
6-31	0,1,3,5,8,9	223431			
6-32(12)	0,2,4,5,7,9	143250			
6-33	0,2,3,5,7,9	143241			
6-34	0,1,3,5,7,9	142422			
6-35(2)	0,2,4,6,8,t	060603			

*Z-related hexachords share the same ic vector; use vector in the third column.

SOURCE: Allen Forte, *The Structure of Atonal Music* (New Haven: Yale University Press, 1973) (adapted)

Credits

Music

Chapter 1: Lennon/McCartney, "Eleanor Rigby." Words and Music by John Lennon and Paul McCartney. Copyright © 1967 Sony/ATV Songs LLC. Copyright Renewed. All Rights Administered by Sony/ATV Music Publishing, 8 Music Square West, Nashville, TN 37203. International Copyright Secured. All Rights Reserved. Webber/Rice, "Don't Cry for Me Argentina" from *Evita*. Copyright 1976 The Really Useful Group, reprinted by permission. Webern, String Quartet, Op. 5, No. 3. Reprinted by permission of Universal Edition.

Chapter 2: Messiaen, *Les corps glorieux*. Reprinted by permission of Theodore Presser Co. Sherman & Sherman, "Feed the Birds" from *Mary Poppins*, Copyright The Walt Disney Music Company. Reprinted by permission.

Chapter 3: Leven, Mel, "Cruella DeVille" from *101 Dalmations*. Copyright The Walt Disney Music Company. Reprinted by permission. Menken/Rice, "A Whole New World" from *Aladdin*. Copyright The Walt Disney Music Company. Reprinted by permission. Rodgers/Hammerstein, "Do-Re-Mi" from *The Sound of Music*. Lyrics by Oscar Hammerstein II. Music by Richard Rodgers. Copyright © 1959 by Richard Rodgers and Oscar Hammerstein II. Copyright Renewed. WILLIAMSON MUSIC owner of publication and allied rights throughout the world. International Copyright Secured. All Rights Reserved. Rodgers/Hammerstein, "The Sound of Music" from *The Sound of Music*. Lyrics by Oscar Hammerstein II. Music by Richard Rodgers. Copyright © 1959 by Richard Rodgers and Oscar Hammerstein II. Copyright Renewed. WILLIAMSON MUSIC owner of publication and allied rights throughout the world. International Copyright Secured. All Rights Reserved. Sherman & Sherman, "Feed the Birds" from *Mary Poppins*. Copyright The Walt Disney Music Company. Reprinted by permission. Webern, "Herr Jesu Mein." Reprinted by permission of Universal Edition.

Chapter 4: Gershwin, George and Ira, "'S Wonderful" from *Funny Face*. Reprinted by permission of Warner Bros/Warner Chappell, all rights reserved. Lennon/McCartney, "Eleanor Rigby." Words and Music by John Lennon and Paul McCartney. Copyright © 1967 Sony/ATV Songs LLC. Copyright Renewed.

All Rights Administered by Sony/ATV Music Publishing, 8 Music Square West, Nashville, TN 37203. International Copyright Secured. All Rights Reserved.

Chapter 5: Bartok, String Quartet, No. 2, Mvt. 1. © Copyright 1920 in the USA by Boosey & Hawkes, Inc. Copyright Renewed. Reprinted by permission. Lennon/McCartney, "Norwegian Wood." Words and Music by John Lennon and Paul McCartney. Copyright © 1965 Sony/ATV Songs LLC. Copyright Renewed. All Rights Administered by Sony/ATV Music Publishing, 8 Music Square West, Nashville, TN 37203. International Copyright Secured. All Rights Reserved. Livingston/Hoffman, "Bibbidi Bobbidi Boo." Copyright The Walt Disney Music Company. Reprinted by permission. Vaughan Williams, "Agnus Dei." Copyright 1922, reprinted by permission of G. Schirmer.

Chapter 6: Gershwin, George and Ira, "'S Wonderful" from *Funny Face*. Reprinted by permission of Warner Bros/Warner Chappell, all rights reserved.

Chapter 7: Copyright 1953 Bourne Co., admin by Music Sales Corporation. Reprinted by permission.

Chapter 8: Webber/Rice, "Don't Cry for Me Argentina" from *Evita*. Copyright 1976 The Really Useful Group, reprinted by permission.

Chapter 10: Corigliano, "Come Now My Darling," from *The Ghosts of Versailles*. Copyright G. Schirmer/Music Sales Corp., reprinted by permission. Ives, "Variations on America" © C. F. Peters.

Chapter 11: Rodgers/Hart, "My Funny Valentine" from *Babes in Arms*. Words by Lorenz Hart. Music by Richard Rodgers. Copyright © 1937 (Renewed) by Chappell & Co. Rights for the Extended Renewal Term in the U.S. Controlled by Williamson Music and WB Music Corp. o/b/o The Estate of Lorenz Hart. International Copyright Secured. All Rights Reserved.

Chapter 12: Lloyd, Normann arr., "Clementine." Reprinted by permission of Simon & Schuster. From *Fireside Book of Folk Songs*.

Chapter 13: Webber/Rice, "Don't Cry for Me Argentina" from *Evita*. © Copyright 1976 The Really Useful Group, reprinted by

Translations

Index of Music Examples

Page numbers in *italics* indicate music examples.

Index of Terms and Concepts

Page numbers in *italics* indicate music examples. Please consult the *Index of Music Examples* for specific compositions.

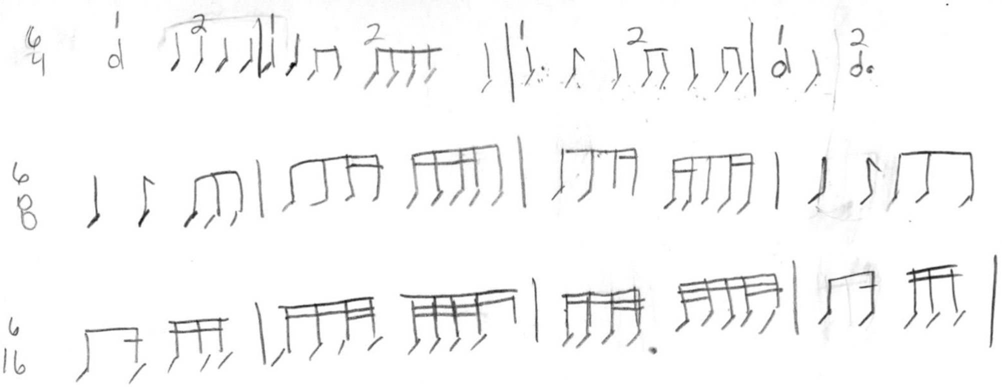
6
4
6
8
6
16

CD Tracks and Performers